The 8th International Conference on Time Series and Forecasting

The 8th International Conference on Time Series and Forecasting

Editors

Ignacio Rojas
Hector Pomares
Olga Valenzuela Cansino
Fernando Rojas
Luis Javier Herrera

MDPI • Basel • Beijing • Wuhan • Barcelona • Belgrade • Manchester • Tokyo • Cluj • Tianjin

Editors

Ignacio Rojas
University of Granada
Spain

Hector Pomares
University of Granada
Spain

Olga Valenzuela Cansino
University of Granada
Spain

Fernando Rojas
University of Granada
Spain

Luis Javier Herrera
University of Granada
Spain

Editorial Office
MDPI
St. Alban-Anlage 66
4052 Basel, Switzerland

This is a reprint of proceeding papers published online in the open access journal *Engineering Proceedings* (ISSN 2673-4591) (available at: https://www.mdpi.com/2673-4591/18/1).

For citation purposes, cite each article independently as indicated on the article page online and as indicated below:

LastName, A.A.; LastName, B.B.; LastName, C.C. Article Title. *Journal Name* **Year**, *Volume Number,* Page Range.

ISBN 978-3-0365-5451-8 (Hbk)
ISBN 978-3-0365-5452-5 (PDF)

Cover image courtesy of MonoDex.

Contents

Preface to "The 8th International Conference on Time Series and Forecasting"

The ITISE 2022 (8th International conference on Time Series and Forecasting) seeks to provide a discussion forum for scientists, engineers, educators and students about the latest ideas and realizations in the foundations, theory, modeling and applications for interdisciplinary and multidisciplinary research encompassing disciplines of computer science, mathematics, statistics, forecasting, econometrics, etc., in the field of time series analysis and forecasting.

Ignacio Rojas, Hector Pomares, Olga Valenzuela Cansino, Fernando Rojas and Luis Javier Herrera
Editors

Editorial

Statement of Peer Review [†]

Olga Valenzuela [1], Fernando Rojas [2], Luis Javier Herrera [2], Hector Pomares [2] and Ignacio Rojas [2,*]

[1] Department of Applied Mathematics, University of Granada, 18071 Granada, Spain
[2] Department of Computer Engineering, Automation and Robotics, University of Granada, 18071 Granada, Spain
* Correspondence: irojas@ugr.es
† Presented at the 8th International Conference on Time Series and Forecasting, Gran Canaria, Spain, 27–30 June 2022.

In submitting conference proceedings to *Engineering Proceedings*, the volume editors of the proceedings certify to the publisher that all papers published in this volume have been subjected to peer review performed by the volume editors. Reviews are conducted by expert referees adhering to the professional and scientific standards expected of a proceedings journal.

- Type of peer review: single-blind; double-blind; triple-blind; open; other (please describe): Single-Blind
- Conference submission management system: Easychair (https://easychair.org/conferences/?conf=itise2022)
- Number of submissions sent for review: 197
- Number of submissions accepted: 101
- Acceptance rate (number of submissions accepted/number of submissions received): 101/197
- Average number of reviews per paper: 3
- Total number of reviewers involved: 274
- Any additional information on the review process: no

check for updates

Citation: Valenzuela, O.; Rojas, F.; Herrera, L.J.; Pomares, H.; Rojas, I. Statement of Peer Review. *Eng. Proc.* **2022**, *18*, 43. https://doi.org/10.3390/engproc2022018043

Published: 6 September 2022

Publisher's Note: MDPI stays neutral with regard to jurisdictional claims in published maps and institutional affiliations.

engineering
proceedings

Proceeding Paper

Evaluating a Recurrent Neural Network Model for Predicting Readmission to Cardiovascular ICUs Based on Clinical Time Series Data [†]

Sobhan Moazemi *[,‡,§] , Sebastian Kalkhoff [§] , Steven Kessler, Zeynep Boztoprak, Vincent Hettlich, Artur Liebrecht, Roman Bibo, Bastian Dewitz, Artur Lichtenberg , Hug Aubin ‖ and Falko Schmid ‖

Digital Health Lab Düsseldorf, Department of Cardiac Surgery, Medical Faculty and University Hospital Düsseldorf, Heinrich-Heine-University Düsseldorf, 40225 Düsseldorf, Germany; sebastian.kalkhoff@med.uni-duesseldorf.de (S.K.); steven.kessler@med.uni-duesseldorf.de (S.K.); zeynep.boztoprak@hhu.de (Z.B.); vincenthendrik.hettlich@med.uni-duesseldorf.de (V.H.); artur.liebrecht@med.uni-duesseldorf.de (A.L.); roman.bibo@med.uni-duesseldorf.de (R.B.); bastian.dewitz@med.uni-duesseldorf.de (B.D.); artur.lichtenberg@med.uni-duesseldorf.de (A.L.); hug.aubin@med.uni-duesseldorf.de (H.A.); falko.schmid@med.uni-duesseldorf.de (F.S.)
* Correspondence: sobhan.moazemi@med.uni-duesseldorf.de
† Presented at the 8th International Conference on Time Series and Forecasting, Gran Canaria, Spain, 27–30 June 2022.
‡ Current address: Moorenstr. 5, 40225 Düsseldorf, Germany.
§ These authors contributed equally to this work.
‖ These authors contributed equally to this work as senior authors.

check for
updates

Citation: Moazemi, S.; Kalkhoff, S.; Kessler, S.; Boztoprak, Z.; Hettlich, V.; Liebrecht, A.; Bibo, R.; Dewitz, B.; Lichtenberg, A.; Aubin, H.; et al. Evaluating a Recurrent Neural Network Model for Predicting Readmission to Cardiovascular ICUs Based on Clinical Time Series Data. *Eng. Proc.* **2022**, *18*, 1. https:// doi.org/10.3390/engproc2022018001

Academic Editors: Ignacio Rojas, Hector Pomares, Olga Valenzuela, Fernando Rojas and Luis Javier Herrera

Published: 16 June 2022

Publisher's Note: MDPI stays neutral with regard to jurisdictional claims in published maps and institutional affiliations.

Abstract: Unexpected readmission to intensive care units (ICUs) endangers patients' lives due to premature patient transfers or prolonged stays at the care units. This can be mitigated by stratification of the readmission risk at discharge times using state-of-the-art machine learning (ML) methods. We fitted two alternative recurrent neural network (RNN) models based on long short-term memory (LSTM) on the Medical Information Mart for Intensive Care (MIMIC-III) dataset and evaluated them with an independent cohort from our hospital's ICU (UKD). The first model processed all the available time series data from each patient's ICU stay, whereas the second model focused on the data from the last 48 hours of the ICU stay prior to transfer. Our readmission prediction on MIMIC data reached an area under the curve of receiver operating characteristic (AUC-ROC) of 0.82. Furthermore, the model with the 48 h time frame outperformed the other model, as both models were applied to the independent test cohort. The results suggest that the RNN model for time series forecasting holds promise for future use as a clinical decision support tool, although follow-up studies with larger cohorts as well as user studies should be conducted to assess the generalizability and usability of the methods, respectively.

Keywords: readmission prediction; intensive care unit (ICU); recurrent neural network (RNN); long short-term memory (LSTM); machine learning (ML); time series analysis; health forecasting

1. Introduction

According to different retrospective and review studies [1–3], the rates of readmission to ICUs in hospitals in developed countries are quantified inconsistently in the range from 0.14 to 14.5 percent. Regardless of the inconsistent readmission rates, patients who are readmitted to ICUs due to inappropriate discharge time are subject to life-threatening risks, with respiratory and cardiac complications as the most common causes of readmission [1,4]. At the same time, prolonged stays at ICUs can also lead to increased mortality or poor long-term prognosis for patients [5]. In particular, patients who undergo cardiac surgery are prone to longer ICU stays due to the invasive nature of heart surgery and the resulting increased risk of postoperative complications [6]. Therefore, it is important to find the optimal point in time for transfer, for this particular vulnerable group of patients. Intensivists need to quantify patients' readmission risks in order to determine this point in time and avoid unplanned readmissions. This implies an increasing need for clinical decision support tools which complement current discharge routines through the use of predictive models taking advantage of artificial intelligence (AI).

AI in general and ML in particular have been widely used in many diagnostic and prognostic domains, such as oncology [7,8] and computational neuroscience [9,10], to provide clinical decision support tools, which either replace or complement established diagnostic and prognostic routines. More specifically, time series analysis has been successfully applied in many medical domains, including management of type 2 diabetes [11], hospital admission prediction [12], age-related death prediction [13] and ICU readmission prediction [3,14].

From a technical point of view, as related works suggest, a variety of techniques ranging from simple probabilistic predictors such as logistic regression (LR) and ML-based classifiers such as support vector machines (SVMs) to more sophisticated models such as convolutional neural networks (CNNs) have shown their potential for the prediction of readmission to ICUs [3,15,16].

In a previous study [17], currently under review, we trained a model with a recurrent architecture on a subset of the MIMIC-III dataset, an open access dataset of time series data from more than 50,000 care unit stays with different health conditions at a single center [18], without any limitation on the time frames of the input time series data, and showed its superiority to logistic regression and a feed forward network in predicting readmission. In the current study, we analyze the performance of a recurrent neural network (RNN) model processing health-related times series data, taking advantage of the long short-term memory (LSTM) method with slight architectural enhancements compared to the previous model, considering time series data from the last 48 h of patients' stays at ICUs, sampled in 60-minute intervals.

The main contribution of our work is to propose and evaluate two alternative ML-based models, which are trained and fit using a publicly available dataset of health-related time series data, with and without concrete time windows (in compliance with state-of-the-art metrics in the domain) prior to patients' discharge from ICUs. Moreover, as a further contribution, the proposed models were evaluated using a real-world hospital cohort with data from our own cardiovascular intensive care unit at UKD to assess how they would generalize against new sets of unseen data.

In the next sections, first, a detailed overview of the patient data and methods is given, and then the results of model training and evaluations are presented and discussed. Finally, the relevance of the findings and possible future follow-ups will be discussed.

2. Materials and Methods

This section explains the methodology of the study. First, the details of the dataset curation for training, validation and test steps will be elaborated, including the selection criteria and cohort statistics, which will be followed by the description of the integrated times series data. Then, the details of the training and validation step using 5-fold cross-validation on the MIMIC-III dataset are discussed. Finally, the details of the test step on an unseen set of data from a held-out MIMIC cohort as well as the UKD database are presented. The entire in-house-developed analysis pipeline is developed in the Python (V3.6.) programming language. The LSTM models for time series data analysis are implemented using the PyTorch library [19].

The inclusion criteria of subjects from both MIMIC and UKD datasets have been defined as follows:

1. **Patients who were transferred from the ICU to a normal station and then returned to the ICU within 48 h.** Due to possible logistical reasons, patients whose first ICU stay was less than 24 h are excluded. These patients are labeled as 'readmitted'.

2. **Patients who died during the hospital stay.** The dead subjects are also labeled as 'readmitted'.
3. **Patients who were transferred from the ICU to a normal station and then were not returned to the ICU within 30 days.** Those who did not return within 30 days after transfer from ICU are labeled as 'non-readmitted'.

2.1. Patient Cohorts

For the training, we focused on the cases of patients from the MIMIC-III dataset who visited cardiovascular care units. As a result, the training subject cohort consisted of 11,513 patients, out of which 966 patients were labeled as readmitted and 10,547 were labeled as non-readmitted. From the MIMIC dataset, the train subjects' ages ranged from 17 to 89 years (mean(M) = 66, standard deviation(SD) = 13.51). For anonymization purposes, the real admission times are not attainable from the MIMIC dataset.

For test purposes, a cohort of 502 patients who visited the cardiovascular ICU at the UKD were retrospectively analyzed. Among these, 100 patients were returned to the ICU within the 48 h after discharge (labeled as 'readmitted') and 402 patients visited the ICU just once, without being readmitted within 30 days after their discharge (labeled as 'non-readmitted'). The ages of the subjects from the UKD database were quantified in the range from 19 to 95 years (M = 67, SD = 12.25). The cohort corresponds to cardiovascular ICU stays in the time period from January 2017 to December 2020. Due to the retrospective character of the study, patient consent was waived.

2.2. Time Series and Patient Data

For each subject in the train or test cohort, 10 vital or laboratory variables (selected by highly qualified cardiovascular surgeons) were captured during the patient's stay at the corresponding intensive care unit. To form the time series data for all the subjects, 60 min time intervals have been taken into account. The missing values were extrapolated using the mean value of the corresponding variable throughout the entire corresponding cohort. Moreover, from the patients' files, the age and weight values were extracted. Finally, the length of stay (LoS) of each subject was quantified from the admission time entries from the corresponding database (MIMIC or UKD) and added to the rest of the features to end up with feature vectors of size 13. Table 1 provides the list of the 10 variables used for the time series data analysis and the 3 extra patient variables.

Table 1. The input parameters including time series data from laboratory or vital values and information from patient files (ABP: ambulatory blood pressure, LoS: length of stay). The table is adapted from [17].

Lab Values	Vital Signs	Patient Information
Creatinine	Body Temperature	Age
Blood PH	ABP	Weight
Sodium	Heart Rate	LoS
Potassium	Oxygenation	
Hematocrit		
Bilirubin		

2.3. Preprocessing

Preprocessing of the input data is applied, similarly to our previous work [17], consisting of the following steps: First, the time series features and patient variables are obtained from the corresponding dataset (MIMIC or UKD). Then, all values are standardized and missing data are replaced with the corresponding distribution's mean value. In the last step, the data are both re-sampled and oversampled before being processed by the corresponding model. Figure 1 gives an overview of the preprocessing pipeline.

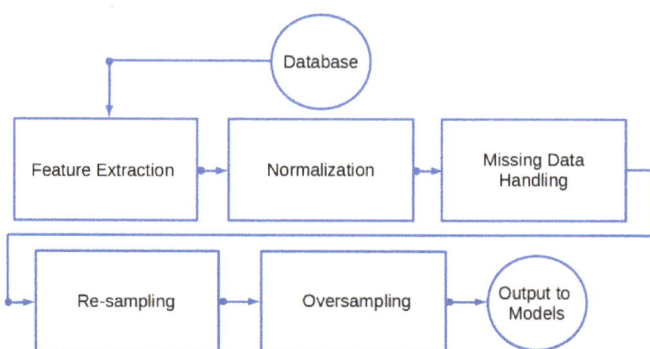

Figure 1. Preprocessing pipeline. First, the data are extracted and standardized, and then the missing data are filled in. Finally, re-sampling and oversampling are applied before the data are fed to the models. This figure is adapted from previous work [17].

In the feature extraction step, the case IDs of the subjects who met our selection criteria have been processed to acquire the feature values from the corresponding database using appropriate queries. Then, the normalization is applied at two different levels. First, the features which might have been stored in different units (such as weight) have been unified and converted accordingly and cases with extreme and outlier values have been removed from the cohorts. In the second step, we applied standardization around the mean value to end up with normalized feature vectors. The standardization of each variable is applied as defined in Equation (1):

$$\hat{s}_i = \frac{s_i - \mu_x}{\sigma_x},\tag{1}$$

where $\hat{s}_i$ is the standardized value, s_i is the original value, μ_x is the mean of the variable over the whole cohort x and σ_x is the standard deviation over x.

As required by the LSTM method, all the input feature vectors must be of equal size before being analyzed. Thus, for all the timestamps without an actual measurement, the missing value was filled in with zero (which is the mean value after standardization). Moreover, as the vital and lab values of patients are usually measured in fragmented timestamps, the feature vectors extracted from the databases were non-uniformly distributed along subject cohorts. Thus, to unify the entire cohorts, the time series parameters are resampled to a frequency of one entry per hour. In case there exist more than one measurement per hour, the mean of each hour is used as the value. Alternatively, if there is no record for a time step, the mean over the whole cohort is used. Furthermore, the imbalance in the label distribution (there are more non-readmitted cases than readmitted ones in both cohorts) might result in the training of a deep learning model that is not able to predict the minority class labels accurately [20]. Therefore, the data for training the LSTM models were oversampled in order to have evenly distributed classes.

2.4. Model Training

In a previous study [17], we have shown the superiority of an RNN model based on LSTM architecture to logistic regression and a feed forward network using the MIMIC-III dataset. Therefore, in the current study, two alternative models with LSTM architecture have been analyzed, compared and further evaluated on unseen sets of data from open access and available in-house data. Both models are trained and validated using a subset of the MIMIC-III dataset, which was selected randomly. The first model, which will be denoted as the 'cropped' model from now on, applies a fixed window of the last 48 h to each ICU stay. The second model, which will be denoted as 'uncropped' in the next parts of the text, applies no limits on the available time series data from each subject.

As a special kind of recurrent neural network (RNN), long short-term memory (LSTM) is able to learn long-term dependencies in time series data. The input to an LSTM is a batch of arrays containing time series data. Although the LSTM model can handle inputs with varying lengths, the input length has to be equal inside each batch. Thus, to pad each time series with zeros until they have equal length, a PyTorch object is used.

To be able to capture non-linear relations between input variables and target labels, a hidden layer with the size of 50 neurons is applied after the LSTM pipeline. The input to the models are the time series data. For the cropped model, a fixed window of 48 h is used, while, for the uncropped model, no constraint on the length of time series data is applied. After processing the input time series batches, the three patient variables (age, weight and LoS) are concatenated to the feature vectors. Then, a rectified linear unit (ReLU) is applied as the activation function, while a dropout layer with a value of 0.3 is used for regularization purposes. The final fully connected layer consists of 2 neurons, which are then passed through to the softmax function, which quantifies the final class probabilities (one for each label).

Figure 2 illustrates the architecture of the LSTM-based models. The x_i input refers to the i-th time step of all time series. Table 2 summarizes the hyperparameters for model fitting.

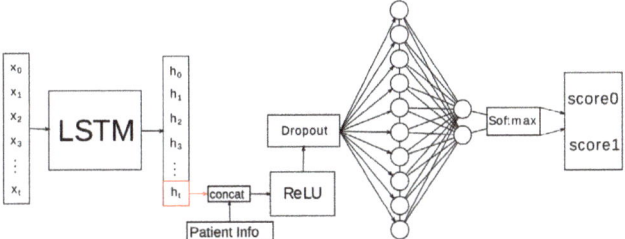

Figure 2. LSTM models' architecture: First, the time series data are passed to the LSTM part. Then, the patient information (age, weight and length of stay) is concatenated to the feature vectors from LSTM output. Next, the ReLU and dropout are applied before the feature vectors are passed through the hidden layers. Finally, the softmax function is used to assign probabilities for each binary label.

Table 2. The hyperparameters of the LSTM-based model. The table is adapted from [17].

Hyperparameters	Values
optimization algorithm	Adam
learning rate	0.003
loss function	cross-entropy
batch size	32
epochs	early stopping

2.5. Model Validation

The training cohort from the MIMIC dataset is first split into separate train and validation cohorts with similar ratios of target labels. Then, to validate the model internally, 5-fold cross-validation is applied with random folds. As a result, the hyperparameters of the best performing models are stored to be used for the corresponding test steps. The training of each model continued until the area under the curve of precision recall (AUC-PR) stopped increasing after several epochs. Subsequently, the model that achieved the highest AUC-PR in the cross-validation was applied to the separate validation set. This procedure was repeated 10 times and the mean and standard deviation of the performance metrics were computed accordingly.

2.6. Model Evaluation

Both of the trained models are evaluated against unseen cohorts from the MIMIC-III and UKD datasets. To this end, two independent test cohorts have acted as representatives of unseen data. To quantify the model performance on each of the held-out test cohorts, each of the cropped and uncropped models, which were trained and fit in the validation step, are applied to the independent test cohorts. Then, the performance of the models is quantified and compared in terms of balanced accuracy, AUC-PR, precision, recall and AUC-ROC.

3. Results

In this section, the results of the model validation and evaluation are presented. First, the results obtained by different models in the training and validation phase will be elaborated. Then, the models' performance on the test cohorts will be quantified and compared.

3.1. Model Training and Validation

The results of the model training with five-fold cross-validation on the MIMIC dataset are summarized in Table 3. Both cropped and uncropped models performed well on held-out validation subsets within the training cohort, with AUC-ROCs of 0.877 and 0.859, respectively.

Table 3. Evaluation metrics for the validation set from MIMIC database.

	Balanced Accuracy	Recall	Precision	AUC-PR	AUC-ROC
cropped to 48 h	0.799	0.694	0.389	0.666	0.877
uncropped	0.778	0.649	0.389	0.636	0.859

3.2. Model Evaluation

The results of the evaluation steps on held-out cohorts from the MIMIC and UKD databases are illustrated in Table 4 and Figures 3 and 4, comparing the models' performance together and to an unskilled classifier. In general, we observe a remarkable gap in the performance of the models as applied to the two groups of held-out data. Both the cropped and uncrpopped models perform reasonably well on the held-out set from MIMIC, with AUC-ROCs of 0.796 and 0.828, respectively. From the test results of the UKD data, the cropped model (AUC-ROC = 0.554) performed better than the uncropped model (AUC-ROC = 0.517).

Table 4. Evaluation metrics for the test sets from UKD and MIMIC databases.

UKD					
	Balanced Accuracy	Recall	Precision	AUC-PR	AUC-ROC
cropped to 48 h	0.514	0.06	0.318	0.223	0.554
uncropped	0.498	0.22	0.196	0.221	0.517
MIMIC					
	Balanced Accuracy	Recall	Precision	AUC-PR	AUC-ROC
cropped to 48 h	0.74	0.575	0.35	0.538	0.796
uncropped	0.766	0.628	0.477	0.571	0.828

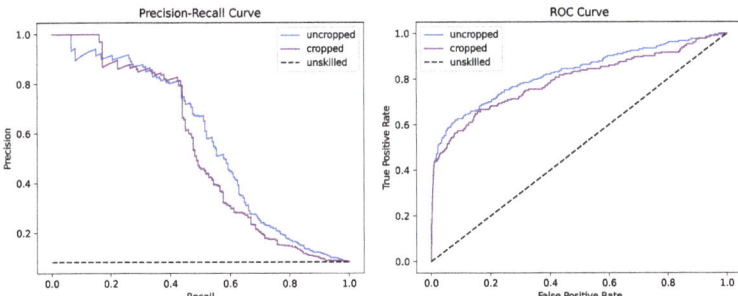

Figure 3. Results of the two alternative models' predictions on the unseen cohort from MIMIC dataset: (**left**) the precision–recall curve; (**right**) the receiver operating characteristic curve. The dashed lines denote the performance expected by an unskilled classifier.

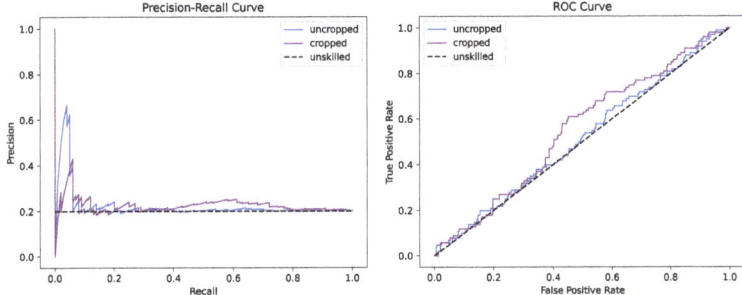

Figure 4. Results of the two alternative models' predictions on the unseen dataset from UKD: (**left**) the precision–recall curve; (**right**) the receiver operating characteristic curve. The dashed lines denote the performance expected by an unskilled classifier.

4. Discussion

Predicting the risk of readmission to intensive care units at discharge times through the use of artificial intelligence can support healthcare systems to manage their resources in a more efficient way. As unplanned readmissions might result in longer stays as well as health hazards for patients [1,4], it is critical to provide quantification of the readmission risks as an additional asset for decision making for the intensivists. Related works suggest that different vital and laboratory values of patients sampled in the last 48 h prior to the patient's discharge from the intensive care unit contribute the most to the fact of whether the patient will return to the care unit [21]. Thus, state-of-the-art time series forecasting methods on health-related data from ICU stays could be of great importance for the analysis of readmission risk for patients. Therefore, the motivation behind this study has been to propose and evaluate two alternative models, based on time series forecasting, for readmission prediction for patients visiting cardiovascular ICUs after heart surgery.

The first model analyzes all available vital and lab values for all the participating subjects during their stays at the corresponding ICU. Alternatively, the second model takes into account only the values in the last 48 h prior to discharge from the care unit. As elaborated in the results, both of the alternate models performed reasonably well in predicting patients who would be readmitted to the ICU when they were applied to an unseen cohort from the MIMIC dataset. Furthermore, we showed that the model with the 48 h time limit outperformed the other model in predicting readmissions for a cohort of unseen cases from UKD, which conforms with the findings from related work [21]. The superiority of the model with a persistent number of timestamps can be justified, as, typically, data-driven ML-based methods perform more efficiently on data cohorts with higher consistency [22]. Moreover, it signifies the relevance of the patients' clinical factors measured in the most recent timestamps prior to transfer for predicting readmission risks.

Overall, the findings reveal the predictive potential of the AI-based approach for health forecasting after evaluating its performance on unseen datasets. However, there are some drawbacks to the currently applied methodology, which should be mitigated in future follow-ups. As for any other time series model, the methodology towards health forecasting as described in this paper would also be affected by the issue of missing data. For this study, we replaced missing measurements with the corresponding mean value throughout the whole cohort. For the future follow-ups, we will consider alternative AI-based imputation methods such as bidirectional recurrent imputation for time series (BRITS) [23], which would most likely help to further improve the robustness of our methods. Furthermore, most of the state-of-the-art ML-based models with deep architectures are less interpretable due to their 'black box' nature. Therefore, one of our future works will be to provide an ML-based approach towards ICU readmission prediction in an explainable manner, i.e., by following explainable AI (XAI) best practices. This will further help to give the medical experts higher levels of interpretability and confidence in AI analyses.

The results of the evaluation step reveal the inconsistency between the time series measurements from the two databases (MIMIC-III and UKD), also known as the dataset shift problem [24]. This might reflect different protocols and standards for patient care and discharge in the corresponding care units and should be diminished in the future using appropriate transfer learning techniques or by training new models on larger cohorts which better fit in protocols. Thus, we are gathering more annotated data to prepare a suitable cohort of ICU stays at UKD for further follow-ups. Nonetheless, even these relatively poor preliminary results on the data from UKD are slightly better than the performance of an unskilled classifier. These findings identify room for improvement in readmission prediction accuracy by the AI model. Although the AI performance might be considered far from perfection, even highly experienced intensivists will not predict ICU readmissions quite perfectly. Therefore, to further quantify how the proposed AI approach would compete with experienced domain experts, we intend to conduct experiments in which the performance of the AI model for ICU readmission prediction is compared to that of a group of experienced intensivists. Nevertheless, it should be noted that the proposed methods are designed as decision support tools for medical experts and therefore should not be used as an autonomous system for decision making.

Another important aspect of any clinical decision support tool is usability. In this regard, as part of the upcoming follow-ups, we intend to conduct proper empirical studies to assess how a provided AI assistant user interface would satisfy user needs in terms of experience and performance. Moreover, to account for better generalizability, the integration of datasets from other hospitals and intensive care units would be a useful next step to take.

5. Conclusions

The aim of the study has been to train and evaluate a deep model with a recurrent architecture to predict the readmission of patients who visited cardiovascular ICUs based on times series data of vital and lab values. To this end, the RNN model based on the LSTM method was trained with open access data and tested using independent hospital data. Our findings revealed the potential of the proposed AI-based methodology to assist domain experts at cardiovascular intensive care units for the better quantification of readmission risks at discharge times. To further address the usability and generalizability aspects of the methods, empirical user studies and experiments with data from other care units should be conducted.

Author Contributions: Conceptualization, S.M., S.K. (Sebastian Kalkhoff), S.K. (Steven Kessler), H.A. and F.S.; methodology, S.M., S.K. (Sebastian Kalkhoff), S.K. (Steven Kessler) and Z.B.; software, S.K. (Steven Kessler) and Z.B.; validation, S.K. (Steven Kessler), Z.B. and H.A.; formal analysis, S.M., S.K. (Sebastian Kalkhoff), H.A., F.S. and A.L. (Artur Lichtenberg); resources, A.L. (Artur Liebrecht), R.B., B.D., H.A., F.S., A.L. (Artur Lichtenberg) and A.L. (Artur Lichtenberg); data curation, V.H., S.K. (Steven Kessler), Z.B. and H.A.; writing—original draft preparation, S.M., S.K. (Sebastian Kalkhoff), S.K. (Steven Kessler), Z.B., A.L. (Artur Liebrecht), R.B. and B.D.; writing—review and editing, A.L. (Artur Liebrecht), R.B., B.D., A.L. (Artur Lichtenberg), H.A. and F.S.; visualization, S.K. (Steven Kessler) and Z.B.; supervision, S.M., S.K. (Sebastian Kalkhoff), A.L. (Artur Lichtenberg), H.A. and F.S.; project administration, A.L. (Artur Lichtenberg), H.A. and F.S.; funding acquisition, A.L. (Artur Lichtenberg), H.A. and F.S. All authors have read and agreed to the published version of the manuscript.

Funding: The authors disclose receipt of the following financial support for the research, authorship and/or publication of this article: This work was supported by the Federal Ministry of Education and Research of Germany (grant number 16SV8601).

Institutional Review Board Statement: The study was conducted according to the guidelines of the Declaration of Helsinki and approved by the Ethics Committee at the Faculty of Medicine of Heinrich Heine University Düsseldorf (Study No. 2021-1388, 5 May 2021).

Informed Consent Statement: Patient consent was waived due to the retrospective nature of the study.

Data Availability Statement: This study applied an open access dataset (MIMIC-III [18]), which is referenced accordingly, as well as an independent cohort from UKD that, according to German data protection policies, cannot be accessed from outside our facilities.

Conflicts of Interest: The authors declare no conflicts of interest.

Abbreviations

The following abbreviations are used in this manuscript:

UKD	University Hospital Düsseldorf
ICU	Intensive Care Unit
RNN	Recurrent Neural Network
LSTM	Long Short-Term Memory
ML	Machine Learning
AI	Artificial Intelligence
MIMIC	Medical Information Mart for Intensive Care
BRITS	Bidirectional Recurrent Imputation for Time Series
XAI	eXplainable AI

References

1. Rosenberg, A.L.; Charles, W. Patients Readmitted to ICUs: A Systematic Review of Risk Factors and Outcomes. *Chest* **2000**, *118*, 492–502. [CrossRef] [PubMed]
2. van Sluisveld, N.; Bakhshi-Raiez, F.; de Keizer, N.; Holman, R.; Wester, G.; Wollersheim, H.; van der Hoven, J.G.; Zegers, M. Variation in rates of ICU readmissions and post-ICU in-hospital mortality and their association with ICU discharge practices. *BMC Health Serv. Res.* **2017**, *17*, 281. [CrossRef] [PubMed]
3. Desautels, T.; Das, R.; Calvert, J.; Trivedi, M.; Summers, C.; Wales, D.J.; Ercole, A. Prediction of early unplanned intensive care unit readmission in a UK tertiary care hospital: A cross-sectional machine learning approach. *BMJ Open* **2017**, *7*, e017199. [CrossRef] [PubMed]
4. Lin, W.T.; Chen, W.L.; Chao, C.M.; Lai, C.C. The outcomes and prognostic factors of the patients with unplanned intensive care unit readmissions. *Medicine* **2018**, *97*, e11124. [CrossRef] [PubMed]
5. Azarfarin, R.; Ashouri, N.; Totonchi, Z.; Bakhshandeh, H.; Yaghoubi, A. Factors influencing prolonged ICU stay after open heart surgery. *Res. Cardiovasc. Med.* **2014**, *3*, e20159. [CrossRef] [PubMed]
6. Almashrafi, A.; Elmontsri, M.; Aylin, P. Systematic review of factors influencing length of stay in ICU after adult cardiac surgery. *BMC Health Serv. Res.* **2016**, *16*, 318. [CrossRef] [PubMed]
7. Andrearczyk, V.; Fontaine, P.; Oreiller, V.; Castelli, J.; Jreige, M.; Prior, J.O.; Depeursinge, A.: Multi-task Deep Segmentation and Radiomics for Automatic Prognosis in Head and Neck Cancer. In *Predictive Intelligence in Medicine. PRIME 2021. Lecture Notes in Computer Science*; Rekik, I., Adeli, E., Park, S.H., Schnabel, J., Eds.; Springer: Cham, Switzerland, 2021. [CrossRef]

8. Moazemi, S.; Essler, M.; Schultz, T.; Bundschuh, R.A. Predicting Treatment Response in Prostate Cancer Patients Based on Multimodal PET/CT for Clinical Decision Support. In *Multimodal Learning for Clinical Decision Support. ML-CDS 2021. Lecture Notes in Computer Science*; Springer: Cham, Switzerland, 2021. [CrossRef]
9. Khatami, M.; Wehler, R.; Schultz, T. Parcellation-Free prediction of task fMRI activations from dMRI tractography. *Med. Image Anal.* **2022**, *76*, 102317. [CrossRef] [PubMed]
10. Khan, A.R.; Wang, L.; Beg, M.F. FreeSurfer-Initiated Fully-Automated Subcortical Brain Segmentation in MRI Using Large Deformation Diffeomorphic Metric Mapping. *NeuroImage* **2008**, *41*, 735–746. [CrossRef] [PubMed]
11. Hsu, G.C. *Using Time-Series and Forecasting to Manage Type 2 Diabetes Conditions (GH-Method: Math-Physical Medicine)*; Universdad de Granada: Granada, Spain, 2019.
12. Spiga, R.; Batton-Hubert, M.; Sarazin, M. Predicting hospital admissions with integer-valued time series. In *ITISE 2019. Proceedings of Papers*; ITISE: Grenade, Spain, 2019. pp. 897–998.
13. Šimpach, O.; Dotlačilová, P. Age-Specific Death Rates Smoothed by the Gompertz–Makeham Function and Their Application in Projections by Lee–Carter Model. In *Time Series Analysis and Forecasting. Contributions to Statistics*; Rojas, I., Pomares, H., Eds.; Springer: Cham, Switzerland, 2016. [CrossRef]
14. Lin, Y.W.; Zhou, Y.; Faghri, F.; Shaw, M.J.; Campbell, R.H. Analysis and prediction of unplanned intensive care unit readmission using recurrent neural networks with long short-term memory. *PLoS ONE* **2019**, *14*, e0218942. [CrossRef] [PubMed]
15. Huang, Y.; Talwar, A.; Chatterjee, S.; Rajender, R.A. Application of machine learning in predicting hospital readmissions: A scoping review of the literature. *BMC Med. Res. Methodol.* **2021**, *21*, 96. [CrossRef] [PubMed]
16. Ashfaq, A.; Sant'Anna, A.; Lingman, M.; Nowaczyk, S. Readmission prediction using deep learning on electronic health records. *J. Biomed. Inform.* **2019**, *97*, 103256. [CrossRef] [PubMed]
17. Kessler, S.; Schroeder, D.; Korlakov, S.; Hettlich, V.; Lichtenberg, A.; Schmid, F.; Aubin, H. Predicting readmission to the cardiovascular ICU using recurrent neural networks. *J. Digital. Health* 2022, *manucript in final decision*.
18. Johnson, A.; Pollard, T.; Shen, L.; Lehman, L.H.; Feng, M.; Ghassemi, M.; Moody, B.; Szolovits, P.; Celi, L.A.; Mark, R.G. MIMIC-III, a freely accessible critical care database. *Sci. Data* **2016**, *3*, 160035. [CrossRef] [PubMed]
19. Paszke, A.; Gross, S.; Massa, F.; Lerer, A.; Bradbury, J.; Chanan, G.; Killeen, T.; Lin, Z.; Gimelsshein, N.; Antiga, L.; et al. PyTorch: An Imperative Style, High-Performance Deep Learning Library. In Proceedings of the 33rd Conference on Neural Information Processing Systems (NeurIPS 2019), Vancouver, Canada, 8–14 December 2019; pp. 8024–8035.
20. Bauder, R.A.; Khoshgoftaar, T.M.; Hasanin, T. An Empirical Study on Class Rarity in Big Data. In Proceedings of the 2018 17th IEEE International Conference on Machine Learning and Applications (ICMLA), Orlando, FL, USA, 17–20 December 2018; pp. 785–790. [CrossRef]
21. Brown, S.E.; Ratcliffe, S.J.; Halpern, S.D. An empirical derivation of the optimal time interval for defining ICU readmissions. *Med. Care* **2013**, *51*, 706–714. [CrossRef] [PubMed]
22. Gudivada, V.; Apon, A.; Ding, J. Data Quality Considerations for Big Data and Machine Learning: Going Beyond Data Cleaning and Transformations. *Int. J. Adv. Softw.* **2017**, *10*, 1–20.
23. Cao, W.; Wang, D.; Li, J.; Zhou, H.; Li, L.; Li, Y. BRITS: Bidirectional Recurrent Imputation for Time Series. *Adv. Neural Inf. Process. Syst.* **2018**, *31*, 6775–6785.
24. Quiñonero-Candela, J.; Sugiyama, M.; Schwaighofer, A.; Lawrence, N.D.; Jordan, M.I.; Dietterich, T.G. *Dataset Shift in Machine Learning*; MIT Press: Cambridge, MA, USA, 2008; ISBN 978-0-262-17005-5.

engineering
proceedings

MDPI

Proceeding Paper

K-Means Clustering Assisted Spectrum Utilization Prediction with Deep Learning Models [†]

Bethelhem S. Shawel [1,2,*] , Frehiwot Bantigegn [3], Tsegamlak T. Debella [1,4] and Sofie Pollin [2] and Dereje H. Woldegebreal [1]

1   School of Electrical and Computer Engineering, Addis Ababa Institute of Technology, Addis Ababa University, Addis Ababa P.O. Box 1176, Ethiopia; tsegamlak.terefe@aait.edu.et (T.T.D.); dereje.hailemariam@aait.edu.et (D.H.W.)
2   Department of Electrical Engineering, KU Leuven, 3001 Leuven, Belgium; sofie.pollin@esat.kuleuven.be
3   Ethio Telecom, Addis Ababa P.O. Box 1047, Ethiopia; frehiwot.bantigegn@ethiotelecom.et
4   ENSISA, Institute for Research in Informatics, Mathematics, Automation and Signal, Université de Haute Alsace, 68093 Mulhouse, France
*   Correspondence: bethelhem.seifu@aait.edu.et
†   Presented at the 8th International Conference on Time Series and Forecasting, Gran Canaria, Spain, 27–30 June 2022.

Abstract: The radio spectrum is a finite and scarce resource needed to transport data generated by existing and emerging wireless mobile networks and services. As the demand for wireless services is increasing, operators look for ways to efficiently utilize their assigned spectrum. While operators do regularly perform spectrum occupancy measurement using an external spectrum analyzer or installing a dedicated sensing network to understand and plan the spectrum utilization level, both in time and spatial dimensions, such a measurement-based approach is expensive, given the dynamic and wide area covered by spectrum utilization. This paper proposes an indirect approach to assess and predict the average spectrum utilization level using data traffic measured from base stations of an operator network. K-Means clustering and deep learning algorithms, namely Convolution Neural Network (CNN) and Long Short Term Memory (LSTM), are used to model and analyze the current and future spectrum utilization in the 900 MHz frequency range. Data collected from 639 base stations of a mobile operator are used to build the spectrum utilization model. The results show that the CNN model trained on clustered data outperforms the model developed on non-clustered data (with a Root Mean Square Error (RMSE) of 0.58), mainly for base station level prediction. In terms of utilization level, the results also show that the operator does not optimally utilize the 900 MHz range.

Keywords: spectrum; utilization; prediction; time-series; clustering; K-Means; LSTM; CNN

check for updates

Citation: Shawel, B.S.; Bantigegn, F.; Debella, T.T.; Pollin, S.; Woldegebreal, D.H. K-Means Clustering Assisted Spectrum Utilization Prediction with Deep Learning Models. *Eng. Proc.* 2022, 18, 2. https://doi.org/10.3390/engproc2022018002

Academic Editors: Ignacio Rojas, Hector Pomares, Olga Valenzuela, Fernando Rojas and Luis Javier Herrera

Published: 17 June 2022

Publisher's Note: MDPI stays neutral with regard to jurisdictional claims in published maps and institutional affiliations.

1. Introduction

Over the last three decades, cellular data traffic has exploded due to the proliferation of attractive telecom services with requirements ranging from high throughput to guaranteed low latency and low error rate. To respond to the demand, mobile network operators (MNOs) continuously upgrade their networks, e.g., by deploying advanced network technologies such as Advanced Fourth Generation Long Term Evolution (LTE+) and Fifth Generation (5G) broadband cellular mobile networks. These networks are designed to efficiently utilize the available spectrum and operate in the previously unutilized spectrum in the GHz range.

As the radio spectrum is one of the key and finite resources to transport the growing traffic, there is an ever-increasing demand for it. Due to its favorable propagation condition in providing high coverage and capacity, some bands (mostly sub-6 GHz) are being intensively utilized at different times of the day and space (e.g., location and service area), creating some sort of "scarcity", in contrast with other bands [1]. In most cases, the non-uniformity of users' spatial distribution and usage patterns within various geographical areas and times limits the full utilization of the available radio spectrum assigned for MNOs [2]. In order to increase the efficient use of spectrum bands, MNOs consider different spectrum harvesting approaches, such as intra or inter-operator spectrum sharing or spectrum refarming that rely on detailed knowledge about the spectrum usage in time and space.

From the MNO's perspective, optimizing the spectrum usage focuses not only on maintaining the quality of service but also on ensuring that the allocated spectral resources can support the demands of subscribers. Thus, operators are expected to understand the dynamics of their spectral resource utilization by continuously monitoring the use in terms of space, time, and the number of channels (in a channelized band) that all users in a certain territory may access. While conducting continuous spectrum measurement by dedicating sensing networks is the most accurate approach to attaining such knowledge, it is costly and resource intensive, given cellular traffic's rising demand and dynamic nature. Rather, an alternative approach is to exploit the correlation between spectrum use and transported data/voice traffic information, which is already available in the operator's network, to understand, estimate, and predict the spectrum utilization.

From these aspects, several literature analyzed efficient spectrum/channel use in spectral and temporal dimensions. Motivated by the lack of knowledge regarding spectrum occupancy in South Africa, the authors of [3] measured the spectrum occupancy for Global System for Mobile Communications (GSM) 900 and 1800 MHz bands. The results indicate a maximum occupancy of 20% for UHF bands and different maximum utilization during peak hours for the GSM 900 (92%) and 1800 (40%) MHz. Similarly, spectrum utilization in Malaysia's TV and cellular bands was carried out in [3] showing the maximum utilization of 35%, 10%, and 26% in GSM900, GSM1800, and 3G bands, respectively, and 11% and 13% utilization for TV broadcasting in VHF and UHF bands.

The practical prowess of time series modeling methodologies are considered for predicting spectrum occupancy in different bands and applications. In this regard, ref. [4] applied Autoregressive Integrated Moving Average (ARIMA) models, Lagrangian Support Vector Machine, and an Elman network (simplified models of Recurrent Neural Networks (RNNs)) are used to predict spectrum occupancy in a TV and cellular bands. The results show that the RNN technique outperforms the other models in prediction accuracy for cellular networks, as it better captures the non-stationarity and several irregularities in the data traffic. In contrast, the ARIMA model works efficiently in the TV band, since the traffic pattern is stationary. A similar analysis is presented in [5] for GSM channel utilization modeling and prediction with Seasonal ARIMA (SARIMA).

On the other hand, traffic volume and resource utilization mapping is presented in [1,6]. Traffic-related measurements such as call success rate, call drop rate, and antenna properties, including antenna height, transmit power, used/unused time, and frequency bandwidth, are used in [6] to indirectly map system/network parameters into spectrum utilization efficiency. Under a multi-MNOs environment, the analysis results showed a heavy under-utilization of the spectrum. In [1], upper limits on the traffic volume and the spectrum resource usage is evaluated for a single LTE cell to ensure seamless video streaming in dense urban environments.

While these papers indicated: (1) the need for analyzing spectrum usage directly from measurement or indirectly from voice/data traffic volume; and (2) the need for prediction or classification models that are capable of understanding random spectrum usage, there is still a limitation of capturing the spatial correlation within various geographical regions.

With the limitations in mind, the main objective of this paper is to develop a machine-learning-based model that captures the spatio-temporal variation of spectrum utilization. The model helps to understand (in an average sense) how the operator utilizes the different spectrum bands allocated to it. For that, 100 days of voice traffic channel data (hourly based frequency utilization per cell in percentage) are collected from 639 base stations operating at the 900 MHz frequency range. Based on the data, the approaches followed in this work are as follows:

1. Map channel utilization measurements into spectrum utilization using an industry practiced utilization formula. Erlang B is used to validate the formula and the mapping in both cases is found to be similar;
2. Temporal clustering with K-mean is applied to classify the spectrum utilization of the 639 base stations. The clustering has two-fold advantages, first to understand the spectrum utilization in decision making, such as load optimization [7] and second, to improve prediction accuracy [8];
3. RNN (specifically, Long Short Term Memory (LSTM)) and Convolutional Neural Network (CNN) are applied to predict future utilization on a per cluster level;

The indirect spectrum usage assessment is of low cost and requires fewer resources, as it uses the operator's already monitored/available data. With knowledge of the average spectrum utilization, operators may follow multiple approaches, such as going for a new frequency band in the case of "full utilization"; reframing frequency, half rate configuration implementation, and spectral efficient technologies to improve the utilization in case of moderate/medium utilization; or in the case of low utilization even allowing other users to utilize its frequency in the context of cognitive radios or spectrum sharing with other operators [9]. To the best of our knowledge, no prior work has investigated spectrum utilization based on the operator's data. Even though our analysis considers voice traffic at 900 MHz of the spectrum channel, it can easily be extended to different spectrum bands and data traffic volume inputs with appropriate traffic-spectrum utilization mapping and more complex learning architecture.

The remainder of the paper is organized as follows. The spectrum utilization concept and its traffic mapping are discussed in Section 2. We present the clustering and prediction approaches used in Section 3, followed by the results and discussion in Section 4. Finally, we conclude the work in Section 5.

2. Spectrum Utilization Analysis

2.1. Spectrum Bands in Cellular Mobile Networks

Radio spectrum is divided into frequency/spectrum bands, e.g., in mobile systems 800 MHz, 900 MHz, 1800 MHz, 2100 MHz, and 2600 MHz bands are allocated for various generations of mobile systems [9]. Each band has different propagation characteristics and bandwidth that, in turn, determine mobile network coverage and capacity [2]. Operators further divide the frequency bands into channels (also called carriers) and are used to transport traffic and control information. As an example in GSM systems operating in the 900 MHz band, the band is further divided into 124 duplex channels (or carriers) of 200 kHz bandwidth.

By systematically spacing base stations in a geographic area, each base station is configured to operate on a certain group/cluster of channels. The configured channels are reused by other base stations as many times as the resulting co-channel interference is within the service requirement [10]. In mobile systems, channels are classified as a physical channel and a logical channel. The physical channel corresponds to one timeslot on one carrier/channel, while the logical channel reflects the specific type of information carried by the physical channel, which could be either a traffic channel or a control channel. A traffic channel in GSM is abbreviated by TCH and is used for either voice or data service. For voice service, each timeslot can carry a full rate TCH of 9600 bit/s, two half-rate TCHs of each 4800 bit/s rates, or one of the control channels.

2.2. Traffic Engineering

As previously stated, the main intention of this work is to use data available in operators' performance report systems (PRS) to estimate current and future channel utilization. When viewed per base station level where measurement is available, channel utilization level, among others, depends on the number of configured channels per base station; the specific geographic area; time of a day; users' behaviors; service delivered; generation of the cellular network; rate, i.e., full- or half rate, supported; and multiplexing scheme used.

Cognizant of these facts, as well as taking the availability of operator's data and operator's understanding, the utilization study is a 2G network providing voice service. The approach is, however, generalizable to other advanced networks and it is one area in which we are working to publish the results in the future. Moreover, from the operator's PRS, one can collect the aggregate offered traffic, measured in Erlang, for the configured channels per base station on an hourly basis and for both full-rate, T_{v_F}, and half-rate, T_{v_H}, TCH channels. For this paper, data available per base station are TCH traffic both for half and full rate, configured channels per base station, and each site's longitude and latitude to analyze the spatial behavior of its utilization. Six hundred and thirty-nine sites (base stations) are used and one-month data with a granularity of 1 hour is collected.

Traffic engineering is then used to map the utilized channels, which in turn will be compared with the configured channels to compute the percentage utilization. Channel utilization, C_U, is defined as:

$$C_U = \frac{T_{v_F}}{C_c \times \left(1 + \frac{T_{v_H}}{T_{v_F}}\right)} \times 100 \qquad (1)$$

The operator understudy designed its voice service assuming Erlang B service with a grade of service of 98% network availability [9]. Figure 1 shows the calculated spectrum/channel utilization, based on Equation (1), for a particular base station.

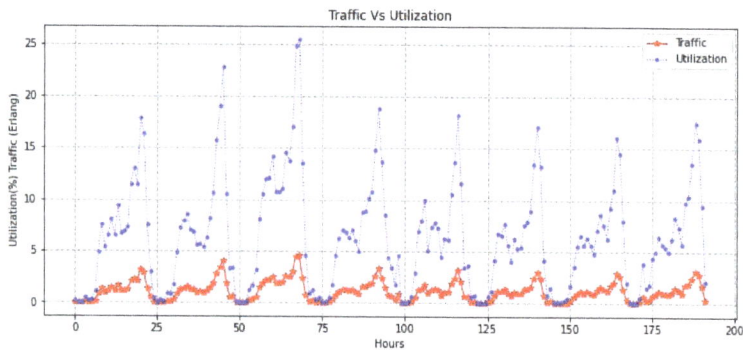

Figure 1. Spectrum/channel utilization.

3. Methodology

As the spectrum utilization data are evaluated from the cellular traffic observed in a timely basis, it is modeled as a non-linear and non-stationarity time series. In order to capture the commonality in users' behaviors and distribution at different times and locations, a cluster-level approach is considered when predicting the utilization. The prediction model is developed using LSTM and CNN for clustered and non-clustered data.

3.1. Utilization Clustering with K-Means

As one of the most popular unsupervised clustering algorithms due to its simplicity and linear complexity, K-Means is widely used in many application areas such as computer vision, image processing, and business analytics [9]. The goal of the algorithm is to group the unlabeled multidimensional data into K clusters by assigning each data point to one unique cluster based on the provided features. With the objective of maximizing intra-cluster similarities and minimizing the inter-cluster similarities in the spectrum usage, we used *Silhouette analysis* to find the optimum number of clusters.

The Silhouette index (SI) is used to distinguish the different unique patterns and measures the distance between the time series and the centroid of the cluster they belong to compared through comparison with other clusters. Base stations might have significant load variation, as shown in Figure 2, due to changes in work or rest time in commercial and residential regions, as well as variations in human behavior through time and in different locations, among other factors. Based on the district pattern on the spectrum utilization time series data, SI can be used to cluster the different spatially distributed base stations. The SI for the time series dataset, y, and k the number of clusters, is defined as [9]:

$$SI(C) = \frac{1}{N} \sum_{c_k \in C} \sum_{y_i \in c_k} \frac{b(c_k, y_i) - a(c_k, y_i)}{max(a(c_k, y_i), b(c_k, y_i))} \tag{2}$$

where $a(c_k, y_j) = \frac{1}{|c_k|} \sum_{y_j \in c_k} ||y_i - y_j||$, is the measure of similarity of the time series to its own cluster and $b(c_k, y_j) = \min_{\substack{c_m \neq c_k \\ c_m \in C}} \frac{1}{|c_k|} \sum_{y_j \in c_k} ||y_i - y_j||$, is the measure of dissimilarity from time series in other clusters.

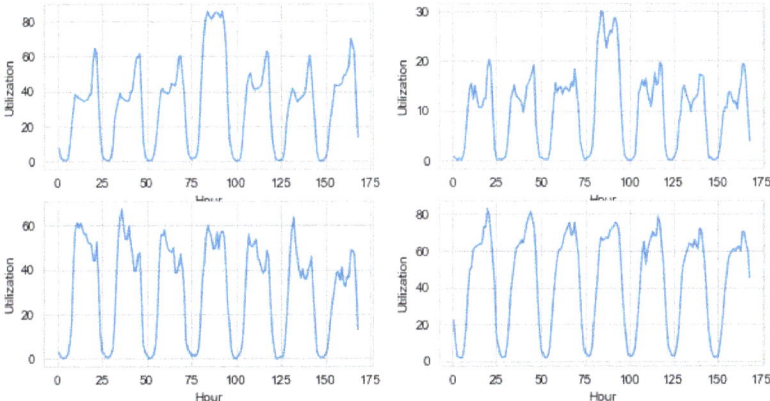

Figure 2. Different channel utilization observed at four base stations.

3.2. Spectrum Utilization Prediction Approach with Deep Learning

The remarkable achievement of deep learning prediction in relation to wireless network problems, including its capability to capture complex nature and its processing of time series information, was achieved with a "time-aware" architecture. Without explicitly decomposing the different time series characteristics of spectrum utilization, deep learning will model/learn its dynamic temporal behavior. We consider the two widely used deep learning networks, CNN and LSTM, for the spectrum utilization problem.

3.2.1. Spectrum Utilization Modeling Using CNN

CNN is a type of deep neural network initially designed for image processing problems, but now it is applied to data that can be represented in a grid-like matrix form. In CNN, time-series and textual data can be represented by a 1D vector and a 2D matrix can be used to represent the pixels in the image data [11]. Unlike image processing, the CNN-based time series analysis/prediction requires extracting information along the time dimension, hence the reason we use the stack 1D CNN model.

To achieve the purpose of extracting features, two layers of a 1D-convolution layer are used. Max pooling layer follows each convolution layer to shirk the input resolution and assist the convolution layer to extract abundant temporal correlated features under the various input resolutions. In addition, a flattening layer for data reshaping and two dense layers are used sequentially to get the required output shape.

3.2.2. Spectrum Utilization Modeling Using LSTM

LSTM network is an advanced recurrent neural network (RNN) and is designed to learn order dependence in sequence prediction. The LSTM contains three parts, namely the Forget gate, f_t, Input gate, i_t, Output gate, O_t, and memory cell, C_t, where each part performs a separate function. The forget gate chooses whether the information coming from the previous timestamp is to be remembered or is irrelevant and can be forgotten. The input gate is used to quantify the importance of the new information carried by the input. While in the output gate, the cell passes the updated information from the current timestamp to the next timestamp. Even with its computational complexity for retaining memory, it is easy to model complex non-linear feature interactions using the LSTM [12].

$$f_t = \sigma(X_t \times U_f + H_{t-1} \times W_f) \tag{3}$$

$$i_t = \sigma(X_t \times U_i + H_{t-1} \times W_i) \tag{4}$$

$$C_t = f_t \odot C_{t-1} + i_t \odot tanh(x_t \times U_c + H_{t-1} \times W_c) \tag{5}$$

$$O_t = \sigma(X_t \times U_o + H_{t-1} \times W_o) \tag{6}$$

$$H_t = O_t \odot tanh(C_t) \tag{7}$$

For our real-valued prediction problem, three layers of LSTM networks are used with ReLU, $\sigma(.) = R(z) = max(0, z)$, as an activation function.

4. Results and Discussion

4.1. Experimental Settings

4.1.1. Data Preprocessing

We considered a dataset from an operator measuring the spectrum utilization of GSM 900 in Ethiopia. The data were collected for 100 days, from 1 January to 10 April 2021, with a granularity of 1 h for 639 base stations. Additionally, each site's longitude and latitude information was taken to analyze the spatial behavior of its utilization. The operator has 61 and 85 channels configured to handle GSM service at 900 Mhz and 1800 Mhz, respectively (Tabel 1). The maximum cell capacity for GSM900 is 8TRX per cell and 12 TRX for DCS 1800 [9].

Table 1. GSM channel configuration.

Network Type	Channel Type	Frequency Number
GSM 900	BCCH	14
	TCH	47
	Guard band	1
GSM 1800	BCCH	24
	TCH	61
	Guard band	1

Data preprocessing techniques, such as handling missing values, standardization, and outlier handling, are applied to the collected dataset. With that, five base stations with a continuous missing value are excluded; the data set is divided into 80% of training data, 10% of validation data, and 10% of test data.

4.1.2. Hyperparameter Tuning

Hyperparameter tuning refers to finding the best parameters to get the best results from models. Hyperparameters are set before training a machine learning model. These hyperparameters need to be optimized to adapt the model to a dataset [6].

When building the LSTM model, how many hidden layers the model will include, the number of LSTM cells that should be used in each layer, and what the dropout should be must be considered, in addition to other parameters. Similarly, the CNN model is defined with various hyperparameters such as kernel size, filter size, hidden layer, optimizer activation function, and Epoch. A grid search algorithm was used for selecting these appropriate combinations of hyperparameters listed in Table 2 as it is critical for building a model with better accuracy.

Table 2. Hyperparameters used in LSTM And CNN Models.

Hyperparameters	Value	
	CNN	LSTM
Hidden Layer	2	3
Number of Filters	(64), (32)	-
Kernel Size	(3), (3)	-
Hidden layer Neurons	-	(48), (32), (32)
Batch Size	64	128
Dropout	0.2%	0.2%
Maxpooling-1D	2	-
Dense layer	(50),(24)	-
Optimizer	Adam	Adam
Activation Function	ReLU	ReLU
Epoch	2000	100

4.1.3. Evaluation Metrics

The Model evaluation aims to estimate the generalization accuracy of a model on future or test data. We jointly used two evaluation metrics to quantify our model performance: Mean Absolute Error (MAE) and Root Mean Squared Error (RMSE).

$$MAE = \frac{1}{N} \sum_{i=1}^{N} |y_i - \hat{y}_i| \tag{8}$$

$$RMSE = \sqrt{\frac{1}{N} \sum_{i=1}^{N} (y_i - \hat{y}_i)^2)} \tag{9}$$

where N is the size of the evaluated set and $\hat{y}_i$ is the predicted utilization for y_i.

4.2. Model Performances

4.2.1. Clustering with K-Means

As the utilization of the spectrum resource at a particular base station relates to the number of channels allocated and the aggregated traffic requested from the users, its temporal pattern resembles, to certain extent, the users' behavior.

In the K-Means analysis, the closeness of the utilization pattern of a particular base station to the mean traffic pattern of a cluster is evaluated for cluster membership. Using preprocessed data, the K-Means algorithm clusters the data into an optimal cluster size of five based on the minimum SI score. Figure 3 illustrates the utilizations pattern and the spatial distribution of the corresponding base stations. The plots illustrate a distinct variation in utilization pattern due to factors such as user behavior (the high call rate during working hours indicated by the high picks) and a higher number of channel allocations (reflected in 3rd cluster,from left to right). Aside from being an input for better spectrum utilization through dynamic spectrum allocation, the clustering based approach averaged out the different patterns observed at a base station level to four, simplifying network-level predictions.

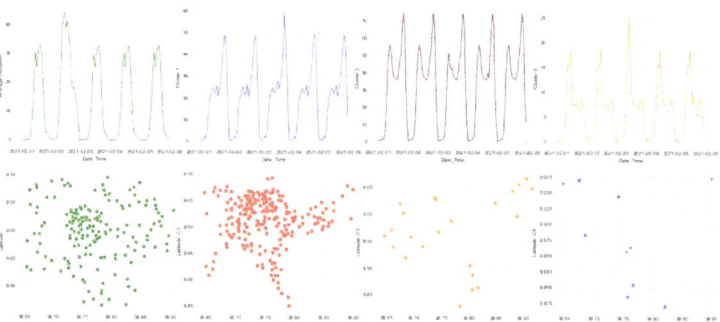

Figure 3. The four clustered base stations based on their average spectrum utilization patterns. The top-row plots representing the average utilization pattern of each cluster in five days duration, and the bottom-row plots represents the spatially distributed base stations of each cluster.

4.2.2. Prediction Performance

The prediction for spectrum utilization at a cluster level and base station level was made considering the two models: LSTM and CNN. Figure 4 and Table 3 present results for cluster-level prediction that showed close performance between the LSTM and CNN models in capturing characteristics of the GSM 900 spectrum usage. Similarly, results for 24 h base station level prediction are shown in Table 4 and Figure 5.

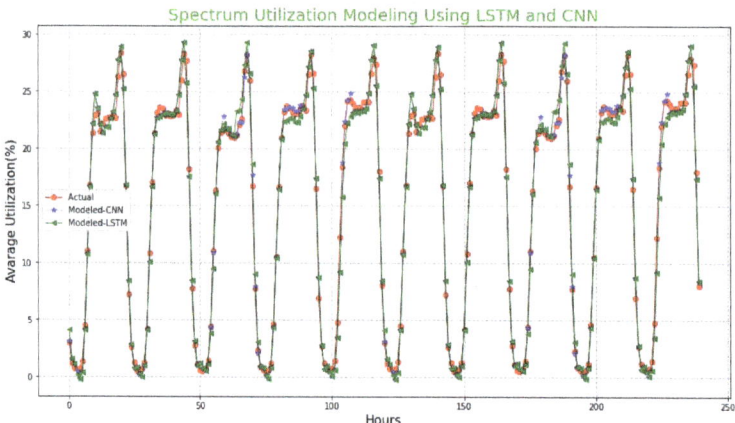

Figure 4. Actual vs. predicted plot for CNN and LSTM.

Table 3. Cluster level prediction performance.

	Clustered		Non-Clustered	
	RMSE	**MAE**	**RMSE**	**MAE**
LSTM	0.8	0.845	1.197	1.057
CNN	0.585	0.26	0.767	0.521

Table 4. Performance evaluation results for base station level prediction.

	RMSE	MAE	MAPE	MSE
LSTM-Prediction	13.34	010.325	7.684	1.434
LSTM-Prediction Clustered	2.4492	2.092	6.872	0.641
CNN-Prediction	7.114	5.058	4.433	0.589
CNN-Prediction Clustered	1.04	0.76	2.3821	0.201

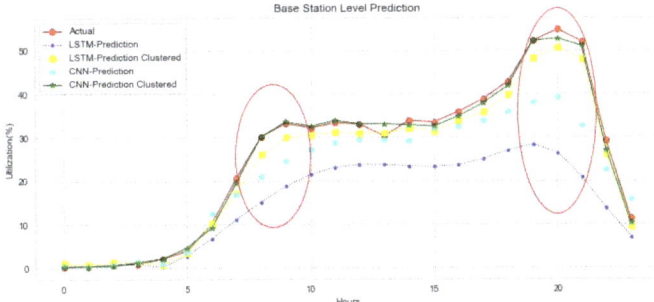

Figure 5. Base station level prediction with both LSTM and CNN.

As noted, the prediction error produced by our LSTM model is much greater than the CNN (RMSE of 0.58) in both cluster and base station levels, showing its limitation was an inability to sufficiently learn the patterns (i.e., trend, seasonalities, and non-linearities) inherent in the data.

Compared to the error generated by the cluster level prediction (RMSE of 1.04), the base station level approaches in both models perform poorly. Especially during high utilization, the prediction error is very significant, which will create network condition and QoS degradation in case of prediction-based network resource allocation and optimization.

5. Conclusions

In wireless network planning and optimization, data-prediction-assisted analysis provides the opportunity for operators to determine the extent to which the resources are utilized and quality of service is attained. As spectrum is the scare resource in wireless communication, it is important for MNOs to understand how the spectrum is utilized over time and space.

In our paper, spectrum utilization data are modeled as time series data during model development, and various strategies for enhancing the model's performance are employed to obtain a better model with the least amount of error. Since the utilization data in practice are not typically measured, we exploit the traffic utilization relation. A cluster-level approach is considered with the help of K-Means to provide network-level spectrum utilization prediction CNN and LSTM algorithms. Based on the temporal pattern, the GSM 900 band utilization is clustered into four. To compare and evaluate the prediction accuracy, four different metrics are used. As shown, the model developed for the cluster data using the CNN outperforms the LSTM algorithm with an RMSE value of 0.58. Similarly, for base-station-level prediction, CNN is found to be the best predicting model with an RMSE value of 1.04.

We hope the presented results provide a new insight for MNOs to understand the utilization level of the spectrum allocated to them that can also be extended to 3G and beyond networks. Moreover, the presented approach is on a per-cluster level, which spans a wider geographic area. How to obtain base-station-level knowledge and for a large number of base stations is another area to explore in future work.

Author Contributions: Conceptualization, B.S.S., F.B. and D.H.W.; methodology, B.S.S., F.B. and D.H.W.; software, B.S.S., F.B. and T.T.D.; validation, B.S.S. and T.T.D.; formal analysis, B.S.S., F.B. and D.H.W.; investigation, B.S.S., F.B. and D.H.W.; resources, F.B. and D.H.W.; data curation, F.B; writing—original draft preparation, B.S.S. and F.B.; writing—review and editing, B.S.S. and D.H.W.; visualization, F.B.; supervision, D.H.W. and S.P. All authors have read and agreed to the published version of the manuscript.

Funding: This research received no external funding.

Data Availability Statement: Restrictions apply to the availability of these data. Data was obtained from Ethio Telecom and are available from the corresponding author with the permission of Ethio Telecom.

Conflicts of Interest: The authors declare no conflict of interest.

References

1. ITU-R. *Spectrum Occupancy Measurements and Evaluation*; Report SM.2256-1; ITU: Geneva, Switzerland, 2016.
2. Dalela, P.K.; Nayak, A.; Tyagi, V.; Sridhara, K. Analysis of spectrum utilization for existing cellular technologies in context to cognitive radio. In Proceedings of the 2011 2nd International Conference on Computer and Communication Technology (ICCCT-2011), Allahabad, India, 15–17 September 2011; pp. 585–588.
3. Barnes, S.D.; Jansen Van Vuuren, P.A.; Maharaj, B.T. Spectrum occupancy Investigation: Measurements in South Africa. *J. Int. Meas. Confed.* **2013**, *46*, 3098–3112. [CrossRef]
4. Agarwal, A.; Sengar, S.; Gangopadhyay, R. Spectrum Occupancy Prediction for Realistic Traffic Scenarios: Time Series versus Learning-Based Models. *J. Commun. Inf. Netw.* **2018**, *3*, 44–51. [CrossRef]
5. Luis, P.; César, H.; Enrique, R.-C. Modeling of GSM Spectrum Based on Seasonal ARIMA model. In Proceedings of the 6th IEEE Latin-American Conference on Communications, Cartagena, Colombia, 5–7 November 2014.
6. Jordan, J. Hyperparameter Tuning for Machine Learning Models. 2017. Available online: https://www.jeremyjordan.me/hyperparameter-tuning/ (accessed on 23 January 2021).
7. Saitwal, M.S. Dynamic Spectrum Sharing between Mobile Network Operators in GSM. Ph.D. Thesis, Indian Institute of Technology Hyderabad, Telangana, India, 2015.
8. Musey, J.A.; Barlow Keener, E. *The Spectrum Handbook*; Summit Ridge Group, LLC: New York, NY, USA, 2018.
9. Bantigegn, F. Hybrid Clustering and Deep Learning-Based Spatio-Temporal Analysis of Spectrum Usage. Master's Thesis, Addis Ababa University, Addis Ababa, Ethiopia, 2021.
10. Marsa-Maestre, I.; Ito, T.; Pollin, S.; Chiumento, A.; Gimenez-Guzman, J.M. Efficient spectrum usage for wireless communication. *Wirel. Commun. Mob. Comput.* **2019**, 8719849. [CrossRef]
11. Maya, M. Convolutional neural networks for forex time series forecasting. In *AIP Conference Proceedings*; AIP Publishing LLC: Melville, NY, USA, 2021; Volume 2459, p. 030024.
12. Staudemeyer, R.C.; Morris, E.R. Understanding LSTM: A tutorial into Long Short-Term Memory Recurrent Neural Networks. *arXiv* **2019**, arXiv:1909.09586.

Proceeding Paper

Alone We Can Do So Little; Together We Cannot Be Detected †

Sergej Korlakov [1,*,‡] , Gerhard Klassen [1,*,‡] , Marcus Bravidor [2] and Stefan Conrad [1]

1   Department of Computer Science, Heinrich Heine University, Universitätsstr. 1, 40225 Düsseldorf, Germany; stefan.conrad@hhu.de
2   Department of Financial Accounting & Auditing, Albert Ludwigs University Freiburg, Rempartstraße 10–16, 79098 Freiburg, Germany; marcus.bravidor@accounting.uni-freiburg.de
*   Correspondence: korlakov@hhu.de (S.K.); klassen@hhu.de (G.K.)
†   Presented at the 8th International Conference on Time Series and Forecasting, Gran Canaria, Spain, 27–30 June 2022.
‡   These authors contributed equally to this work.

Abstract: It is no longer possible to imagine our everyday life without time series data. This includes, for example, market developments, COVID-19 cases, electricity prices, and other data from a wide variety of domains. An important task in the analysis of these data is the detection of anomalies. In most cases, this is accomplished by examining individual time series. In our work, we use the techniques of cluster analysis to establish a relationship between time series and groups of time series. This relationship allows us to observe the development of time series in their entirety, thereby gaining additional insights. Our approach identifies outliers with a real-world reference and enables the user to locate outliers without prior knowledge. To underline the strengths of our approach, we compare our method with another known method on two real-world datasets. We found that our solution needs significantly fewer calculations, produces more reasonable results, and can be applied to real-time data. Moreover, our method detected additional outliers, whose occurrence could be explained by real events.

Keywords: outlier detection; outlier detection in time series; time series analysis; time series clustering; time series cluster evaluation

Citation: Korlakov, S.; Klassen, G.; Bravidor, M.; Conrad, S. Alone We Can Do So Little; Together We Cannot Be Detected. *Eng. Proc.* **2022**, *18*, 3. https://doi.org/10.3390/engproc2022018003

Academic Editors: Ignacio Rojas, Hector Pomares, Olga Valenzuela, Fernando Rojas and Luis Javier Herrera

Published: 17 June 2022

Publisher's Note: MDPI stays neutral with regard to jurisdictional claims in published maps and institutional affiliations.

1. Introduction

Outlier or anomaly detection in time series is the problem of identifying rare or deviating observations in (univariate or multivariate) time series. Those observations may occur once or form a sequence when arising multiple times in a row. Finding anomalies in time series can be beneficial in a variety of applications, such as fraud detection in stock markets [1,2], anomaly detection in network data [3,4], and the detection of unusual time series in medical data [5,6]. The sheer number of possible applications of anomaly detection in time series makes it important for industry; therefore, it has been implemented in a number of business applications released by Google (https://cloud.google.com/blog/products/data-analytics/ (accessed on 10 April 2022)), RapidMiner (https://rapidminer.com/glossary/anomaly-detection/ (accessed on 10 April 2022)), Microsoft, and IBM [7,8]. The broad diversity of applications and products indicates a variation in the underlying data, which requires specific solutions in order to detect meaningful anomalies. Furthermore, outliers may also be defined differently, depending on the context at hand.

Most approaches focus on the detection of anomalous observations or subsequences in a single time series. This is useful for many applications but does not include a comparison to other time series from the same domain. However, assuming that time series from the same context are influenced by similar framework conditions, such a comparison becomes necessary. The idea of outlier detection by comparing time series is part of recent research and often applies Dynamic Time Warping (DTW) techniques [9,10] or the Granger Causality [11,12]. Although, these approaches are able to identify anomalous data points or even subsequences, they are limited to the comparison of only two time series at a time. The comparison of one time series to a group of other time series at the same time is, therefore, the next logical step; however, it also requires techniques to localize corresponding groups. The latter is well researched and is referred to as cluster analysis in time series.

In general, the goal of cluster analysis is to group objects with the objects in the same group being as similar as possible to each other and the objects from different groups being as dissimilar as possible. The similarity between two objects is usually expressed by a distance function (e.g., Euclidean distance). The number of existing clustering algorithms is very large; hence, which one should be used depends, among other things, on the given data and performance requirements. There are also different approaches for the clustering of time series. Examples of these are clustering using common methods with an explicit distance function for time series, clustering of multiple time series at each point in time, or using a clustering algorithm that was specifically developed for time series.

An example of a clustering algorithm developed for time series (based on K-means [13]) is the method of Chakrabarti et al. [14]. The authors claim that their algorithm can preserve a certain consistency of clusters in consecutive points in time. A recent study by Tatusch et al. [15], however, has shown, that the development of time-series adapted algorithms is not implicitly required to preserve this consistency. Instead, it is sufficient to find corresponding parameters for existing not-time-adjusted clustering algorithms. In a different work, the authors also demonstrate the use of this technique to find behavioral outliers in time series. Although the results are convincing, the given method is not applicable to streaming data because it is decidedly computationally intensive. Furthermore, the approach of Tatusch et al. [16] requires the user to set a threshold, which is based on the time-series over-time stability. However, the construct of this stability measure is not intuitive; therefore, it may be very difficult to find appropriate values for the threshold.

In this paper, we present an alternative approach based on a **c**luster **o**ver-time **s**tability **e**valuation measure called *CLOSE* [15] that is significantly less computationally expensive. Moreover, the results are based on a much more intuitive threshold that incorporates the cluster membership of time series. We compare the obtained results with those of Tatusch et al. [16].

In the remainder of this section, we provide the necessary notations and definitions (Section 1.1). In the next section, we first introduce a categorization of machine learning methods to time series analysis. Based on this categorization, we present the related work with the respective fundamental concepts and discuss the limitations in comparison to our solution. In Section 3, we describe our method mathematically with examples for every introduced definition. Then, we propose an optimization to reduce the number of computations required and, thus, to improve the performance of our method. In Section 4, we compare the results of our method with the results of Tatusch et al. [16], a solution with a similar key idea. To ensure a fair comparison, we use the same data set and hyperparameters as in [16]. Finally, we conclude and discuss possible future work in Section 5.

1.1. Notation and Definitions

Since we compared our procedure with that of Tatusch et al. [16], we adapted the definitions they provided.

Definition 1 (Time Series). *A time series $TS_x = x_1, \ldots, x_n$ is an ordered set of n real-valued data points of any dimension. The data points are ordered chronologically by time. The order is represented by the corresponding indices of the data points.*

Definition 2 (Subsequence). *A subsequence* $S_{x,[k,m]} = x_k, \dots, x_m$ *of a time series* TS_x *is an ordered subset of* $m - k$ *real-value data points of* TS_x *with* $k < m$ *and* $\forall x_l \in TS_x : k < l < m :$ $x_l \in S_{x,[k,m]}.$

Definition 3 (Data Set). *A data set* $D = \{TS_1, \dots, TS_m\}$ *is a set of m time series of the same length n and equivalent points in time.*

Definition 4 (Cluster). *A cluster* $C_{i,t}$ *at time t with* $i \in 1, \dots, p$ *being an unique identifier, is a set of similar data points, identified by a clustering algorithm. All clusters have distinct labels regardless of time.*

Definition 5 (Cluster Member). *A cluster* $C_{i,t}$ *at time t with* $i \in 1, \dots, p$ *being an unique identifier, is a set of similar data points identified by a clustering algorithm. All clusters have distinct labels regardless of time.*

2. Related Work

The different nature of data and approaches has led to a variety of diverse definitions of outliers; however, the general definition according to Douglas M. Hawkins is often used: "An observation which deviates so much from other observations as to arouse suspicions that it was generated by a different mechanism" [17]. The observations mentioned may have been made at one point in time or over a period of time and refer to univariate or multivariate time series. To capture the differences in both data and methods, Blázquez-García et al. [18] proposed a taxonomy that categorizes methods for anomaly detection in time series by three axes: input data (i.e., univariate, multivariate), outlier type (i.e., point, subsequence, time series) and nature of the method (i.e., univariate, multivariate). The latter describes whether a technique converts a multivariate time series into multiple univariate time series before further processing of the data. In the following, the described taxonomy is used to categorize the methods presented in the remainder of this section.

One method that can be categorized according to the described taxonomy under methods of univariate nature with the support of point and subsequence outliers was presented by Sun et al. [19]. The goal of the method is to detect anomalies in character sequences. Therefore, a probabilistic suffix tree is first constructed from character sequences, which is then used to estimate the probability of a point or subsequence being an anomaly. Due to the fact that the method takes univariate character sequences as input, a time series must first be converted into such a sequence, e.g., by SAX [20], in order to be processed in the following steps. In contrast, our proposed method can process time series without first having to convert them into a different (reduced) representation.

Alternatively, Munir et al. [21] introduced a method, that is multivariate in nature and can be applied equally to both types of time series. It consists of two modules: a CNN-based event predictor and a distance-function-based anomaly detector. As the name suggests, the event predictor predicts the next event based on all given time series, and the anomaly detector determines whether the deviation between the prediction and the occurred event is higher than a certain threshold. Thus, the outlier type handled by this method is a point in time. Compared to the supervised CNN-based event predictor, our proposed method is unsupervised, so that a training phase is not required. Moreover, the approach presented here has a white box character, which allows a more detailed analysis of outlier formation.

In contrast to the black box model of Munir et al. [21], Hyndman et al. [22] proposed a white box method exclusively for anomaly detection in multivariate time series. In their study, they extracted 18 features from each time series first. Then, principal components were determined from the data points of these features. Finally, a density based multidimensional anomaly detection algorithm [23] was applied to the first two principal components to detect anomalous time series. Although the method has a good performance and accuracy compared to other presented models, the approach contains a number of drawbacks. On one hand, the feature extraction from time series and the dimension reduction by PCA

(Principal Component Analysis) can lead to a loss of important information. On the other hand, principal components generally have a low interpretability. In this context, it can be difficult to determine the impact of features on the outlier detection. Since we consider the dimensions of the time series as a whole in our approach, there is no loss of information. In addition, based on cluster transitions and the reasons for those transitions, our method allows a detailed analysis of the occurrence of anomalous subsequences.

In response to the fact that several approaches (including those described here) focused on the deviation of one time series from the others, Tatusch et al. [16] presented a method for anomalous subsequence detection, which examines the behavior of a time series relative to their peers. For this, all time series are first clustered per timestamp; then, the transitions of time series between clusters are analyzed. If a time series or its subsequence frequently moves to different clusters compared to its peers from previous clusters, it will obtain a higher outlier score. According to this method, a time series or its subsequence is an outlier, if the outlier score exceeds a threshold, which must be specified by the user. In other words, if a time series changes its group often enough over time, it will be identified as an outlier.

As for any threshold that has to be set by a user, the approach of Tatusch et al. [16] raises the question of what value to set it to. Thus, the problem arises that the outlier score is not intuitive. While an outlier score of zero states that the corresponding time series is consistently in the same clusters with its peers over time, an outlier score from an interval $I = [0, 1]$ can be much more difficult to interpret. Further, under the assumption that all time series of a dataset D have the same length l, the proposed method requires K computations to find all anomalous subsequences in D, where K is defined as:

$$K = \frac{(l-1)^2 + (l-1)}{2} * |D|$$

Finally, Tatusch et al. [16] differentiate between two outlier types: outliers by distance and intuitive outliers. Outliers by distance can be detected based on their outlier score, and intuitive outliers are subsequences consisting of noise which can arise during clustering per timestamp. This distinction is necessary to be able to categorize the latter type of subsequences as outlier as well, since the outlier score for these would be zero.

In our work, we present an alternative definition of an outlier, which is also based on a clustering of the time series per timestamp; however, it addresses the problems listed for the approach of Tatusch et al. [16]. Thus, the threshold of our method is more intuitive, contains no need to differentiate between any types of outliers, and the number of computations K', based on the same assumptions as above, is smaller with:

$$K' = (l-1) * |D|$$

For this purpose, the given time series are clustered per timestamp first. Then, scores are calculated for each time series between consecutive timestamps, indicating the number of peers with which the time series remains in the same cluster. Finally, a threshold is defined to indicate how unique a path between two clusters in consecutive timestamps must be for the corresponding subsequence to be classified as an anomaly.

3. Method

Building on the described fundamentals, this section first introduces further terminology that is necessary to understand the method. This is followed by the definition of an anomalous subsequence of a time series. Finally, a way to find all anomalous subsequences within a time series is presented.

For a better illustration of the equations and corresponding calculations, we refer to the example given in Figure 1, which represents multiple time series clustered per timestamp. In the context of this work, data points defined as noise are considered as separate clusters. Thus, the data points of the time series TS_f are assigned to the clusters $C_{r,1}$ and $C_{v,2}$ at timestamps one and two.

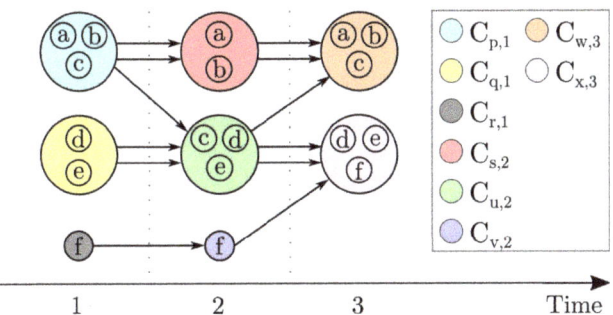

Figure 1. Example: clustering per timestamp.

The first term which will be relevant in the rest of this section is the cluster transitions set ct. A single cluster transition of a time series TS_y is a tuple of two cluster labels indicating in which clusters two adjacent data points of TS_y are located. Thus, a set of cluster transitions ct has the following definition:

$$ct(TS_y) = \{(C_{i,t}, C_{j,t+1}) \mid \exists y_t, y_{t+1} \in TS_y : y_t \in C_{i,t} \wedge y_{t+1} \in C_{i,t+1}\}. \tag{1}$$

For example, in Figure 1, the cluster transition sets of the time series TS_c are:

$$ct(TS_c) = \{(C_{p,1}, C_{u,2}), (C_{u,2}, C_{w,3})\}.$$

Given the description of the cluster transition set, we next define a multiset M that contains all cluster transitions for all time series TS_i of the data set D:

$$M_D = \bigcup_{TS_i \in D} ct(TS_i). \tag{2}$$

Regarding Figure 1, the multiset M_D is:

$$M_D = \{(C_{p,1}, C_{s,2}), (C_{p,1}, C_{s,2}), (C_{p,1}, C_{u,2}),$$
$$(C_{q,1}, C_{u,2}), (C_{q,1}, C_{u,2}), (C_{r,1}, C_{v,2}),$$
$$(C_{s,2}, C_{w,3}), (C_{s,2}, C_{w,3}), (C_{u,2}, C_{w,3}),$$
$$(C_{u,2}, C_{x,3}), (C_{u,2}, C_{x,3}), (C_{v,2}, C_{x,3})\}_b.$$

In combination with the equation for the cluster transition set, the given multiset description is then used to define a conformity score, which indicates how often a particular cluster transition p occurs in all time series of a data set D:

$$conformity\_score(p, M_D) = M_D(p). \tag{3}$$

With respect to this equation, the conformity score of the cluster transition $(C_{p,1}, C_{s,2})$ of the data set D presented in Figure 1 is:

$$conformity\_score((C_{p,1}, C_{s,2}), M_D) = M_D((C_{p,1}, C_{s,2})) = 2.$$

Using Equations (1)–(3), a set of anomalous transitions at for a time series $TS_y \in D$ is defined as follows:

$$at(TS_y) = \{p \mid p \in ct(TS_y) \wedge conformity\_score(p, M_D) \leq \sigma\}, \tag{4}$$

where σ is a threshold for the conformity score of a single cluster transition. Thus, if the conformity score is less than or equal to σ, then the corresponding transition is categorized as anomalous. Consequently, a subsequence $S_{y,[k,m]}$ of a time series TS_y is anomalous if and only if:

$$at(S_{y,[k,m]}) = ct(S_{y,[k,m]}).$$ (5)

According to Equations (4) and (5), the entire time series TS_c of the data set D shown in Figure 1 is anomalous due to:

$$at(TS_c) = \{(C_{p,1}, C_{u,2}), (C_{u,2}, C_{w,3})\} = ct(TS_c).$$

Using Equation (5), anomalous subsequences of a time series TS_y can be identified by iterating over all possible subsequences of TS_y. As an alternative to this approach, a set of tuples can be derived based on the set of anomalous cluster transitions, where the first element of each tuple indicates the beginning of an anomalous subsequence, and the second one specifies the end of the corresponding subsequence. Given a lower number of required iterations through a time series, this alternative is intended to optimize the performance of the method presented in this paper. This first requires the definition of an order relation $\leq$:

$$(C_{i,t_a}, C_{j,t_b}) \leq (C_{k,t_c}, C_{l,t_d}) :\Leftrightarrow (t_a \leq t_b) \wedge (t_c \leq t_d).$$ (6)

Based on the presented order relation, a set of tuples can be defined with respect to a time series TS_y, where each tuple consists of two anomalous cluster transitions. The first transition indicates the beginning of an anomalous subsequence of the time series TS_y, and the last one specifies the end of the corresponding subsequence. The formal description for this set of anomalous transition boundaries atb is given by:

$$atb(TS_y) = \{(p, p') \,|\, (p, p' \in at(TS_y)) \wedge$$
$$(\nexists \tilde{p} \in ct(TS_y) \wedge \tilde{p} \notin at(TS_y) : p \leq \tilde{p} \leq p') \wedge$$
$$(\nexists (C_{i,t}, C_{j,t+1}) \in at(TS_y) : p' = (C_{h,t-1}, C_{i,t}))\}.$$

In the case of the time series TS_c from Figure 1, the set of anomalous transition boundaries for $\sigma = 1$ is:

$$atb(TS_c) = \{((C_{p,1}, C_{u,2}), (C_{u,2}, C_{w,3}))\}.$$

Further, to obtain data point-based outlier boundaries for a time series TS_y, a mapping $dp_y(C_{i,t}, C_{j,t'}) = (y_t, y_t')$ is required that maps cluster tuples to a tuple of data points based on TS_y, such that:

$$y_t \in TS_y \wedge y_t \in C_{i,t} \wedge y_{t'} \in TS_y \wedge y_{t'} \in C_{j,t'}.$$

Finally, the outlier boundaries set ob within a time series TS_y is defined as a element-wise merge of tuples of the set of the anomalous transition boundaries, which is then mapped to the data points of TS_y:

$$ob(TS_y) = \{dp_y(C_{w,t}, C_{z,t'+1}) | \forall((C_{w,t}, C_{x,t+1}), (C_{y,t'}, C_{z,t'+1})) \in atb(TS_y)\}.$$

In this context, the set of outlier boundaries consists of tuples, where the first element of each tuple marks the beginning of an anomalous subsequence, and the second one indicates the end of that subsequence. Consequently, the outlier boundaries set of the time series $TS_c = c_1, c_2, c_3$ shown in Figure 1 for $\sigma = 1$ is:

$$ob(TS_c) = \{dp_c(C_{p,1}, C_{w,3})\} = \{(c_1, c_3)\}.$$

4. Experiments

In this section, we evaluate the method presented in this work. Since the method for detection of outliers in time series (*DOOTS* (https://github.com/tatusch/ots-eval/blob/main/doc/doots.md (accessed on 20 April 2022))) of Tatusch et al. [22] also detects anomalous subsequences based on time series transitions between different clusters, we used their method for comparison with our approach. In addition, we used the identical data sets and the same clustering method. This is intended to make the comparison of the two methods as fair as possible. In both approaches, DBSCAN with euclidean distance was used for timestamp-based clustering, with *minPts* and ε set differently for each data set but equally for both methods. In order to identify the best cluster parameters, we made use of the cluster over-time stability evaluation measure called *CLOSE* [15] and found that these were the same as Tatusch et al. used in their study [16]. Furthermore, we used the same thresholds for *DOOTS* as proposed in Tatusch et al. In order to make a meaningful comparison with our method, we chose the conformity score threshold in a way to ensure the results of both methods were as similar as possible. Overall, we used two real world data sets to compare both methods.

4.1. Eikon Financial Data Set

One of the real world data sets Tatusch et al. used for the evaluation of their work was an extract from the EIKON database. This database contains financial data from over 150,000 sources worldwide, and the information includes the previous 65 years. The extract contained annual values from the features' net sales and expected return for 30 (originally) random selected companies. The values of both features were normalized by min–max-normalization. The parameters used for the clustering by DBSCAN were $\varepsilon = 0.15$ and $minPts = 2$.

Figure 2a shows the result of *DOOTS* [16] for the threshold $\tau = 0.6$, and Figure 2b illustrates the result of our outlier detection method for the conformity score threshold of $\sigma = 1$. The black dashed boxes in Figure 2a mark intuitive outliers, which by definition consist of noise, and the red boxes represent outliers found by analyzing cluster transitions (outlier by distance). In contrast, in Figure 2b, each black dashed box highlights the beginning of an anomalous subsequence and each red dashed box marks the remainder of that subsequence.

The most noticeable fact when comparing the results of both methods is the different number of detected subsequences. While *DOOTS* [16] found only two anomalous subsequences ($S_{GM,[2008,2009]}$ and $S_{KR,[2009,2013]}$), our solution identified four of them ($S_{GM,[2008,2009]}$, $S_{KR,[2008,2013]}$, $S_{TJX,[2008,2009]}$, and $S_{UPS,[2012,2013]}$). A detailed analysis of $S_{TJX,[2008,2009]}$ and $S_{UPS,[2012,2013]}$ showed that both of them had a unique cluster transition with a conformity score of one each. Since the threshold σ was set to the same value, both subsequences were identified as anomalous by our method.

The explanation for why $S_{TJX,[2008,2009]}$ and $S_{UPS,[2012,2013]}$ were not considered anomalous by *DOOTS* [16] is more complex. In the case of UPS, neither a subsequence score nor the best score can be calculated, due to the lack of a cluster membership of the last data point of the time series. The inclusion of such a case requires an additional case differentiation. This can be seen as a disadvantage of the method of Tatusch et al. [16]. The reason for the missing detection of $S_{TJX,[2008,2009]}$ was the small size of the cluster in which TJX was located in 2008. Therefore, the calculation of the subsequence score for $S_{TJX,[2008,2009]}$ resulted in 0.5. Since the best score for this subsequence was one, the outlier score for it was $(1 - 0.5) = 1$, thus lower than the threshold τ of 0.6. From this case, the dependence of the outlier detection result on the corresponding cluster sizes can be derived, which can be considered as another disadvantage of the method of *DOOTS* [16].

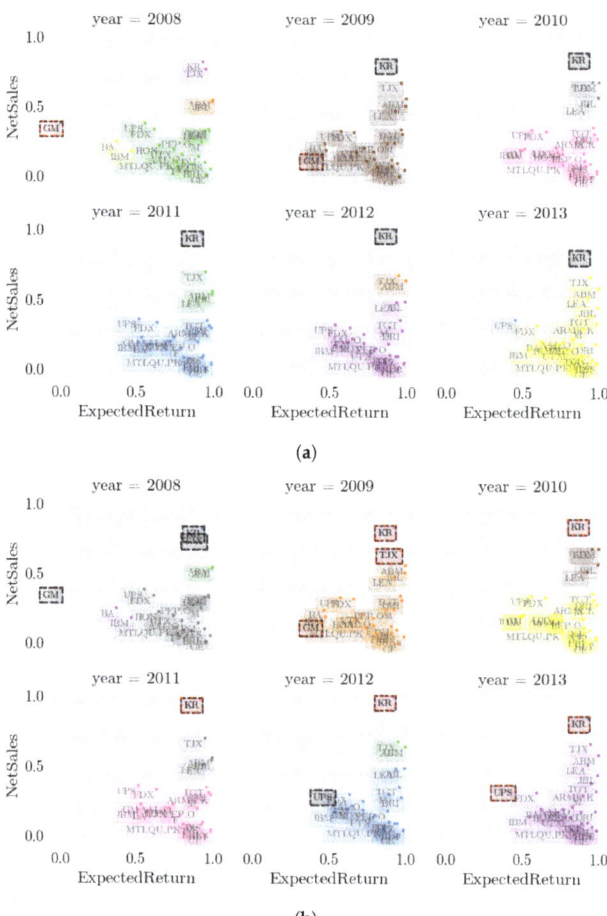

Figure 2. (**a**) Result of Tatusch et al. Colors: cluster memberships, red dashed boxes: outlier by distance, black dashed boxes: intuitive outliers. (**b**) Result of our method. Colors: cluster memberships, red dashed boxes: outliers, black dashed boxes: preoutliers.

Most interesting with regard to the identification of UPS (2012–2013) and TJX (2008–2009) as outliers is probably the realization that they can be explained by related events. Unlike the companies with which UPS was clustered in 2012, UPS had to lower its expected return in 2013. This was probably attributable to the crash of UPS Airlines Flight 1354 (https://www.bbc.com/news/world-us-canada-23698279; accessed on 25 April 2022) 14 August 2013. TJX Companies is a multinational department store corporation that in 2009 was still struggling with the consequences of the recession triggered by the economic crisis in 2008 (https://www.bizjournals.com/denver/stories/2009/07/06/daily63.html; accessed on 25 April 2022). For this reason, sales fell sharply, as they did for all retail traders. The reason why TJX was identified as an outlier here was that it was the only retail company in the data set.

4.2. Airline On-Time Performance Data Set

The other real world data set that Tatusch et al. [16] used in their publication was called "Airline on-time performance". It was originally created for a challenge with the goal to predict delayed and canceled flights. Therefore, the authors included flight data on all commercial flights in the USA between October 1987 and April 2008, resulting in a total of 120 million records. Based on this data set, Tatusch et al. [16] generated one dimensional time series with the feature "distance". As described in their work, they took eight days of every month and calculated the average distance for each airline in the data set. Before the authors clustered the created data set with DBSCAN, they normalized the distances by the min–max normalization. The parameters for the applied clustering algorithm were $minPts = 3$ and $\epsilon = 0.03$.

The result of *DOOTS* [16] for $\tau = 0.4$ is displayed in Figure 3a. Here, the black solid lines represent outliers by distance, and the black dashed lines are both outliers by distance and intuitive outliers. Our result for $\sigma = 1$ is shown in Figure 3b, where the black solid lines mark anomalous subsequences. In both figures, the colors of the dots set at each time point represent the cluster membership, with the red color representing noise found by DBSCAN. The results of both methods show strong similarities regarding the detection of anomalous subsequences, but there are also some differences. The most relevant of them are discussed below.

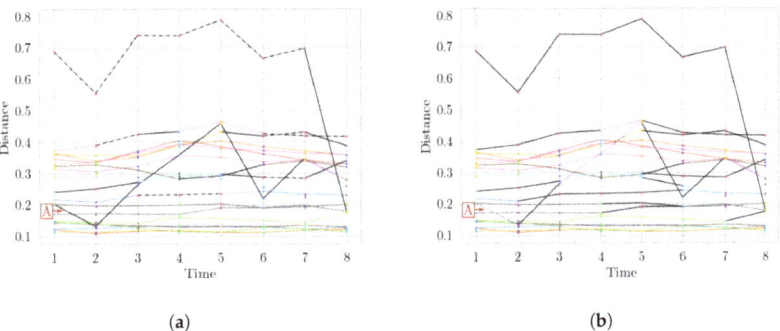

(a)   (b)

Figure 3. Airline on-time performance data set. (**a**) Outlier detection result of the method of Tatusch et al. (**b**) Result of our method.

Foremost, the subsequences $S_{A,[1,2]}$ and $S_{A,[3,4]}$ of the time series marked as A in Figure 3 were detected as anomalous by *DOOTS* [16], while they were not detected as such by our method. In the context of our approach, these subsequences were not detected as anomalous, because the number of equal cluster transitions and, therefore, the conformity score of $S_{A,[1,2]}$ as well as of $S_{A,[3,4]}$ was higher than the threshold $\sigma = 1$. In contrast, explaining the results of *DOOTS* [16] requires detailed calculations. First, the subsequence score for $S_{A,[1,2]}$ is:

$$subseq\_score(S_{A,[1,2]}) = 3/4 = 0.75.$$

Given that the best score for the last cluster of $S_{A,[1,2]}$ is one, the outlier score for this subsequence is:

$$outlier\_score(S_{A,[1,2]}) = 1 - 0.75 = 0.25 < \tau.$$

Based on this result, $S_{A,[1,2]}$ should not be labeled as anomalous. However, if we take the subsequence $S_{A,[1,3]}$, which in addition to $S_{A,[1,2]}$ contains a further value at $time = 3$, the subsequence score for $S_{A,[1,3]}$ becomes smaller compared to $S_{A,[1,2]}$ with:

$$subseq\_score(S_{A,[1,3]}) = 0.5 * (0.5 + 0.1) = 0.3.$$

Since the best score for the corresponding cluster at $time = 3$ is one, the outlier score for $S_{A,[1,3]}$ is:

$$outlier\_score(S_{A,[1,3]}) = 1 - 0.3 = 0.7 > \tau.$$

Thus, the subsequence $S_{A,[1,3]}$, was marked as anomalous. The same type of calculations led to the detection of the subsequence $S_{A,[3,5]}$ as anomalous, which contained the not anomalous subsequence $S_{A,[3,4]}$.

The detection of $S_{A,[1,2]}$ and $S_{A,[3,4]}$ by *DOOTS* [16] leads to two possible conclusions. On one hand, it can be concluded that the approach of Tatusch et al. [16] considers anomalous subsequences in a broader context with respect to the length of a time series than our method, which would be an advantage of *DOOTS*. On the other hand, this solution leads to subsequences that are not anomalous within their interval being detected as anomalous. This can be seen as a disadvantage of *DOOTS* [16]. In contrast, our method detects only those subsequences that exhibit suspicious behavior within their time interval. However, a broader context regarding our detection method can be achieved by additionally considering non-anomalous subsequences that are adjacent to detected anomalous subsequences.

A more general observation is that our method detected every subsequence of length two as anomalous if it contained one or more noisy data points. The reason for this is that the conformity score of such sequences was one and thus smaller or equal to the chosen threshold σ. In contrast, the solution of Tatusch et al. [16] follows a different approach. Even if a subsequence of length two had a noisy data point, it does not mean that *DOOTS* [16] would detect this subsequence as anomalous. In addition to the subsequence score, the detection of outliers by the method of Tatusch et al. [16] also depends on the value of the corresponding best score and whether both scores can be calculated for the given subsequence. In summary, we can conclude that *DOOTS* [16] has a much more complex set of rules than our method, whereby the results of both methods are similar.

5. Conclusions and Future Work

In this paper, we introduced a new approach for detecting outliers in multiple multivariate time series. For this purpose, we first clustered the time series data at each time point and then calculated conformity scores for each subsequence of length two. Finally, we determined whether the conformity scores were less than or equal to the specified threshold and labeled them as outliers if they were.

Since we found only one alternative algorithm (called *DOOTS*) [16] based on a similar idea, we compared the two in detail. The application of both methods led to similar results, although our solution had a much simpler rule set and, therefore, required fewer calculations (the runtime estimation is provided in Section 2). On one hand, this simplified the understanding of the origin of the outliers and, on the other hand, the better performance of our method allows it to be used on real time data. In addition, our rule set seems to be more consistent in contrast to *DOOTS* [16]. This statement is supported, among other things, by comparing the thresholds of both methods. While for our method the same minimum conformity score threshold was used in each dataset, the threshold set in *DOOTS* [16] varied without much difference between the results of both methods. Furthermore, our solution detected subsequences even if they ended with a noisy data point.

The most important drawback of our method is that the outlier detection result depends highly on the result of previous clustering. This implies that a poor clustering result would lead to a poor detection result of our method. Since the analysis of cluster transitions is the core idea of our method, we have to rely on approaches such as *CLOSE* [15] to obtain reasonable clustering results for our solution. Furthermore, while our method can be applied to real-time data due to its performance, this requires prior clustering in real-time with reasonable results for time series data. Here, *CLOSE* [15] provides good results, but the procedure is not applicable to real-time data because of the high number of needed computations. Given that, the most important aspect for future work is to optimize *CLOSE* [15] for real-time application. In addition, the freely selectable threshold σ in our work has a high impact on the detection result of our method. Every increment of σ leads to a superset of detected outliers regarding the result of the previous threshold. Although in this work we set this parameter to one for each dataset in order to obtain results that were as similar as possible and thus comparable to *DOOTS* [16], the optimal value for σ can be determined in several ways, and each determination should depend on the dataset in question. One way to determine the optimal σ is to count the cluster transitions that occur, sort them in ascending order, and choose the value for σ at which the slope change is greatest. However, the analysis of this and other possible methods is beyond the scope of this work and should therefore be addressed in future work. Another aspect is that not all detected anomalous subsequences may be useful in the context of given requirements. Since this case requires further analysis, our method could be applied to multiple data sets in which the outliers have already been labeled.

Author Contributions: Conceptualization, S.K. and G.K.; methodology, S.K. and G.K.; software, S.K. and G.K.; validation, S.K. and G.K.; formal analysis, S.K. and G.K.; investigation, S.K. and G.K. and S.C.; data collection, S.K., G.K. and M.B.; writing—original draft preparation S.K. and G.K.; writing—review and editing, S.K., G.K., M.B. and S.C.; visualization, S.K. and G.K.; project administration S.C., M.B. All authors have read and agreed to the published version of the manuscript.

Funding: This work was funded by the Jürgen Manchot Foundation.

Institutional Review Board Statement: Not applicable.

Informed Consent Statement: Not applicable.

Data Availability Statement: Data available in a publicly accessible repository that does not issue DOIs (https://github.com/YellowOfTheEgg/mldp-outlier_detection (accessed on 16 June 2022)). Publicly available datasets were analyzed in this study. This data can be found here: EIKON dataset: https://www.refinitiv.com/ (accessed: 20 April 2020); Airline on-time performance dataset: https://community.amstat.org/jointscsg-section/dataexpo/dataexpo2009 (accessed on 20 April 2020).

Acknowledgments: We would like to thank the Jürgen Manchot Foundation, which supported this work by financing the AI research group Decision-making with the help of Artificial Intelligence at Heinrich Heine University Düsseldorf.

Conflicts of Interest: The authors declare no conflict of interest.

Abbreviations

The following abbreviations are used in this manuscript:

DOOTS	Detecton of outliers in time series (method)
CLOSE	cluster over-time stability evaluation (measure)
DTW	dynamic time warping

References

1. Ferdousi, Z.; Maeda, A. Unsupervised Outlier Detection in Time Series Data. In Proceedings of the 22nd International Conference on Data Engineering Workshops Atlanta, GA, USA, 3–7 April 2006; IEEE: New York, NY, USA, 2006.
2. Golmohammadi, K.; Zaiane, O.R. Time series contextual anomaly detection for detecting market manipulation in stock market. In Proceedings of the 2015 IEEE International Conference on Data Science and Advanced Analytics (DSAA), Paris, France, 19–21 October 2015; IEEE: New York, NY, USA, 2015.
3. Gao, J.; Liang, F.; Fan, W.; Wang, C.; Sun, Y.; Han, J. On community outliers and their efficient detection in information networks. In Proceedings of the 16th ACM SIGKDD International Conference on Knowledge Discovery and Data Mining KDD'10, Washington, DC, USA, 25–7 July 2010; ACM Press: New York, NY, USA, 2010
4. Ghoting, A.; Otey, M.; Parthasarathy, S. LOADED: Link-Based Outlier and Anomaly Detection in Evolving Data Sets. In Proceedings of the Fourth IEEE International Conference on Data Mining (ICDM'04), Brighton, UK, 1–4 November 2004; IEEE: New York, NY, USA, 2004.
5. Keogh, E.; Lin, J.; Fu, A.; Herle, H.V. Finding Unusual Medical Time-Series Subsequences: Algorithms and Applications. *IEEE Trans. Inf. Technol. Biomed.* **2006**, *10*, 429–439. [CrossRef] [PubMed]
6. Nouira, K.; Trabelsi, A. Time Series Analysis and Outlier Detection in Intensive Care Data. In Proceedings of the 2006 8th international Conference on Signal Processing, Guilin, China, 16–20 November 2006; IEEE: New York, NY, USA, 2006.
7. Biem, A.; Feng, H.; Riabov, A.V.; Turaga, D.S. Real-time analysis and management of big time-series data. *IBM J. Res. Dev.* **2013**, *57*, 8:1–8:12. [CrossRef]
8. Ren, H.; Xu, B.; Wang, Y.; Yi, C.; Huang, C.; Kou, X.; Xing, T.; Yang, M.; Tong, J.; Zhang, Q. Time-Series Anomaly Detection Service at Microsoft. In Proceedings of the 25th ACM SIGKDD International Conference on Knowledge Discovery & Data Mining, Anchorage, AK, USA, 4–8 August 2019; ACM Press: New York, NY, USA, 2019.

9.   Benkabou, S.E.; Benabdeslem, K.; Canitia, B. Unsupervised outlier detection for time series by entropy and dynamic time warping. *Knowl. Inf. Syst.* **2017**, *54*, 463–486. [CrossRef]
10. Diab, D.M.; AsSadhan, B.; Binsalleeh, H.; Lambotharan, S.; Kyriakopoulos, K.G.; Ghafir, I. Anomaly Detection Using Dynamic Time Warping. In Proceedings of the 2019 IEEE International Conference on Computational Science and Engineering (CSE) and IEEE International Conference on Embedded and Ubiquitous Computing (EUC), New York, NY, USA, 1–3 August 2019; IEEE: New York, NY, USA, 2019.
11. Granger, C.W.J. Investigating Causal Relations by Econometric Models and Cross-spectral Methods. *Econometrica* **1969**, *37*, 424. [CrossRef]
12. Qiu, H.; Liu, Y.; Subrahmanya, N.A.; Li, W. Granger Causality for Time-Series Anomaly Detection. In Proceedings of the 2012 IEEE 12th International Conference on Data Mining, Brussels, Belgium, 10 December 2012; IEEE: New York, NY, USA, 2019.
13. Lloyd, S. Least squares quantization in PCM. *IEEE Trans. Inf. Theory* **1982**, *28*, 129–137. [CrossRef]
14. Chakrabarti, D.; Kumar, R.; Tomkins, A. Evolutionary clustering. In Proceedings of the 12th ACM SIGKDD International Conference on Knowledge Discovery Furthermore, Data Mining—KDD'06, Philadelphia, PA, USA, 20–23 August 2006; ACM Press: New York, NY, USA, 2006.
15. Tatusch, M.; Klassen, G.; Bravidor, M.; Conrad, S. How is your team spirit? cluster over-time stability evaluation. In *Machine Learning and Data Mining in Pattern Recognition, Proceedings of the 16th International Conference on Machine Learning and Data Mining, MLDM 2020, New York, NY, USA, 18–23 July 2020*; IBAI Publishing: Leipzig, Germany, 2020; pp. 155–170.
16. Tatusch, M.; Klassen, G.; Bravidor, M.; Conrad, S. Show Me Your Friends and I will Tell You Who You Are. Finding Anomalous Time Series by Conspicuous Cluster Transitions. In *Communications in Computer and Information Science*; Springer: Singapore, 2019; pp. 91–103.
17. Hawkins, D.M. *Identification of Outliers*; Springer: Cham, The Netherlands, 1980.
18. Blázquez-García, A.; Conde, A.; Mori, U.; Lozano, J.A. A review on outlier/anomaly detection in time series data. *ACM Comput. Surv.* **2021**, *54*, 56:1–56:33. [CrossRef]
19. Sun, P.; Chawla, S.; Arunasalam, B. Mining for Outliers in Sequential Databases. In Proceedings of the 2006 SIAM International Conference on Data Mining. Society for Industrial and Applied Mathematics, Bethesda, MD, USA, 20–22 April 2006.
20. Lin, J.; Keogh, E.; Wei, L.; Lonardi, S. Experiencing SAX: A novel symbolic representation of time series. *Data Min. Knowl. Discov.* **2007**, *15*, 107–144. [CrossRef]
21. Munir, M.; Siddiqui, S.A.; Dengel, A.; Ahmed, S. DeepAnT: A Deep Learning Approach for Unsupervised Anomaly Detection in Time Series. *IEEE Access* **2019**, *7*, 1991–2005. [CrossRef]
22. Hyndman, R.J.; Wang, E.; Laptev, N. Large-Scale Unusual Time Series Detection. In Proceedings of the 2015 IEEE International Conference on Data Mining Workshop (ICDMW), Atlantic City, NJ, USA, 14–17 November 2015; IEEE: New York, NY, USA, 2019.
23. Hyndman, R.J. Computing and Graphing Highest Density Regions. *Am. Stat.* **1996**, *50*, 120.

Proceeding Paper

ODIN TS: A Tool for the Black-Box Evaluation of Time Series Analytics †

Niccolò Zangrando *, Rocio Nahime Torres , Federico Milani and Piero Fraternali

Department of Electronics Information and Bioengineering, Politecnico di Milano, 20133 Milano, Italy;
rocionahime.torres@polimi.it (R.N.T.); federico.milani@polimi.it (F.M.); piero.fraternali@polimi.it (P.F.)
* Correspondence: niccolo.zangrando@polimi.it
† Presented at the 8th International Conference on Time Series and Forecasting, Gran Canaria, Spain,
27–30 June 2022.

Abstract: The increasing availability of time series datasets enabled by the diffusion of IoT architectures and the progress in the analysis of temporal data fostered by Deep Learning methods are boosting the interest in anomaly detection and predictive maintenance applications. The analysis of performance for these tasks relies on standard metrics applied to the entire dataset. Such indicators provide a global performance assessment but might not provide a deep understanding of the model weaknesses. A complementary diagnostic approach exploits error categorization and ad hoc visualizations. In this paper, we present ODIN TS, an open source diagnosis framework for time series analysis that lets developers compute performance metrics, disaggregated by different criteria, and visualize diagnosis reports. ODIN TS is agnostic to the training platform and can be extended with application- and domain-specific meta-annotations and metrics with almost no coding. We show ODIN TS at work through two time series analytics examples.

Keywords: time series; anomaly detection; predictive maintenance; model evaluation; error diagnosis

Citation: Zangrando, N.; Torres, R.N.;
Milani, F.; Fraternali, P. ODIN TS: A
Tool for the Black-Box Evaluation of
Time Series Analytics. *Eng. Proc.*
2022, *18*, 4. https://doi.org/10.3390/
engproc2022018004

Academic Editors: Ignacio Rojas,
Hector Pomares, Olga Valenzuela,
Fernando Rojas and Luis Javier
Herrera

Published: 20 June 2022

Publisher's Note: MDPI stays neutral
with regard to jurisdictional claims in
published maps and institutional affiliations.

1. Introduction

Time series datasets collect observations sampled at different times. Recording can be continuous, when data are collected continuously in a given interval, or discrete, when data are recorded at set time intervals [1]. Based on the number of observations at each timestamp, the time series can be univariate or multivariate. Univariate time series log values generated by a single sensor, whereas multivariate time series record signals from multiple sensors simultaneously. Time series are used to study time-varying phenomena in many fields: in the economy [2] (e.g., stock price trends), in medicine [3] (e.g., the progress of health variables) or in industry [4] (e.g., the status or energy consumption of a machine). Given a time series dataset, different tasks can be performed to predict a specific attribute or event at a given timestamp or assign a label to a particular observation. The most common tasks can be summarized as follows:

- Classification: assigning a class label to a time series [5]. An example of this task is the classification of the human heartbeat to detect diseases [6].
- Forecasting: predicting future event/s. An example is to predict the future energy consumption of an appliance based on historical data [7].
- Anomaly Detection: identifying deviations from normal behavior [8–10]. An example is the identification of anomalies in HVAC systems [11].
- Predictive Maintenance: predicting when a piece of equipment is likely to fail and deciding which maintenance activity to perform to obtain a good tradeoff between maintenance frequency and cost [10]. This objective could be pursued with classification approaches (identify if the appliance will fail within n days) or regression approaches (predict the Remaining Useful Life, RUL, of an appliance).

The different tasks are usually evaluated by means of standard metrics such as the Mean Absolute Error (MAE) or Precision and Recall. While these metrics are useful global indicators of the model performances, they provide little insight into the weaknesses of the models. For example, predicting a false positive close to a real anomaly is a less severe error than predicting it at a very distant time. Furthermore, information collected but not used during the model training phase could help understand the model performance. For example, in an industrial application it could be interesting to analyze if the performances vary across appliance versions or install locations. A similar analysis could be performed on any other attribute not exploited for training but available at diagnosis time.

This paper introduces ODIN TS, the extension for anomaly detection and predictive maintenance of the ODIN machine learning diagnosis tool. ODIN [12] is an open-source, Python-based, black-box framework for error diagnosis initially conceived for generic classification and computer vision tasks. Contrary to explainability techniques that aim at "opening" the box by exploring the internals of the models (e.g., CNNs), black-box approaches study only the results of the model with regard to the input and its characteristics. ODIN TS adds the implementation of the most widely adopted metrics for the anomaly detection and predictive maintenance tasks and proposes new analyses for anomaly detection, such as false positive error categorization. ODIN TS also enables the inspection of the time series dataset and of the related predictions by means of a visualizer with different functionalities.

The contributions of the paper can be summarized as follows:

- We summarize the most widely used metrics for time series analysis.
- We describe their implementation in ODIN TS, an extensible framework for time series analytics error diagnosis.
- We introduce the novel analysis and visualizations supported by ODIN TS and exemplify them in an anomaly detection and a predictive maintenance task.

The paper is organized as follows: Section 2 summarizes the most common metrics used for time series analysis, Section 3 describes the proposed framework and its functionalities, Section 4 presents some examples of how the tool can be employed, and Section 5 concludes and provides insight into the future work.

2. Related Work

The evaluation of inference models applies standard metrics to compute performance indicators based on a comparison between the ground truth (what is expected) and the model predictions. Table 1 presents a by-task summary of the metrics and performance indicators found in the literature for time series analytics and provides a reference to the definition of each index. Different works have focused on the evaluation of time series tasks by proposing novel metrics and assessment procedures or by providing efficient implementations of the classical indicators. In [13], the authors presented a new benchmarking metric, the Numenta Anomaly Benchmark (NAB) score, which augmented traditional indices by incorporating time explicitly so as to reward early detection and introduced the concept of an anomaly window. The work in [14] illustrated the benefits of decomposing performance metrics based on the characteristics of the observations. As a use case, a model to detect illicit use of computational resources was created and assessed. The evaluation considered how the performances of the predictor changed in servers with a specific attributes (low or high profile). Other contributions proposed novel time series evaluation frameworks. The work [15] introduced Darts, a python framework for handling time series, which implemented some state-of-the-art machine learning methods and provided off-the-shelf a subset of the standard metrics reported in Table 1. Another example is the RELOAD tool proposed in [16] to identify the most informative features of a dataset, run anomaly detection algorithms, and apply a set of evaluation metrics on the results. While both tools aim to support training and evaluation with standard metrics, ODIN TS extends the support to time series analytics with a black-box error diagnosis approach focused on the anomaly detection and predictive maintenance tasks. It enables error categorization, predictions decomposition, and visualizations. The decomposition and visualization functionalities exploit the meta-annotations of the data set, i.e., features not used during model training that can contribute to the interpretation of the model results.

Table 1. Metrics and analysis found in the literature for time series based on the different tasks. The value "yes" is used to indicate the metric applies to the specific task, whereas "n/a" is used to indicate the contrary.

	Classification	Forecasting	Anomaly Detection	Predictive Maintenance	
				Classification	Regression
Accuracy [17]	yes	n/a	yes	yes	n/a
Precision [17]	yes	n/a	yes	yes	n/a
Recall [17]	yes	n/a	yes	yes	n/a
F1 Score [17]	yes	n/a	yes	yes	n/a
Miss Alarm Rate [18]	yes	n/a	yes	yes	n/a
False Alarm Rate [19]	yes	n/a	yes	yes	n/a
NAB Score [13]	n/a	n/a	yes	n/a	n/a
Mean Absolute Error (MAE) [15]	n/a	yes	n/a	n/a	yes
Mean Squared Error (MSE) [15]	n/a	yes	n/a	n/a	yes
Root Mean Squared Error (RMSE) [15]	n/a	yes	n/a	n/a	yes
Matthews Coefficient [20]	yes	n/a	yes	yes	n/a
Mean Absolute Percentage Error (MAPE) [15]	n/a	yes	n/a	n/a	yes
Precision–Recall Curve [21]	yes	n/a	yes	yes	n/a
ROC Curve [17]	yes	n/a	yes	yes	n/a
Gain and Lift Analysis [22]	yes	n/a	yes	yes	n/a
Residuals Analysis [23]	n/a	yes	n/a	n/a	yes
Coefficient of Variation [15]	n/a	yes	n/a	n/a	yes
Mean Absolute Ranged Relative Error (MARRE) [15]	n/a	yes	n/a	n/a	yes
Mean Absolute Scaled Error (MASE) [15]	n/a	yes	n/a	n/a	yes
Overall Percentage Error (OPE) [15]	n/a	yes	n/a	n/a	yes
Coefficient of Determination R2 [15]	n/a	yes	n/a	n/a	yes
Rho-risk [15]	n/a	yes	n/a	n/a	yes
Root Mean Squared Log Error (RMSLE) [15]	n/a	yes	n/a	n/a	yes
Symmetric Mean Absolute Percentage Error (sMAPE) [15]	n/a	yes	n/a	n/a	yes

3. The ODIN TS Framework

The ODIN TS framework supports the development of predictive maintenance and anomaly detection tasks enabling designers to evaluate standard metrics on inputs and outputs grouped by meta-annotation values, perform error categorization, evaluate the confidence calibration error, and visualize a variety of diagnostic reports. ODIN TS also includes a Visualizer module for the inspection of the dataset and of the model predictions. ODIN TS is supported by the extension of classes in the Python-based ODIN framework, and publicly released (https://github.com/rnt-pmi/odin (accessed on 15 June 2022)).

3.1. Dataset Input and Output Formats

ODIN TS supports the import of time series data, of ground truth (GT) annotations, and the output of inference results. The artifacts should follow the guidelines common to most publicly available datasets (summarized in Table 2):

- Anomaly Detection Task
  - Time Series data: a CSV file with the column "timestamp" of the observation and one additional column for each "signal".
  - Ground Truth: a JSON file containing a list of the "timestamp" in which the anomalies appear.
  - Predictions: a CSV file where the first column specifies the "timestamp" and the following column(s) the "confidence" value, or the reconstructed/predicted "signal" values.

- Predictive Maintenance Task
  - Time Series data: a CSV with the columns "observation_id" for the unique identifier of the observation, "unit_id" for the machine or appliance identifier, and one additional column for each "signal".
  - Ground Truth: it is embedded in the previous CSV file as an additional column ("label") with a Boolean value denoting if the machine is going to fail within n timestamps (for classification) or with the RUL value (for regression).
  - Predictions: a CSV file (named "unit_id.csv") for each machine or appliance mentioned in the ground truth. The file contains one column with the identifier of the observation and one column with the "confidence" score (for classification) or with the RUL value (for regression).

In both cases if additional metaproperties are associated to the time series, these are input as a CSV, where the first column is the identifier of the time series observation ("timestamp" or "observation_id"), and there is one column per metaproperty.

Table 2. Dataset format for ODIN time series. The value "n/a" indicates that a field is not used.

	Anomaly Detection			Predictive Maintenance		
	Format	Row Identifier	Signals/Values	Format	Row identifier	Signals/Values
Time Series	CSV	timestamp	a column per signal	CSV	observation_id, unit_id	a column per signal
Ground Truth	JSON	n/a	list of timestamps when the anomalies occur	embedded in TS CSV	n/a	label column (class) or RUL column (regr)
Properties	CSV	timestamp	a column per property	CSV	observation_id, unit_id	a column per property
Predictions	CSV	timestamp	confidence column or a column per signal	CSV	observation_id	confidence column (class) or RUL column (regr)

3.2. Supported Types of Dataset Analysis

ODIN TS supports the following types of analysis of the observations and of the ground truth annotations:

Distribution of classes. For classification, a plot displays the percentage of samples for each category.

Distribution of properties. A plot displays the percentage of the observations associated with each property value. For example, it visualizes if an observation is associated with a certain period of the day (morning, evening, or night) or with a specific type of anomaly (point, contextual, or collective).

Stationarity analysis. A stationary time series is one whose properties do not depend on the time at which the series is observed. The implementation of ODIN TS uses the Augmented Dickey–Fuller statistical test [24].

Seasonality, trend, and residual decomposition. These analyses expose the repeating short-term cycles (seasonal) and the general movement over time (trend) of the series [25]. Residuals include everything not captured by the previous two types of decomposition. Decomposition can be realized with an additive model (addition of the decomposed values restores the original times series) or with a multiplicative one (the original series is obtained by multiplying the decomposed values).

3.3. Supported Types of Prediction Analysis

ODIN TS implements all the metrics of Table 1. To the best of our knowledge, there is no other framework that offers all of them off-the-shelf. Based on the implemented metrics, ODIN TS implements multiple performance reports and types of prediction analysis, summarized in Table 3.

Table 3. Types of analysis in ODIN TS for the different tasks. The value "n/a" specifies the type is not relevant for the specific task.

	Anomaly Detection	Predictive Maintenance	
		Classification	Regression
Summary report	yes	yes	yes
Performance per threshold value	yes	yes	n/a
Per property analysis	yes	yes	yes
FP anomaly categorization	yes	n/a	n/a
Error distance distribution	yes	n/a	n/a
RUL variation distribution	n/a	n/a	yes
Calibration analysis	yes	yes	n/a

Summary report. A report that tabulates the results of all the metrics. The total shows both the micro- and macro-averaged values: the first computes the value without distinguishing the categories; the latter computes the metrics for each class and then performs an unweighted mean.

Performance per threshold value. The classification metrics of interest are computed and shown in a graph for each value of the confidence threshold.

Per property analysis. The values of the metrics of interest are decomposed by property value and contrasted with the average across all the property values. For example, the RUL value prediction or probability of failure in the next N timestamps could be distinguished per appliance brand or installation location.

FP anomaly categorization. The analysis of incorrectly predicted anomalies is supported, including their categorization into the following cases:

- Affected: an FP anomaly prediction is assigned to this category if its timestamp lies within an anomaly window. The anomaly window, introduced in [13], is an interval centered at the GT anomaly timestamp. The window extension (i.e., between, number of points) is a customizable parameter set by default to 10% of the data points divided by the number of anomalies.
- Continuous: this category contains FP anomalies that occur at contiguous timestamps outside the anomaly window.
- Generic: all the other FP anomalies.

FP error distance distribution. A distribution plot of the distance (measured as a number of timestamps) between an FP and the closest GT anomaly, color-coded with the FP anomaly category (affected, continuous, or generic).

RUL variation distribution. Given that a machine or appliance degrades over time, the predicted RUL should decrease by 1 at each timestamp. In a perfectly consistent model, the following formula should apply:

$$\hat{y}_t - \hat{y}_{t-1} = -1 \tag{1}$$

where $\hat{y}_t$ is the predicted RUL at time t, and $\hat{y}_{t-1}$ is the predicted RUL at time $t-1$. This type of analysis plots the distribution of the differences of the predicted RUL between the current cycle and the previous one to assess the consistency of the model predictions.

Calibration analysis. It exploits the confidence histogram and the reliability diagram [26]. Both plots assign the confidence values to buckets (e.g., 0–0.1, 0.1–0.2, . . ., 0.90–1) on the abscissa. The confidence histogram shows the percentage of positive predicted samples that fall into each confidence range. The reliability diagram indicates, for each confidence range, the average accuracy of the positive samples in that range. When a classifier is well-calibrated, its probability estimates can be interpreted as correctness likelihood, i.e., of all the samples that are predicted with a probability estimate of 0.6, around 60% should belong to the positive class [27]. ODIN reports the Expected Calibration Error (ECE) (Equation (2)) and the Maximum Calibration Error (MCE) (Equation (3))

$$ECE = \sum_{m=1}^{M} \frac{B_m}{n} acc(B_m) - conf(B_m) \tag{2}$$

$$MCE = max_{m\epsilon(1..M)} |acc(B_m) - conf(B_m)| \tag{3}$$

where n is the number of samples in the data set, M is the number of buckets (each of size $1/M$), and B_m denotes the set of indices of observations whose prediction confidence falls into the interval m.

3.4. Supported Visualizations

ODIN TS allows one to visualize the dataset and the corresponding model predictions, if provided. The dataset visualization offers the following functionalities:

* Feature filter: one can choose which features to visualize of a multivariate dataset.
* Aggregation: data can be aggregated by minute, hour, day, week, month, or year and visualized at different granularity.
* Pagination: some datasets span a large interval. A pagination function with custom data points size and step can be used to browse the dataset.
* GT display toggle: the GT annotations can be shown or hidden. For anomaly detection, it can be a single point or an anomaly window. For predictive maintenance, it can be the class labels or the RUL values.

If the predictions are available, the following functionalities can be used:

* Predictions' visualization and model comparison: the predictions are visualized along with the GT. If multiple models are selected, their predictions are color-coded.
* FP errors' visualization: the FP predictions are displayed and, in the case of FP anomalies, color-coded by their type.

4. ODIN TS in Action

This section exemplifies ODIN TS at work on an anomaly detection and a predictive maintenance case. The first example from the NAB datasets [13] used the "ambient temperature system failure" data, which contain ≈5000 hourly temperature measurements in an office and feature two anomalies. To detect the anomalies, an LTSM model was trained as in [9]. It comprised two LSTM modules with four hidden layers and a 0.2 dropout rate. The training set included the first 30% of the data (of which 10% was used for validation) while the remaining 70% was used for testing. The model was trained for 100 epochs, with a batch size of 32 and an input window length of 30. The scenario was relatively small given the few anomalies, but it was still useful to highlight some of the ODIN TS capabilities.

Figure 1 shows the distribution of the FP error categories. For the computation of the "affected" errors, an anomaly window of length 34 was used. Most FPs were within a short distance from the real anomalies ("affected", in orange), which suggests that the anomaly was perceived before its reported occurrence time and continued to be perceived shortly after. Furthermore, the "continuous" FPs were more numerous than the generic ones, which shows that the model tends to identify prolonged anomalies rather than instantaneous exceptions. Figure 2 shows the distance of each FP from the closest anomaly to confirm that the "affected" FPs were the closest to a GT anomaly. These errors are better appreciated in Figure 3 in which the Visualizer helps show the findings of the analysis more intuitively.

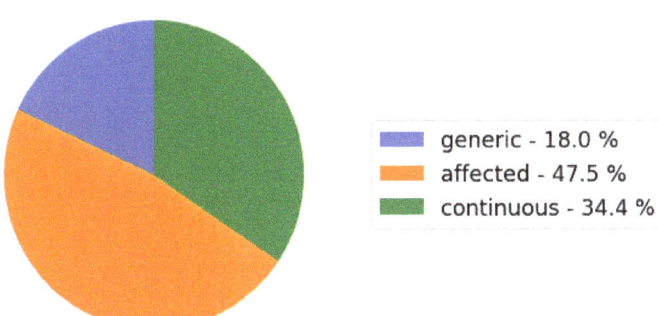

Figure 1. False Positive distribution plot.

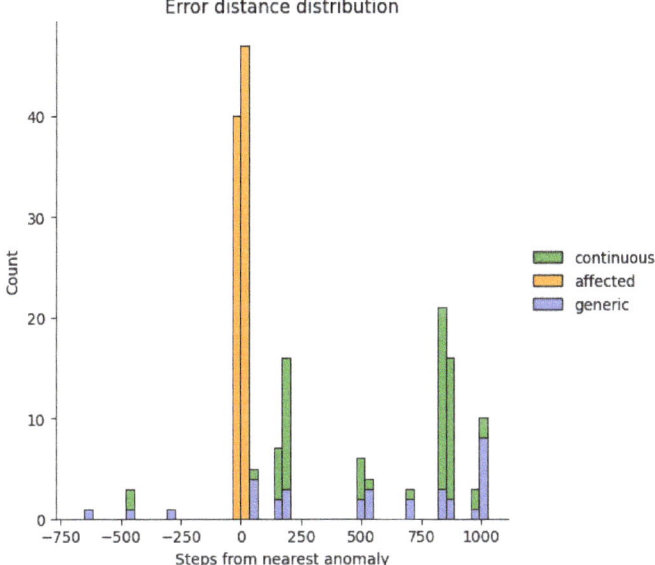

Figure 2. False positive distribution of the distance of each FP from the closest anomaly.

To illustrate a case of predictive maintenance, we used a NASA dataset of turbofan engine degradation [28]. The dataset comprised samples from 100 engines, whose state was represented by 24 variables. The GT consisted of the RUL at each inter-observation interval (called "cycle"). The authors provided the dataset in two splits: training (with 20,631 observations among 100 machines) and testing (13,096 observations among 100 machines). In the testing split, the cycles for each machine ranged from 31 to 303. To predict the RUL at each cycle, a two-layer LSTM was employed, with 128 and 64 hidden layers, respectively, and the same dropout rate of 0.3. The LSTM was trained for 10 epochs with a batch size of 150 and a window input length of 60 cycles.

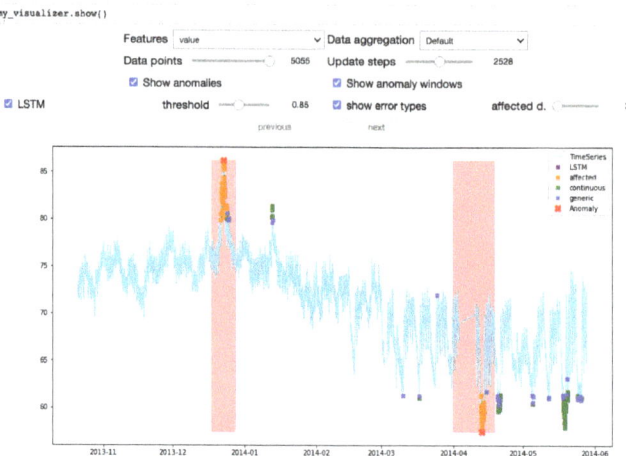

Figure 3. The ODIN TS Visualizer showing the actual data and the model predictions color-coded by error type.

The model had an RUL estimation error of 20 cycles (provided by the MAE) and an MAPE of ≈0.17, which denote good performance. Further analysis helps understand where the model can be improved. Figure 4 shows the residual analysis and enables a visual interpretation of the deviation of the predictions from the GT. Two plots report the predicted RUL on the X-axis. The Y-axis of the left plot reports the GT RUL value, while the Y-axis of the right plot reports the standardized difference between the prediction and the GT. Each color represents a different engine. From the analysis, it can be seen that most errors occurred when the component was still in good condition (with an RUL value greater than 100), which highlights the inability of the model to predict the engine's remaining life in the long term. In particular, the highest predicted RUL was 160, while the corresponding GT value was 260. This suggests that the model is not able to learn high RUL values properly. In scenarios where analysts are more interested in correctly predicting the RUL when the engine is close to a failure, it makes sense to set a maximum GT RUL value to reduce the relevance of large values during training [29].

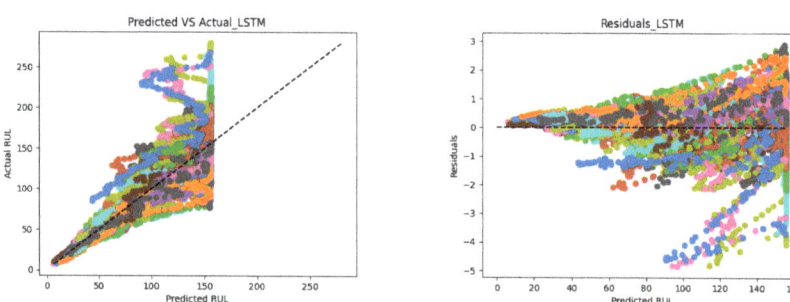

Figure 4. Residuals analysis. The colors indicate the different engines.

Figure 5 illustrates the RUL variation distribution analysis, which shows that the model predictions were not very consistent. The model sometimes increased the estimated RUL by 10 cycles instead of decreasing it by 1. This finding can help improve the prediction; for example, if the variation among consecutive cycles was high, one might interpolate or average the RUL values of previous cycles to mitigate the noise.

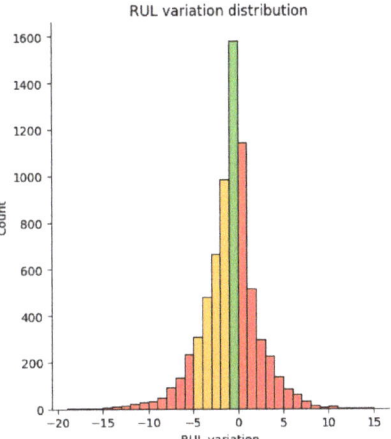

Figure 5. RUL variation distribution: the green bar represents a perfect variation of the RUL estimation, the yellow bars an acceptable variation, and the red bars an inconsistent prediction.

5. Conclusions

This paper described the addition of time series analysis functions into a black-box error diagnosis framework originally conceived for CV tasks. The novel version of ODIN includes an ODIN TS module, which supports performance diagnosis for two analytics tasks on time series: anomaly detection and predictive maintenance. ODIN TS implements all the most widely adopted metrics for the addressed tasks and introduces new types of analysis for anomaly detection, such as FP error categorization. ODIN TS also enables the inspection of the dataset and of the predictions by means of a Visualizer with rich functionalities. ODIN TS is implemented in Python and released as an open-source project, which developers can easily extend with their own metrics, reports, and visualizations. To conclude we have illustrated the tool at work on two use cases, so as to give a glimpse of its utility. Future work will focus on extending the implemented metrics and on supporting more tasks (e.g., time series classification and forecasting). We also plan to extend the Visualizer with novel functions and to integrate a time series annotator for enriching the GT or generating it from scratch (e.g., by annotating the anomalies in a dataset). Finally, we plan to create automatic property extractors (e.g., for assigning to each anomaly the proper type [8]).

Author Contributions: Conceptualization, N.Z., R.N.T., F.M. and P.F.; Methodology, N.Z., R.N.T., F.M. and P.F.; Validation, N.Z., R.N.T., F.M. and P.F.; Writing—original draft, N.Z., R.N.T., F.M. and P.F. All authors have read and agreed to the published version of the manuscript.

Funding: This work was partially supported by the project "PRECEPT—A novel decentralized edge-enabled PREsCriptivE and ProacTive framework for increased energy efficiency and well-being in residential buildings" funded by the EU H2020 Programme, grant agreement No. 958284.

Institutional Review Board Statement: Not applicable.

Informed Consent Statement: Not applicable.

Data Availability Statement: Not applicable.

Conflicts of Interest: The authors declare no conflict of interest. The funders had no role in the design of the study; in the collection, analyses, or interpretation of data; in the writing of the manuscript, or in the decision to publish the results.

References

1. Brockwell, P.J.; Davis, R.A. *Time Series: Theory and Methods*; Springer Science & Business Media: Berlin/Heidelberg, Germany, 2009.
2. Centoni, M.; Cubadda, G. *Modelling Comovements of Economic Time Series: A Selective Survey*; Statistica: Bologna, Italy, 2011.
3. Radhakrishnan, N.; Gangadhar, B. Estimating regularity in epileptic seizure time-series data. *IEEE Eng. Med. Biol. Mag.* **1998**, *17*, 89–94. [CrossRef] [PubMed]
4. Qiao, H.; Wang, T.; Wang, P.; Qiao, S.; Zhang, L. A time-distributed spatiotemporal feature learning method for machine health monitoring with multi-sensor time series. *Sensors* **2018**, *18*, 2932. [CrossRef] [PubMed]
5. Fawaz, H.I.; Forestier, G.; Weber, J.; Idoumghar, L.; Muller, P.A. Deep learning for time series classification: A review. *Data Min. Knowl. Discov.* **2019**, *33*, 917–963. [CrossRef]
6. Kampouraki, A.; Manis, G.; Nikou, C. Heartbeat time series classification with support vector machines. *IEEE Trans. Inf. Technol. Biomed.* **2008**, *13*, 512–518. [CrossRef] [PubMed]
7. Ahmad, A.S.; Hassan, M.Y.; Abdullah, M.P.; Rahman, H.A.; Hussin, F.; Abdullah, H.; Saidur, R. A review on applications of ANN and SVM for building electrical energy consumption forecasting. *Renew. Sustain. Energy Rev.* **2014**, *33*, 102–109. [CrossRef]
8. Choi, K.; Yi, J.; Park, C.; Yoon, S. Deep Learning for Anomaly Detection in Time-Series Data: Review, Analysis, and Guidelines. *IEEE Access* **2021**, *9*, 120043–120065. [CrossRef]
9. Braei, M.; Wagner, S. Anomaly detection in univariate time-series: A survey on the state-of-the-art. *arXiv* **2020**, arXiv:2004.00433.
10. Ran, Y.; Zhou, X.; Lin, P.; Wen, Y.; Deng, R. A survey of predictive maintenance: Systems, purposes and approaches. *arXiv* **2019**, arXiv:1912.07383.
11. Beghi, A.; Brignoli, R.; Cecchinato, L.; Menegazzo, G.; Rampazzo, M.; Simmini, F. Data-driven fault detection and diagnosis for HVAC water chillers. *Control Eng. Pract.* **2016**, *53*, 79–91. [CrossRef]
12. Torres, R.N.; Milani, F.; Fraternali, P. ODIN: Pluggable Meta-annotations and Metrics for the Diagnosis of Classification and Localization. In Proceedings of the International Conference on Machine Learning, Optimization, and Data Science, Grasmere, UK, 4–8 October 2021; pp. 383–398.
13. Lavin, A.; Ahmad, S. Evaluating real-time anomaly detection algorithms–the Numenta anomaly benchmark. In Proceedings of the 2015 IEEE 14th International Conference on Machine Learning and Applications (ICMLA), Miami, FL, USA, 9–11 December 2015; pp. 38–44.
14. Gomes, G.; Dias, L.; Correia, M. CryingJackpot: Network flows and performance counters against cryptojacking. In Proceedings of the 2020 IEEE 19th International Symposium on Network Computing and Applications (NCA), Cambridge, MA, USA, 24–27 November 2020; pp. 1–10.
15. Herzen, J.; Lässig, F.; Piazzetta, S.G.; Neuer, T.; Tafti, L.; Raille, G.; Van Pottelbergh, T.; Pasieka, M.; Skrodzki, A.; Huguenin, N.; et al. Darts: User-friendly modern machine learning for time series. *arXiv* **2021**, arXiv:2110.03224.
16. Zoppi, T.; Ceccarelli, A.; Bondavalli, A. Evaluation of Anomaly Detection algorithms made easy with RELOAD. In Proceedings of the 2019 IEEE 30th International Symposium on Software Reliability Engineering (ISSRE), Berlin, Germany, 28–31 October 2019; pp. 446–455.
17. Hossin, M.; Sulaiman, M.N. A review on evaluation metrics for data classification evaluations. *Int. J. Data Min. Knowl. Manag. Process* **2015**, *5*, 1.
18. An, N.; Weber, S. Impact of sample size on false alarm and missed detection rates in PCA-based anomaly detection. In Proceedings of the 2017 51st Annual Conference on Information Sciences and Systems (CISS), Baltimore, MD, USA, 22–24 March 2017; pp. 1–6.
19. Pokrywka, R. Reducing false alarm rate in anomaly detection with layered filtering. In *International Conference on Computational Science*; Springer: Berlin/Heidelberg, Germany, 2008; pp. 396–404.
20. Chicco, D.; Jurman, G. The advantages of the Matthews correlation coefficient (MCC) over F1 score and accuracy in binary classification evaluation. *BMC Genom.* **2020**, *21*, 6. [CrossRef] [PubMed]
21. Miao, J.; Zhu, W. Precision–recall curve (PRC) classification trees. *Evol. Intell.* **2021**, 1–25. [CrossRef]
22. Jaffery, T.; Liu, S.X. Measuring campaign performance by using cumulative gain and lift chart. In Proceedings of the SAS Global Forum, Washington, DC, USA, 22–25 March 2009; p. 196.
23. Sheather, S. *A Modern Approach to Regression with R*; Springer Science & Business Media: Berlin/Heidelberg, Germany, 2009.
24. Cheung, Y.W.; Lai, K.S. Lag order and critical values of the augmented Dickey–Fuller test. *J. Bus. Econ. Stat.* **1995**, *13*, 277–280.
25. Hyndman, R.J.; Athanasopoulos, G. *Forecasting: Principles and Practice*; OTexts: Melbourne, Australia, 2018.
26. DeGroot, M.H.; Fienberg, S.E. The comparison and evaluation of forecasters. *J. R. Stat. Soc. Ser. D* **1983**, *32*, 12–22. [CrossRef]
27. Guo, C.; Pleiss, G.; Sun, Y.; Weinberger, K.Q. On calibration of modern neural networks. In *International Conference on Machine Learning*; JMLR: Brookline, MA, USA, 2017; pp. 1321–1330.
28. Saxena, A.; Goebel, K. Turbofan engine degradation simulation data set. *NASA Ames Progn. Data Repos.* **2008**, 1551–3203.
29. Song, Y.; Shi, G.; Chen, L.; Huang, X.; Xia, T. Remaining useful life prediction of turbofan engine using hybrid model based on autoencoder and bidirectional long short-term memory. *J. Shanghai Jiaotong Univ. (Sci.)* **2018**, *23*, 85–94. [CrossRef]

Proceeding Paper

Cloud-Base Height Estimation Based on CNN and All Sky Images †

Emanuele Ogliari [1,*,‡] , **Alfredo Nespoli** [1,‡] , **Elena Collino** [2,‡] and **Dario Ronzio** [2,‡]

1. Department of Energy, Politecnico di Milano, Via Giuseppe La Masa, 34, 20156 Milano, Italy; alfredo.nespoli@polimi.it
2. Ricerca sul Sistema Energetico (RSE S.p.A.), Via R. Rubattino, 54, 20134 Milano, Italy; dario.ronzio@rse-web.it (E.C.); elena.collino@rse-web.it (D.R.)
* Correspondence: emanuelegiovanni.ogliari@polimi.it
† Presented at the 8th International Conference on Time Series and Forecasting, Gran Canaria, Spain, 27–30 June 2022.
‡ These authors contributed equally to this work.

Abstract: Among several meteorological parameters, Cloud-Base Height is employed in many applications to provide operational and real-time cloud-base information to the aviation industry, to initialize Numeric Weather Prediction models and to validate climate models. Moreover, Cloud-Base Height is also useful in the nowcasting (very short-term forecasting) of solar radiation. As cloud movements mainly affect the solar irradiance availability, their characterization is extremely important for solar power applications; an accurate estimation of the ground shadowing requires the knowledge of cloud height and extent. In the present work, the Cloud-Base Height value is estimated starting from sky images acquired from a single All Sky Imager. In order to fulfill this task, a Convolutional Neural Network model is chosen and developed.

Keywords: convolutional neural network; CNN; all sky images; cloud-base height; machine learning

Citation: Ogliari, E.; Nespoli, A.; Collino, E.; Ronzio, D. Cloud-Base Height Estimation Based on CNN and All Sky Images. *Eng. Proc.* **2022**, *18*, 5. https://doi.org/10.3390/engproc2022018005

Academic Editors: Ignacio Rojas, Hector Pomares, Olga Valenzuela, Fernando Rojas and Luis Javier Herrera

Published: 20 June 2022

Publisher's Note: MDPI stays neutral with regard to jurisdictional claims in published maps and institutional affiliations.

1. Introduction

Cloud-Base Height (CBH) estimation is an increasingly crucial task: this parameter is required in many applications [1]. It is exploited to validate climate models [2] and to improve Numeric Weather Prediction (NWP) models [3]; for instance, it improves the definition of the cloud-drift vector field, allowing a more effective modeling of the atmosphere dynamics [4]. Moreover, CBH is also useful in the nowcasting (very short-term forecasting) of solar resources [5] and photovoltaic power plant energy outputs [6]. As clouds are the primary cause of intermittency in solar irradiance, they are of interest for solar power applications: an accurate calculation of the ground shadowing requires the knowledge of cloud height and extent [7].

In the scientific literature, several studies are aimed at estimating CBH through different procedures. In [1], seven All Sky Imagers (ASIs) belonging to the Eye2Sky ASI network, located in the city of Oldenburg, are exploited to estimate CBH. In detail, an independent CBH estimation is derived considering each possible pair of ASIs, and then all the different estimations are properly merged into a final and more reliable one. In [8], the authors combined infrared satellite images and spectral information derived from meteorological sounders to improve the accuracy of the cloud height estimation task. In [9], a method for CBH estimation was developed starting from successions of images captured by ground-based imagers with a hemispherical view of the sky. In [10], a model capable of detecting and tracking individual clouds aimed at creating a 3D model providing cloud attributes such as height, position, size, optical properties and motion was developed. In [11], a newly developed temporal height-tracking (THT) algorithm to the backscatter profiles of two ceilometers led to retrieved cloud bases that are statistically consistent with each other and ensured reliable detection of CBH, particularly when inhomogeneous cloud fields were present and changing rapidly in time. However, in situ measurements of cloud properties are essential, but they are quite expensive and typically limited in time and spatial location. On the contrary, Machine Learning-based models are capable overcoming physical model limitations, as for solar power plant energy estimation [12]. A CNN is a classification model specifically designed to detect patterns within images. Since the goal of the work was the evaluation of the possibility of using All Sky Imagers in order to detect the Cloud-Base Height, and considering the complexity of the cloud characteristics, this approach was considered ideal to approach this kind of problem. Therefore, the objective of the present work is to estimate, with a Machine Learning algorithm, the CBH value starting from sky images acquired from a single ASI. In order to fulfill this task, a Convolutional Neural Network (CNN) model was chosen and developed.

2. Convolutional Neural Network

The method selected to fulfill the objective of the current work is the so-called CNN, a classification model specifically designed to detect patterns within images. In the following, the model is first described from a theoretical point of view. Then, all the characteristics of the model implemented in the present work are discussed and explained.

2.1. General Description

CNNs are classification Machine Learning models, nowadays involved, for example, in image search services, self-driving cars, automatic video classification systems, etc. Moreover, their utilization is not restricted to visual tasks: they power many other applications such as voice recognition or natural language processing.

The structure of CNNs derives from the studies of the brain's visual cortex. Several studies and experiments demonstrated that neurons dedicated to vision present a small local receptive field, hence they process only information deriving from a limited region of the visual field. Moreover, the receptive fields of different neurons may overlap, and together they cover the entire visual field. This structure, capable of detecting complex patterns in any region of the visual field, inspired the researcher to develop a Neural Network architecture that gradually evolved into into the current CNN.

In further detail, the typical CNN structure consists of a sequence of convolutional and pooling layers:

- The convolutional layer is the crucial building block of CNNs: neurons in this type of layer are not connected to every pixel in the input image but only to pixels in their corresponding receptive fields. The weight of a neuron is represented by a filter (or convolution kernel) that, when applied to the image, is able to extract features from it. During the training phase, the convolutional layer learns the best suited filters for a specific task.
- The pooling layer has the goal of subsampling the input image in order to reduce the computational load, the memory usage, and the number of network parameters to be tuned. As in convolutional layers, each neuron is connected to a restricted region of the previous layer. Moreover, neurons in this layer do not have weights: all they perform is the aggregation of the inputs according to a specific aggregation function, such as max or mean.

After being processed in the cascade of convolutional and pooling layers, the information flow is flattened, i.e., it is structured in a suitable format to be further processed. The last step of the classification process takes place in one or more dense layers, providing the final output.

2.2. Adopted Structure

The CNN structure adopted is represented in Figure 1. The combination between a convolutional and a pooling layer is exploited two times in order to grant a reasonably deep feature extraction from the input images. Then, the information flow is flattened and delivered to the final dense layer, aimed at providing the output label corresponding to an unlabeled input image.

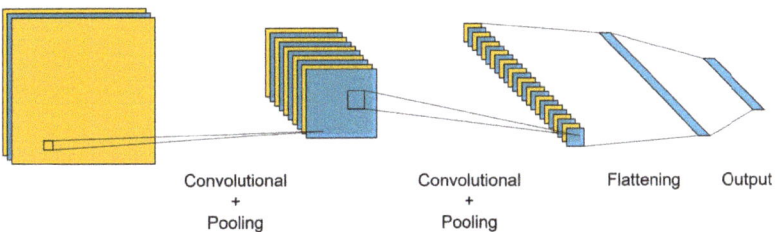

Figure 1. Adopted CNN structure.

Some characteristic parameters of the CNN structure need to undergo an optimization procedure in order to grant the best possible performance on the considered case study. In detail, a sensitivity analysis is carried out on the number of filters involved in the convolutional layers. The dimension of the dense layer is kept fixed at 16 hidden neurons. This study is aimed at selecting the configuration representing the optimal compromise between model accuracy and complexity. The results of the sensitivity analysis depend primarily on the amount of data involved in training and are reported in the results section.

3. Case Study and Available Data

The CBH is a crucial parameter in the characterization of the cloud features and consequently on the determination of the attenuation of solar radiation on the ground. Unfortunately, there are few instruments (ceilometers), which are very expensive, that are able to detect, in an objective way, this parameter. The alternative, considered in this work, is the exploitation of the atmospheric sounding obtained in the correspondence of some airports by means of a radio sounding. This measurement is made with low frequency (generally twice a day at 00 and 12 UTC) because of the weather balloon launch cost which hosts the battery-powered telemetry instrument. In the presented case study, the problem was also to have the radio sounding in proximity of the All Sky Imager. For this reason, the observed dataset was not too large and, therefore, it has been necessary to consider a reduced number of classes. In presence of a consistent dataset of CBH measurements obtained from a ceilometer, it would be possible to increase the number of the classes. Furthermore, in order to train a supervised Machine Learning model, a proper set of data is required. More in detail, it is necessary to have some target data, i.e., representing the quantity that the model is going to estimate, and some input data, i.e., the information on which the estimation is performed. As input data, sky images from an ASI are used. On the other hand, as target data, information derived from radio soundings is available.

3.1. Input Data

All available sky images are acquired through a whole-sky cam and constitute the input to perform the estimation. The images cover two time periods, one comprised between the months of May and September 2020 and one between January 2014 and February 2015, and present an initial resolution of 1124 × 1124 pixels. In order to reduce the computational burden of the estimation algorithm developed, the images are down-sampled to a 256 × 256 pixels resolution.

3.2. Target Data

Target data consist of the CBH cloud cover depicted in each image. This value is computed starting from the Pressure of Lifted Condensation Level (PLCL) values, recorded through a radio sounding sensor. However, PLCL alone is not enough to properly estimate the CBH value because the atmosphere pressure is not constant throughout the year. In order to address this issue, the difference between pressure at sea level and PLCL, representative of the height of the bottom layer of the cloud, must be used to estimate the CBH target value. In the presented case study, radio soundings are carried out once a day, at 12:00: therefore, the useful time frames for CNN training, i.e., those where both PLCL value and the corresponding sky image are available, are not numerous; only 109 sky images with a corresponding target label are available. The CNN is applied, in the present work, as a classification method, while the CBH is a continuous variable; this means it cannot be used as a target variable as it is. However, it was possible to divide the range of the registered CBH values into classes corresponding to a range of values and to train the model to assign each image to its corresponding class. Therefore, the available dataset is divided into 3 classes. The identification of more than 3 classes leads to a critical issue: the number of samples inside each group becomes too small, strongly affecting the classification accuracy. In that case, the algorithm would struggle in recognizing the classes because it does not have a sufficient number of examples to infer their characteristic pattern. On the contrary, if only 2 classes are defined, the range of CBH values corresponding to each class would become too large, reducing the usefulness of the classification.

CBH classes within the interval comprised between the maximum (970) and the minimum (670), can be defined according to different strategies leading to different partitioning of samples. The strategies considered in the current work, and the relevant thresholds, are represented in Figure 2 and are described as:

- Linear: the interval comprised between the maximum and the minimum registered CBH values is divided in 3 evenly spaced intervals (770 and 870).
- Logarithmic: the interval comprised between the logarithm (base 10) of the maximum and the minimum registered CBH values is divided in 3 evenly spaced intervals (764 and 863).
- Equal number of samples: the thresholds dividing CBH classes are set to make three classes with an equal number of samples (848 and 875); this latter partitioning strategy is defined in order to verify the results obtainable with balanced classes in terms of the same number of samples.

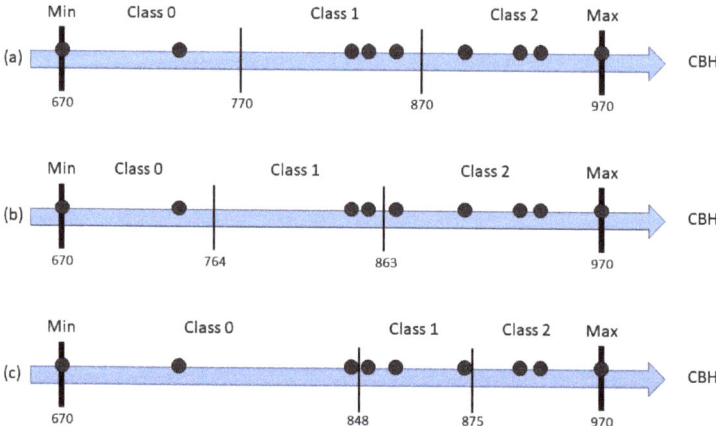

Figure 2. Different strategies for CBH classes definition and relevant thresholds: (**a**) linear; (**b**) logarithmic; (**c**) equal number of samples.

The different partitioning strategies lead to a different number of samples in each class, as reported in Table 1:

Table 1. Number of samples in each class according to different partitioning strategies.

Strategy	Class 0	Class 1	Class 2
Linear	39	66	4
Logarithmic	15	70	24
Equal num samples	39	36	34

3.3. Oversampling

CNNs, in order to be trained, require a large amount of input images. However, in our case study, the available dataset is not that large. In order to address this issue, an oversampling is performed in order to obtain additional generated input samples, useful to improve the training process of the model. Assuming a negligible time variation of the vertical profile of atmosphere, it is possible to assign to a single radio sounding all the images acquired in the surrounding time frames, as graphically represented in Figure 3.

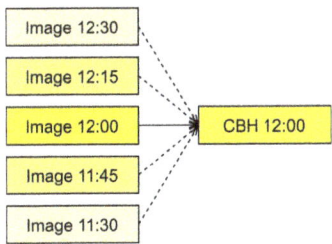

Figure 3. Oversampling strategy adopted to enlarge the amount of training data available.

The impact of oversampling on class population is reported in Table 2:

Table 2. Samples per class of the adopted partitioning strategy after oversampling.

Strategy	Class 0	Class 1	Class 2
Linear	201	330	19
Logarithmic	73	360	117
Equal num samples	201	182	167

4. Results

The performance evaluation is a crucial step to assess the capability of the model to correctly identify the target classes. Here, the classification performances of a CNN are presented and discussed according to specific evaluation metrics after the class definition strategies previously listed in Section 3.2.

4.1. Evaluation Metrics

The evaluation metrics adopted in order to assess the model performances are presented in the following. The Global Accuracy (A) measures "how good" a classification model is, returning the fraction of right predictions. It is calculated as in Equation (1):

$$A = \frac{TP}{TP + TN + FP + FN} \tag{1}$$

where:
- TP (True Positives) are samples correctly classified by the model as positive;
- TN (True Negatives) are samples correctly classified by the model as negative;
- FP (False Positives) are samples that the model incorrectly classifies as belonging to class C, while they belong to a different class;

- *FN* (False Negatives) are samples belonging to class C that are incorrectly classified as belonging to a different class.

Precision, also denoted as Positive Predictive Value (PPV), for a class C is calculated as in Equation (2):

$$Precision = PPV = \frac{TP}{TP + FP} \tag{2}$$

Recall, also denoted as sensitivity, for a class C is calculated as it is stated in the Equation (3):

$$Recall = Sensitivity = \frac{TP}{TP + FN} \tag{3}$$

4.2. Linear Classes Definition

In this case, the classes are defined according to the linear strategy, meaning that samples are defined according to linear partition strategies in the boundary thresholds of the classes, as it is previously described in Section 3.2. The sensitivity analysis carried out in order to identify the optimal network structure indicates the number of filters equal to 64 for both the first and the second convolutional layers. Figure 4 depicts the confusion matrix representing the classification performances in the considered case. A generic cell in row i and column j represents the number of samples belonging to class i that are assigned to class j during classification. Table 3 represents the classification performance evaluated through the metrics previously defined.

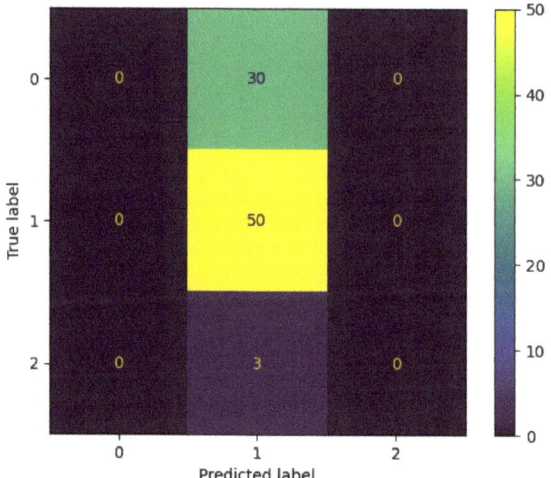

Figure 4. Confusion matrix for the Linear Classes Definition.

Table 3. Classification performances in the Linear Classes Definition.

Class	PPV	Recall
0	-	0.00
1	0.60	1.00
2	-	0.00

In this case, the developed classification model is unable to recognize the presence of two classes (classes 0 and 2) out of three. As a matter of fact, the only class appearing in the model output is class 1, i.e., the most numerous one. The performance metrics numerically confirm the coherent results represented by the confusion matrix.

4.3. Logarithmic Classes Definition

In this case, the classes are defined according to the logarithmic strategy. The sensitivity analysis carried out in order to identify the optimal network structure indicates the number of filters equal to 64 for both the first and the second convolutional layers.

Figure 5 depicts the confusion matrix representing the classification performances in the considered case. A generic cell in row i and column j represents the number of samples belonging to class i that are assigned to class j during classification. Table 4 represents the classification performance evaluated through the metrics previously defined.

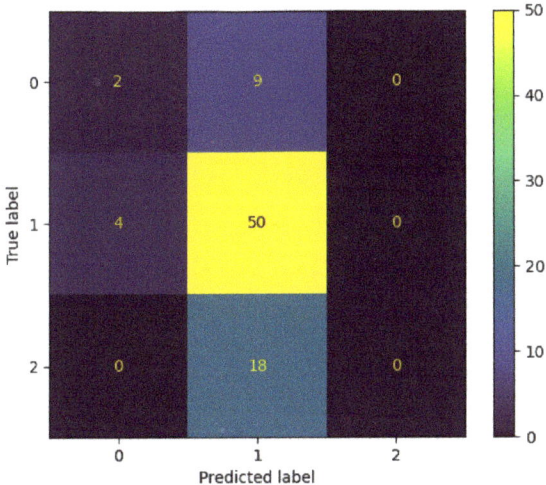

Figure 5. Confusion matrix for the Logarithmic Classes Definition.

Table 4. Classification performances for the Logarithmic Classes Definition.

Class	PPV	Recall
0	0.33	0.18
1	0.65	0.93
2	-	0.00

Unlike the previous case, the CNN recognizes the presence of two classes (classes 0 and 1) instead of only one. A small number of samples are assigned to class 0, but only a couple of them really belong to that class. Evaluation metrics highlight coherently the small number of correct classifications in class 0.

4.4. Classes with Equal Number of Samples

In this case, the classes are defined in a way that an equal number of samples belongs to each class. The sensitivity analysis carried out in order to identify the optimal network structure indicates the number of filters equal to 64 for both the first and the second convolutional layers.

Figure 6 depicts the confusion matrix representing the classification performances in the considered case. A generic cell in row i and column j represents the number of samples belonging to class i that are assigned to class j during classification. Table 5 represents the classification performance evaluated through the metrics previously defined.

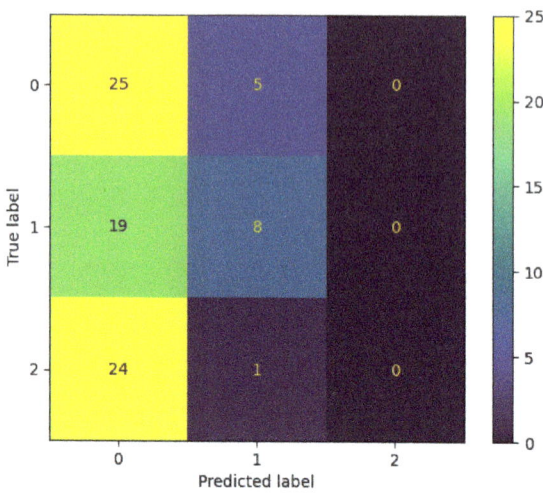

Figure 6. Confusion matrix for classes defined with an equal number of samples.

Table 5. Classification performance for classes with an equal number of samples.

Class	PPV	Recall
0	0.36	0.83
1	0.57	0.30
2	-	0.00

This last case demonstrates that, even with an equal number of samples, the classification performances are slightly worsened compared with the logarithmic class definition. Once again, the CNN recognizes the presence of only two classes out of three and a large number of test samples are misclassified, as highlighted also by the performance metrics. Finally, the Global Accuracy (A) for the different class definitions together with the other evaluation metrics adopted in this work is reported in Table 6. In this study case, the strategy of the logarithmic partition of the samples within classes scores the best result in terms of global accuracy (0.63%), even if the limited amount of samples strongly affects the classification precision PPV. On the contrary, linear class definition shows the worst classification results with a global accuracy equal to 0.4, and it is unable to classify samples belonging to class 0 and class 2, while the Equal Amount of Samples strategy indicates almost comparable results (0.6) to the logarithmic partition of the samples within classes. Finally, samples in class 2 are incorrectly classified, allegedly due to the lack of samples belonging to that class, especially in the linear partition strategy.

Table 6. Classification performances for the different class definitions.

Class Definition Strategy	Linear		Logarithmic		Equal Number of Samples	
Class	PPV	Recall	PPV	Recall	PPV	Recall
0	-	0.00	0.33	0.18	0.36	0.83
1	0.60	1.00	0.65	0.93	0.57	0.30
2	-	0.00	-	0.00	-	0.00
Global Accuracy	0.60		0.63		0.40	

5. Conclusions

The present work aims at estimating the CBH (Cloud-Base Height) value through a CNN (Convolutional Neural Network) model processing sky images acquired from a single ASI. The CBH value for each of the training images is estimated starting from the PLCL (Pressure of Lifted Condensation Level) value recorded by radio soundings and the pressure at sea level. Moreover, the model output was not a specific CBH value but a class corresponding to a range of possible CBH values. In total, three classes were defined according to different strategies, namely: linear, logarithmic, and an equal number of samples partition in each group. In order to increase the number of available training samples, an oversampling procedure was carried out. The final best classification accuracy is 63% with the logarithmic classes definition. The reduced number of samples does not allow generalized conclusions to be drawn, even if the classification obtained with the logarithmic class definition seems to be the most promising. Future works will aim at adding more data and will combine the here-presented information contained in sky images with additional exogenous parameters (i.e., from sensors located in situ) to further improve the accuracy of the model.

Author Contributions: Conceptualization, E.O., A.N., E.C., and D.R.; methodology, E.O. and A.N.; software, A.N.; validation, E.C. and D.R.; formal analysis, E.O.; investigation, E.O. and A.N.; resources, E.C. and D.R.; data curation, A.N.; writing—original draft preparation, E.O.; writing—review and editing, E.C. and D.R.; visualization, E.O., A.N., E.C., and D.R.; supervision, E.O., E.C., and D.R.; project administration, E.O. and E.C.; funding acquisition, E.C. and D.R. All authors have read and agreed to the published version of the manuscript.

Funding: This work has been partly financed by the Research Fund for the Italian Electrical System with the Decree of 16 April 2018.

Institutional Review Board Statement: Not applicable.

Informed Consent Statement: Not applicable.

Data Availability Statement: Not applicable.

Conflicts of Interest: The authors declare no conflict of interest.

References

1. Blum, N.B.; Nouri, B.; Wilbert, S.; Schmidt, T.; Lünsdorf, O.; Stührenberg, J.; Pitz-Paal, R. Cloud height measurement by a network of all-sky imagers. *Atmos. Meas. Tech.* **2021**, *14*, 5199–5224. [CrossRef]
2. Costa-Surós, M.; Calbó, J.; González, J.A.; Martin-Vide, J. Behavior of Cloud-Base Height from ceilometer measurements. *Atmos. Res.* **2013**, *127*, 64–76. [CrossRef]
3. Hogan, R.J.; O'Connor, E.J.; Illingworth, A.J. Verification of cloud-fraction forecasts. *Q. J. R. Meteorol. Soc. J. Atmos. Sci. Appl. Meteorol. Phys. Oceanogr.* **2009**, *135*, 1494–1511. [CrossRef]
4. Kassianov, E.; Long, C.N.; Christy, J. Cloud-base-height estimation from paired ground-based hemispherical observations. *J. Appl. Meteorol.* **2005**, *44*, 1221–1233. [CrossRef]
5. Rodríguez-Benítez, F.J.; López-Cuesta, M.; Arbizu-Barrena, C.; Fernández-León, M.M.; Pamos-Ureña, M.Á.; Tovar-Pescador, J.; Santos-Alamillos, F.J.; Pozo-Vázquez, D. Assessment of new solar radiation nowcasting methods based on sky-camera and satellite imagery. *Appl. Energy* **2021**, *292*, 116838. [CrossRef]
6. Nespoli, A.; Niccolai, A.; Ogliari, E.; Perego, G.; Collino, E.; Ronzio, D. Machine Learning techniques for solar irradiation nowcasting: Cloud type classification forecast through satellite data and imagery. *Appl. Energy* **2022**, *305*, 117834. [CrossRef]
7. Nguyen, D.A.; Kleissl, J. Stereographic methods for Cloud-Base Height determination using two sky imagers. *Sol. Energy* **2014**, *107*, 495–509. [CrossRef]
8. Heidinger, A.K.; Bearson, N.; Foster, M.J.; Li, Y.; Wanzong, S.; Ackerman, S.; Holz, R.E.; Platnick, S.; Meyer, K. Using sounder data to improve cirrus cloud height estimation from satellite imagers. *J. Atmos. Ocean. Technol.* **2019**, *36*, 1331–1342. [CrossRef]
9. Savoy, F.M.; Lemaitre, J.C.; Dev, S.; Lee, Y.H.; Winkler, S. Cloud-Base Height estimation using high-resolution whole sky imagers. In Proceedings of the 2015 IEEE International Geoscience and Remote Sensing Symposium (IGARSS), Milan, Italy, 26–31 July 2015; pp. 1622–1625.
10. Nouri, B.; Kuhn, P.; Wilbert, S.; Hanrieder, N.; Prahl, C.; Zarzalejo, L.; Kazantzidis, A.; Blanc, P.; Pitz-Paal, R. Cloud height and tracking accuracy of three all sky imager systems for individual clouds. *Sol. Energy* **2019**, *177*, 213–228. [CrossRef]
11. Martucci, G.; Milroy, C.; O'Dowd, C. Detection of Cloud-Base Height Using Jenoptik CHM15K and Vaisala CL31 Ceilometers. *J. Atmos. Ocean. Technol.* **2010**, *27*, 305–318. [CrossRef]
12. Ogliari, E.; Dolara, A.; Manzolini, G.; Leva, S. Physical and hybrid methods comparison for the day ahead PV output power forecast. *Renew. Energy* **2017**, *113*, 11–21. [CrossRef]

Proceeding Paper

A Hybrid Model of VAR-DCC-GARCH and Wavelet Analysis for Forecasting Volatility [†]

Maryam Nafisi-Moghadam and Shahram Fattahi *[ID]

Department of Economics, Razi University, Kermanshah 6714414971, Iran; nafisi1988@gmail.com
* Correspondence: sh_fattahi@yahoo.com
† Presented at the 8th International Conference on Time Series and Forecasting, Gran Canaria, Spain, 27–30 June 2022.

Abstract: The purpose of this study is to investigate the time-varying co-movement between the volatility of gold, exchange rate, and stock market returns in Iran, using weekly data from 27 September 2013 to 3 December 2021. The results of the wavelet-based random forest show that the performance of VAR-DCC-GARCH model is better than that of DCC-GARCH model in predicting financial market volatilities. Furthermore, the results of the VAR-DCC-GARCH model indicate that a positive and relatively high conditional correlation exists in the daily exchange rate and gold-return volatility. The conditional correlation is lower between the exchange rate–stock market returns and the daily gold–stock market returns. In short and long terms, there is no correlation between the exchange rate and the stock market volatilities as well as gold and stock market volatilities, while the correlation between the paired markets exists in the medium term.

Keywords: financial market volatility; VAR-DCC-GARCH; wavelet-based random forest; forecasting

check for updates

Citation: Nafisi-Moghadam, M.; Fattahi, S. A Hybrid Model of VAR-DCC-GARCH and Wavelet Analysis for Forecasting Volatility. *Eng. Proc.* **2022**, *18*, 6. https://doi.org/10.3390/engproc2022018006

Academic Editors: Ignacio Rojas, Hector Pomares, Olga Valenzuela, Fernando Rojas and Luis Javier Herrera

Published: 20 June 2022

Publisher's Note: MDPI stays neutral with regard to jurisdictional claims in published maps and institutional affiliations.

1. Introduction

Among the important topics of financial economics are the modeling of volatility, the interdependence of volatility in financial markets, and forecasting. Volatility in financial markets occurs when these markets are at risk [1]. With the spread of information in financial markets, the correlation between markets and their volatility has increased. Investors predict price changes based on the price changes of other markets. In other words, an increase in the return of a market may change the return of the other markets at the same time. This change is called the "Spillover Effect". Therefore, besides accurate modeling and forecasting of financial market volatility, examining their dependence can help investors, risk managers, and traders to create sustainable profits [2].

The exchange rate is determined by the trade balance or current account balance of countries. Since the exchange-rate changes affect international competition and trade balance, these changes affect real incomes and input prices. An increase in the input cost leads to a decrease in profit firms and a decline in stock price [3]. On the other hand, the exchange rate is determined by the supply and demand of financial assets such as equities and bonds, since expectations of relative changes in domestic currency have a significant effect on the price of financial assets. Bodnar and Gentry [4] show that the relationship between firm profitability and exchange-rate changes depends on the nature and type of industrial activity. An increase in the exchange rate leads to a decline in the price of exported goods in the importing country, and if demand is high in the importing country, the export rate will increase and the exporting company will benefit. Conversely, an increase in the exchange rate will make imported goods more expensive and reduce the value of the importing company (Unless the importer's firms can transfer the price increase to the end consumer). The empirical literature provides conflicting findings of the dynamic relationship between the exchange rate and the stock market. Aggarwal [5], Kim [6], Doong et al. [7], and Dahir et al. [3] showed a positive relationship between the exchange rate and the stock market index. Erdogan et al. [8] showed that there were significant volatility spillover effects on the Islamic stock market to the foreign exchange market. According to Gavins [9] and Zhao [10], there is no relationship between exchange rates and stock prices. Hashim et al. [11] showed a negative relationship between the exchange rate and the stock market.

Since individuals hold their financial assets in a combination of cash, gold, currency, bonds, and equities, changes in each market can affect individuals' investment portfolios. Rising inflation, exchange-rate fluctuations, or political instability can lead to some form of market excitement and increase demand for gold. Various studies have been conducted on the relationship between gold prices and stock indices, some of which are as follows: Gilmore et al. [12] showed that there is a cointegration between the gold price, the stock-market price of gold, and the US stock index. Mishra et al. [13] showed that there is no correlation between the gold price and stock index in India. Srinivasan [14] investigated the causal nexus between gold price, stock price, and exchange rate in India using ARDL. He showed that there exists no causality from gold price to stock price or vice versa in the short run. Arouri et al. [15] examine the relationship between the global price of gold and the Chinese stock market over the period of 22 March 2004 through to 31 March 2011 in China. For this purpose, they used VAR-GARCH and other multivariate GARCH models such as DCC and CCC. Their research results show that past gold returns play an important role in explaining the dynamics of conditional returns and stock-market volatility. Jain and Biswal [16], using a DCC-GARCH model, showed that falling gold and crude oil prices were causing the Indian stock market to decline. Yousaf and Ali [17] showed that there are return and volatility spillovers between the gold and emerging Asian stock markets during the global financial crisis. Moreover, several studies in the literature exist about the relationship between gold and the exchange rate. Sjaastad [18] found that since the dissolution of the Bretton Woods international monetary system, floating exchange rates among the major currencies have been a major source of price instability in the world gold market. Qureshi et al. [19] using a wavelet approach showed that gold acts as a consistent short-run hedge against the exchange rate. Wang et al. [20] argued that gold can partly hedge against the depreciation of the currency in the long run.

The purpose of this paper is to investigate the correlation between the volatility of gold, foreign exchange, and stock markets in Iran, using weekly average data from 27 September 2013 to 3 December 2021. For this purpose, this study compares two approaches, VAR-DCC-GARCH and DCC-GARCH, using out-of-sample evaluation by the wavelet-based random forest (WRF) model. Then, the co-movement of the volatility is analyzed using a continuous wavelet (CWT) in the timescale. Iran had been subjected to sanctions, a sharp increase in liquidity, and structural problems that caused inflation. Therefore, investors generally turned to invest in stocks, buying foreign currency, and gold. Given the increasing volatility in the underlying markets, this paper contributes to the literature on the Iranian financial market in the following ways:

1. It shows whether a conditional correlation exists in the weekly exchange rate, gold, and stock market returns by using DCC-GARCH and VAR-DCC-GARCH.
2. It reveals that performance of VAR-DCC-GARCH model is better than that of DCC-GARCH model using out-of-sample prediction by WRF.
3. It identifies the time-varying nature of the correlation among the Iranian financial market's volatilities indexes using CWT.
4. This study helps investors identify the optimal portfolio by identifying asset-return volatility and portfolio diversification.

2. Materials and Methods

2.1. VAR-DCC-GARCH

In the VAR-DCC-GARCH model, the VAR method is used to estimate the conditional mean equation of the DCC-GARCH model. In this study, we consider the conditional mean equation VAR(1) according to the Schwartz and Akaike criterion. The conditional mean equation is written as Equation (1):

$$R_t = \mu + \Phi R_{t-1} + + e_t \, with \, e_t = D_t^{\frac{1}{2}} \eta_t \tag{1}$$

R_t is the 4×1 vector of returns of each variable, t is time, μ denotes a 4×1 vector of constants, and $\Phi = \begin{pmatrix} \varphi_{11} & \varphi_{12} & \varphi_{13} & \varphi_{14} \\ \varphi_{21} & \varphi_{22} & \varphi_{23} & \varphi_{24} \\ \varphi_{31} & \varphi_{32} & \varphi_{33} & \varphi_{34} \\ \varphi_{41} & \varphi_{42} & \varphi_{43} & \varphi_{44} \end{pmatrix}$ is a 4×4 matrix of parameters measuring the influence of each variable with own-lagged and the other. e_t is a residual of mean equation for four returns variables. η_t indicates a 4×1 vector of independenctly and identically distributed random vectors, and

$$D_t^{1/2} = diag\left(\sqrt{h_t^{oil}}, \sqrt{h_t^{TEPIX}}, \sqrt{h_t^{er}}, \sqrt{h_t^{gold}} \right) \tag{2}$$

where h_t indicate the conditional variance of returns variables. The conditional variance equation of the DCC-GARCH model is written as Equation (3):

$$H_t = D_t R D_t \tag{3}$$

The H_t matrix is an MGARCH process that can be modeled using dynamic conditional correlation (DCC) [21,22]. According to Engel's [21] model, a DCC model is defined as (4):

$$R_t = diag\left(q_{11\,t}^{\frac{1}{2}} \cdots q_{NN\,t}^{\frac{1}{2}} \right) \varrho_t diag\left(q_{11\,t}^{\frac{1}{2}} \cdots q_{NN\,t}^{\frac{1}{2}} \right) \tag{4}$$

where ϱ_t is the positive symmetric definite matrix of $N \times N$ and

$$\varrho_t = (1 - \alpha - \beta)\overline{\varrho} + \alpha u_{t-1} u'_{t-1} + \beta \varrho_{t-1} \tag{5}$$

$u_{it} = \frac{\varepsilon_{it}}{\sqrt{h_{iit}}}$, $\overline{\varrho}$, a nonconditional variance matrix of ut, α and β is nonnegative numerical parameters that satisfy $\alpha + \beta < 1$.

2.2. Wavelet-Based Random Forest

In this paper, we consider wavelet-based random forest as a prediction approach. WRF is built based on maximal overlap discrete wavelet transform (MODWT) function and random forest algorithm learning approach. The model structure is flexible and efficient [23].

The wavelet-based random forest (WRF) is based on the method originally proposed by Breiman [24]. The WRF has two stages: The first stage is the bootstrap aggregation, or bagging samples, which is performed with two-thirds of the inputs. Second, for each node of the individual decision tree, a random selection of decision trees is chosen, and those variables belonging to the best split will be allowed to grow. To identify the best split, the Gini impurity function, first introduced by Breiman et al. [25], is used to minimize the effect of impurities and maximize homogeneity of the selected subsets. Each tree will undergo this process of selecting the best subset and minimizing impurity until it is halted by reaching the best possible training performance for each training process [26].

We use this model to be able to select the best model for evaluating volatilities. The WRF performances are measured with three error metrics including root-mean-squared error (RMSE), mean-squared error (MSE), and mean-absolute error (MAE).

$$MSE = \frac{1}{n} \sum_{i=1}^{n} (O_i - P_i)^2 \tag{6}$$

$$RMSE = \sqrt{\frac{1}{n}\sum_{i=1}^{n}(O_i - P_i)^2} \tag{7}$$

$$R = \frac{\sum_{i=1}^{n}(O_i - O_{avg}) \times (P_i - P_{avg})}{(\sum_{i=1}^{n}(O_i - O_{avg})^2)^{0.5} \times (\sum_{i=1}^{n}(P_i - P_{avg})^2)^{0.5}} \tag{8}$$

$$MAE = \frac{1}{n}\sum_{i=1}^{n}|O_i - P_i| \tag{9}$$

2.3. Continuous Wavelet Analysis

Continuous wavelet transform is a method used to investigate the relationship between two time series. In mathematics, a continuous wavelet function for the time series xt whose integral is squared, is defined by the scale a > 0 and the place B∈R as relation (10):

$$X(a,b) = \frac{1}{\sqrt{a}}\int_{-\infty}^{\infty} x(t)\psi^*\left(\frac{t-b}{a}\right)dt \tag{10}$$

In this relation, $\psi(t)$ is a continuous function in both time and frequency domains. We use Morlet wavelet to define the $\psi(t)$ function as follows:

$$\psi^M(t) = \frac{1}{\pi^{\frac{1}{4}}}\left(e^{i\omega t} - e^{-\omega/2}\right)e^{-t/2} \tag{11}$$

where $\psi^M(t)$ is the continuous Morlet function, t is time, and ω is frequency.

3. Discussion

The study employs weekly data on the Tehran Price Index, gold price, and Unofficial Free Exchange Rate (US Dollar) in the period from 27 September 2013 to 3 December 2021. The weekly return of the above variables can be defined as follows:

$$y_t = 100\left[\ln(p_t) - \ln(p_{t-1})\right] \tag{12}$$

where pt represents each variable under study. The descriptive statistics for the return series are shown in Table 1. Accordingly, the mean returns on TEPIX, USD, and gold are 0.87, 0.55, and 0.636, respectively. All of the returns series exhibit positive skewness and asymmetry. According to the Jarque–Bera test, the null of normality is strongly rejected for all returns series.

Table 1. Descriptive statistics.

	TEPIX	USD	Gold
Mean	0.87	0.5507	0.636
Maximum	15.71	16.80	15.88
Minimum	−10.74	−10.87	−11.71
Sd	3.29	2.96	3.12
skewness	0.91	1.28	0.85
kurtosis	6.51	10.22	7.59
Jb	260.08	976.08	399.15

The results of Pearson's correlation coefficient are shown in Table 2. Accordingly, the unconditional correlation between the returns on TEPIX–USD, TEPIX–gold and USD– gold returns are positive. Since this analysis is straightforward and does not consider the effect of time on the correlation between the series of returns, the conditional correlation method is used.

Table 2. Pearson's correlation coefficient.

	Gold	Dollar	TEPIX
gold	1		
USD	0.777	1	
TEPIX	0.1899	0.1552	1

This study employs the VAR-DCC-GARCH and DCC-GARCH method to calculate the volatility of all returns. In order to estimate VAR-DCC-GARCH, it is necessary to determine the optimal lag. In this research, it is chosen a VAR(1) for the mean equation using Akaike and Schwartz Bayesian criteria. The results of this estimation model are reported in Table 3.

Table 3. Determination of optimal Lag.

	Akaike	Bayes	Hannan-Quinn
1	13.045	13.305	13.148
2	13.092	13.442	13.231
3	13.151	13.591	13.325

The results of estimating the mean equation are presented in Table 4. φ_{11}, φ_{22}, φ_{33} are the coefficients of own-mean spillover. φ_{11} and φ_{33} are significantly positive. In other words, the lag of the return of the time series has a direct effect on the current indicators of the returns of the total stock index TEPIX and gold. φ_{22} is significantly positive. This is not unexpected, because the exchange rate is controlled by the Iranian government. The coefficient of φ_{21} and φ_{31} indicate unidirectional and positive return spillover from USD and gold to TEPIX. In other words, when the prices of USD and gold rise, investors tend to increase their investment in the stock market. Moreover, the gold–USD return results (φ_{23}; φ_{32}) indicate unidirectional and positive return spillover from USD to gold. This indicates that when the returns of USD increase, investors tend to increase their investment in gold as well.

Table 4. Estimates of conditional mean VAR-DCC-GARCH model.

		Coefficient	p-Value
TEPIX	c_1	0.327	0.02
	φ_{11}	0.5058	0.000
	φ_{12}	0.087	0.24
	φ_{13}	−0.005	0.94
USD	c_2	0.362	0.000
	φ_{21}	0.0678	0.000
	φ_{22}	−0.0591	0.000
	φ_{23}	0.2856	0.000
gold	c_3	0.470	0.003
	φ_{31}	0.1376	0.004
	φ_{32}	−0.097	0.23
	φ_{33}	0.1924	0.01

In the following, the variance equations of the VAR-DCC-GARCH and DCC-GARCH are estimated.

Table 5 present the results of the variance equations of the VAR-DCC-GARCH and DCC-GARCH model. In this study, Ω_1, Ω_2, and Ω_3 indicate intercept of TEPIX, USD, and gold, respectively. GARCH parameters (α and β) in two models are statically significant, and the α and β coefficients in the estimated equations are non-negative and satisfy the condition $\alpha + \beta < 1$. The sum of coefficients in two models are in close unity, implying that shocks are strongly persistent. In other words, this condition guarantees that the volatility of the previous period affects the volatility of the current period.

Table 5. Estimates of conditional variance VAR-DCC-GARCH model.

		VAR-DCC-GARCH		DCC-GARCH	
		Coefficient	p-Value		
	Ω_1	0.358	0.21	1.07	0.14
TEPIX	α_1	0.1399	0.05	0.29	0.03
	β_1	0.808	0.000	0.527	0.01
	Ω_2	0.47	0.11	0.47	0.18
USD	α_2	0.216	0.003	0.44	0.05
	β_2	0.719	0.000	0.56	0.000
	Ω_3	0.1599	0.08	0209	0.05
gold	α_3	0.1703	0.001	0.309	0.001
	β_3	0.8234	0.000	0.689	0.000
DCC	α	0.095	0.006	0.028	0.02
	β	0.639	0.02	0.956	0.000

For conditional correlation analyses, we use VAR-DCC-GARCH model. The estimated conditional correlation graphs in VAR-DCC-GARCH between the returns of variables are used in this paper. Therefore, Figures 1–3 show the dynamic conditional correlation trend between USD–TEPIX, gold–TEPIX, and USD-gold, respectively.

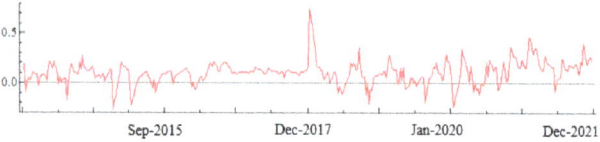

Figure 1. Dynamic conditional correlation between USD–TEPIX in VAR-DCC-GARCH model.

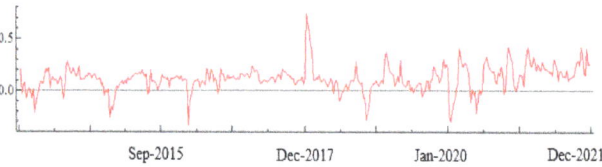

Figure 2. Dynamic conditional correlation between gold–TEPIX in VAR-DCC-GARCH model.

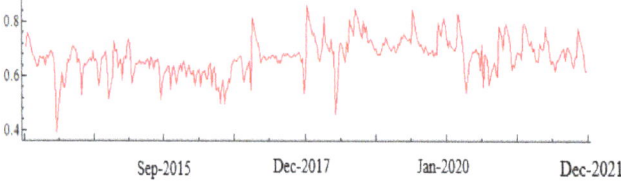

Figure 3. Dynamic Conditional Correlation between USD–gold in VAR-DCC-GARCH model.

The dynamic conditional correlation volatility between USD–TEPIX in the range of −0.2657 and 0.7558. The mean correlation coefficient of volatility is 0.1068. These volatilities are positive for most years. Figure 2 shows the dynamic conditional correlation between the returns of gold and TEPIX. The mean correlation coefficient volatility in the period under study is 0.12098. The highest and lowest correlation coefficients between gold–TEPIX are 0.7458 and −0.3338, respectively. Figure 3 shows the dynamic conditional correlation of the returns of USD and gold. The mean correlation coefficient is 0.67409. The highest and the lowest correlation coefficients are 0.8626 and 0.3924, respectively.

The results show that the correlations between gold–TEPIX, USD–TEPIX, and gold–USD are positive. In addition, the correlation between gold–USD is the biggest than the others. It means that investing in the stock market can be considered as an appropriate investment against gold and USD and vice versa. Moreover, these figures show that co-movement between conditional correlations variables exist from early 2018 to December 2021.

3.1. Forecasting Performance

In this section, the wavelet-based random forest is used to select the best model for forecasting. In fact, we compare out-of-sample forecasting of two approaches, VAR-DCC-GARCH and DCC-GARCH, using the wavelet-based random forest (WRF). For this purpose, the time series of volatilities are calculated using the VAR-DCC-GARCH and DCC-GARCH methods, then these volatilities in the financial markets are predicted using the wavelet-based random forest. Table 6 shows the performance metrics of the WRF modeling approach employed in this study. Comparing the RMSE, MSE, R-squared, and MAE, it indicates that the VAR-DCC-GARCH model outperforms the DCC-GARCH model.

Table 6. Model performance metrics.

		VAR-DCC-GARCH				DCC-GARCH			
		MSE	RMSE	R-Sq	MAE	MSE	RMSE	R-Sq	MAE
USD	Train	19.40	4.4	0.93	1.8	66.85	8.17	0.88	3.2
	Test	3.4	1.8	0.98	1.16	13.03	3.6	0.97	2.11
gold	Train	10.5	3.2	0.97	1.62	28.61	5.35	0.93	2.44
	Test	3.5	1.87	0.98	1.21	9.46	3.07	0.97	1.96
TEPIX	Train	3.47	1.86	0.89	0.96	22.52	4.74	0.86	2.20
	Test	13.27	3.64	0.95	2.27	50.7	7.07	0.94	3.96

3.2. Results of Wavelet Coherence Estimation

Applying volatilities extracted from VAR-DCC-GARCH model, the wavelet approach is used to examine the interconnected relationships between markets. The results of the coherence estimation are shown in Figures 4–6. The color of the graph shows the strength of coherency, ranging from blue (low coherency) to red (high coherency). Therefore, the more the color spectrum trends to red, the higher the correlation. The horizontal axis represents the time scale and the vertical axis represents the frequency. The graphs also show the frequency of the period (short, medium, and long term). In this way, the shortest period is 4 days and the longest is 256 days.

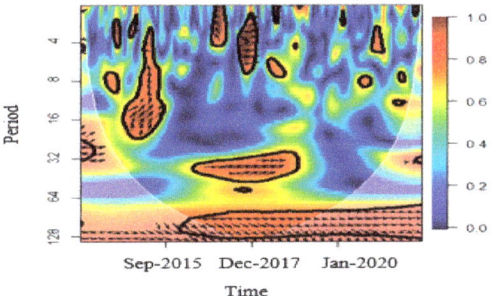

Figure 4. The continuous wavelet power spectrum of volatilities in USD–TEPIX.

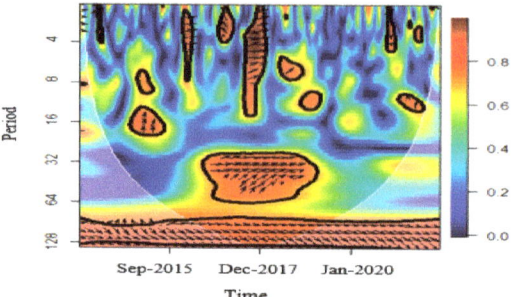

Figure 5. The continuous wavelet power spectrum of volatilities in gold–TEPIX.

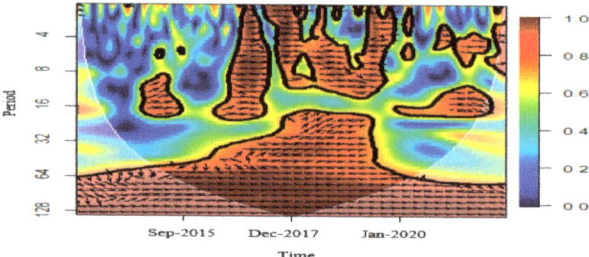

Figure 6. The continuous wavelet power spectrum of volatilities in gold–USD.

Figure 4 shows the correlation wavelet of volatilities in USD–TEPIX. According to the Figure, the color blue dominates for the most part in the short run, so there is no high correlation in the short run between volatilities in USD–TEPIX. However, in the medium term, despite the orange and red color spectrum between 2014 and 2015, it can be said that the correlation between USD–TEPIX volatilities has increased in the medium term. In the long run, there is correlation from 2016 to 2021.

The wavelet correlation analysis in gold–TEPIX volatilities is presented below in Figure 5. In the short run, given that the blue color spectrum is predominant in most of the periods, there is a low correlation between volatilities in the pairs of gold and TEPIX. In the medium term, given the dominance of the orange and yellow spectrum, especially in the period between 2017, there is a correlation between the volatility of the two markets. In the long run, there is correlation between the volatility of these two markets.

Finally, Figure 6 shows the correlation wavelet analysis on USD–gold volatilities. According to this figure, in the short and medium term from early 2016 to January 2020, given the dominant red color spectrum, a high correlation is observed in the volatilities of the returns of gold–USD. In the long run, the correlation trend in the volatilities of gold–USD has been increasing.

4. Conclusions

This study investigated the time-varying co-movement between the volatility of gold, exchange rate, and stock market returns in Iran. To do so, we first modelled the conditional correlations of financial markets using VAR-DCC-GARCH and DCC-GARCH models. Then, we compared the out-of-sample forecasting of these models. Finally, the CWT was used to study the co-movement between financial markets' volatilities. The results of the wavelet-based random forest model showed that the forecasting performance of VAR-DCC-GARCH model is better than that of DCC-GARCH model. Furthermore, there are positive correlations between the returns of gold–TEPIX and USD–TEPIX, as well as the returns of USD–gold. On the other hand, the correlation between the returns of USD–gold is higher than the other paired markets. This result implies that investors can use stocks as a suitable investment against gold and USD to increase profitability and reduce risk in their portfolio, and vice versa. In addition, the existence of gold and USD in their portfolio can significantly eliminate the benefits of portfolio diversification and increase their portfolio risk. The results of the wavelet analysis showed that the correlation process of the volatilities in the returns of gold–USD is increasing in the medium and long term. This result helps investors to maximize profitability in the short, medium, and long terms by choosing different assets in their portfolios.

Author Contributions: Conceptualization and methodology, S.F. and M.N.-M.; software, S.F and M.N.-M.; validation, S.F. and M.N.-M.; writing—original draft preparation, S.F. and M.N.-M.; writing—review and editing, S.F. and M.N.-M.; visualization, S.F. All authors have read and agreed to the published version of the manuscript.

Funding: This research received no significant external funding for the submitted work.

Institutional Review Board Statement: Not applicable.

Informed Consent Statement: Not applicable.

Data Availability Statement: The data are available on request from the corresponding author.

Conflicts of Interest: The authors have no conflicts of interest to declare that are relevant to the content of this paper.

References

1. Ping, P.Y.; Ahmad, M.H.; Ismail, N. Analysis of Volatility Spillover Effects Using Trivariate GARCH Model. *Rep. Econ. Financ.* **2016**, *2*, 61–68. [CrossRef]
2. Koo, E.; Kim, G. A Hybrid Prediction Model Integrating GARCH Models with a Distribution Manipulation Strategy Based on LSTM Networks for Stock Market Volatility. *IEEE Access* **2022**, *10*, 34743–34754. [CrossRef]
3. Dahir, A.M.; Mahat, F.; Ab Razak, N.H.; Bany-Ariffin, A.N. Revisiting the dynamic relationship between exchange rates and stock prices in BRICS countries: A wavelet analysis. *Borsa Istanb. Rev.* **2018**, *18*, 101–113. [CrossRef]
4. Bodnar, G.M.; Gentry, W.M. Exchange rate exposure and industry characteristics: Evidence from Canada, Japan, and the USA. *J. Int. Money Financ.* **1993**, *12*, 29–45. [CrossRef]
5. Aggarwal, R. Exchange rates and stock prices: A study of the United States capital markets under floating exchange rates. *Akron Bus. Econ. Rev.* **1981**, *12*, 7–12.
6. Kim, K. Dollar exchange rate and stock price: Evidence from multivariate cointegration and error correction model. *Rev. Financ. Econ.* **2003**, *12*, 301–313. [CrossRef]
7. Doong, S.C.; Yang, S.Y.; Wang, A.T. The dynamic relationship and pricing of stocks and exchange rates: Empirical evidence from Asian emerging markets. *Acad. Bus. J.* **2005**, *7*, 118–123.
8. Erdogan, S.; Gedikli, A.; Cevik, E.İ. Volatility spillover effects between Islamic stock markets and exchange rates: Evidence from three emerging countries. *Borsa Istanb. Rev.* **2020**, *20*, 322–333. [CrossRef]
9. Gavin, M. The stock market and exchange rate dynamics. *J. Int. Money Financ.* **1989**, *8*, 181–200. [CrossRef]
10. Zhao, H. Dynamic relationship between exchange rate and stock price: Evidence from China. *Res. Int. Bus. Financ.* **2010**, *24*, 103–112. [CrossRef]
11. Hashim, K.K.; Masih, M. *Stock Market Volatility and Exchange Rates: MGARCH-DCC and Wavelet Approaches*; MPRA Paper No. 65234; MPRA: Munich, Germany, 2015.
12. Gilmore, C.G.; McManus, G.M.; Sharma, R.; Tezel, A. The dynamics of gold prices, gold mining stock prices and stock market prices comovements. *Res. Appl. Econ.* **2009**, *1*, 1–19. [CrossRef]
13. Mishra, P.K.; Das, J.R.; Mishra, S.K. Gold price volatility and stock market returns in India. *Am. J. Sci. Res.* **2010**, *9*, 47–55.
14. Srinivasan, P.; Karthigai, P. Gold Price, Stock Price and Exchange Rate Nexus: The Case of India. *IUP J. Financ. Risk Manag.* **2014**, *11*, 1–12.
15. Arouri, M.E.H.; Lahiani, A.; Nguyen, D.K. World gold prices and stock returns in China: Insights for hedging and diversification strategies. *Econ. Model.* **2015**, *44*, 273–282. [CrossRef]
16. Jain, A.; Biswal, P.C. Dynamic linkages among oil price, gold price, exchange rate, and stock market in India. *Resour. Policy* **2016**, *49*, 179–185. [CrossRef]
17. Yousaf, I.; Ali, S. Linkages between gold and emerging Asian stock markets: New evidence from the Chinese stock market crash. *Stud. Appl. Econ.* **2021**, *39*, 26. [CrossRef]
18. Sjaastad, L.A. The price of gold and the exchange rates: Once again. *Resour. Policy* **2008**, *33*, 118–124. [CrossRef]
19. Qureshi, S.; Rehman, I.U.; Qureshi, F. Does gold act as a safe haven against exchange rate fluctuations? The case of Pakistan rupee. *J. Policy Model.* **2018**, *40*, 685–708. [CrossRef]

20. Wang, K.M.; Thi, T.B.N.; Lee, Y.M. Is gold a safe haven for the dynamic risk of foreign exchange? *Future Bus. J.* **2021**, *7*, 56. [CrossRef]
21. Engle, R. Dynamic conditional correlation: A simple class of multivariate generalized autoregressive conditional heteroskedasticity models. *J. Bus. Econ. Stat.* **2002**, *20*, 339–350. [CrossRef]
22. Tse, Y.K.; Tsui, A.K.C. A multivariate generalized autoregressive conditional heteroscedasticity model with time-varying correlations. *J. Bus. Econ. Stat.* **2002**, *20*, 351–362. [CrossRef]
23. Prieto, C.; Le Vine, N.; Kavetski, D.; García, E.; Medina, R. Flow prediction in ungauged catchments using probabilistic random forests regionalization and new statistical adequacy tests. *Water Resour. Res.* **2019**, *55*, 4364–4392. [CrossRef]
24. Breiman, L. Random forests. *Mach. Learn.* **2001**, *45*, 5–32. [CrossRef]
25. Breiman, L.; Friedman, J.H.; Olshen, R.A.; Stone, C.J. *Classification and Regression Trees*; Chapman and Hall/CRC: Boca Raton, FL, USA, 1984.
26. Woznicki, S.A.; Baynes, J.; Panlasigui, S.; Mehaffey, M.; Neale, A. Development of a spatially complete floodplain map of the conterminous United States using random forest. *Sci. Total Environ.* **2019**, *647*, 942–953. [CrossRef]

Proceeding Paper

Synthetic Subject Generation with Coupled Coherent Time Series Data †

Xabat Larrea [1,2,*], **Mikel Hernandez** [1,*], **Gorka Epelde** [1,3], **Andoni Beristain** [1,3], **Cristina Molina** [1], **Ane Alberdi** [2], **Debbie Rankin** [4], **Panagiotis Bamidis** [5,‡] and **Evdokimos Konstantinidis** [5,6,‡]

1   Vicomtech Foundation, Basque Research and Technology Alliance (BRTA), 20009 Donostia-San Sebastian, Spain; gepelde@vicomtech.org (G.E.); aberistain@vicomtech.org (A.B.); cmolina@vicomtech.org (C.M.)
2   Biomedical Engineering Department, Mondragon Unibertsitatea, 20500 Arrasate-Mondragon, Spain; aalberdiar@mondragon.edu
3   eHealth Group, Biodonostia Health Research Institute, 20014 Donostia-San Sebastian, Spain
4   School of Computing, Engineering and Intelligent Systems, Ulster University, Derry-Londonderry BT48 7JL, UK; d.rankin1@ulster.ac.uk
5   Laboratory of Medical Physics and Digital Innovation, School of Medicine, Aristotle University of Thessaloniki, 54124 Thessaloniki, Greece; pdbamidis@gmail.com (P.B.); evdokimosk@gmail.com (E.K.)
6   European Network of Living Labs, 1210 Brussels, Belgium
*   Correspondence: xlarreal@vicomtech.org (X.L.); mhernandez@vicomtech.org (M.H.)
†   Presented at the 8th International Conference on Time Series and Forecasting, Gran Canaria, Spain, 27–30 June 2022.
‡   These authors contributed equally to this work.

Citation: Larrea, X.; Hernandez, M.; Epelde, G.; Beristain, A.; Molina, C.; Alberdi, A.; Rankin, D.; Bamidis, P.; Konstantinidis, E. Synthetic Subject Generation with Coupled Coherent Time Series Data. *Eng. Proc.* **2022**, *18*, 7. https://doi.org/10.3390/engproc2022018007

Academic Editors: Ignacio Rojas, Hector Pomares, Olga Valenzuela, Fernando Rojas and Luis Javier Herrera

Published: 21 June 2022

Publisher's Note: MDPI stays neutral with regard to jurisdictional claims in published maps and institutional affiliations.

Abstract: A large amount of health and well-being data is collected daily, but little of it reaches its research potential because personal data privacy needs to be protected as an individual's right, as reflected in the data protection regulations. Moreover, the data that do reach the public domain will typically have under-gone anonymization, a process that can result in a loss of information and, consequently, research potential. Lately, synthetic data generation, which mimics the statistics and patterns of the original, real data on which it is based, has been presented as an alternative to data anonymization. As the data collected from health and well-being activities often have a temporal nature, these data tend to be time series data. The synthetic generation of this type of data has already been analyzed in different studies. However, in the healthcare context, time series data have reduced research potential without the subjects' metadata, which are essential to explain the temporal data. Therefore, in this work, the option to generate synthetic subjects using both time series data and subject metadata has been analyzed. Two approaches for generating synthetic subjects are proposed. Real time series data are used in the first approach, while in the second approach, time series data are synthetically generated. Furthermore, the first proposed approach is implemented and evaluated. The generation of synthetic subjects with real time series data has been demonstrated to be functional, whilst the generation of synthetic subjects with synthetic time series data requires further improvements to demonstrate its viability.

Keywords: time series; synthetic data; shareable data; privacy

1. Introduction

Time series data are defined as a class of temporal data objects, a collection of chronological observations [1]. Time series data tend to be large in size and with high dimensionality. Time series data are characterized by their numerical and continuous nature, always considered as a whole, instead of a numerical field.

The motivation to investigate synthetic time series generation (STSG) is born from the VITALISE H2020 project [2]. One of the main objectives of this project is to provide virtual transnational access to data generated from several living labs (LLs) throughout Europe and beyond. To provide this transnational access, synthetic data generation (SDG) techniques have been incorporated into the controlled data processing workflow to generate shareable data for external researchers in compliance with the General Data Protection Regulation (GDPR) [3]. LLs are research infrastructures that enable research studies to take place in real-life environments. Those research studies generate data that are potentially interesting for the research community. However, given that these data contain human personal or sensitive information, they are stored internally in LL infrastructures and cannot be externally shared outside the original research context.

Traditionally, anonymization techniques have been used to allow sensitive data to be made publicly available whilst preserving privacy, but traditional anonymization techniques tend to suppress useful data because many of them add noise to the real data or delete attributes from them. In this scenario, SDG is presented as a game-changing anonymization technique, as it has the potential to create data without erasing potentially interesting data.

In this context, a workflow to make LL data accessible for external researchers by generating synthetic data (SD) has been proposed by Hernandez et al. [4]. As explained in the proposed workflow, SD is created with a clear purpose, enabling researchers to develop algorithms and analyses locally using it. Subsequently, the locally developed algorithms and analyses are remotely executed with the real data stored in LL infrastructures. This approach enables external researchers to conduct and validate experiments with GDPR compliance.

When evaluating SD quality, the following three dimensions are most commonly considered: privacy, utility, and resemblance. The main aim of the use case mentioned above is to remotely develop algorithms with SD to test them with real data later. Therefore, the utility dimension will be more relevant than resemblance when generating SD. Once the privacy of SD is ensured, in the context described above, more importance should be given to the utility dimension of the SD in contrast to its resemblance with real data.

2. Related Work

SDG has been gaining importance for privacy-preserving data publishing. It enables the creation of artificial data with a high statistical resemblance to real data without containing potentially private data [5]. In this context, Hernandez et al. reviewed the SDG approaches proposed as an alternative to anonymization techniques for health domain applications [6]. Furthermore, there are also studies in which STSG has been researched and used [7–14].

In 2018, Norgaard et al. [7] proposed the use of a supervised generative adversarial network (GAN), which is a variation in the originally proposed GAN approach [15]. In 2019, Yoon et al. [8] presented a time series specific GAN model, named Time-GAN, whose focus was on preserving the temporal dynamics of data. TimeGAN has later been used in the medical time series context by Dash et al. [9]. In 2020, Wang et al. [10] proposed a privacy-preserving augmentation and releasing scheme for time series data via a GAN (PART-GAN). This approach added differential privacy to the conditional temporal GAN (CT-GAN) [16], an approach that was proposed for generating videos. In addition, in 2020, an update on the Synthetic Data Vault (SDV) [11], a Python package used for generating synthetic data, added a specific model for generating time series data. This model is a probabilistic autoregressive (PAR) model, but its mathematical principles are still unpublished. In 2021, Hyun et al. [13] proposed NeuralProphet, a neural network variation in the forecasting tool Prophet [17], as a method for STSG to create synthetic diabetic foot patients. In 2022, Li et al. [14] presented the transformer-based time-series GAN (TTS-GAN) based on a transformer-encoder architecture.

Although the number of proposed STSG approaches is considerable, most of them do not consider the metadata of the subjects, as are focused on generating highly realistic sequences of data. Furthermore, some of the approaches mentioned above transform time series data into the latent space, without analyzing the option to transform the generated synthetic time series back to the data format of the real data.

3. Proposed Approaches

This section presents two approaches for generating synthetic subjects containing temporal data. The first approach assumes that time series data do not require further transformations to ensure patient privacy. The second approach requires time series data to be synthesized. Thus, well-performing STSG techniques that consider the metadata of subjects are required. On this section, both approaches are presented on a general theoretical basis and the specific data generation models that have been used are specified in Section 4.

3.1. Synthetic Subjects with Real Time Series Data

This approach, as depicted in Figure 1, has been proposed to generate useful partially synthetic multi-subject datasets containing time series data. The approach of adding time series data to synthetically generated patients, by using synthetic tabular data generation techniques, was inspired by Schiff et al. [18], who proposed to enrich synthetic patients' data with real time series data. In their approach, tabular data of synthetic patients are generated from a dataset, creating patients that have their illnesses labelled with diagnostic codes. Then, time series data, which are also labelled with diagnostic codes and do not have any relationship with the first dataset, are added to enrich patients' information. This process is carried out by comparing the diagnostic codes of both datasets. Our approach improves Schiff et al.'s proposed approach, by linking (with a meaningful relationship) time series data with synthetically generated tabular subject metadata, starting from real cohort data containing such links.

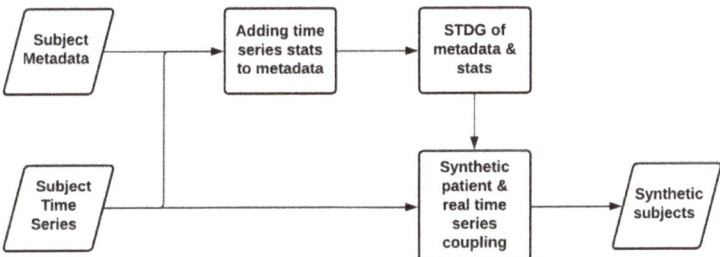

Figure 1. Workflow for generating a synthetic patient containing real time series data.

The first and obvious step in this approach is to perform a basic exploratory data analysis. Then, data preprocessing is performed to remove missing values and inconsistencies, such as negative age values. The next step is to extract meaningful statistics from each time series and append them in a table to each subject's metadata.

Once the multi-subject tabular data, including subject metadata and basic time series statistics, have been created, synthetic tabular data generation (STDG) techniques [6] are applied to generate a synthetic patient table with synthetic metadata and synthetic time series statistics. The last step is to couple the synthetic statistics with the statistics of real time series. This process matches each synthetic patient with the fitting time series.

3.2. Synthetic Subjects with Synthetic Time Series Data

The second approach depicted in Figure 2 could be considered the ideal approach, as its outcome is a fully synthetic dataset. This approach can be understood as an evolution of the approach introduced in Section 3.1, since it incorporates STSG techniques.

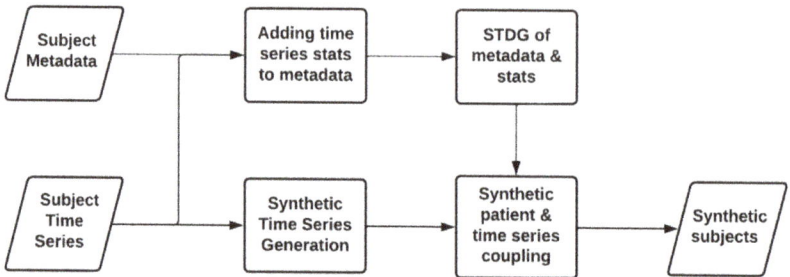

Figure 2. Workflow for generating a synthetic patient containing synthetic time series data.

The process of generating synthetic subjects and synthetic statistics is the same as the previously explained approach. However, in this approach, time series data are synthetically generated instead of using the real time series. Once STSG techniques have been applied, the same basic statistics computed from the real time series are extracted. Considering the statistics generated with the synthetic patients and the statistics obtained from the synthetic time series data, the best fitting synthetic time series is selected for each synthetic subject, using a distance-based metric.

4. Implementation

Attempts have been made to implement the approaches presented in Section 3, but the quality of synthetic time series generated for the approach presented in Section 3.2 are not yet suitable for the target use. Thus, the approach introduced in Section 3.1, the approach that generates synthetic patient datasets and then couples them with the real time series data, has been implemented. In this section, the steps followed for the implementation of this approach are explained.

4.1. Dataset Selection

To implement the proposed approach, a dataset with a high patient volume, simple metadata, and manageable time series data that is not extremely long has been chosen. The treadmill maximal exercise tests (TMET) database [19,20] was selected from PhysioNet [21] as it fulfills the aforementioned requirements.

The TMET database is an ensemble of cardiorespiratory measurements acquired during 992 treadmill maximal graded exercise tests (GET) performed in the Exercise Physiology and Human Performance Lab of the University of Malaga. During maximal effort tests, heart rate (HR), oxygen uptake (VO2), carbon dioxide elimination (VCO2), respiration rate (RR), and pulmonary ventilation (VE) were measured on a breath-to-breath premise alongside the treadmill speed. All these measures are measured and time-stamped (Time) every 2–5 s.

The dataset is composed of two files. The first one contains all the subjects' metadata and environmental metadata (humidity and temperature) in a tabular format. It contains data from 992 effort tests from 857 subjects, as there are subjects with several tests. These metadata are organized as shown in Table 1. The second file contains the results obtained from the treadmill experiments, i.e., the time series data. The mean length of these effort tests is 580 data rows; being each row, a measurement taken every two seconds. The time series data are organized as shown in Table 2. In this approach, each test has been considered as a subject.

Table 1. Subject metadata variables.

Age	Weight	Height	Humidity	Temperature	Sex	ID	ID_test

Table 2. Time series variable organization.

Time	Speed	HR	VO2	VCO2	RR	VE	ID_test	ID

4.2. EDA and Data Preprocessing

Before applying the proposed approach to the selected dataset, an exploratory data analysis (EDA) has been carried out to identify missing values and inconsistencies.

Once these undesired values have been identified, a criterion to decide how to treat them has been established. If missing values are found in the time series data, a threshold of 30 data points, a 5% of the mean length of time series data, has been established to decide if the time series must be kept or rejected. Therefore, if a time series contains less than 30 missing values, imputation is made by linear interpolation. However, if more than 30 missing values are found, the time series, and the subjects they are related to, are excluded. In case missing values are found in the metadata, the exclusion of the subject, and its related time series, has been considered.

The exploratory analysis found that the environmental data were missing for 30 subjects. Those subjects were excluded from the dataset. No unexpected values were found on the metadata. The time series data analysis found that 942 HR datapoints and 4871 VO2 and VCO2 datapoints had missing values. Following the criteria described above, 12 subjects were excluded due to the amount of missing data in the time series.

Upon completing the preprocessing stage, 950 subjects remained in the dataset from the original 992 subjects.

4.3. Time Series Feature Extraction

Before selecting the appropriate statistics that need to be extracted, it is important to consider the nature of the tests from which the time series data were obtained. For the selected dataset, the data were obtained from a treadmill test. The treadmill effort test began at a speed of 5 km/h, a speed that increased 1 km/h per minute until the subject went beyond exhaustion [21]. Once the subject's maximal effort had been reached, the treadmill speed was reduced to 5 km/h, and the recovery was recorded for 200 s.

Considering that each test has a different duration and maximal speed, the following statistics have been selected: maximal speed, test duration (last time value), and maximal, minimal, and mean values of the physiological variables (HR, VO2, VCO2, RR, and VE). These statistics have been extracted for each time series, identified with the ID_test variable, and appended to the corresponding subject in the metadata table.

4.4. Synthetic Subject Generation

The synthetic subject, and the synthetic time series statistics, have been generated by applying a STDG technique. Specifically, the Synthetic Data Vault (SDV) [11] Python package has been used. Using this approach, the generation of a cohort of synthetic subjects with their metadata and the statistics that their effort test should have were enabled. SDV contains several STDG models, from which the tabular variational auto encoder (TVAE) model with default parameters has been used to generate SD.

4.5. Time Series Coupling with Synthetic Subject

Considering that the synthetically generated statistics and the statistics extracted from the real time series do not have the same values, a strategy to couple the real effort test to the synthetic subjects is proposed. The mean value of all Euclidean distances between each synthetic time series statistics and all real time series statistics is computed. Then, the time series that brings the lowest value is selected.

Firstly, all the statistics are normalized to avoid some variables being more influential than others when calculating the mean of the distances. Subsequently, distances between each pair of statistics are calculated to compute the sum of all the distances. The ID_test of the best fitting, lowest distance sum valued, time series data are appended to each synthetic subject. Once all the synthetic subjects are assigned a time series, another dataset containing those time series is created. Finally, new identifiers linking synthetic subjects with the time series data are created. The pseudocode of this coupling can be observed in Algorithm 1.

Algorithm 1. Coupling method.

```
def coupler(synth_row):
    i = 'null'
    Tid = 'null'
    for row in stats:
        curr = stats(row)
        temp = curr − synth_row
        dst = sum(absolute(temp))
        if dst < i or i == 'null':
            i = dst
            Tid = stats ('ID_test')
    return Tid

assigned_ID = []
for row in synth_stats:
    Test = coupler (synth_stats (row))
    assigned_ID.append(Test)
synth_info ['ID_test'] = assigned_ID
```

4.6. Validation of Subjects

To validate the metadata of the cohort of synthetic subjects, some standardized metrics and methods proposed by Hernandez et al. [22] have been used.

Firstly, the mean and standard deviation values for each variable of real data and SD have been obtained. These values are collected in Table 3. From there, it can be observed that the mean and standard deviation values of the attributes of SD are similar to those of real data.

Table 3. Mean and standard deviation (mean $\pm$ std) values for real data and SD (where SD is generated using SDV).

Variable	Real Data	SD
Age	28.95 $\pm$ 10.19	27.67 $\pm$ 9.94
Weight	73.14 $\pm$ 11.96	72.12 $\pm$ 11.56
Height	174.82 $\pm$ 7.99	174.39 $\pm$ 7.73
Humidity	48.14 $\pm$ 8.54	45.4 $\pm$ 6.86
Temperature	22.82 $\pm$ 2.79	23.92 $\pm$ 1.5
Sex	Male ($n = 806$) Female ($n = 104$)	Male ($n = 810$) Female ($n = 110$)

A dimensionality reduction method, specifically principal component analysis (PCA), has been used to analyze whether the dimensional properties of the real cohort are preserved in the synthetic one. Figure 3 indicates that the generated cohort of synthetic subjects is quite similar in dimensionality. There are only a few points that differ from the cohort of real subjects.

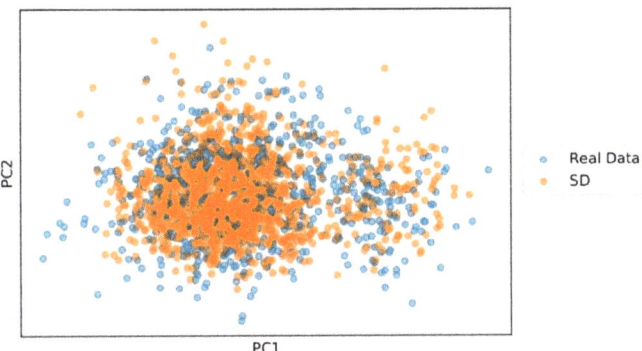

Figure 3. PCA plot of real data (blue) and SD (orange).

Figure 4 shows the pairwise Pearson correlation (PPC) matrices for both the cohort of real subjects and the cohort of synthetic subjects. From there, it can be observed that the correlations between the attributes are very similar for both cohorts. A few correlations in the cohort of synthetic subjects are weaker than the correlations from the cohort of real subjects.

Figure 4. Pairwise PPC matrices for real data (**left**) and SD (**right**).

A pairwise distance has been computed between each pair of real and synthetic subjects to evaluate how private the cohort of synthetic subjects is. The Hamming distance metric is used for this, which represents the proportion of attributes that are different between the two sets of records. Therefore, the higher the pairwise distance is, the better the privacy is preserved, since fewer attributes of the SD subjects are exactly equal to the attributes of the real subjects.

After computing the Hamming distance for each pair of real data and SD subjects, the distribution of those pairwise distances has been analyzed. As shown in Figure 5, most of the pairwise distance values are higher than 0.9, which indicates that for most synthetic subjects, the attributes are different from the real subject. This result indicates that privacy has been quite well preserved in the cohort of synthetic subjects.

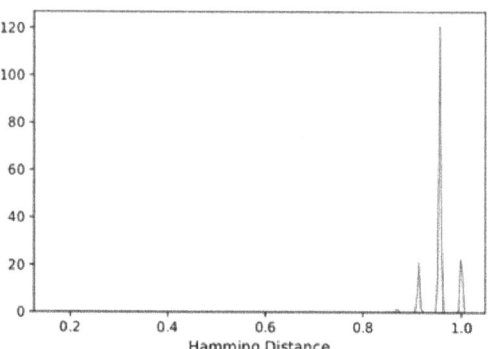

Figure 5. Distribution of pairwise Hamming distances between real data and SD.

5. Conclusions

The main conclusion derived from this work is that the proposed approach for the generation of synthetic subjects with real time series data can be used to generate a synthetic, thus shareable dataset. Hence, it can be demonstrated that with the selected dataset, the proposed methodology can be used to generate synthetic patients and then combine them with real time series data. Furthermore, the generated cohort of synthetic subjects preserves the privacy of the cohort of real subjects, while maintaining correlations and dimensional properties.

However, the developed work has a few limitations. Firstly, more evaluation with other time series datasets should be performed to validate the generalizability of the approach used. Secondly, despite some trials implementing the second proposed approach described in Section 3.2 (using the SDV PAR for STSG), the results obtained with this model and applied to the selected dataset did not meet the minimum similarity requirements to present them. More favorable results may be obtained using this approach with other datasets. Thirdly, the privacy of the generated subject cohort has not been extensively analyzed, nor has the quality of the coupling. A more extensive evaluation of the generated synthetic cohorts should be carried out to compare different STDG or STSG techniques to select the ones that yield better results. Fourthly, this approach has been generated with only one cohort of subjects and temporal data. More research with more cohorts of subjects and time series data should be carried out to validate the generalizability and improve the approach used and the other proposed approach.

The limitations mentioned above can be taken as guidelines for future work. Firstly, other missing time series data imputation techniques, such as forecasting, will be incorporated into the data processing step. Secondly, a strategy to evaluate the coupling process will be ideated, for example, using some forecasting analysis methods. Then, the approach utilized will be evaluated with more datasets. In addition, the second approach, in which synthetic time series data are generated, will be implemented and validated, together with better performing STSG techniques and more datasets to generate multivariate time series. Concerning this approach, a method to validate the temporal nature of synthetic time series will be established, since the time series data will be fully synthetic. Furthermore, a complete strategy to evaluate the subject's resemblance and privacy will be defined. For multivariate resemblance, the comparison of eigenvalues, the percentage of variance explained by each component and coordinates of the PCA analysis will be considered. In terms of privacy, the use of Wilcoxon signed-rank tests, the analysis of re-identification risks and computation of similarity to real data will be considered. Finally, it is intended to incorporate the proposed approaches in the VITALISE controlled data processing workflow presented by Hernandez et al. [4]. This workflow enables researchers to develop algorithms and perform analyses locally using SD and then request their execution remotely with the real data.

Author Contributions: Conceptualization, X.L., M.H., G.E. and A.B.; Data curation, X.L. and M.H.; Funding acquisition, G.E., P.B. and E.K.; Investigation, X.L., M.H. and G.E.; Methodology, G.E.; Project administration, G.E. and E.K.; Software, X.L., M.H., G.E., A.B. and C.M.; Supervision, G.E.; Validation, X.L. and M.H.; Visualization, X.L. and M.H.; Writing—original draft, X.L. and M.H.; Writing—review and editing, X.L., M.H., G.E., A.B., C.M., A.A., D.R. and E.K. All authors have read and agreed to the published version of the manuscript.

Funding: This research was partly funded by the VITALISE (Virtual Health and well-being Living Lab Infrastructure) project, funded by the Horizon 2020 Framework Program of the European Union for Research Innovation (grant agreement 101007990).

Institutional Review Board Statement: Not applicable.

Informed Consent Statement: Not applicable.

Data Availability Statement: The data used in this study are openly available in Physionet at https://doi.org/10.13026/7ezk-j442 (accessed on 17 June 2022).

Acknowledgments: VITALISE Consortium partners and external people participating in requirements shaping open sessions.

Conflicts of Interest: The authors declare no conflict of interest.

References

1. Fu, T. A review on time series data mining. *Eng. Appl. Artif. Intell.* **2011**, 24, 164–181. [CrossRef]
2. VITALISE H2020. Available online: https://vitalise-project.eu/about/ (accessed on 6 March 2022).
3. Regulation (EU) 2016/679 of the European Parliament and of the Council of 27 April 2016—on the Protection of Natural Persons with Regard to the Processing of Personal Data and on the Free Movement of Such Data, and Repealing Directive 95/46/EC (General Data Protection Regulation). Available online: https://eur-lex.europa.eu/eli/reg/2016/679/oj (accessed on 22 March 2022).
4. Hernandez, M.; Epelde, G.; Beristain, A.; Álvarez, R.; Molina, C.; Larrea, X.; Alberdi, A.; Timoleon, M.; Bamidis, P.; Konstantinidis, E. Incorporation of Sythetic Data Generation Techniques within a Controlled Data Processing Workflow in the Health and Wellbeing Domain. *Electronics* **2022**, 11, 812. [CrossRef]
5. Emam, K.E.; Hoptroff, R. The synthetic data paradigm for using and sharing data. *Cut. Exec. Update* **2019**, 19, 6.
6. Hernandez, M.; Epelde, G.; Alberdi, A.; Cilla, R.; Rankin, D. Synthetic data generation for tabular health records: A systematic review. *Neurocomputing* **2022**, 493, 28–45. [CrossRef]
7. Norgaard, S.; Saeedi, R.; Sasani, K.; Gebremedhin, A.H. Synthetic Sensor Data Generation for Health Applications: A Supervised Deep Learning Approach. In Proceedings of the 2018 40th Annual International Conference of the IEEE Engineering in Medicine and Biology Society (EMBC), Honolulu, HI, USA, 18–21 July 2018; pp. 1164–1167.
8. Yoon, J.; Jarrett, D.; van der Schaar, M. Time-series Generative Adversarial Networks. In *Advances in Neural Information Processing Systems*; Wallach, H., Larochelle, H., Beygelzimer, A., Alché-Buc, F.d', Fox, E., Garnett, R., Eds.; Curran Asociates, Inc.: New York, NY, USA, 2019.
9. Dash, S.; Yale, A.; Guyon, I.; Bennett, K.P. Medical Time-Series Data Generation Using Generative Adversarial Networks. In *Artificial Intelligence in Medicine*; Michalowski, M., Mokovitch, R., Eds.; Springer International Publishing: Cham, Switzerland, 2020; pp. 382–391.
10. Wang, S.; Rudolph, C.; Nepal, S.; Grobler, M.; Chen, S. PART-GAN: Privacy-preserving time-series sharing. In *Artificial Neural Networks and Machine Learning—ICANN 2020, Proceedings of the 29th International Conference on Artificial Neural Networks, Bratislava, Slovakia, 15–18 September 2020, Part I*; Springer: Cham, Switzerland, 2020; pp. 578–593.
11. Patki, N.; Wedge, R.; Veeramachaneni, K. The Synthetic Data Vault. In Proceedings of the 2016 IEEE International Conference on Data Science and Advanced Analytics (DSAA), Montreal, QC, Canada, 17–19 October 2016; pp. 399–410.
12. Li, Z.; Ma, C.; Shi, X.; Zhang, D.; Li, W.; Wu, L. TSA-GAN: A Robust Generative Adversarial Networks for Time Series Augmentation. In Proceedings of the 2021 International Joint Conference on Neural Networks (IJCNN), Shenzhen, China, 18–22 July 2021; pp. 1–8.
13. Hyun, J.; Lee, Y.; Son, H.M.; Lee, S.H.; Pham, V.; Park, J.U.; Chung, T.-M. Synthetic Data Generation System for AI-Based Diabetic Foot Diagnosis. *SN Comput. Sci.* **2021**, 2, 345. [CrossRef]
14. Li, X.; Metsis, V.; Wang, H.; Ngu, A.H.H. TTS-GAN: A Transformer-based Time-Series Generative Adversarial Network. *arXiv* **2022**, arXiv:2202.02691.
15. Goodfellow, I.; Pouget-Abadie, J.; Mirza, M.; Xu, B.; Warde-Farley, D.; Ozair, S.; Courville, A.; Bengio, Y. Generative Adversarial Nets. In *Advances in Neural Information Processing Systems*; Ghahramani, Z., Welling, M., Cortes, C., Lawrence, N., Weinberger, K.Q., Eds.; Curran Associates, Inc.: New York, NY, USA, 2014.
16. Saito, M.; Matsumoto, E.; Saito, S. Temporal Generative Adversarial Nets with Singular Value Clipping. In Proceedings of the 2017 IEEE International Conference on Computer Vision (ICCV), Venice, Italy, 22–29 October 2017; pp. 2849–2858.

17. Taylor, S.J.; Letham, B. Forecasting at Scale. *Am. Stat.* **2018**, *72*, 37–45. [CrossRef]
18. Schiff, S.; Gehrke, M.; Möller, R. Efficient Enriching of Synthesized Relational Patient Data with Time Series Data. *Procedia Comput. Sci.* **2018**, *141*, 531–538. [CrossRef]
19. Mongin, D.; García Romero, J.; Alvero Cruz, J.R. Treadmill Maximal Exercise Tests from the Exercise Physiology and Human Performance Lab of the University of Malaga (version 1.0.1). *PhysioNet* **2021**. [CrossRef]
20. Mongin, D.; Chabert, C.; Courvoisier, D.S.; García-Romero, J.; Alvero-Cruz, J.R. Heart rate recovery to assess fitness: Comparison of different calculation methods in a large cross-sectional study. *Res. Sports Med.* **2021**, 1–14. [CrossRef] [PubMed]
21. Goldberger, A.L.; Amaral, L.A.N.; Glass, L.; Hausdorff, J.M.; Ivanov PCh Mark, R.G.; Mietus, J.E.; Moody, G.B.; Peng, C.-K.; Stanley, H.E. PhysioBank, PhysioToolkit, and PhysioNet: Components of a New Research Resource for Complex Physiologic Signals. *Circulation* **2000**, *101*, e215–e220. [CrossRef] [PubMed]
22. Hernandez, M.; Epelde, G.; Alberdi, A.; Cilla, R.; Rankin, D. Standardised Metrics and Methods for Synthetic Tabular Data Evaluation. *TechRxiv* **2021**. [CrossRef]

Proceeding Paper

Price Dynamics and Measuring the Contagion between Brent Crude and Heating Oil (US-Diesel) Pre and Post COVID-19 Outbreak †

Claudio Marcio Cassela Inacio, Jr. *‡ and Sergio Adriani David *‡

Institute of Mathematics and Computer Science, University of São Paulo, Av. Trabalhador São-Carlense 400, São Carlos 13566-590, Brazil

* Correspondence: claudio.inacio@usp.br (C.M.C.I.J.); sergiodavid@usp.br (S.A.D.)
† Presented at the 8th International Conference on Time Series and Forecasting, Gran Canaria, Spain, 27–30 June 2022.
‡ These authors contributed equally to this work.

Abstract: The objective of this work is to analyze the price dynamics and the level of association between the Brent crude oil prices and heating oil (HO), i.e., US diesel. The data series are obtained from daily future contract prices of Chicago Mercantile Exchange (CME) group exchanges and the Intercontinental Exchange (ICE). A continuous evaluation of the Detrended Cross-Correlation Analysis (DCCA) between Brent crude oil prices vis-a-vis HO is proposed by means of the rolling window approach, allowing a dynamic analysis of their cross-correlations covering two periods, namely from January 2018 to December 2019 (before the COVID-19 pandemic) and from January 2020 to December 2021 (during the COVID-19 pandemic). The results indicate that there is a strong evidence of contagion in cross-correlation due to the initial impact of the pandemic, but the HO–Brent correlation fully recovered after approximately 200 days. However, lower time scales (n) are also sensitive to supply shortages in the short term and can be most reliable for agents that might not take long positions. Measuring this dynamic cross-correlation can provide useful information for investors and agents in the oil and energy markets.

Keywords: cross-correlation; DCCA method; oil derivatives; energy

Citation: Inacio, C.M.C., Jr.; David, S.A. Price Dynamics and Measuring the Contagion between Brent Crude and Heating Oil (US-Diesel) Pre and Post COVID-19 Outbreak. *Eng. Proc.* 2022, 18, 8. https://doi.org/10.3390/engproc2022018008

Academic Editors: Ignacio Rojas, Hector Pomares, Olga Valenzuela, Fernando Rojas and Luis Javier Herrera

Published: 21 June 2022

Publisher's Note: MDPI stays neutral with regard to jurisdictional claims in published maps and institutional affiliations.

1. Introduction

Since the first propositions about the relationship between oil prices and economic activity proposed by Hamilton [1], a significant number of researchers have dedicated themselves to exploring the connection between variations in its price and its effects on global economic activities. According to Zhang, Lai and Wang [2], oil is a resource known for large price fluctuations, where prices increases usually cause an increase in inflation and harm the economies of importing countries. On the other hand, price drops usually cause economic recessions and political instability in exporting countries, as their economic development can be jeopardized or delayed. In addition to price levels, another relevant factor is their volatility, since a relatively small increase can cause considerable economic losses [3]. Oil price variations are influenced by several factors. The dynamics between supply and demand is one of the main factors that affect price movement, which is also sensitive to exogenous factors such as the weather and irregular events [4,5] and also to political aspects and the expectations of market agents [6,7]. Such factors make the price movement non-linear and non-stationary, which makes its analysis more challenging and an important strategy for importers, exporters, investors and governments. While crude oil prices have historically been a fundamental component of economic analysis, the variation in crude oil prices also affects a country's economy and politics [8]. For this reason, it is pertinent to understand how crude oil prices relate to its derivatives. In this context, the objective of this work is to analyze the relationship between Brent crude and heating oil (US diesel) prices, covering two periods. The first period (P1) precedes the COVID-19 crisis and includes data from January 2018 to December 2019. The second (P2) addresses the period from January 2020 to December 2021, covering the COVID-19 crisis period. The present study expands the existing literature, empirically examining the relationship between the price of oil and its derivatives in light of a continuous evaluation by means of adoption of the rolling window approach [9–11] applied to the DCCA (Detrended Cross-Correlation Analysis) method [11–20]. Such a perspective becomes relevant as the price of oil and its derivatives is the basis for decision-making in many countries. Indeed, in practical terms, the knowledge of the level of association between the prices of these products can help in the anticipation and formulation of strategies for companies and consumers. This paper is organized as follows: in Section 2, the data are introduced and the DCCA method and statistical test are presented. In Section 3, the results of the DCCA analysis are discussed. Finally, in Section 4, the main conclusions are outlined.

2. Methods

2.1. Data Characteristics

In this study, we use time series (TS) to represent daily prices of future market settlements related to the first available contract (C1) from CME group exchanges (NYMEX) and the ICE exchange for the HO and Brent, respectively. Each contract of the selected pair represents the most negotiated future contracts for diesel and crude oil worldwide. In general, price imbalances in the crude oil market tend to rapidly transfer to its derivatives. The reason is that the HO–Brent differential, also known as 'crack-spread', can be applied as a representation of the refinery margin to buy crude oil and produce diesel/heating oil.

In order to analyze the price dynamics of such pairs, we considered two distinguished periods, P_1 and P_2, where the first denotes the two-year period prior to the COVID-19 outbreak (January 18 to December 2019) and the second denotes the two-year period after the COVID-19 outbreak (January 20 to December 2021).

2.2. Detrended Cross-Correlation Analysis

In recent years, the concept of fractals in TS has been investigated by means of the Hurst exponent (H) and Auto-Regressive Fractional Integrated Moving Average (ARFIMA) processes [7,21–30]. Several computational algorithms have been proposed to explore this field [31–36]. For example, when it comes to non-stationary TS, the Detrended Fluctuation Analysis (DFA) and its respective scaling coefficients yield satisfactory results to avoid the spurious detection of correlations or self-similarity [31,32]. This process is related to the Brownian and fractional Brownian motions, which allow us to quantify the long-range dependence in the analyzed TS.

A generalization of the DFA method was proposed by Podobnik and Stanley in 2008 [37], the so-called Detrended Cross-Correlation Analysis (DCCA), which is based on the detrended covariance between two TS. This method provides the quantification of long-range cross-correlations in the presence of non-stationarity. Considering two long-range cross-correlated TS y_i and y'_i of equal length N, the values can be approached in the integrated form:

$$Y_k = \sum_{i=1}^{k} y_i \tag{1}$$

$$Y'_k = \sum_{i=1}^{k} y'_i \tag{2}$$

where $k = 1, \ldots, N$. The entire TS are fractioned into $N - n$ overlapping boxes with $n + 1$ values. The box starting at the position i and landing at the position $i + n$ is defined as the "local trend". Moreover, we can define the $\hat{Y}_{k,i}$ and $\hat{Y'}_{k,i}(i \leq k \leq i + n)$ as the ordinate points of the linear least-squares fit. For each box, it is possible to calculate the covariance of the residual as follows:

$$f_{DCCA}^2(n,i) = \frac{1}{(n-1)} \sum_{k=i}^{i+n} (Y_k - \hat{Y}_{k,i})(Y'_k - \hat{Y'}_{k,i}) \tag{3}$$

Hence, the detrended covariance is calculated by summing over all overlapping $N - n$ boxes of size n as:

$$F_{DCCA}^2(n) = \frac{1}{(N-n)} \sum_{N-n}^{i=1} f_{DCCA}^2(n,i) \tag{4}$$

When a long-range cross-correlation appears between the two TS, then $F_{DCCA} \sim n^\lambda$, where $\lambda \approx (H_{DFA} + H'_{DFA})/2$. The λ exponent quantifies the long-range power-law correlations, but does not quantify the level of cross-correlation [37–39]. For this matter, Zebende [39] proposed the DCCA cross-correlation coefficient, defined by:

$$\rho_{DCCA} \equiv \frac{F_{DCCA}^2}{F_{DFA}\{y_i\}} F_{DFA}\{y'_i\} \tag{5}$$

These coefficient values are interpreted similarly to Pearson's correlation and can be summarized as follows: (a) $-1 \leq \rho_{DCCA} \leq 1$, (b) $\rho_{DCCA} = 1$ for a perfect cross-correlation, (c) $\rho_{DCCA} = 0$ for no cross-correlation presented between the TS, and (d) $\rho_{DCCA} = -1$ for a perfect anti-cross-correlation.

2.3. Rolling Window Approach and the Statistical Test for $\Delta\rho_{DCCA}$

Different statistical tests have been adopted to evaluate the detrended cross-correlation coefficients [30,38,40,41]. In this work, we applied the statistical test proposed by Guedes et al. [9] to evaluate $\Delta\rho_{DCCA}$. This test allows us to analyze two distinct moments separated by a phenomenon, such as the economic crisis caused by the COVID-19 pandemic. The coefficient is represented by:

$$\Delta\rho_{DCCA}(n) = \rho_{DCCA}^{P_2}(n) - \rho_{DCCA}^{P_1}(n) \tag{6}$$

where $\rho_{DCCA}^{P_2}(n)$ and $\rho_{DCCA}^{P_1}(n)$ are the DCCA coefficients for the periods P_1 and P_2, respectively. The subsequent test consists in calculating the probability distribution function (PDF) of the $\Delta\rho_{DCCA}(n)$, supposing that they obey a normal distribution and follow the below steps [9]:

- Generate two TS with long-range cross-correlation by ARFIMA process [37];
- Divide the TS for periods P_1 and P_2 and shuffle these pairs;
- Estimate $\rho_{DCCA}(n)$ and the periods' difference $\Delta\rho_{DCCA}(n)$;
- Repeat step 2 several times;
- Obtain the distribution of $\Delta\rho_{DCCA}(n)$, and
- (Additional step) Evaluate the normality of the distribution.

In general, the PDF of $\Delta\rho_{DCCA}(n)$ converges to a normal distribution, as shown by [9]. However, we decided to conduct D'Agostino and Pearson's normality test [42,43] to verify the normality of the distribution. Hereafter, the following contagion hypothesis is tested with a T-test for the mean of the $\Delta\rho_{DCCA}(n)$ parametric group and the Wilcoxon signed-rank test for the non-parametric group:

$H_0: \Delta\rho_{DCCA}(n) = \langle\Delta\rho_{DCCA}\rangle$ (contagion does not exist);

$H_1: \Delta\rho_{DCCA}(n) \neq \langle\Delta\rho_{DCCA}\rangle$ (contagion exists);

where $\langle\Delta\rho_{DCCA}\rangle$ is the sample mean, which is approximately equal to zero. Thus, for each PDF defined by window size N (in this study, W1 = 50 days, W2 = 100 days, W3 = 150 days, W4 = 200 days, W5 = 250 days) and n time scales, we can obtain the positive critical point defined as $\Delta\rho_c(n)$ for 90%, 95%, and 99% confidence levels as follows:

$$\langle \Delta \rho_{DCCA} \rangle \pm Z_{\alpha 1/2} \frac{SD}{\sqrt{N}} \tag{7}$$

where $Z_{\alpha 1/2}$ is the value for the chosen confidence level α, SD is the standard deviation, and N is the sample size.

3. Results and Discussion

Figure 1 shows the $\rho_{DCCA}(n)$ behavior for HO–Brent during periods P_1 and P_2 for every presented time scale (n) and different sliding window sizes (W1–W5). From Figure 1a,c, one can note that considering a window size of 50 and 100 days, the prices showed a weaker relation during the beginning of 2019, which is not applied to larger sizes of W, and it is an indication of short-term effects. Moreover, we can notice that all the window sizes (W1–W5) exhibited a fall in cross-correlation in the period that preceded the COVID-19 outbreak.

Regarding the COVID-19 period (P_2), Figure 1b,d,f,h,j allow us to observe a loss of cross-correlation from March to April of 2020, when both markets presented an intense fall in prices due to lockdowns worldwide, especially the US market. Moreover, a considerable amount of market agents took a bearish (selling) position in these contracts due to the lack of global demand predictability during this period. However, one of the reasons for the price dissolution likely may have come from the specific characteristics of the diesel market. For example, heating oil—as the name suggests—can be used for heating purposes during severe US cold winters. Differently, the same product in Europe—namely gasoil—is applied for driving, such as gasoline for the US market. Therefore, during the lockdowns and with a lack of driving demand for fuel, the HO's price movement may have diverged from that of crude oil, gasoline, and gasoil.

Moreover, the 50-day and 100-day rolling windows are shown in Figure 1b,d, which showed another strong price dissolution between May and June of 2020. In addition, one can also observe that shorter window sizes are sensitive to short-term effects, which one can note during the year 2021. These effects are related to the US Gulf diesel supply shortage presented during the cold weather at the beginning of 2021 and also during the Ida hurricane effects in the second half of 2021 [44]. This might suggest that short-term supply shortages of diesel in the US Gulf can affect the HO–Brent cross-correlation, similarly to the restricted demand period caused by COVID-19. However, the supply short-term effects are not observed when using larger rolling window sizes, which is not the case for the initial pandemic effects that are displayed for every tested window. In general, the larger windows presented a cross-correlation recovery for the pair after the first half of 2020 until the end of 2021. One can also note that the greater time scales (n) diverge from the lower time scales and cannot encapsulate the complete price dynamics of both periods, since both markets are mostly interdependent in the long term compared to the short term [10].

Table 1 summarizes the descriptive statistics for the $\Delta \rho_{DCCA}$ distributions as a function of n with different sizes of W. As suggested by Guedes et al. [9], the observed mean values are approximately close to zero and the standard deviation (SD) decreases for greater W sizes. However, mostly skewness and kurtosis diverged from values observed from normal distributions, i.e., *Kurtosis* ≈ 3 and *Skewness* ≈ 0 for different combinations of n and W, which tends to affect the normality of the distributions. For this reason, we conducted D'Agostino and Pearson's normality test and the results are shown in Table 2. It can be seen that all the applied window sizes (W) presented non-normality for most tested time scales (n).

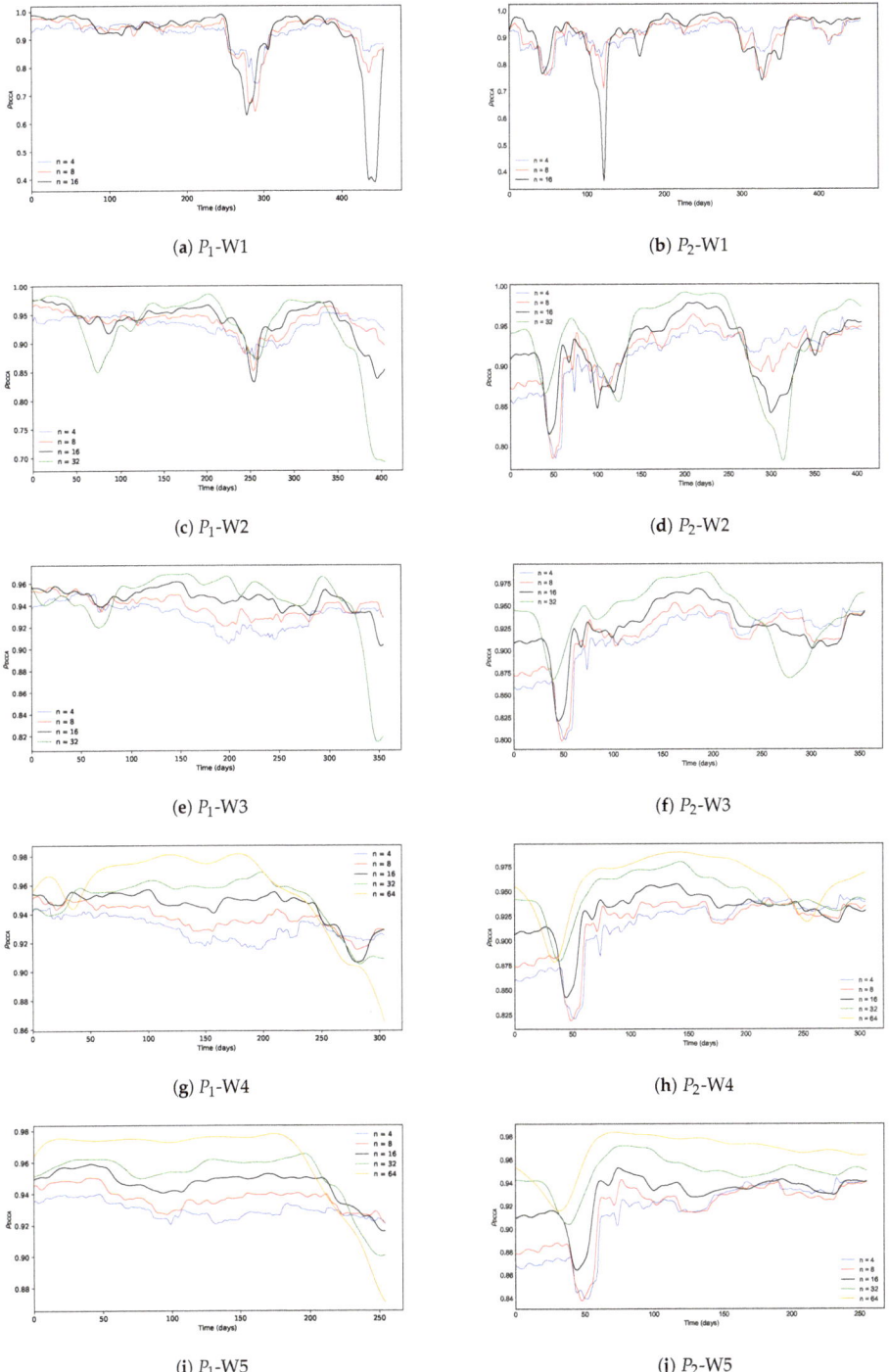

(a) P_1-W1

(b) P_2-W1

(c) P_1-W2

(d) P_2-W2

(e) P_1-W3

(f) P_2-W3

(g) P_1-W4

(h) P_2-W4

(i) P_1-W5

(j) P_2-W5

Figure 1. The Brent–HO ρ_{DCCA} TS comparison of P_1 vs. P_2 for W1 to W5.

Table 1. The *Brent-HO* descriptive summary of $\Delta\rho_{DCCA}$ for W1 to W5.

Descriptive Statistics					
Statistics	$n = 4$	$n = 8$	$n = 16$	$n = 32$	$n = 64$
W1 = 50					
Mean	0.0469	0.0478	0.0606	-	-
SD	0.0519	0.0585	0.0949	-	-
Skewness	0.7747	1.3477	2.7715	-	-
Kurtosis	0.4957	1.3932	9.5141	-	-
W2 = 100					
Mean	0.0336	0.0314	0.0233	0.0012	-
SD	0.0513	0.0519	0.0492	0.0546	-
Skewness	0.3688	0.4340	−0.6524	−0.0903	-
Kurtosis	−0.3147	0.0274	0.0166	−0.3943	-
W3 = 150					
Mean	0.0276	0.0289	0.0216	0.0033	-
SD	0.0475	0.0422	0.0330	0.0232	-
Skewness	0.8434	1.1727	1.3479	1.2184	-
Kurtosis	−0.0618	0.8768	2.4628	1.5078	-
W4 = 200					
Mean	0.0213	0.0245	0.0197	0.0071	0.0062
SD	0.0393	0.0351	0.0261	0.0215	0.0199
Skewness	0.9908	1.3799	1.6650	1.4585	1.6720
Kurtosis	−0.3018	0.9029	2.9319	2.2209	1.8339
W5 = 250					
Mean	0.0165	0.0211	0.0170	0.0030	−0.0043
SD	0.0335	0.0308	0.0242	0.0232	0.0310
Skewness	1.1137	1.3311	1.2920	−0.1065	−0.4814
Kurtosis	−0.2545	0.6427	1.8523	0.4632	0.8582

Table 2. The *Brent-HO* normality test of $\Delta\rho_{DCCA}$ for W1 to W5. Significance level of 95% (*p*-value < 0.05) rejects the null hypothesis of normality.

D'Agostino and Pearson's Normality Test					
Statistics	$n = 4$	$n = 8$	$n = 16$	$n = 32$	$n = 64$
W1 = 50					
χ^2	24.1151	59.8950	171.8440	-	-
p-value	5.80×10^{-6}	9.86×10^{-14}	4.84×10^{-38}	-	-
W2 = 100					
χ^2	6.7952	7.873	0.9515	9.0797	-
p-value	0.0335	0.0195	0.6214	0.0107	-
W3 = 150					
χ^2	24.8080	46.5804	68.8323	54.3651	-
p-value	4.10×10^{-6}	7.68×10^{-11}	1.13×10^{-15}	1.57×10^{-12}	-
W4 = 200					
χ^2	32.8813	57.2596	88.2648	72.4758	79.9174
p-value	7.24×10^{-8}	3.68×10^{-13}	6.82×10^{-20}	4.43×10^{-18}	3.89×10^{-20}
W5 = 250					
χ^2	38.6335	52.6530	61.0372	2.7892	14.8160
p-value	4.08×10^{-9}	3.69×10^{-12}	5.57×10^{-14}	0.2479	0.0010

Thus, the contagion hypothesis can be tested for each $\Delta\rho_{DCCA}$ distribution. Table 3 depicts the significance test, where the T-test is applied to parametric (normal) distributions and the Wilcoxon signed-rank test for non-parametric (non-normal) distributions. One can note that there is evidence of a contagion predominance for time scales $n < 32$, which suggests short-term effect spillover when comparing P_1 and P_2. However, there is no strong evidence of the contagion effect for values of $n \geq 32$ days, which suggests that the market imbalances caused by COVID-19 did not affect the HO–Brent cross-correlation in the long term as much as the short term. Figure 2a–c confirms the alternative hypothesis ($\Delta\rho_{DCCA}(n) \neq 0$), where it is possible to notice a prevalence of $\Delta\rho_{DCCA}(n) > 0$ for the first 150 days of comparison. The $\Delta\rho_{DCCA}(n)$ overpasses the critical limits for most parts of the periods (see Table 4). On the other hand, from Figure 2d,e, one can observe that greater values of n and W tend to smooth the curves and have no clear pattern. However, for every time scale (n), the correlations are shown to be lower during the beginning of P_2 if compared to the same period in P_1, in addition to the lower $\Delta\rho_{DCCA}(n)$ in the last 50 days of the curves, which indicates that the HO–Brent fully recovered in terms of correlation after 200 days of the COVID-19 outbreak.

Table 3. The *Brent-HO* significance test of $\Delta\rho_{DCCA}$ for W1 to W5. Significance level of 95% (p-value < 0.05) rejects the null hypothesis of $\Delta\rho_{DCCA} = 0$.

	t-Test or Wilcoxon Signed-Rank Test for Significance at Differences				
Statistics	$n = 4$	$n = 8$	$n = 16$	$n = 32$	$n = 64$
			W1 = 50		
Statistic	W = 2924	W = 1744	W = 2325	-	-
p-value	1.03×10^{-29}	6.42×10^{-35}	2.67×10^{-32}	-	-
			W2 = 100		
Statistic	W = 5951	W = 6600	t = 7.5491	W = 16,146	-
p-value	2.37×10^{-18}	2.73×10^{-16}	7.94×10^{-13}	0.9683	-
			W3 = 150		
Statistic	W = 7050	W = 4865	W = 4547	W = 15,694	-
p-value	6.16×10^{-15}	4.25×10^{-22}	2.90×10^{-23}	0.6706	-
			W4 = 200		
Statistic	W = 9763	W = 3956	W = 2472	W = 11,748	W = 15,046
p-value	4.12×10^{-8}	1.62×10^{-25}	1.18e-31	0.0001	0.3280
			W5 = 250		
Statistic	W = 11094	W = 3623	W = 3942	t = 2.0720	W = 12,846
p-value	1.36×10^{-5}	7.81×10^{-27}	1.43×10^{-25}	0.0393	0.0043

Table 4. The *Brent-HO* critical values of $\Delta\rho_{DCCA}$ with 90%, 95% and 99% confidence level (CL) for W1 to W5.

Critical Values	$n = 4$	$n = 8$	$n = 16$	$n = 32$	$n = 64$
CL = 95%					
W1	0.1321	0.1464	0.2342	-	
W2	0.1229	0.1189	0.1111	0.0885	-
W3	0.1059	0.0971	0.0747	0.0363	-
W4	0.0863	0.0834	0.0651	0.0429	0.0500
W5	0.0751	0.0736	0.0584	0.0436	0.0511

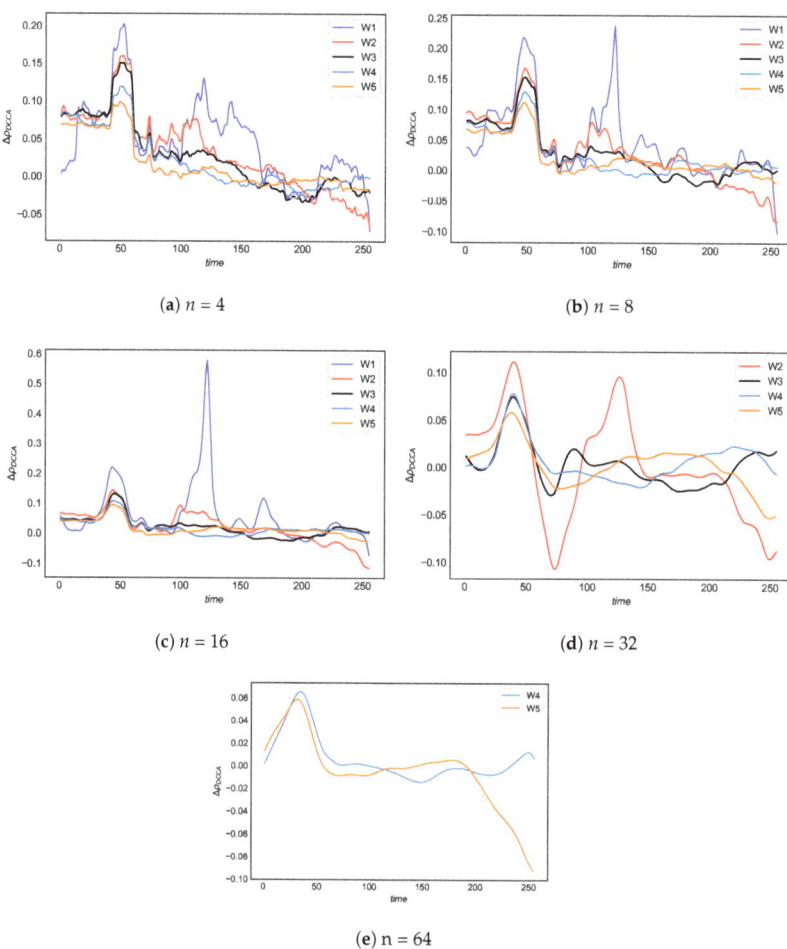

Figure 2. The *Brent-HO* $\Delta\rho_{DCCA}$ TS for different time scales (n).

4. Conclusions

This work employed Detrended Cross-Correlation Analysis in the study of the future contract price dynamics between the US diesel (HO) and Brent crude oil during the periods pre- and post-COVID-19. The results indicate that there is strong evidence of contagion in cross-correlation due to the initial impact of the pandemic, but the HO–Brent correlation fully recovered after approximately 200 days. However, lower time scales (n) are also sensitive to supply shortages in the short term and can be most reliable for agents that might not take long positions. Therefore, this indicates that, despite the pair being highly correlated, the initial global lack of crude oil demand generated by the lockdowns caused a fall in crude oil prices, but the same dynamics appeared in the US diesel market only after a delay.

Author Contributions: Conceptualization, S.A.D.; methodology, C.M.C.I.J. and S.A.D.; software, C.M.C.I.J.; formal analysis, C.M.C.I.J. and S.A.D.; writing—original draft preparation, C.M.C.I.J. and S.A.D.; writing—review and editing, C.M.C.I.J. and S.A.D.; visualization, C.M.C.I.J.; supervision, S.A.D. All authors have read and agreed to the published version of the manuscript.

Funding: This research received no external funding.

Institutional Review Board Statement: Not applicable.

Informed Consent Statement: Not applicable.

Data Availability Statement: Not applicable.

Acknowledgments: The authors wish to acknowledge the Institute of Mathematics and Computer Science of the University of São Paulo (ICMC-USP), CeMEAI-USP and MECAI-USP for the general and financial support.

Conflicts of Interest: The authors declare no conflicts of interest.

Abbreviations

The following abbreviations are used in this manuscript:

HO	Heating Oil (US Diesel)
TS	Time Series
SD	Standard Deviation
DCCA	Detrended Cross-Correlation Analysis
DFA	Detrended Fluctuation Analysis
P_1	First Period
P_2	Second Period
ARFIMA	Auto-Regressive Fractional Integrated Moving Average
H	Hurst Exponent

References

1. Hamilton, J. Oil and the Macroeconomy since World War II. *J. Political Econ.* **1983**, *91*, 228–248. [CrossRef]
2. Zhang, X.; Lai, K.; Wang, S. A new approach for crude oil price analysis based on Empirical Mode Decomposition. *Energy Econ.* **2008**, *30*, 905–918. [CrossRef]
3. Sauter, R.; Awerbuch, S. Oil price volatility and economic activity: A survey and literature review. *Iea Res. Pap.* **2003**, *28*, 550–577.
4. Lu, Q.; Li, Y.; Chai, J.; Wang, S. Crude oil price analysis and forecasting: A perspective of "new triangle". *Energy Econ.* **2020**, *87*, 104721. [CrossRef]
5. Ji, Q.; Guo, J. Oil price volatility and oil-related events: An Internet concern study perspective. *Appl. Energy* **2015**, *137*, 256–264. [CrossRef]
6. Matutinović, I. Oil and the political economy of energy. *Energy Policy* **2009**, *37*, 4251–4258. [CrossRef]
7. David, S.; Inácio, C.; Quintino, D.; Machado, J. Measuring the Brazilian ethanol and gasoline market efficiency using DFA-Hurst and fractal dimension. *Energy Econ.* **2020**, *85*, 104614. [CrossRef]
8. Chen, H.; Liao, H.; Tang, B.; Wei, Y. Impacts of OPEC's political risk on the international crude oil prices: An empirical analysis based on the SVAR models. *Energy Econ.* **2016**, *57*, 42–49. [CrossRef]
9. Guedes, E.; Zebende, G. DCCA cross-correlation coefficient with sliding windows approach. *Phys. A Stat. Mech. Appl.* **2019**, *527*, 121286. [CrossRef]
10. Tilfani, O.; Ferreira, P.; Boukfaoui, M. Dynamic cross-correlation and dynamic contagion of stock markets: A sliding windows approach with the DCCA correlation coefficient. *Empir. Econ.* **2021**, *60*, 1127–1156. [CrossRef]
11. Ferreira, P.; Kristoufek, L.; Area Leão Pereira, E. DCCA and DMCA correlations of cryptocurrency markets. *Phys. A Stat. Mech. Appl.* **2020**, *545*, 123803. [CrossRef]
12. Wang, B.; Wei, Y.; Xing, Y.; Ding, W. Multifractal detrended cross-correlation analysis and frequency dynamics of connectedness for energy futures markets. *Phys. A Stat. Mech. Appl.* **2019**, *527*, 121194. [CrossRef]
13. Prass, T.; Pumi, G. On the behavior of the DFA and DCCA in trend-stationary processes. *J. Multivar. Anal.* **2021**, *182*, 104703. [CrossRef]
14. He, L.; Chen, S. Multifractal Detrended Cross-Correlation Analysis of agricultural futures markets. *Chaos Solitons Fractals* **2011**, *44*, 355–361. [CrossRef]
15. Cai, Y.; Lu, X.; Ren, Y.; Qu, L. Exploring the dynamic relationship between crude oil price and implied volatility indices: A MF-DCCA approach. *Phys. A Stat. Mech. Appl.* **2019**, *536*, 120973. [CrossRef]
16. Paiva, A.; Rivera-Castro, M.; Andrade, R. DCCA analysis of renewable and conventional energy prices. *Phys. A Stat. Mech. Appl.* **2018**, *490*, 1408–1414. [CrossRef]
17. Malik, A.; Brönnimann, S. Factors affecting the inter-annual to centennial timescale variability of Indian summer monsoon rainfall. *Clim. Dyn.* **2018**, *50*, 4347–4364. [CrossRef]
18. Lin, M.; Wang, G.; Xie, C.; Stanley, H. Cross-correlations and influence in world gold markets. *Phys. A Stat. Mech. Appl.* **2018**, *490*, 504–512. [CrossRef]

19. Zebende, G.; Silva, M.; Filho, A. DCCA cross-correlation coefficient differentiation: Theoretical and practical approaches. *Phys. A Stat. Mech. Appl.* **2013**, *392*, 1756–1761. [CrossRef]
20. Ferreira, P.; Dionísio, A.; Guedes, E.; Zebende, G. A sliding windows approach to analyse the evolution of bank shares in the European Union. *Phys. A Stat. Mech. Appl.* **2018**, *490*, 1355–1367. [CrossRef]
21. David, S.; Inacio, C., Jr.; Nunes, R.; Machado, J. Fractional and fractal processes applied to cryptocurrencies price series. *J. Adv. Res.* **2021**, *32*, 85–98. [CrossRef] [PubMed]
22. Valentim, C.; Inacio, C.; David, S. Fractal Methods and Power Spectral Density as Means to Explore EEG Patterns in Patients Undertaking Mental Tasks. *Fractal Fract.* **2021**, *5*, 225. [CrossRef]
23. Kristoufek, L.; Vosvrda, M. Commodity futures and market efficiency. *Energy Econ.* **2014**, *42*, 50–57. [CrossRef]
24. David, S.; Machado, J.; Trevisan, L.; Inácio, C., Jr.; Lopes, A. Dynamics of commodities prices: Integer and fractional models. *Fundam. Inform.* **2017**, *151*, 389–408. [CrossRef]
25. David, S.; Machado, J.; Inácio, C.; Valentim, C. A combined measure to differentiate EEG signals using fractal dimension and MFDFA-Hurst. *Commun. Nonlinear Sci. Numer. Simul.* **2020**, *84*, 105170. [CrossRef]
26. David, S.; Inácio, C.; Machado, J. Quantifying the Predictability and Efficiency of the Cointegrated Ethanol and Agricultural Commodities Price Series. *Appl. Sci.* **2019**, *9*, 5303. [CrossRef]
27. Ayadi, O.; Williams, J.; Hyman, L. Fractional dynamic behavior in Forcados Oil Price Series: An application of detrended fluctuation analysis. *Energy Sustain. Dev.* **2009**, *13*, 11–17. [CrossRef]
28. Shang, P.; Lu, Y.; Kamae, S. Detecting long-range correlations of traffic time series with multifractal detrended fluctuation analysis. *Chaos Solitons Fractals* **2008**, *36*, 82–90. [CrossRef]
29. Teng, Y.; Shang, P. Detrended fluctuation analysis based on higher-order moments of financial time series. *Phys. A Stat. Mech. Appl.* **2018**, *490*, 311–322. [CrossRef]
30. Kristoufek, L. Testing power-law cross-correlations: Rescaled covariance test. *Eur. Phys. J.* **2013**, *86*, 1–11. [CrossRef]
31. Peng, C.; Buldyrev, S.; Havlin, S.; Simons, M.; Stanley, H.; Goldberger, A. Mosaic organization of DNA nucleotides. *Phys. Rev. E* **1994**, *49*, 1685–1689. [CrossRef] [PubMed]
32. Shieh, S. Long Memory and sampling frequencies: Evidence in stock index futures markets. *Int. J. Theor. Appl. Financ.* **2006**, *9*, 787–799. [CrossRef]
33. Carbone, A. Detrending moving average algorithm: A brief review. *Dimension* **2009**, *49*, 59.
34. Simonsen, I.; Hansen, A.; Nes, O. Determination of the Hurst exponent by use of wavelet transforms. *Phys. Rev. E* **1998**, *58*, 2779. [CrossRef]
35. Mandelbrot, B. Statistical methodology for nonperiodic cycles: From the covariance to R/S analysis. *Ann. Econ. Soc. Meas.* **1972**, *1*, 259–290.
36. Mandelbrot, B.; Wallis, J. Robustness of the rescaled range R/S in the measurement of noncyclic long run statistical dependence. *Water Resour. Res.* **1969**, *5*, 967–988. [CrossRef]
37. Podobnik, B.; Stanley, H. Detrended cross-correlation analysis: A new method for analyzing two nonstationary time series. *Phys. Rev. Lett.* **2008**, *100*, 084102. [CrossRef] [PubMed]
38. Podobnik, B.; Jiang, Z.; Zhou, W.; Stanley, H. Statistical tests for power-law cross-correlated processes. *Phys. Rev. E Stat. Nonlinear Soft Matter Phys.* **2011**, *84*, 066118. [CrossRef] [PubMed]
39. Zebende, G. DCCA cross-correlation coefficient: Quantifying level of cross-correlation. *Phys. A Stat. Mech. Appl.* **2011**, *390*, 614–618. [CrossRef]
40. Guedes, E.; Brito, A.; Filho, F.; Fernandez, B.; Castro, A.; Silva Filho, A.; Zebende, G. Statistical test for $\Delta\rho$DCCA cross-correlation coefficient. *Phys. A Stat. Mech. Appl.* **2018**, *501*, 134–140. [CrossRef]
41. Silva, M.; Area Leão Pereira, É.; Silva Filho, A.; Castro, A.; Miranda, J.; Zebende, G. Quantifying the contagion effect of the 2008 financial crisis between the G7 countries (by GDP nominal). *Phys. Stat. Mech. Appl.* **2016**, *453*, 1–8. [CrossRef]
42. D'Agostino, R.; Pearson, E. Tests for departure from normality. Empirical results for the distributions of b2 and b1. *Biometrika* **1973**, *60*, 613–622. [CrossRef]
43. D'Agostino, R. An Omnibus Test of Normality for Moderate and Large Size Samples. *Biometrika* **1971**, *58*, 341. [CrossRef]
44. French, M. *Hurricane Ida Disrupted Crude Oil Production and Refining Activity*; U.S. Energy Information Administration (EIA): Washington, DC, USA, 2021. Available online: https://www.eia.gov/todayinenergy/detail.php?id=49576 (accessed on 14 April 2022).

Proceeding Paper

Hybrid K-Mean Clustering and Markov Chain for Mobile Network Accessibility and Retainability Prediction [†]

Amel Salem Omer [1,*], Tesfaye Addisie Yemer [2] and Dereje Hailemariam Woldegebreal [1]

1   School of Electrical and Computer Engineering, Addis Ababa University, Addis Ababa P.O. Box 385, Ethiopia; dereje.hailemariam@aait.edu.et

2   Ethio Telecom, Addis Ababa P.O. Box 1047, Ethiopia; tesfaye.addisie@ethiotelecom.et

*   Correspondence: amel.salem@yenepay.com

†   Presented at the 8th International Conference on Time Series and Forecasting, Gran Canaria, Spain, 27–30 June 2022.

Abstract: To provide reliable services, mobile network operators (MNOs) continuously collect vital mobile network performance data to monitor and analyze the functioning of their radio access networks (RANs). RAN is a critical infrastructure for mobile networks and its performance is measured by key performance indicators (KPIs) such as accessibility, retainability, availability, integrity, and mobility. The standard practice is that network managers utilize KPIs to identify failures or unusual events that can significantly degrade the quality of service delivery and the end-users' experiences. However, taking corrective steps based on monitored performance parameters is a reactive approach that contributes to network and service degradations until corrective actions are taken. With the monitoring and automation of RAN infrastructure performance in mind, this paper presents the Markov chain, a widely used probabilistic modeling approach, as a systematic method for jointly predicting network accessibility and retainability status, two of the crucial RAN performance measures. The novel joint prediction is proposed to have a single operation for both accessibility and retainability. Real-time hourly KPIs data was collected from 1530 cells (base stations) run by an operator's network in Addis Ababa, Ethiopia, for 4 months, from 1 November 2020 to 28 February 2021. The cells are scattered across the capital city, where factors such as land use, settlement patterns, and customers behaviors differ. To capture the spatial variation of the KPIs without escalating the computational complexity much, the dataset is separated into six clusters using the K-mean clustering approach. The Markov chain KPIs status prediction models are formulated on a cluster level. The results reveal that the proposed models can predict the KPIs status with 94.61 percent accuracy. Because the data is already available and can be collected at any time using the operator's network management system (NMS), this is a cost-effective technique to proactively improve mobile network performance.

Keywords: accessibility; retainability; Markov chain; K-mean clustering

Citation: Omer, A.S.; Yemer, T.A.; Woldegebreal, D.H. Hybrid K-Mean Clustering and Markov Chain for Mobile Network Accessibility and Retainability Prediction. *Eng. Proc.* **2022**, *18*, 9. https://doi.org/10.3390/engproc2022018009

Academic Editors: Ignacio Rojas, Hector Pomares, Olga Valenzuela, Fernando Rojas and Luis Javier Herrera

Published: 21 June 2022

Publisher's Note: MDPI stays neutral with regard to jurisdictional claims in published maps and institutional affiliations.

1. Introduction

The demand for dependable mobile network services is growing and is projected to continue to grow in the coming years. To meet this rising service demand, mobile network operators (MNOs) are expanding their networks and use a centralized network management system (NMS) to monitor the performance of the radio access network (RAN) and core network, two critical components of mobile network infrastructure. NMS is a network monitoring and control tool, with fault management and performance management its two essential functionalities [1]. Fault management is the need for fault-free operation and has three aspects, namely fault identification, fault isolation, and fault correction. The fault identification is conducted with the help of network alarms, while fault isolation of the network's remaining components from the failure is needed so that the isolated network can continue to function normally. Fault correction requires repairing or replacing failed components. Performance management, on the other hand, includes network monitoring to observe network activities and network control to take mitigations that increase network performance. Some of the network manager's performance concerns include determining the amount of capacity utilization, traffic monitoring, throughput status, and reaction time status, among others [1].

Although the NMS offers critical information through various management subsystems, most operators find it challenging to manage the data collected from the system and take corrective actions in a timely manner. Operators select key performance indicators (KPIs) and monitor them at hourly, daily, weekly, or monthly intervals to discover problems or unusual events that might drastically affect service delivery and end-user experience. KPIs are further grouped to assess network performance, and the widely used performance measures are accessibility, retainability, availability, integrity, and mobility. NMS holds vast amounts of historical network performance data, from which possible trends and patterns can be revealed using cutting-edge data mining techniques.

In mobile networks, Markov chain is used for call admission control [2], quality of experience (QoE) modeling [3], quality of service (QoS) modeling [4], efficient resource utilization [5], prediction of user mobility [6], handover management, and network operation status monitoring [7]. In [8,9], Markov chain is proposed to forecast radio resource controller (RRC) setup success and call setup success rates (CSSR) for the Long-term Evolution (LTE) mobile network. The status or state as per Markov's terminology of a cell (base stations) is classified as "Good/High," "Moderate/Acceptable," or "Bad/Low" based on the RRC success rate. Data collected from an operator's network is used to create the Markov chain–based models for RRC and CSSR future state predictions. A given cell is in one of the three states depending on the time of a day, the cell's geographic location, network capacity, and other user- and network-related factors. In addition to the Markov chain, cluster-based approaches, decision trees, and artificial neural networks were employed in [10–12] to estimate a network accessibility-related parameters. These and papers such as [13–15] addressed related performance measures for various generations of cellular mobile systems.

This paper's primary goal is to forecast mobile network accessibility and retainability status using real-time data gathered from the NMS of a major network operator in the capital city of Addis Ababa, Ethiopia. Specifically, the data were collected on an hourly basis from 1530 cells for 4 months' duration, from 1 November 2020 to 28 February 2021. The states of these two critical RAN performance parameters are defined based on the International Telecommunication Union's (ITU's) recommendations for network accessibility and retainability. As the cells are scattered across different geographic regions of the capital city, K-mean clustering technique is used to group cells having spatially correlated performances. The per-cluster averaged data are used to construct the Markov chain prediction model. Two approaches are used for the model formulation, and one is a separate approach so that two Markov models are built for accessibility and retainability. In the joint modeling, a single model is used to predict both parameters. Using either of the two approaches, we can compute the state of the network and the number of transitions until a steady-state is reached. The essential contributions of the research are mentioned here.

- In contrast to prior attempts, we established four states [16], namely "Idle," "Good," "Acceptable," and "Bad" states, to conform to the ITU's recommendations. Furthermore, the Markov chain is constructed to jointly estimate accessibility and retainability in a single operation, yielding a model with 16 states. Four-state separate estimation is employed as a benchmark for comparison. Incorporating ITU's recommendations for state definition and the joint prediction proposal are the unique contributions of this research.
- Previous models only operate for a single cell, leaving out the correlated nature of accessibility and retainability in the spatial domain. Including more cells, however, increases the number of combined states; thus, the Markov model may not scale as the number of cells increases. As an alternative to replicating the prediction method as

many times as the number of cells, we employed K-mean clustering to identify related cells. The Markov chain is then applied to the per-cluster averaged data. Prediction aids in analyzing the status of the considered mobile network.

The remaining paper is organized as follows. Section two discusses fundamental concepts and formulas in accessibility and retainability. Section three introduces some basic concepts of discrete Markov chains. Section four presents and discusses the results obtained. Finally, Section five concludes the paper by identifying possible future directions.

2. Accessibility and Retainability KPIs

KPIs obtained from network counters can be grouped into accessibility, retainability, integrity, mobility, and other factors in order to manage and track the performance of the network [17]. According to ITU, service accessibility is *"the ability of a service to be obtained, within specified tolerances and other given conditions, when requested by the user."* Service retainability is *"the ability of a service, once obtained, to continue to be provided under given conditions for a requested duration"* [18].

2.1. Accessibility

The accessibility KPI is expressed in probabilities, which indicate how likely a user is able to access the mobile service during specific service times and conditions. Accessibility measures the network's performance during call setup or before establishing a bearer [19]. For data availability reason, this paper focuses on the Third Generation (3G) mobile networks. RRC, radio access bearer (RAB), Enhanced Universal Terrestrial RAN RAB (ERAB), and CSSR are critical accessibility parameters, as presented below.

- RRC setup success rate (RRC SSR) evaluates the call success rate in a cell or cluster. The formula for this KPI is:

$$RRC\ SSR = \frac{Number\ of\ RRC\ setup\ success}{number\ of\ RRC\ connection\ attempt} \times 100\%. \tag{1}$$

- RAB setup success rate (RAB SSR) evaluates the success rate of assigning a RAB during a call setup procedure. The formula for this KPI is given as follows:

$$RAB\ SSR = \frac{Number\ of\ RAB\ setup\ success}{number\ of\ RAB\ setup\ attempt} \times 100\%. \tag{2}$$

- CSSR is used to evaluate the call setup success at the cell or cluster level. This KPI is calculated based on RRC SSR and RAB SSR for the case of third generation (3G) networks and ERAB SSR for the case of LTE networks.

$$Accessibility = CSSR = RRC\ SSR \times RAB\ SSR \times 100\%. \tag{3}$$

2.2. Retainability

Retainability assesses a network's performance after RAB is established and indicates the proportion of calls that serve the essential service without call drops.

$$Retainability = \left(1 - \frac{Number\ of\ RAB\ abnormal\ release}{d\ total\ number\ of\ RAB\ release}\right) \times 100\%. \tag{4}$$

Equation (4) fraction shows the call drop rate (CDR) value.

3. Discrete-Time Markov Chain

A Markov chain is a particular class of a stochastic process with random variables designating the states or outputs of the system [7,20]. The probability of the system transitioning from its current state to a future state depends only on the current state. The collection of states forms a state space of alphabet size N. Let $\{a_1, a_2, \ldots, a_N\}$ designate the state space and let a sequence of states $S_1, \ldots, S_n \ldots$, generated by the system in time, where $S_n \in \{a_1, a_2, \ldots, a_N\}$ and n in S_n indicates the discrete-time index.

For the Markov chain fulfilling the memoryless assumption, the transition probability is expressed as [21]:

$$
\begin{aligned}
P(S_{n+1} &= a_j | S_n = a_i, S_{n-1} = a_h, \ S_{n-2} = a_g, \ldots.) \\
&= P(S_{n+1} = a_j | S_n = a_i),
\end{aligned}
\tag{5}
$$

where $1 \leq i, j \leq N$. We learn from the Markov property that only the most recent state matters to predict the next or future state. From Equation (5), the transition probability from state a_i to state a_j is designated as:

$$
P_{ij} = P(S_{n+1} = a_j | S_n = a_i).
\tag{6}
$$

For all i and j, the summation of all transition probabilities in a row must be equal to one, i.e.,

$$
\sum_{j=1}^{n} P_{ij} = 1.
\tag{7}
$$

3.1. Transition Probability Matrix

The collection of the transition probabilities P_{ij} forms the probability transition matrix (TPM), P (See Equation (8)). Each entry of the matrix shows the probability that the system will transition or remain in the same state. P is a square matrix with the same dimension as the number of states.

$$
P = \begin{bmatrix}
P_{11} & P_{12} & P_{13} & .. & P_{1N} \\
P_{21} & P_{22} & P_{23} & .. & P_{2N} \\
. & . & . & .. & . \\
. & . & . & .. & . \\
P_{N1} & P_{N2} & P_{N3} & .. & P_{NN}
\end{bmatrix}
\tag{8}
$$

The transition probability P_{ij} is computed from empirical data by counting the number of transitions from state i to state j and dividing the result by the count of all transitions from state i [7].

3.2. Initial (Probability or State) Distribution

The initial state distribution is usually expressed as a probability distribution vector, U of dimension $1 \times n$, as shown in Equation (9), with entries that indicate the probability that the system is in a given state at a given initial time. Each entry of the vector is non-negative and the sum of the all entries should be unity.

$$
U = [P_1, P_2, \ldots., P_N].
\tag{9}
$$

Without accurate knowledge of the initial distribution, the system can be considered to be in one state with absolute certainty, i.e., probability of unity.

3.3. Steady-State Distribution

One of the fascinating aspects of systems that obey the Markov chain is that, after a sufficient number of iterations/transitions, the chain converges to a steady-state, stable, equilibrium, or static distribution [7]. A steady-state condition is one in which the probability of the next state is the same regardless of the present state.

With knowledge of the transition matrix P and the initial probability vector U, the probability distribution of the chain after k transitions in the future is given by [7].

$$
U^{(k)} = UP^k
\tag{10}
$$

P^k is the result of multiplying the transition matrix k times by itself. Each element of $U^{(k)}$, designated as $P_{ij}^{(k)}$, is the probability of going from state i to state j in k iteration. As we keep iterating through state transitions by applying P^k, the probability vectors $U^{(k)}$ converge to some fixed value, say $\pi_{(k)}$. That is called the *steady-state distribution* and mathematically written in the form as in Equation (11) below.

$$\lim_{k\to\infty} U^{(k)} = UP^k = \pi_{(k)}. \tag{11}$$

We note from Equation (11) that the Markov chain probabilistically predicts the system's future state based on knowledge of state space, initial distribution, and transition matrix.

3.4. Transition Diagram

A transition diagram, which illustrates all of the system's transitions, is another way to display the TPM. A directed arrow shows the presence of a transition from one state to another state, and each node represents a state of the Markov chain. The edge represents the current state, and the arrow points towards the next state [7].

4. Results and Discussions

This section covers data collection and accessibility and retainability status prediction using a four- and sixteen-state Markov chain model.

4.1. Data Collection and Preprocessing

The performance report system (PRS) installed in the operator's network was used to collect real-time hourly data from 1530 cells for 4 months' duration.

- Linear interpolation is used to fill data gaps caused by factors such as cell outages and connection problems among cells and central radio network controller (RNC).
- If no voice or data service attempts are made in a cell for one hour, the accessibility and retainability values are zero. This situation is handled separately, and the accessibility or retainability status is "Idle." Figure 1 shows RRC and RAB attempt values for Cluster 6 throughout a week, and both values are zero at midnight.

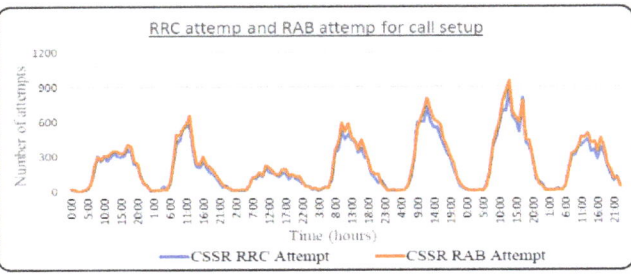

Figure 1. One-week RRC and RAB attempts.

- The data are split into two, with 60% utilized for training and 40% for model validation/testing. The training data are used to generate the transition matrix, and the process of constructing such a matrix from data are described in [7]. Combinations of 70/30 and 80/20 are also utilized for comparison purposes.
- The system predicts the next probability vector given the current state probability distribution and the transition matrix. The operation is then continued until a steady-state condition is reached. Following step/iteration prediction, results are compared to the validation data to assess prediction accuracy.

4.2. Clustering

It takes time to analyze individual cell performance and patterns. In this research, we suggest K-mean clustering as a method for grouping cells with similar accessibility and retainability properties. Model construction and prediction are based on per-cluster averaged accessibility and retainability. The Elbow approach in K-mean clustering is used to identify the number of clusters by changing the parameter from 2 to 18. Each cell was randomly assigned to several clusters to vary the centroid of each center. The procedure was repeated until the cluster variation in the data could no longer be reduced by adjusting the cluster centroid. We discovered that a clustering value of 6 is adequate. Hourly data acquired from each cell varies from 0% to 100%; however, if no voice or data service requests are received in a cell for 1 h, all counter values for that hour are zero, as illustrated in Figure 1.

4.3. KPI Threshold for States Definition

Operators set threshold values for several KPIs based on the ITU's recommendations, considering variables such as capital expenditures, operational expenses, QoS, and customer satisfaction. Tables 1 and 2 display a threshold value for the considered operator's accessibility and retainability. Based on the values in the two tables, the states of accessibility and retainability are generated.

Table 1. Possible values of call setup attempt and CSSR.

Call Setup Attempt	Value	State of a Cell
>0.0	CSSR ≥ 98.0%	Good (G)
>0.0	95.0% ≤ CSSR ≤ 98.0%	Acceptable (A)
>0.0	0.0% ≤ CSSR ≤ 95.0%	Bad (B)
=0.0	-	Idle (I)

Table 2. Possible values of RAB setup success and CDR.

RAB Setup Attempt	Value	State of a Cell
>0.0	0.0% ≤ CDR ≤ 1.0%	Good (G)
>0.0	1.0% ≤ CDR ≤ 3.0%	Acceptable (A)
>0.0	3.0% ≤ CDR	Bad (B)
=0.0	-	Idle (I)

4.4. Separate Prediction

As indicated above, the accessibility and retainability predictions at the cluster level can be made separately and jointly. Four states are required for the separate case. Hence, the corresponding transition matrices are 4 × 4. The state transition probability diagram for the sixth cluster is given in Figure 2 below, which is obtained after developing the model.

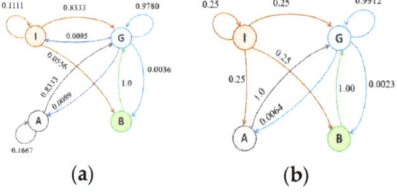

(a)   (b)

Figure 2. Transition probability diagram of cluster 6. (**a**) Accessibility. (**b**) Retainability.

Note that there are missing arrows in the two figures. As an example, there is no arrow in Figure 2a pointing from state A to state I, indicating that such a transition does not exist or the system has never landed in an idle state if it was initially in the Acceptable state.

4.5. Joint Prediction

The different state combinations of accessibility and retainability can be seen via joint estimation. For example, a Bad state of in accessibility and a Bad state in retainability can occur at the same time. When all possible combinations are considered, the total number of states rises to 16, and the resulting transition matrix is shown in Figure 3.

	II	IG	IA	IB	GI	GG	GA	GB	AI	AG	AA	AB	BI	BG	BA	BB
II	0.0625	0.0625	0.0625	0.0625	0.0625	0.0625	0.0625	0.0625	0.0625	0.0625	0.0625	0.0625	0.0625	0.0625	0.0625	0.0625
IG	0.0000	0.1176	0.0000	0.0000	0.0000	0.7647	0.0588	0.0000	0.0000	0.0000	0.0000	0.0000	0.0000	0.0588	0.0000	0.0000
IA	0.0000	0.0000	0.0000	0.0000	0.0000	1.0000	0.0000	0.0000	0.0000	0.0000	0.0000	0.0000	0.0000	0.0000	0.0000	0.0000
IB	0.0625	0.0625	0.0625	0.0625	0.0625	0.0625	0.0625	0.0625	0.0625	0.0625	0.0625	0.0625	0.0625	0.0625	0.0625	0.0625
GI	0.0625	0.0625	0.0625	0.0625	0.0625	0.0625	0.0625	0.0625	0.0625	0.0625	0.0625	0.0625	0.0625	0.0625	0.0625	0.0625
GG	0.0000	0.0090	0.0006	0.0000	0.0000	0.9707	0.0048	0.0024	0.0000	0.0090	0.0000	0.0000	0.0000	0.0030	0.0006	0.0000
GA	0.0000	0.0000	0.0000	0.0000	0.0000	1.0000	0.0000	0.0000	0.0000	0.0000	0.0000	0.0000	0.0000	0.0000	0.0000	0.0000
GB	0.0000	0.0000	0.0000	0.0000	0.0000	1.0000	0.0000	0.0000	0.0000	0.0000	0.0000	0.0000	0.0000	0.0000	0.0000	0.0000
AI	0.0625	0.0625	0.0625	0.0625	0.0625	0.0625	0.0625	0.0625	0.0625	0.0625	0.0625	0.0625	0.0625	0.0625	0.0625	0.0625
AG	0.0000	0.0000	0.0000	0.0000	0.0000	0.8333	0.0000	0.0000	0.0000	0.1667	0.0000	0.0000	0.0000	0.0000	0.0000	0.0000
AA	0.0625	0.0625	0.0625	0.0625	0.0625	0.0625	0.0625	0.0625	0.0625	0.0625	0.0625	0.0625	0.0625	0.0625	0.0625	0.0625
AB	0.0625	0.0625	0.0625	0.0625	0.0625	0.0625	0.0625	0.0625	0.0625	0.0625	0.0625	0.0625	0.0625	0.0625	0.0625	0.0625
BI	0.0625	0.0625	0.0625	0.0625	0.0625	0.0625	0.0625	0.0625	0.0625	0.0625	0.0625	0.0625	0.0625	0.0625	0.0625	0.0625
BG	0.0000	0.0000	0.0000	0.0000	0.0000	1.0000	0.0000	0.0000	0.0000	0.0000	0.0000	0.0000	0.0000	0.0000	0.0000	0.0000
BA	0.0000	0.0000	0.0000	0.0000	0.0000	1.0000	0.0000	0.0000	0.0000	0.0000	0.0000	0.0000	0.0000	0.0000	0.0000	0.0000
BB	0.0625	0.0625	0.0625	0.0625	0.0625	0.0625	0.0625	0.0625	0.0625	0.0625	0.0625	0.0625	0.0625	0.0625	0.0625	0.0625

Figure 3. Sixteen-state TPM of cluster 6.

4.6. State Prediction

After creating the transition matrices and knowing the current/initial state distribution, the next state and steady state distributions are predicted using Equation (10). If the current state is (assumed to be) in a Good state, then the value of π_0 is,

$$\pi_0 = [\, I\, G\, A\, B\,] = [\, 0\, 1\, 0\, 0\,] \tag{12}$$

Then, using Equations (10) and (12), the next accessibility probability is π_1 for one of the clusters when computed, and the result is:

$$[0\,1\,0\,0] \times \begin{pmatrix} 0.1111 & 0.8333 & 0.0000 & 0.0556 \\ 0.0095 & 0.9780 & 0.0089 & 0.0036 \\ 0.0000 & 0.8333 & 0.1667 & 0.0000 \\ 0.0000 & 1.0000 & 0.0000 & 0.0000 \end{pmatrix}$$
$$= [\, 0.0095 \quad 0.9780 \quad 0.0089 \quad 0.0036 \,] \tag{13}$$

According to the result, the system has a 0.95 percent chance of going to the Idle state, a 97.80 percent chance of staying in a Good state, a 0.89 percent chance of going to the Acceptable state, and a 0.36 percent chance of going to the Bad state.

Equation (11) is used to find the steady-state distribution calculated iteratively until the next and previous state values are equal. Tables 3 and 4 display the steady-state results for the four-state Markov chain regarding accessibility and retainability. Table 5 depicts the cluster 1 steady-state distribution using the sixteen-state Markov chain. For both scenarios, 70% of the data are used as a training set.

Table 3. Steady-state vector of accessibility using four-state Markov chain.

Cluster	Steady-State Vector of Accessibility			
	I	G	A	B
1	0.0000	0.9926	0.0060	0.0015
2	0.0000	0.9722	0.0149	0.0129
3	0.0000	0.9911	0.0079	0.0010
4	0.0000	0.9782	0.0179	0.0040
5	0.0000	0.9916	0.0055	0.0030
6	0.0109	0.9722	0.0114	0.0055

Table 4. Steady-state vector of retainability using four-state Markov chain.

Cluster	Steady-State Vector of Retainability			
	I	G	A	B
1	0.0000	0.9980	0.0020	0.0000
2	0.0000	0.9955	0.0035	0.0010
3	0.0000	1.0000	0.0000	0.0000
4	0.0000	0.9980	0.0020	0.0000
5	0.0000	0.9965	0.0030	0.0005
6	0.0000	0.9901	0.0079	0.0020

Table 5. Steady-state vector of Cluster 1 using sixteen-state Markov chain.

Cluster	Steady-State Vector			
	[II IG IA IB	GI GG GA GB	AI AG AA AB	BI BG BA BB]
1	[0.0000	0.0000	0.0000	0.0000
	0.0000	0.9926	0.0000	0.0000
	0.0000	0.0040	0.0020	0.0000
	0.0000	0.0015	0.0000	0.0000]

In Table 3, the maximum value in the Good state from the six clusters is 99.26% in cluster 1, and the minimum value is 97.22% in clusters 2 and 6. The maximum value of the Bad state is 1.29% in cluster 2, and the minimum value is 0.1% in cluster 3. From this cluster, one cell is at the top in the Good state, and cluster 2 cells are at the top in the Bad state. Though cluster 6 cells are the least in the Good state, they are not at the top in the Bad state because, next to the Good state, cluster 6 cells have a high probability (1.09%) of being in the Idle state. So, if optimization or maintenance work is needed, the schedule and priority should be given based on the steady-state vector values of each cluster.

Steady state distribution for the sixteen-state Markov chain follows the same approach. Cluster 1's steady-state outcome is shown in Table 5. The first letter stands for accessibility, while the second stands for retainability, and 99.26% of the time, accessibility and retainability were in the Good state, while for 0.4% of the time accessibility was in the Acceptable state and retainability was in the Good state. Furthermore, for 0.2% of the time, accessibility and retainability were both in the Acceptable state, while 0.15% of the time, accessibility was Bad, and retainability was in the Good state. As a result, the table provides cell information relating to accessibility and retainability, allowing operators to quickly sort cells that perform poorly in either or a combination of the two performance measures.

4.7. Evaluation Metric

The accuracy of a model was assessed using Equation (14) [21], which calculates the percentage of correctly forecasting the next state given the current state.

$$Accuracy = \frac{Correct\ predictions}{Total\ number\ of\ examples} \times 100\%. \tag{14}$$

Table 6 below shows the accuracy results for different combinations of training data proportion, clusters, four vs sixteen states modeling and the two KPIS considered. As an example, we note that a minimum value of 96.09% prediction accuracy is achieved in cluster 2 in predicting accessibility when 60% training set is used, while 96.87% prediction accuracy is achieved in cluster 5 in predicting retainability when the 80% training set is used. A 94.61% prediction accuracy is achieved in cluster 6 in predicting both accessibility and retainability when 80% of the data are used for training and when the modeling is the case of the sixteen-state Markov chain.

Table 6. Prediction accuracy for sixteen-state Markov chain.

Cluster	Training Set	Accessibility Accuracy Using Four States	Retainability Accuracy Using Four States	[(Column 3 × Column 4)/100] (%)	Accessibility and Retainability Accuracy Using Sixteen States
1	60%	98.7837	99.1312	97.9254	97.8280
	70%	98.3796	98.8426	97.2410	97.1065
	80%	98.0870	98.2609	96.3811	96.1739
2	60%	96.0904	98.6968	94.8381	95.5691
	70%	96.7593	98.3796	95.1914	96.1806
	80%	96.1739	97.7391	93.9995	95.4783
3	60%	98.5230	100.0000	98.5230	98.5230
	70%	98.4954	100.0000	98.4954	98.4954
	80%	98.6087	100.0000	98.6087	98.6087
4	60%	98.5230	100.0000	98.5230	98.5230
	70%	98.3796	100.0000	98.3796	98.3796
	80%	98.6087	100.0000	98.6087	98.6087
5	60%	97.7411	98.4361	96.2126	97.0460
	70%	97.3380	97.9167	95.3101	96.4120
	80%	96.1739	96.8696	93.1633	94.7826
6	60%	96.5248	98.0886	94.6798	94.7871
	70%	96.8750	98.0324	94.9689	95.0231
	80%	96.6957	97.7391	94.5095	94.6087

5. Conclusions

In this paper, the two important mobile network KPI parameters of accessibility and retainability are predicted by formulating the Markov chain in four states and sixteen states. The sixteen-state Markov chain is formulated in a bid to jointly estimate both KPIs in a single operation. Moreover, in order to capture the spatial behaviors of these KPIs, K-mean clustering is applied to cluster the data from 1530 cells into 6 clusters. States are created based on threshold values set by operators and the developed models are validated by splitting the data for training and testing. We hope the approach provides significant insight on how to use data available within an operator's NMS to better understand the status of a network.

This work might be improved in some ways. Conducting the prediction for a large number of cells in a computationally efficient manner and to obtain per-cell level information is one research area. The clustering and joint approach may not scale well as the number of cells grows. Moreover, applying the approach for other KPIs, network types, and services is an area worth exploring. Finally, future research should employ the hidden Markov model for status modeling and prediction.

Author Contributions: Conceptualization, T.A.Y. and D.H.W.; methodology, T.A.Y. and D.H.W.; software, T.A.Y. and A.S.O.; validation, A.S.O. and T.A.Y.; formal analysis, A.S.O., T.A.Y. and D.H.W.; investigation, A.S.O., T.A.Y. and D.H.W.; resources, T.A.Y.; data curation, T.A.Y.; writing—original draft preparation, A.S.O. and T.A.Y.; writing—review and editing, A.S.O. and D.H.W.; visualization, A.S.O.; supervision, D.H.W. All authors have read and agreed to the published version of the manuscript.

Funding: This research received no funding.

Institutional Review Board Statement: Not applicable.

Informed Consent Statement: Not applicable.

Data Availability Statement: Restrictions apply to the availability of the data used for the research. Data was obtained from ethio telecom and are available from the second author with the permission of ethio telecom.

Conflicts of Interest: The authors declare no conflict of interest.

References

1. Yemer:, T.A. Mobile Networks Accessibility, and the Retainability States Prediction Using Markov Chain. Master's Thesis, Addis Ababa University, Addis Ababa, Ethiopia, January 2022.
2. Huawei Technologies Co., Ltd. *HUAWEI RAN KPI for Performance Management (RNC V100R006)*; Huawei Technologies Co., Ltd.: Shenzhen, China, 2006.
3. Machine Learning Glossary. Available online: https://developers.google.com/machine-learning/glossary#multi-class (accessed on 19 May 2021).
4. International Telecommunication Union. *Quality of Service and Dependability Vocabulary*; The International Telegraph and Telephone Consultative Committee: Geneva, Switzerland, 1988; Volume E.800, p. 16.
5. Tolver, A. *An Introduction to Markov Chain*; Department of Mathematical Sciences, University of Copenhagen: Copenhagen, Denmark, November 2016.
6. Ng, H.Y.; Ko, K.T.; Tsang, K.F. 3G Mobile Network Call Admission Control Scheme Using Markov Chain. In Proceedings of the Ninth International Symposium on Consumer Electronics, Macau, China, 14–16 June 2005. [CrossRef]
7. Mitra, K.; Ahlund, C.; Zaslavsky, A. QoE Estimation and Prediction Using Hidden Markov Models in Heterogeneous Access Networks. In Proceedings of the Australasian Telecommunication Networks and Applications Conference (ATNAC), Brisbane, Australia, 7–9 November 2012. [CrossRef]
8. Wu, Q.; Zhang, M.; Zheng, R.; Lou, Y.; Wei, W. A QoS-satisfied Prediction Model for Cloud-Service Composition Based on a Hidden Markov Model, Special issue on Applied Mathematics and Algorithms for Cloud Computing and IoT, Hindawi, July 2013. *Math. Probl. Eng.* **2013**, *2013*, 387083. [CrossRef]
9. Hendrawan. RRC success rate accessibility prediction on SAE/LTE network using Markov chain model. In Proceedings of the 2017 11th International Conference on Telecommunication Systems Services and Applications (TSSA), Lombok, Indonesia, 26–27 October 2017. [CrossRef]
10. Amirrudin, N.A.; Ariffin, S.H.S.; Abd Malik, N.N.N.; Ghazali, N.E. Mobility Prediction via Markov Model in LTE Femtocell. *Int. J. Comput. Appl.* **2013**, *65*, 18.
11. Wang, Y. Evaluating Wireless Network Accessibility Performance Via Clustering-Based Model: An analytic methodology. In Proceedings of the Wireless Telecommunications Symposium (WTS), London, UK, 18–20 April 2016. [CrossRef]
12. Hendrawan, N.A. Accessibility Degradation Prediction on LTE/SAE Network Using Discrete-Time Markov Chain (DTMC) Model. *J. ICT Res. Appl.* **2019**, *13*, 1–18. [CrossRef]
13. Iyer, A.P.; Li, L.E.; Stoica, I. Automating Diagnosis of Cellular Radio Access Network Problems. In Proceedings of the 23rd Annual International Conference on Mobile Computing and Networking, Snowbird, UT, USA, 16–20 October 2017. [CrossRef]
14. Oluwafemi, E.O.; Nnonye, O.E.; Okechukwu, U.; Adewale, A.L. Prediction of Call Drops in GSM Network using Artificial Neural Network. *J. Teknol. Syst. Comput.* **2019**, *7*, 38–46.
15. Akanbasiam, J.A.; Ngala, D.K. The Study of Quality of Service on a Major Mobile Network Operator in Ghana. *IOSR J. Electron. Commun. Eng. (IOSR-JECE)* **2017**, *12*, 21–25. [CrossRef]

16. Olayinka, O.O.; Olukemi, S.O.; Chukwuemeka, O. Assessment of Quality of Service of Mobile Network Operators in Akure. *Int. J. Bus. Adm.* **2019**, *10*, 3. [CrossRef]
17. ETSI TS 132 410, Version 9.0.0, Release 9. 2010. Available online: https://cdn.standards.iteh.ai/samples/32882/33cf7e8727da4bf7bb448687b19604f9/ETSI-TS-132-410-V9-0-0-2010-01-.pdf (accessed on 19 May 2022).
18. Porod, U. Dynamics of Markov Chains for Undergraduates. 19 February 2021. Available online: https://www.math.northwestern.edu/documents/book-markov-chains.pdf (accessed on 17 June 2022).
19. Abdulkareem, H.A.; Tekanyi, M.S.; Kassim, A.Y.; Zakariyya, Z.M.; Almustapha, M.D.; Abdu-Aguye, U.F.; Adamu, H. Analysis of a GSM Network Quality of Service Using Call Drop Rate and Call Setup Success Rate as Performance Indicators. *Eur. J. Electr. Eng.* **2020**, *9*, 113–121.
20. Omer, A.S.; Woldegebreal, D.H. Review of Markov Chain and Its Applications in Telecommunication Systems. In *E-Infrastructure and E-Services for Developing Countries*; Sheikh, Y.H., Rai, I.A., Bakar, A.D., Eds.; AFRICOMM 2021; Lecture Notes of the Institute for Computer Sciences, Social Informatics and Telecommunications Engineering; Springer: Cham, Switzerland, 2022; Volume 443. [CrossRef]
21. Paranthaman, V.V.; Mapp, G.; Shah, P.; Nguyen, H.X.; Ghosh, A. Exploring Markov Models for the Allocation of Resources for Proactive Handover in a Mobile Environment. In Proceedings of the IEEE 40th Local Computer Networks Conference Workshops (LCN Workshops), Clearwater Beach, FL, USA, 26–29 October 2015. [CrossRef]

Proceeding Paper

A Multivariate Approach for Spatiotemporal Mobile Data Traffic Prediction [†]

Bethelhem S. Shawel [1,2,*], Endale Mare [3], Tsegamlak T. Debella [1,4], Sofie Pollin [2] and Dereje H. Woldegebreal [1]

1   School of Electrical and Computer Engineering, Addis Ababa Institute of Technology, Addis Ababa University, Addis Ababa 386, Ethiopia; tsegamlak.terefe@aait.edu.et (T.T.D.); dereje.hailemariam@aait.edu.et (D.H.W.)
2   Department of Electrical Engineering, KU Leuven, 3001 Leuven, Belgium; sofie.pollin@esat.kuleuven.be
3   Ethio Telecom, Addis Ababa 1047, Ethiopia; endale.mare@ethiotelecom.et
4   ENSISA, Institute for Research in Informatics, Mathematics, Automation and Signal, Université de Haute Alsace, 68093 Mulhouse, France
*   Correspondence: bethelhem.seifu@aait.edu.et
†   Presented at the 8th International Conference on Time Series and Forecasting, Gran Canaria, Spain, 27–30 June 2022.

Abstract: Widespread deployment of spectrally efficient mobile networks, advancements in mobile devices, and proliferation of attractive applications has led to an exponential increase in mobile data traffic. Mobile Network Operators (MNOs) benefit from the associated revenue generation while putting efforts to meet customers' expectations of delivered services. Having a clear knowledge of the traffic demand is critical for network dimensioning, optimization, resource allocation, market planning, and the like. As the traffic demand, among others, is a function of customers' behavior and settlement patterns, land use, and time of the day, capturing traffic characteristics in both temporal and spatial dimensions is needed. Moreover, other parameters, such as the number of users and data throughput, inherently contain traffic-related information, necessitating a multivariate approach for understanding the traffic demand. Realizing the multidimensional and multivariate nature of the mobile data traffic, in this paper, we propose a multivariate and hybrid Convolutional Neural Network and Long Short-Term Memory network (CNN-LSTM) data traffic prediction model. The model is built on mobile traffic data collected from a Network Operator for Long-Term Evolution (LTE) network. The results confirm that the proposed model outperforms its univariate counterparts in Root Mean Square Error (RMSE) and Mean Absolute Percentage Error (MAPE) by 58% and 50%, respectively. Moreover, the model is further compared with CNN-only univariate and multivariate models, which it also outperforms. The comparisons substantiate the achievable improvements because of the hybrid and multivariate nature of the prediction algorithm.

Keywords: mobile data traffic; multivariate prediction; temporal; spatial; CNN; LSTM

Citation: Shawel, B.S.; Mare, E.; Debella, T.T.; Pollin, S.; Woldegebreal, D.H. A Multivariate Approach for Spatiotemporal Mobile Data Traffic Prediction. *Eng. Proc.* **2022**, *18*, 10. https://doi.org/10.3390/engproc2022018010

Academic Editors: Ignacio Rojas, Hector Pomares, Olga Valenzuela, Fernando Rojas and Luis Javier Herrera

Published: 21 June 2022

Publisher's Note: MDPI stays neutral with regard to jurisdictional claims in published maps and institutional affiliations.

1. Introduction

The global need for mobile data traffic is increasing for a variety of reasons, including the continuous growth of smarter mobile phones, emergence of machine-to-machine connections, and the availability of appealing and data-intensive applications [1]. Constant optimization, capacity enhancement, and efficient utilization of scarce resources are approaches by Mobile Network Operators (MNOs) to maintain service quality and avoid capacity crunch because of this ever-growing data demand. Moreover, network densification, traffic offloading, spectral efficiency improvement, and using more radio spectrum are techniques to improve the poor quality of service (QoS) that rises due to capacity crunch [2]. MNOs select the appropriate method based on their customer demand and financial capability. Current and future data traffic demand knowledge is one critical input for the design and implementation of the above-mentioned approaches.

Time-series prediction methods play a vital role to forecast future demands for several real-world applications, including mobile data traffic demand. Data prediction models are broadly grouped as conventional and computational intelligence models [3]. Autoregressive Integrated Moving Average (ARIMA) and its extensions such as Seasonal ARIMA (SARIMA) are conventional methods. Computational intelligence techniques, on the other hand, include machine learning and deep learning-based models such as Long Term Short Memory (LSTM) and Convolutional Neural Network (CNN) networks. The time-series prediction method can be deveoped based on univariate or multivariate variables (or features). In the univariate case, there is one observation (a dependent feature, which in our case is data traffic) available for different time instants, while in the multivariate case there are multiple observations observed over different time instants. Multivariate time series prediction becomes popular in many real-world applications such as energy, finance, and weather and smoothens model building by increasing the model's performance [4].

Several researchers used machine learning methods, such as deep learning and data clustering, and multivariate approaches to model the dynamics of mobile data traffic in temporal and spatiotemporal domains. Based on data collected from an operator's network, ref. [3] proposed LSTM and Gated Recurrent Unit (GRU) to capture the dynamics in mobile data traffic. By comparing with Adaptive Neuro-Fuzzy Inference System (ANFIS) and Artificial Neural Network (ANN), the authors demonstrated the performance gain by using the proposed model. Similar to [3], ref. [5] also applied LSTM and Recurrent Neural Network (RNN) to predict data traffic demand of a 4G network run by an operator. In both papers, the prediction is done on a per-base-station basis and in temporal dimension only.

To separately estimate the linear and non-linear part of mobile data traffic, ref. [6] proposed a hybrid model using Double SARIMA (DSARIMA) and LSTM in which the DSARIMA handles the linear part whereas the LSTM predicts the nonlinear part of data traffic. To capture correlation among temporal traffic data taken from different bases stations that are spatially separated, K-Means clustering is used to group the base stations having similar data traffic. The result shows that the hybrid model outperforms the DSARIMA and LSTM-only models. A similar clustering-based approach was also used in [7] to assess the effectiveness of different time series prediction models for efficient deployment of base stations.

A multivariate and LSTM-based prediction approach is proposed in [8] to collect scheduling information of users. The multivariate features considered are: number of resource blocks, transport block size, and modulation and coding schemes. The results show the effectiveness of the LSTM network in capturing temporal variation for multivariate input features. Though for different applications, refs. [9–11] demonstrated the capability of multivariate and hybrid CNN-LSTM model to predict residential energy consumption and forecasting particulate matter, respectively. Univariate models are used as a benchmark for comparison and the results confirm that multivariate features greatly improve the model performance.

In summary, in a bid to improve prediction accuracy, from the survey we understood the need to incorporate multiple variables, data clustering, and blend LSTM and CNN to capture traffic dynamics in spatiotemporal dimensions. In this work, a hybrid CNN-LSTM mobile data traffic-prediction model that takes multiple traffic-related variables is proposed. A total of 4 months of Long-Term Evolution (LTE) network data traffic that is collected from the network operator is used to build and validate the model. To the best of our knowledge, there is no prior work that applies a hybrid CNN-LSTM model for such types of neural networks. Understandably, the multivariate features are technology- and application-dependent. Hence, we used our experience and availability of data to determine the features.

The remainder of the paper is organized as follows. The characteristics of mobile data traffic and associated data preprocessing are described in Section 2, followed by the discussions of mobile data traffic prediction approaches in Section 3. Section 4 contains the results and discussion, while the conclusion of the paper is presented in Section 5.

2. Analysis of Mobile Data Traffic

2.1. Mobile Data Traffic Characteristics

Mobile data traffic exhibits different properties in both time and spatial domains. Trend and seasonality are used to demonstrate the temporal properties of time-series data. The trend shows a long-term increase or decrease in the data, whereas seasonality is a repeating pattern with a fixed period such as daily, weekly and yearly. Figure 1 illustrates sample downlink data traffic, measured in Gigabytes, from two LTE radio base stations, called eNodeBs, measurement taken for a duration of 9 days. We observe that, even if the average daily traffic differs for different days, there is a daily seasonality observed in the data.

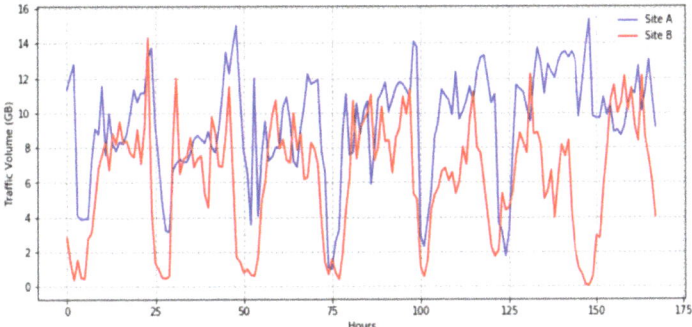

Figure 1. Data traffic pattern for sample LTE sites located at A and B.

2.2. Data Traffic in Spatial Dimension

We observe from Figure 1 a variation in data traffic demand at the two locations, motivating the need for additional investigation of the traffic pattern in the spatial dimension. Since mobile users constantly move within a given cellular network, the traffic pattern across neighboring base stations are correlated or complemented, such that developing in both the spatial and temporal dimensions would provide better information for telecom operators [12]. Spatiotemporal data traffic prediction incorporates different user behavior such as mobility and network behavior, such as the number of handovers in the network [13].

For spatial analysis, a grid-based or cluster-based approach can be used. In the former approach, a given service area is partitioned into (usually) uniform grids, and eNodeBs that fall into one cell of a grid are considered as one unit. However, because of the non-uniform distribution of eNodeBs, it is difficult to formulate models for large areas with fine-granularity grids.

The clustering approach is another option to incorporate all eNodeBs. In this approach, eNodeBs with similar traffic load patterns are grouped together and those eNodeBs within the same cluster have similar characteristics. The eNodeBs can be clustered based on either geographical location, also called spatial clustering, or on temporal behavior [6,7]. The assumption in spatial clustering is that neighboring eNodeBs exhibit similar temporal properties. In temporal-based clustering, the clustering is done based on temporal behavior irrespective of geographical location [6]. Considering more than one eNodB in time series clustering incorporates the spatial information of the data traffic. After clustering the base stations, the data traffic prediction model is developed per cluster level. In this paper, we have applied the temporal-based clustering approach.

2.3. Multivariate Features Selection

The data used in this paper is collected from an operator's LTE network for 4 months from October 2020 to January 2021 in an hourly granularity. The multivariate dataset incorporates eight features: download downlink (DL) traffic, which is the traffic to be predicted; DL throughput; average and maximum number of users in a cell; number of attempted, successful, and setup failure Radio Access Bearers (RABs); uplink (UL) data traffic; and location information of the eNodeBs.

Pearson's-based correlation analysis is applied to select features and the result of the correlation analysis is illustrated in Figure 2. A correlation threshold value of 0.5 and above is used to select features. Moreover, for features whose correlation coefficient values are closer, e.g., cell average user of 0.83 value and cell maximum user of 0.82, only one is considered. Among the multivariate features DL traffic, a number of successful RABs, cell average user, and UL traffic are selected as they are highly correlated with downlink data traffic.

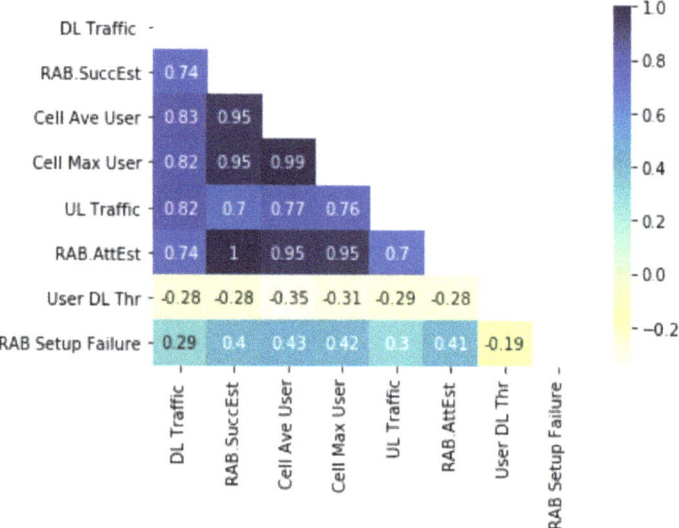

Figure 2. Feature correlation results.

2.4. Data Preparation for CNN-LSTM Model

In data preparation, missing values in the multivariate dataset are imputed with the Kalman filter, preserving the strong seasonality and trend of the data traffic. The features in the dataset are scaled with a standard scaler so all data points fall within a certain range. Since some machine learning algorithms that use distance metrics are affected by the span of the value found in the dataset, feature scaling is critical for improving model performance. Furthermore, the time series prediction problem is framed as supervised learning makes it suitable to train and test deep learning models.

2.5. Time Series-Based Clustering

Clustering a dynamic dataset differs from static data since the former changes over time. Different approaches such as Hierarchical Clustering, K-Means Clustering, and Fuzzy C Means Clustering are used for time series data clustering. Each method has its advantages and disadvantages. Among those methods, K-Means Clustering is used in several works for fast convergence even for a large number of datasets [14]. In this work, K-Means clustering is used to group the eNodeBs according to the daily data traffic volume and four distinct clusters are obtained based on K-Means clustering for the dataset.

3. Mobile Data Traffic Prediction Methods

Deep learning models such as LSTM, GRU, and CNN are becoming popular in dealing with sequential or time-series data such as text, speech, and often images [15]. The basics of LSTM and CNN networks that are used to develop the proposed model are revised in the following subsections.

3.1. One Dimensional CNN Model

CNN models are typically employed to analyze spatial or multidimensional data. However, one-dimensional CNN (1D CNN) can also be used to analyze texts and time-series data [16]; 1D CNN can extract salient and representative features of time-series data by performing 1D convolution operations using multiple filters [17]. Figure 3 shows the difference between 1D CNN and 2D CNN. The kernel (filter) in 2D moves in both directions while it moves only in one direction for 1D CNN. The input for 2D CNN is an image, while multivariate time series features can be inputs for 1D CNN.

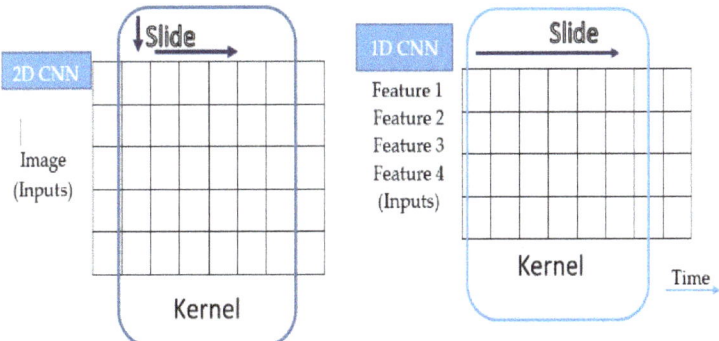

Figure 3. 2D and 1D CNN model input type and kernel slide direction [18].

3.2. LSTM Model

RNN is designed for handling sequential data by feeding the output of the previous layer as an input to the next layer, allowing the network to capture the dependency of sequential data [19]. LSTM is a type of RNN network that was modeled to solve short-term dependency problems as well as exploding and vanishing gradient problems. LSTM network has three gates (*Forget gate* f_t, *Input gate* i_t and *Output gate* o_t) that decide which information to add or remove from the cell state, and the *Cell state*, C_t, memory stores the desired information. The mathematical expression for the LSTM network at time t, is described as follows:

$$f_t = \sigma(W_f \cdot X_t + U_f \cdot h_{t-1} + b_f) \tag{1}$$

$$i_t = \sigma(W_i \cdot X_t + U_i \cdot h_{t-1} + b_i) \tag{2}$$

$$S_t = \tanh(W_c \cdot X_t + U_c \cdot h_{t-1} + b_c) \tag{3}$$

$$C_t = i_t \odot S_t + f_t \odot S_{t-1} \tag{4}$$

$$o_t = \sigma(W_o \cdot X_t + U_o \cdot h_{t-1} + V_o \cdot C_t + b_o) \tag{5}$$

$$h_t = o_t \odot \tanh(C_t) \tag{6}$$

where $\tanh(\cdot)$ and σ are activation functions while i_t, f_t, and o_t represent input gate, the forget gate, and the output gate values at time t, whereas b_i, b_f, b_c, and b_o are bias vectors for the input gate, forget gate, cell state, and output gate, respectively. X_t is the input vector to the memory cell at time t while the parameters $W_f, W_i, W_c, W_o, U_f, U_i, U_c, U_o$, and V_o are weight matrices for gates and cell state.

3.3. Proposed CNN-LSTM Model

The CNN model is well known for its ability to automatically learn and extract features from raw sequence or time-series data. It is possible to combine this capability of the CNN model with the LSTM model. The LSTM network captures long-term and short-term dependency of temporal features more efficiently. The CNN model accepts input data sequences and extracts important feature information, whereas the LSTM model connected in tandem interprets and provides an output [20]. This combination of CNN and LSTM models is called a CNN-LSTM model. The general approach followed in this paper is illustrated in Figure 4.

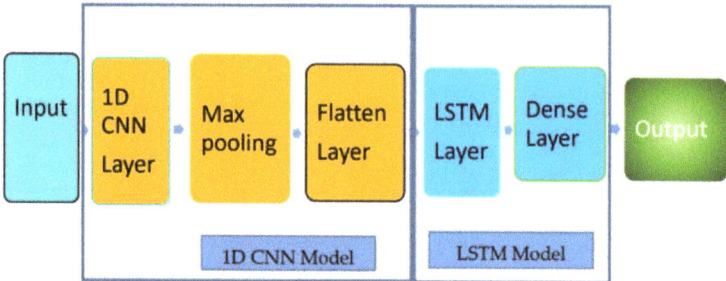

Figure 4. Proposed CNN-LSTM Hybrid Model.

Common performance evaluation metrics for regression models are Root Mean Square Error (RMSE) and Mean Absolute Percentage Error (MAPE). In this work, RMSE and MAPE are used as evaluation metrics, and the formula for those metrics are:

$$RMSE = \sqrt{\frac{1}{n}\sum_{i=1}^{n}(y_i - \hat{y}_i)^2} \tag{7}$$

$$MAPE = \frac{1}{n}\sum_{i=1}^{n}\left|\frac{y_i - \hat{y}_i}{y_i}\right| \tag{8}$$

where $\hat{y}_i$ and y_i corresponds to the actual and predicted values and n is the number of predicted instances.

4. Experimental Results and Discussion

4.1. Clustering

Among different clustering methods, in this work K-Means clustering is selected. Elbow method and silhouette score are used to determine the optimal number of clusters in K-Means clustering and to evaluate the goodness of a clustering technique, respectively. For our data, the optimal number of clusters is selected to be four and the sites are grouped into four clusters, as shown in Figure 5. We note how sites from various geographical areas are grouped into the same cluster because of similarities in their traffic patterns. Moreover, some base stations found in the same locations are grouped into different clusters.

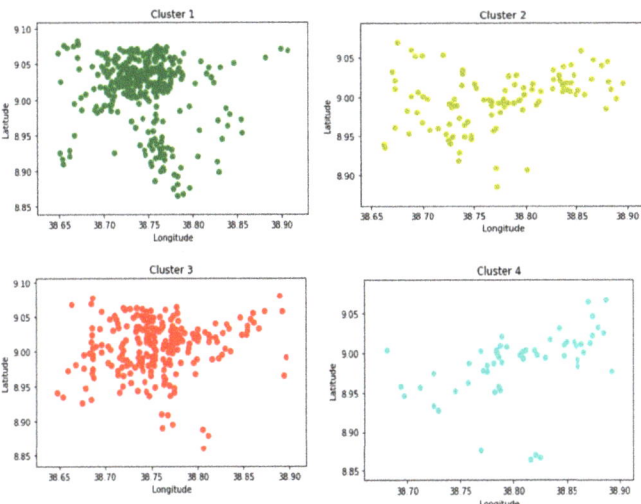

Figure 5. 4G eNodeBs geographical distribution in each cluster.

4.2. Per Cluster Time-Series Predictions

Figure 6 shows the actual and predicted values of mobile data traffic, using multivariate features in Figure 6a, and univariate feature Figure 6b. In both cases, the predicted data traffic has a similar pattern, in terms of daily seasonality, when compared with the actual data traffic. Comparing predicted results in (a) and (b), we note that including multiple features in a multivariate manner helps to capture the irregularities and edges that occur during peak hours. The improved result with multivariate features also demonstrates the ability of the deep learning model, CNN-LSTM, to extract salient information from complex data required for prediction. Table 1 depicts a comparison in terms of RMSE and MAPE.

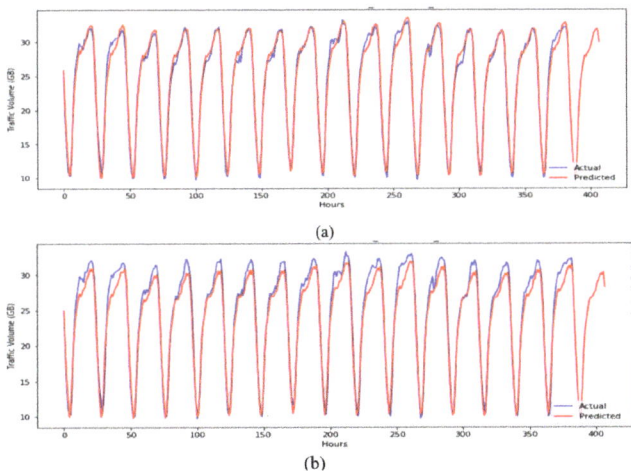

Figure 6. Mobile data traffic prediction with CNN-LSTM model (**a**) multivariate features (**b**) univariate feature.

The proposed model performance is compared with the CNN-only model with univariate and multivariate features models as also summarized in Table 1. The result confirms the performance improvements because of the hybrid CNN-LSTM model as well as the consideration of multivariate features.

Table 1. Model performance comparison.

Features	RMSE	MAPE
Proposed CNN-LSTM Model, Multivariate	0.81	2.97
Proposed CNN-LSTM Model, Univariate	1.28	4.48
CNN Model Multivariate	1.34	4.44
CNN Model Univariate	1.53	6.20

Furthermore, the impact of filling the missing values and input time steps are analyzed. The results in Figure 7 and Table 2 show the model performance with and without imputing the missing values in the datasets. The model output shows that, while the model captures traffic variation for the imputed dataset well, not filling in the missing values degrades the prediction result.

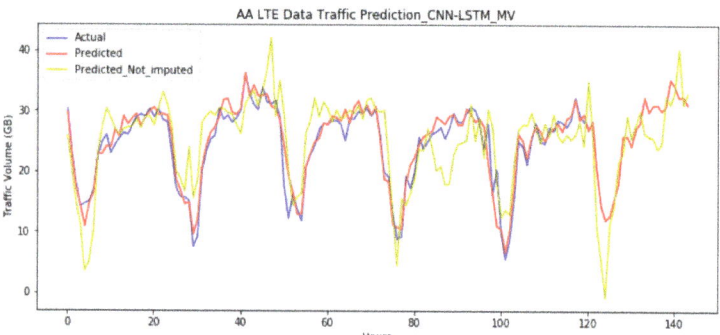

Figure 7. Model prediction for with and without imputation of missing value.

Table 2. Effect of filling missing value.

CNN-LSTM	RMSE	MAPE
With missing values imputation	2.01	6.88
Without missing values imputation	4.56	19.01

The effect of the input time steps while developing a prediction model is investigated with two input time steps of 24 h and 168 h. Figure 8 and Table 3 illustrate the data traffic prediction for the CNN-LSTM model using 168 h input time steps compared to the actual data traffic, and it captures the data traffic variation well, including for irregular shapes and sharp edges at both ends. However, this modest performance improvement comes at the expense of computational time. The model with 168 input time steps took more time to train the model.

Table 3. Model performance comparison for 24 and 168 input time steps.

Input Time Step	RMSE	MAPE
24 h	0.81	2.97
168 h	0.78	2.69

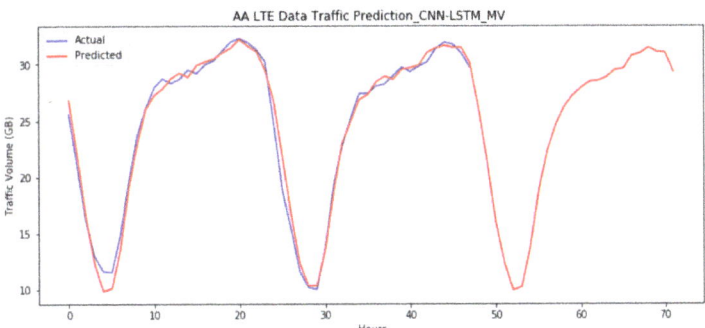

Figure 8. CNN-LSTM model prediction output for 168 input time steps.

5. Conclusions

Due to the increasing demand for mobile data traffic, the cellular network capacity is changing continuously and predictive models become inevitable in capturing the dynamics of mobile data traffic. In this paper, a deep learning-based model, CNN-LSTM, is proposed for mobile data traffic prediction using multivariate features. The hybrid CNN-LSTM networks leverage the power of the CNN model to extract salient features in the complex and nonlinear dataset as well as an LSTM to capture long–short dependency for time series data. The study shows the prediction capability of the CNN-LSTM model for mobile data traffic demand along with multivariate input features as compared to univariate features.

Future studies could include investigating the impact of other variants of clustering methods on model performance improvement. Furthermore, incorporating more specific multivariate features such as the amount of spectrum used and RAB attributes such as maximum source data, traffic type, and maximum bit rate might increase model performance and further improve the prediction accuracy.

Author Contributions: Conceptualization, B.S.S., E.M. and D.H.W.; methodology, B.S.S., E.M. and D.H.W.; software, B.S.S., E.M. and T.T.D.; validation, B.S.S. and T.T.D.; formal analysis, B.S.S., E.M. and D.H.W.; investigation, B.S.S. and E.M.; resources, E.M. and D.H.W.; data curation, E.M.; writing—original draft preparation, B.S.S. and E.M.; writing—review and editing, E.M. and D.H.W.; visualization, B.S.S. and E.M.; supervision, D.H.W. and S.P. All authors have read and agreed to the published version of the manuscript.

Funding: This research received no external funding.

Data Availability Statement: Restrictions apply to the availability of these data. Data was obtained from Ethio Telecom (a Mobile Network Operator) and are available from the corresponding author with the permission of Ethio Telecom.

Conflicts of Interest: The authors declare no conflict of interest.

References

1. Shi, W. Almost One Zettabyte of Mobile Data Traffic in 2022—Cisco. *Telecoms.com*, 20 February 2019. Available online: https://telecoms.com/495666/almost-one-zettabyte-of-mobile-data-traffic-in-2022-cisco/ (accessed on 3 October 2020).
2. GSMA. Data Demand Explained. June 2015. Available online: https://www.gsma.com/spectrum/wp-content/uploads/2015/06/GSMA-Data-Demand-Explained-June-2015.pdf (accessed on 6 August 2021).
3. Do, Q.H.; Doan, T.T.H.; Nguyen, T.V.A.; Duong, N.T.; Linh, V.V. Prediction of Data Traffic in Telecom Networks based on Deep Neural Networks. *J. Comput. Sci.* **2020**, *16*, 1268–1277. [CrossRef]
4. Bhanja, S.; Das, A. Deep Neural Network for Multivariate Time-Series Forecasting. In Proceedings of the 2nd International Conference on Frontiers in Computing and Systems, Singapore, 29 September–1 October 2021; pp. 267–277.
5. Dalgkitsis, A.; Louta, M.; Karetsos, G.T. Traffic forecasting in cellular networks using the LSTM RNN. In Proceedings of the 22nd Pan-Hellenic Conference on Informatics, New York, NY, USA, 29 November–1 December 2018; pp. 28–33.

6. Shawel, B.S.; Debella, T.T.; Tesfaye, G.; Tefera, Y.Y.; Woldegebreal, D.H. Hybrid Prediction Model for Mobile Data Traffic: A Cluster-Level Approach. In Proceedings of the International Joint Conference on Neural Networks (IJCNN), Glasgow, UK, 19–24 July 2020; pp. 1–8.

7. Mahdy, B.; Abbas, H.; Hassanein, H.; Noureldin, A.; Abouzeid, H. A Clustering-Driven Approach to Predict the Traffic Load of Mobile Networks for the Analysis of Base Stations Deployment. *J. Sens. Actuator Netw.* **2020**, *9*, 53. [CrossRef]

8. Trinh, H.D.; Giupponi, L.; Dini, P. Mobile Traffic Prediction from Raw Data Using LSTM Networks. In Proceedings of the IEEE 29th Annual International Symposium on Personal, In-Door and Mobile Radio Communications (PIMRC), Bologna, Italy, 9–12 September 2018; pp. 1827–1832.

9. Kim, T.Y.; Cho, S.B. Predicting residential energy consumption using CNN-LSTM neural networks. *Energy* **2019**, *182*, 72–81. [CrossRef]

10. Li, T.; Hua, M.; Wu, X. A Hybrid CNN-LSTM Model for Forecasting Particulate Matter (PM2.5). *IEEE Access* **2020**, *8*, 26933–26940. [CrossRef]

11. Mohammed, B.; Krishnaswamy, N.; Kiran, M. Multivariate Time-Series Prediction for Traffic in Large WAN Topology. In Proceedings of the ACM/IEEE Symposium on Architectures for Networking and Communications Systems (ANCS), Cambridge, UK, 24–25 September 2019; pp. 1–4.

12. Zhang, J.; Zheng, Y.; Qi, D.; Li, R.; Yi, X. DNN-based prediction model for spatio-temporal data. In Proceedings of the SIGSPACIAL '16: Proceedings of the 24th ACM SIGSPATIAL International Conference on Advances in Geographic Information Systems, Burlingame, CA, USA, 31 October–3 November 2016; pp. 1–4.

13. Wang, X.; Zhou, Z.; Yang, Z.; Liu, Y.; Peng, C. Spatio-temporal analysis and prediction of cellular traffic in metropolis. In Proceedings of the IEEE 25th International Conference on Network Protocols (ICNP), Toronto, ON, Canada, 10–13 October 2017; pp. 1–10.

14. Aghabozorgi, S.; Seyed Shirkhorshidi, A.; Ying Wah, T. Time-series clustering: A decade review. *Inf. Syst.* **2015**, *53*, 16–38. [CrossRef]

15. Rajagukguk, R.; Ardiansyah Ramadhan, R.A.; Lee, H.J. A Review on Deep Learning Models for Forecasting Time Series Data of Solar Irradiance and Photovoltaic Power. *Energies* **2020**, *13*, 6623. [CrossRef]

16. Terefe, T.; Devanne, M.; Weber, J.; Hailemariam, D.; Forestier, G. Time Series Averaging Using MultiTasking Autoencoder. In Proceedings of the IEEE 32nd International Conference on Tools with Artificial Intelligence (ICTAI), Baltimore, MD, USA, 9–11 November 2020; pp. 1065–1072.

17. Xu, G.; Ren, T.; Chen, Y.; Che, W. A One-Dimensional CNN-LSTM Model for Epileptic Seizure Recognition Using EEG Signal Analysis. *Front. Neurosci.* **2020**, *14*, 1253. [CrossRef] [PubMed]

18. Mare, E. Mobile Data Traffic Prediction Using Multivariate Time Series Data: The Case of LTE Network in Addis Ababa. Master's Thesis, Addis Ababa University, Addis Ababa, Ethiopia, 2021.

19. Cecaj, A.; Lippi, M.; Mamei, M.; Zambonelli, F. Comparing Deep Learning and Statistical Methods in Forecasting Crowd Distribution from Aggregated Mobile Phone Data. *Appl. Sci.* **2020**, *10*, 6580. [CrossRef]

20. Brownlee, J. *Deep Learning for Time Series Forecasting: Predict the Future with MLPs, CNNs and LSTMs in Python*; Machine Learning Mastery: Vermont, Australia, 2018.

engineering proceedings

MDPI

Proceeding Paper

An Application of Neural Networks to Predict COVID-19 Cases in Italy †

Lorena Saliaj * and Eugenia Nissi

Department of Economic Studies, School of Economic, Business, Legal and Sociological Sciences, Università degli Studi "G. d'Annunzio", 65127 Pescara, Italy; eugenia.nissi@unich.it

* Correspondence: lorena.saliaj@unich.it

† Presented at the 8th International Conference on Time Series and Forecasting, Gran Canaria, Spain, 27–30 June 2022.

Abstract: COVID-19 pandemic has become the greatest worldwide threat, as it has spread rapidly among individuals in most countries around the world. This study concerns the problem of weekly prediction of new COVID-19 cases in Italy, aiming to find the best predictive model for daily infection number in countries with a large number of confirmed cases. We compare the forecasting performance of linear and nonlinear forecasting models using weekly COVID-19 data for the period between 24 February 2020 until 16 May 2022. We discuss various forecasting approaches, including a Nonlinear Autoregressive Neural Network (NARNN) model, an Autoregressive Integrated Moving Average (ARIMA) model, a TBATS model, and Exponential Smoothing on the collected data and compared their accuracy using the data collected from 23 March 2020 to 20 April 2020, choosing the model with the lowest Mean Absolute Percentage Error (MAPE) value. Since the linear models seem to not easily follow the nonlinear patterns of daily confirmed COVID-19 cases, Artificial Neural Network (ANN) have been successfully applied to solve problems of forecasting nonlinear models. The model has been used for weekly prediction of COVID-19 cases for the next 4 weeks without any additional intervention. The prediction model can be applied to other countries struggling with the COVID-19 pandemic, to any possible future pandemics, and also help make better decisions in future.

Keywords: COVID-19; time series forecasting; NARNN; ARIMA

check for updates

Citation: Saliaj, L.; Nissi, E. An Application of Neural Networks to Predict COVID-19 Cases in Italy. *Eng. Proc.* **2022**, *18*, 11. https://doi.org/10.3390/engproc2022018011

Academic Editors: Ignacio Rojas, Hector Pomares, Olga Valenzuela, Fernando Rojas and Luis Javier Herrera

Published: 21 June 2022

Publisher's Note: MDPI stays neutral with regard to jurisdictional claims in published maps and institutional affiliations.

1. Introduction

The World Health Organization has recognized the COVID-19 virus as a global threat, declaring it a universal epidemic. Predicting COVID-19 infections' future trend is very important, as it has been having a significant worldwide negative impact on economics, medicine, finance, life expectancy, etc. The chance of having data in advance on its spread may enhance public health decision-making, allowing countries to avoid possible future crises by better allocating health resources.

Different forecasting models have been proposed for predicting the global or local spread of the pandemic, since 2020.

In our work, we provide forecasts for the confirmed Italian regions' new COVID-19 cases, using linear and nonlinear time series forecasting models and comparing their accuracy to analyze their advancement based on the daily reported data. Our aim is to forecast new confirmed COVID-19 cases through a comparison of the performance of these models, with the aim to have clear expectations of future new cases.

The purpose of our work is to determine the best COVID-19 new cases forecasting model.

Several studies try to predict the evolution of the COVID-19 pandemic. Batista [1] predicted the number of cases in China, South Korea, and the rest of the world during the first semester of 2020 using a logistic model. Safi and Sanusi [2] applied an ARIMA model on data collected during the first and second pandemic wave. Khan and Gupta [3] chose an ARIMA (1,1,0) model for predicting Indian COVID-19 infection cases considering data that followed a linear trend. Abotaleb and Makarovskikh [4] proposed a combined ARIMA, Exponential Smoothing, BATS, and TBATS hybrid model for data collected until March 2021 in Russia. Gecili et al. [5] proposed an ARIMA model for American and Italian data collected from February 2020 until April 2020. Salaheldin and Abotaleb [6] chose the exponential growth model for daily COVID-19 forecasting in China, Italy, and USA.

In this paper, we aim to choose the best model among the most known time series forecasting models. Since the COVID-19 new-cases curve follows a nonlinear trend and considering that we have collected more recent pandemic data, this work emphasizes the importance of using nonlinear methods for modeling these time series, as classical linear models would not be able to identify the traits of nonlinear time series and, subsequently, would not give reliable predicted values. We have considered data from the beginning of the spread of the pandemic in Italy (24 February 2020) to 16 May 2022 in the Italian regions, months which were thought, according to previous proposed forecasting models, would correspond to quiet months from the point of the spread of the pandemic.

2. Materials and Methods

In this work, we considered data published online from Superior Health Institute on Epidemiology for Public Health related to COVID-19 infection cases in Italian regions for the period between 24 February 2020 and 16 May 2022 considering:

- new daily regional infections from 24 February 2020 to 16 May 2022;
- the last 8 days for testing daily cases (11 May 2022 to 16 May 2022);
- the last 30 days for testing the forecasting accuracy of the third wave.

The forecasting was conducted through the R package "forecasting", which provides methods and tools for forecasting univariate time series. We implemented an ARIMA model, a NNAR model, as well as a TBATS and Holt's linear model, and chose the best model considering the Mean Average Percentage Error (MAPE) for each of them as follows:

$$\text{MAPE} = \frac{1}{n} \sum_{t=1}^{n} \left| \frac{A_t - F_t}{A_t} \right| \tag{1}$$

where, n is the total number of observations, A_t is the actual value at time t, and F_t is the forecast value at time t.

2.1. ARIMA Model

The first model is ARIMA (Auto-Regressive Integrated Moving Average), which is the most common linear model for time series forecasting. It represents a time series as a function of its past values, its own lags, and the lagged errors, to forecast future values. An ARIMA model is compound by three terms: p, d, q:

$$y_t = \varphi_0 + \varphi_1 y_{t-1} + \varphi_2 y_{t-2} + \cdots + \varphi_p y_{t-p} + \varepsilon_t + \theta_1 \varepsilon_{t-1} + \theta_2 \varepsilon_{t-2} + \ldots + \theta_p \varepsilon_{t-q} \tag{2}$$

where, p is the order of the Auto-Regressive (AR) term and refers to the number of y lags, which should be used as predictors; q is the order of the Moving Average (MA) term and it refers to the number of lagged errors used as predictors; while d is the number of differentiating required to make the time series stationary.

Although ARIMA is widely used for time series analysis, it is not easy to choose appropriate orders for its components, so we proceeded to determine them automatically, using the *auto.arima* function to obtain the best ARIMA model for each region (Table 1).

Table 1. The chosen ARIMA model for each region.

Region	ARIMA
Abruzzo	ARIMA (3,1,2)
Basilicata	ARIMA (0,1,5)
Calabria	ARIMA (3,1,2)
Campania	ARIMA (0,1,5)
Emilia-Romagna	ARIMA (2,1,3)
Fiuli-Venezia Giulia	ARIMA (2,1,3)
Lazio	ARIMA (0,1,5)
Liguria	ARIMA (5,0,0)
Lombardia	ARIMA (0,1,5)
Marche	ARIMA (0,1,5)
Molise	ARIMA (2,1,3)
Piemonte	ARIMA (0,1,5)
Puglia	ARIMA (3,1,2)
Sardegna	ARIMA (2,1,3)
Sicilia	ARIMA (0,1,5)
Toscana	ARIMA (2,1,3)
Trentino Alto-Adige	ARIMA (3,1,2)
Umbria	ARIMA (0,1,5)
Valle D'Aosta	ARIMA (3,1,2)
Veneto	ARIMA (2,1,3)

The model estimation concerns the use of statistical techniques to derive the coefficients that better fit the chosen ARIMA model. Once the model was identified and the parameters were estimated, it was used for forecasting. It is checked using statistical tests and residual plots that can be used to analyze the suitability of various models to historical data.

2.2. TBATS Model

The TBATS (Trigonometric Exponential smoothing state space model with Box-Cox transformation, ARMA errors, Trend, and Seasonal component) model uses a combination of Fourier terms with an exponential smoothing state space model and a Box-Cox transformation, in an automated manner. The unit of time used in modeling was day.

2.3. Holt's Linear Trend

This model includes a prediction equation and two smoothing equations. It uses double exponential smoothing parameters to forecast future values: The first parameter is used for the overall smoothing, while the other for the trend smoothing equation. We obtained the current value considering the adjusted last smoothed value for the last period's trend and updated the trend over time, expressing it as the difference between the last two smoothed values.

Holt's forecast equation:

$$\hat{y}_{t+h|t} = l_t + hb_t \tag{3}$$

where

$$l_t = \alpha y_t + (1 - \alpha)(l_{t-1} + b_{t-1}) \tag{4}$$

indicates the first equation (level equation), while

$$b_t = \beta(l_t - l_{t-1}) + (1 - \beta)b_{t-1} \tag{5}$$

indicates the trend equation, where:

$0 \leq \alpha \leq 1$ is the smoothing parameter for the trend, $0 \leq \beta \leq 1$; l_t indicates the time series value at time t; b_t is the time series trend at time t.

2.4. ANN Model

Artificial Neural Networks forecasting models are nonlinear models inspired by biological neural networks that identify and model nonlinear relationships between the variables. They are compounds of a collection of neurons, grouped in input, hidden, and output layers, and map a set of inputs into a set of output variables, through hidden layers of neurons. Their ability to learn from a training procedure and previous examples makes them a powerful forecasting tool. They have the ability to analyze new data based on previous results.

An ANN is composed of several layers:

- The first layer, known as the input layer, is the one that takes the data in input.
- The last layer, called the output layer, gives the results of the analysis or the solution to the problem.
- The hidden layers, through which data flows from the input layer to the output. This is where the data is analyzed and the outputs are taken. The nodes of the hidden layers detect the features in the pattern of the data and the relationships between them. Then, the requested output is sent from the hidden layer to the output layer.

In our study, the NAR network was developed using the "nnetar" function of R software "caret" package that fits a neural network model to a time series [7] developed by Hyndman, O'Hara, and Wang. A NNAR (p,k), where p indicates the number of non-seasonal lags used as inputs and k the number of nodes in the hidden layer, can be described as an AR process with nonlinear functions. Considering the traits of the new COVID-19 cases trend for Italian regions, we chose a (28-5-1) network, with 28 lags as input nodes and 1 hidden layer with 5 nodes. It has the form of a feedforward three-layer ANN, where neurons have a one-way connection with the neurons of the next layers. The data set was divided into training set (70%) and testing set (15%), while the last 8 days data were used for the validation.

The forecasting performance of all these models was evaluated using the Mean Absolute Percentage Error (MAPE), while the model fits were evaluated using AIC (Akaike Information Criterion), reported in Table 2.

Table 2. MAPE (%) for forecasting models' accuracy.

Region	ARIMA	TBATS	Holt's	ANN
Abruzzo	47.07	65.68	58.68	14.56
Basilicata	45.13	60.02	71.24	12.28
Calabria	40.23	54.10	46.53	28.07
Campania	62.11	69.36	55.81	25.64
Emilia-Romagna	39.62	50.08	49.31	34.15
Fiuli-Venezia Giulia	29.56	44.37	40.65	20.18
Lazio	33.85	43.78	53.12	24.52
Liguria	39.41	52.44	44.18	22.46
Lombardia	47.54	65.13	46.24	32.14
Marche	44.25	41.28	51.23	13.54
Molise	40.68	44.76	50.04	11.37
Piemonte	38.72	60.81	65.13	30.16
Puglia	33.15	47.85	44.32	26.45
Sardegna	39.87	44.65	49.16	27.09
Sicilia	22.45	42.11	45.02	20.33
Toscana	24.03	47.16	60.87	24.18
Trentino Alto-Adige	25.39	52.64	55.71	27.89
Umbria	20.48	54.54	54.39	18.52
Valle D'Aosta	32.18	53.07	47.85	19.15
Veneto	33.30	48.79	50.69	20.05

3. Results

Selection and accuracy measures for the forecasting models are reported in Table 2. MAPE was used to measure the performance of the models. We chose the best forecasting model according to the MAPE value, as it is recommended as an accuracy comparing unit when using different methods on a time series, considering as the most accurate model the one with the lowest MAPE value.

In addition to the graph, where it can be clearly seen, the above values of the table show that the ANN model has given more accurate forecasting values than the other linear forecasting models, for every region. According to MAPE, ANN improved the forecasting accuracy compared with ARIMA, TBATS, and Holt's.

The NARNN model gives better results in almost all the considered regions, with a considerable difference from the indicators of the other models. ANN model has the lowest MAPE for the considered period for all the regions, improving the forecasting performance up to 36.47%, considering Campania. TBATS model has the highest MAPE values for the considered period, indicating that it cannot appropriately follow our data's traits.

In Table 3 we present the MAPE value for the last 6 days data, considered as testing data. Once again, we can observe that the ANN model is the best for forecasting COVID-19 new cases in Italian regions. This fact confirms once again our assumption about choosing the best model for our time series, considering the nonlinear trend our data follow.

Table 3. MAPE (%) for 6 days' accuracy of ANN forecasting model for Italian regions.

Region	11 MAY 2022	12 MAY 2022	13 MAY 2022	14 MAY 2022	15 MAY 2022	16 MAY 2022
Abruzzo	13.54	14.42	10.28	12.96	13.08	12.84
Basilicata	12.52	10.85	12.27	13.63	11.05	12.71
Calabria	25.32	24.12	16.05	22.41	15.33	20.82
Campania	23.45	18.96	17.05	21.21	26.84	20.36
Emilia-Romagna	28.97	32.12	30.54	33	29.06	31.80
Fiuli-Venezia Giulia	20.45	17.33	19.56	17.84	19.07	21.32
Lazio	21.46	22.30	27.18	19.36	20.08	22.18
Liguria	20.97	21.54	19.75	21.13	16.33	19.54
Lombardia	31.84	30.46	32.56	28.72	31.88	32.99
Marche	12.72	14.56	16.22	15.02	13.21	11.88
Molise	10.76	11.64	12.12	10.98	12.54	10.35
Piemonte	28.12	25.12	22.31	20.64	29.22	31.60
Puglia	23.40	21.44	20.16	25.39	22.48	24.56
Sardegna	21.39	17.96	17.75	23.41	24.84	20.36
Sicilia	22.83	21.78	20.05	21.44	26.45	22.02
Toscana	22.18	18.56	19.34	21.12	20.88	20.52
Trentino Alto-Adige	26.59	23.17	16.75	24.31	15.42	20.78
Umbria	18.52	21.56	16.45	19.02	23.21	20.82
Valle D'Aosta	19.15	17.33	26.02	15.25	13.54	15.65
Veneto	20.05	24.06	26.69	18.43	18.28	17.98

We performed the forecasting for new COVID-19 cases in Italian regions using the above models. We conducted a 30-days-ahead forecast (until 16 June 2022) and compared the forecasting data with the testing data for 6 days (11 May 2022–16 May 2022), applying the forecasting models to the confirmed cases for the last 8 days data and compared the results with the actual COVID-19 data. We calculated the MAPE values as the difference between actual data and forecast values. The MAPE values for ANN forecasting model are represented in Table 3. Based on our analysis, we concluded that the prediction performance of the models was similar to the real data. In particular, the ANN model gave more accurate predictions, as its MAPE values were lower compared to the other models. We observed decreasing MAPE values, in particular for the last 6 days' testing values, as its values decreased from about 7% to 1%. Higher MAPE values were observed for the other predictive models. ARIMA had a worse predicting performance for the first 3 days and the last day, while TBATS was the worst forecasting model when comparing the 6 days' training data MAPE values.

Figure 1 presents the forecasting results of ANN model for the following 30 days for COVID-19 new confirmed cases in Italian regions. The NARNN model values follow very well the time series' trend thanks to the training process, which enables the model to better understand the time series' features. Once trained, the ANN decides itself on the importance of the variables, as it keeps learning continuously, performing quite well with unfamiliar data, thanks to its ability to work with multiple parallel inputs, as well as nonlinearity and plasticity in finding the most suitable model for time-series forecasting [8].

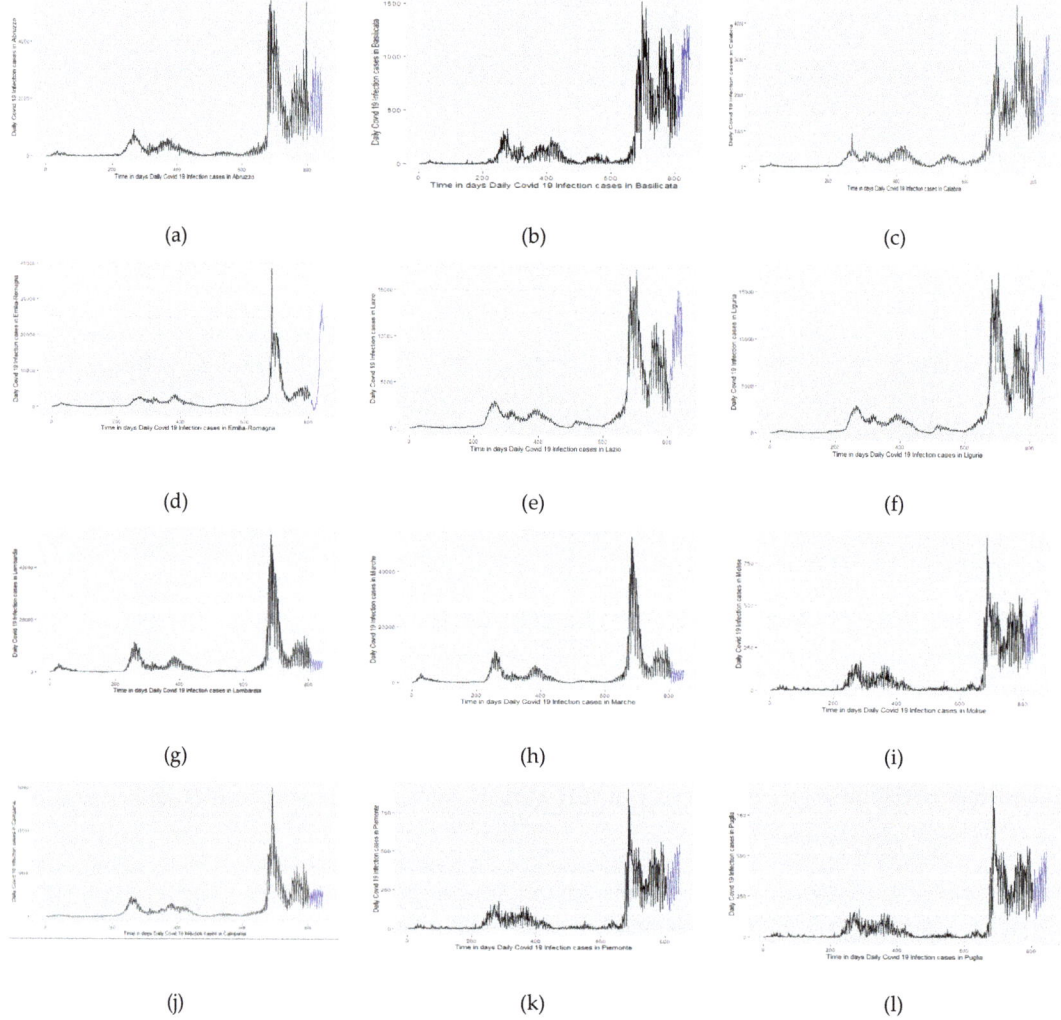

(a)   (b)   (c)

(d)   (e)   (f)

(g)   (h)   (i)

(j)   (k)   (l)

Figure 1. *Cont.*

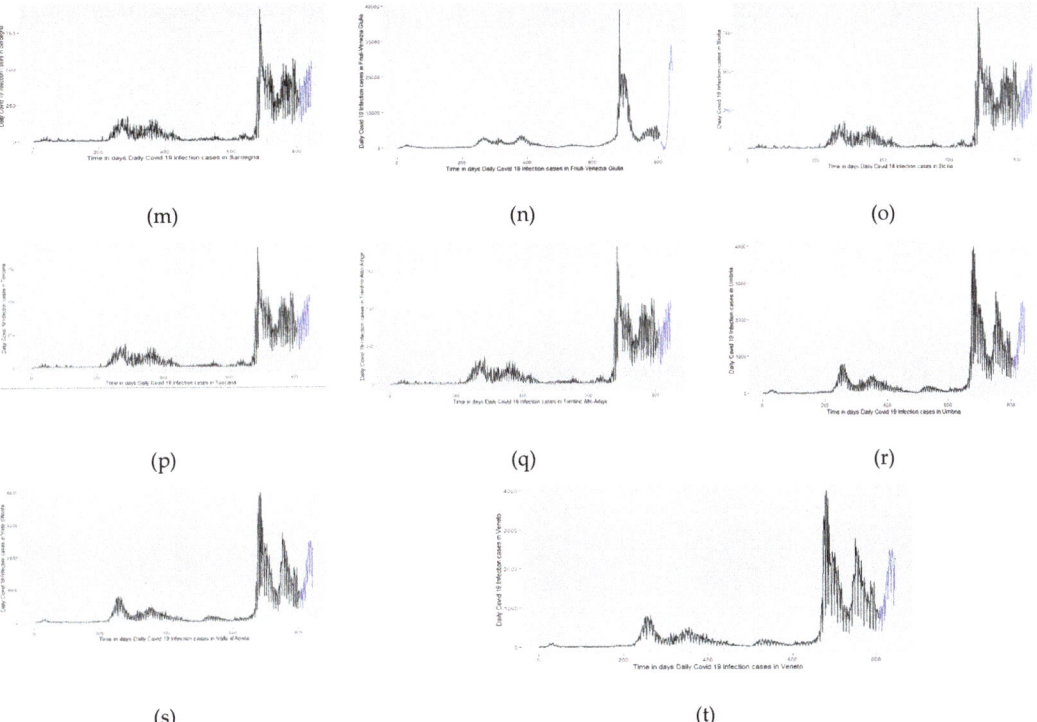

(m)   (n)   (o)

(p)   (q)   (r)

(s)   (t)

Figure 1. Daily COVID-19 Italian regions' new cases prediction with ANN model: (**a**) Abruzzo; (**b**) Basilicata; (**c**) Calabria; (**d**) Emilia-Romagna,(**e**) Lazio; (**f**) Liguria; (**g**) Lombardia; (**h**) Marche; (**i**) Molise; (**j**) Campania; (**k**) Piemonte; (**l**) Puglia; (**m**) Sardegna; (**n**) Friuli-Venezia Giulia; (**o**) Sicilia; (**p**) Toscana; (**q**)Trentino Alto-Adige; (**r**) Umbria; (**s**) Valle D'Aosta; (**t**) Veneto.

Figure 1 shows the trend of the number of new cases predicted by the ANN model for each region, obtained considering 28 lags as inputs and 5 nodes in the hidden layer. From the results obtained by the predictions of NARNN model, we can say that this model's predictions of the new COVID-19 confirmed cases are closer to the observed time series values. This is also emphasized by the value of MAPE for the test set, which is much lower than other forecasting models' MAPE values. According to the ANN (28-5-1) model, there will be an increasing trend in the number of new COVID-19 infections by the end of May, until 16 June in the following regions: Abruzzo, Basilicata, Calabria, Lazio, Liguria, Molise, Piemonte, Trentino Alto-Adige, and Veneto, while for the rest of them the ANN model predicted a constant to decreasing trend for the next 30 days.

4. Discussion

In this work, we evaluated four different time series forecasting models for predicting daily Italian regions' COVID-19 confirmed new cases. Using various models let us compare their forecasting accuracy and make an optimal selection. For our time series, the ANN model was preferred over the other linear forecasting models. It was chosen based on MAPE value, as it had the lowest value among all the forecasting models. The ANN (28-5) model gives better results in all the considered indicators with a considerable difference from the indicators of the other linear models. It predicted an increase in the number of new COVID-19 infections by the end of May 2022, in almost all the Italian regions. The results are valid for a short period of time because in the long run they can be influenced by other factors such as vaccination, immunization of the population, and measures taken by government authorities to limit the spread of the infection, etc.

The above-considered models can be implemented on new data as they become available for possible future COVID-19 new confirmed cases forecasting, in order to improve forecasting accuracy, maybe taking into consideration other patients' parameters as possible inputs for the ANN model, since additional data would improve forecasting performance. Predictions about possible future new cases would be very helpful for the allocation of medical resources, handling the spread of the pandemic, and getting more prepared in terms of health care systems. People that deal with decision-making could find it very helpful for future projections regarding intervention for reducing and controlling the spread of the infection.

Author Contributions: Conceptualization, E.N. and L.S.; methodology, E.N.; software, L.S.; validation E.N.; formal analysis, E.N. and L.S.; investigation, L.S.; resources, L.S.; data curation, E.N.; writing—original draft preparation, L.S.; writing—review and editing, E.N.; visualization, E.N.; supervision, E.N. All authors have read and agreed to the published version of the manuscript.

Funding: This research received no external funding.

Institutional Review Board Statement: Not applicable.

Informed Consent Statement: Not applicable.

Data Availability Statement: Data are available at: https://www.iss.it/ (accessed on 5 May 2022).

Conflicts of Interest: The authors declare no conflict of interest.

References

1. Batista, M. Estimation of the final size of the COVID-19 epidemic. *MedRxiv* 2020, *Preprint*. [CrossRef]
2. Safi, S.K.; Sanusi, O.I. A hybrid of artificial neural network, exponential smoothing, and ARIMA models for COVID-19 time series forecasting. *Model Assist. Stat. Appl.* **2021**, *16*, 25–35. [CrossRef]
3. Khan, F.M.; Gupta, R. ARIMA and NAR based prediction model for time series analysis of COVID-19 cases in India. *J. Saf. Sci. Resil.* **2020**, *1*, 12–18. [CrossRef]
4. Abotaleb, M.; Makarovskikh, T. System for Forecasting COVID-19 Cases Using Time-Series and Neural Networks Models. *Eng. Proc.* **2021**, *5*, 46. [CrossRef]
5. Gecili, E.; Ziady, A.; Szczesniak, R.D. Forecasting COVID-19 confirmed cases, deaths and recoveries: Revisiting established time series modeling through novel applications for the USA and Italy. *PLoS ONE* **2021**, *16*, e0244173. [CrossRef] [PubMed]
6. Abotaleb, M.S.A. Predicting COVID-19 Cases using Some Statistical Models: An Application to the Cases Reported in China Italy and USA. *Acad. J. Appl. Math. Sci.* **2020**, *6*, 32–40. [CrossRef]
7. Reilly, D.L.; Cooper, L.N. An overview of Neural Networks: Early models to real world systems. In *How We Learn; How We Remember: Toward an Understanding of Brain and Neural Systems*; World Scientific Series in 20th Century Physics; World Scientific Publishers: Singapore, 1990; Volume 10, pp. 300–321. [CrossRef]
8. Zhang, G.; Patuwo, B.E.; Hu, M.Y. Forecasting with artificial neural networks:: The state of the art. *Int. J. Forecast.* **1998**, *14*, 35–62. [CrossRef]

Proceeding Paper

Relationship between Stationarity and Dynamic Convergence of Time Series †

Gerardo Covarrubias and Xuedong Liu *

Faculty of Higher Studies Aragon, National Autonomous University of Mexico,
Ciudad Netzahualcóyotl 57000, Mexico; gerardo_covarrubias_lopez@hotmail.com
* Correspondence: xdong@comunidad.unam.mx; Tel.: +52-1-5626293891
† Presented at the 8th International Conference on Time Series and Forecasting,
  Gran Canaria, Spain, 27–30 June 2022.

Abstract: In economic science, when a stochastic process is studied from an econometric approach, it focuses on stationarity and the reference approach to dynamic equilibrium is ignored. Although both approaches are theoretically closely linked through the common purpose of making forecasts, in existing methodologies they are studied in a mutually exclusive way. Therefore, in this paper the consistency between dynamic equilibrium and stationarity is analyzed. In practice, the theoretical correspondence between these two important properties could present some inconsistency due to misspecification in an autoregressive model or the presence of spuriousness, generated by the components of the series.

Keywords: time series; dynamic convergence; stationarity; unit root

check for
updates

Citation: Covarrubias, G.; Liu, X. Relationship between Stationarity and Dynamic Convergence of Time Series. *Eng. Proc.* **2022**, *18*, 12. https://doi.org/10.3390/engproc2022018012

Academic Editors: Ignacio Rojas, Hector Pomares, Olga Valenzuela, Fernando Rojas and Luis Javier Herrera

Published: 21 June 2022

Publisher's Note: MDPI stays neutral with regard to jurisdictional claims in published maps and institutional affiliations.

1. Introduction

In recent years, economists have been mainly interested in the study of successions of random variables that change over time and that give rise to stochastic processes; in which, from the econometric approach, stationarity, as a particular state of equilibrium, is considered an elementary assumption in the specification of a model that has the purpose of forecasting. On the other hand, if the stochastic processes are studied from the dynamic stability approach, the fundamental assumption is convergence, which will determine the behavior of the time series through the construction of difference equations.

Although both approaches are theoretically linked, forecasting studies are carried out in different ways.

In this regard, when time series are analyzed, the estimated models aim to understand the series around its dynamic structure to make a forecast as an extrapolation of the stochastic process or time series [1–4]. The origin of the study focuses on the understanding of predictable components and time lags in dynamic analysis, which is based on the estimation of stochastic equations in differences.

From a theoretical point of view, it is accepted that there is a correspondence between dynamic convergence and stationarity, since both properties are a key point in the forecast of a realization; that is, a time series is stationary if and only if its dynamics are stable or convergent to equilibrium. For this reason, this research aims to open a line of empirical research on this correspondence.

It should be noted that in all the textbooks on the subject it is assumed that stationarity is a sufficient condition to estimate an autoregressive type model and as a result the projection of a realization is obtained.

In this regard, if the assumption of ergodicity is assumed, there is uncertainty or ambiguity in the estimation due to the high degree of complexity involved in building the probability distribution structure of a stochastic process. Consequently, when doing an empirical study, it is likely that both properties are not consistent, in an issue that has not been addressed in the conventional literature.

A solution to resolve the inconsistency may be to extract the components of the series and model only the irregular component.

2. Theoretical and Conceptual Approach on the Stationarity–Convergence Relationship

From the econometric point of view, when we talk about stationarity, the first difference of a time series is fundamental (Equation (1)), which from the dynamic stability approach represents an equation in differences. This implies that the problem of forecasting a realization in econometric terms is widely linked to the formulation and estimation of difference equations from the dynamic stability approach.

The following equation represents a stochastic process without intercept:

$$\Delta y_t = y_{t+1} - y_t \tag{1}$$

In this way, if the series is first order stationary, it should converge towards the dynamic stability of the process, and vice versa.

The Importance of Stationarity and Convergence in a Stochastic Process

Stationarity is a particular state of statistical equilibrium and is a fundamental part of the study of time series [5]. The probability distributions corresponding to these series remain stable over time. This is because, for any subset of the time series, the joint probability distribution must remain unchanged [6]. Furthermore, the fact that a series is stationary implies that the system is impacted by some type of shock in each instance, it will adjust to equilibrium again [7] or the consequences of impact will gradually disappear; that is, a shock in period t will have a small effect at time $t + 1$ and a smaller one at $t + 2$, and so on [8].

Since there is no variation in the probability distribution, if the time series is non-stationary, the results derived from classical linear regression are invalid or simply may not have theoretical meaning, which is known as spurious correlation [9].

To solve this problem, as defined by Granger and Newbold [10] based on the study by Yule [11], the application of cointegration models and error correction mechanism (ECM) for the long term emerged, applying the Engle and Granger [12] cointegration model for equations with two or more variables and the Johansen [13,14] model for systems of equations with autoregressive vectors. In these cases, it should be noted that, if the series are not stationary, they must be adjusted by differentiation, and with the same order to guarantee cointegration. Consequently, when we analyze the time series or stochastic process, it is of vital importance to determine stationarity by applying tests such as Phillips–Perron [15] and Augmented Dickey–Fuller [16], which are explained below.

$$Y_t = \rho Y_{t-1} + u_t \tag{2}$$

If $\rho = 1$ it is a random walk model without intercept with the presence of a unit root; that is, the serie is not stationary; in contrast, if $|\rho| < 1$ it is a stationary serie and is also convergent.

In this regard, Gujarati and Porter [17] pose an interesting question: why not simply regress Y_t on its lagged value over a period Y_{t-1} and find that ρ is statistically equal to 1?

If this happens, Y_t would not be stationary. Nevertheless, it is not convenient to estimate the regression by ordinary least squares (OLS) and test the hypothesis that $\rho = 1$ through the usual t-test, since this test has a very marked bias in the case of a unit root; for this reason, Equation (2) is manipulated by subtracting Y_{t-1} from both sides simultaneously to obtain Equation (3).

$$Y_t - Y_{t-1} = \rho Y_{t-1} - Y_{t-1} + u_t$$
$$\Delta Y_t = (\rho - 1)Y_{t-1} + u_t$$
$$\Delta Y_t = \delta Y_{t-1} + u_t \tag{3}$$

Therefore, the regression is not estimated on Equation (2), but on Equation (3), and the null hypothesis $\delta = 0$ is tested.

As Equation (2) is a first-order difference equation, it is required that it meets the stability condition $|\rho| < 1$ as mentioned [4].

From the dynamic stability approach, the solution of a random walk model without drift seen as a difference equation is:

$$y_t = Ab^t \qquad (4)$$

where $A = y_0$, $b = a_0$.

Thus, the path described by Equation 4 depends on the value of b. In this case, if the complementary function tends to zero when t grows indefinitely, the equilibrium is dynamically stable; that is, the trajectory expressed in Equation (4) must be analyzed as t increases as shown in Table 1 [18].

Table 1. Trajectory behaviors.

b-Value	Behavior
$b > 0$	Non-oscillatory
$b < 0$	Oscillatory
$|b| > 1$	Divergent
$|b| < 1$	Convergent

In the same way, derived from Equation (4), when stipulating the convergence condition of the time trajectory y_t towards the equilibrium y_p we must rule out the case of $b = \pm 1$, which means that there is a unit root from the point of view econometric.

In general terms, the necessary and sufficient equilibrium condition is confirmed for a trajectory to be convergent if and only if $|b| < 1$, according to the stationarity condition.

3. Empirical Evidence of Bias in the Stationarity–Convergence Relationship

In order to find possible empirical inconsistencies between dynamic convergence and stationarity in a time series, three stochastic processes corresponding to trade between Mexico and China were analyzed to which the unit root test was applied and their convergence was analyzed at equilibrium using first-order autoregressive models.

3.1. Case 1: Trade Balance of Mexico with China: An Explosive Deficit Balance

In this first case, the trade balance between Mexico and China was analyzed, explained by the difference between Mexico and China in millions of dollars per year in the period 1993–2020. Figure 1 shows that the deficit for Mexico systematically increases explosively over time, so it is evidently a non-stationary and divergent stochastic process.

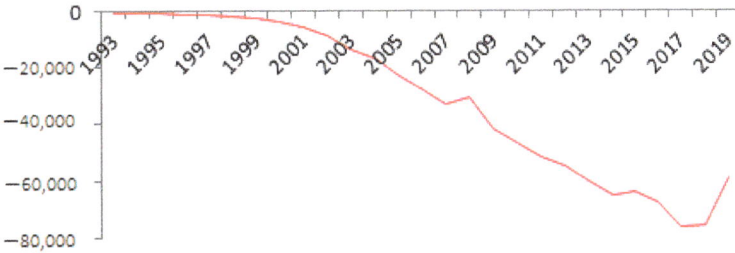

Figure 1. Trade balance between Mexico and China in millions of USD 1993–2020.

Table 2 shows the results obtained in the Dickey–Fuller augmented (DFA) test using the E-views software, with the t-statistic in parentheses.

Table 2. DFA test results.

Case 1	Coefficient	Confidence	*t*-Statistics	*p*_Value
Y(−1)	0.0330		1.2890	0.9459
	(1.28)	1%	−2.6534	
		5%	−1.9539	
		10%	−1.6096	

Case 2	Coefficient	Confidence	*t*-Statistics	*p*_Value
Y(−1)	−0.0162		−0.4544	0.8856
	(−0.45)	1%	−3.6999	
C	−2639.322	5%	−2.9762	
	(1.878)	10%	−2.6274	

Case 3	Coefficient	Confidence	*t*-Statistics	*p*_Value
Y(−1)	−0.2525		−1.8578	0.6481
	(−1.85)	1%	−4.3393	
C	2325.362	5%	−3.5875	
	(0.75)	10%	−3.2292	
@Trend	−837.7699			
	(− 1.79) *			

* *t*-statistic for statistical significance in parentheses.

The case 1 is discarded since = $(\rho - 1) = 0.0330$. $\rho = 1.0330 > 1$. In the remaining cases, we can verify that, according to the hypothesis test, the null hypothesis is not rejected; consequently, the series has a unit root; additionally, despite the fact that the coefficient is negative and greater than −2, they are not statistically significant, so we can conclude that it is a divergent and non-stationary stochastic process in congruence with what is stipulated in the theory.

3.2. Case 2: Trade Balance of Mexico with China: An Estimate in Relative Terms

In this second case, it is proposed to use the trade balance in relative terms; that is, the quotient between imports and exports made by Mexico with its second trading partner on a monthly basis (Figure 2).

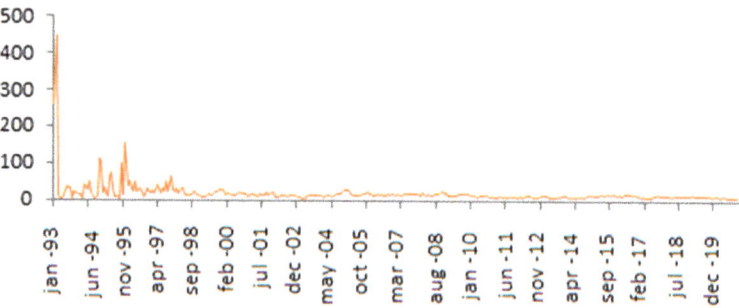

Figure 2. Monthly fluctuation of trade between China and Mexico, 1993–2020.

Similarly, Table 3 shows the results obtained in the unit root test with δ coefficients between −2 and 0, which is why not one of them is discarded. The best model that describes the trajectory is case 2, according to the criteria of Akaike, Schwartz, and Hannan-Quinn and it is obtained that $\rho = 0.3907$, which shows that the convergence and stability condition is met, $|\rho| < 1$ and similarly, from the econometric approach, δ is statistically significant, in addition, the *p*-value of the test is 0.0000, so the existence of a unit root is rejected. We can then conclude that it is a stationary and convergent stochastic process.

Table 3. DFA test results.

Case 1	Coefficient	Confidence	t-Statistics	p_Value
Y(−1)	−0.4609		−11.3628	0.0000
	(−11.36)	1%	−2.5719	
		5%	−1.9418	
		10%	−1.6161	
Case 2	**Coefficient**	**Confidence**	**t-Statistics**	**p_Value**
Y(−1)	−0.6093		−13.6917	0.0000
	(−13.69)	1%	−3.4497	
C	10.3563	5%	−2.8700	
	(6.52)	10%	−2.5713	
Case 3	**Coefficient**	**Confidence**	**t-Statistics**	**p_Value**
Y(−1)	−0.6500		−14.1956	0.0000
	(−14.19)	1%	−3.9857	
C	18.7574	5%	−3.4233	
	(6.05)	10%	−3.1346	
@Trend	−0.0456			
	(− 3.14) *			

* t-statistic for statistical significance in parentheses.

3.3. An Empirical Inconsistency in the Fluctuation of Trade between Mexico and China

In a third case, the behavior of the trade balance between Mexico and China in the period 1993–2020 was analyzed with annualized data.

In the first instance, if we inspect the graph in Figure 3, we can see that the series is possibly stationary and convergent.

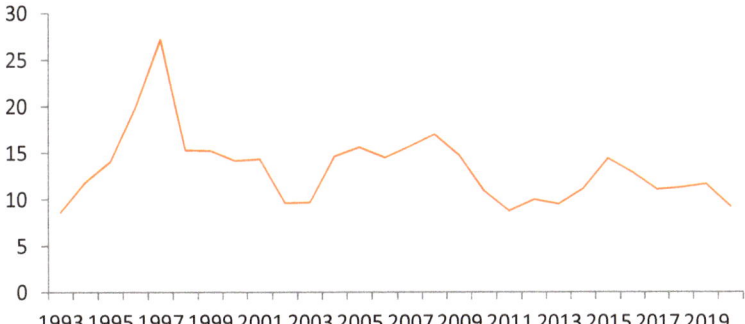

Figure 3. Annual fluctuation of trade between China and Mexico 1993–2020.

Table 4 shows that for the three cases a negative value of δ and greater than −2 was obtained.

Table 4. DFA test results.

Case 1	Coefficient	Confidence	t-Statistics	p_Value
Y(−1)	−0.0321		−0.6413	0.4300
	(−0.64)	1%	−2.6534	
		5%	−1.9539	
		10%	−1.6096	
Case 2	**Coefficient**	**Confidence**	**t-Statistics**	**p_Value**
Y(−1)	−0.4470		−2.7081	0.0857
	(−2.70) *	1%	−3.6999	
C	6.0326	5%	−2.9763	
	(2.61) *	10%	−2.6274	
Case 3	**Coefficient**	**Confidence**	**t-Statistics**	**p_Value**
Y(−1)	−0.5746		−3.4853	0.0613
	(−3.48) *	1%	−4.3393	
C	10.21	5%	−3.5875	
	(−3.53) *	10%	−3.2292	
@Trend	−0.1756			
	(− 2.16) *			

* t-statistic for statistical significance in parentheses.

As can be seen, the p value in all three cases is greater than 0.05; therefore, at 95% confidence, the null hypothesis that there is a unit root is not rejected, thus, the analyzed series is not stationary.

However, if we analyze in detail the dynamic equilibrium in the three cases, the value of δ is negative, greater than −2 and statistically significant for cases 2 and 3, which means that the series in question is convergent.

If we opt for case 3, according to the value of the t statistic and the p value, we can assert that the coefficient of δ is statistically significant at 95% confidence; likewise, we determine the value of ρ which is 0.4254, implies that the series is convergent and stable. It is important to mention that by choosing case 3 convergence is guaranteed but around a deterministic trend, and consequently the stability of the series is questioned.

For case 2, the coefficient δ is also statistically significant from which a value of p of 0.5530 is derived; that is, the convergence and stability of the series is confirmed again. However, when applying the unit root test, it was shown that the series is non-stationary, both at 99% and 95% confidence level.

From the econometric approach, in the case of annual figures, the stability of the series would be ambiguous since it is not a stationary series since it is not possible to reject the null hypothesis of the unit root test.

4. Concluding Remarks

When theoretically analyzing the stochastic processes, the results obtained were consistent for the divergent case; however, for the convergent case certain ambiguities were found.

We can then assert that there is a double causal relationship between stationarity and dynamic stability theoretically. Because the forecasts about the behavior of the series are the result of making estimates using a stationary series, in autoregressive models, this statement is of great importance. However, the problem arises when there is no stationarity.

Then, we can conclude that the non-stationarity of a series could mean a wrong specification of the model, including a spurious correlation. So, when applying the model for projections of series or forecasts, in the bias with respect to the true values, the impact is not necessarily lost over time. In other words, the possible dynamical convergence that follows from a non-stationary series might not be the closest to the true trajectory; in short, it could be classified as a false dynamic convergence.

Let us also consider that within the process to determine stationarity, if we assume the assumption of ergodicity, stationarity implies a simplification of various assumptions; in general, that a sample preserves the properties of the population.

In other words, the ergodicity assumption implies that the series is stationary, which induces a considerable homogeneity in the stochastic process, reduces the uncertainty as a simplification of the suppositions. So, if the analyzed series is not stationary, the ergodicity is not satisfied; therefore, the assumptions are not simplified and, consequently, there would be no stability and convergence in the series, so the coefficients obtained from the regression are the result of spuriousness or an erroneous specification of the model.

Finally, since the simplification of the assumptions is not met, the mean and variance of the series vary with respect to time; then, being non-stationary, the ergodic process is not fulfilled, and they should not be used for forecasts.

Author Contributions: Conceptualization, G.C. and X.L.; methodology, G.C. and X.L.; software, G.C.; validation, X.L.; formal analysis, G.C. and X.L.; investigation, G.C. and X.L.; resources, X.L.; data curation, G.C. and X.L.; writing—original draft preparation, G.C. and X.L.; writing—review and editing, G.C. and X.L.; visualization, G.C. and X.L.; supervision, X.L.; project administration, X.L.; funding acquisition, X.L. All authors have read and agreed to the published version of the manuscript.

Funding: PAPIIT Program of DGAPA, UNAM Number IN31102.

Institutional Review Board Statement: Not applicable.

Informed Consent Statement: Not applicable.

Data Availability Statement: Sistema de Consulta de Información Estadística por País. Available online: http://www.economia-snci.gob.mx/sic_php/pages/estadisticas/ (accessed on 21 February 2021).

Acknowledgments: For the preparation of this research, the Postdoctoral Scholarship Program at UNAM and the PAPIIT Program of DGAPA, UNAM are widely appreciated and recognized.

Conflicts of Interest: The authors declare no conflict of interest.

References

1. Harvey, A. *Time Series Model*, 2nd ed.; Harvester Wheatsheaf: Hemel Hemstead, UK, 1993.
2. Maddala, G. *Introduction to Econometrics*, 3rd ed.; Jhon Wiley and Sons Chichester: London, UK, 2001.
3. Guerrero, C. *Introducción a la Econometría Aplicada*; Editorial Trillas: Mexico City, Mexico, 2011.
4. Enders, W. *Applied Econometrics Time Series*, 4th ed.; Wiley: Hoboken, NJ, USA, 2015.
5. Box, G.; Jenkins, G. *Time Series Analysis: Forecasting and Control*, Revised ed.; Holden Day: San Francisco, CA, USA, 1976.
6. Wooldridge, J. *Introducción a la Econometría: Un Enfoque Moderno*, 4th ed.; Cengage Learning: Mexico City, Mexico, 2010.
7. Juselius, K. *The Cointegrated VAR Model. Methodology and Applications*; Advanced Texts in Econometrics; Oxfrod University Press: Oxfrod, NY, USA, 2006.
8. Brooks, C. *Introductory Econometrics for Finance*, 2nd ed.; Cambridge University Press: Cambridge NY, USA, 2008.
9. Asteriou, D.; Hall, S. *Applied Econometrics. A Modern Approach*; Palgrave McMillan: New York, NY, USA, 2007.
10. Granger, C.W.; Newbold, P. Spurious regressions in econometrics. *J. Econom.* **1974**, 2, 111–120. [CrossRef]
11. Yule, G. Why do we Sometimes get Nonsense-Correlations between Time-Series? A Study in Sampling and the Nature of Time-Series. *J. R. Stat. Soc.* **1926**, 89, 1–63. [CrossRef]
12. Engle, R.; Granger, C.W.J. Cointegration and error correction representation, estimation and testing. *Econometrica* **1987**, 55, 251–276. [CrossRef]
13. Johansen, S. Statistical Analysis of Cointegration Vectors. *J. Econ. Dyn. Control* **1988**, 12, 231–254. [CrossRef]
14. Johansen, S. The role of the constant and linear terms in cointegration analysis of nonstationary variables. *Econom. Rev.* **1994**, 13, 205–229. [CrossRef]
15. Phillips, P.; Perron, P. Testing for a Unit Root in Time Series Regression. *Biometrika* **1988**, 75, 335–346. [CrossRef]
16. Dickey, D.A.; Fuller, W.A. Distribution of Estimators for Autoregressive Time Series with a Unit Root. *J. Am. Stat. Assoc.* **1979**, 74, 427–431. [CrossRef]
17. Gujarati, D.N.Y.; Porter, D. *Econometría*, 5th ed.; McGrawHill: Mexico City, Mexico, 2010.
18. Chiang, A.; Wainwright, K. *Fundamentos de Economía Matemática*, 4th ed.; McGrawHill: Mexico City, Mexico, 2006.

engineering
proceedings

MDPI

Proceeding Paper

Partitioning of Net Ecosystem Exchange Using Dynamic Mode Decomposition and Time Delay Embedding [†]

Maha Shadaydeh [1,*] , Joachim Denzler [1] and Mirco Migliavacca [2]

1   Department of Mathematics and Computer Science, Friedrich Schiller University Jena, 07743 Jena, Germany; joachim.denzler@uni-jena.de
2   European Commission Joint Research Centre, 1050 Brussels, Belgium; mirco.migliavacca@ec.europa.eu
*   Correspondence: maha.shadaydeh@uni-jena.de
†   Presented at the 8th International Conference on Time Series and Forecasting, Gran Canaria, Spain, 27–30 June 2022.

Abstract: Ecosystem respiration (Reco) represents a major component of the global carbon cycle. An accurate estimation of Reco dynamics is necessary for a better understanding of ecosystem–climate interactions and the impact of climate extremes on ecosystems. This paper proposes a new data-driven method for the estimation of the nonlinear dynamics of Reco using the method of dynamic mode decomposition with control input (DMDc). The method is validated on the half-hourly Fluxnet 2015 data. The model is first trained on the night-time net ecosystem exchange data. The day-time Reco values are then predicted using the obtained model with future values of a control input such as air temperature and soil water content. To deal with unobserved drivers of Reco other than the user control input, the method uses time-delay embedding of the history of Reco and the control input. Results indicate that, on the one hand, the prediction accuracy of Reco dynamics using DMDc is comparable to state-of-the-art deep learning-based methods, yet it has the advantages of being a simple and almost hyper-parameter-free method with a low computational load. On the other hand, the study of the impact of different control inputs on Reco dynamics showed that for most of the studied Fluxnet sites, air temperature is a better long-term predictor of Reco, while using soil water content as control input produced better short-term prediction accuracy.

Keywords: ecosystem respiration; dynamic mode decomposition with control; time delay embedding

check for
updates

Citation: Shadaydeh, M.; Denzler, J.; Migliavacca, M. Partitioning of Net Ecosystem Exchange Using Dynamic Mode Decomposition and Time Delay Embedding. *Eng. Proc.* **2022**, *18*, 13. https://doi.org/10.3390/engproc2022018013

Academic Editors: Ignacio Rojas, Hector Pomares, Olga Valenzuela, Fernando Rojas and Luis Javier Herrera

Published: 21 June 2022

Publisher's Note: MDPI stays neutral with regard to jurisdictional claims in published maps and institutional affiliations.

1. Introduction

Carbon losses from ecosystems affect climate change. Ecosystem respiration (Reco), the sum of autotrophic and heterotrophic respiration, represents a major component of the global carbon cycle. Accurate estimation of Reco dynamics is necessary for a better understanding of ecosystem–climate interactions and the impact of climate extremes on ecosystems. This paper proposes a new data-driven method for the estimation of the nonlinear dynamics of Reco using the method of dynamic mode decomposition (DMD), an emerging tool for the analysis of nonlinear dynamical systems.

Ecosystem respiration is typically described as an exponential function of temperature based on the law of thermodynamics [1]. This function is defined based on certain parameters, such as temperature sensitivity, which are assumed to remain constant. However, several studies have pointed to the dependence of these parameters on other drivers of Reco [2] . Such issue is partially compensated in regression models by the use of temporal moving windows for parameters estimation [3].

The Eddy Covariance (EC) technique is widely used to measure the net ecosystem exchange (NEE) which is the difference between Reco, the total CO_2 release due to all respiration processes, and the gross carbon uptake by photosynthesis (GPP). The two CO_2 fluxes Reco and GPP are derived from NEE by applying partitioning methods. Recently deep learning-based methods have been proposed for modeling Reco dynamics [4,5] using EC measurement of night-time NEE when photosynthesis, and therefore GPP, is assumed to be 0. These approaches provide data-driven equation-free estimates of Reco with the flexibility to include other meteorological and biological drivers affecting Reco during the daytime to achieve the NEE partitioning task. In spite of their improved performance compared to state-of-the-art empirical methods, they require a sufficient amount of training data as well as extensive tuning of the used deep networks' hyper-parameters. Accordingly, the trained model cannot take into account some short-term variations in ecosystem respiration.

2. Methods

The Koopman operator [6] enables the transformation of finite-dimensional nonlinear system dynamics to an infinite-dimensional linear dynamical system. Finding the eigenfunctions of the Koopman operator, however, remains a major obstacle to its implementation. DMD is a simple numerical algorithm that approximates the Koopman operator with a best-fit linear model that advances measurements from one time step to the next ([7], [8]. It is an equation-free system identification method where the underlying dynamics of the system are learned from snap-shot in time of measurement data. DMD decomposes system dynamics into temporal modes whereby each mode represents a fixed oscillation frequency and decay/growth rate. It has been extended to deal with dynamical systems with exogenous control input (DMDc) [9].

In this paper, we propose a new data-driven yet physics-aware method for the dynamical modeling of Reco, which can serve as an NEE partitioning method. The proposed approach is based on using DMDc in a sliding temporal window approach. The system state Reco is represented as a linear dynamical model with an autonomous component in addition to an exogenous component which is a function of control input. The control input to the system can be soil or air temperature (Tair) in accordance with the thermodynamics law or any other observed drivers such as soil water contents (SWC). Such modeling of Reco dynamics allows to disentangle the exogenous effect of the control input, e.g., Tair, from the autonomous dynamics of Reco, and hence allows to intervene on the control input to study its effect on the system. To deal with unobserved drivers of Reco other than temperature or any user control input, we make use of time-delay embedding (TDE) of the history of the system's state and control input. According to the Takens theory [10], such an embedding guarantees, under certain conditions, that the system will learn the trajectories of the original system. The TDE in DMDc has been shown to facilitate the treatment of nonlinear systems with linear models [11]. Another advantage of using TDE in the proposed method is that it allows for learning Reco dynamics from short data as it compensates for using advanced measurement in time. This is relevant as it enables ecosystem forecast taking into account short-term variations in the system dynamics.

3. Results

We used the half-hourly EC Fluxnet 2015 data [12] measured at multiple Fluxnet sites with different vegetation types and average temperatures to investigate the impact of different control inputs, e.g., Tair and SWC, on Reco dynamics. The model is trained on night-time NEE which is assumed to be the ground-truth values of night-time Reco. The day-time Reco values are then predicted using the obtained model with future values of control input. The method is validated on Reco short-term and long-term forecast periods with different control inputs. The obtained results indicate that: (1) The performance of the proposed method is comparable to the recently proposed deep learning-based NEE partitioning methods, yet it has the advantages of being a simple and almost hyper-parameter-free method with a very low computational load. (2) The use of TDE facilitates learning Reco dynamics from very short data, i.e., up to one night samples of NEE. (3) For most of the studied Fluxnet sites, Tair is a better long-term predictor of Reco, while using SWC as control input produced better short-term forecast accuracy.

Author Contributions: Conceptualization, M.S., J.D. and M.M; methodology, M.S.; writing—original draft preparation, M.S.; writing—review and editing, M.S., J.D. and M.M.; funding acquisition, M.S. J.D. All authors have read and agreed to the published version of the manuscript.

Funding: This research is funded by the Carl Zeiss Foundation within the scope of the program line "Breakthroughs: Exploring Intelligent Systems" for "Digitization — explore the basics, use applications" and the German Research Foundation (DFG) grant SH 1682/1-1.

Institutional Review Board Statement: Not applicable.

Informed Consent Statement: Not applicable.

Data Availability Statement: We used the Fluxnet 2015 datasets publicaly available at https://doi.org/10.1038/s41597-020-0534-3, accessed on 15 April 2022.

Conflicts of Interest: The authors declare no conflict of interest.

References

1. Lloyd, J.; Taylor, J.A. On the Temperature Dependence of Soil Respiration. *Funct. Ecol.* **1994**, *8*, 315–323. [CrossRef]
2. Mahecha, M.D.; Reichstein, M.; Carvalhais, N.; Lasslop, G.; Lange, H.; Seneviratne, S.I.; Vargas, R.; Ammann, C.; Arain, M.A.; Cescatti, A.; et al. Global Convergence in the Temperature Sensitivity of Respiration at Ecosystem Level. *Science* **2010**, *329*, 838–840. [CrossRef] [PubMed]
3. Reichstein, M.; Falge, E.; Baldocchi, D.; Papale, D.; Aubinet, M.; Berbigier, P.; Bernhofer, C.; Buchmann, N.; Gilmanov, T.; Granier, A.; et al. On the separation of net ecosystem exchange into assimilation and ecosystem respiration: review and improved algorithm. *Glob. Chang. Biol.* **2005**, *11*, 1424–1439. [CrossRef]
4. Tramontana, G.; Migliavacca, M.; Jung, M.; Reichstein, M.; Keenan, T.F.; Camps-Valls, G.; Ogee, J.; Verrelst, J.; Papale, D. Partitioning net carbon dioxide fluxes into photosynthesis and respiration using neural networks. *Glob. Chang. Biol.* **2020**, *26*, 5235–5253. [CrossRef] [PubMed]
5. Trifunov, V.T.; Shadaydeh, M.; Runge, J.; Reichstein, M.; Denzler, J. A Data-Driven Approach to Partitioning Net Ecosystem Exchange Using a Deep State Space Model. *IEEE Access* **2021**, *9*, 107873–107883. [CrossRef]
6. Koopman, B.O. Hamiltonian Systems and Transformation in Hilbert Space. *Proc. Natl. Acad. Sci. USA* **1931**, *17*, 315–318. [CrossRef] [PubMed]
7. Mezić, I. Spectral Properties of Dynamical Systems, Model Reduction and Decompositions. *Nonlinear Dyn.* **2005**, *41*, 309–325. [CrossRef]
8. Schmid, P.J. Dynamic mode decomposition of numerical and experimental data. *J. Fluid Mech.* **2010**, *656*, 5–28. [CrossRef]
9. Proctor, J.L.; Brunton, S.L.; Kutz, J.N. Dynamic Mode Decomposition with Control. *SIAM J. Appl. Dyn. Syst.* **2016**, *15*, 142–161. [CrossRef]
10. Takens, F. Detecting strange attractors in turbulence. In *Dynamical Systems and Turbulence, Warwick 1980*; Rand, D.; Young, L.S., Eds.; Springer: Berlin/Heidelberg, Germany, 1981; pp. 366–381.
11. Brunton, S.L.; Brunton, B.W.; Proctor, J.L.; Kaiser, E.; Kutz, J.N. Chaos as an intermittently forced linear system. *Nat. Commun.* **2017**, *8*, 19. [CrossRef] [PubMed]
12. Pastorello, G.; Trotta, C.; Canfora, E.; Chu, H.; Christianson, D.; Cheah, Y.-W.; Poindexter, C.; Chen, J.; Elbashandy, A.; Humphrey, M.; et al. The FLUXNET2015 dataset and the ONEFlux processing pipeline for eddy covariance data. *Sci. Data* **2020**, *7*, 225. [CrossRef] [PubMed]

Proceeding Paper

An Ordinal Procedure to Detect Change Points in the Dependence Structure between Non-Stationary Time Series [†]

Alexander Schnurr [1] and Svenja Fischer [2],*

1 Department of Mathematics, Emmy-Noether Campus, University Siegen, Walter-Flex-Str. 3, 57068 Siegen, Germany; schnurr@mathematik.uni-siegen.de
2 SPATE Research Unit, Ruhr-University Bochum, 44801 Bochum, Germany
* Correspondence: svenja.fischer@rub.de
† Presented at the 8th International Conference on Time Series and Forecasting, Gran Canaria, Spain, 27–30 June 2022.

Abstract: The presence of non-stationarity can have crucial effects on statistical tests on correlation between two or more data sets. We present a procedure to detect changes in the strength of dependence between data sets that is based solely on a comparison of the ordinal structures within a moving window and thus compares the up-and-down behavior only. Hence, it is not distracted by changes within a single data set, such as change-points and trends or even nonlinear transformations, leading to non-stationarity. The applicability of the method is demonstrated for a hydrological data set of runoff time series which are impacted by a reservoir. It is demonstrated that the method overcomes problems of classical methods when non-stationarity is present.

Keywords: ordinal patterns; structural breaks; non-stationary time series; hydrological data

Citation: Schnurr, A.; Fischer, S. An Ordinal Procedure to Detect Change Points in the Dependence Structure between Non-Stationary Time Series. *Eng. Proc.* **2022**, *18*, 14. https://doi.org/10.3390/engproc2022018014

Academic Editors: Ignacio Rojas, Hector Pomares, Olga Valenzuela, Fernando Rojas and Luis Javier Herrera

Published: 21 June 2022

Publisher's Note: MDPI stays neutral with regard to jurisdictional claims in published maps and institutional affiliations.

1. Introduction

In various applications, the co-movement of different data sets is a desirable property. More often, it is a source of risk:

- If a trader holds a portfolio of various assets which are strongly 'correlated', it is more likely that several of them fall into the abyss at the same time.
- If a company produces parts for cars (for different brands), this company will be in trouble if the whole car industry goes through rough times.
- If several catchments in a basin are affected by extreme floods or extreme low flows at the same time, severe damage can be expected for the downstream catchments by flood superposition or spatial drought.
- If many requests are made to the same server at the same time, it becomes overloaded.

In all of these cases, it is important to monitor the strength of the interdependence between the data sets. This interdependence or co-movement is often modeled using the mathematical concept of correlation. However, sometimes it is not clear whether the time series admit second moments. Hence, it might be the case that correlation between the random variables (of which the time series consist) is not even defined. Another drawback of this mathematical concept is that it is well known to measure mostly *linear* dependence whilst the dependence in our applications could be far from being linear.

Our aim in the present article is to detect changes within the dependence structure between data sets. Since co-monotonic behavior might be a source of risk, we would like to detect whether this becomes (at a certain point in time) stronger or weaker. An additional difficulty arises since some of the data examples we have in mind are known to be non-stationary. Usually, tests for change points in the dependence structure require that the single time series *are* stationary (cf. e.g., [1,2]). If this was not the case, the tests would falsely detect a change in the dependence, which in fact might be a change in one of the single time series while the dependence between the time series remains constantly strong.

Due to climate change, the demand of being able to detect changes in the dependence structure in non-stationary settings has increased. Several data sets (like temperature) which were known to be stationary (up to some seasonal components) have started to increase systematically. Sometimes, it is not known how strong the incline of the new deterministic component is. Even worse: the incline itself is subject to change and increases stronger and stronger.

In the following, we will always use the term 'time series' if we consider the mathematical model, that is, a stochastic process $(X_i)_{i \in \mathbb{N}}$ defined on a probability space $(\Omega, \mathcal{F}, \mathbb{P})$. In contrast to this, we write 'data set' for the real or simulated data we are using. Here, and in what follows, we always consider two time series or two data sets at a time. If we want to analyze the dependence of more than two time series or data sets, we consider them pairwise.

Let us start with a simulated example illustrating the above idea. Consider two correlated ARMA(1,1) time series, i.e.,

$$X_i^{(1)} = \mu_1 + \phi_1 X_{i-1}^{(1)} + \epsilon_i^{(1)} - \theta_1 \epsilon_{i-1}^{(1)}$$
$$X_i^{(2)} = \mu_2 + \phi_2 X_{i-1}^{(2)} + \epsilon_i^{(2)} - \theta_2 \epsilon_{i-1}^{(2)},$$

where $\mu_1, \mu_2 \in \mathbb{R}$, $\phi_1, \phi_2, \theta_1, \theta_2 \in (0,1)$ and $\epsilon \sim \mathcal{N}_2(\mu, \Sigma)$ with $\Sigma = \begin{pmatrix} \sigma_1 & \rho \\ \rho & \sigma_2 \end{pmatrix}$. Here, we chose $\mu_1 = 5$, $\mu_2 = 6$, $\phi_1 = 0.7$, $\phi_2 = 0.8$, $\theta_1 = 0.3$, $\theta_2 = 0.2$, $\sigma_1 = \sigma_2 = 1$ and $\rho = 0.9$ to simulate $n = 600$ data points from a short-range dependent time series with a high cross-correlation (Figure 1). Artificially, two change-points were included in the data set: first, an exponential drift was added to the second part of $X^{(2)}$, i.e., $X_i'^{(2)} = X_i^{(2)} + \exp(i/300)$ for $i = 301, \ldots, 600$ and $X_i'^{(2)} = X_i^{(2)}$ for $i = 1, \ldots, 300$. Secondly, another 400 data points were added (third part) by simulating once again two cross-correlated ARMA(1,1) time series $\widetilde{X}^{(1)}$ and $\widetilde{X}^{(2)}$ with the same parameters as before but $\rho = 0.6$. These two data sets were added to the first two data sets such that each set consists of 1000 data points, e.g., $X_i'^{(1)} = X_i^{(1)}$ for $i = 1, \ldots, 600$ and $X_i'^{(1)} = \widetilde{X}_i^{(1)}$ for $i = 601, \ldots, 1000$. Moreover, the mean of the second time series was adjusted to match the exponential drift, that is, $X_i'^{(2)} = \widetilde{X}_i^{(2)} + \exp(2)$ for $i = 601, \ldots, 1000$. The exponential drift in the second series led to significant non-stationarity (detected with Mann–Kendall test for short-range dependent data; [3]). In a way, this is more than just a random simulated example: think about a data set of monthly temperature and the corresponding discharges of a river. While it is known that temperature tends to increase for most parts of the world, this was not detected yet for discharge [4], though both data sets are clearly cross-correlated. Application of the classical correlation measures such as Pearson's correlation coefficient, ρ_P, or Spearman's Rho, denoted by ρ_S, leads to a significant drop of the estimated correlation coefficients when applying the measure to the first and second part of the data. For the first part of the time series, both correlation measures detected significant correlation, where $\rho_P(X_{1:300}'^1, X_{1:300}'^2) = 0.786$ and $\rho_S(X_{1:300}'^{(1)}, X_{1:300}'^{(2)}) = 0.837$. However, when considering also the part with the exponential drift, significant correlation was no longer detected: $\rho_P(X_{1:600}'^{(1)}, X_{1:600}'^{(2)}) = 0.201$ and $\rho_S(X_{1:600}'^{(1)}, X_{1:600}'^{(2)}) = 0.303$. This implies that, though the correlation between both time series is still high, in the sense that they show the same up-and-down behavior, the drift masks this correlation for the classical correlation measures.

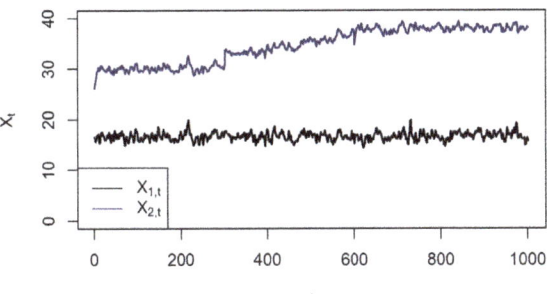

Figure 1. Simulated cross-correlated ARMA(1,1) series with exponential drift in the middle part of the second time series.

We would like to overcome this problem. To this end, we use so-called ordinal patterns in order to analyze the up-and-down behavior of the data sets (and time series) under consideration.

The most common approach in *ordinal pattern analysis* works as follows: One decides for a small number $d \in \mathbb{N}$, that is, for the length of the data windows under consideration. In each window, only the ordinal information is considered. There are various ways to encode the ordinal information of a d-dimensional vector in a pattern. Here, we use the following: Let S_d denote the set of permutations of $\{1, \ldots, d\}$, which we write as d-tuples containing each of the numbers $1, \ldots, d$ exactly one time. By the *ordinal pattern of order d* of the vector $x = (x_1, \ldots, x_d)$, we refer to the permutation

$$\Pi(x_1, \ldots, x_d) := (\pi_1, \ldots, \pi_d) \in S_d$$

which satisfies

$$x_{\pi_1} \geq \ldots \geq x_{\pi_d}.$$

When using this definition, it is often assumed that the probability of coincident values within the vector $(x_1, \ldots, x_d)$ is zero. Allowing for coincident values would require an additional convention like $\pi_{j-1} > \pi_j$ if $x_{\pi_{j-1}} = x_{\pi_j}$ for $j \in \{2, \ldots, d\}$ or an approach as in [5].

Roughly speaking, *ordinal pattern dependence* measures how often we encounter the same patterns at the same time considering our two data sets (cf. Figure 2); the theoretical counterpart is the probability

$$\mathbb{P}(\Pi(X_1, \ldots, X_d) = \Pi(Y_1, \ldots, Y_d))$$

for the underlying models, that is, the time series we consider.

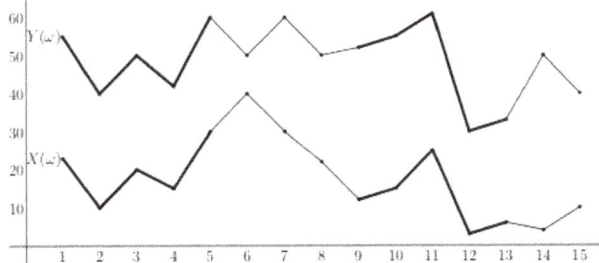

Figure 2. Two data sets with partially co-monotonic behavior.

In fact, one subtracts the probability for the hypothetical case of independence and divides by some normalizing factor in order to obtain values between zero and one in the case of positive dependence. The mathematical definition of ordinal pattern dependence can be found in the subsequent section.

In our simulated toy example above, the ordinal pattern dependence (we have chosen $d = 5$) is not impacted by the exponential drift. In fact, the ordinal pattern dependence (here, we use the sample version $\overline{OPD}$ defined below Equation (2)) does not change significantly with $\overline{OPD}_5(X_{1:300}^{\prime(1)}, X_{1:300}^{\prime(2)}) = 0.366$ and $\overline{OPD}_5(X_{1:600}^{\prime(1)}, X_{1:600}^{\prime(2)}) = 0.300$. However, the change of dependency between both time series in the last part is clearly detected with $\overline{OPD}_5(X_{601:1000}^{\prime(1)}, X_{601:1000}^{\prime(2)}) = 0.105$. This change can also be detected by the classical correlation measures ρ_P and ρ_S, but less clearly with $\rho_P(X_{601:1000}^{\prime(1)}, X_{601:1000}^{\prime(2)}) = 0.592$ and $\rho_S(X_{601:1000}^{\prime(1)}, X_{601:1000}^{\prime(2)}) = 0.601$. Recall that, although the up-and-down-behavior remains the same in the second part, the classical measures do not detect this any more due to the moderate exponential drift in the background.

The origin of the concept of ordinal patterns lies in the theory of dynamical systems [6,7]. They have been used in order to analyze the entropy of data sets [8] and to estimate the Hurst-parameter of long-range dependent time series [9,10]. Furthermore, related methods have proved to be useful in the context of EEG-data in medicine [11], index data in finance [12] and flood data in extreme value theory [13]. Already in [14], we have suggested using ordinal patterns for the analysis of hydrological time series. Changes in the dependence have not been considered in that article. However, changes in a *single* data set have been analyzed in [15] via ordinal patterns. Analyzing changes in the dependence between time series/data sets is a topic that has attained considerable interest over the last few years (cf. [1,2,16]). There exists an approach (cf. [17]) that was developed to detect changes in the dependence structure despite having non-stationarity of the single time series using the concept of local stationarity, but the assumptions are rather technical and make it hard to apply to short time series in practice.

Using ordinal patterns in order to analyze the dependence between time series, instead, has several advantages: we do not need to assume the existence of second moments and the time series do not necessarily have to be stationary. Furthermore, the method is robust against small noise and/or measurement errors and the intuitive concept makes it easy to apply in practice. Since only the order structure is considered, the algorithms are quick.

The notation we are using is more or less standard. $(\Omega, \mathcal{F}, \mathbb{P})$ denotes a probability space in the background. We write $\mathbb{E}$ for the expected value w.r.t. $\mathbb{P}$, while $\mathbb{N}$ denotes the positive integers starting with one.

The paper structure is as follows: first, we describe the methodology in the subsequent section. In Section 3, our method is used on hydrological data sets. The Section 4 consists of a short discussion and an outlook.

2. Methodology

Let $X = (X_i)_{i \in \mathbb{N}}$ and $Y = (Y_i)_{i \in \mathbb{N}}$ be two time series defined on a common probability space $(\Omega, \mathcal{F}, \mathbb{P})$. We describe our analysis step-by-step:

(I) Preparation and first analysis.

Check whether the whole time series are stationary. Maybe even the bivariate time-series (X, Y) is stationary. In this case, both single time series are stationary and the dependence structure remains the same over time. In this case, we are done. If the single time series are stationary, but the bivariate one is not stationary, one can use our method or one of those found in the literature (cf. [1,2,16]) to detect changes in the dependency. The most interesting case for us is if the two time series X and Y or at least one of them is not stationary. Then, the classical methods cannot be applied. Still, one might be interested in the analysis of co-monotonic behavior and in changes of this behavior.

(II) Calculate the ordinal pattern dependence of the whole time series.

At first, we have to check whether the two time series admit ordinal pattern dependence.

Definition 1. *We define the ordinal pattern dependence between two random vectors* $\mathbf{X} = (X_1, \ldots, X_d)$ *and* $\mathbf{Y} = (Y_1, \ldots, Y_d)$ *by*

$$\text{OPD}_d(\mathbf{X}, \mathbf{Y}) = \frac{\mathbb{P}(\Pi(\mathbf{X}) = \Pi(\mathbf{Y})) - \sum_{\pi \in S_d} \mathbb{P}(\Pi(\mathbf{X}) = \pi)\mathbb{P}(\Pi(\mathbf{Y}) = \pi)}{1 - \sum_{\pi \in S_d} \mathbb{P}(\Pi(\mathbf{X}) = \pi)\mathbb{P}(\Pi(\mathbf{Y}) = \pi)}. \tag{1}$$

This definition of ordinal pattern dependence only considers positive dependence, which is in line with our considerations in the present article. Negative dependence could be included by analyzing the co-movement of $\mathbf{X}$ and $-\mathbf{Y}$ or by using an analogous definition taking inverse patterns into account. Usually, one is interested in measuring either positive *or* negative dependence. If one wants to consider both dependencies at the same time, the quantity

$$\text{OPD}_d(\mathbf{X}, \mathbf{Y})^+ - \text{OPD}_d(\mathbf{X}, -\mathbf{Y})^+, \tag{2}$$

where $a^+ := \max\{a, 0\}$ for every $a \in \mathbb{R}$, is useful (cf. [18]).

For data sets, we use the estimators

$$\frac{1}{n} \sum_{i=1}^{n-d+1} 1_{\{\Pi(X_i, \ldots, X_{i+d-1}) = \Pi(Y_i, \ldots, Y_{i+d-1})\}}$$

for $\mathbb{P}(\Pi(\mathbf{X}) = \Pi(\mathbf{Y}))$ and $(\pi \in S_d)$

$$\frac{1}{n} \sum_{i=1}^{n-d+1} 1_{\{\Pi(X_i, \ldots, X_{i+d-1}) = \pi\}}$$

for $\mathbb{P}(\Pi(\mathbf{X}) = \pi)$. For OPD in Equation (1), we use these plug-in estimators and denote it with $\overline{\text{OPD}}_d$.

(III) Check whether the dependence changes over time.

Using a test statistic of the following kind, we analyze whether the ordinal pattern dependence between the time series remains more or less the same

$$T_{OPD} = \max_{1 \leq k \leq n} \left| \overline{\text{OPD}}_d(X_{1:k}, Y_{1:k}) - \overline{\text{OPD}}_d(X_{1:n}, Y_{1:n}) \right|, \tag{3}$$

which is a CUSUM type test statistic. In the examples of the subsequent section, we already have a good candidate for the time of the structural break. If this was not the case, the argmax could be used in order to find this point in time.

3. Results

As a real life example, we consider the six runoff data sets of catchments of the mesoscale in Bavaria, Southern Germany. Four of the measuring gauges, Windischeschenbach, Unterköblitz, Münchshofen, and Heitzenhofen, are located at the main river Naab, a large tributary of the Danube river (Figure 3a). Between Unterköblitz and Münchshofen gauges, the tributary river Schwarzach flows into the Naab. Two gauges are located at the Schwarzach river: Rötz and Warnbach. In November 1975, a large reservoir was built at the Schwarzach river, called the Eixendorfer See, located directly downstream of the Rötz gauge. It serves flood protection, low water elevation (water regulation), hydropower generation, and recreation, and, with a storage of 19.30 million m^3, it is among the largest reservoirs in Southern Germany. We consider the monthly maximum discharges of the period from 1959–2018, which often serve as a basis for flood frequency analyses. Due to their temporal resolution, monthly maximum discharges are usually considered to be short-range dependent [19] and affected by seasonality (Figure 3b).

We apply the methods to analyze the data sets as described in Section 2.

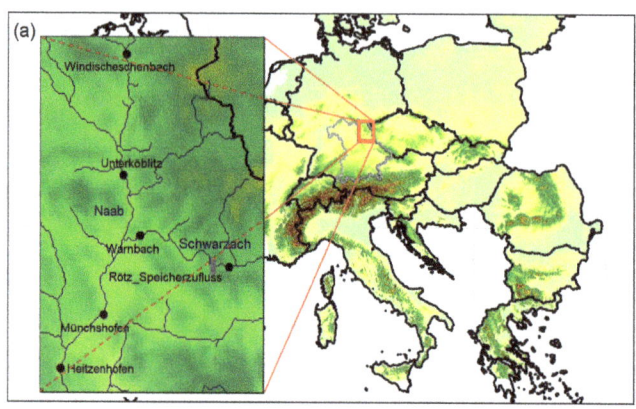

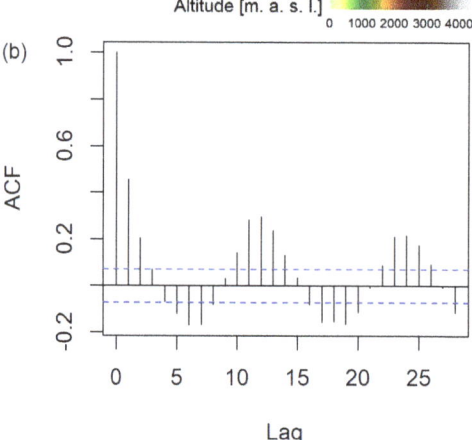

Figure 3. (**a**) Map of the location of the gauges considered in the application with Bavarian borders (grey) and location of the zoom-in map in Europe (red); (**b**) auto-correlation of the monthly maximum discharges at Münchshofen gauge.

(I) Preparation and first analysis.

The available discharge data sets are checked for consistency and trimmed to a joint time period between 1959 and 2018, therefore consisting of $n = 730$ data points each. For each data series, the Wilcoxon test for short-range dependent data [20] is applied to test whether there is a significant change-point in the mean. For the gauges Münchshofen and Heitzenhofen in the Naab river as well as Warnbach in the Schwarzach river, such a significant change-point (5% significant level) was detected in the period of 1975 till 1977. This change-point can be directly related to the beginning of operation of the dam in the Schwarzach, which has a large impact on the mean since the largest discharge peaks are reduced by the reservoir for flood protection. Therefore, all gauges located downstream of the reservoir can be considered as non-stationary. Hence, the classical tests for structural breaks in the dependence structure cannot be applied.

(II) Calculate the ordinal pattern dependence of the whole time series.

In the next step, we calculate the ordinal pattern dependence between the discharge series of all six gauges as given in Definition 1 with $d = 5$. A similar pattern length was chosen before in the case of hydrological data and proved to be sufficient (cf. [5,14]). One could also think about using $d = 12$ and thus taking into account the annual cycle. However, this would increase the number of patterns and thus the computational effort significantly. Moreover, the annual cycle is not equally strong everywhere, e.g., due to different periods of snowmelt, and thus a general definition could be difficult. We can assume a positive dependence in this application since discharges will most likely increase and fall similarly due to spatial extension of weather patterns such as rainfall.

The ordinal pattern dependence between all six gauges is given in Table 1.

Table 1. Ordinal pattern dependence of all six gauges for the time period 1959-2018. Since the OPD is symmetric, only the upper half of the table is shown.

Gauge	Windischeschenbach	Unterköblitz	Rötz	Warnbach	Münchshofen	Heitzenhofen
Windischeschenbach	1.000	0.326	0.151	0.170	0.250	0.221
Unterköblitz		1.000	0.179	0.249	0.507	0.462
Rötz			1.000	0.278	0.209	0.205
Warnbach				1.000	0.317	0.343
Münchshofen					1.000	0.670
Heitzenhofen						1.000

The results reveal that there is a high dependence between the gauges of the main river, decreasing with distance. This can be related to weather patterns such as rainfall events which are spatially extended and affect several catchments at the same time as well as routing. Interestingly, the gauges of the tributary are less correlated, neither with each other nor with the main river. However, dependency increases for the gauges downstream of the tributary, which is hydrologically reasonable.

(III) Check whether the dependence changes over time.

The commissioning of the dam in 1975 may not only affect the mean of the discharge series. Indeed, it is also likely that the dependence structure between the discharge series of the gauges is altered by it. It can be assumed that especially the dependency between the gauges upstream of the dam and therefore those not affected by the regulation have a higher dependency to the gauges downstream after commissioning of the dam since the incoming tributary discharge is regulated and smoother and thus does not alter the main river discharge as much as before. The dam may also affect the low dependency between the gauges in the tributary given in Table 1. This hypothesis is tested in the following by applying the ordinal pattern dependence to the time series before as well as after the assumed change-point in 1975 (Table 2). Due to the nature of ordinal patterns, this change-point detection is not affected by the previously detected change in mean.

There are clear differences between the dependency before and after the commissioning of the dam. It is not straight-forward to determine if the differences are significant, since classical tests like Fisher's Z-test cannot be applied. However, it was shown in previous studies that such differences appear to be significant ([14]). Indeed, the dependency between the upstream main river gauges, Windischeschenbach and Unterköblitz, increases or stays the same compared to the period before the commissioning of the dam. The dependency between the gauge upstream of the dam, Rötz, and downstream of the dam, Warnbach, instead decreases since the discharge is no longer transferred directly between the gauges, but the dam now regulates the runoff. Instead, the discharge of the downstream gauge is mostly impacted by inter flow. We also tested possible change-points in 1976 and 1977, taking into account a possible delayed reaction, but the general tendency of all results stayed the same. The ordinal pattern dependence, therefore, was able to detect the changes in the dependence structure caused by the commissioning of the dam despite the change in mean at the exact same position in the time series.

Table 2. Ordinal pattern dependence of all six gauges for the time period 1959–1975 (upper table) and 1976–2018 (lower table).

Gauge	Windischeschenbach	Unterköblitz	Rötz	Warnbach	Münchshofen	Heitzenhofen
Windischeschenbach	1.000	0.222	0.095	0.115	0.179	0.179
Unterköblitz		1.000	0.164	0.240	0.525	0.486
Rötz			1.000	0.390	0.181	0.187
Warnbach				1.000	0.289	0.317
Münchshofen					1.000	0.746
Heitzenhofen						1.000
Windischeschenbach	1.000	0.372	0.175	0.191	0.273	0.241
Unterköblitz		1.000	0.191	0.259	0.517	0.465
Rötz			1.000	0.246	0.224	0.205
Warnbach				1.000	0.337	0.356
Münchshofen					1.000	0.655
Heitzenhofen						1.000

4. Discussion

Our method shows how the commissioning of the dam has changed the dependence between the discharge data sets. In a similar way, it could be used on the other frameworks described in the Introduction. If we had not known in advance when the dam was built, we could have analyzed this by calculating the argmax of the test statistic (3) above.

The data analysis shows that ordinal pattern dependence can indeed be used in order to derive changes in the dependence structure between time series. The method is robust, easy to implement and has the advantage that the concept behind it has a simple intuitive meaning: if the ordinal patterns are often the same at the same time points, the up-and-down-behavior of the two data sets is similar.

We have chosen here $d = 5$. This value has proven to be useful in the context of discharge data. Smaller values of d are more often used in statistical frameworks, while higher values are used in the analysis of dynamical systems. Finding an optimal choice for d is part of ongoing research.

In a way, our toy example and the real world data analysis of Section 3 serve as a pilot study, showing the applicability of the method. By now, it is not possible to derive critical values or confidence bands. This is not in the scope of the present paper, since it is very technical and still a work in progress: in order to leave classical stationarity behind, a standing assumption would be 'ordinal pattern stationarity'. One needs to show that both data sets might be realizations of ordinal pattern stationary time series. Then, and that is a point being missing in the existing literature, one needs to derive limit theorems for, say, a short range dependent time-series on the space of ordinal patterns (which is a discrete space without canonical order). Finally, one might be able to derive exact change point tests in this framework. If the original time series can be assumed to be stationary, limit results like in [18] could be applied. However, the above example shows how nicely the method can deal with *non-stationary* time series.

Author Contributions: Conceptualization, A.S. and S.F.; methodology, A.S.; software, S.F.; writing—original draft preparation, A.S. and S.F.; writing—review and editing, A.S. and S.F.; visualization, A.S. and S.F. All authors have read and agreed to the published version of the manuscript.

Funding: This research was funded by the German Reserach Foundation (DFG) Grant No. FOR 2416 (research unit SPATE) for Svenja Fischer and Grant No. SCHN 1231-3/2 for Alexander Schnurr.

Institutional Review Board Statement: Not applicable.

Informed Consent Statement: Not applicable.

Data Availability Statement: Publicly available datasets were analyzed in this study. These data can be found here: https://www.nid.bayern.de/abfluss (accessed on 12 May 2022).

Acknowledgments: We are grateful to Bayerisches Landesamt für Umwelt, www.lfu.bayern.de (accessed on 12 May 2022), for providing the discharge data. We would like to thank three anonymous referees for their valuable comments.

Conflicts of Interest: The authors declare no conflict of interest.

References

1. Aue, A.; Hörmann, S.; Horvath, L.; Reimherr, M. Break detection in the covariance structure of multivariate time series models. *Ann. Stat.* **2009**, *37*, 4046–4087. [CrossRef]
2. Dehling, H.; Vogel, D.; Wendler, M.; Wied, D. Testing for changes in Kendall's tau. *Econom. Theory* **2017**, *33*, 1352–1386. [CrossRef]
3. Hamed, K.H.; Rao, A.R. A modified Mann–Kendall trend test for autocorrelated data. *J. Hydrol.* **1998**, *204*, 182–196. [CrossRef]
4. Sharma, A.; Wasko, C.; Lettenmaier, D.P. If Precipitation Extremes Are Increasing, Why Aren't Floods? *Water Resour. Res.* **2018**, *54*, 8545–8551. [CrossRef]
5. Schnurr, A.; Fischer, S. Generalized ordinal patterns allowing for ties and their applications in hydrology. *Comput. Stat. Data Anal.* **2022**, *171*, 107472. [CrossRef]
6. Bandt, C. Ordinal time series analysis. *Ecol. Model.* **2005**, *182*, 229–238. [CrossRef]
7. Bandt, C.; Shiha, F. Order Patterns in Time Series. *J. Time Ser. Anal.* **2007**, *28*, 646–665. [CrossRef]
8. Bandt, C.; Pompe, B. Permutation entropy: A natural complexity measure for time series. *Phys. Rev. Lett.* **2002**, *88*, 174102. [CrossRef] [PubMed]
9. Sinn, M.; Keller, K. Estimation of ordinal pattern probabilities in Gaussian processes with stationary increments. *Comp. Stat. Data Anal.* **2011**, *55*, 1781–1790. [CrossRef]
10. Betken, A.; Buchsteiner, J.; Dehling, H.; Münker, I.; Schnurr, A.; Woerner, J. Ordinal Patterns in Long-Range Dependent Time Series. *Scand. J. Stat.* **2020**, *48*, 969–1000. doi:10.1111/sjos.12478. [CrossRef]
11. Keller, K.; Unakafov, A.; Unakafova, V. Ordinal Patterns, Entropy, and EEG. *Entropy* **2014**, *16*, 6212–6239. [CrossRef]
12. Schnurr, A. An Ordinal Pattern Approach to Detect and to Model Leverage Effects and Dependence Structures between Financial Time Series. *Stat. Pap.* **2014**, *55*, 919–931. [CrossRef]
13. Oesting, M.; Schnurr, A. Ordinal Patterns in Clusters of Extremes of Regularly Varying Time Series. *Extremes* **2020**, *23*, 521–545. [CrossRef]
14. Fischer, S.; Schumann, A.; Schnurr, A. Ordinal Pattern Dependence Between Hydrological Time Series. *J. Hydrol.* **2017**, *548*, 536–551. [CrossRef]
15. Unakafov, A.; Keller, K. Change-point detection using the conditional entropy of ordinal patterns. *Entropy* **2018**, *20*, 709. [CrossRef] [PubMed]
16. Wied, D.; Dehling, H.; van Kampen, M.; Vogel, D. A fluctuation test for constant Spearman's rho with nuisance-free limit distribution. *Comput. Stat. Data Anal.* **2014**, *76*, 723–736. [CrossRef]
17. Dette, H.; Wu, W.; Zhou, Z. Change point analysis of correlation in non-stationary time series. *Stat. Sin.* **2019**, *29*, 611–643. [CrossRef]
18. Schnurr, A.; Dehling, H. Testing for Structural Breaks via Ordinal Pattern Dependence. *JASA* **2017**, *112*, 706–720. [CrossRef]
19. Wu, C.L.; Chau, K.W.; Li, Y.S. Predicting monthly streamflow using data-driven models coupled with data-preprocessing techniques. *Water Resour. Res.* **2009**, *45*. [CrossRef]
20. Dehling, H.; Fried, R.; Wendler, M. A robust method for shift detection in time series. *Biometrika* **2020**, *107*, 647–660. [CrossRef]

engineering proceedings

Proceeding Paper

On the Prospective Use of Deep Learning Systems for Earthquake Forecasting over Schumann Resonances Signals [†]

Carlos Cano-Domingo [1,*] , Ruxandra Stoean [2] , Nuria Novas-Castellano [1] , Manuel Fernandez-Ros [1] , Gonzalo Joya [3] and Jose A. Gázquez-Parra [1]

1 Ceia3, Departamento de Ingenieria, Universidad de Almeria, 04120 Almeria, Spain; nnovas@ual.es (N.N.-C.); mfernandez@ual.es (M.F.-R.); jgazquez@ual.es (J.A.G.-P.)
2 Department of Computer Science, University of Craiovar, 200585 Craiova, Romania; rstoean@inf.ucv.ro
3 Departamento de Tecnologia Electronica, Universidad de Málaga Telecommunications Institute of the University of Malaga (TELMA), 29071 Malaga, Spain; gjoya@uma.es
* Correspondence: carcandom@ual.es
† Presented at the 8th International Conference on Time Series and Forecasting, Gran Canaria, Spain, 27–30 June 2022.

Abstract: The relationship between Schumann resonances and earthquakes was proposed more than 50 years ago; however, the experimental support has not been fully established. A considerable amount of recent studies have focused on the relationship between a single earthquake and the Schumann resonance signal variation around this earthquake, obtaining preliminary support for the existence of the link. Nonetheless, they all lack a systematic and general approach. In this research, we propose a novel methodology to detect the presence of relevant earthquakes based on the Schumann resonance. The methodology is based on a deep learning framework composed of a pretrained variational auto-encoder followed by an LSTM network and a fully connected layer with a sigmoid output. The results reveal the uncovered relationship between earthquake activity and Schumann resonance signal using the novel methodology, being the first automatic earthquake detector based on Schumann resonance signal.

Keywords: Schumann resonance; earthquake detection; deep learning; autoencoder; LSTM; RNN; forecasting; dimension reduction

check for updates

Citation: Cano-Domingo, C.; Stoean, R.; Novas-Castellano, N.; Fernandez-Ros, M.; Joya, G.; Gázquez-Parra, J.A. On the Prospective Use of Deep Learning Systems for Earthquake Forecasting over Schumann Resonances Signals. *Eng. Proc.* **2022**, *18*, 15. https://doi.org/10.3390/engproc2022018015

Academic Editors: Ignacio Rojas, Hector Pomares, Olga Valenzuela, Fernando Rojas and Luis Javier Herrera

Published: 21 June 2022

Publisher's Note: MDPI stays neutral with regard to jurisdictional claims in published maps and institutional affiliations.

1. Introduction

Schumann resonance (SR) are extremely low frequency (ELF) electromagnetic signals generated mainly through the lightning iteration, which propagates along the Earth–ionosphere Electromagnetic Cavity [1]. The electromagnetic cavity is formed by two electromagnetic media with a high level of conductivity (the Earth and the ionosphere) and an insulator (the atmosphere). The electromagnetic resonance produced has multiple modes in which the intensity of higher modes are considerably lower than the first modes [2]. Experimentally, the average central frequency for the first six modes is agreed to be around 7.8 Hz, 14 Hz, 20 Hz, 26 Hz, 33 Hz, and 39 Hz. Despite that, no theoretical characterization of the frequency of the SRs modes manages to accurately fit the experimental results. For example, in [3], the authors detailed a novel method for estimating the central values; however, the results do not agree accurately with the experimental worldwide data. Other studies have approached the central frequency estimation using a 3D electromagnetic simulator with very promising results [4,5]. Although the results are consistent with the experimental data, they are not completely equal to them. It is important to remark that all these approaches are centered on the central frequency estimation in a steady condition, the analytical or simulated behavior of the SR frequency variation remains undiscovered.

In light of the above, it is clear that there is difficulty involved in the estimation of the SR signal parameters, even for one of the simplest parameters, e.g., the central frequency for the first mode in the steady condition. This fact has led this team to introduce deep learning (DL) techniques in order to analyze it.

Over the last five years, one of the most studied parts of SR has been the diurnal and seasonal patterns of SR and their evolution over the time. The importance of this pattern is mainly driven by the fact that many observatories have been set up during these years. The diurnal and seasonal patterns of a UK observatory is fully explained in [6]. They explain the specific frequency registered by their observatory based on the proximity to the African thunderstorm. In [7], the researchers detailed this regular pattern and its relation with the most important lightning hot spots during specific hours of the day. Slight differences are also expected between observatories. Some aspects of the electromagnetic composition of the Earth–ionosphere cavity can be explained based on the little differences between observatories. For example, in [1], the authors use two distant stations and focus on the comparison between their spectrum and the differences between the central frequency of the first mode. In recent years, a growing interest in their relationship with other natural phenomena has received more attention; for example, the connection with the lightning activity [8,9], the relation with geomagnetic storms in [10], or with a solar proton event in [11]. Due to the complexity of the SR signals, the characteristics of the previously mentioned relationship have not been dealt with in depth, although the auspicious results point out a highly possible connection.

In relation with the presented research, earthquake (EQ) detection using SR signals has become a central issue in the last five years in the SR research. Experiments on detecting individual EQ were performed in the last two years with encouraging results. Some papers have centered their investigation on the relationship between individual events and their impact on the SR signal.

The study of the relation with two huge EQs in Japan is presented in [12]. The results discussed the effect of EQs both in the transient domain and in the frequency domain, along with a compelling theoretical explanation. In [13], the researchers point out the statistical link between frequency and intensity values of the first SR mode around individual seismic events. The work was centered on the study of the SR signal variations around important EQs, fifteen days before and five days after each EQ event. The study of the relation between two important EQ and their affectation in the SR signal in Greece can be found in [14]. They exposed the statistical interconnection between these two EQ events and the variation of the ELF background signal. Although this approach is interesting, it does not allow for establishing a systematical methodology that can detect EQ events using the continuous SR signal.

Other authors have focused on describing the prerequisites and modeling the electromagnetic (EM) iteration between SR signal and EQ. A model treatment to estimate the EQ magnitude based on the variation of the SR spectrum is fully explained in [15]. The results show substantial evidence of the usage of SR signal variation for detecting EQ above 7 and at a distance up to 3 Mn. A model of the electromagnetic manifestation in the SR band by close EQ events is described in [16]. The most promising result that emerges from their research is that nearby EQs provoke noticeable modification of the SR signal. In [17], the authors studied the prerequisites to record seismic activity in the SR band in the time domain. The results using two distant stations are promising; however, the system does not fulfill the needed accuracy for the EQ prediction. The study of the possibility of forecasting EQ using a narrow transient window is explored in [18], with a machine learning (ML) approach.

To the best of our knowledge, the evidence proposed by these studies are not conclusive. The detection of EQ events is mainly performed by the analysis of individual EQ; however, a more generalized framework would be needed to established an experimental link between SR and EQ.

It is also important to mention the lack of previous studies exploring the usage of the latest advances in computational intelligence applied to SR signals, which is more than important due to the vast amount of data and the difficulty involved in detecting variation in the regular patterns, as was mentioned before.

This research presents a new approach to exploring the possibility of using the time evolution of the SR signal to detect the occurrence of high-intensity nearby EQs. The methodology is constituted of three parts: A pretrained variation auto-encoder (VAE) focuses on reducing the data dimension, followed by a long short-term memory (LSTM) network, with the aim of taking into account the temporal trend of the SR codified data and a fully connected layer to classify the interaction based on the LSTM neuron states. The aim of this paper is to use the DL advances to design a method for establishing a correlation between SR signal and EQ.

2. Materials and Methods

The methodology used in this research is composed by a deep encoder followed by an LSTM for studying the correlation between the EQ and the SR signal. A complete description of the methodology can be seen in Figure 1.

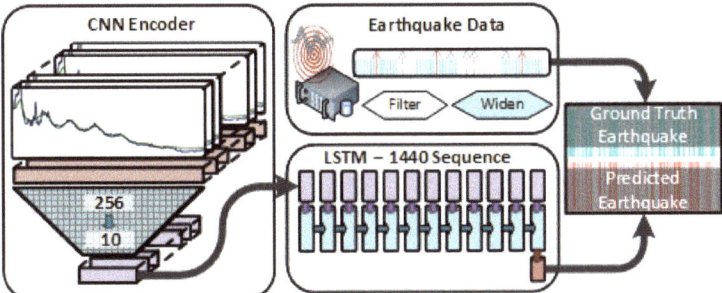

Figure 1. Summary of the methodology used composed by a CNN encoder followed by an LSTM network.

The SR signal is obtained by the ELF Sierra de Los Filabres observatory. The observatory has been recording SR signals continuously from 2016, although, due to maintenance problems, some registers were not captured. This observatory contains two sensors, one for the $\mathcal{H}_{NS}$ and the other for the $\mathcal{H}_{EW}$. The digital part is composed of an ADC with 24 bits of resolution and 187 samples per second. A detailed description of the observatory can be found in [19]. The data are recorded in 30-min segments. Each segment is processed and the Welch algorithm fetches the spectral information of each segment. Finally, each segment is reduced to a 256 length vector, which contains the frequency information from 0 Hz to 42 Hz. For the sake of concreteness, we have selected only the $\mathcal{H}_{NS}$ sensor. Considering the data from January 2016 to December 2020, the total number of 30-min intervals is 87,697; however, due to the maintenance problem, the real number of 30 min intervals is 79,281.

The EQ data have been obtained through a public EQ Repository [20]. The total number of EQ with a Richter magnitude greater than 4.5 during the five year period is 35,023; however, not all EQs have been considered for this research, as the system will be focused on detecting the EQ, which can have more impact on the SR of our observatory. The EQ events have been filtered by an ad hoc criterium based on the expert knowledge of this group and the previous literature:

- Richter magnitude greater than 5.0.
- Distance between the EQ and the observatory less than 30 km.
- Depth less than 40 km.

By selecting only the EQ that fulfills these criteria, the number of EQ is reduced to 161.

The time step used in this paper is 30 min due to the resolution of the SR signal. Consequently, the EQ event has been adjusted to its corresponding 30 min time step. The duration of the EQ has been widened to 24 h, which means 48 registers around the actual event. This widened process is performed to allow the DL model to learn about the influence of the EQ on the SR signal; therefore, the widened register can no longer be considered the EQ event, but we consider the positive values as a representation of the EQ affection in the SR register.

To sum up, the ground truth comprises 87,697 registers, in which, 5459 are labeled as 1 (meaning that an EQ affected the SR register) and 82,238 are labeled as 0 (no affection).

The data set has been split into two parts:

- Training data set: from January 2016 to June 2019—60,129 samples.
- Test data set: from July 2019 to December 2020—27,568 samples.

The first step in our methodology is the usage of a pretrained DL encoder, framed in a VAE methodology. A schematic representation can be seen in Figure 2. The deep encoder is composed of three convolutional layers and two fully connected layers. The first convolutional layer takes a 1D vector of 256 positions and outputs 32 vectors of length 128. The second convolutional layer outputs 64 vectors of length 64. The last convolutional layer converts the input to 64 vectors of length 32. The last part of the encoder is composed of two fully connected layers that take the output of the last convolutional and output a code vector of 10 components. The code data set is composed of 87,692 codes of 10 values, out of which 79,281 are the output of the deep encoder plus 8000 zeros codes, which correspond with the SR lost segments due to maintenance problems. The main purpose of using the encoder is to focus on the variability of the signal, but not to take into account the common structure of the SR signal. The method selected for this purpose is a VAE, which tries to reconstruct the original signal but reduces the dimension of the input from 256 to 10; however, retaining the most critical information, while removing the record's common part. The variational term refers to the randomization of the learned space [21]. The VAE is also reinforced by the Lorentzian fit algorithm in the cost function.

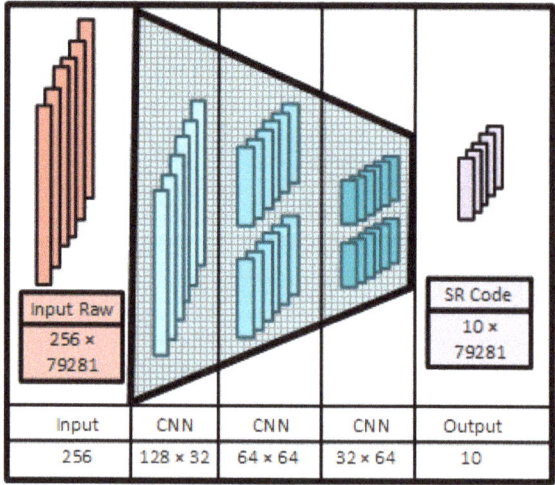

Figure 2. Deep encoder and data description. The encoder is composed of three CNN layers, which output a code of 10 values for each SR segment.

The next step is composed of an LSTM network, which sequentially takes the inputs composed by the five-year outputs of the DL encoder. The LSTM architecture is composed of an LSTM layer with 32 features in the hidden state. The LSTM network is fed with 1440 values, which correspond to 30 days of 30-min segments. After the 1440 sequence registers have been introduced into the LSTM network, the hidden state of the network is processed by a fully connected layer made of two layers. The first layer takes 32 values as the input and produces a vector of 128 values as output. The last layer processes the

128 values and outputs a code of only 1 value. In order to calculate a binary output, the last layer is followed by a sigmoid function.

The binary output of the LSTM layer is compared to the SR affectation of this register. The DL LSTM system is trained to predict the affectation of the EQ in the first 25% of the 1440 sequences. In Figure 3, a description of our LSTM methodology is outlined. The sequence is compared after 1440 values have been fed to the network (30 days). The result is compared against the EQ affectation of the 360 registers (7.5 days). In order to add more generalization to the model, an L1 regularization and a dropout of 0.4 have been added. The hyper-parameters of the LSTM network have been selected using an automatic tool.

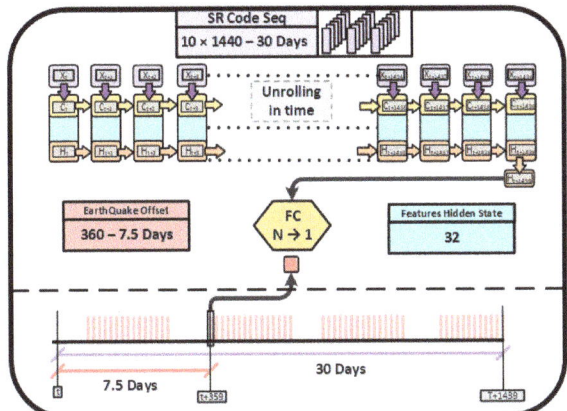

Figure 3. Diagram of the LSTM network used in this research.

The DL system is trained to predict the affectation of the EQ in the middle of the 1440 sequence. A summary of this methodology can be found in Figure 1.

3. Results

The results have been obtained after applying the pre-trained deep encoder to the previously mentioned training data set and the decoded output has been fed to the LSTM network. The LSTM network is trained until a 96.5% accuracy is obtained in the training data set. In Figure 4, the results applied to the training data set can be observed. It can be seen that the system has learned completely and is able to recognize the pattern of the codified SR evolution. As was explained in the methodology section, this approach first used a training data set for supervised learning and then an extensive test data set to evaluate the performance of the model. This test data set is composed of patterns that have not been presented to the network before. The results can be seen in Figure 5. It can be observed that the system is able to generalize the EQ detection when the test data set is used. There are some clear matches, although other times, the system predicts an EQ but there is no clear reference register. It is also important to notice that at the end of the test data set the system is not able to detect the EQ affectation in general.

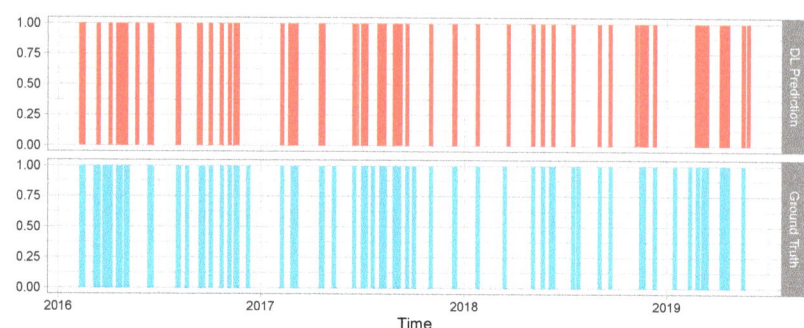

Figure 4. Results of the model applied to the training data set. 1st Row: DL output. 2nd Row: reference.

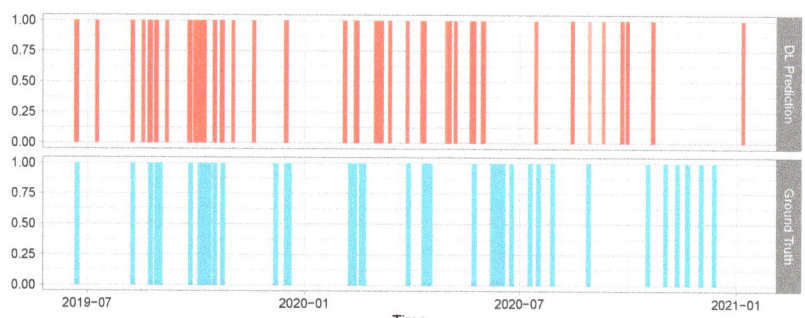

Figure 5. Results of the model applied to the test data set. 1st Row: DL output. 2nd Row: reference.

In Table 1, the confusion matrix of both the training and test data set is exhibited. The results have to be taken carefully because the methodology is based on the assumption that the SR affection lasts around 24 h and the offset between the SR and the EQ is fixed. It leads to two issues. The DL do not have the constraint of 48 consecutive "1" and also the detection does not have to start twelve hours before the EQ event constantly. Considering these two factors, even the test results are very promising with a high detection rate. Table 2 gathers the summary of the results obtained for both data sets. Considering that the number of segments labeled as EQ affectation is around 7%, the system is able to recognize a pattern in more than 18% of cases. It is also important to remark that the balance accuracy greatly supports the fact that this methodology can be seen as the first step in the EQ DL detection research.

Table 1. Confusion matrix for training and test data sets.

	Train Data Set		Test Data Set	
	Reference		Reference	
Predicted	0	1	0	1
0	55,865	777	24,989	607
1	1472	2014	1614	359

Table 2. Summary of results for training and test data sets.

	Train Data Set	Test Data Set
Accuracy	0.9626	0.9194
Sensitivity	0.72161	0.37164
Specificity	0.97433	0.93933
Pos Pred Value	0.57774	0.18196
Balanced Accuracy	0.84797	0.65548

The criteria used for selecting which EQ events are considered for training purposes is based on earlier literature as it was explained previously; however, a possible discrepancy can be expected as an explanation for the false positive detection of the DL algorithm. In Figure 6, the predicted result is presented along with a higher number of EQ events. The 2nd row shows the distance between the observatory and the EQ and the 3rd row outlines their magnitude. To expose the possible discrepancies for selecting EQ, more flexible criteria have been used: 5 Richter magnitude and 4500 km max distance. The results show that for some DL prediction with no correspondence in the expected register, the system is able to recognize the pattern as a SR affectation. This is very clear for the last DL forecast.

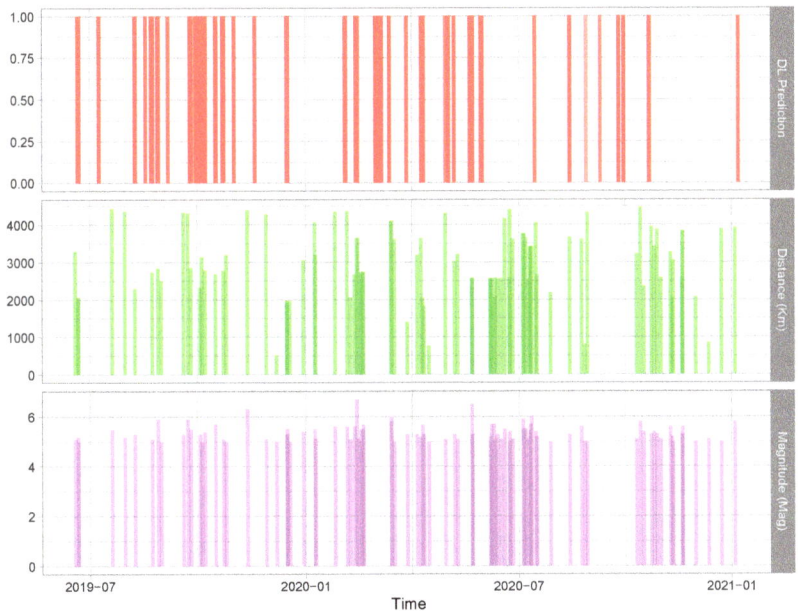

Figure 6. Results of the model applied to the test data set with more EQ considered. 1st Row: DL output. 2nd Row: distance. 3rd Row: magnitude.

A total of 27 EQ can be recognized from the test data set, each EQ event is composed of a set of at least 15 consecutive "1" values. The middle point of each consecutive segment has been chosen to evaluate the behavior of these EQ events.

In Figure 7, the minimum time difference between the prediction of the EQ event and all the expected ones can be seen. The 50 h can be considered a reasonable limit in which it can be ensured that the prediction does not match with any EQ expected event. The time difference distribution performs substantially better when the values are close to the training data set; however, when it comes to a far distant SR, the register is not able to predict with the same level of accuracy.

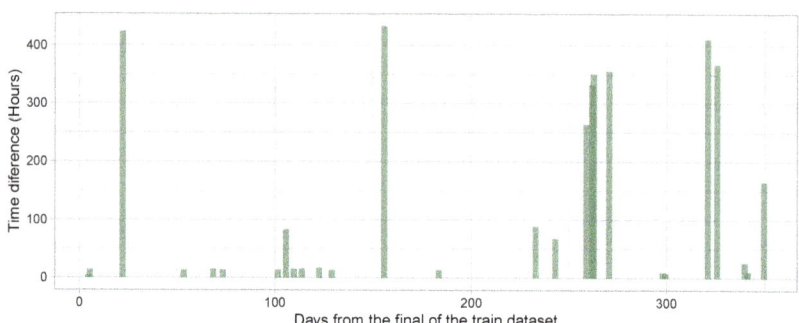

Figure 7. Relation between the time difference and the days from the last point of the training data set.

The correlation between time difference and intensity of the EQ event is worth mentioning because it means that the proposed DL methodology is effectively learning to detect EQ events with lower error values when the EQ event is more powerful. In Figure 8, the correlation between the time difference and the magnitude or distance for the EQ events with less than 50 h of time difference can be observed. It is interesting to notice that EQ events with lower magnitude values are detected with more delay than higher values, contrary to our suppositions. On the other hand, the relation between time difference and distance follows our expectation. The prediction of closer EQ events is produced sooner than for the more distant ones.

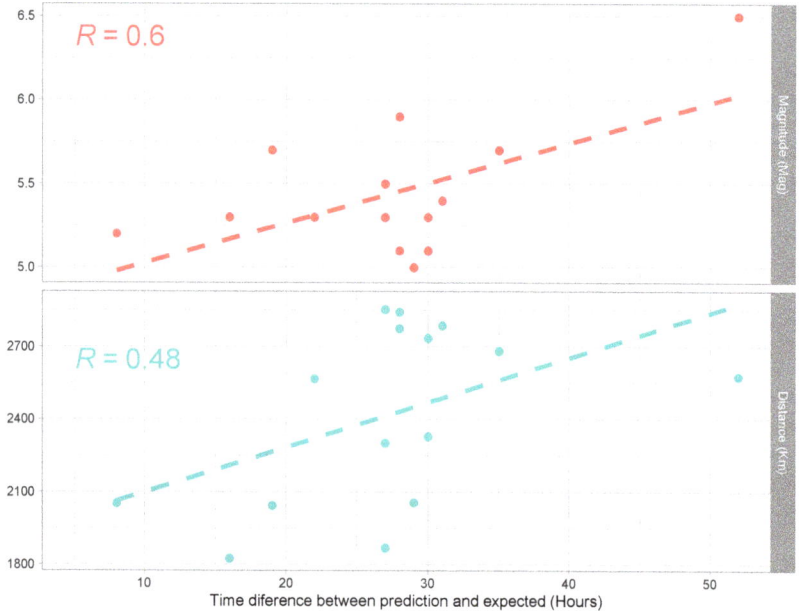

Figure 8. Correlation between the time difference and the magnitude or distance. Points: results-Dashed Line: Linear Regression.

Finally, a comparison without using the DL encoder was performed for validation purposes. In Table 3, the results are summarized. It can be seen that the LSTM methodology is not enough to detect EQ events using SR signals. The balanced accuracy is even worse than the pure random option.

Table 3. Summary of result for training and test data sets using the LSTM with the raw SR registers.

	Train Data Set	Test Data Set
Accuracy	0.5031	0.645
Sensitivity	0.07941	0.08230
Specificity	0.94543	0.91576
Pos Pred Value	0.61299	0.31974
Balanced Accuracy	0.51342	0.49903

4. Conclusions

Our work led us to conclude that the usage of DL for processing SR and for exploring their relationship with other phenomena is more than promising. We have managed to develop a novel methodology for studying the SR signal based on two aspects: the dimension reduction using VAE and the study of the SR variation with a recurrent neural network (RNN) network.

These results have gone some way towards enhancing our understanding of the relationship between EQ events and the variation of the SR signal. This work has highlighted that the codification of the SR using VAE extracts valuable information at least for detecting changes in the SR pattern. Contrary to most of the literature, in this study, we have used the central peak frequency of each of the first six SR modes, which could help find these unexpected results. Our investigation into this area is still ongoing and seems likely to confirm our hypothesis; however, due to the lack of data from other observatories to compare, this finding might not be generalized to other SR registers. To further our research, we are planning to use the information from the two sensors of our observatory and also obtain SR data from observatories that were substantially distant from the Sierra de Los Filabres one, so as to enhance the accuracy of our prediction. We will also have to construct new DL architectures in order to improve the characteristics of our EQ detector models, such as temporal convolutional network (TCN) or temporal fusion transformer (TFT).

Author Contributions: Conceptualization: C.C.-D., R.S., N.N.-C. and J.A.G.-P.; methodology: C.C.-D., R.S. and G.J.; software: C.C.-D.; hardware: J.A.G.-P. and M.F.-R.; investigation: C.C.-D., N.N.-C. and J.A.G.-P.; resources: J.A.G.-P.; writing—original draft preparation: C.C.-D. and R.S.; writing—review and editing: N.N.-C., G.J., M.F.-R. and J.A.G.-P.; visualization: C.C.-D. and R.S.; supervision: J.A.G.-P. and N.N.-C.; project administration: J.A.G.-P. All authors have read and agreed to the published version of the manuscript.

Funding: This research received funding by "Proyecto Puente 2021/001" of the University of Almeria (Spain), I+D+I Project UAL18-TIC-A025-A, the University of Almeria, and the European Regional Development Fund (FEDER). And the Ministry of Economics and Competitiveness of Spain financed this work, under Project TEC2014-60132-P, in part by Innovation, Science and Enterprise, Andalusian Regional Government through the University of Almeria, Spain and in part by the European Union FEDER Program.

Institutional Review Board Statement: Not applicable.

Informed Consent Statement: Not applicable.

Data Availability Statement: Not applicable.

Acknowledgments: We thank the Andalusian Institute of Geophysics, the Electronics, Communications, and Telemedicine TIC019 Research Group of the University of Almeria, Spain, CIAMBITAL Group. The European Regional Development Fund (FEDER) and the Technologies Electronics Department and the Telecommunication Research Institute (TELMA) from the University of Malaga.

Conflicts of Interest: The authors declare no conflict of interest.

References

1.   Koloskov, A.V.; Nickolaenko, A.P.; Yampolsky, Y.M.; Hall, C.; Budanov, O.V. Variations of global thunderstorm activity derived from the long-term Schumann resonance monitoring in the Antarctic and in the Arctic. *J. Atmos. Sol.-Terr. Phys.* **2020**, *201*, 105231. [CrossRef]
2.   Nickolaenko, A. *Resonance for Tyros*; Springer: Tokyo, Japan, 2014.
3.   Perotoni, M.B. Eigenmode prediction of the schumann resonances. *IEEE Antennas Wirel. Propag. Lett.* **2018**, *17*, 942–945. [CrossRef]
4.   Goncharov, E.S.; Lyakhov, A.N.; Loseva, T.V. 3D-FEM simulation model of the Earth-ionosphere cavity. *J. Electromagn. Waves Appl.* **2019**, *33*, 734–742. [CrossRef]
5.   Kwisanga, C.; Fourie, C.J. 3-D modeling of electromagnetic wave propagation in the uniform earth-ionosphere cavity using a commercial FDTD software package. *IEEE Trans. Antennas Propag.* **2017**, *65*, 3275–3278. [CrossRef]
6.   Pizzuti, A.; Bennett, A.; Füllekrug, M. Long-term observations of schumann resonances at portishead (UK). *Atmosphere* **2022**, *13*, 38. [CrossRef]
7.   Cano-Domingo, C.; Fernandez-Ros, M.; Novas, N.; Gazquez, J.A. Diurnal and seasonal results of the Schumann Resonance Observatory in Sierra de Filabres, Spain. *IEEE Trans. Antennas Propag.* **2021**, *69*, 6680–6690. [CrossRef]
8.   Tatsis, G.; Sakkas, A.; Christofilakis, V.; Baldoumas, G.; Chronopoulos, S.K.; Paschalidou, A.K.; Kassomenos, P.; Petrou, I.; Kostarakis, P.; Repapis, C.; et al. Correlation of local lightning activity with extra low frequency detector for Schumann Resonance measurements. *Sci. Total Environ.* **2021**, *787*, 147671. [CrossRef] [PubMed]
9.   Prácser, E.; Bozóki, T.; Sátori, G.; Williams, E.; Guha, A.; Yu, H. Reconstruction of Global Lightning Activity Based on Schumann Resonance Measurements: Model Description and Synthetic Tests. *Radio Sci.* **2019**, *54*, 254–267. [CrossRef]
10. Pazos, M.; Mendoza, B.; Sierra, P.; Andrade, E.; Rodríguez, D.; Mendoza, V.; Garduño, R. Analysis of the effects of geomagnetic storms in the Schumann Resonance station data in Mexico. *J. Atmos. Sol.-Terr. Phys.* **2019**, *193*, 105091. [CrossRef]
11. Sanfui, M.; Biswas, D. First Mode Schumann Resonance Frequency Variation During a Solar Proton Event. *Terr. Atmos. Ocean. Sci.* **2016**, *27*, 253. [CrossRef]
12. Hayakawa, M.; Izutsu, J.; Schekotov, A.Y.; Nickolaenko, A.P.; Galuk, Y.P.; Kudintseva, I.G. Anomalies of Schumann resonances as observed near Nagoya associated with two huge (M7) Tohoku offshore earthquakes in 2021. *J. Atmos. Sol.-Terr. Phys.* **2021**, *225*, 105761. [CrossRef]
13. Figueredo, P.S.; Ortega, B.M.; Pazos, M.; Osorio, D.R.; Mascote, E.A.; Mendoza, V.M.; Garduño, R. Schumann Resonance anomalies possibly associated with large earthquakes in Mexico. *Indian J. Phys.* **2021**, *95*, 1959–1966. [CrossRef]
14. Florios, K.; Contopoulos, I.; Christofilakis, V.; Tatsis, G.; Chronopoulos, S.; Repapis, C.; Tritakis, V. Pre-seismic Electromagnetic Perturbations in Two Earthquakes in Northern Greece. *Pure Appl. Geophys.* **2020**, *177*, 787–799. [CrossRef]
15. Galuk, Y.P.; Kudintseva, I.G.; Nickolaenko, A.P.; Hayakawa, M. Modifications of Schumann resonance spectra as an estimate of causative earthquake magnitude: The model treatment. *J. Atmos. Sol.-Terr. Phys.* **2020**, *209*, 105392. [CrossRef]
16. Nickolaenko, A.; Hayakawa, M.; Galuk, Y.; Kudintseva, I. *Model of Electromagnetic Manifestations of Nearby Moderate Earthquakes*; Institute of Electrical and Electronics Engineers Inc.: Kharkiv, Ukraine, 2020; pp. 954–957. [CrossRef]
17. Tritakis, V.; Contopoulos, I.; Mlynarczyk, J.; Christofilakis, V.; Tatsis, G.; Repapis, C. How Effective and Prerequisite Are Electromagnetic Extremely Low Frequency (ELF) Recordings in the Schumann Resonances Band to Function as Seismic Activity Precursors. *Atmosphere* **2022**, *13*, 185. [CrossRef]
18. Florios, K.; Contopoulos, I.; Tatsis, G.; Christofilakis, V.; Chronopoulos, S.; Repapis, C.; Tritakis, V. Possible earthquake forecasting in a narrow space-time-magnitude window. *Earth Sci. Inform.* **2021**, *14*, 349–364. [CrossRef]
19. Gazquez, J.A.; Garcia, R.M.; Castellano, N.N.; Fernandez-Ros, M.; Perea-Moreno, A.J.; Manzano-Agugliaro, F. Applied engineering using Schumann Resonance for earthquakes monitoring. *Appl. Sci.* **2017**, *7*, 1113. [CrossRef]
20. U.S. Geological Survey. Earthquake Lists, Maps, and Statistics. 2020. Available online: https://www.usgs.gov/natural-hazards/earthquake-hazards/lists-maps-and-statisti2 (accessed on 1 June 2022).
21. Kingma, D.P.; Welling, M. Auto-Encoding Variational Bayes. *arXiv* **2013**, arXiv:1312.6114.

Proceeding Paper

Probabilistic Forecasting for Oil Producing Wells Using Seq2seq Augmented Model [†]

Hadeel Afifi [1,*], Mohamed Elmahdy [2], Motaz El Saban [2,3] and Mervat Abu-Elkheir [1]

1   Faculty of Media Engineering and Technology, German University in Cairo, Cairo 11511, Egypt; mervat.abuelkheir@guc.edu.eg
2   Raisa Energy LLC, Cairo 11728, Egypt; melmahdy@raisaenergy.com (M.E.); melsaban@raisaenergy.com (M.E.S.)
3   Faculty of Computers and Artificial Intelligence, Cairo University, Cairo 11562, Egypt
*   Correspondence: hadeel.mostafa@guc.edu.eg
†   Presented at the 8th International Conference on Time Series and Forecasting, Gran Canaria, Spain, 27–30 June 2022.

Abstract: Time series forecasting is a challenging problem in the field of data mining. Deterministic forecasting has shown limitations in the field. Therefore, researchers are now more inclined towards probabilistic forecasting, which has shown a clear advantage by providing more reliable models. In this paper, we utilize seq2seq machine learning models in order to estimate prediction intervals (PIs) for a large oil production dataset. To evaluate the proposed models, Prediction Interval Coverage Probability (PICP), Prediction Interval Normalized Average Width (PINAW), and Coverage Width-based Criterion (CWC) metrics are used. Our results show that the proposed model can reliably estimate PIs for production forecasting.

Keywords: time series forecasting; prediction intervals; seq2seq; oil production

check for updates

Citation: Afifi, H.; Elmahdy, M.; El Saban, M.; Abu-Elkheir, M. Probabilistic Forecasting for Oil Producing Wells Using Seq2seq Augmented Model. *Eng. Proc.* **2022**, *18*, 16. https://doi.org/10.3390/engproc2022018016

Academic Editors: Ignacio Rojas, Hector Pomares, Olga Valenzuela, Fernando Rojas and Luis Javier Herrera

Published: 21 June 2022

Publisher's Note: MDPI stays neutral with regard to jurisdictional claims in published maps and institutional affiliations.

1. Introduction and Background

A time series is a sequence of observations that is captured through time, and forecasting is the process of estimating future trends or values based on present and past values. Time series forecasting has applications in various fields, such as electricity consumption and price forecasts [1,2], wind forecasting [3], temperature forecasting [4], and several other real-life applications [5].

There are two main forecasting methods: deterministic forecasting and probabilistic forecasting [6]. Deterministic forecasting, also known as point forecasting, is the process of predicting a single deterministic value in the future, which is then compared against the target real value. However, deterministic forecasting has shown limitations in the field because no information is available about the dispersion of the actual values around the estimated values, and it is hard to tell by how much the actual value would deviate from the predicted value, which could be especially disadvantageous for complex data. Therefore, probabilistic forecasting is being explored as a forecasting method that produces potentially substantial improvement over deterministic forecasting by providing more reliable models [7]. In probabilistic forecasting, a range under which the target value should be present is predicted. This range is referred to as Prediction interval (PI).

The goal of time series analysis is to create a model that attempts to describe the behavior of the series and predict its future values. In order to facilitate the inference of information about time series, the series should be transformed to be a stationary one [8]. Moreover, most of the statistical approaches to analyzing time series data require the series to be stationary [9]. A stationary series is loosely defined as a series which has statistical properties that do not vary over time, such as mean and variance. A strict stationary series definition is too restricting; thus, a weaker version is usually used instead [10]. In order to make the series stationary, we need to remove the trend and the seasonality. Trend represents a varying mean which can be observed in the series by the values that either keep on increasing or decreasing over time. On the other hand, seasonality is represented by a pattern which repeats itself over time, which can indicate a varying variance.

Both time series forecasting statistical and deep learning models have been discussed in the literature. Statistical models such as ARIMA are used for more precise prediction, but need experts and deep domain knowledge with vigorous analysis. On the other hand, deep learning models such as Long short-term memory (LSTM) require less knowledge in the field and less time in investigation, as there is no need to discover optimal features and parameters for the model [11]. Time series models have also adapted an attention mechanism. Attention was first introduced to solve a machine translation task [12]. The goal of attention was to overcome the shortcomings in recurrent neural networks (RNNs), as they struggled to remember long sequences. This is achieved by retaining the hidden stats at each step during decoding. Attention gives more importance to some features over the others by using weights for the features. Then, weighted sum is taken using soft max to get the sequence context for each feature.

The application of interest in this study is oil production. Oil is a traditional fossil fuels which is studied by many researchers. Even with the emergence of renewable energy such as wind, oil is still an important factor that affects the economy and plays an important role in energy investment due to the high risk, a long cost payback period and other factors accompanied by the investment in renewable energy [13].

State-of-the-art reservoir engineering forecasting techniques rely on Arps' Decline Curve Analysis (DCA) equations [14]. To estimate oil and gas reserves for current and future wells, DCA has been used as one of the prominent techniques for such a task. Arps divides the well production into two main partitions:

1. A hyperbolic curve representing the segment after an initial ramp-up period until the curve reaches a peak.
2. An exponential curve representing the decline behavior after the peak.

The curve function is summarized as follows:

$$q(t) = \begin{cases} \dfrac{q_i}{(1+bd_it)^{\frac{1}{b}}} & t < t_h \\ q_h e^{-d_f t} & t \geq t_h \end{cases} \tag{1}$$

where $q(t)$ is the oil production rate in barrels/day, q_i is the initial production, d_i is the initial decline in the hyperbolic part of the equation, t is time, and b is the hyperbolic factor controlling the rate of change of the decline. After reaching a certain decline rate d_f, the curve is represented by an exponential one using q_h, the production reached by time t_h.

Decline curve modeling has been used to predict production data where the curve is fitted to the data to estimate future points. In [15], different decline models are evaluated, namely the Exponential Decline Model (SEDM) and the Logistic Growth Model (LGM), followed by the Extended Exponential Decline Model (EEDM), the Power Law Exponential Model (PLE), Doung's Model, and the Arps Hyperbolic Decline Model.

In [16], unlike the traditional trend stationarity techniques, a new method was adopted which utilizes the Arps decline curve. The trend found in the oil datasets is removed, utilizing the Arps fitted curve in an attempt to make the series stationary.

In this study, we propose a machine learning model that estimates a prediction interval for a large dataset composed of monthly oil production data of unconventional oil-producing wells. Accurate estimation of prediction intervals can play a critical role in quantifying uncertainty and to support investment and divestment decisions. The following sections are organized as follows: Section 2 discusses the experiment details and the setups used. Section 3 describes the data. Section 4 describes the evaluation metrics used to assess the prediction intervals. Section 5 includes the results and their visualization, and presents some insights. We finally conclude in Section 6.

2. Model

The machine learning model utilized in this study is a sequence-to-sequence (seq2seq) model. seq2seq is an encoder–decoder-based deep learning model. Two LSTM models are used separated by a repeat vector, which repeats the input three times. It is used as multi-step ahead forecasting, since it forecasts several steps (three) ahead in the future (future sequence). It is followed by two layers of densely connected NN of 100 units and 1 unit applied using TimeDistributed layers.

Using the model, we test different setups, which include trend removal and attention mechanism. Quantile loss is utilized to create the upper and lower bounds of the PIs, as well as the 0.5 quantile (p50).

Trend removal is used to make the series stationary by utilizing the special trend accompanied by oil production series. First, the sequence is fitted using a hyperbolic-to-exponential Arps decline curve. Then, trend removal is simply achieved by taking the difference between the original series with the Arps fitted curve, as shown in Figure 1. Regarding the attention mechanism, we implemented a simple attention layer using keras [17] following the attention mechanism introduced in [12].

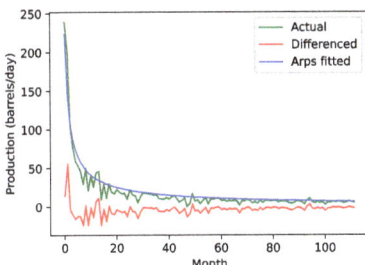

Figure 1. Trend removal by taking the difference between the actual curve and the Arps fitted curve.

3. Data

Experiments are conducted on a dataset consisting of sequences of production data obtained over successive months for producing wells from all US oil and gas basins. These sequences are represented by the number of oil barrels per day from oil horizontal wells. Only the data post the peak production are used, bearing in mind that typically, the data prior to the peak production in the reservoir engineering domain are studied independently of the rest of the data. The total number of wells in our experiment is 60,000, where 50,000 were used to train the model and 10,000 are withheld for the testing phase. The sliding window technique is leveraged to cover all months and make the input sequence consistent in size where sequences of nine consecutive months are taken; six months are used as features, and three as targets. Accordingly, the training set consists of 1,596,240 sequences and the test set consists of 46,386 sequences. We aim to estimate an interval by employing the quantile loss using the 0.5 quantile for the lower bound and the 0.95 quantile for the upper one to achieve 90% of the prediction interval.

4. Evaluation Metrics

Different metrics are utilized to evaluate the predicted prediction intervals. The most commonly used metrics are: Prediction Interval Coverage Probability (PICP) and Prediction Interval Normalized Average Width (PINAW) [2,18]. PICP is a method that measures the probability of a specific target existing within the predicted interval. It is defined as follows:

$$PICP = \frac{1}{N} \sum_{i=1}^{N} \epsilon_i \qquad (2)$$

where ϵ_i is defined as

$$\epsilon_i = \begin{cases} 1, & \text{if } x_i \in [L_i, U_i] \\ 0, & \text{if } x_i \notin [L_i, U_i] \end{cases}$$

L_i and U_i represent the lower and upper bound of the prediction interval, respectively; N is the number of samples, and x_i is the target.

The results are enhanced significantly by increasing the PICP value. However, the width of the PI has an impact on the prediction. Increasing the PI width by moving the lower and upper bounds further apart to include more targets negatively affects the prediction significance, as the decision-makers will have little information to base their decision upon. PINAW, also known in the literature as Normalized Mean Prediction Interval Width (NMPIW), was introduced to overcome this flaw; it is a metric that measures the width of the interval. It is commonly used in the literature with the investigation of probabilistic forecasting. PINAW is the average width of the several predicted PIs normalized by the width of the target, and it is defined as follows:

$$PINAW = \frac{1}{N * R} \sum_{i=1}^{N} (U_i - L_i) \tag{3}$$

where R is the range of the target; in other words, it is the maximum minus the minimum target.

Hence, the smaller the value of the PINAW, the better the results are.

It is desirable to have a narrow PI, which can be obtained by targeting a narrower interval while considering the quantiles. However, that has conflicted interests with having a large number of target points, which can be obtained by making the PI wider. Therefore, a Coverage Width-based Criterion (CWC) is introduced in the literature [19]. CWC is defined as

$$CWC = PINAW * (1 + \gamma(PICP) * e^{-\eta(PICP - \mu)}) \tag{4}$$

where $\gamma(PICP)$ is defined as follows:

$$\gamma(PICP) = \begin{cases} 1, & \text{if } PICP < \mu \\ 0, & \text{if } PICP \geq \mu \end{cases}$$

While the hyper-parameter μ is the target PICP value and η is the penalty for having a PICP value less than the target.

The value of η should be large to provide a high penalty for non-sufficiently-informative PIs. Having reached the target PICP, the CWC will have the same value as the PINAW and, in that case, it is safe to assume an informative PI. On the other hand, a smaller PICP will lead to high CWC values caused by the penalty η in the exponential term in equation 4. Hence, a small CWC is targeted.

5. Results and Discussion

The results are shown in Table 1. Adding attention only and 90% PI by choosing 0.05 and 0.95 quantiles, we are able to obtain 90.5% PICP, 9.4% for PINAW and, 0.094 CWC when the expected PICP is set to 90% and the penalty parameter is equal to 50 [20]. On the other hand, by applying trend removal only, we obtain 85.9% PICP, 6.9% PINAW, and 0.605 CWC. Additionally, when using both trend removal and attention, we get 85.4% PICP, 6.7% PINAW and 0.729 CWC. The CWC value increases with non-satisfactory PICP, which means when PICP is less than the expected value, the CWC will be significantly greater than PINAW. CWC will be equal to PINAW when the PICP value is greater than or equal to the expected value. Thus, we can deduce that the smaller the CWC value is, the better the prediction is. The very slight improvement upon using the attention can be attributed to the sequence under investigation; the sequence is not long enough to emphasize the enhancement.

Table 1. Seq2seq results for different setups in percentage using PICP, PINAW and CWC evaluation metrics. Arps in the set-up means trend is removed using Arps differencing. The μ is set to 0.9 for 90% PI and 0.8 for 80% PI.

Set-Up	PICP	PINAW	CWC $\eta = 50$
90 PI + Arps	85.9	6.9	60.5
90 PI + Attention	90.49	9.4	9.4
90 PI + Arps + Attention	85.42	6.7	72.9
90 PI	90.93	9.8	9.8
80 PI	82.16	6.4	6.4

The result in our work regarding using Arps differencing confirms the results in [16], which can be found in Table 2. From our results in Table 1, it is clear that using Arps differencing yields a narrower width compared to keeping the trend. We can also see that using Arps differencing is better than choosing a narrower PI in regards to PICP, which represents the coverage probability of the PI when both yield a narrower width, as shown in Figure 2.

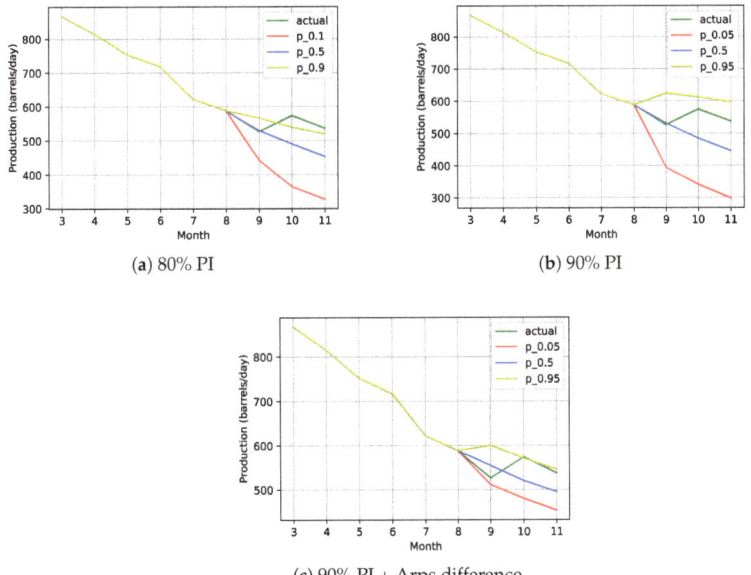

Figure 2. Arps differencing yields a narrower width compared to keeping the trend. It also has more PI coverage probability compared to a narrower width.

Table 2. Gradient Boosting for regression results in percentage for different setups using PICP and PINAW evaluation metrics in [16]. Each step represents a predicted month.

Set-Up	Step 1		Step 2		Step 3		Aggregation	
	PICP	PINAW	PICP	PINAW	PICP	PINAW	PICP	PINAW
Direct 80	82.4	4.7	81.4	6.6	81.0	8.0	81.64	5.2
Direct 90	91.1	7.9	90.7	11.0	90.6	12.9	90.80	8.6
Arps Difference Direct 90	86.6	6.1	85.1	8.3	84.1	9.7	85.23	6.5

6. Conclusions and Future Work

The proposed machine learning model uses monthly production data as features. The sliding window technique is utilized to cover all production months. The model applies the Arps differencing technique to reduce the variation in the statistical properties that make the series non-stationary. Moreover, we investigate the effect of applying the attention mechanism to the model. The seq2seq deep learning model is utilized by taking the first n production points starting from the peak production to predict a p50 production curve, as well as a prediction interval in which the next m production points observed will most likely lie. Prediction intervals are estimated besides the p50 in order to capture uncertainties lacking in the deterministic forecasts. Further investigation applying different architectures and machine learning models and observing the outcome after removing other special trends that may accompany other datasets is warranted.

Author Contributions: Conceptualization, H.A., M.E., M.E.S. and M.A.-E.; methodology, H.A., M.E. and M.E.S.; software, H.A.; validation, H.A.; resources, H.A., M.E., M.E.S.; writing original draft preparation, H.A.; writing—review and editing, M.E., M.E.S. and M.A.-E.; visualization, H.A.; supervision, M.E., M.E.S. and M.A.-E.; project administration, M.E., M.E.S. and M.A.-E. All authors have read and agreed to the published version of the manuscript.

Funding: This research received no external funding.

Data Availability Statement: Production data are publicly available but a third party service (Conduit Resources) was used to collect the scattered data from many sources.

Conflicts of Interest: The authors declare no conflict of interest.

References

1. Zeng, Y.-R.; Zeng, Y.; Choi, B.; Wang, L. Multifactor-influenced energy consumption forecasting using enhanced back-propagation neural network. *Energy* **2017**, *127*, 381–396. [CrossRef]
2. Khosravi, A.; Nahavandi, S.; Creighton, D. Quantifying uncertainties of neural network-based electricity price forecasts. *Appl. Energy* **2013**, *112*, 120–129. [CrossRef]
3. Soman, S.S.; Zareipour, H.; Malik, O.; Mandal, P. A review of wind power and wind speed forecasting methods with different time horizons. In Proceedings of the North American Power Symposium 2010, Arlington, TX, USA, 26–28 September 2010; pp. 1–8.
4. Romeu, P.; Zamora-martínezz, F.; Botella-Rocamora, P.; Pardo, J. Time-series forecasting of indoor temperature using pre-trained deep neural networks. In *Proceedings of the International Conference on Artificial Neural Networks*; Springer: Berlin/Heidelberg, Germany, 2013; pp. 451–458.
5. Gooijer, J.G.D.; Hyndman, R.J. 25 years of time series forecasting. *Int. J. Forecast.* **2006**, *22*, 443–473. [CrossRef]
6. Wang, H.; Yi, H.; Peng, J.; Wang, G.; Liu, Y.; Jiang, H.; Liu, W. Deterministic and probabilistic forecasting of photovoltaic power base don deep convolutional neural network. *Energy Convers. Manag.* **2017**, *153*, 409–422. [CrossRef]
7. Camporeale, E.; Chu, X.; Agapitov, O.; Bortnik, J. On the generation of probabilistic forecasts from deterministic models. *Space Weather* **2019**, *17*, 455–475. [CrossRef]
8. Kirchgässner, G.; Wolters, J.; Hassler, U. *Introduction to Modern Time Series Analysis*; Springer Science & Business Media: Berlin/Heidelberg, Germany, 2012.
9. Chang, F.; Huang, H.; Chan, A.H.; Man, S.S.; Gong, Y.; Zhou, H. Capturing long-memory properties in road fatality rate series by an autoregressive fractionally integrated moving average model with generalized autoregressive conditional heteroscedasticity: A case study of florida, the united states, 1975–2018. *J. Saf. Res.* **2022**, *81*, 216–224. [CrossRef] [PubMed]
10. Nason, G.P. Stationary and non-stationary time series. In *Statistics in Volcanology*; Geological Society of London: London, UK, 2006; Volume 60.
11. Cecaj, A.; Lippi, M.; Mamei, M.; Zambonelli, F. Comparing deep learning and statistical methods in forecasting crowd distribution from aggregated mobile phone data. *Appl. Sci.* **2020**, *10*, 6580. [CrossRef]
12. Bahdanau, D.; Cho, K.; Bengio, Y. Neural machine translation by jointly learning to align and translate. *arXiv* **2014**, arXiv:1409.0473.
13. Zhang, Y.-J.; Chen, M.-Y. Evaluating the dynamic performance of energy portfolios: Empirical evidence from the dea directional distance function. *Eur. J. Oper. Res.* **2018**, *269*, 64–78. [CrossRef]
14. Ma, X.; Liu, Z. Predicting the oil production using the novel multivariate nonlinear model based on arps decline model and kernel method. *Neural Comput. Appl.* **2018**, *29*, 579–591. [CrossRef]
15. Manda, P.; Nkazi, D.B. The evaluation and sensitivity of decline curve modelling. *Energies* **2020**, *13*, 2765. [CrossRef]

16. Afifi, H.; Elmahdy, M.; Saban, M.E.; Abu-Elkheir, M. Probabilistic time series forecasting for unconventional oil and gas producing wells. In Proceedings of the 2020 2nd Novel Intelligent and Leading Emerging Sciences Conference (NILES), Giza, Egypt, 24–26 October 2020; pp. 450–455.
17. The Base Layer Class. Available online: https://keras.io/api/layers/baselayer/layer-class (accessed on 30 May 2021).
18. der Meer, D.W.V.; Widén, J.; Munkhammar, J. Review on probabilistic forecasting of photovoltaic power production and electricity consumption. *Renew. Sustain. Energy Rev.* **2018**, *81*, 1484–1512. [CrossRef]
19. Khosravi, A.; Nahavandi, S.; Creighton, D.; Atiya, A.F. Lower upper bound estimation method for construction of neural network-based prediction intervals. *IEEE Trans. Neural Netw.* **2010**, *22*, 337–346. [CrossRef] [PubMed]
20. Petneházi, G. Recurrent neural networks for time series forecasting. *arXiv* **2019**, arXiv:1901.00069.

engineering proceedings

Proceeding Paper

Towards Time-Series Feature Engineering in Automated Machine Learning for Multi-Step-Ahead Forecasting [†]

Can Wang [1,*], Mitra Baratchi [1], Thomas Bäck [1], Holger H. Hoos [1], Steffen Limmer [2] and Markus Olhofer [2]

1   Leiden Institute of Advanced Computer Science, Leiden University, 2333 CA Leiden, The Netherlands; m.baratchi@liacs.leidenuniv.nl (M.B.); t.h.w.baeck@liacs.leidenuniv.nl (T.B.); h.h.hoos@liacs.leidenuniv.nl (H.H.H.)
2   Honda Research Institute Europe, 63073 Offenbach am Main, Germany; steffen.limmer@honda-ri.de (S.L.); markus.olhofer@honda-ri.de (M.O.)
*   Correspondence: c.wang@liacs.leidenuniv.nl
†   Presented at the 8th International Conference on Time Series and Forecasting, Gran Canaria, Spain, 27–30 June 2022.

Citation: Wang, C.; Baratchi, M.; Bäck, T.; Hoos, H.H.; Limmer, S.; Olhofer, M. Towards Time-Series Feature Engineering in Automated Machine Learning for Multi-Step-Ahead Forecasting. *Eng. Proc.* **2022**, *18*, 17. https://doi.org/10.3390/engproc2022018017

Academic Editors: Ignacio Rojas, Hector Pomares, Olga Valenzuela, Fernando Rojas and Luis Javier Herrera

Published: 21 June 2022

Publisher's Note: MDPI stays neutral with regard to jurisdictional claims in published maps and institutional affiliations.

Abstract: Feature engineering is an essential step in the pipelines used for many machine learning tasks, including time-series forecasting. Although existing AutoML approaches partly automate feature engineering, they do not support specialised approaches for applications on time-series data such as multi-step forecasting. Multi-step forecasting is the task of predicting a sequence of values in a time-series. Two kinds of approaches are commonly used for multi-step forecasting. A typical approach is to apply one model to predict the value for the next time step. Then the model uses this predicted value as an input to forecast the value for the next time step. Another approach is to use multi-output models to make the predictions for multiple time steps of each time-series directly. In this work, we demonstrate how automated machine learning can be enhanced with feature engineering techniques for multi-step time-series forecasting. Specifically, we combine a state-of-the-art automated machine learning system, auto-sklearn, with tsfresh, a library for feature extraction from time-series. In addition to optimising machine learning pipelines, we propose to optimise the size of the window over which time-series data are used for predicting future time-steps. This is an essential hyperparameter in time-series forecasting. We propose and compare (i) auto-sklearn with automated window size selection, (ii) auto-sklearn with tsfresh features, and (iii) auto-sklearn with automated window size selection and tsfresh features. We evaluate these approaches with statistical techniques, machine learning techniques and state-of-the-art automated machine learning techniques, on a diverse set of benchmarks for multi-step time-series forecasting, covering 20 synthetic and real-world problems. Our empirical results indicate a significant potential for improving the accuracy of multi-step time-series forecasting by using automated machine learning in combination with automatically optimised feature extraction techniques.

Keywords: automated machine learning; machine learning; time-series forecasting

1. Introduction

Time-series (TS) data, such as electrocardiograms, music, exchange rates, and energy consumption, is everywhere in our daily life and business world. Multi-step-ahead forecasting is an important task in time-series modeling with many industrial applications, such as crude oil price forecasting [1] and flood forecasting [2]. Both ML models [3,4] and statistical models [5,6] are used for this purpose. Creating an ML pipeline for such TS data analysis is, however, difficult for many domain experts with limited machine learning expertise, due to the complexity of the data sets and the ML models.

To reduce the complexity of creating machine learning pipelines, automated machine learning (AutoML) research has recently focused on developing algorithms that can automatically design ML pipelines optimised for a given data set without human input [7,8]. The components in a pipeline may include a data cleaning component, feature engineering component, ML model component, and ensemble construction component. While there has been work proposed in the past that used AutoML for TS analysis [9], the current AutoML systems do not support specialised techniques used for designing machine learning pipelines for TS data, such as TS feature engineering. As demonstrated by Christ et al. [10], including such specialized techniques for extracting TS features or feature importance filtering could significantly improve the accuracy of ML models. Therefore, our goal in this paper is to study if extending AutoML systems by including such techniques can improve the quality of automatically generated machine learning pipelines for multi-step forecasting.

This paper presents a study of AutoML for time-series multi-step TS forecasting implemented through (i) multi-output modeling, and (ii) recursive modeling. We combine the state-of-the-art AutoML system of auto-sklearn with tsfresh, a well-known library for feature extraction from TS. We implement three AutoML variants and state-of-the-art baseline models, including auto-sklearn, SVM, GBM, N-BEATS, and Auto-Keras. More specifically, our contributions are as follows:

- We adapt the auto-sklearn AutoML system to the task of forecasting and introduce three AutoML forecasting variants for multi-step-ahead TS forecasting.
- We demonstrate the importance of feature selection and window size selection in forecasting problems and further show that by incorporating such approaches, our TS AutoML techniques outperform available AutoML methods.
- We evaluate our methods on 20 benchmarking data sets from 20 different categories and against the baselines. We found that our proposed AutoML method outperformed the traditional ML baseline on 14 out of 20 data sets and N-BEATS on 15 out of 20 data sets.

The remainder of this paper is structured as follows: Section 2 covers related work on TS forecasting, TS feature engineering and AutoML. Section 3 introduces the problem statement of AutoML for multi-step TS forecasting. In Section 4, the methodology of our newly proposed models is explained. Section 5 presents the results of the empirical performance comparison of different ML models for multi-step TS forecasting. A summary of our work and directions for future work are given in Section 6.

2. Related Work

Multi-step TS Forecasting: different ML methods and statistical methods have been used for both single-step and multi-step TS analysis in the past few decades [11]. These include artificial neural networks [3], support vector machines [4], gradient boosting machine [12], random forest [13], auto-regressive moving average models [5], and exponential smoothing models [6]. To use these models for multi-step forecasting, two major approaches are used: direct and recursive strategies [14]. The first of these uses multi-output regression models to predict multiple TS steps into the future directly or use multiple models (one for each time step) to make multi-step forecasting. Multi-output models show good performance and require less computational resources than training multiple models to realise multi-step forecasting [15]. The second approach uses a single model recursively, using the predicted values as an additional input to forecast the next step. In this case, the error in the prediction may be accumulated [14]. Recursive strategies only require one model, which saves significant computational time [14]. Other methods based on these two approaches are also used, such as the DirRec strategy [16], which combines the recursive strategies and direct strategies.

TS feature engineering: Feature engineering is an essential component in ML pipelines. Feature extraction methods have also been used for TS analysis tasks [17,18]. There are a number of TS feature extraction libraries that are widely used for TS analysis, including tsfresh [19], Catch22 [20], and hctsa [21]. Catch22 extracts a selected list of the 22 most useful features of the 4791 features of hctsa from a TS. Extracting features with Catch22 is more computationally efficient than hctsa, with only a 7% reduction in accuracy on average. In the following, we use tsfresh, which extracts more than 700 TS features in parallel and has previously shown strong performance [19], since it does not require huge computational resources like hctsa, or suffers from an accuracy reduction like Catch22.

AutoML: AutoML systems have been used in many domains, such as image classification [22], language processing [23] and energy consumption forecasting [9]. However, TS features are not well-studied in AutoML systems. In our earlier work [9], we studied AutoML for short-term load forecasting demonstrating the competitive performance of AutoML systems. However, we did not investigate the use of TS features. In another work [24], we studied AutoML with TS features for single-step TS forecasting. Our experimental results indicate that AutoML with TS features can further improve the accuracy of AutoML systems. In this work, we focus on studying how to improve the performance of AutoML systems on multi-step forecasting tasks by using TS features. Many AutoML systems have been recently developed, including Auto-sklearn [25], AutoGluon [8] and Auto-Keras [26] . Auto-sklearn is used in our experiments, since it supports various algorithms (e.g., SVMs) that are not available in the other systems, and it is easy to extend. Auto-Keras is used to create a deep learning baseline in our experiments.

3. Problem Statement

Given a univariate TS $\mathbf{x} = [x_1, \ldots, x_i]$ composed of i observations. We are interested in predicting the next k values $\mathbf{x} = [x_{i+1}, \ldots, x_{i+k}]$, where $k > 1$ denotes the forecasting window. Usually not all the data points show the same influence on the predictions of $[x_{i+1}, \ldots, x_{i+k}]$. The more recent data points tend to be more important. Specifically, given a TS segment $[x_{i-w+1}, \ldots, x_i]$, we are interested in forecasting of $[x_{i+1}, \ldots, x_{i+k}]$; the window size w indicates how much historical data are used to make the prediction. In our previous work [24], we found that the window size w plays an essential role in single-step TS forecasting; specifically, if an ML model gets too much or too little information, this may reduce the model's performance. Here, we extend the automated window size selection technique to multi-step forecasting. Besides this, we use tsfresh to automatically extract features from TS data within these windows.

AutoML for Multi-Step TS Forecasting

We define the *Combined Algorithm Selection and Hyperparameter optimisation (CASH)* problem [27] for multi-output TS forecasting as the following joint optimisation problem: Given a TS data set $\mathbf{x} = [x_1, \ldots, x_n]$ that is split into $\mathbf{x}_{train}$ and $\mathbf{x}_{valid}$, we are interested in building an optimised model using $\mathbf{x}_{train}$ by minimising loss on $\mathbf{x}_{valid}$. Formally, we define the **automated TS forecasting problem** as:

Let $\mathcal{A} = \{A^{(1)}, \ldots, A^{(k)}\}$ *be a set of algorithms with associated hyperparameter spaces* $\Lambda^{(1)}, \ldots, \Lambda^{(k)}$. *Let* $\mathbf{w} = \{w^{(1)}, \ldots, w^{(l)}\}$ *be the set of the possible window sizes. Furthermore, let* $\mathbf{x}_{train}$ *be a training set, and* $\mathbf{x}_{valid}$ *be a validation set. Finally, let* $\mathcal{L}(A_\lambda^{(i)}, w^{(j)}, \mathbf{x}_{train}, \mathbf{x}_{valid})$ *denote the loss that algorithm* $A^{(i)}$ *achieves on* $\mathbf{x}_{valid}$ *when trained on* $\mathbf{x}_{train}$ *with hyperparameters* $\lambda \in \Lambda^{(i)}$ *and window size* $w^{(j)}$. *Then the automated TS forecasting problem is to find the window size, algorithm, and hyperparameter setting that minimises this loss, i.e., to determine:*

$$(A^*, \lambda^*, w^*) \in \underset{A \in \mathcal{A}, \lambda \in \Lambda, w \in \mathbf{w}}{\arg\min} \; \mathcal{L}(A_\lambda, w, \mathbf{x}_{train}, \mathbf{x}_{valid}) \tag{1}$$

4. Methodology

This section presents the two multi-step forecasting techniques and the AutoML technique enhanced with TS features we use later in our experiments.

4.1. Multi-Step Forecasting

Recursive strategy: In this strategy, given a univariate TS $\mathbf{x} = [x_1, \ldots, x_n]$ composed of n observations, a model f is trained to perform a single-step ahead forecast:

$\hat{x}_{i+1} = f(x_{i-w+1}, ..., x_i)$ with $i \in \{w, ..., n-1\}$. Then we use $\hat{x}_{i+1}$ as an input to predict x_{i+2}. $\hat{x}_{i+2} = f(x_{i-w+2}, ..., x_i, \hat{x}_{i+1})$ with $i \in \{w, ..., n-1\}$. We continue recursively, making new predictions in this manner until we forecast x_{i+k}.

Direct Multi-Output strategy: A multi-output strategy has been proposed by Taieb and Bontempi [28] to solve multi-step TS forecasting tasks. In this strategy, one multi-output model f is learned, i.e., $[\hat{x}_{i+1}, ..., \hat{x}_{i+k}] = f(x_{i-w+1}, ..., x_i)$ with $i \in \{w, ..., n-k\}$.

4.2. Auto-Sklearn with TS Feature Engineering

In this work, we study how we can extend auto-sklearn [25] to perform automatic feature extraction on TS data. Originally, the pipelines constructed by auto-sklearn include a preprocessor, feature preprocessor and ML components. The ensemble construction used in auto-sklearn uses a greedy algorithm to build the ensembles. The workflow of auto-sklearn is illustrated in Figure 1. Auto-sklearn has a powerful feature preprocessor component. However, it does not support any specialised TS feature extractors. In our work, we use our newly proposed TS feature extractors in the search space instead of the feature extractor in auto-sklearn. Automated feature extraction in this case considers both the selection of the window size and extraction of relevant features. Therefore, we propose three variants of auto-sklearn that are specially designed for TS forecasting tasks by replacing the feature extractors of auto-sklearn with one of the following.

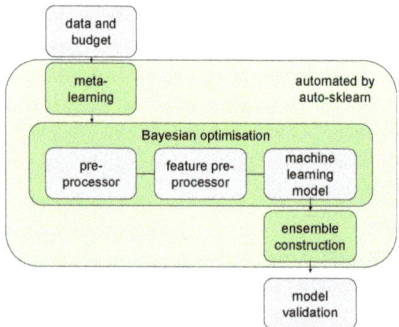

Figure 1. Workflow of auto-sklearn. Auto-sklearn uses Bayesian optimisation to search the space of ML pipelines, including a preprocessor, feature preprocessor and ML components.

1. **Auto-sklearn with automated window size selection (W):** the first variant of auto-sklearn for TS forecasting optimises the window size w. The TS $\mathbf{x} = [x_{i-w+1}, ..., x_i]$ are used to train a model that predicts $[x_{i+1}, ..., x_{i+k}]$.
2. **Auto-sklearn with tsfresh features (T):** the second variant of auto-sklearn extracts tsfresh TS features from the TS segment $\mathbf{x} = [x_{i-w+1}, ..., x_i]$ to predict $[x_{i+1}, ..., x_{i+k}]$. In this case, the window size w is predefined and fixed. The TS features $g(\mathbf{x}) = g([x_{i-w+1}, ..., x_i])$ are calculated using the TS feature extractor g. Feature importance is calculated using the Benjamini-Hochberg procedure [29] to select the important features. The Benjamini-Hochberg procedure selects important features for each step in the TS separately. We then use the union of all the important features to predict $[x_{i+1}, ..., x_{i+k}]$.
3. **Auto-sklearn with automated window size selection and tsfresh features (WT):** this approach combines the two previously mentioned approaches. Both window size w and the TS extractor g are optimised in this variant.

5. Experimental Results

Our key empirical results are based on aggregate performance over 20 data sets and 8 models. More detailed descriptions of the data sets and models are described in the section.

5.1. Data Sets

The open-source datasets from CompEngine [30] are used in our experiments. CompEngine is a TS data engine containing 197 types of data sets comprising 29,514 in total. These data sets include both real-world and synthetic data sets. We chose ten real-world and ten synthetic data sets from different categories. These are comprised of the following 20 categories: Audio: Animal sounds, Human speech, Music; Ecology: Zooplankton growth; Economics: Macroeconomics, Microeconomics; Finance: Crude oil prices, Exchange rate, Gas prices; Medical: Electrocardiography ECG; Flow: Driven pendulum with dissipation, Duffing-van der Pol Oscillator, Driven van der Pol oscillator, Duffing two-well oscillator, Diffusionless Lorenz Attractor; Stochastic Process: Autoregressive with noise, Correlated noise, Moving average process, Nonstationary autoregressive, Random walk.

Since there are usually more than one data set in each category, we choose the first one of each category. We split every data set into 67% training and 33% test set, based on temporal order, since the data sets are TS.

5.2. Experimental Setup

All the experiments were executed on 8 cores of an Intel Xeon E5-2683 CPU (2.10 GHz) with 10 GB RAM. In the experiments, version 0.8.0 of auto-sklearn and version 0.16.1 of tsfresh were used. To evaluate the quality of an ML pipeline, we used quantified error/accuracy. *RMSE* was used as a performance metric in the optimisation. The maximum evaluation time for one ML pipeline was set to 20 min wall-clock time. The time budget for every AutoML optimisation on each data set was set to 3 h wall-clock time. In these experiments, we used hold-out validation (training:validation = 67:33), the default validation technique in auto-sklearn. The split was carried out only on the training data, such that the optimisation process never sees the test data. However, we did not shuffle the data set in order to preserve the temporal structure of the TS data. All remaining choices were left at their default settings. Since experiments are very time-consuming, we used bootstrapping to create distributions of performance results in order to investigate their variability. Every experiment was run 25 times. We then randomly sampled 5 out of the 25 results and selected the model with the lowest *RMSE* on the training set out of these five models and reported the *RMSE* on the test set. We repeated this process 100 times per model and data set. The distributions we showed are based on these 100 values.

We compared the AutoML methods, including Auto-Keras, auto-sklearn and our proposed variants, with traditional ML baselines and N-BEATS. Both recursive and multi-output techniques are used in the ML baselines (GBM and SVM). All other models use the multi-output approach.

5.3. Baselines

- **Gradient Boosting Machine (GBM):** Gradient Boosting Machine is a classical ML model used for TS analysis tasks that has shown promising performance in the M3, M4 competitions [31]. For hyperparameter optimisation, we performed a random search on GBM with 30 iterations and window size $w = 100$ [32]. In this case, the search space is the same as the search space of GBM in auto-sklearn. In this experiment, we did not split the training set into the training set and validation sets.

- **Support vector machine (SVM):** SVM is another classical ML model that has been used for TS forecasting (e.g., [13]). Similar to GBM experiments, we use 30 iterations of random search and window size $w = 100$. The search space is the same as the search space of SVM in auto-sklearn.

- **N-BEATS:** N-BEATS [33] uses fully-connected layers with residual links to improve 3% over the winner of the M4 competition, which demonstrates state-of-the-art performance. We used the default hyperparameter settings in the implementation provided by Oreshkin et al. [33] and the bootstrapping approach mentioned in Section 5 to create distributions of results. The number of epochs was set to 500.

- **Auto-Keras:** Auto-Keras [26] is a neural architecture search system that uses Bayesian optimisation to search for high-performance neural network architectures. Some neural network units available in its search space (e.g., LSTM, GRU), have been used for TS forecasting (see, e.g., [34,35]). Vanilla Auto-Keras does not support multi-output models. To deal with multi-step forecasting tasks, we designed our new search space using three types of blocks available in Auto-Keras: Input block, RNN Block and Regression Head (see Figure 2). The RNN Block is the critical component in our networks. We use RNN as a baseline, as it has been recently studied in the literature on TS forecasting (see, e.g., [34,36]). Several hyperparameters need to be considered for this block, including bidirectionality, the number of layers and layer type (LSTM or GRU). Auto-Keras cannot choose the window size w automatically. We manually preprocessed the data with window size $w = 100$. We used Bayesian optimisation for architecture search. The number of epochs was set to 100, and we left the remaining settings of Auto-Keras at their default values.
- **Vanilla auto-sklearn (VA):** We manually preprocessed the data with window size $w = 100$ and then fed it to the auto-sklearn. The time budget for the optimisation was set to 3 h.

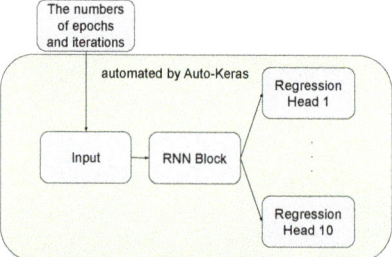

Figure 2. Workflow of our customised search space of Auto-Keras for TS forecasting. The input data flows through the RNN Block. Hyperparameters, such as the number of layers and learning rate, will be optimised during the search. The Regression Head then generates output based on the information from the RNN Block.

5.4. Our Methods

- **Auto-sklearn with automated window size selection (W):** For the W variant, we did not need to manually preprocess the data, since the window size w is selected automatically. The window size ranges from 50 to 200.
- **Auto-sklearn with tsfresh features (T):** In the T variant, the TS feature extractor tsfresh was used as an internal component of auto-sklearn. Auto-sklearn used these TS features as input data to search over ML pipelines. The window size was set to $w = 100$.
- **Auto-sklearn with automated window size selection and tsfresh features (WT):** In WT, we set the window size w to range from 50 to 200. The TS features were extracted from these input data.

Tables 1 and 2 compare the performance achieved by different methods in terms of *RMSE* on the test set. Table 1, shows the results for traditional ML baseline models, while Table 2 presents the results for AutoML techniques and N-BEATS. To present the results in these tables, we calculated the statistical significance of the results by the non-parametric Mann–Whitney U-test [37] with a standard significance level set to 0.05. The bold-faced entries show the lowest mean *RMSE* achieved on a given data set, and the ∗ means the *RMSE* is statistically best.

Table 1. *RMSE* on test set acquired from traditional ML baselines. GBM-recursive, GBM-multiout, SVM-recursive, and SVM multioutput win on 6, 6, 0, and 8 out of 20 data sets respectively.

Dataset	RMSE (GBM -Recursive)	RMSE (GBM -Multioutput)	RMSE (SVM -Recursive)	RMSE (SVM -Multioutput)
Autoregre noise	**0.458890**	0.461558	0.484516	0.459410
Correlated noise	1.872176	**1.862137**	2.012916	2.004572
Lorenz Attractor	0.102323	**0.088045**	0.188223	0.152384
Pendulum	0.112041	0.104519	0.172118	**0.035350**
Driven oscillator	**0.121606**	0.124701	0.231661	0.224206
Two-well oscillator	0.033950	0.032462	0.075318	**0.007772**
Duffing oscillator	0.025830	0.021330	0.075308	**0.013762**
Moving average	0.629791	0.627176	0.641453	**0.622803**
Nonstationary	6.049796	**5.987631**	6.796246	6.448516
Random walk	**12.766561**	13.690753	30.594553	25.654821
Crude oil prices	28.215008	32.909490	42.278003	**20.867176**
ECG	**79.209558**	103.881034	128.420743	126.1525026
Exchange rate	0.006880	0.006823	0.028571	**0.005433**
Gas prices	102.819893	**100.612148**	166.021626	172.605827
Human speech	0.059365	**0.054838**	0.085002	0.057631
Macroeconomics	779.515969	806.704035	713.073168	**713.363569**
Microeconomics	**647.432403**	705.051879	3500.094238	3865.235605
Music	0.082864	0.076047	0.068341	**0.052978**
Tropical sound	0.009468	**0.006285**	0.034925	0.008820
Zooplankton	**312.033380**	385.377067	319.839856	320.049399

Table 2. *RMSE* on test set acquired from different AutoML methods including vanilla auto-sklearn (VA), our proposed variants (W, T, and WT), Auto-Keras and the state-of-the-art method N-BEATS. The accuracy of N-BEATS, Auto-Keras, VA, W, T, WT are statistically significant on 5, 0, 2, 8, 3, and 3 out of 20 data sets, respectively.

	RMSE (N-BEATS)	RMSE (Auto-Keras)	RMSE (VA)	RMSE (W)	RMSE (T)	RMSE (WT)
Autoregre noise	0.491133 ± 0.001470	0.468036	0.454026 ± 0.000502	**0.453002 ± 0.000137 ***	0.464252 ± 0.000286	0.463611 ± 0.000302
Correlated noise	1.949831 ± 0.012037	1.848905	1.832344 ± 0.003727	**1.822611 ± 0.0009631 ***	1.841418 ± 0.000878	1.843744 ± 0.000858
Lorenz Attractor	0.076379 ± 0.007143	1.248956	0.050628 ± 0.009272	**0.039705 ± 0.003994 ***	0.140621 ± 0.081695	0.249406 ± 0.012638
Pendulum	0.113806 ± 0.010232	0.512860	0.055285 ± 0.020322	**0.021416 ± 0.022933 ***	0.154815 ± 0.100197	0.177645 ± 0.048287
Driven oscillator	0.101795 ± 0.006627	0.232306	0.094895 ± 0.010350	0.085300 ± 0.005317	**0.061014 ± 0.001292 ***	0.149184 ± 0.003854

Table 2. *Cont.*

	RMSE (N-BEATS)	RMSE (Auto-Keras)	RMSE (VA)	RMSE (W)	RMSE (T)	RMSE (WT)
Two-well oscillator	0.010395 ± 0.000897 *	0.201339	0.032185 ± 0.006572	0.033103 ± 0.000724	0.019638 ± 0.001726	0.057722 ± 0.009568
Duffing oscillator	0.004316 ± 0.001006 *	0.500197	0.011301 ± 0.011301	0.010777 ± 0.000844	0.020875 ± 0.000919	0.019648 ± 0.001661
Moving average	0.662554 ± 0.002471	0.610291	0.615606 ± 0.000661	0.614169 ± 0.000080	0.609240 ± 0.000326	**0.608775 ± 0.000241 ***
Nonstationary	6.253612 ± 0.034291	9.888761	**5.775404 ± 0.048135 ***	5.783582 ± 0.012927 *	6.720498 ± 0.023618	6.826646 ± 0.022398
Random walk	3.099224 ± 0.058073 *	19.385011	13.478998 ± 0.172438	13.240742 ± 0.138406	14.765951 ± 0.843100	15.411989 ± 0.368020
Crude oil prices	32.199970 ± 0.846056 *	44.305246	34.766214 ± 0.702608	34.669098 ± 0.374047	33.134671 ± 0.228864	35.373982 ± 0.209542
ECG	143.617378 ± 7.120182	149.577016	**96.577900 ± 3.258370 ***	102.0317220 ± 14.282081	104.228003 ± 1.6258357	103.260689 ± 2.110540
Exchange rate	0.004831 ± 0.001875	0.013859	0.006049 ± 0.000130	**0.003627 ± 0.001326 ***	0.006886 ± 0.000237	0.004569 ± 0.001505
Gas prices	59.147486 ± 3.122861 *	126.112217	118.033606 ± 25.754493	101.514037 ± 0.021932	109.711360 ± 4.170307	121.133289 ± 1.387935
Human speech	0.089423 ± 0.001085	0.065285	0.061140 ± 0.001988	0.061280 ± 0.002512	0.058722 ± 0.000191	**0.057920 ± 0.000288 ***
Macroeconomics	755.905175 ± 11.131619	711.622796	791.586127 ± 37.469871	766.036513 ± 31.082581	682.959633 ± 3.559769	**662.098158 ± 24.511173 ***
Microeconomics	2179.375169 ± 6643.906258	5545.979242	805.637017 ± 61.049526	**733.760632 ± 12.795080 ***	1295.531031 ± 34.305972	1348.425680 ± 264.961810
Music	0.078767 ± 0.001062	0.091060	0.085224 ± 0.005985	0.072422 ± 0.002119	**0.068895 ± 0.000906 ***	0.084715 ± 0.002951
Tropical sound	0.010038 ± 0.000203	0.010660	0.008483 ± 0.000072	**0.008407 ± 0.000013 ***	0.008930 ± 0.000029	0.008717 ± 0.000044
Zooplankton	306.329197 ± 2.591637	310.290963	297.091504 ± 2.118263	282.485896 ± 1.234165	**278.597102 ± 1.237304 ***	301.160979 ± 4.331423

5.5. Research Questions

Q1: How do recursive and multi-output techniques compare in terms of accuracy?

To determine the answer to this question, we compared the recursive and multi-output versions of GBM and SVM algorithms. Among the baselines we consider, N-BEATS as described in the original work is not a recursive model. Therefore, we do not consider it for this analysis. Looking at Table 1, we generally observe that GBM-multioutput performs better than GBM-recursive on 12 out of 20 data sets, while SVM-multioutput outperforms SVM-recursive on 17 out of 20 data sets in terms of *RMSE*. As we have observed that multi-output models tend to perform better, which is in line with the results from [14]. Therefore, we only use the multi-output technique in our next experiments.

Q2: To what extent can AutoML techniques (Auto-Keras, auto-sklearn, and our variants) beat the traditional baselines (GBM, SVM)?

Looking at Tables 1 and 2, one can compare the performance achieved by different methods in terms of *RMSE* on the test set. We observe that Auto-Keras beats all the traditional ML baseline models (GBM-recursive, GBM-multioutput, SVM-recursive, and SVM-multioutput) on 4 out of 20 data sets. Vanilla auto-sklearn outperforms all the traditional ML baselines on 8 out of 20 data sets. Our three variants W, T, WT show lower error than all the traditional ML baselines on 10, 5, and 5 out of 20 data sets, respectively. The best AutoML (W) outperforms the best traditional ML baseline (SVM-multioutput) on 14 out of 20 data sets.

Q3: To what extent can AutoML techniques beat N-BEATS?

Looking at Table 2, we observe that the best AutoML (W) outperforms N-BEATS on 14 out of 20 data sets. For other AutoML techniques we observe that Auto-Keras, VA, T, and WT beat N-BEATS on 5, 12, 11, and 10 out of 20 data sets, respectively. AutoML methods that are based on standard machine learning are beating this neural networks based model.

6. Conclusions

In this paper, we extend AutoML for multi-step TS forecasting with TS features. We found that AutoML can achieve significantly higher accuracy than the traditional ML baselines on 14 out of 20 data sets in terms of *RMSE*. Although N-BEATS performs better than Auto-Keras and vanilla auto-sklearn on many data sets, our AutoML TS variants still managed to beat it on 14 out of 20 data sets. We found that the multi-output technique tends to perform better with the same budget than the recursive technique in the multi-step TS forecasting tasks. Overall, these results clearly demonstrate that the use of AutoML techniques and multi-output strategies for multi-step TS forecasting is promising.

Interesting avenues for future work include AutoML for online learning and TS classification. Most AutoML systems focus on a stable data set. Characteristics of TS data might change over time and consequently, the best configuration of data sets may vary over time. We see potential value in extending AutoML on evolving data streams. Furthermore, in TS classification typically classification with a fixed-sized sliding window has been studied. However, the best window size might not be easily determined. Our automated window size selection technique may help to improve the performance of the classification tasks.

Author Contributions: Conceptualization, C.W., M.B. and H.H.H.; methodology, C.W., M.B. and H.H.H.; software, C.W.; validation, C.W.; formal analysis, C.W.; investigation, C.W., M.B. and H.H.H.; resources, C.W., M.B. and H.H.H.; data curation, C.W.; writing—original draft preparation, C.W.; writing—review and editing, M.B., T.B., H.H.H., S.L. and M.O.; visualization, C.W.; supervision, M.B., T.B., H.H.H., S.L. and M.O.; project administration, T.B., H.H.H., S.L. and M.O.; funding acquisition, T.B., H.H.H., S.L. and M.O. All authors have read and agreed to the published version of the manuscript.

Funding: This work is part of the research programme C2D–Horizontal Data Science for Evolving Content with project name DACCOMPLI and project number 628.011.002, which is (partly) financed by the Netherlands Organisation for Scientific Research (NWO).

Institutional Review Board Statement: Not applicable.

Informed Consent Statement: Not applicable.

Data Availability Statement: The data sets used in our experiments are available in https://github.com/wangcan04/AutoML-multistep-forecasting, accessed on 1 June 2022.

Conflicts of Interest: The authors declare no conflict of interest.The funders had no role in the design of the study; in the collection, analyses, or interpretation of data; in the writing of the manuscript, or in the decision to publish the results.

Abbreviations

The following abbreviations are used in this manuscript:

TS	Time-series
ML	Machine Learning
AutoML	Automated Machine Learning

References

1. Xiong, T.; Bao, Y.; Hu, Z. Beyond one-step-ahead forecasting: Evaluation of alternative multi-step-ahead forecasting models for crude oil prices. *Energy Econ.* **2013**, *40*, 405–415. [CrossRef]
2. Chang, F.J.; Chiang, Y.M.; Chang, L.C. Multi-step-ahead neural networks for flood forecasting. *Hydrol. Sci. J.* **2007**, *52*, 114–130. [CrossRef]
3. Chen, P.; Liu, S.; Shi, C.; Hooi, B.; Wang, B.; Cheng, X. NeuCast: Seasonal Neural Forecast of Power Grid Time Series. In Proceedings of the Twenty-Seventh International Joint Conference on Artificial Intelligence, IJCAI 2018, Stockholm, Sweden, 13–19 July 2018; pp. 3315 3321.
4. Nie, H.; Liu, G.; Liu, X.; Wang, Y. Hybrid of ARIMA and SVMs for Short-Term Load Forecasting. *Energy Procedia* **2012**, *16*, 1455–1460. [CrossRef]
5. Box, G.E.; Jenkins, G.M.; Reinsel, G.C.; Ljung, G.M. *Time Series Analysis: Forecasting and Control*; John Wiley & Sons: Hoboken, NJ, USA, 2015.
6. Nedellec, R.; Cugliari, J.; Goude, Y. GEFCom2012: Electric load forecasting and backcasting with semi-parametric models. *Int. J. Forecast.* **2014**, *30*, 375–381. [CrossRef]
7. Guyon, I.; Sun-Hosoya, L.; Boullé, M.; Escalante, H.J.; Escalera, S.; Liu, Z.; Jajetic, D.; Ray, B.; Saeed, M.; Sebag, M.; et al. Analysis of the AutoML Challenge Series 2015–2018. In *Automated Machine Learning*; Springer: Berlin, Germany, 2019; pp. 177–219.
8. Shi, X.; Mueller, J.; Erickson, N.; Li, M.; Smola, A. Multimodal AutoML on Structured Tables with Text Fields. In Proceedings of the 8th ICML Workshop on Automated Machine Learning (AutoML), Virtual, 23–24 June 2021.
9. Wang, C.; Bäck, T.; Hoos, H.H.; Baratchi, M.; Limmer, S.; Olhofer, M. Automated Machine Learning for Short-term Electric Load Forecasting. In Proceedings of the 2019 IEEE Symposium Series on Computational Intelligence (SSCI), Xiamen, China, 6–9 December 2019; pp. 314–321.
10. Christ, M.; Kempa-Liehr, A.W.; Feindt, M. Distributed and parallel time series feature extraction for industrial big data applications. *arXiv* **2016**, arXiv:1610.07717.
11. Hong, T.; Fan, S. Probabilistic electric load forecasting: A tutorial review. *Int. J. Forecast.* **2016**, *32*, 914–938. [CrossRef]
12. Li, L.; Dai, S.; Cao, Z.; Hong, J.; Jiang, S.; Yang, K. Using improved gradient-boosted decision tree algorithm based on Kalman filter (GBDT-KF) in time series prediction. *J. Supercomput.* **2020**, *76*, 6887–6900. [CrossRef]
13. Candanedo, L.M.; Feldheim, V.; Deramaix, D. Data driven prediction models of energy use of appliances in a low-energy house. *Energy Build.* **2017**, *140*, 81–97. [CrossRef]
14. Taieb, S.B.; Bontempi, G.; Atiya, A.F.; Sorjamaa, A. A review and comparison of strategies for multi-step ahead time series forecasting based on the NN5 forecasting competition. *Expert Syst. Appl.* **2012**, *39*, 7067–7083. [CrossRef]
15. Ferreira, L.B.; da Cunha, F.F. Multi-step ahead forecasting of daily reference evapotranspiration using deep learning. *Comput. Electron. Agric.* **2020**, *178*, 105728. [CrossRef]
16. Sorjamaa, A.; Lendasse, A. Time series prediction using DirRec strategy. In Proceedings of the ESANN 2006, 14th European Symposium on Artificial Neural Networks, Bruges, Belgium, 26–28 April 2006; pp. 143–148.
17. Coyle, D.; Prasad, G.; McGinnity, T.M. A time-series prediction approach for feature extraction in a brain-computer interface. *IEEE Trans. Neural Syst. Rehabil. Eng.* **2005**, *13*, 461–467. [CrossRef] [PubMed]
18. Phinyomark, A.; Quaine, F.; Charbonnier, S.; Serviere, C.; Tarpin-Bernard, F.; Laurillau, Y. Feature extraction of the first difference of EMG time series for EMG pattern recognition. *Comput. Methods Programs Biomed.* **2014**, *117*, 247–256. [CrossRef] [PubMed]
19. Christ, M.; Braun, N.; Neuffer, J.; Kempa-Liehr, A.W. Time series feature extraction on basis of scalable hypothesis tests (tsfresh—A python package). *Neurocomputing* **2018**, *307*, 72–77. [CrossRef]
20. Lubba, C.H.; Sethi, S.S.; Knaute, P.; Schultz, S.R.; Fulcher, B.D.; Jones, N.S. catch22: CAnonical Time-series CHaracteristics. *arXiv* **2019**, arXiv:1901.10200.
21. Fulcher, B.D.; Jones, N.S. hctsa: A computational framework for automated time-series phenotyping using massive feature extraction. *Cell Syst.* **2017**, *5*, 527–531. [CrossRef] [PubMed]
22. Zoph, B.; Vasudevan, V.; Shlens, J.; Le, Q.V. Learning Transferable Architectures for Scalable Image Recognition. In Proceedings of the 2018 IEEE Conference on Computer Vision and Pattern Recognition, CVPR 2018, Salt Lake City, UT, USA, 18–22 June 2018; pp. 8697–8710.
23. Bisong, E. Google automl: Cloud natural language processing. In *Building Machine Learning and Deep Learning Models on Google Cloud Platform*; Springer: Berlin, Germany, 2019; pp. 599–612.
24. Wang, C.; Baratchi, M.; Bäck, T.; Hoos, H.H.; Limmer, S.; Olhofer, M. Towards time-series-specific feature engineering in automated machine learning frameworks. 2022, *under review*.
25. Feurer, M.; Klein, A.; Eggensperger, K.; Springenberg, J.; Blum, M.; Hutter, F. Efficient and Robust Automated Machine Learning. In *Advances in Neural Information Processing Systems 28*; Curran Associates, Inc.: Montreal, QC, Canada, 7–12 December 2015; pp. 2962–2970.
26. Jin, H.; Song, Q.; Hu, X. Auto-Keras: An Efficient Neural Architecture Search System. In Proceedings of the 25th ACM SIGKDD International Conference on Knowledge Discovery & Data Mining, Anchorage, AK, USA, 4–8 August 2019; ACM: New York, NY, USA, 2019; pp. 1946–1956.

27. Thornton, C.; Hutter, F.; Hoos, H.H.; Leyton-Brown, K. Auto-WEKA: Combined Selection and Hyperparameter Optimization of Classification Algorithms. In *KDD'13, Proceedings of the 19th ACM SIGKDD International Conference on Knowledge Discovery and Data Mining, Chicago, IL, USA, 11–14 August 2013*; ACM: New York, NY, USA, 2013; pp. 847–855.
28. Taieb, S.B.; Bontempi, G. Recursive Multi-step Time Series Forecasting by Perturbing Data. In Proceedings of the 11th IEEE International Conference on Data Mining, ICDM 2011, Vancouver, BC, Canada, 11–14 December 2011; pp. 695–704. [CrossRef]
29. Benjamini, Y.; Hochberg, Y. Controlling the false discovery rate: A practical and powerful approach to multiple testing. *J. R. Stat. Soc. Ser. B (Methodol.)* **1995**, *57*, 289–300. [CrossRef]
30. Fulcher, B.D.; Lubba, C.H.; Sethi, S.S.; Jones, N.S. CompEngine: A self-organizing, living library of time-series data. *arXiv* **2019**, arXiv:1905.01042.
31. Januschowski, T.; Gasthaus, J.; Wang, Y.; Salinas, D.; Flunkert, V.; Bohlke-Schneider, M.; Callot, L. Criteria for classifying forecasting methods. *Int. J. Forecast.* **2020**, *36*, 167–177. [CrossRef]
32. Bergstra, J.; Bengio, Y. Random Search for Hyper-Parameter Optimization. *J. Mach. Learn. Res.* **2012**, *13*, 281–305.
33. Oreshkin, B.N.; Carpov, D.; Chapados, N.; Bengio, Y. N-BEATS: Neural basis expansion analysis for interpretable time series forecasting. *arXiv* **2019**, arXiv:1905.10437.
34. Siami-Namini, S.; Tavakoli, N.; Namin, A.S. A Comparison of ARIMA and LSTM in Forecasting Time Series. In Proceedings of the 17th IEEE International Conference on Machine Learning and Applications, ICMLA, Orlando, FL, USA, 17–20 December 2018; pp. 1394–1401.
35. Zhang, X.; Shen, F.; Zhao, J.; Yang, G. Time Series Forecasting Using GRU Neural Network with Multi-lag After Decomposition. In Proceedings of the Neural Information Processing—24th International Conference, ICONIP 2017, Guangzhou, China, 14–18 November 2017; Springer: Berlin, Germany, 2017; Volume 10638, pp. 523–532.
36. Yamak, P.T.; Yujian, L.; Gadosey, P.K. A comparison between arima, lstm, and gru for time series forecasting. In Proceedings of the 2019 2nd International Conference on Algorithms, Computing and Artificial Intelligence, Sanya, China, 20–22 December 2019; pp. 49–55.
37. Mann, H.B.; Whitney, D.R. On a test of whether one of two random variables is stochastically larger than the other. *Ann. Math. Stat.* **1947**, *18*, 50–60. [CrossRef]

engineering
proceedings

Proceeding Paper

PV Fault Diagnosis Method Based on Time Series Electrical Signal Analysis †

Carole Lebreton, Fabrice Kbidi *, Frédéric Alicalapa, Michel Benne and Cédric Damour

Energy Lab, Université de La Réunion, 15, Avenue René Cassin CS 92003, CEDEX 9, 97744 Saint-Denis, France; carole.lebreton@univ-reunion.fr (C.L.); frederic.alicalapa@univ-reunion.fr (F.A.); michel.benne@univ-reunion.fr (M.B.); cedric.damour@univ-reunion.fr (C.D.)
* Correspondence: fabrice.kbidi@univ-reunion.fr
† Presented at the 8th International Conference on Time Series and Forecasting, Gran Canaria, Spain, 27–30 June 2022.

Abstract: With the objectives of energy self-sufficiency and zero emissions in La Reunion, photovoltaics are becoming an increasingly important part of the local energy mix. Installation reliability and safety are crucial to ensure network stability and security, therefore PV system fault diagnosis is an essential tool in the expansion of this electricity production method. The DETECT Project (Diagnosis onlinE of sTate of health of EleCTric systems) is a research project aiming at diagnosis method development. In this way, signal processing provides us with promising tools in the form of decomposition algorithms. Thanks to their low computation cost, empirical mode decomposition (EMD) and variational mode decomposition (VMD) allow undertaking a real-time diagnosis, with on-line PV electrical signal time-series data analysis.

Keywords: PV systems; faults; diagnosis; signal processing; time series data

check for
updates

Citation: Lebreton, C.; Kbidi, F.; Alicalapa, F.; Benne, M.; Damour, C. PV Fault Diagnosis Method Based on Time Series Electrical Signal Analysis. *Eng. Proc.* **2022**, *18*, 18. https://doi.org/10.3390/engproc2022018018

Academic Editors: Ignacio Rojas, Hector Pomares, Olga Valenzuela, Fernando Rojas and Luis Javier Herrera

Published: 21 June 2022

Publisher's Note: MDPI stays neutral with regard to jurisdictional claims in published maps and institutional affiliations.

1. Introduction

The current ecological and environmental situation has led to an international awareness of greenhouse gas emissions. Renewable and natural energy sources have been widely used and developed over the last 20 years. The production of electrical energy from photovoltaic energy in territories with a high solar potential has increased considerably. As Reunion Island is located in a tropical zone with a high annual productivity (1314 h of full-power equivalent in 2019 [1]), the energy policy of France and of the island encourages the development of photovoltaic solar energy. In this context, the production of electrical energy by photovoltaic means has increased from 0 to 206.3 MW in 15 years [1] in order to counter the massive importation of fossil fuels. As a non-interconnected grid territory, the Reunion Island grid is prone to instability due to strong variations in intermittent energy production. Thereby, maintenance and forecasting of photovoltaic production are necessary. The tropical conditions induce an increase in faults and premature aging of photovoltaic systems [2]. Moreover, the photovoltaic park in Reunion Island includes a wide range of sizes of power plants. There is a large proportion of small installations (62.66% of the number of photovoltaic plants are below 9 kVA), which are unequally equipped for diagnosis and fault detection.

The DETECT project aims to implement innovative technical solutions to detect, isolate, and identify faults that may lead to failures. These solutions allow improvement of the energy efficiency of PV systems by anticipating maintenance operations. The deployment of these solutions on a large scale relies on the use of low-cost technologies, allowing the implementation of diagnostic modules while limiting the installation of additional sensors in situ. The objective of the project is to develop distributed technical solutions to analyze the health status of hybrid systems, in particular PV systems, installed in humid tropical environments such as Reunion Island. The innovative character of this project is based on several elements:

- development of a diagnostic system based on the electrical signals available on the photovoltaic installations (voltage, current, and power),
- real-time diagnosis without system interruption,
- facilitation of the deployment of these solutions by promoting low-cost technologies.

2. Method Presentation

When a fault occurs, symptoms will appear in the PV system, the behavior of the voltage or current curves can be affected in a more or less visible way [3]. Advanced diagnosis methods collect the information available on the production site and process it in order to highlight the characteristic behavior, i.e., the fault symptoms.

The development of a diagnosis method consists of three steps:

1. identification of measured variables that are sensitive to faults,
2. selection of the most suitable tool to highlight the symptoms (data processing),
3. interpretation of the symptoms in order to make a diagnosis.

In order to meet the constraints of the DETECT project, the following options are retained:

- permanent shading, hotspots, and bypass diode faults will be studied,
- the input variables of the diagnostic method are current and voltage collected by the inverters, and weather data simulated by the regional climate model (WRF models),
- signal processing tools with low computational cost are selected.

3. Time Series Decomposition and Preliminary Results

Signal processing methods are used to extract additional features from time series. Among the most known, the fast Fourier transform (FFT) transforms discrete time domain data into the frequency domain. The information collected comprises the gain and the phase of the signal for each frequency value. These characteristics carry information not available for data in the time domain. Unlike FFT, whose scope is limited to stationary or periodic signals, the wavelet transform (WT) is applicable to non-stationary and transient signals. The signal is decomposed into distinct details with determined bandwidths. The analysis of the information then extracted is used for fault diagnosis.

In order to extract information from PV output time series, these well-known decomposition tools have already been applied to PV fault diagnosis, as well as more recent tools. FFT [4], EMD (empirical mode decomposition) [5], discrete wavelet transform decomposition [6], and PCA (principal component analysis) [7] can be cited. Diagnosis of PV system faults warrants special attention for these tools in order to, e.g., detect arc faults, define PV system health status, quantify power quality disturbances in a PV-based microgrid, or discern shading faults.

Variational mode decomposition (VMD) is a decomposition algorithm, developed in 2014 by Dragomiretskiy [8], that demodulates non-recursively a signal $x(t)$ in a finite number of distinct amplitude-modulated-frequency-modulated (AM-FM) signals $x_k(t)$, called intrinsic mode functions (IMFs).

The superiority of EMD or VMD has been studied in cases of structural health monitoring [9] and medical time series [10]. The latter highlights that EMD is more sensitive to low frequencies than VMD and conversely for VMD and high frequencies. Regarding signal noise, VMD filters high-frequency noise in a more effective way without signal characteristic changes, unlike EMD, which reduces signal amplitude.

It is important to note that EMD's or VMD's superiority and advantages highly depend on the time series characteristics.

VMD has already been used in other application domains for diagnosis [11], and it is a promising tool for electrical system diagnosis [12]. In the next subsections, EMD and VMD are applied to PV output current for healthy, cloudy, and faulty data.

3.1. Experimental Data Selection

Three types of experimental conditions were applied on a 4kWc real rooftop PV plant consisting of 2 lines of twelve panels, corresponding to healthy conditions during clear and cloudy sky, and faulty conditions during clear sky weather.

3.2. Preliminary Results

The following figures illustrate EMD and VMD analysis of the selected data. The different time series are shown in Figure 1. The selected windows defined in red are decomposed by EMD and VMD. Figures 2 and 3 exhibit the different IMFs for the three conditions.

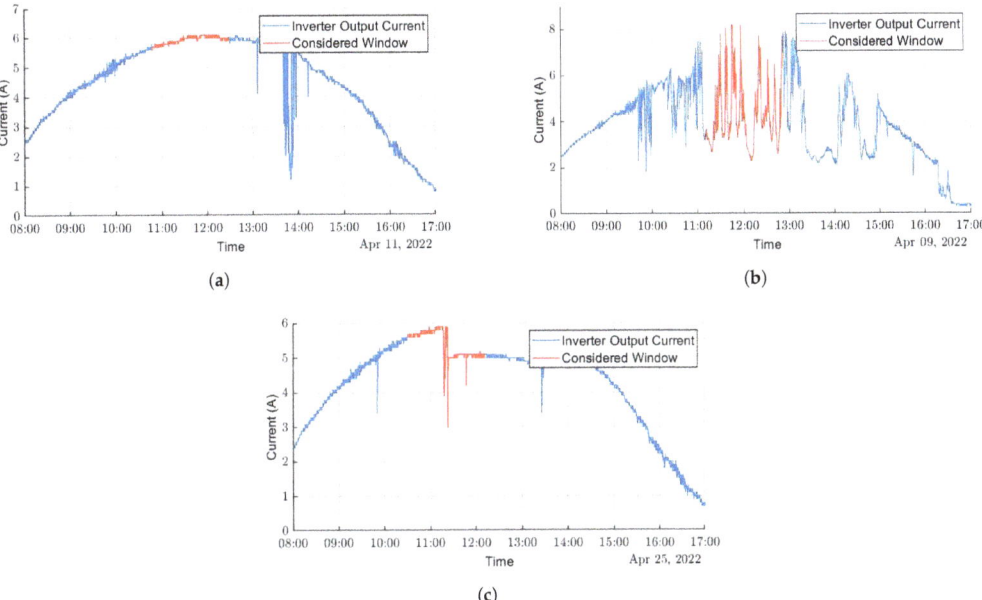

Figure 1. Experimental dataset. (**a**) Healthy conditions: clear sky. (**b**) Healthy conditions: cloudy sky. (**c**) Faulty conditions: partial shading.

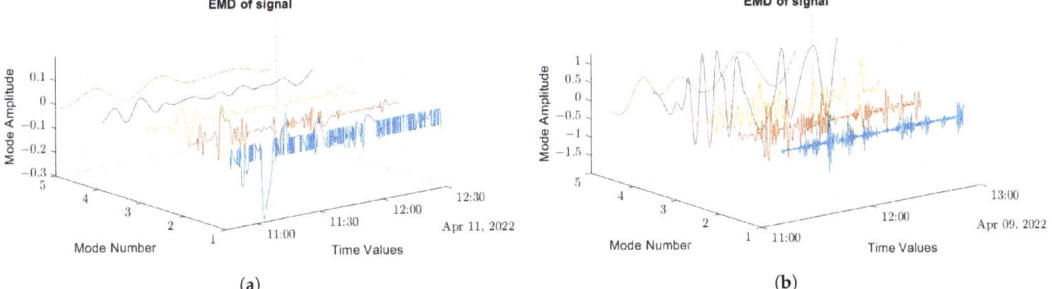

Figure 2. *Cont.*

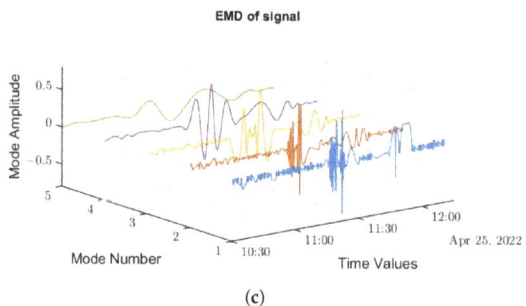

(c)

Figure 2. Empirical mode decomposition. (**a**) Healthy conditions: clear sky. (**b**) Healthy conditions: cloudy sky. (**c**) Faulty conditions: partial shading.

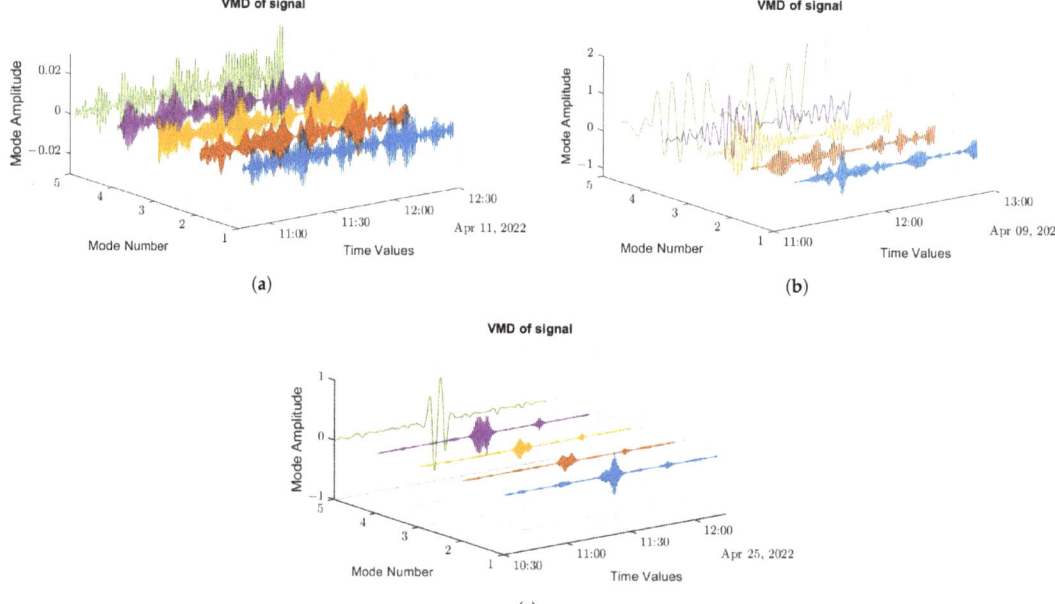

(c)

Figure 3. Variational mode decomposition. (**a**) Healthy conditions: clear sky. (**b**) Healthy conditions: cloudy sky. (**c**) Faulty conditions: partial shading.

In order to extract more information regarding the IMF characteristics, an analysis of each IMF was conducted. For each IMF, its energetic contribution was calculated, as well as its central frequency being collected and the coefficient of correlation being calculated between the current IMF and the original signal. These preliminary results suggest that some IMFs react differently according to experimental conditions. The analysis and the study of these IMFs could allow determination of the occurring conditions with accuracy, and discrimination of a faulty state from a healthy state.

4. Conclusions and Perspectives

The DETECT Project aims to develop real-time, low cost, and accurate PV system fault diagnosis. In this context, EMD and VMD are promising signal processing tools with a low computational cost. This advantage allows undertaking an on-line PV time-series data analysis.

The proposed targeted method should combine high-efficiency and low-cost technologies, yet minimize human and material effort deployment on photovoltaic parks. The first results have been confirmed on a set of experimental data. The analysis of IMF characteristics and the selection of the most significant ones are in progress. A comparative study of EMD and VMD performance associated with another step of the fault diagnosis tool is being undertaken. In parallel, different research domains are being investigated, in the context of signal processing and information theory. The main perspective is to build an indicator coming from IMF characteristics, aiming to precisely detect, isolate, and diagnose possible faults.

Author Contributions: Conceptualization, C.L., C.D. and F.K.; methodology, C.L., C.D. and F.K.; software, C.L. and C.D.; validation, C.L., C.D., F.K., F.A. and M.B.; formal analysis, C.L., C.D., F.K., F.A. and M.B.; investigation, C.L., C.D., F.K., F.A. and M.B.; resources, C.D., F.A. and M.B.; writing—original draft preparation, C.L. and F.K.; writing—review and editing, C.L., C.D. and F.K.; supervision, C.D., F.A. and M.B.; project administration, C.D., F.A. and M.B.; funding acquisition, C.D., F.A. and M.B. All authors have read and agreed to the published version of the manuscript.

Funding: This research work was funded by the ERDF (European Regional Development Fund) and the Region Council of La Réunion.

Institutional Review Board Statement: Not applicable.

Informed Consent Statement: Not applicable.

Data Availability Statement: Not applicable.

Acknowledgments: Special acknowledgments go to the European Regional Development Fund (ERDF) and the Regional council of Reunion for DETECT project funding. We also thank the project's partner, the Femto-ST laboratory.

Conflicts of Interest: The authors declare no conflict of interest.

References

1. SPL Énergie Réunion. *Bilan Energétique de La Réunion Année 2020*; Technical Report; Observatoire Énergie Réunion (OER), Horizon Réunion: Saint-Pierre, France, 2020.
2. Jordan, D.C.; Silverman, T.J.; Wohlgemuth, J.H.; Kurtz, S.R.; VanSant, K.T. Photovoltaic failure and degradation modes. *Prog. Photovolt. Res. Appl.* **2017**, *25*, 318–326. [CrossRef]
3. Pillai, D.S.; Blaabjerg, F.; Rajasekar, N. A Comparative Evaluation of Advanced Fault Detection Approaches for PV Systems. *IEEE J. Photovoltaics* **2019**, *9*, 513–527. doi: 10.1109/JPHOTOV.2019.2892189. [CrossRef]
4. Wang, Z.; McConnell, S.; Balog, R.S.; Johnson, J. Arc fault signal detection—Fourier transformation vs. wavelet decomposition techniques using synthesized data. In Proceedings of the 2014 IEEE 40th Photovoltaic Specialist Conference (PVSC), Denver, CO, USA, 8–13 June 2014; pp. 3239–3244.
5. Ding, K.; Feng, L.; Zhang, J.; Chen, X.; Chen, F.; Li, Y. A health status-based performance evaluation method of photovoltaic system. *IEEE Access* **2019**, *7*, 124055–124065. [CrossRef]
6. Yılmaz, A.; Bayrak, G. A real-time UWT-based intelligent fault detection method for PV-based microgrids. *Electr. Power Syst. Res.* **2019**, *177*, 105984. [CrossRef]
7. Rouani, L.; Harkat, M.F.; Kouadri, A.; Mekhilef, S. Shading fault detection in a grid-connected PV system using vertices principal component analysis. *Renew. Energy* **2021**, *164*, 1527–1539. [CrossRef]
8. Dragomiretskiy, K.; Zosso, D. Variational mode decomposition. *IEEE Trans. Signal Process.* **2014**, *62*, 531–544. [CrossRef]
9. Civera, M.; Surace, C. A comparative analysis of signal decomposition techniques for structural health monitoring on an experimental benchmark. *Sensors* **2021**, *21*, 1825. [CrossRef] [PubMed]
10. Maji, U.; Pal, S. Empirical mode decomposition vs. variational mode decomposition on ECG signal processing: A comparative study. In Proceedings of the 2016 International Conference on Advances in Computing, Communications and Informatics, ICACCI 2016, Jaipur, India, 21–24 September 2016; pp. 1129–1134. [CrossRef]
11. Shang, H.; Li, F.; Wu, Y. Partial discharge fault diagnosis based on multi-scale dispersion entropy and a hypersphere multiclass support vector machine. *Entropy* **2019**, *21*, 81. [CrossRef] [PubMed]
12. Achlerkar, P.D.; Samantaray, S.R.; Manikandan, M.S. Variational Mode Decomposition and Decision Tree Based Detection and Classification of Power Quality Disturbances in Grid-Connected Distributed Generation System. *IEEE Trans. Smart Grid* **2018**, *9*, 3122–3132. [CrossRef]

Proceeding Paper

Early Detection of Flash Floods Using Case-Based Reasoning †

Enrique Fernádez [1,‡], José R. Villar [1,*] , Alberto Navarro [2] and Javier Sedano [2]

1   Computer Science Department, University of Oviedo, 33005 Oviedo, Spain; uo257742@uniovi.es
2   Instituto Tecnológico de Castilla y León, 09001 Burgos, Spain; alberto.navarro@itcl.es (A.N.);
    javier.sedano@itcl.es (J.S.)
*   Correspondence: villarjose@uniovi.es
†   Presented at the 8th International Conference on Time Series and Forecasting, Gran Canaria, Spain,
    27–30 June 2022.
‡   Current address: Computer Science Department, University of Oviedo, Campus de Viesques, s/n,
    33204 Gijón, Spain.

Abstract: A flash flood is the sudden increase in the water level of a basin due to an abrupt change in weather conditions. The importance of early flash flood detection is given by reducing its consequences, either in infrastructure damage or human losses. Interestingly, the studies in the literature focus on the dynamics of the basins, determining how the water levels in a basin would be in a considered scenario, and leaving the early and online flash flood detection unaddressed. This research addresses this latter problem and proposes a case-based reasoning that estimates the flooding map for a given prediction horizon. Provided enough data are available, this CBR tool would perfectly deal with different basins and locations. This research is being designed and developed on two concrete basins, one from Spain and one from France. We expect that the performance of the CBR tool will satisfactorily assess the decision making of the public safety experts.

Keywords: flash flood; case-based reasoning; risk prediction

check for
updates

Citation: Fernádez, E.; Villar, J.R.; Navarro, A.; Sedano, J. Early Detection of Flash Floods Using Case-Based Reasoning. *Eng. Proc.* **2022**, *18*, 19. https://doi.org/10.3390/engproc2022018019

Academic Editors: Ignacio Rojas, Hector Pomares, Olga Valenzuela, Fernando Rojas and Luis Javier Herrera

Published: 21 June 2022

Publisher's Note: MDPI stays neutral with regard to jurisdictional claims in published maps and institutional affiliations.

1. Introduction

The abrupt changes in the weather conditions and climate change are inducing more and more flash floods, which are sudden increments in the water level in a basin due to a sudden change in the weather conditions, among other variables, such as soil conditions. A great effort in the risk assessment has been performed, aiming to evaluate the risk of flooding for certain scenarios in different basins. The risk assessment identifies those areas of a basin that are susceptible to flooding to define efficient management policies [1,2], to design a new infrastructure that avoids the flooding [3] or to design complementary infrastructures to mitigate the effects of these flash floods [4].

Nevertheless, the early and online detection of flash floods has not yet gathered the focus of the research community [5]. Such a tool would allow public safety experts to make decisions in advance in the event of a flash flood, reducing as much as possible its consequences. Solving this latter application, that is, aiding the public safety experts in the flash flood detection, needs the use of data not only from the basin's geomorphological and hydrological information, but also information concerning the current scenario—for example, the water level of the rivers at certain points, the amount of rain in the last relevant period—together with weather forecast information.

In this research, a prototype for the online detection of flash floods is proposed. To do so, information from the sensory systems deployed on the basin is queried, as well as the weather forecast system, to obtain a clear picture of the basin's current state. These time series are used to estimate the height of water at any point in the basin. The water's height can be superimposed on a map, providing information about what geographical points in the basin are in danger of a sudden flood.

Features are extracted from the above-mentioned time series, and case-based reasoning (CBR), such as the intelligent paradigm, finds similarities among the retrieved and selected cases from the case base. The outcome of the CBR is the above-mentioned map containing the height of the water for every single point in the basin. Together with a web application, a novel online flash flood tool can guide public safety teams in their decision-making.

The structure of this research is as follows. Section 2 discusses the related work section concerning flash flood risk assessment. Section 3 describes the prototype that has been developed. Section 4 shows the results obtained for a real basin in Spain. Finally, the conclusions from this research are drawn.

2. Related Work

Risk assessment aims to identify basin's susceptible to flooding areas; it is a widely used term in the flood detection literature. A risk assessment measurement uses, among other possibilities, Machine Learning (ML) and artificial intelligence methods and techniques; however, the majority of the research proposed off-line numerical approaches [6]; the off-line characteristics come from the computation requirements for the simulations.

When talking about ML, either unsupervised and supervised learning have been applied. With respect to unsupervised learning, the main developed idea is to design or select a set of risk indexes or features by means of clustering the instances from the available GIS (Global Information System) points—which introduces a risk label per group—then, the risk label of the most suitable group labels every new GIS point instance. For example, the study in [7] proposes merging the improved analytic hierarchy process, which hybridizes the iterative self-organizing data analysis and the Maximum Likelihood (ISO-Maximum) clustering algorithm. With these methods, a risk index that reflects its geomorphical and geographical characteristic labels every possible position.

Moreover, supervised learning methods, such as decision trees or support vector machines, have also been used for risk assessment. In [8], flood susceptibility mapping of GIS points in the Kelantan basin (Malaysia) was addressed using rule-based decision trees and the combination of frequency ration and logistic regression statistical methods. Up to 10 features called conditional factors were calculated in the first stage devoted to feature selection from GIS and remote sensing data. Afterwards, ML and the statistical methods computed a risk value for each position in a basin map. This scheme has been also used in different studies, such as in [9], where random forest and boosted regression trees were compared.

Neural networks have also been reported for risk assessment [10,11]. As before, a set of features were extracted from GIS positions to train and test the neural model. Each GIS position is evaluated when deploying the model, computing the corresponding set of features and calculating the risk assessment using the trained neural model for the basin. Support vector machines were proposed instead of neural networks using a rather similar procedure reported in [12].

Furthermore, the study in [13] used multicriteria decision making in the evaluation of the risk assessment. This research proposed analytical hierarchy process to generate the decision-making process and assign a risk label to each GIS position. A similar study was reported in [14] for the assessment in the Mashhad Plain basin, Iran.

Additionally, the Dempster–Shafer-based evidential belief function has been proposed for the assessment and spatial prediction of flood-susceptible areas [15]. A set of features is extracted from each GIS location and these features are used as inputs to the Dempster–Shafer method. Interestingly, this probabilistic-based reasoning method overtook other methods used in the literature, such as logistic regression and frequency ratio. A similar conclusion is presented in [9], where a comparison between the Dempster–Shafer of two different decision trees was performed- In this latter case, the features and the method varies from the former studio, but the conclusions are similar.

These studies show that perhaps ML is not the most interesting technique for this type of problem because of the difficulties to obtain enough valid and representative data from all the basin, so training the model could lead to generalized models. Furthermore, the evidence that the Dempster–Shafer theory could compete with the ML methods suggests that what is needed is an artificial intelligence technique that can represent the knowledge from the experts, extrapolating this knowledge to the different positions in the basin.

It is worth recalling that all of these approaches are focused on off-line risk assessment. Nonetheless, if we also consider the case of on-line information, not only GIS information is needed but also the sensory data and the weather forecasts could be needed in order to assess a certain scenario. With all these premises, this research proposes to use an alternative that has never been used in this context.

3. A Flash Flood Detection System: Using CBR as Reasoning Paradigm

The main idea is to develop a web application to assist public safety experts in their decision-making process. This web application requests basic information about the corresponding basin; then, it queries a CBR web service for a sequence of maps representing the mm of water in the area, with one map per prediction horizon. The CBR, on the other hand, performs the first three stages in this type of system (retrieve, recall, and reuse) to merge the maps from the most relevant cases considering a similarity measurement between the stored cases and the current scenario or status of the basin. For the purpose of this research, the retain stage will not be implemented as is explained when discussing the case representation.

This study analyses the behavior of hydrological basins, each basin including one or more locations where the prediction would be requested. A requested prediction would predict the state of the basin (in millimeters of water level) for up to six prediction horizons. A prediction horizon is a time step that is a function of the dynamics of the concrete basin; for instance, for some quick response basins, this time could be in minutes, while for more steady basins, this period could be 1 hour.

The following subsections provide details on the different parts of the system. Section 3.1 deals with the web interface; Section 3.2 explain how a case, representing a basin state, is stored. Finally, the different CBR stages are detailed in Section 3.3.

3.1. Exploiting the CBR Tool

Figure 1 shows the interface of the web application that has been developed for the INUNDATIO project; this interface is where the expert interacts with the system. Firstly, the user must introduce the basin and location, then the weather forecast. Then, by clicking on the button, the CBR service is requested and a sequence of maps will be delivered and shown. The tool visualizes the map of the mm of water as a layer on top of an open-layers map from the corresponding basin.

There are two main options in this interface: automatic weather forecast—requesting the values to the designated forecast service—and manual forecasting. In this latter case, the user chooses between a linear, a quadratic, or Gaussian forecast by setting the function's parameters. This realistic forecast allows for evaluating the basin behavior in case of extreme events.

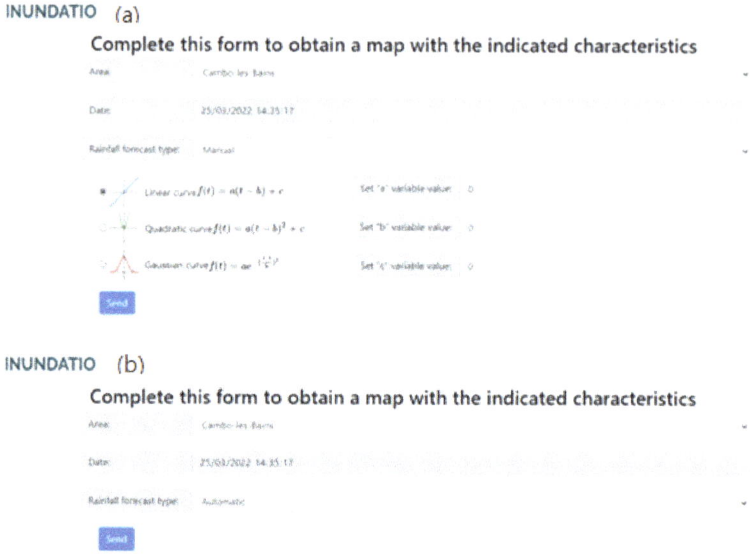

INUNDATIO (a)

Complete this form to obtain a map with the indicated characteristics

Area: Cambo les Bains

Date: 25/03/2022 14:35:17

Rainfall forecast type: Manual

 Linear curve $f(t) = a(t - b) + c$ Set 'a' variable value: 0

 Quadratic curve $f(t) = a(t - b)^2 + c$ Set 'b' variable value: 0

 Gaussian curve $f(t) = ae^{-\frac{(t-b)^2}{c}}$ Set 'c' variable value: 0

Send

INUNDATIO (b)

Complete this form to obtain a map with the indicated characteristics

Area: Cambo les Bains

Date: 25/03/2022 14:35:17

Rainfall forecast type: Automatic

Send

Figure 1. Example of the web interface for the CBR deployment. (**a**) In the upper part, the manual rainfall forecast is shown. (**b**) In the bottom part, the automatic weather forecast interface is depicted.

3.2. Case Representation of the Basin State

As mentioned before, a case in the case base represents the state of a certain basin. The state of the basin is defined by a set of variables; each of them is a time series. According to the hydrodynamic experts, these time series can be represented using a window of values; the length of each window varies with the variable and the specific basin as a function of its dynamics: faster basins require smaller windows and vice versa. Moreover, each window is split into intervals, and the average of the values of the variable is computed for each interval. Then, each time series is represented as a sequence of aggregated values.

Furthermore, each basin includes information such as its list of deployed sensors and sensor types, and whether the values from a sensor type should be aggregated or not. For instance, the Rain Gauges (RG) are usually aggregated among all the rain gauges in the basin, whereas the Water Discharge Levels (WDL) are usually considered individually. Figure 2 shows the variables and the number of intervals that are considered in this study. Additionally, each case also stores maps of the basin with the millimeters of water at any point for a set of prediction horizons, as also shown in the Figure.

It is worth mentioning that these maps and information are gathered from the results of the simulations of the basin using the hydrological models. For sure, there are well-defined hydrological models of the basins; however, running a simulation takes too much time and the outcomes are not expected to be available in such a small period of time to be useful for an online request from public safety experts. Hence, that is the reason why the whole CBR is designed: mimicking the performance of the hydrological models for the prediction of a basin's behavior.

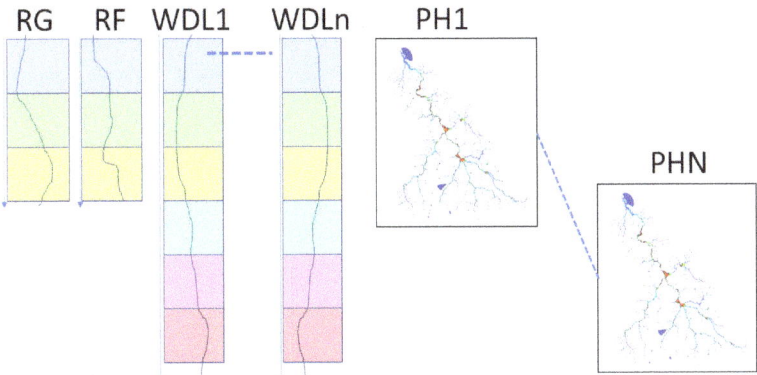

Figure 2. The case representation used in this research. The colored boxes represent the intervals in which each window is split. A map with the mm of water is stored for each prediction horizon.

3.3. CBR Stages

A case includes maps with the mm of water for each prediction horizon. This means that, in the case of requiring the CBR to retain cases, these flood maps must be gathered for each prediction horizon so the CBR system could store them within the case. Nevertheless, this information is not available for the system: there is no method to recollect the mm of water for each point in a basin; therefore, the retain phase of the CBR can not be completed and the CBR would only rely on the information extracted from simulations. How to use ideas such as concept drift to include extra information in the case base is left for future research.

Hence, only three stages are to be defined: retrieve, reuse, and revise. For the retrieval phase, simple queries were performed to retrieve the cases for the current location and basin. This might not be efficient in terms of computation; however, the scheme allows us to define different distance measurements without the need of designing complex queries.

The reuse stage is the one that performs the calculation of the distances between the retrieved cases from the case database and the current scenario. For this research, the square root of the weighted sum of the differences between the values for the variables describing the current scenario and a case is used as the distance measurement. Single criteria sorting using the distance measurement, together with a maximum number of neighbors, define the selection of the most relevant cases. Moreover, it is expected that more distance measurements can be defined, such as using the Sobol' [16] indexes or introducing not only single criteria but multi-criteria sorting—for instance, using the Pareto non-dominance concept.

Finally, the revise stage generates the outcome of each case. To do so, the distance between each relevant case and the current scenario is used as a weight to calculate the weighted map among the maps from each relevant case (see Equation (1)). The idea is that the smaller the distance, the higher the weight should be; therefore, each reused case is assigned with the product of the distances of the remaining cases; this value is then scaled in [0.0, 1.0]. Using these weights, and for each prediction horizon, the CBR calculates a weighted map as the agreement among the cases.

$$w_i = \frac{\prod_{j \neq i} d(c_j, \text{current scenario})}{\sum_j \prod_{j \neq i} d(c_j, \text{current scenario})} \tag{1}$$

4. Experimentation and Discussion

The INUNDATIO project focuses on two basins: Venero Claro and Nive; however, this study has only been analyzed with the Venero Claro basin, in Spain. The Venero Claro represents a small torrential hydrographical basin in Sierra de Gredos, Ávila. The Cabrera creek is a torrential-rain current and a tributary to the Alberche river belonging to the Tajo basin. It refers to a series of small creeks on the northern side of Sierra del Valle; its vegetation is 45% Pinus Pinaster, but also includes Pinus Sylvestris and Alnus Glutinosa. The behavior of this basin is a very active fluvial(torrential hydrodynamics) with relatively short dynamic time periods, between 15 min to 45 min.

During the implementation of the INUNDATIO project, a set of sensors was deployed in the basin to develop the hydrodynamic models; these models, unfortunately, will not be available during the project. As a consequence, for testing this CBR, the research team produced a realistic case base.

To generate the realistic case base, two main criteria have been defined in agreement with the experts: soil saturation and weather forecast; these criteria were a sort of look-up table to set the initial conditions and the evolutionary rules of the generated cases. Up to three different possible soil saturation states were considered: non-saturated soil, mid-saturated soil, and highly saturated soil. Furthermore, three possible forecasts were proposed: scarce rain forecast, soft rain forecast, and heavy rain forecast. The evolution of the sensors' measurements and the rain forecast sequences were standardized for each pair of soil saturation and weather forecast. With these assumptions, a realistic case was generated by randomly biasing the standardized sensors functions and the rain forecast. Finally, the maps of the basin for each of the prediction horizons containing the millimeters of water were generated; these maps were carefully chosen to represent plausible states of the basin given the basin variables and rain forecast.

To evaluate this prototype of the CBR, different queries were performed by manually setting the rain forecast. The outcome of the tool must be such that the maps resemble the variances in mm of water in the basin. Because the tool automatically queries the online databases for the basin sensory information, tests with different basin initial conditions were not available.

The performance of the CBR is briefly outlined in Figures 3 and 4. The former figure depicts the web interface, showing the CBR output map overlapped with the basin map. The user can easily zoom in and out as well as pan over the map. This outcome comes from a scenario where the basin was suffering strong rain and then it stopped raining; the area in the upper-left corner of the studied basin of Venero Claro is completely flooded; this area is a low height plain.

In Figure 4, the maps for each of the 6 prediction horizons are included, limiting the view to the surroundings of the basin's flooded area. As mentioned, the outcome is generated for a transition from heavy rain to a dry period. Consequently, the expectation is that the basin stabilizes and starts draining water. This is actually what the outcome shows, although due to the zoom that is necessary to notice the draining, it is almost unnoticeable.

Figure 3. CBR results' visualization in the web interface for one prediction horizon, with the common facilities for zoom and pan. Notice that the limits of the study abruptly end at the flooding.

Figure 4. CBR outcome for the six prediction horizons, varying from 1 to 6 prediction horizons from left to right and top to bottom (left-top and right-bottom stand for 1 and 6 prediction horizons, respectively.

5. Conclusions

In this research, a web application that uses a case-based reasoning intelligent service has been proposed for the prediction of the behavior of the basins; the goal is to assist the safety experts when flash floods are more possible according to the basin state. This proposal covers different types of basins, from those with fast responses to those with a slower dynamic.

Results only include the evolution of the Venero Claro basin in Spain and were obtained using realistic data and cases. This is because the data from the different basins—that is, the relevant cases, the sources of information, and forecasts—are still in development; therefore, work is still pending and, hopefully, a complete test could be available by the end of this year. Nevertheless, the CBR has shown its capacity to predict what the experts expect from a given set of initial conditions, merging the information from the most relevant stored cases.

In future work, the implementation of different extensions, such as multi-criteria sorting using Pareto dominance or the availability of different distance measurements, will be addressed.

Author Contributions: All the authors have equally contributed in the development of this research. All authors have read and agreed to the published version of the manuscript.

Funding: This research has been funded by the SUDOE Interreg Program under the grant INUNDA-TIO SOE3/P4/E0929. Furthermore, this research has been funded by European Union's Horizon 2020 research and innovation programme (project DIH4CPS) under the Grant Agreement no 872548, by the Spanish Ministry of Economics and Industry under the grant PID2020-112726RB-I00, by the Spanish Research Agency (AEI, Spain) under the grant agreement RED2018-102312-T (IA-Biomed), by CDTI (Centro para el Desarrollo Tecnológico Industrial) under projects CER-20211003 and CER-20211022, by the Missions Science and Innovation project MIG-20211008 (INMERBOT). Further, by Principado de Asturias, grant SV-PA-21-AYUD/2021/50994 and by ICE (Junta de Castilla y León) under project CCTT3/20/BU/0002.

Data Availability Statement: Not applicable.

Conflicts of Interest: The authors declare no conflict of interest.

Abbreviations

The following abbreviations are used in this manuscript:

CBR	Case-Based Reasoning
GIS	Global Information System
RG	Rain Gauge
WDL	Water Discharge Level

References

1. Li, W.; Lin, K.; Zhao, T.; Lan, T.; Chen, X.; Du, H.; Chen, H. Risk assessment and sensitivity analysis of flash floods in ungauged basins using coupled hydrologic and hydrodynamic models. *J. Hydrol.* **2019**, *572*, 108–120. [CrossRef]
2. Țîncu, R.; Zêzere, J.L.; Crăciun, I.; Lazăr, G.; Lazăr, I. Quantitative micro-scale flood risk assessment in a section of the Trotuș River, Romania. *Land Use Policy* **2020**, *95*, 103881. [CrossRef]
3. Terêncio, D.; Fernandes, L.S.; Cortes, R.; Moura, J.; Pacheco, F. Flood risk attenuation in critical zones of continental Portugal using sustainable detention basins. *Sci. Total. Environ.* **2020**, *721*, 137727. [CrossRef] [PubMed]
4. Wyżga, B.; Kundzewicz, Z.W.; Konieczny, R.; Piniewski, M.; Zawiejska, J.; Radecki-Pawlik, A. Comprehensive approach to the reduction of river flood risk: Case study of the Upper Vistula Basin. *Sci. Total. Environ.* **2018**, *631–632*, 1251–1267. [CrossRef] [PubMed]
5. Acosta-Coll, M.; Ballester-Merelo, F.; Martinez-Peiró, M.; la Hoz-Franco, E.D. Real-Time Early Warning System Design for Pluvial Flash Floods—A Review. *Sensors* **2018**, *18*, 2255. [CrossRef] [PubMed]
6. Zhang, Y.; Wang, Y.; Chen, Y.; Liang, F.; Liu, H. Assessment of future flash flood inundations in coastal regions under climate change scenarios—A case study of Hadahe River basin in northeastern China. *Sci. Total. Environ.* **2019**, *693*, 133550. [CrossRef] [PubMed]
7. Lin, K.; Chen, H.; Xu, C.Y.; Yan, P.; Lan, T.; Liu, Z.; Dong, C. Assessment of flash flood risk based on improved analytic hierarchy process method and integrated maximum likelihood clustering algorithm. *J. Hydrol.* **2020**, *584*, 124696. [CrossRef]
8. Tehrany, M.S.; Pradhan, B.; Jebur, M.N. Spatial prediction of flood susceptible areas using rule based decision tree (DT) and a novel ensemble bivariate and multivariate statistical models in GIS. *J. Hydrol.* **2013**, *504*, 69–79. [CrossRef]
9. Rahmati, O.; Pourghasemi, H.R. Identification of Critical Flood Prone Areas in Data-Scarce and Ungauged Regions: A Comparison of Three Data Mining Models. *Water Resour. Manag.* **2017**, *31*, 1473. [CrossRef]
10. Ngo, P.T.T.; Hoang, N.D.; Pradhan, B.; Nguyen, Q.K.; Tran, X.T.; Nguyen, Q.M.; Nguyen, V.N.; Samui, P.; Tien Bui, D. A Novel Hybrid Swarm Optimized Multilayer Neural Network for Spatial Prediction of Flash Floods in Tropical Areas Using Sentinel-1 SAR Imagery and Geospatial Data. *Sensors* **2018**, *18*, 3704. [CrossRef] [PubMed]
11. Pradhan, B.; Lee, S. Landslide susceptibility assessment and factor effect analysis: Backpropagation artificial neural networks and their comparison with frequency ratio and bivariate logistic regression modelling. *Environ. Model. Softw.* **2010**, *25*, 747–759. [CrossRef]
12. Tehrany, M.S.; Pradhan, B.; Mansor, S.; Ahmad, N. Flood susceptibility assessment using GIS-based support vector machine model with different kernel types. *CATENA* **2015**, *125*, 91–101. [CrossRef]
13. Mishra, K.; Sinha, R. Flood risk assessment in the Kosi megafan using multi-criteria decision analysis: A hydro-geomorphic approach. *Geomorphology* **2020**, *350*, 106861. [CrossRef]
14. Shadmehri Toosi, A.; Calbimonte, G.H.; Nouri, H.; Alaghmand, S. River basin-scale flood hazard assessment using a modified multi-criteria decision analysis approach: A case study. *J. Hydrol.* **2019**, *574*, 660–671. [CrossRef]
15. Tehrany, M.S.; Kumar, L. The application of a Dempster–Shafer-based evidential belief function in flood susceptibility mapping and comparison with frequency ratio and logistic regression methods. *Environ. Earth Sci.* **2018**, *77*, 490. [CrossRef]
16. Sobol, I. Global sensitivity indices for nonlinear mathematical models and their Monte Carlo estimates. *Math. Comput. Simul.* **2001**, *55*, 271–280. [CrossRef]

Proceeding Paper

Inland Areas, Protected Natural Areas and Sustainable Development †

Antonio Bertini, Immacolata Caruso and Tiziana Vitolo *

Consiglio Nazionale delle Ricerche (CNR), Istituto di Studi sul Mediterraneo (ISMed), 80134 Naples, Italy;
antonio.bertini@ismed.cnr.it (A.B.); immacolata.caruso@ismed.cnr.it (I.C.)
* Correspondence: tiziana.vitolo@ismed.cnr.it
† Presented at the 8th International Conference on Time Series and Forecasting, Gran Canaria, Spain, 27–30 June 2022.

Abstract: In recent years, policies implemented by many countries have resulted in the deterioration of the Earth's environment rather than the protection of environmental resources. The impact on the environment and territories, particularly those in the Mediterranean basin, is now evident in all its gravity. Even in Italy, the development policies pursued until 2010 favored urban settlements, neglecting the rest of the territory and, in particular, areas far from the traffic flows of people and goods. In the last decade, Italy has also begun to invest in 'inland areas' and protected natural areas that, if well analyzed, organized and managed, can become the promoter of sustainable development for the entire country. Starting from the potential expressed by local communities, landscape resources, cultural, intangible and tangible heritage, the aim is to provide direction and potential scenarios for enhancing economic opportunities, unexpressed and possible drivers of sustainable development.

Keywords: Italian inland areas; protected natural areas; sustainable development

Citation: Bertini, A.; Caruso, I.; Vitolo, T. Inland Areas, Protected Natural Areas and Sustainable Development. *Eng. Proc.* **2022**, *18*, 20. https://doi.org/10.3390/engproc2022018020

Academic Editors: Ignacio Rojas, Hector Pomares, Olga Valenzuela, Fernando Rojas and Luis Javier Herrera

Published: 21 June 2022

Publisher's Note: MDPI stays neutral with regard to jurisdictional claims in published maps and institutional affiliations.

1. Introduction

Over the last 60 years, the Italian development model has focused mainly on urban settlements, neglecting the rest of the territory and, in particular, areas far from the traffic flows of goods and people. It is only recently that non-densely urbanized areas have been taken into consideration, analyzed and observed, and that organic decisions have been made that respond to true and proper concerted programming and planning that affects the entire country. In Italy, areas that are distant, both from the most important urban centers and from communication infrastructures—in particular the digital one—have been defined as 'inland areas' since 2013, and have been illustrated in a comprehensive planning document drawn up by the Ministry for Territorial Cohesion and the South, called '*National Strategy for Inland Areas*' [1,2].

Inland areas are 'fragile' areas from a socio-demographic point of view, due to the ageing process of the population. They are unstable areas from an environmental, physical and eco-systemic point of view, due to widespread hydrogeological instability, loss of biodiversity and a slow but cumulative process of degradation of landscape values. The municipalities concerned number 3101; the population involved amounts to 4,171,667 inhabitants; and the available resources are 210 million euros [3].

To ensure that the analyses of the '*National Strategy for Inland Areas*' had effective consequences, the 'Support Fund for Economic, Artisan and Commercial Activities' was established, for each of the years from 2020 to 2022 [4].

In this context, some municipalities have initiated cooperation processes, involving local communities, for the production of essential services, and for the protection of environmental and cultural resources to enhance them. At the same time, other inland areas—many of which are located in the central and northern regions of Italy, and a few in southern Italy—have generated good policies and good practices that have made it possible to retain the population, in some cases even recording an increase in the number of settled inhabitants. In central and northern Italy, inland areas are not synonymous with depressed or poor areas: as a result of national public policies such as the expansion of the welfare state and the promotion of local development projects, together with private initiative, some areas have reached an adequate level of per capita material well-being. In the south of Italy, on the other hand, despite having significant territorial capital (buildings and settlement systems, cultivable surface area, practical knowledge, landscapes and ecosystems), it has not been possible to create that virtuous circle capable of promoting and enhancing the territory [5].

This study, after outlining a brief examination of the current situation, examines the potential and problems of inland areas, in order to define a framework of guidance for sustainable planning in areas rich in raw materials—i.e., biodiversity and cultural, material and intangible heritage—but scarce in initiatives. The aim is to help create real sustainable development, considering that future generations must be handed down not only heritage but a civilization—our civilization [6].

2. National and International Policies and Strategies for Inland Areas

A recent report by the Intergovernmental Science-Policy Platform on Biodiversity and Ecosystem Services (IPBES) notes that the current rate of species extinction is a thousand times higher than the average rate for the entire history of life on Earth. Nevertheless, eight years after the approval of the 2030 Agenda, and after the 10-year World Biodiversity Strategy 2011–2020, the state of planetary biodiversity continues to deteriorate.

The theme of environmental quality has been the center of debate at key world summits (Earth Summit, Climate Convention, Kyoto Protocol, Agenda 21) and in most policies conducted in recent years. In Europe, 2% of agricultural land has been lost since 1970—in Italy, 20%—and an irreversible process has been generated that impacts not only the territories suffering transformation but also the entire national territory, due to the fragmentation that ecosystems are facing [7]. The global context provides reference for policies on the conservation and management of the natural and environmental heritage, derived from a more consolidated and articulated programmatic regulatory apparatus at international and EU level, which has been developing for almost thirty years, and which has undergone powerful acceleration in recent years. Progressively, the subject is better-understood, and studied as a complex reality, formed by natural resources, potentials, risks, sedimentation of culture, economic activities and history [8]. The subject is considered a particularly diverse one, and in this sense it must be studied, because in it the works and transformations of the environment—planned and executed for the needs of society—interact with the rules of nature [9]. On a European scale, protected areas show strong connections with land management because they are key elements of environmental policies, although there is a known lack of systematic information on planning and management experiences.

However, in recent years, policy and planning coordination in Europe has made significant progress, which can be outlined as follows: a growth of protected areas is taking place on the continent; conflicts between parks and local contexts have been alleviated due to a shift from the concept of constrained resources to resources for development; the relationship between planning and management has been consolidated, with the integration of the different dimensions present in protected areas. The quantitative increase in protected areas has implied, and will increasingly imply, the overlapping of parks with areas affected by strong processes of urbanization and productive development. This is leading to an increase in the number of issues relating to protected areas in the overall management of these territories, which can no longer be separated from the reference contexts in which they are located. At the same time, a widespread process of environmental degradation and alteration is ongoing, with global repercussions. These facts generate conflicts between economic, social and cultural interests and the protection of natural resources that are profoundly different than those faced at the birth of nature conservation policies [10]. This has also led to the development of environmental law, and the spread of the need for sustainable growth and territorial identities [11]. However, it is possible to highlight some negative trends that profoundly affect these policies and more general land policies:

-   difference in procedures between planning of protected areas and 'ordinary' territory, which also negatively affects the parks and reserves themselves;
-   underestimation of local development plans;
-   lack of appropriate integration between plans and programs.

A balance must exist between the environmental conditions of protected areas and the needs of tourism development. European indications also point towards an integrated approach that is able to meet the needs of protecting the natural environment, increasing tourist flows and managing the flow of new inhabitants who choose to live in protected areas [12].

3. Protected Natural Areas in Italy

In Italy, many of the protected natural areas fall within the 'inland areas', and cover 3,100,000 hectares or approximately 10% of the national land surface. There are also 27 protected marine areas and the 'International Marine Mammal Sanctuary', which is shared between Italy, France and the Principality of Monaco, while the two underwater archaeological parks of Baia and Gaiola, both in the Gulf of Naples, constitute two rarities of considerable interest [13].

The number of residents in all the Italian parks is a total of 4,407,741, while the population accounts for 23.7% of the total (around 14 million inhabitants) [14]. At the same time, 68% of Italian municipalities have a territory that contributes in part or in full to the formation of the protected area, whether at national or regional level, and of these, 35% are municipalities with less than 5,000 inhabitants.

The system of Italy's protected natural areas is characterized by remarkable biodiversity, which coexists with an extraordinary cultural heritage made up of historical-architectural-artistic emergencies and intangible assets. The 'Law on Protected Natural Areas' No. 394 of 1991, one of the best nature conservation laws in Europe, defined an integrated system of national protected areas and introduced the concepts of valorization and experimentation of productive activities compatible with the conservation of natural heritage and biodiversity. The law aimed to combine the conservation of nature, landscape, history, anthropology and local culture with economic opportunities and sustainable development possibilities.

However, especially in southern Italy, the policy, strategies and opportunities indicated by the law were only partially implemented. In southern Italy in particular, most parks are having difficulty getting developed, due to a lack of participation by local communities in the pursuit of sustainable development objectives, and a lack of capacity on the part of the park authorities and the park community to be proactive, driving forces in addressing the realities involved [15].

Inland areas and protected natural areas, especially Italian parks when analyzed as a whole, are not just synonymous with depressed or poor areas. In fact, the residents in these areas have a reasonable standard of living commensurate with their needs. Most of the people who live in these somewhat secluded areas do not have much incentive to improve their economic condition, as they find their standard of living balanced against their expectations. For the most part, they are people who prefer to live away from the hectic life of densely populated areas, in an environment where the environmental quality is better, and where human relationships are daily and constant over time, and therefore more satisfying. This condition has not led to a social and economic crisis, as many think, but has relegated these communities to a sort of limbo in which there are few incentives to invest in activities that create growth, change the status quo, and develop and therefore also enhance the rich heritage of these places [16].

4. For Sustainable Tourism in Inland and Protected Areas

In 1995, at the World Conference on Sustainable Tourism held in Lanzarote (Canary Islands, Spain), the World Charter for Sustainable Tourism was signed, which represents a reference for defining the priorities, objectives and instruments needed to promote future tourism.

The World Tourism Organisation (WTO) has defined tourism activities as sustainable when they "develop in such a way that they remain viable in a tourist area for an unlimited time, do not alter the natural, social and artistic environment and do not hinder or inhibit the development of other social and economic activities".

On 19 October 2007, 'The Agenda for a Sustainable and Competitive European Tourism' marked the official start of planning for such tourism, which aims at economic prosperity, equity and social cohesion, and environmental and cultural protection.

In line with the Lisbon Treaty and the commitments ratified by EU ministers at the Madrid Conference on 14 April 2010, a new framework for EU action on European tourism was defined, which included, among other things, the development of sustainable management of tourist destinations and local enterprises.

In the wake of these premises and shared regulatory and cultural references, many and diverse attempts have been made to revive the fortunes of protected areas, but with scarce and, above all, limited results. In many areas of Italy, investments have been made in tourism activities, a sector that accounts for about 10% of European GDP, and is the third sector, with the greatest potential for economic growth in the Union, rightly considered a powerful driver of local development and employment in European countries. The factors of tourist interest in Italy have often been treated as separate compartments, which instead could have had a greater attractive force precisely from their coexistence: lakes and rivers, wine and food routes, religious tourism, ancient and historical centers, archaeological nature sites, archaeological nature trails, craft activities, including identity activities, more than 50 UNESCO sites, etc. Environments were rich in diversified tourist proposals, in which to study and propose ideas while avoiding the environmental depauperate [17,18].

In the context of protected natural areas falling within the inland areas, another widespread, consistent and culturally relevant heritage is constituted by the 'small towns' where, in some cases, a few hundred families live, and which for the most part maintain a close environmental, morphological and landscape relationship, if not still functional, with the surrounding territory. The number of small towns is substantial, and reaches 72% of Italy's municipalities; their surface area covers 55% of the national territory, and 17% of the Italian population lives there (on average there are 64 inhabitants per km). Small towns also have a significant economic, settlement and infrastructural value. The relatively recent affirmation of new policies tending to promote local dimensions, networking the widespread and articulated diversities of experience, culture and identity, and constituting a tendentially multifaceted offer, has determined a favorable climate for a relaunch of the issue of small towns in new development contexts, making previously unusual resources, instruments and availability accessible [19].

5. Conclusions for the Sustainable Development of The Protected Inland Areas of Southern Italy

One of the most agreeable and convincing approaches to dealing more effectively with the problem of a concerted strategy of actions in the inland and protected areas is that of the 'Smart land', i.e., a territorial sphere of diffuse and shared experimental policies which have the objective of increasing the attractiveness of the territory, taking due account of social cohesion, the diffusion of knowledge, accessibility, freedom of movement, the usability of the environment, the quality of the landscape and the daily life of the local communities that live in those places. The aim is to attempt to rebuild a 'middle society' made up of those residents interested in and capable of transforming the premises into real economic, social and cultural practices capable of turning local potential into economic activities [20].

Most local regeneration and development projects remain hetero-directed and top-down because the involvement of the communities occurs later, thus lacking the direct involvement of local populations, especially for the implementation of specific projects. More successful, and growing more successful still, is the implementation of bottom-up projects, which arise from the mechanisms of protection and enhancement of local identities, which constitute a driver of lasting and sustainable development according to the logic of sharing [21].

In this context, in recent years, some administrations of those municipalities suffering from significant depopulation (this phenomenon does not spare the south or even central and northern Italy, concentrating in small and mountainous centers) are offering economic and social incentives, giving away abandoned houses to encourage the return of emigrants, or welcoming new communities to revive agricultural and craft activities. Nevertheless, the conditions of peripheral location persist, not only because of geographical issues but also because of the lack of socio-economic and political connections between metropolitan and urban areas in general and inland areas. After having created the material conditions for a return to the inland areas, the next step, where possible, is to transform the community into a 'project community', a partnership, that is, between those who plan, those who reside, and those who benefit from the services offered [22].

In our opinion, it is in the encounter between the top-down and bottom-up processes that a balance that generates real development opportunities can be achieved. Furthermore, targeted policies and direct funding for the development of essential services are crucial if good practices are to become an effective incentive for communities to remain in inland and protected areas. This process is also contemplated in the '*National Recovery and Resilience Plan*', which could help to bridge the existing gaps between northern, central and southern Italy, and demonstrate institutions' renewed awareness of marginal areas.

Author Contributions: Conceptualization, A.B., I.C. and T.V.; methodology, A.B., I.C. and T.V.; software, T.V.; validation, A.B., I.C. and A.B.; formal analysis, T.V.; investigation, I.C.; resources, A.B.; data curation, A.B.; writing—original draft preparation, T.V; writing—review and editing, A.B.; visualization, T.V.; supervision, T.V. All authors have read and agreed to the published version of the manuscript.

Funding: This research received no external funding.

Institutional Review Board Statement: Not applicable.

Informed Consent Statement: Not applicable.

Data Availability Statement: Not applicable.

Conflicts of Interest: The authors declare no conflict of interest.

References

1. Documento di Lavoro dei Servizi Della Commissione. Analisi del Piano per la Ripresa e la Resilienza dell'Italia. Available online: https://italiadomani.gov.it/it/strumenti/documenti/archivio-documenti/documento-di-lavoro-dei-servizi-della-commissione--analisi-del-p.html? (accessed on 2 June 2022).
2. Ministero per la Coesione Territoriale e il Mezzogiorno. "Strategia Nazionale per le Aree Interne". 2013. Available online: https://www.miur.gov.it/documents/20182/890263/strategia_nazionale_aree_interne.pdf/d10fc111-65c0-4acd-b253-63efae626b19 (accessed on 2 June 2022).
3. De Rossi, A. *Riabitare l'Italia. Le Aree Interne Tra Abbandoni E Riconquiste*; Progetti Donzelli: Padova, Italy, 2020.
4. Il Presidente del Consiglio dei Ministri. Available online: https://www.gazzettaufficiale.it/eli/id/2020/12/04/20A06526/sg (accessed on 2 June 2022).
5. Rodríguez-Pose, A. The revenge of the places that don't matter (and what to do about it). *Camb. J. Reg. Econ. Soc.* **2018**, *11*, 189–209. [CrossRef]
6. Giacomini, V.; Romani, V. *Uomini e Parchi*; Franco Angeli: Milano, Italy, 1982.
7. Bock, B.B. Rural Marginalisation and the Role of Social Innovation; A Turn Towards Nexogenous Development and Rural Reconnection. *Soc. Rural.* **2016**, *56*, 552–573. [CrossRef]
8. Borghi, E. *Piccole Italie. Le Aree Interne e la Questione Territoriale*; Donzelli: Roma, Italy, 2017.
9. Hicks, J. *Capital and Time*; Clarendon Press: Oxford, UK; Etas libri: Milano, Italy, 1973.

10. Carrosio, G. *I margini al Centro. L'Italia Delle Aree Interne Fra Fragilità E Innovazione*; Donzelli: Roma, Italy, 2019.
11. Lewanski, R. La politica ambientale. In *Le Politiche Pubbliche in Italia*; Dente, B., Ed.; Il mulino: Bologna, Italy, 1990; pp. 281–314.
12. Pinto, M.R.; Viola, S.; Fabbricatti, K.; Pacifico, M.G. Adaptive reuse process of the Historic Urban Landscape Post-COVID-19. The Potential of the Inner Areas for a "New Normal". *Vitr. Int. J. Arch. Technol. Sustain.* **2020**, *5*, 87–105. [CrossRef]
13. Bertini, A.; Nicoletti, D.; Russo, G.F.; Vitolo, T. *Aree Protette in Italia. Il caso della Campania*; Rubbettino: Soveria Mannelli, Italy, 2015.
14. Ortis, I. La Riforma Della Legge Quadro Sulle Aree Naturali Protette. p. 3. Available online: https://www.italianostra.org/wp-content/uploads/ortis_OK.pdf (accessed on 2 June 2022).
15. D'Alessandro, S.; Salvatore, R.; Bortoletto, N. *Ripartire Dai Borghi, Per Cambiare le città. Modelli e Buone Pratiche per Ripensare lo Sviluppo Locale*; Franco Angeli: Milano, Italy, 2020.
16. Bertini, A. Per i centri abitati "poco noti". In *Turismi e Turisti. Politica, Innovazione, Economia in Italia in Età Contemporanea*; Avallone, P., Strangio, D., Eds.; Franco Angeli: Milano, Italy, 2015; pp. 207–226.
17. Sommella, R. *Una Strategia per le Aree Interne Italiane*; AGEI—Geotema: Bologna, Italy, 2017; pp. 76–79.
18. Sommella, R.; Viganoni, L. Territorio e sviluppo locale nel Mezzogiorno. In *Territorialità, Sviluppo Locale, Sostenibilità: Il Modello SlOT*; Dematteis, G., Governa, F., Eds.; Franco Angeli: Milano, Italy, 2005; pp. 189–210.
19. Lupoli, R.; Bonfanti, A.; Dossier Legambiente. Scatti di Futuro. Storie di Piccoli Comuni Che Innovano. 2018. Available online: https://www.legambiente.it/sites/default/files/docs/scatti_di_futuro_storie_di_piccoli_comuni_che_innovano.pdf (accessed on 2 June 2022).
20. Bonomi, A.; Masiero, R. *Dalla Smart City Alla Smart Land*; Marsilio: Venezia, Italy, 2014.
21. Vitolo, T. Sostenibilità ed aree protette, le comunità ed i luoghi: Valori da tutelare. In *Aree Protette in Italia. Il Caso Della Campania*; Bertini, A., Nicoletti, D., Russo, G.F., Vitolo, T., Eds.; Rubbettino: Soveria Mannelli, Italy, 2015; pp. 55–82.
22. Lang, G. The Dialectic between the Urban Dimension and Inland Areas: A Response to the Pandemic. Available online: https://www.pandorarivista.it/artico-li/la-dialettica-tra-dimensione-urbana-e-aree-interne-una-risposta-alla-pandemia (accessed on 2 June 2022).

*engineering
proceedings*

MDPI

Proceeding Paper

Expectation-Maximization Algorithm for Autoregressive Models with Cauchy Innovations †

Monika S. Dhull * and Arun Kumar

Department of Mathematics, Indian Institute of Technology Ropar, Rupnagar 140001, India;
arun.kumar@iitrpr.ac.in
* Correspondence: 2018maz0005@iitrpr.ac.in
† Presented at the 8th International Conference on Time Series and Forecasting, Gran Canaria, Spain,
27–30 June 2022.

Abstract: In this paper, we study the autoregressive (AR) models with Cauchy distributed innovations. In the AR models, the response variable y_t depends on previous terms and a stochastic term (the innovation). In the classical version, the AR models are based on normal distribution which could not capture the extreme values or asymmetric behavior of data. In this work, we consider the AR model with Cauchy innovations, which is a heavy-tailed distribution. We derive closed forms for the estimates of parameters of the considered model using the expectation-maximization (EM) algorithm. The efficacy of the estimation procedure is shown on the simulated data. The comparison of the proposed EM algorithm is shown with the maximum likelihood (ML) estimation method. Moreover, we also discuss the joint characteristic function of the AR(1) model with Cauchy innovations, which can also be used to estimate the parameters of the model using empirical characteristic function.

Keywords: autoregressive model; Cauchy innovations; EM algorithm

check for
updates

Citation: Dhull, M.S.; Kumar, A. Expectation-Maximization Algorithm for Autoregressive Models with Cauchy Innovations. *Eng. Proc.* **2022**, *18*, 21. https://doi.org/10.3390/engproc2022018021

Academic Editors: Ignacio Rojas, Hector Pomares, Olga Valenzuela, Fernando Rojas and Luis Javier Herrera

Published: 21 June 2022

Publisher's Note: MDPI stays neutral with regard to jurisdictional claims in published maps and institutional affiliations.

1. Introduction

Autoregressive (AR) models with stable and heavy-tailed innovations are of great interest in time series modeling. These distributions can easily assimilate the asymmetry, skewness, and outliers present in time series data. The Cauchy distribution is a special case of stable distribution with undefined expected value, variance, and higher order moments. The Cauchy distribution and its mixture has many applications in the field of economics [1], seismology [2], biology [3], and various other fields, but only a few studies have been conducted concerning time series models with Cauchy errors. In [4], the maximum likelihood (ML) estimation of AR(1) model with Cauchy errors is studied.

The standard estimation techniques for the AR(p) model with Cauchy innovations, particularly the Yule–Walker method and conditional least squares method, cannot be used due to the infinite second order moments of the Cauchy distribution. Therefore, it is worthwhile to study and assess the alternate estimation techniques for the AR(p) model with Cauchy innovations. In the literature, several estimation techniques have been proposed to estimate the parameters of AR models with infinite variance errors (see e.g., [5–7]).

In this paper, we propose to use the EM algorithm to estimate the parameters of the distribution and model simultaneously. It is a general iterative algorithm for model parameter estimation which iterates between two steps, namely the expectation step (E-step) and the maximization step (M-step) [8]. It is an alternative to the numerical optimization of the likelihood function which is proven to be numerically stable [9]. We also provide the formula based on the characteristic function (CF) and empirical characteristic function (ECF) of Cauchy distribution for AR(p) model estimation. The idea to use ECF in a time series stable ARMA model has been discussed in [10].

The remainder of the paper is organized as follows. In Section 2, we present a brief overview of the Cauchy AR(p) model, followed by a discussion of estimation techniques, namely the EM algorithm and estimation by CF and ECF. Section 3 checks the efficacy of the estimation procedure on simulated data. We also present the comparative study, where the proposed technique is compared with ML estimation for Cauchy innovations. Section 4 concludes the paper.

2. Cauchy Autoregressive Model

We consider the AR(p) univariate stationary time-series $\{Y_t\}$, $t \in \mathbb{N}$ with Cauchy innovations defined as

$$Y_t = \sum_{i=1}^{p} \rho_i Y_{t-i} + \varepsilon_t = \rho^T Y_{t-1} + \varepsilon_t, \tag{1}$$

where $\rho = (\rho_1, \rho_2, \cdots, \rho_p)^T$ is a p-dimensional column vector, $Y_{t-1} = (Y_{t-1}, Y_{t-2}, \cdots, Y_{t-p})^T$ is a vector of p lag terms, and $\{\epsilon_t\}$, $t \in \mathbb{N}$ are i.i.d. innovations distributed as Cauchy(α, γ). The pdf of Cauchy(α, γ) [11] is

$$f(x; \alpha, \gamma) = \frac{\gamma}{\pi}\left[\frac{1}{\gamma^2 + (x - \alpha)^2}\right], \quad \gamma > 0,\ \alpha \in \mathbb{R},\ x \in \mathbb{R}. \tag{2}$$

The conditional distribution of Y_t given the preceding data $\mathcal{F}_{t-1} = (Y_{t-1}, Y_{t-2}, \cdots, Y_1)^T$ is given by [4]

$$p(Y_t|\mathcal{F}_{t-1}) = f(y_t - \rho^T y_{t-1}; \alpha, \gamma) = \frac{\gamma}{\pi}\left[\frac{1}{\gamma^2 + (y_t - \rho^T y_{t-1} - \alpha)^2}\right],$$

where y_{t-1} is the realization of Y_{t-1}. In the next subsection, we propose the methods to estimate the model parameters ρ and innovation parameters α and γ simultaneously.

2.1. Parameter Estimation Using EM Algorithm

We estimate the parameters of the AR(p) model using an EM algorithm which maximizes the likelihood function iteratively. Further, we discuss the time series $\{Y_t\}$ using the characteristic function (CF) and estimation method using CF and ECF. Recently [7], the exponential-squared estimator for AR models with heavy-tailed errors was introduced and proven to be $\sqrt{n}$-consistent under some regularity conditions; similarly, the self-weighted least absolute deviation estimation method was also studied for the infinite variance AR model [12]. The ML estimation of AR models with Cauchy errors with intercept and with linear trend is studied, and the AR coefficient is shown to be $n^{3/2}$-consistent under some conditions [4]. For the AR(p) model with Cauchy innovations with n samples, the log likelihood is defined as

$$l(\Theta) = (n - p)\log(\gamma) - (n - p)\log(\pi) - \sum_{t=p+1}^{n} \log(\gamma^2 + (y_t - \rho^T Y_{t-1} - \alpha)^2),$$

where $\Theta = \left(\alpha,\ \gamma,\ \rho^T\right)$.

Proposition 1. *Consider the AR(p) time-series model given in Equation (1) where error terms follow Cauchy(α, γ). The maximum likelihood estimates of the model parameters using EM algorithm are as follows*

$$\hat{\rho}^T = \left(\sum_{t=p+1}^{n} \frac{(y_t - \alpha) Y_{t-1}^T}{s_t^{(k)}} \right) \left(\sum_{t=p+1}^{n} \frac{Y_{t-1} Y_{t-1}^T}{s_t^{(k)}} \right)^{-1} ;$$

$$\hat{\alpha} = \frac{\displaystyle\sum_{t=p+1}^{n} \frac{(y_t - \rho^T Y_{t-1})}{s_t^{(k)}}}{\sum_{t=p+1}^{n} \frac{1}{s_t^{(k)}}} ; \tag{3}$$

and

$$\hat{\gamma} = \sqrt{\frac{n - p}{2 \sum_{t=p+1}^{n} \frac{1}{s_t^{(k)}}}},$$

where $s_t^{(k)} = (y_t - \rho^{T(k)} Y_{t-1} - \alpha^{(k)})^2 + \gamma^{(k)2}$.

Proof. Consider the AR(p) model

$$Y_t = \rho^T Y_{t-1} + \varepsilon_t, \ t = p + 1, 2, \cdots, n,$$

where ε_t follows Cauchy distribution Cauchy(α, γ). Let (ε_t, V_t) for $t = 1, 2, \cdots, n$ denote the complete data for innovations ε. The observed data ε_t are assumed to be from Cauchy(α, γ) and the unobserved data V_t follow inverse gamma IG($1/2, \gamma^2/2$). A random variable $V \sim$ IG(a, b) if the pdf is given by

$$f_V(v; a, b) = \frac{b^a}{\Gamma(a)} \frac{e^{-b/v}}{v^{a+1}}, \ a > 0, \ b > 0, \ v > 0.$$

We can rewrite ε_t as $\varepsilon_t = Y_t - \rho^T Y_{t-1}$, for $t = 1, 2, \cdots, n$. The stochastic relation $\varepsilon = \alpha + \sqrt{V}Z$ with $Z \sim N(0, 1)$ i.e., standard normal and $V \sim$ IG($1/2, \gamma^2/2$) is used to generate Cauchy(α, γ) distribution. Then, the conditional distribution is

$$f(\varepsilon = \varepsilon_t | V = v_t) = \frac{1}{\sqrt{2\pi v_t}} \exp\left(-\frac{1}{2v_t} (\varepsilon_t - \alpha))^2 \right).$$

Now, we need to estimate the unknown parameters $\Theta = (\alpha, \gamma, \rho^T)$. To apply the EM algorithm for estimation, we first find the conditional expectation of log-likelihood of complete data (ε, V) with respect to the conditional distribution of V given ε. As the unobserved data are assumed to be from IG($1/2, \gamma^2/2$), the posterior distribution is again an inverse gamma i.e.,

$$V | \varepsilon = e, \Theta \sim \text{IG}\left(1, \frac{(e - \alpha)^2 + \gamma^2}{2} \right).$$

The following conditional inverse first moment and $\mathbb{E}(\log(V) | \varepsilon = e)$ will be used in calculating the conditional expectation of the log-likelihood function:

$$\mathbb{E}(V^{-1} | \varepsilon = e) = \frac{2}{(e - \alpha)^2 + \gamma^2},$$

$$\mathbb{E}(\log(V) | \varepsilon = e) = \log((e - \alpha)^2 + \gamma^2) - \log 2 + 0.5776.$$

The complete data likelihood is given by

$$L(\Theta) = \prod_{t=p+1}^{n} f(\epsilon_t, v_t) = \prod_{t=p+1}^{n} f_{\epsilon|V}(\epsilon_t|v_t) f_V(v_t)$$

$$= \prod_{t=p+1}^{n} \frac{\gamma}{2\pi v_t^2} \exp\left(-\frac{(\epsilon_t - \alpha)^2 + \gamma^2}{2v_t}\right).$$

The log likelihood function will be

$$l(\Theta) = (n-p)\log(\gamma) - (n-p)\log(2\pi) - 2\sum_{t=p+1}^{n}\log(v_t) - \sum_{t=p+1}^{n}\frac{(\epsilon_t - \alpha)^2 + \gamma^2}{2v_t}.$$

Now, we will use the relation $\epsilon_t = Y_t - \rho^T Y_{t-1}$ in further calculations. In the first step at kth iteration, E-step of EM algorithm, we need to compute the expected value of the complete data log likelihood known as $Q(\Theta|\Theta^{(k)})$, which is expressed as

$$Q(\Theta|\Theta^{(k)}) = \mathbb{E}_{V|\epsilon,\Theta^{(k)}}\left[\log f(\epsilon, V|\Theta)|\epsilon_t, \Theta^{(k)}\right] = \mathbb{E}_{V|\epsilon,\Theta^{(k)}}\left[l(\Theta|\Theta^{(k)})\right]$$

$$= (n-p)\log\gamma - (n-p)\log 2\pi - \sum_{t=p+1}^{n}\mathbb{E}(\log v_t|\epsilon_t, \Theta^{(k)})$$

$$- \frac{\gamma^2}{2}\sum_{t=p+1}^{n}\mathbb{E}(v_t^{-1}|\epsilon_t, \Theta^{(k)}) - \frac{1}{2}\sum_{t=p+1}^{n}(\epsilon_t - \alpha)^2\mathbb{E}(v_t^{-1}|\epsilon_t, \Theta^{(k)})$$

$$= (n-p)\log\gamma - (n-p)\log 2\pi - (n-p)\log 2 + 0.5776(n-p) - \sum_{t=p+1}^{n}\log((\epsilon_t - \alpha^{(k)})^2 + \gamma^{(k)^2})$$

$$- \frac{\gamma^2}{2}\sum_{t=p+1}^{n}\frac{1}{(\epsilon_t - \alpha^{(k)})^2 + \gamma^{(k)2}} - \sum_{t=p+1}^{n}\frac{(\epsilon_t - \alpha)^2}{(\epsilon_t - \alpha^{(k)})^2 + \gamma^{(k)2}}$$

$$= (n-p)\log\gamma - (n-p)\log 2\pi - (n-p)\log 2 + 0.5776(n-p) - \sum_{t=p+1}^{n}\log(s_t^{(k)})$$

$$- \frac{\gamma^2}{2}\sum_{t=p+1}^{n}\frac{1}{s_t^{(k)}} - \sum_{t=p+1}^{n}\frac{(\epsilon_t - \alpha)^2}{s_t^{(k)}}.$$

where $s_t = (y_t - \rho^T Y_{t-1} - \alpha)^2 + \gamma^2$. In the next M-step, we estimate the parameters α, γ, and ρ^T by maximizing the Q function using the equations below:

$$\frac{\partial Q}{\partial \rho} = 4\sum_{t=p+1}^{n}\frac{(y_t - \rho^T Y_{t-1} - \alpha Y_{t-1}^T)}{s_t^{(k)}},$$

$$\frac{\partial Q}{\partial \alpha} = \sum_{t=p+1}^{n}\frac{(y_t - \rho^T Y_{t-1} - \alpha)}{s_t^{(k)}},$$

$$\frac{\partial Q}{\partial \gamma} = \frac{n-p}{\gamma} - 2\gamma\sum_{t=p+1}^{n}\frac{1}{s_t^{(k)}}.$$

Solving the above equations at each iteration, we find the following closed form estimates of the parameters at $k + 1$th iteration:

$$\rho^T = \left(\sum_{t=p+1}^{n} \frac{(y_t - \alpha)Y_{t-1}^T}{s_t^{(k)}} \right) \left(\sum_{t=p+1}^{n} \frac{Y_{t-1}Y_{t-1}^T}{s_t^{(k)}} \right)^{-1};$$

$$\hat{\alpha} = \frac{\sum_{t=p+1}^{n} \frac{(y_t - \rho^T Y_{t-1})}{s_t^{(k)}}}{\sum_{t=p+1}^{n} \frac{1}{s_t^{(k)}}}; \tag{4}$$

and

$$\hat{\gamma} = \sqrt{\frac{n-p}{2\sum_{t=p+1}^{n} \frac{1}{s_t^{(k)}}}},$$

where $s_t^{(k)} = (y_t - \rho^{T(k)}Y_{t-1} - \alpha^{(k)})^2 + \gamma^{(k)2}$. $\square$

2.2. Characteristic Function for Estimation

Thus far, we have considered the conditional distribution of Y_t given the preceding data $\mathcal{F}_{t-1}$. Now, we include the dependency of time series $\{Y_t\}$ by defining the variable $d_j = (y_j, \cdots, y_{j+p})$ for $j = 1, \cdots, n - p$. In each variable $\{d_j\}$, there are p terms the same as adjacent variable. The distribution of $\{d_j\}$ will be multivariate Cauchy with dimension $r = p + 1$.

The CF of each d_j is $c(\Theta, s) = \mathbb{E}(\exp(i s^T d_j))$ and the ECF is $c_n(s) = \frac{1}{n} \sum_{j=1}^{n-p} \exp(i s^T d_j)$ where $s = (s_1, \cdots, s_{p+1})^T$.

To estimate the parameters using CF and ECF, we make sure that the joint CF of the AR(p) model has a closed form. In the next result, the closed form expression for the joint CF of the AR(1) model with Cauchy innovations is given.

Proposition 2. *The joint CF of stationary AR(1) model with Cauchy innovations is*

$$c(s_1, s_2; \Theta) = \exp\left[i\alpha(s_1 + s_2)\left(\frac{1}{1-\rho} \right) \right] \times \exp\left[-\gamma\left(|s_2| + |s_1 + \rho s_2|\left(\frac{1}{1-|\rho|} \right) \right) \right].$$

Proof. For stationary AR(1) model $y_t = \rho y_{t-1} + \varepsilon_t$, we can rewrite it as

$$y_t = \varepsilon_t + \rho\varepsilon_{t-1} + \rho^2\varepsilon_{t-2} + \rho^3\varepsilon_{t-3} + \cdots.$$

Note that $\{\varepsilon_t\}$ are i.i.d from Cauchy(α, γ) distribution, and the CF of Cauchy(α, γ) is $\mathbb{E}(\exp(i\, s\varepsilon_t)) = \exp(i\, \alpha s - \gamma|s|)$ [11]. Then, the joint CF of (y_t, y_{t-1}) is calculated as follows:

$$
\begin{aligned}
c(s_1, s_2; \Theta) &= \mathbb{E}[\exp(i\, s_1 y_{t-1} + i\, s_2 y_t)] \\
&= \mathbb{E}[\exp(i\, s_1(\varepsilon_{t-1} + \rho\varepsilon_{t-2} + \rho^2\varepsilon_{t-3} + \cdots)) + i\, s_2(\varepsilon_t + \rho\varepsilon_{t-1} + \rho^2\varepsilon_{t-2} + \cdots)] \\
&= \mathbb{E}[\exp(i\, s_2\varepsilon_t + i(s_1 + s_2\rho)\varepsilon_{t-1} + i\rho(s_1 + \rho s_2)\varepsilon_{t-2} + \cdots)] \\
&= \exp(i\alpha s_2 - \gamma|s_2|) \times \exp(i\alpha(s_1 + \rho s_2) - \gamma|s_1 + \rho s_2|) \\
&\quad \times \exp(i\alpha(\rho s_1 + \rho^2 s_2) - \gamma|\rho s_1 + \rho^2 s_2|) \times \cdots. \\
&= \exp(i\alpha(s_1 + s_2)(1 + \rho + \rho^2 + \rho^3 + \cdots)) \\
&\quad \times \exp(-\gamma(|s_2| + |s_1 + \rho s_2| + |\rho||s_1 + \rho s_2| + |\rho^2||s_1 + \rho s_2| + \cdots)) \\
&= \exp(i\alpha(s_1 + s_2)\left(\frac{1}{1-\rho}\right) \times \exp(-\gamma(|s_2| + |s_1 + \rho s_2|(1 + |\rho| + |\rho^2| + \cdots))) \\
&= \exp\left[i\alpha(s_1 + s_2)\left(\frac{1}{1-\rho}\right)\right] \times \exp\left[-\gamma\left(|s_2| + |s_1 + \rho s_2|\left(\frac{1}{1-|\rho|}\right)\right)\right].
\end{aligned}
$$

□

The joint CF for a higher dimension can be obtained in similar manner. Now, the model parameters can be estimated by solving the following integral with CF and ECF as defined in [10]:

$$
\int \cdots \int w_\Theta(s)(c_n(s) - c(s;\Theta))ds = 0. \tag{5}
$$

where optimal weight function

$$
w_\Theta^*(s) = \frac{1}{2\pi}\int \cdots \int \exp(-i\, s^T d_j)\frac{\partial \log f(y_{j+p}|y_j, \cdots, y_{j+p-1})}{\partial\Theta}dy_j \ldots dy_{j+p}. \tag{6}
$$

Remark 1. *For a stationary AR(l) process $\{Y_t\}$ with $p = l$, the ECF estimator defined by Equation (5) with optimal weight function defined in Equation (6) is a conditional ML (CML) estimator and hence asymptotically efficient. The conditional log pdf for Cauchy distribution is:*

$$
\log f(y_{j+p}|y_j, \cdots, y_{j+p-1}) = \log\gamma - \log\pi - \log\left(\gamma^2 + (y_t - \rho^T Y_{t-1} - \alpha^2)^2\right).
$$

The proof is similar to the proof of Proposition 2.1 in [10].

3. Simulation Study

In this section, we assess the proposed model and the introduced estimation technique using a simulated data set. We discuss the estimation procedure for the AR(2) model with Cauchy innovations. The AR(2) model defined in (1) is simulated with ρ_1 and ρ_2 as model parameters. We generate 1000 trajectories, each of size $N = 500$ of Cauchy innovations using the normal variance-mean mixture form $\varepsilon = \alpha + \sqrt{V}Z$ with $Z \sim N(0,1)$, i.e., standard normal and $V \sim IG(1/2, \gamma^2/2)$. We then use the following simulation steps to generate the Cauchy innovations:

step 1: Generate standard normal variate Z;

step 2: Generate inverse gamma random variate $IG(1/2, \gamma^2/2)$ with $\gamma = 2$;

step 3: Using the relation $\varepsilon = \alpha + \sqrt{V}Z$, we simulate the Cauchy innovations with $\alpha = 1$;

step 4: The time series data y_t is generated with model parameters $\rho_1 = 0.5$ and $\rho_2 = 0.3$.

The exemplary time series data plot and scatter plot of innovation terms are shown in Figure 1. We apply the discussed EM algorithm to estimate the model parameters and distribution parameters. The relative change in the parameters is considered to terminate the algorithm. The following is the stopping criteria which is commonly used in literature:

$$\max\left\{\left|\frac{\alpha^{(k+1)} - \alpha^{(k)}}{\alpha^{(k)}}\right|, \left|\frac{\gamma^{(k+1)} - \gamma^{(k)}}{\gamma^{(k)}}\right|, \left|\frac{\rho_1^{(k+1)} - \rho_1^{(k)}}{\rho_1^{(k)}}\right|, \left|\frac{\rho_2^{(k+1)} - \rho_2^{(k)}}{\rho_2^{(k)}}\right|\right\} < 10^{-4}. \quad (7)$$

We compare the estimation results of Cauchy(α, γ) with the EM algorithm and maximum likelihood (ML) estimation. The ML estimates are computed using the inbuilt function "mlcauchy" in R, which uses the exponential transform of the location parameter and performs non-linear minimization by a Newton-type algorithm. The comparison of the estimates of Cauchy(α, γ) are shown in boxplots in Figure 2. From the boxplots, we find that the EM algorithm converges near to the true value of the Cauchy(α, γ) as compared to the ML estimation. There is a possibility of achieving a better result from ML method if a different algorithm or inbuilt function for optimization are used for estimation.

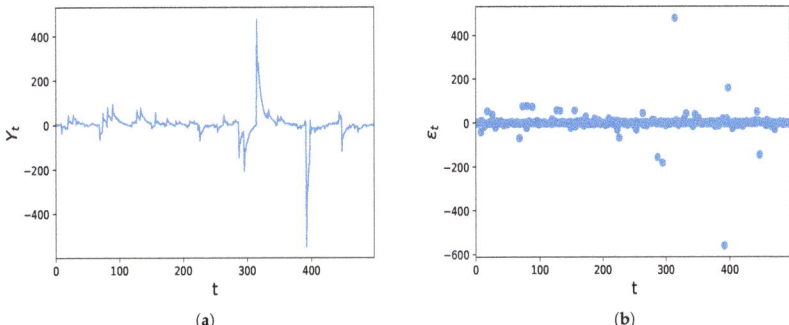

(a) (b)

Figure 1. (a) The data plot of exemplary time series of length $N = 500$ and (b) the scatter plot of the corresponding innovation terms of the AR(2) model with Cauchy innovations. The chosen parameters of the model are $\rho_1 = 0.5$, $\rho_2 = 0.3$, $\alpha = 1$, and $\gamma = 2$.

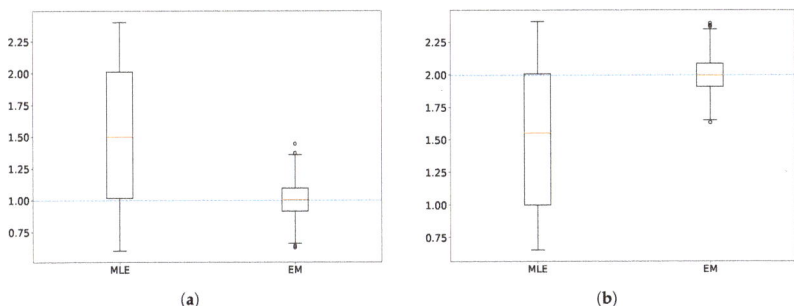

(a) (b)

Figure 2. Boxplots of the estimates of the AR(2) model's parameters with theoretical values (a) $\alpha = 1$ and (b) $\gamma = 2$ represented with blue dotted lines. The boxplots are created using 1000 trajectories, each of length 500.

4. Conclusions and Future Scope

In this work, we derive the closed form of estimates of AR model with Cauchy innovations using an EM algorithm. The performance of the proposed algorithm is compared with the ML method using simulated data. The ML estimation is found using an inbuilt function in R. Another benefit of using the EM algorithm is that it calculates the model as well as the innovation parameters simultaneously. It is evident from the boxplot that the EM algorithm outperforms the ML method. Further, we discuss another approach based on CF to estimate the AR model parameters with stable distribution. In the future, we plan to study and compare the proposed algorithm and ECF based estimation method with the existing techniques in [5–7] for an AR model with infinite variance. Further, the real life phenomena can be studied using the proposed model and methods.

Author Contributions: Conceptualization, A.K. and M.S.D.; Methodology, A.K. and M.S.D.; Writing-Original Draft Preparation, M.S.D. and A.K.; WritingReview & Editing, A.K. and M.S.D. All authors have read and agreed to the published version of the manuscript.

Funding: This research received no external funding.

Institutional Review Board Statement: Not applicable.

Informed Consent Statement: Not applicable.

Data Availability Statement: Not applicable.

Acknowledgments: M.S.D. would like to thank her institute Indian Institute of Technology Ropar, India and the Ministry of Education (MoE), Government of India, for supporting her research work.

Conflicts of Interest: The authors declare no conflict of interest.

References

1. Liu, T.; Zhang, P.; Dai, W.S.; Xie, M. An intermediate distribution between Gaussian and Cauchy distributions. *Phys. A Stat. Mech. Appl.* **2012**, *391*, 5411–5421. [CrossRef]
2. Kagan, Y.Y. Correlations of earthquake focal mechanism. *Geophys. J. Int.* **1992**, *110*, 305–320. [CrossRef]
3. Bjerkedal, T. Acquisition of resistance in guinea pigs infected with different doses of virulent tubercle bacilli. *Am. J. Hyg.* **1960**, *72*, 130–148. [PubMed]
4. Choi, J.; Choi, I. Maximum likelihood estimation of autoregressive models with a near unit root and Cauchy errors. *Ann. Inst. Stat. Math.* **2019**, *71*, 1121–1142. [CrossRef]
5. Jiang, Y. An exponential-squared estimator in the autoregressive model with heavy-tailed errors. *Stat. Interface* **2016**, *9*, 233–238. [CrossRef]
6. Li, J.; Liang, W.; He, S.; Wu, X. Empirical likelihood for the smoothed LAD estimator in infinite variance autoregressive models. *Statist. Probab. Lett.* **2010**, *80*, 1420–1430. [CrossRef]
7. Tang, L.; Zhou, Z.; Wu, C. Efficient estimation and variable selection for infinite variance autoregressive models. *J. Appl. Math. Comput.* **2012**, *40*, 399–413. [CrossRef]
8. Dempster, A.P.; Laird, N.M.; Rubin, D.B. Maximum likelihood from incomplete data via EM Algorithm. *J. R. Stat. Soc. Ser. B* **1977**, *39*, 1–22. .
9. McLachlan, G.J.; Krishnan, T. *The EM Algorithm and Extensions*, 2nd ed.; John Wiley & Sons: Hoboken, NJ, USA, 2007.
10. Yu, J.; Knight, J.L. Empirical characteristic function in time series estimation. *Econom. Theory* **2002**, *18*, 691–721.
11. Feller, W. *An Introduction to Probability Theory and Its Applications*, 2nd ed.; John Wiley & Sons: New York, NY, USA, 1991; Volume 2.
12. Ling, S. Self-weighted least absolute deviation estimation for infinite variance autoregressive models. *J. R. Stat. Soc. Ser. B* **2005**, *67*, 381–393. [CrossRef]

Proceeding Paper

Deep Representation Learning for Cluster-Level Time Series Forecasting †

Tsegamlak T. Debella [1,2,*], Bethelhem S. Shawel [1,3], Maxime Devanne [2], Jonathan Weber [2],
Dereje H. Woldegebreal [1], Sofie Pollin [3] and Germain Forestier [2]

1   Addis Ababa Institute of Technology, School of Electrical & Computer Engineering, Addis Ababa University,
    Addis Ababa 386, Ethiopia; bethelhem.seifu@aait.edu.et (B.S.S.); dereje.hailemariam@aait.edu.et (D.H.W.)
2   École Nationale Supérieure d'Ingénieurs Sud-Alsace, Institut de Recherche en Informatique, Mathématiques,
    Automatique et Signal, Université de Haute Alsace, 68093 Mulhouse, France; maxime.devanne@uha.fr (M.D.);
    jonathan.weber@uha.fr (J.W.); germain.forestier@uha.fr (G.F.)
3   Department of Electrical Engineering, KU Leuven, 3001 Leuven, Belgium; sofie.pollin@esat.kuleuven.be
*   Correspondence: tsegamlak.terefe@aait.edu.et or tsegamlak-terefe.debella@uha.fr
†   Presented at the 8th International Conference on Time Series and Forecasting, Gran Canaria, Spain,
    27–30 June 2022.

Citation: Debella, T.T.; Shawel, B.S.;
Devanne, M.; Weber, J.; Woldegebre,
D.H.; Pollin, S.; Forestier, G. Deep
Representation Learning for
Cluster-Level Time Series Forecasting.
Eng. Proc. **2022**, *18*, 22. https://
doi.org/10.3390/engproc2022018022

Academic Editors: Ignacio Rojas,
Hector Pomares, Olga Valenzuela,
Fernando Rojas and Luis Javier
Herrera

Published: 21 June 2022

Publisher's Note: MDPI stays neutral
with regard to jurisdictional claims in
published maps and institutional affiliations.

Abstract: In today's data-driven world, time series forecasting is an intensively investigated temporal data mining technique. In practice, there is a range of forecasting techniques that have been proven to be efficient at capturing different aspects of an input. For instance, classic linear forecasting models such as seasonal autoregressive integrated moving average (S-ARIMA) models are known to capture the trends and seasonality evident in temporal datasets. In contrast, neural-network-based forecasting approaches are known to be best at capturing nonlinearity. Despite such differences, most forecasting techniques inherently assume that models are fitted using a single input. In practice, there are often cases where we cannot deploy forecasting models in this manner. For instance, in most wireless communication traffic forecasting problems, temporal datasets are defined by taking samples from hundreds of base stations. Moreover, the base stations are expected to have spatial correlation due to user mobility, land use, settlement patterns, etc. Thus, in such cases, it is often advised that forecasting should be approached using clusters that group the base stations based on their traffic patterns. However, when this approach is used, the quality of the cluster centroids and the overall cluster formation process is expected to have a significant impact on the performance of forecasting models. In this paper, we show the effectiveness of representation learning for cluster formation and cluster centroid definition, which in turn improves the quality of cluster-level forecasting. We demonstrate this concept using data traffics collected from 729 wireless base stations. In general, based on the experimental results, the representation learning approach outperforms cluster-level forecasting models based on classical clustering techniques such as K-means and dynamic time warping barycenter averaging K-means (DBA K-means).

Keywords: clustering; forecasting; representation learning; time series; multitasking

1. Introduction

Time series forecasting (prediction) is a well-developed temporal data mining technique [1–4]. The theory of time series forecasting often relies on the data having recognizable patterns that can either be captured or learned. In practice, patterns or components within a time series dataset include trends, seasonality, cycles, and irregular (error) components [2,5,6]. In general, given a set of time series denoted by $\mathcal{S} = \{X_1, X_2, X_3, \ldots X_{t-1}\}$: $X_i \in \mathbb{R}^N$, the forecasting task can be formalized as:

$$\hat{X}_{i,t:t+p} = f(X_{i,t-L:t-1}, Y_{i,t-L:t-1}) \tag{1}$$

where, $\hat{X}_{i,t:t+p} = \{\hat{X}_{i,t}, \hat{X}_{i,t+1}, \dots, \hat{X}_{i,t+p}\}$ is the forecast for the ith series for p forward steps or horizons. Moreover, $X_{i,t-L:t-1} = \{X_{i,t-L}, \dots, X_{i,t-1}\}$ are past observations over a look-back window L. In most practical cases, different forecasting techniques often aim to provide predictions for a range of future time stamps [1,2,5]. However, when this is the case, it is important to carefully address the propagation of errors and the size of the look-back window. In this regard, some forecasting techniques often incorporate exogenous variables that are presumed to add value to (improve) the prediction accuracy [6]. In Equation (1), the possibility of incorporating exogenous variables is indicated using the parameter $Y_{i,t-L:t-1}$. In practice, we can broadly categorize forecasting models based on different factors. For instance, we can categorize them into univariate or multivariate models based on their ability to incorporate either a single or multiple time series. We can also categorize them, based on their mathematical formulation, as linear or nonlinear [1]. In general, on deployment, the underlying data often govern which of the different forecasting models is to be utilized. For instance, if forecasting is performed on a group of input time series that have some degree of correlation, then multivariate techniques are more fitting [6–8]. In contrast, if forecasting is performed on a group of series that show a sense of independence, standard univariate techniques are often considered [9].

In practice, despite the differences among forecasting approaches, we must overcome certain challenges and limitations that are associated with either the underlying data or a forecasting model [1]. For instance, a limited number of training samples often leads to the overfitting problem. In reality, overfitting is a problem in both univariate and multivariate forecasting approaches [2,5,10]. However, in reality, there are also challenges (limitations) that are specific to a given forecasting approach. For example, in some practical cases, univariate forecasting models often fail to capture the dynamic nature of the underlying data [3,11]. This is because, in these approaches, the model's locality with respect to an individual time series will restrict its scalability in the context of other correlated time series [5,7]. For instance, in most wireless communication forecasting problems, temporal datasets are collected from a range of base stations that share a certain geographical area [6,11]. In these cases, deploying univariate forecasting models on an individual base station is often not advised for two reasons [3,11]. Firstly, due to the presence of user mobility, settlement patterns, land use, etc., base stations cannot be treated as isolated entities. Consequently, a given base station is expected to have a piece of inherent hidden information about its neighbors [12,13]. In addition to this, in wireless communication networks, the base stations number hundreds if not thousands. Therefore, the sheer number alone makes it challenging to deploy univariate forecasting models. In order to overcome these and other additional challenges, most univariate time series forecasting tasks make use of pre-processing techniques. For instance, prior to fitting most univariate linear forecasting models, an input series is often processed in the context of identifying seasonal patterns, extracting external explanatory variables, putting a limit on the forecasting horizon, and using a "global" approach, which clusters the time series based on similarity [1,2,5,6,11,14]. Among such pre-processing steps, clustering is often considered to be useful in capturing the spatial correlations and reducing the number of required forecasting models [11,14]. This is because, while clustering, we often group base stations that have similar traffic patterns around a centroid (average). Thus, given an optimal cluster centroid, the patterns observed within cluster members can be generalized. This, in turn, provides a way to embed the information a base station has about its neighbors. Moreover, it has been shown to be possible to further incorporate spatial correlation by defining a cluster correlation matrix [11].

Although pre-processing techniques have proved to be useful, they often induce challenges of their own. In reality, this will be evident if the techniques are not properly configured or if the right technique is not utilized. In this respect, the quality of cluster-level forecasting is often dependent on the separability of clusters, the correlation among cluster members, and the quality of cluster centroids [11,14]. If, for instance, we focus on the cluster centroids (averages), we at times find them being utilized as representatives while fitting univariate or multivariate forecasting models [11]. However, in practice, time series cluster centroids are often significantly affected by temporal distortion, which misaligns patterns (shapes) [15,16]. For instance, in Figure 1, we show a cluster of 50-Hertz sinusoids (sin signals) that have phase differences of $0, \pi/3, \pi/6, \frac{2\pi}{3}, and \pi$. We also show the cluster centroids (averages) that are estimated using an arithmetic mean (shown in Figure 1a) and the soft dynamic time warping barycenter averaging (SDBA) (shown in Figure 1b) [17]. The average estimated using the arithmetic mean is smaller, due to the presence of a phase shift (temporal distortion). In general, in practice, temporal distortion often forces the arithmetic mean to aggregate shapes in a destructive manner [17,18]. Therefore, we often expect a cluster-level forecasting model that is based on an arithmetic mean to be affected by underprediction. In addition to this, the impact of a temporal shift is not limited to the distortion of the cluster centroids. A sub-optimal cluster centroid could also lead to the grouping of members that have no significant correlation (similarity). This in turn could affect the quality of cluster-level predictions that aim at capturing spatial correlations via clustering [11,14].

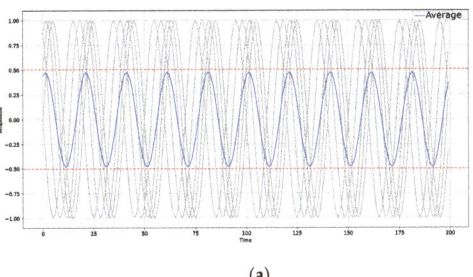 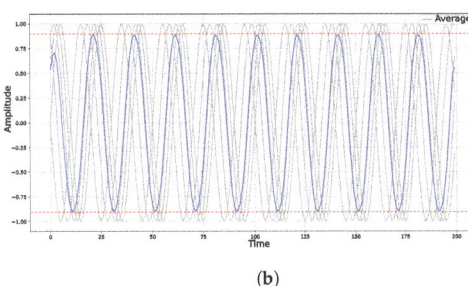

(a) (b)

Figure 1. A demonstration of the impact of temporal distortion on the estimation of cluster centroids. (a) An arithmetic mean. (b) An average estimated using SDBA.

With these observations in mind, in this paper, we propose to utilize a neural network arrangement for cluster formation and centroid estimation. In this regard, we show the advantage of utilizing representation learning, which aims to identify patterns that are presumed to be useful for cluster formation in the latent space of neural networks [19]. Moreover, we also propose to utilize a neural network architecture that is able to estimate time-domain cluster centroids from latent representations [18]. In reality, the utilization of neural networks for the cluster formation and centroid estimation is expected to be advantageous as a result of at least one factor, i.e., transfer learning [20]. In this regard, neural networks are known to be good at generalizing for a range of unseen datasets. Therefore, well-organized and trained clustering and centroid estimation networks are capable of generating clusters and centroids without the need for costly re-runs, i.e., if additional datasets (base stations) become available.

We have organized the rest of the paper into three additional sections. In Section 2, we give a brief review of different clustering and forecasting techniques. Following this, i.e., in Section 3, we present the methodology used in this study. In Section 4, we present the experimental evaluations. Finally, in Section 5, we present our concluding remarks.

2. Background

2.1. A Brief Review of Common Time Series Forecasting Techniques

On a holistic level, the different time series forecasting methods can be grouped into [1,5,10]:

- Statistical models that aim to explicitly model time series patterns using domain knowledge.
- Deep-learning-based models that learn temporal dynamics in a purely data-driven way and without explicit formulations.

In practice, we find both categories of forecasting approaches deployed in wireless network traffic prediction problems. Forecasting models that are deployed in this application domain could be either one of the two or a hybrid of both approaches [2,9–12]. In general, in this domain, one of the dominant knowledge-driven forecasting approaches is the S-ARIMA forecasting model. The main driving force behind this dominance is the seasonal nature of most mobile traffic data [2,6,9]. For instance, we expect base stations located in residential areas to have a cyclic peak traffic demand in the early mornings, late at night, and at weekends. The S-ARIMA model is found to be capable of modeling such seasonalities by linearly combining the forecasts of autoregressive (AR) and moving average (MA) models (θ) [1,5]. However, in practice, increasing (decreasing) trends within datasets have been found to introduce offsets into predicted values. Consequently, S-ARIMA incorporates a difference operation, which is indicated with the keyword I(d). Moreover, to account for seasonality, it treats the seasonal and non-seasonal parts of the data independently. In general, assuming a $(1 - L)$ lag operator, a S-ARIMA model is mathematically represented as [1]:

$$(\phi_p(L)\Phi_P(L^{s_k}))(1 - L)^d(1 - L)^{D_{s_k}}(X_t - \mu) = (\theta_q(L))(\Theta_Q(L^{s_k}))\varepsilon_t \tag{2}$$

where the $(p; P_{(.)})$ and $(q; Q_{(.)})$ orders of polynomials are used for AR(ϕ; Φ) and MA(θ; Θ) coefficients, i.e., for the non-seasonal and seasonal parts. The parameters d and D are also used to represent the differencing operation performed on the non-seasonal and seasonal parts of the data. Moreover, X_t, ε_t, and μ are the value of a series at t, its residual term, and a constant.

In practice, there are also cases where the underlying data could have patterns that cannot be captured with linear models [8,11]. When this is the case, researchers often propose deploying neural networks that are capable of performing nonlinear transformations. In this regard, neural networks that are based on the long short-term memory (LSTM) method are often found to be efficient [2,10]. This is because these networks are capable by design of capturing the dependencies between time stamps, which is a useful characteristic in time series forecasting. However, in some cases, combining S-ARIMA and neural networks has been proposed, to better capture the seasonal, linear, and nonlinear aspects of an underlying series [8,11]. We now conclude this section and proceed to the discussion of time series clustering techniques.

2.2. A Brief Review of Time Series Clustering Techniques

Like time series forecasting, time series clustering is also an intensively investigated temporal data mining technique [15,21,22]. In general, we can broadly categorize time series forecasting as either distance- or features-based. In distance-based approaches, clustering techniques utilize distance metrics either to group series around their centroids or to group them in a hierarchical manner [22,23]. However, in practice, distance-based approaches are often expected to incorporate some type of temporal alignment technique, to overcome the impact of temporal distortion. When this is the case, the most frequently proposed alignment technique is dynamic time warping (DTW) [24]. However, the incorporation of DTW into the clustering process often increases the computational complexity of the clustering process [16]. With this understanding, in recent years, researchers have proposed performing clustering by utilizing latent space embedding of neural networks [19,21]. For instance, in [19], the authors proposed deep embedding clustering (DEC), which uses a denoising autoencoder to extract latent features from the input series. The latent features are then grouped into K clusters by first computing the soft cluster assigning given in (3).

$$q_{i,j} = \frac{\left(\frac{1+||Z_i - \mu_j)||_{l2}}{\alpha}\right)^{\frac{-\alpha+1}{2}}}{\sum_{j=1}^{K}\left(\frac{1+||Z_i - \mu_j)||_{l2}}{\alpha}\right)^{\frac{-\alpha+1}{2}}} \tag{3}$$

In (3), $Z_i \in \mathbb{R}^\tau$ is a latent embedding corresponding to a time series $X_i \in \mathbb{R}^N$, where $\tau < N$. Moreover, $\mu_i \in \mathbb{R}^\tau$ is the arithmetic mean of the latent embedding corresponding to a cluster. In reality, the soft cluster assignment computes cluster labels based on the likelihood of latent features under the Student t-distribution. In order to make the soft assignments meaningful, the authors proposed to define the auxiliary distribution ($p_{i,j}$) given in (4). Finally, the network was forced to minimize the Kullback–Leibler (KL) divergence between its soft assignments and the auxiliary distribution (4).

$$L = KL(P||Q) = \sum_i \sum_j p_{i,j} \log \frac{p_{i,j}}{q_{i,j}} \,, \ where \ \ p_{i,j} = \frac{\frac{q_{i,j}^2}{\sum_{j=1}^K q_{i,j}}}{\sum_{j=1}^K \frac{q_{i_j}^2}{\sum_{j=1}^K q_{i,j}}} \tag{4}$$

In this paper, we propose to cluster base stations using the DEC setup. However, one minor inconvenience is that the DEC setup cannot generate time-domain cluster centroids. We propose to overcome this limitation by utilizing a multitasking autoencoder, which is set to perform multi-class classification and reconstruction. This configuration was proposed in [18], in order to estimate the averages of multi-class temporal datasets from their latent embedding. With this in mind, we will next present the methodology used.

3. Methodology

3.1. Proposed Network Architecture

In this study, we utilized the multitasking architecture shown in Figure 2, in order to estimate time-domain cluster centroids. Moreover, we also used the architectures shown at the encoder for deep embedding clustering under the DEC arrangement. In general, the multitasking setup optimizes for reconstruction and the multi-class classification losses given in (5), where X_i, $\hat{X}_i$ are input and reconstructed time series in $\mathbb{R}^N$. Moreover, $p_{i,j}$ are the softmax activation values (the likelihood) of a series X_i belonging to category (Cat) [18]. In terms of layer arrangements, the multitasking network is constructed from transposed and normal convolutional, max-pooling, flattening, and dense layers [25].

$$L_{Multi}(X_i, \hat{X}_i, Cat, p_{cat}) = \frac{1}{N} \sum_{i=1}^N ||X_i - \hat{X}_i||_{l2} - \frac{1}{N} \sum_{i=1}^N \sum_{j=1}^C Cat_{i,j} \ln^{p_{i,j}} \tag{5}$$

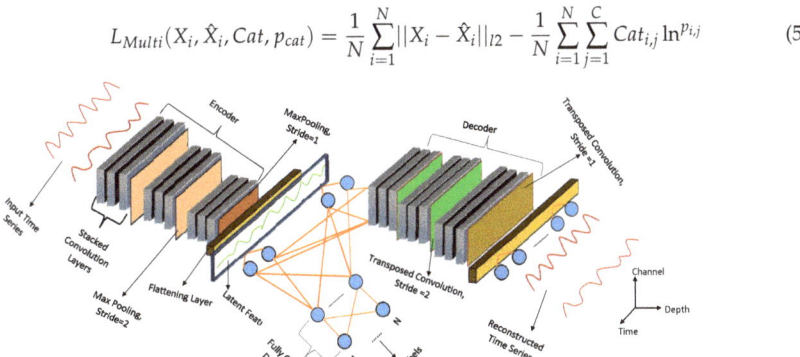

Figure 2. Neural network architecture utilized for cluster centroid estimation.

In reality, the layer arrangements are motivated by the layer configurations observed in the Visual Geometry Group-16 (VGG16) architecture [26]. Overall, we configured the convolutional and max-pooling layers with a kernel size of 3. Moreover, we configured the transposed convolutions to have a stride of 2. In contrast, the non-transposed convolutional layer and the encoder's last max-pooling layer had a stride of 1. Furthermore, the number of neurons in the encoder's dense layer was set to $\lfloor \frac{2688}{4} \rfloor$. Moreover, we configured the dense layers of the three classifiers to have $\lfloor \frac{0.9 \times 2688}{8} \rfloor$, $\lfloor \frac{0.8 \times 2688}{16} \rfloor$, and K neurons, where

K is the number of clusters. Finally, we set the number of neurons for the decoder's dense layer to 2688. In terms of layer activation, we utilized a rectified linear unit (ReLU) activation function on most of the proposed neural network's layers. However, for the first encoder's convolutional layer and the last decoder's dense layer, we utilized a linear activation function. Finally, we set the classifier's last dense layer to use a softmax activation function [20,25].

3.2. Datasets

The datasets used were collected from 729 base stations providing wireless data services to regions located within Addis Ababa, Ethiopia. In order to define the temporal datasets, 24 h of data traffic measurements were taken for four consecutive months, i.e., from September 2019 to the end of December 2019. Hence, we obtained 729 temporal datasets that were 2688 time stamps long.

3.3. Experimental Setup

In order to evaluate the proposed approach, we first converted the datasets from terabytes to gigabytes by dividing by 1024. We then took the encoder and decoder portion of the multitasking setup and trained it for a reconstruction loss, i.e., using the first part of (5). Following this, we took the encoder portion of the trained autoencoder and trained it for 1500 epochs using the objective function given in (4). We then used the network to predict cluster labels for the latent embedding of input datasets. Next, we used the labeled series to train the full multitasking setup using (5). This training was performed in order to generate time-domain centroids (averages) for the clustered latent space representations. After training, we estimated time-domain cluster centroids using the decoder portion of the multitasking autoencoder and by taking the arithmetic mean of the latent space represenations. We then took the estimated centroids and fitted a D-SARIMA model, which was implemented in R [27]. The model fitting was performed using a segment of the estimated cluster centroids, i.e., a segment that corresponded to $3\frac{1}{4}$ months of traffic measurements. However, in addition to segmenting the centroids, we also identified the most strongly correlated cluster centroids. We used these centroids as exogenous variables of one another while fitting the D-SARIMA model. This, in turn, becomes useful for capturing the spatial correlation among base stations that is evident due to land use.

Finally, we used the D-SARIMA models that were fitted to the cluster centroids to generate $1\frac{1}{2}$ weeks of predictions for individual cluster members. However, in order to generate the predictions, we substituted the centroid segments used for model fitting with the corresponding segments of the individual cluster members. In this way, it is possible to test the representativeness of the coefficients learned using the segments of the cluster centroids. Finally, we assessed the quality of the predictions using the root mean square (RMS) error and mean absolute error (MAE), as given in (6). As a comparison, we performed the same evaluations using the TSLearner implantation of K-means and its variant, DBA K-means [16,23,28].

$$RMSE = \sqrt{\frac{1}{N}\sum_{i=0}^{N-1}(y_{t_i} - \hat{y}_{t_i})^2} \quad MAE = \frac{1}{N}\sum_{i=0}^{N-1}|y_{t+i} - \hat{y}_{t+i}| \quad (6)$$

4. Experimental Results and Discussion

Prior to any model training or fitting, we first assessed the inter-cluster inertia of the traffic datasets, i.e., we determined the optimal number of clusters (K). In this regard, we first conducted a basic K-means clustering for different values of K. We then observed the average within-group squared sum (WGSS) for different values of K. From this observation, we found that five clusters sufficiently minimized the inter-cluster inertia. Next, we decomposed the datasets into their trend, seasonal, and residue components. Moreover, we conducted autocorrelation (AC) and partial autocorrelation (PAC) analyses of the datasets in order to determine the period of the seasonalities. Figure 3a,b show that the datasets have seasonal and trend components. Moreover, Figure 3c,d show that there are two seasons, i.e., a daily (24 h) season and a weekly (168 h) season. Therefore, we decided to deploy a double seasonal ARIMA (D-SARIMA) model rather than an S-ARIMA model.

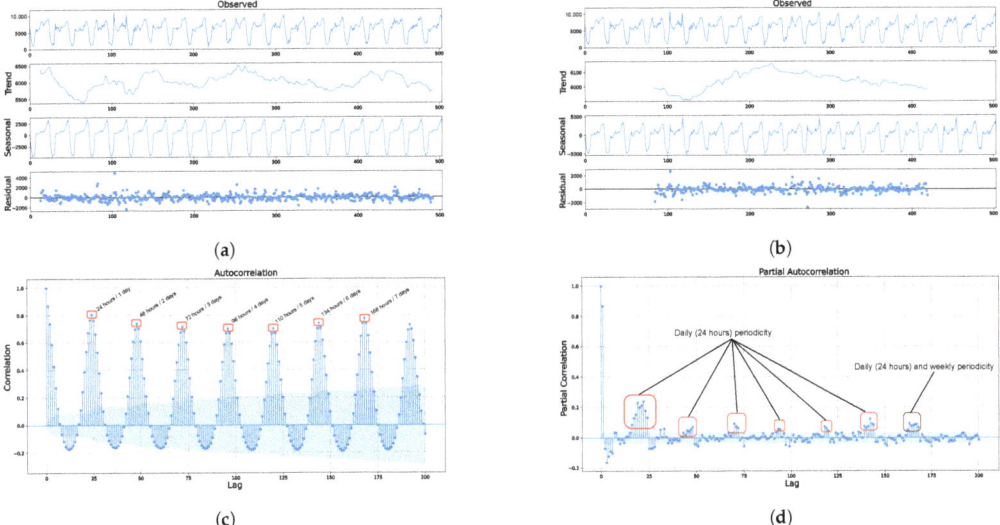

Figure 3. Demonstration of the seasonality of the data traffic. (**a**) Daily seasonality. (**b**) Weekly seasonality. (**c**) Autocorrelation. (**d**) Partial autocorrelation.

We then used R's auto.sarima package to determine the optimal model parameters for D-SARIMA $\{S_1(P, Q, D), S_2(P, Q, D), \text{and } (p, q, d)\}$. In this regard, we found that D-SARIMA $\{(2, 1, 2), (2, 0, 0)_{24}, (2, 0, 0)_{168}\}$ gave a better validation error. Therefore, we first clustered the base stations into five groups using the DEC arrangement. We then plotted the clusters on the map of Addis Ababa in order to visually assess whether the clusters had a geographical meaning, as shown in Figure 4.

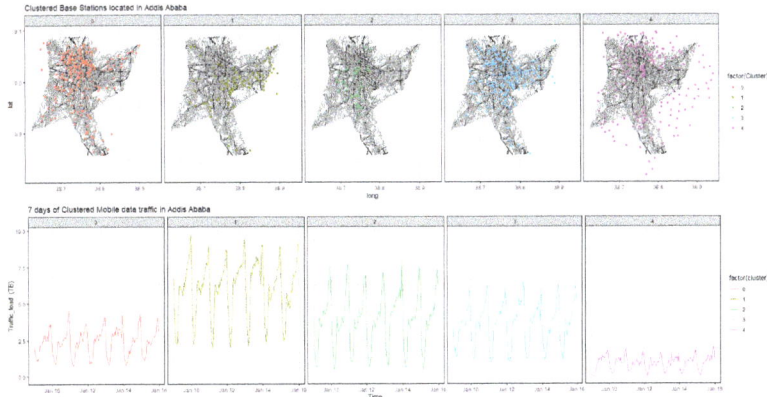

Figure 4. Geographical location of clusters corresponding to base stations within Addis Ababa.

In general, the clustering algorithm identified geographical locations that correlated with the offered traffic demand. For instance, cluster 1 corresponded to the areas locally known as *"Megenagna"* and *"Bole"*. These locations are known to accommodate large entertainment facilities and the country's largest airport. Additionally, the locations corresponding to cluster 2 accommodate governmental and non-governmental institutions, universities, residential areas, and embassies. Furthermore, cluster 0 and cluster 3 corresponded to mixed use areas that are densely populated, such as *"Cherkos"* and *"Autobis Tera"*. Finally, cluster 4 was a purely residential area that is sparsely populated. Overall, the DEC arrangement identified geographical locations that correlated with the amplitudes of the centroids. The alternative clustering also identified similar patterns. However, we observed minor distortions in the centroids of the DBA K-means clustering. We associated these distortions with the sensitivity of DBA to the offset (trend) that is evident in the datasets. Figure 5 demonstrates DBA's response to the offsets, which are manifested as sharp spikes.

Figure 5. Clusters and cluster centroids estimated by DBA K-means.

We next compared the performances of the D-SARIMA models fitted on the cluster centroids estimated using the different clustering techniques. In this regard, we made two types of predictions. First, we predicted cluster members using D-SARIMA models that were fitted on the cluster centroids, as discussed in the Experimental Setup section. In Table 1, these predictions are differentiated using the keyword CS. In addition to this, as a benchmark, we made similar predictions using D-SARIMA models that were fitted on the individual cluster members. In Table 1, these prediction are differentiated using the keyword BS.

We can interpret the results shown in Table 1 from two different angles. First, we can note that whatever the utilized clustering technique, cluster-level forecasting approaches better captured the dynamics of the underlying data. This is evident, because we have incorporated the spatial information by using highly correlated cluster centroids as exogenous variables. In addition to this, we can also note that the representation learning approach had the lowest aggregate prediction error. This, in turn, implies that the approach is able to overcome the impact of temporal distortion either on cluster formation or on centroid estimation. We conclude this section by presenting the forecasts generated by the three approaches for one of the base stations. For the forecasts shown in Figure 6, the D-SARIMA based on representation learning achieved RMSE and MAE values of 0.758 and 0.596. In contrast, the DBA K-means and basic K-means approaches achieved RMSE and MAE values of 0.802 and 0.617, and 0.669 and 0.847.

Table 1. Comparison of cluster-level and data-level forecasting.

Techniques	Errors	Cluster 0	Cluster 1	Cluster 2	Cluster 3	Cluster 4	Average
DEC_CS	RMSE	1.104	1.050	0.409	1.524	0.863	0.990
	MAE	0.816	0.778	0.305	1.145	0.671	0.743
DEC_Clust_BS		1.417	1.205	0.426	1.867	0.992	1.181
		1.092	0.932	0.308	1.158	0.758	0.909
DBA K-Means_CS	RMSE	0.714	2.129	1.079	0.416	1.468	1.161
	MAE	0.524	1.715	0.789	0.318	1.156	0.901
DBA_K-Means_Clust_BS		0.868	2.012	1.205	0.330	1.652	1.214
		0.664	0.565	0.919	0.239	1.288	0.935
K-Means_CS	RMSE	1.131	0.938	0.389	1.774	1.906	1.228
	MAE	0.859	0.739	0.293	1.452	1.522	0.973
K-Means_Clust_BS		1.263	0.961	0.388	1.664	1.993	1.254
		0.968	0.735	0.282	1.289	1.562	0.967

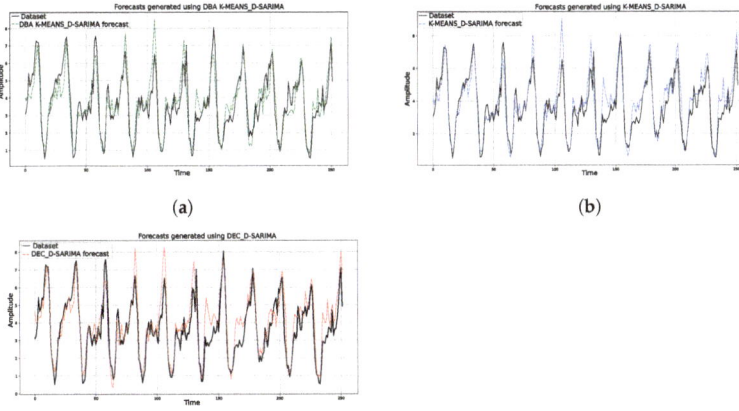

(a)

(b)

(c)

Figure 6. Example forecasts generated using K-means, DBA K-means, and DEC clustering multitasking autoencoder centroid estimation. (**a**) DBA-K-means-based forecasts. (**b**) K-means-based forecasts. (**c**) DEC and multitasking autoencoder based forecasts.

5. Conclusions

In this paper, we argued that the effect of temporal distortion on cluster formation and cluster centroid estimation cannot be ignored. With this in mind, we proposed a representation-learning-based clustering and cluster centroid estimation approach for cluster-level forecasting. We showed that this approach has the ability to better capture the spatial correlation evident among base stations within wireless communication networks. In general, to validate our argument we only utilized a basic linear forecasting model. However, in reality, the potential of the proposal is not limited to this. In our future work, we aim to assess the improvement in the quality of forecasts using either neural-network-based forecasting techniques or a hybrid of linear and neural-network-based forecasting approaches.

Author Contributions: Conceptualization, Methodology, Software, Validation, Formal Analysis, Investigation, and Data Curation: T.T.D. and B.S.S.; Original Draft Preparation: T.T.D.; Supervision, Review, and Editing: M.D., J.W., D.H.W., S.P. and G.F. All authors have read and agreed to the published version of the manuscript.

Funding: This research was conducted under the Ethio-France PhD. program.

Data Availability Statement: The datasets utilized for experimental evaluation are obtained from Ethio Telecom. The authors could make the datasets available up on request and with the consent of the network operator.

Acknowledgments: The authors would like to thank the French Embassy for Ethiopia and the African Union and the former Ethiopian Ministry of Science and Higher Education (MOSHE) for supporting the PhD program under which this research was conducted.

Conflicts of Interest: The authors declare no conflict of interest.

References

1. Fotios, P.; Daniele, A.; Vassilios, A.; Babai, M.Z.; Barrow, D.K.; Taieb, S.B.; Bergmeir, C.; Bessa, R.J.; Bijak, J.; Boylan, J.E.; et al. Forecasting: Theory and practice. *Int. J. Forecast.* **2022**, *38*, 705–871.
2. Azari, A.; Papapetrou, P.; Denic, S.; Peters, G. Cellular Traffic Prediction and Classification: A Comparative Evaluation of LSTM and ARIMA. In *Discovery Science*; Kralj Novak, P., Šmuc, T., Džeroski, S., Eds.; Springer International Publishing: Cham, Switzerland, 2019; pp. 129–144.
3. Chen, G. *Spatiotemporal Individual Mobile Data Traffic Prediction*; Technical Report RT-0497; INRIA Saclay—Ile-de-France: Leyon, France, 2018.
4. Xu, F.; Lin, Y.; Huang, J.; Wu, D.; Shi, H.; Song, J.; Li, Y. Big Data Driven Mobile Traffic Understanding and Forecasting: A Time Series Approach. *IEEE Trans. Serv. Comput.* **2016**, *9*, 796–805. [CrossRef]
5. Wei, W. *Time Series Analysis: Univariate and Multivariate Methods*; Pearson Addison Wesley: Boston, MA, USA, 2006.
6. Shu, Y.; Yu, M.; Liu, J.; Yang, O. Wireless traffic modeling and prediction using seasonal ARIMA models. In Proceedings of the IEEE International Conference on Communications, Anchorage, AK, USA, 11–15 May 2003; Volume 3, pp. 1675–1679.
7. Montero-Manso, P.; Hyndman, R.J. Principles and algorithms for forecasting groups of time series: Locality and globality. *Int. J. Forecast.* **2021**, *37*, 1632–1653. [CrossRef]
8. Zeng, D.; Xu, J.; Gu, J.; Liu, L.; Xu, G. Short Term Traffic Flow Prediction Using Hybrid ARIMA and ANN Models. In Proceedings of the 2008 Workshop on Power Electronics and Intelligent Transportation System, Guangzhou, China, 2–3 August 2008; pp. 621–625.
9. Zhou, B.; He, D.; Sun, Z. Traffic Modeling and Prediction using ARIMA/GARCH Model. In *Modeling and Simulation Tools for Emerging Telecommunication Networks*; Springer: Boston, MA, USA, 2006; pp. 101–121.
10. Zhang, C.; Patras, P.; Haddadi, H. Deep Learning in Mobile and Wireless Networking: A Survey. *IEEE Commun. Surv. Tutor.* **2019**, *21*, 2224–2287. [CrossRef]
11. Shawel, B.S.; Debella, T.T.; Tesfaye, G.; Tefera, Y.Y.; Woldegebreal, D.H. Hybrid Prediction Model for Mobile Data Traffic: A Cluster-level Approach. In Proceedings of the 2020 International Joint Conference on Neural Networks (IJCNN), Glasgow, UK, 19–24 July 2020; pp. 1–8.
12. Jaderberg, M.; Simonyan, K.; Zisserman, A.; Kavukcuoglu, K. Spatial Transformer Networks. In *Advances in Neural Information Processing Systems*; Curran Associates, Inc.: Jose, CA, USA, 2015; Volume 28.
13. John, G.P.; Masoud, S. *Fundamentals of Communication Systems*; Prentice Hall: Upper Saddle River, NJ, USA, 2002.
14. Sfetsos, A.; Siriopoulos, C. Time series forecasting with a hybrid clustering scheme and pattern recognition. *IEEE Trans. Syst. Man Cybern. Part A Syst. Humans* **2004**, *34*, 399–405. [CrossRef]
15. Aghabozorgi, S.; Shirkhorshidi, A.S.; Wah, T.Y. Time-series clustering–a decade review. *Inf. Syst.* **2015**, *53*, 16–38. [CrossRef]
16. Petitjean, F.; Forestier, G.; Webb, G.I.; Nicholson, A.E.; Chen, Y.; Keogh, E. Faster and more accurate classification of time series by exploiting a novel dynamic time warping averaging algorithm. *Knowl. Inf. Syst.* **2016**, *47*, 1–26. [CrossRef]
17. Petitjean, F.; Gançarski, P. Summarizing a set of time series by averaging: From Steiner sequence to compact multiple alignment. *Theor. Comput. Sci.* **2012**, *414*, 76–91. [CrossRef]
18. Terefe, T.; Devanne, M.; Weber, J.; Hailemariam, D.; Forestier, G. Time Series Averaging Using Multi-Tasking Autoencoder. In Proceedings of the 2020 IEEE 32nd International Conference on Tools with Artificial Intelligence (ICTAI), Baltimore, MD, USA, 9–11 November 2020; pp. 1065–1072.
19. Xie, J.; Girshick, R.; Farhadi, A. Unsupervised Deep Embedding for Clustering Analysis. In Proceedings of the 33rd International Conference on International Conference on Machine Learning, New York, NY, USA, 19–24 June 2016; Volume 48, pp. 478–487.
20. Vasilev, I.; Slater, D.; Spacagna, G.; Roelants, P.; Zocca, V. *Python Deep Learning: Exploring Deep Learning Techniques and Neural Network Architectures with PyTorch, Keras, and TensorFlow*, 2nd ed.; Packt Publishing: Birmingham, UK, 2019.
21. Lafabregue, B.; Weber, J.; Gançarski, P.; Forestier, G. End-to-end deep representation learning for time series clustering: A comparative study. *Data Min. Knowl. Discov.* **2021**, *36*, 29–81. [CrossRef]

22. Leonard, K.; Peter, J.R. *Finding Groups in Data: An Introduction to Cluster Analysis*; John Wiley: Hoboken, NJ, USA, 1990.
23. Bock, H.H. Origins and extensions of the -means algorithm in cluster analysis. *J. Électron. d'Histoire Probab. Stat.* **2008**, *4*, 18.
24. Sakoe, H.; Chiba, S. Dynamic programming algorithm optimization for spoken word recognition. *IEEE Trans. Acoust. Speech Signal Process.* **1978**, *26*, 43–49. [CrossRef]
25. Chollet, F. Keras. 2015. Available online: https://keras.io (accessed on 1 May 2022).
26. Simonyan, K.; Zisserman, A. Very Deep Convolutional Networks for Large-Scale Image Recognition. In Proceedings of the 3rd International Conference on Learning Representations, San Diego, CA, USA, 7–9 May 2015.
27. Hyndman, R.J.; Khandakar, Y. Automatic Time Series Forecasting: The forecast Package for R. *J. Stat. Softw.* **2008**, *27*, 1–22. [CrossRef]
28. Tavenard, R.; Faouzi, J.; Vandewiele, G.; Divo, F.; Androz, G.; Holtz, C.; Payne, M.; Yurchak, R.; Rußwurm, M.; Kolar, K.; et al. Tslearn, A Machine Learning Toolkit for Time Series Data. *J. Mach. Learn. Res.* **2020**, *21*, 1–6.

Proceeding Paper

Autoencoders for Anomaly Detection in an Industrial Multivariate Time Series Dataset [†]

Theodoros Tziolas [1], Konstantinos Papageorgiou [1,*], Theodosios Theodosiou [1], Elpiniki Papageorgiou [1], Theofilos Mastos [2] and Angelos Papadopoulos [2]

1 Department of Energy Systems, University of Thessaly, 38221 Volos, Greece; ttziolas@uth.gr (T.T.); dozius@uth.gr (T.T.); elpinikipapageorgiou@uth.gr (E.P.)
2 KLEEMANN HELLAS S.A., Kilkis Industrial Area, 61100 Kilkis, Greece; t.mastos@kleemannlifts.com (T.M.); ag.papadopoulos@kleemannlifts.com (A.P.)
* Correspondence: konpapageorgiou@uth.gr; Tel.: +30-2410-684587
† Presented at the 8th International Conference on Time Series and Forecasting, Gran Canaria, Spain, 27–30 June 2022.

Abstract: In smart manufacturing, the automation of anomaly detection is essential for increasing productivity. Timeseries data from production processes are often complex sequences and their assessment involves many variables. Thus, anomaly detection with deep learning approaches is considered as an efficient and effective methodology. In this work, anomaly detection with deep autoencoders is examined. Three autoencoders are employed to analyze an industrial dataset and their performance is assessed. Autoencoders based on long short-term memory and convolutional neural networks appear to be the most promising.

Keywords: autoencoders; deep learning; LSTM; 1DCNN; anomaly detection; elevator industry

Citation: Tziolas, T.; Papageorgiou, K.; Theodosiou, T.; Papageorgiou, E.; Mastos, T.; Papadopoulos, A. Autoencoders for Anomaly Detection in an Industrial Multivariate Time Series Dataset. *Eng. Proc.* **2022**, *18*, 23. https://doi.org/10.3390/engproc 2022018023

Academic Editors: Ignacio Rojas, Hector Pomares, Olga Valenzuela, Fernando Rojas and Luis Javier Herrera

Published: 22 June 2022

Publisher's Note: MDPI stays neutral with regard to jurisdictional claims in published maps and institutional affiliations.

1. Introduction

The collection and the processing of timeseries data in industrial procedures is an essential task in smart manufacturing. Exploitation of these data enables data holders to engage complex strategies and processes such as process optimization and predictive maintenance within the context of Industry 4.0. A key asset towards zero-defect manufacturing (ZDM) is timeseries anomaly detection (AD), which can reveal misconfigurations in manufacturing lines and eminent faults. Manual AD requires expert technicians to monitor sensor signals from manufacturing lines, identify faults in real-time, and trigger proper actions. As the volume of production and data increases, manual operations become ineffective. This task becomes more complicated if multiple measurements need to be assessed simultaneously and in combination. To alleviate such issues, artificial intelligence (AI) methods are considered.

The first step in AD in a manufacturing line is to determine what an anomaly is. Clearly, this is a case-dependent issue and makes AD in industrial timeseries an extremely wide area; thus, this work focuses on a specific case study using data from manufacturing and testing elevators. The investigated production line uses sensors to capture real-time data regarding hydraulic pressure, elevator velocity and the noise produced. Actual data for a two-year period (2019–2021) were provided by KLEEMANN (KLEE) one of the most important lift manufacturers in the European and global markets. According to KLEE expert technicians, the signal attributes that reveal anomalies in the production line are duration, the magnitude and the direction of the acquired curves.

Conventional AD methods include clustering-based and statistical-based [1,2] methods; the k-NN [3] and the K-means [4] methods are probably the most popular clustering methods, while the autoregressive-moving-average models are typical statistical choices [5]. However, conventional methods demonstrate poor performance and face challenges such as low anomaly recall rate, noise-resilient anomaly detection, difficulty to deal with complex anomalies and in high-dimensional date—especial in case of interdependencies [2], etc. Many of these challenges are addressed by deep learning (DL).

Common DL approaches include prediction-based models [6]. These assume strong correlation between neighbor values and employ past values to predict the current and future ones. DL methods are usually based on artificial neural networks (ANN) and their variants to perform AD. In timeseries processing, the recurrent neural networks (RNN) and the convolutional neural networks (CNN) are the most efficient architectures as the they were designed targeting data sequences. Stacked layers of long short-term memory (LSTM) RNNs were employed in [7] for AD in engine datasets. Similarly, an LSTM predictor was used in [8] for a system of two industrial robotic manipulators using simulated data. A Bayesian neural network based on dropout and CNN was proposed in [9] for an industrial dataset to process pressure profiles. Despite their success, predictive models still have limitations in actual industrial environments due to the complexity involved in the production process [10]. Furthermore, defective products and anomalies in the signals are rather rare, making it difficult to train the AI models.

Autoencoders (AE) were proposed to overcome these shortcomings. AEs are composed of two different networks in series: an encoder that compresses the input in a lower dimensional space and a decoder that attempts to reconstruct the input from the compressed representation [11]. A key-feature of AEs is that they can be trained using only normal data, thus, overcoming the lack of anomalies in the data in an actual manufacturing line. An LSTM-based AE was proposed in [10] for application on engine datasets. Both the encoder and the decoder consisted of a single layer. This architecture could detect anomalies even when the values in a sequence change very frequently. A deeper LSTM-based AE with eight hidden layers and five LTSM units in each layer was proposed in [12]. The performance of this model was efficiently confirmed for the detection of rare sound events. CNN-based architectures are also found in literature, as an alternative to the LSTM-based. A more complex architecture was proposed in [13] to learn features from complex vibration signals and perform gearbox fault diagnosis; this architecture employed a residual connection and a deeper 1DCNN-based AE. It is evident that AD with AEs is a promising methodology that can capture underlying correlations that often exist in industrial multivariate datasets.

For a similar case study of AD in timeseries produced by elevators, an approach of supervised learning was proposed in [14]. In this work, a multi-head CNN-RNN was trained to classify the timeseries in normal and including anomalies. Even though the operation of the elevator was monitored from 20 sensors, due to the complexity in labeling all possible scenarios from real data, expertise knowledge was used to generate a simulated dataset of 20 variables. In this approach, the model is processing each variable independently. The model showed good performance with a trade off in long training times.

This work takes from successful AE-based AD practices and investigates the performance of different AE-based architectures for AD in datasets acquired from actual elevator production lines. To the best of our knowledge, there are no similar implementations of AE-based AD. The contributions of this work include: (i) the assessment of three different AE-based architectures, namely ANN-, LSTM- and CNN-based AE, for the analysis of the provided industrial dataset, (ii) the capture of underlying correlations, possibly missed if each signal was considered independently from the others, (iii) the demonstration of a simple, yet effective, methodology for inducing realistic anomalies in timeseries data, which is also applicable to optimized production lines.

2. Theoretical Background

2.1. Long Short-Term Memory Recurrent Neural Networks

Traditional ANNs treat inputs and outputs as individual values. RNNs account for information from previous inputs as well, and, therefore, can efficiently treat sequences of data. While standard RNNs apply a pointwise nonlinearity to the affine transformation of inputs and recurrent units, LSTMs use "gates" to control what information is used to update the cell state [7]. LSTM units (see Figure 1) are composed of a cell c_t, an input gate i_t, an output gate o_t and a forget gate f_t.

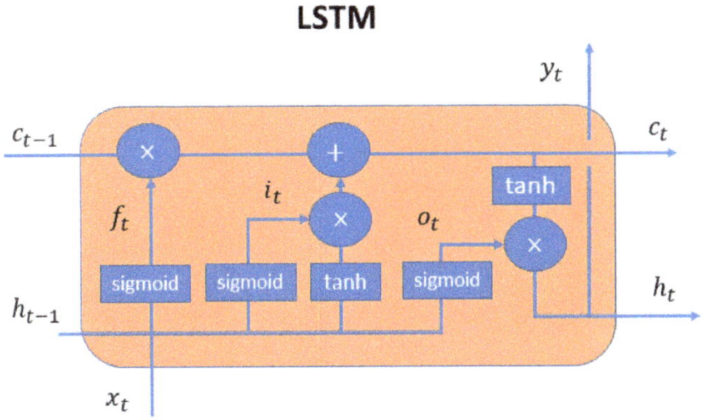

Figure 1. LSTM unit.

The equations for the forward pass of an LSTM are:

$$f_t = (W_f \cdot x_t + U_f \cdot h_{t-1} + b_f), \tag{1}$$

$$i_t = \sigma(W_i \cdot x_t + U_i \cdot h_{t-1} + b_i), \tag{2}$$

$$o_t = \sigma(W_o \cdot x_t + U_f \cdot h_{t-1} + b_f), \tag{3}$$

$$c_t = f_t c_{t-1} + i_t \tanh(W_c \cdot x_t + U_c \cdot h_{t-1} + b_c), \tag{4}$$

$$h_t = \tanh(c_t) o_t, \tag{5}$$

where σ, W, U, b, respectively denote the activation function (sigmoid in this work), the input weights, the recurrent weights, and the biases.

2.2. One-Dimensional Convolutional Neural Networks

CNNs are widely used to perform feature extraction and selection from the input in an unsupervised way. A CNN consists of convolutional layers to extract features, and pooling layers to perform down-sampling. 1DCNNs is a special CNN targeting timeseries data. For an input vector $x = \{x_0, x_1, \ldots, x_{n-1}\}, n \in \mathbb{N}^*$, the output of the convolutional operation (cross-correlation) with a kernel $k = \{k_0, k_1, \ldots, k_{m-1}\}, m \in \mathbb{N}^*$, and $m < n$ at a timestep t, is defined as:

$$y(t) = (x * k)(t) = \sum_{i=0}^{m-1} x(t + i + (t * s)) k(i). \tag{6}$$

In Equation (6), $s \in \mathbb{N}$ is the stride, i.e., the number of timesteps omitted in the cross-correlation operation; it resembles a sliding window over time. Zero-padding is typically employed to avoid the shrinking of the input at the boundaries. The output typically passes through a non-linear activation function like sigmoid or ReLU [15]. The output of a max-pooling operation with *pooling size* $= p$, $p \in \mathbb{N}^*$ at a timestep t can be defined as:

$$y(t) = \max_{i=0,\ldots p-1} x(t + i + (t * s)). \tag{7}$$

2.3. Anomaly Detection with Autoencoders

AEs attempt to reconstruct their input signal. If an AE is trained with optimal inputs only, its hyperparameters will be tuned to reconstruct optimal signals. Thus, when fed with timeseries which include anomalies, it is expected to fail reconstruction; this will be realized as high values in the loss function, quantified by typical error metrics, like the Mean Square Error (MSE) and the Mean Absolute Error (MAE).

Given a dataset of normal samples $X \in R^{t \times m}$ with $t \in \mathbb{N}^*$ the time steps and $m \in \mathbb{N}^*$ the measurements, the AE uses an encoding function $E : X \to Z$ to compress its input to the latent space Z, and a decoding function $D : Z \to \hat{X}$ to recover samples from the latent space. Ideally, the original samples X and the reconstructed samples $(\hat{X})$, i.e., the output of the AE, should be identical. However, in practical cases suitable E, D functions are pursued such that the $Loss(X, \hat{X})$ becomes minimal; the MSE or MAE metrics are typical employed as Loss functions. In case a dataset $A \in R^{t \times m}$ containing synthetic samples (with artificial anomalies in the data) is fed into a trained AE, it is expected that

$$Loss(X, \hat{X}) < Loss(A, \hat{A}), \ \forall x \in X, \ \hat{x} \in \hat{X}, a \in A, \hat{a} \in \hat{A}. \tag{8}$$

Each sample is classified as 'Normal' or 'Anomalous' based on the values of the loss function. However, Equation (8) poses a strong condition that is difficult to satisfy for all samples, therefore, a soft margin threshold is employed to quantify the AD capabilities of the network.

$$c(A) = \begin{cases} Normal & Loss(A, \hat{A}) < e_{th} \\ Anomalous & Loss(A, \hat{A}) \geq e_{th} \end{cases}, \tag{9}$$

where e_{th} is a predetermined threshold value. The optimal threshold is properly selected to maximize the usual metrics, namely the Accuracy (A), the Precision (P) and the Recall (R) [5].

3. Implementation on Industrial Dataset

3.1. Description of the Dataset

An industrial dataset was provided by KLEEMANN Greece containing historical measurements of elevator hydraulic power units (HPU). These measurements correspond to quality tests, that monitor the speed of the elevator, the developed pressure in the hydraulic unit, and noise produced during operation. The dataset contains 7200 different cases, corresponding to different client orders and employing various configurations and setups. An indicative example is shown in Figure 2.

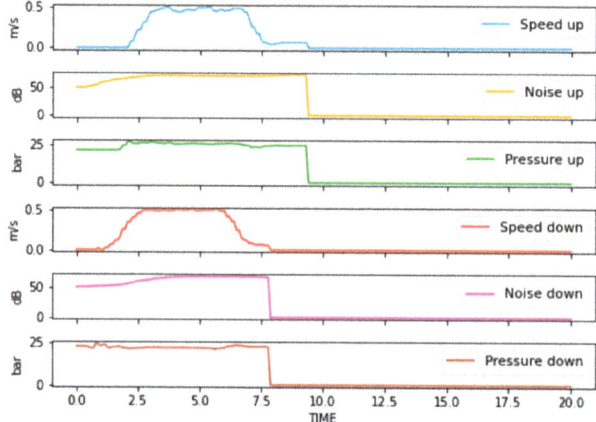

Figure 2. Indicative diagram from a HPU quality test. Speed, pressure and noise are captured for both translational directions.

Investigation of the provided dataset revealed that the acquired curves are not affected by the translational direction. Thus, directional information was not regarded as a classification parameter and measured curves for all direction were merged into a single dataset with $2 \times 7200 = 14,400$ samples. On the other hand, discrepancies were observed on testing parameters, e.g., some tests last longer than others, or the HPU operated in a different speed range, etc. Such deviations occur due to the different client requirements for each individual order, and cannot be avoided; therefore, some data preprocessing is needed, as described in the following section.

3.2. Data Preprocessing

The number of captured time steps in each HPU varied from 201 to 1035, albeit most samples (ca. 80%) consisted of only 201 time-steps. Therefore, all data sequences were brought to the same length (i.e., 201 time-steps), to enable mini-batch processing. The values of speed were all in the same range $[0, 0.91]$, thus, no treatment was necessary. Noise and pressure were in very different ranges, namely $[0, 91.2]$ and $[0, 53.98]$ respectively, thus, they were normalized by dividing with their maximum value.

The derived dataset was split for training (90%) and testing (10%). The sizes of the datasets involved were (samples × time steps × variables) (see Table 1):

Table 1. Employed datasets for training and testing.

Dataset	Population
Training	$12.960 \times 201 \times 3$
Testing (w/o anomalies)	$1.440 \times 201 \times 3$
Testing (with anomalies)	$1.440 \times 201 \times 3$

3.3. Synthetic Data for Anomaly Detection

As already mentioned, a well-configured manufacturing line rarely produces measurements with anomalies. This was also the case with the provided dataset; all timeseries correspond to optimal operation. Thus, a synthetic dataset for anomaly detection testing was created to test the model and assess its performance. To prevent biasing, communications with expert technicians were conducted to establish realistic deviations and criteria for identification of sub-optimal operation. According to the technical experts, anomalies in measured timeseries should be identified by (a) deviations more than ± 1.9 bar in pressure, and (b) noise values higher than 68 dB. No hard indicator could be provided for speed. Furthermore, the noise value was treated as a weak indicator, since there were samples with noise value higher than 68 dB and still treated as normal.

To tackle these ambiguities, the provided dataset was further explored to establish more strict and realistic thresholds; these thresholds were then exploited to induce artificial anomalies. An example is shown in Figure 3 (Graphs 1–3), where it is clear that speed is not constant but exhibits fluctuations; thus, such curves can be used to extract the fluctuation threshold, beyond which, the operation is considered sub-optimal. The same applies for pressure (Graphs 4–6). Following this approach, the following factors were accounted for during generation of artificial anomalies:

- **Duration.** Point anomalies seem to be of minor importance, at least in the beginning of testing. Hence, anomalies of finite duration were chosen randomly with a minimum of 10 time-steps.
- **Magnitude.** Both positive and negative deviations were induced, with addition or subtraction of random numbers with magnitude: [1.6 bar, 2.6 bar] for pressure, [1 dB, 4 dB] for noise and [5, 20]% of the maximum speed value of the curve for speed.
- **Location.** Location of the anomalies was chosen randomly between the timesteps that the test is performed (operational values > 0).

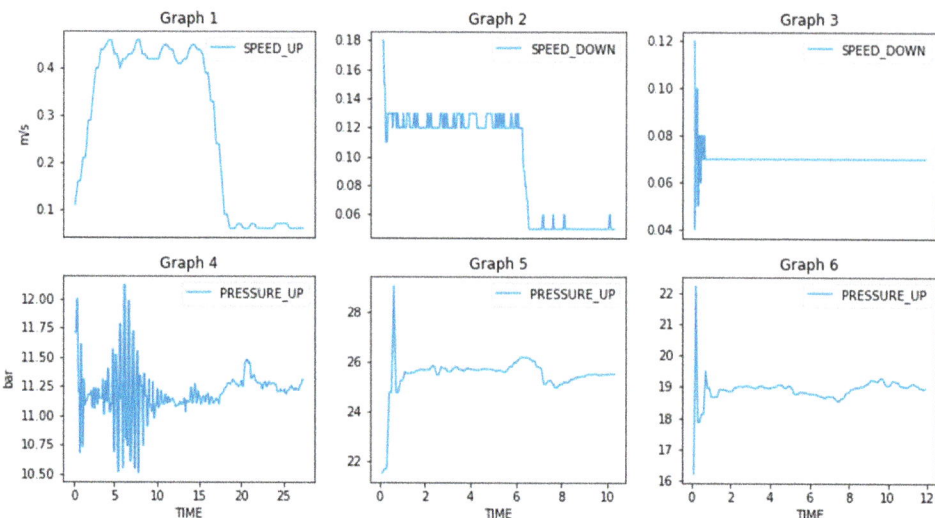

Figure 3. Examples of time series during optimal operation.

To create the synthetic dataset for anomaly detection for testing, each measured curve of the normal testing dataset was processed. Therefore, each curve in the testing dataset for anomalous detection is the counterpart of a curve which includes anomalies in the normal testing dataset. Examples of normal and synthetic curve-pairs including artificial anomalies are shown in Figure 4.

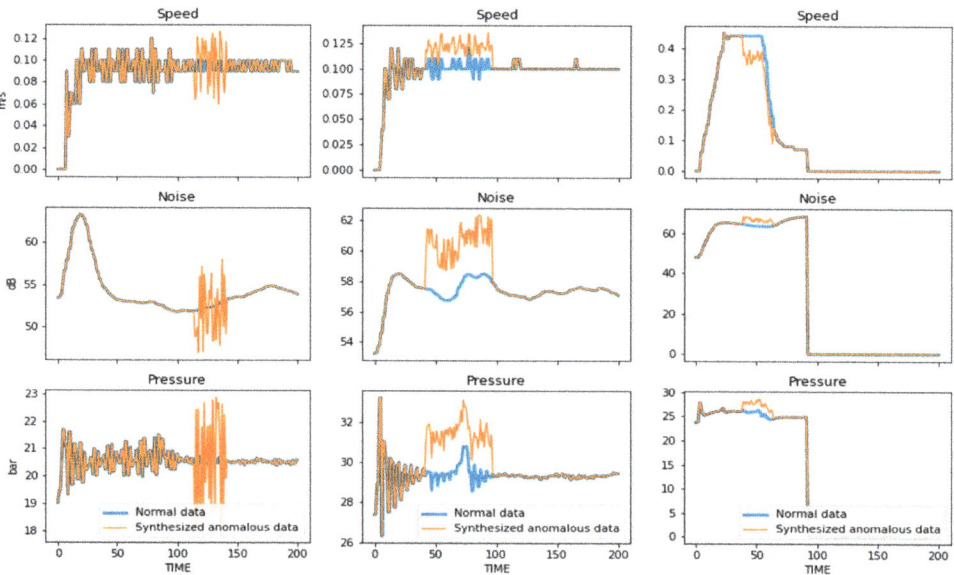

Figure 4. Examples of normal-synthetic/anomalous pair of curves.

3.4. Description of the AE Architectures

To acquire the most appropriate AE for AD in this industrial dataset, three different AE architectures were considered, namely ANN-, LSTM- and CNN-based AEs. Thus, some popular architectures found in literature were explored and assessed using the training and testing datasets described.

ANN-based AE. The first implementation was an ANN-based AE. It consisted of 10 fully connected (dense) layers, a layer that flattens the matrix and a reshape layer in the decoding operation that transforms the vector back to a matrix. In particular, the architecture is as follows: Input (128-64-32)-flatten-1024-latent space (128)-(1024-6432)-reshape (64-128)-output. For all hidden layers ReLU activation function was used.

LSTM-based AE. The LSTM-based AE is a shallower network compared to the previous one. It consists of 4 LSTM layers, a layer that repeats the vector in the corresponding timesteps and a skip connection layer. Hyperbolic tangent and sigmoid activation functions were used in LSTM units for the input and the recurrent state respectively. Skip-connections were employed in the stacked LSTM layers, following the practice of [16–18], to boost model's reconstruction performance. The architecture is shown in Figure 5.

LSTM AE

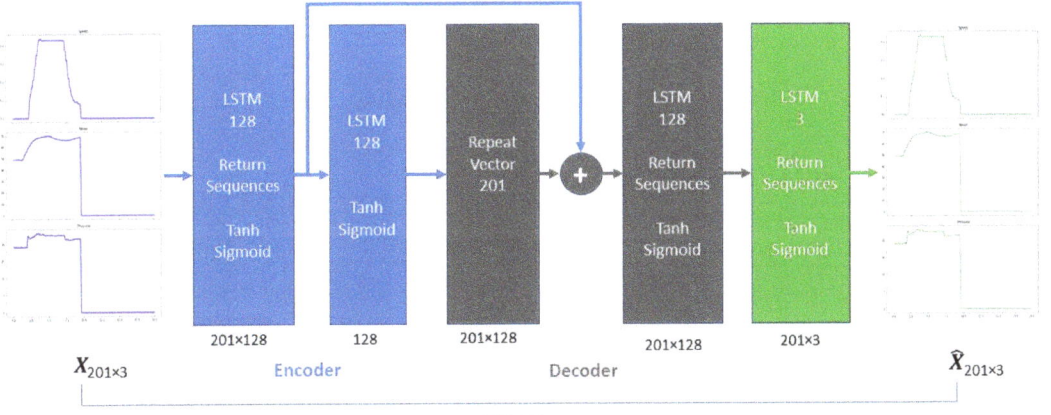

Figure 5. Architecture of the LSTM-based AE.

CNN-based AE. The CNN-based AE consists of convolutions, transpose convolutions and pooling operation. Convolutions and pooling operation were part of the encoding process while transpose convolutions [19] were used to perform up-sampling during decoding. Convolutional and transpose convolutional layers employed the "same-padding" method, so that the size of the output matched the size of input. ReLU was used as the activation function. The complete architecture is presented in Figure 6.

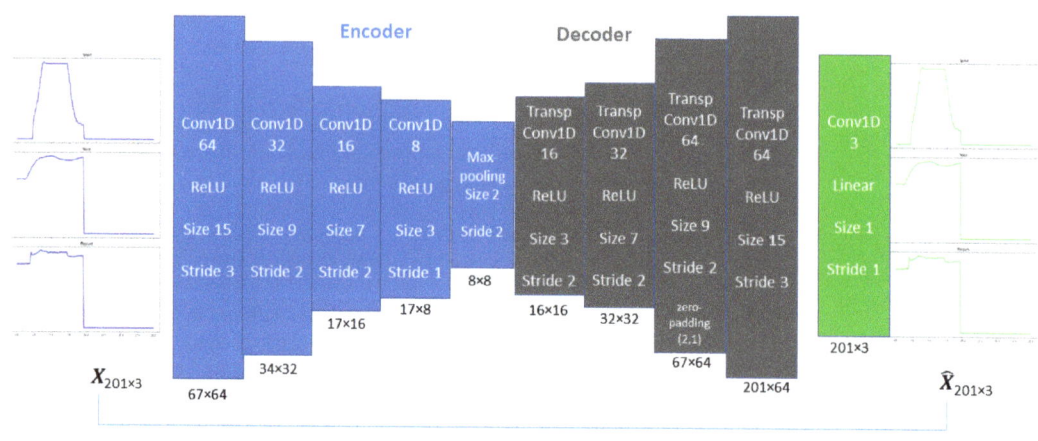

Figure 6. Architecture of the CNN-Based AE.

3.5. Results

All the experiments were conducted on a custom-built workstation to accommodate the computational needs of OPTIMAI; the workstation was equipped with an Intel Core i9-11900KF @ 3.5 GHz CPU, 16 GB RAM and NVIDIA GeForce RTX 3080 Ti with 12 GB of GDDR6X memory, running on Windows 10 Pro. The proposed AEs were implemented in Python 3.8.3, with the Keras API framework of TensorFlow 2.0 [20].

The dataset was split by random selection for training (90%, 12,960 records) and testing (10%, 1440 records) so as to acquire a larger representative training dataset that will assist the network to learn the variety of operational values [21]. A smaller testing dataset is produced considering both synthetic anomalies and normal cases.

The L2 loss was chosen as the training cost function. In all experiments, both 5-fold and 10-fold cross validation were used, with the hold-out group of data being exploited as a validation dataset during training. The early stopping setup of Keras was used to avoid overfitting. As shown in Table 2, there was a considerable difference in the running times and number of epochs required for AEs to converge. The ANN-based AE was the fastest model to train despite it involved significantly more parameters than the others. CNN-based AE on the other hand, combines both computational efficiency and low training time.

Table 2. Computational characteristics for each proposed architecture.

AE	Training Time (s)	Epochs	Total Parameters	Threshold	Accuracy	Precision	Recall
ANN-based	81	122	13,465,155	0.0063	84.79	91.27	76.94
LSTM-based	677	91	332,336	0.00048	91.38	96.05	86.31
CNN-based	101	99	109,611	0.00514	94.09	97.10	90.90

To determine the most suitable AE type, one critical parameter needs to be considered: the classification threshold. To determine the classification threshold of signals as normal or anomalous, the mean reconstruction error values were investigated. Both the MSE and MAE metrics were considered, but the MSE curves was prone to outliers; thus, the classification threshold was selected based on MAE. The distribution of MAE for both normal and synthetic samples in the data is presented in Figure 7. An ideal model would perfectly reconstruct its input; thus, no overlap (zero error) should be observed in the diagrams; or equivalently, the higher the overlap the worse the performance.

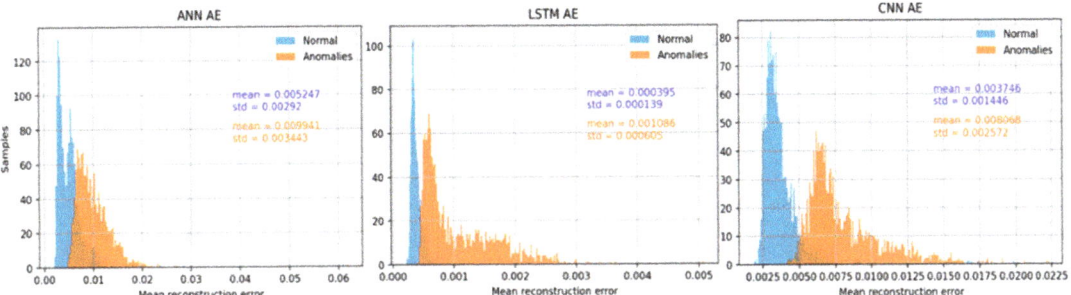

Figure 7. Distributions of MAE for each AE architecture.

Optimal performance was achieved by setting the threshold to 0.0063, 0.00048, and 0.00514 for the ANN-based, the LSTM-based and the CNN-based AEs, respectively.

The CNN-based AE achieved the highest scores according to the classification metrics (see Table 2). Its reconstruction capabilities are presented for two types of anomalies in Figures 8 and 9, with the corresponding MAE for both normal- anomalous pairs. Oscillations (Figure 8) produced higher MAE errors than dips/rises failures (Figure 9). However, further research is needed regarding localization using DL methods.

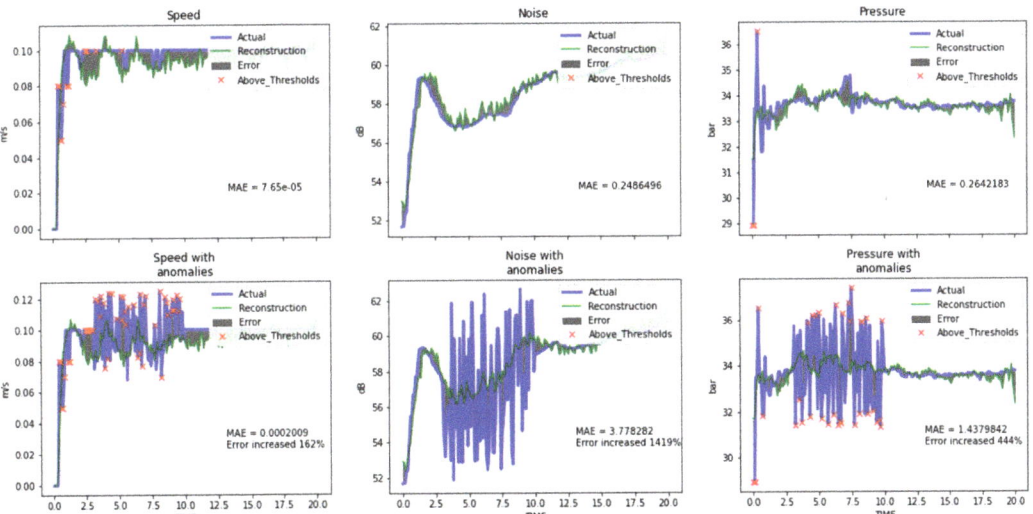

Figure 8. The reconstruction of the proposed model for a pair of normal and the corresponding with oscillation anomalies sample.

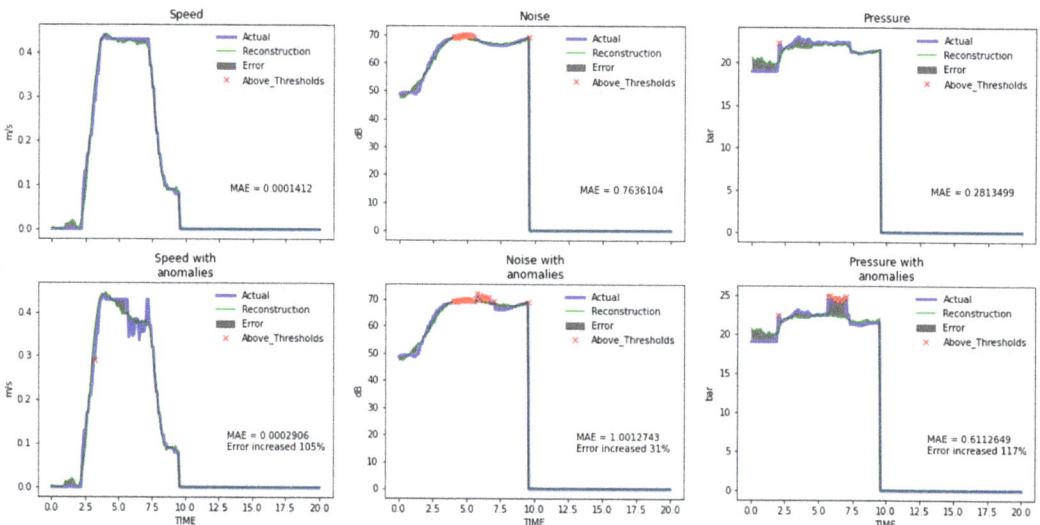

Figure 9. The reconstruction of the proposed model for a pair of normal and the corresponding with dips/rises anomalies sample.

All three examined AEs architectures demonstrated enhanced anomaly detection capabilities by producing a higher reconstruction error when fed with data including anomalies. According to the provided results, LSTM-based AE achieved the lowest reconstruction error for both cases of input data (normal or synthetic with artificial anomalies) which reveals that CNN-based AEs present higher sensitivity to anomalies. In terms of classification capability, the LSTM-based AE provided worse classification metrics than those achieved by the CNN-based AE, according to the MAE distribution graphs and the observed overlap, which also limited the range for the selection of the classification threshold. Overall, it emerges that the CNN-based AE shows better performance with regard to accuracy, also requiring less training time due to the reduced number of parameters.

4. Conclusions

To tackle the absence of anomalies in the data that is a common problem of real industrial datasets, a simple methodology of inducing anomalies based on expert's knowledge and data analysis was deployed. The AE based on 1DCNN layers outperformed in terms of classification accuracy, both LSTM-based and ANN-based AE. In addition, the ability of the CNN layers to share weights reduced the parameters-depth analogy of the proposed model and resulted in fast training times. The model achieved distinction of normal data and data including anomalies with 94% accuracy in an industrial dataset enhanced with artificial anomalies. Moreover, this work presented a methodology for inducing artificial anomalies, in order to generate samples that deviate from the normal operational thresholds of the examined industrial dataset.

Regarding the limitations with our approach, the possibility that the artificial dataset might not be representative for all possible outcomes including anomalies, is one of them. Thus, the classification threshold that selected with our approach can be considered optimal just for this test dataset. For future work, the consideration of real anomalies and the examination of other methodologies in classification threshold estimation, are essential.

Author Contributions: Conceptualization, T.T. (Theodoros Tziolas), K.P. and E.P.; methodology, T.T. (Theodoros Tziolas) and K.P.; software, T.T. (Theodoros Tziolas); validation, T.T. (Theodosios Theodosiou), T.T. (Theodoros Tziolas) and T.M.; formal analysis, T.T. (Theodoros Tziolas) and T.T. (Theodosios Theodosiou); investigation, T.T. (Theodoros Tziolas); resources, T.M. and A.P.; data curation, T.T. (Theodoros Tziolas) and T.M.; writing—original draft preparation, T.T. (Theodoros Tziolas), T.T. (Theodosios Theodosiou) and K.P.; writing—review and editing, E.P., T.M. and A.P.; visualization, T.T. (Theodoros Tziolas); supervision, E.P.; project administration, E.P.; funding acquisition, E.P. All authors have read and agreed to the published version of the manuscript.

Funding: This research was funded by OPTIMAI, European project, grant number GA 958264.

Institutional Review Board Statement: Not applicable.

Informed Consent Statement: Not applicable.

Data Availability Statement: The datasets analyzed during the current study are available from the KLEEMAN co-authors on reasonable request.

Conflicts of Interest: The authors declare no conflict of interest.

References

1. Chandola, V.; Banerjee, A.; Kumar, V. Anomaly Detection: A Survey. *ACM Comput. Surv. (CSUR)* **2009**, *41*, 1–58. [CrossRef]
2. Gupta, M.; Gao, J.; Aggarwal, C.C.; Han, J. Outlier Detection for Temporal Data: A Survey. *IEEE Trans. Knowl. Data Eng.* **2014**, *26*, 2250–2267. [CrossRef]
3. Breunig, M.; Kriegel, H.-P.; Ng, R.; Sander, J. LOF: Identifying Density-Based Local Outliers. *ACM SIGMOD Rec.* **2000**, *29*, 93–104. [CrossRef]
4. Lei, D.; Zhu, Q.; Chen, J.; Lin, H.; Yang, P. Automatic K-Means Clustering Algorithm for Outlier Detection. In Proceedings of the International Conference on Information Engineering and Applications, Chongqing, China, 26–28 October 2012; Zhu, R., Ma, Y., Eds.; Springer: London, UK, 2012; pp. 363–372.
5. Kozitsin, V.; Katser, I.; Lakontsev, D. Online Forecasting and Anomaly Detection Based on the ARIMA Model. *Appl. Sci.* **2021**, *11*, 3194. [CrossRef]
6. Pang, G.; Shen, C.; Cao, L.; Hengel, A.V.D. Deep Learning for Anomaly Detection: A Review. *ACM Comput. Surv. (CSUR)* **2021**, *54*, 1–38. [CrossRef]
7. Malhotra, P.; Vig, L.; Shroff, G.; Agarwal, P. Long Short Term Memory Networks for Anomaly Detection in Time Series. *Proceedings* **2015**, *89*, 89–94.
8. Ding, S.; Morozov, A.; Vock, S.; Weyrich, M.; Janschek, K. Model-Based Error Detection for Industrial Automation Systems Using LSTM Networks. In Proceedings of the 7th International Symposium, IMBSA 2020, Lisbon, Portugal, 14–16 September 2020; Zeller, M., Höfig, K., Eds.; Springer International Publishing: Cham, Switzerland, 2020; pp. 212–226.
9. Carletti, M.; Masiero, C.; Beghi, A.; Susto, G.A. A Deep Learning Approach for Anomaly Detection with Industrial Time Series Data: A Refrigerators Manufacturing Case Study. *Procedia Manuf.* **2019**, *38*, 233–240. [CrossRef]
10. Malhotra, P.; Ramakrishnan, A.; Anand, G.; Vig, L.; Agarwal, P.; Shroff, G. LSTM-Based Encoder-Decoder for Multi-Sensor Anomaly Detection. *arXiv* **2016**, arXiv:1607.00148.
11. Hinton, G.E.; Salakhutdinov, R.R. Reducing the Dimensionality of Data with Neural Networks. *Science* **2006**, *313*, 504–507. [CrossRef] [PubMed]
12. Provotar, O.I.; Linder, Y.M.; Veres, M.M. Unsupervised Anomaly Detection in Time Series Using LSTM-Based Autoencoders. In Proceedings of the 2019 IEEE International Conference on Advanced Trends in Information Theory (ATIT), Kyiv, Ukraine, 18–20 December 2019; pp. 513–517.
13. Yu, J.; Zhou, X. One-Dimensional Residual Convolutional Autoencoder Based Feature Learning for Gearbox Fault Diagnosis. *IEEE Trans. Ind. Inform.* **2020**, *16*, 6347–6358. [CrossRef]
14. Canizo, M.; Triguero, I.; Conde, A.; Onieva, E. Multi-Head CNN–RNN for Multi-Time Series Anomaly Detection: An Industrial Case Study. *Neurocomputing* **2019**, *363*, 246–260. [CrossRef]
15. Krizhevsky, A.; Sutskever, I.; Hinton, G.E. Imagenet Classification with Deep Convolutional Neural Networks. *Adv. Neural Inf. Processing Syst.* **2012**, *25*, 1097–1105. [CrossRef]
16. He, K.; Zhang, X.; Ren, S.; Sun, J. Deep Residual Learning for Image Recognition. In Proceedings of the 2016 IEEE Conference on Computer Vision and Pattern Recognition (CVPR), Las Vegas, NV, USA, 27–30 June 2016; pp. 770–778.
17. Rasmus, A.; Berglund, M.; Honkala, M.; Valpola, H.; Raiko, T. Semi-Supervised Learning with Ladder Networks. In Proceedings of the 28th International Conference on Neural Information Processing Systems, Montreal, QC, Canada, 7–12 December 2015.
18. Zhang, S.; Qiu, T. Semi-Supervised LSTM Ladder Autoencoder for Chemical Process Fault Diagnosis and Localization. *Chem. Eng. Sci.* **2022**, *251*, 117467. [CrossRef]
19. Zeiler, M.D.; Krishnan, D.; Taylor, G.W.; Fergus, R. Deconvolutional Networks. In Proceedings of the 2010 IEEE Computer Society Conference on Computer Vision and Pattern Recognition, San Francisco, CA, USA, 13–18 June 2010; pp. 2528–2535.
20. Kingma, D.P.; Ba, J. Adam: A Method for Stochastic Optimization. *arXiv* **2014**, arXiv:1412.6980.
21. Shahin, M.A.; Maier, H.R.; Jaksa, M.B. Data Division for Developing Neural Networks Applied to Geotechnical Engineering. *J. Comput. Civ. Eng.* **2004**, *18*, 105–114. [CrossRef]

engineering proceedings

Proceeding Paper

Time Series Clustering of High Gamma Dose Rate Incidents †

Mohammed Al Saleh [1,2,3,*], Beatrice Finance [1], Yehia Taher [1], Ali Jaber [2] and Roger Luff [4]

1 David Laboratory, PARIS-SACLAY University, 45 Avenue des Etats-Unis, 78035 Versailles, France; beatrice.finance@uvsq.fr (B.F.); yehia.taher@uvsq.fr (Y.T.)
2 Rafic Hariri University Campus, Lebanese University, Beirut 6573, Lebanon; ali.jaber@ul.edu.lb
3 Lebanese Atomic Energy Commission (LAEC), National Council for Scientific Research (CNRS), Airport Road, P.O. Box 11-8281 Beirut, Lebanon
4 Federal Office for Radiation Protection (BfS), D-24768 Rendsburg, Germany; rluff@bfs.de
* Correspondence: mhdalsaleh@gmail.com
† Presented at the 8th International Conference on Time Series and Forecasting, Gran Canaria, Spain, 27–30 June 2022.

Abstract: In this paper, we proposed an unsupervised machine-learning-based framework to automate the process of extracting suspicious gamma dose rate incidents from the real unlabeled raw historical data measured in the German Radiation Early Warning Network and identify the underlying events behind each. This raised the research problem of clustering unlabeled time series data with varying lengths and scales. Based on the many evaluations, we demonstrated that the state-of-the-art's most popular time series clustering models were not suitable to perform this task. This motivated us to introduce our own approach. Through this approach we were able to perform online classification for gamma dose rate incidents of varying lengths and scales.

Keywords: machine learning algorithms; predictive model; time series clustering; gamma dose rate; Radiation Early Warning Network

check for updates

Citation: Al Saleh, M.; Finance, B.; Taher, Y.; Jaber, A.; Luff, R. Time Series Clustering of High Gamma Dose Rate Incidents. *Eng. Proc.* **2022**, *18*, 24. https://doi.org/10.3390/engproc2022018024

Academic Editors: Ignacio Rojas, Hector Pomares, Olga Valenzuela, Fernando Rojas and Luis Javier Herrera

Published: 22 June 2022

Publisher's Note: MDPI stays neutral with regard to jurisdictional claims in published maps and institutional affiliations.

1. Introduction

Time series analysis is gaining more and more interest in so many domains. That is because, with the proliferation of the use of sensors and IoT (Internet of Things) devices that continuously produce massive amounts of real-time data, special care has been given for analyzing that data to understand past events and patterns and predict future ones. Medical heart monitor's data, stock market prices, weather conditions, etc., are all examples of such time series data.

In this paper, we are interested in analyzing the gamma dose rate (background radiation level) in the environment. Some incidents can cause an abrupt increase in the gamma dose rate, such as what happened in the Chernobyl accident where the biggest short-term leak of radioactive materials was ever recorded in history [1]. Such an event has to be intercepted at the earliest point possible to take the proper measures and precautions and notify the concerned authorities to minimize the effects of such a hazardous situation. It is a very critical task, as long term or acute exposure to a high gamma dose rate can have many hazardous consequences on humans as well as on the ecosystem.

Around the globe, there are thousands of probes (sensors) that collect gamma dose rates in real time. A Radiation Early Warning System (REWS) collects and analyses data while raising alarm in case of an increase in the local gamma dose rate. Whenever an event occurs (i.e., the gamma dose rate goes above the accepted threshold, provided by experts), an alarm is triggered, and a team of experts and personnel have to unite to investigate the reasons behind this rise. Currently, analyzing the incoming incidents is performed manually while relying on the expert efforts. Such a method is time-consuming and risky, knowing that the factors affecting the gamma dose rate are not always known immediately. Fortunately, most of the incoming incidents are mainly innocent as they remain in an acceptable range value for humans health and this value returns to normal after a period of time.

The objective of our research is to propose an *Intelligent Radiation Early Warning System* that automatically finds the cause behind an incident and its classification into *real or innocent* in real time. In order to build such an intelligent system, we first need to understand and learn from the past by using the historical databases produced by REWS. These databases contain raw unlabeled data (i.e., time series) corresponding to the gamma dose rate monitoring at each probe. Second, we need to identify, in real time, situations already encountered or not in the past to predict the cause behind an incident as quick as possible.

In this paper, we are only interested in describing the challenges of the first phase. We aim at proposing an unsupervised machine learning model that will help us to automatically identify the reasons behind incidents. Since we do not have full knowledge regarding the incident causes (neither their number), or the incident behavior patterns, we solicited the help of experts to validate the result quality of our model and to label the obtained clusters. Another challenge we run into was finding the right unsupervised machine learning model, which is a highly challenging mission. We have run experiments on real data in order to come up with the most suitable approach that is described in this paper. Surprisingly, the most popular approaches found in the state-of-the-art were not the ones selected for our proposal.

The remaining sections of the paper are organized as follows. In Section 2, we address the context and problem statement. Section 3 recalls the background related to the state-of-the-art. Section 4 describes the methodology and the different evaluations we conducted to find the best model for our data. Finally, we conclude in Section 4.

2. Context and Problem Statement

For a long time now, time series data analysis has been a center of attention in research as it is used in different applications such as weather prediction, motion capture processing, analyzing insect behavior, pattern discovery on health-care data, and so on. Similarly, intelligence can be extracted from the gamma dose rate time series data in the radiation monitoring domain.

Although gamma dose rate is in theoretically affected by real incidents, it may also be affected by other factors such as weather conditions (rain, lightning, snow...), environmental factors (sun's cosmic radiations), and many other events as shown in Figure 1. Depending on the type of event, they cause the gamma dose rate to go above an acceptable value for a short or long period of time. These kinds of incidents, such as the ones caused by the rain, we call them *soft parabolas*, which are incidents that stay above the acceptable value of gamma dose rate for a considerable period of time. Incidents such as the ones caused by lightning are called *hard parabolas* and are hardly confused with real incidents or cause alarm. Usually, they are either caused by instantaneous events or a malfunctioning probe.

Note that even these *innocent* events trigger the system's alarm (depicted in red in Figure 1) and ensue a technically useless investigation; they have to be recognized and discarded by the experts after manually searching through and analyzing the multiple data sources (rain data, temperature data, wind data, even transportation data, etc.), which may not be available for inspection at any time and which elongates the useless process of evaluating the event as not alarming.

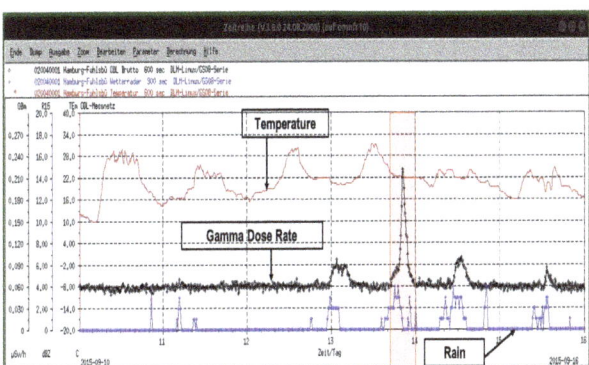

Figure 1. Increased gamma dose rate due to the deposits of Radon by-products from the atmosphere by rain.

To build our *Intelligent Radiation Early Warning System*, we faced the following problems. Firstly, the historical databases only maintain the gamma dose rate for each probe, unfortunately the experts' evaluations of the incidents are not maintained in the historical databases. We are not dealing with multivariate time series, as the different sources, such as precipitation and temperature, are not stored in some databases. Here, we deal with univariate time series, which are unlabeled as shown in the Figure 2. Secondly, incidents that are caused by the same event may not have a recognizable temporal trace or characteristics but more common behavior. For example, a particular event may cause peaks of increasing amplitudes that decrease over a longer period of time; another may cause an abrupt increase and maintain its amplitude for a period of time, and so on. Note that incidents caused by the same event can last for a varying length of time and reach different amplitudes. Thus, grouping the discovered incidents into similar patterns to explore their causes is deemed to be a big challenge.

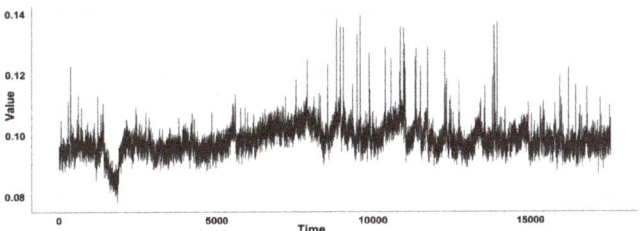

Figure 2. Typical gamma dose rate time series.

Although the literature on time series analysis is prolific, the aforementioned challenge still remains an open question that can be formulated as follows: *"What is the best-fit unsupervised machine learning model that should be used for clustering our time series of varying lengths and different scales?"*

We propose to answer this question in this paper; this can be achieved thanks to the Germany REWS System [2], which offer their data to run all experiments; we thank all the experts we are in contact with, to validate or invalidate the results found by applying the different time series clustering algorithms. The data used in this work comprise the past ten years minute-by-minute gamma dose rate real data for over a thousand probes.

3. Background and State-of-the-Art

In this section, we briefly recall the four main phases for defining a time series clustering approach. First, there is the time series data preprocessing. Second, the similarity measure should be chosen. Then, the clustering algorithm must be selected. Finally, the optimal number of clusters should be determined. Based on these, we enumerate the approaches proposed in the state-of-the-art for univariate time series clustering, especially those for the ones of varying length.

3.1. Time Series Clustering Generic Model

1. Time Series Data Preprocessing Data normalization and missing data imputation are the basic data preprocessing activities to be applied on time series data. Both kinds of techniques have a significant impact on the performance of a model, and they should be chosen based on the problem and model at hand.

   Missing data imputation: Missing values may cause problems for machine learning algorithms as they will perform better with complete well-formed data. Some of the most popular approaches to deal with this problem are dropping rows with missing values, statistical imputation, and model imputation.

   Normalization: The most common normalization methods used during data transformation include min-max, decimal scaling, and z-normalization [3]. The first two methods rely entirely on the minimum and/or maximum values that should be predefined from the data and upon which normalization will be performed. This is not the case with gamma dose rate time series data because the minimum and the maximum values are unknown.

2. Similarity Measure Similarity measures are algorithms used to determine the resemblance between different samples. In time series clustering, it is the determining factor used by the clustering algorithm to decide which cluster each sample belongs to. Shape-based distances evaluate the similarity of samples based on the actual or the normalized values, whereas feature-based distances evaluate similarity based on extracted features. In our context, we are only interested in shape-based measures. They fall into one of two categories:

   Lock-step measures are metrics that evaluate the distance between two time series sequences as the overall difference between each point and its counterpart in the other sequence. These measures require data sequences to be of equal length. Minkowski (L_p norm) distances, specifically Euclidean [4], are the most favored lock-step metrics in machine learning. Their popularity is derived from their simplicity and success in machine learning literature as well as their being parameter-free.

   Elastic measures on the other hand, provide better flexibility as they permit one-to-many and one-to-none point evaluation. Due to this flexibility, these measures provide a better comparison. This flexibility, however, comes at the price of increased time complexity.

   Dynamic Time Warping (DTW) [5] is the most famous elastic measure in the literature, specifically introduced for time series analysis. As its name suggests, it warps the two considered sequences in time to deal with time shift and speed variations. DTW is a good similarity measure for comparing samples of varying lengths. It produces a scale-like effect, stretching and contracting, by accepting many-to-one matching; however, this also makes it sensitive to outliers.

3. Clustering Algorithm Despite the major role each part plays in the process, a recent study has shown that the choice of the proper similarity measure is considered to be more fundamental than that of the clustering algorithm itself in time series clustering. As a result, the majority of time series clustering fall back on classic clustering algorithms where either the choice of distance measure is modified as befits the time series data (raw-based methods), or the data are transformed to fit the clustering algorithm (feature and model-based) [6]. The raw-based approach is often preferable to the feature and model-based approaches. The latter are generally domain-dependent, where the features or models have to be altered depending on the application in the different domains. On the other hand, the main catch of

the raw-based algorithms is the *curse of dimensionality*, [7] where specs with high dimensionality are considered.

In our study, we focus on raw-based approaches as the results can be better generalized across the different applications and domains. We therefore only consider hierarchical and partitional clustering methods, as they are the most commonly used clustering methods in the literature on time series clustering [6,8].

Hierarchical clustering takes no parameters other than the linkage criteria [9]. Depending on the linkage criteria, a tree-like nested "hierarchy" of clusters is built, which can be visualized by a dendrogram. Hierarchical clustering's main advantage is that it does not require the number of clusters as input. Once the dendrogram is obtained, the clusters can be decided by making a cut at a certain point. On the other hand, it requires the distance matrix of all possible pairs of observations. This makes it very computationally expensive and not a favorable option for huge data sets.

Partitional clustering, as its name implies, partitional clustering partitions the data into k different clusters where k is specified a priori. Partitional clustering's aim is to minimize intra-cluster distance and maximize the inter-cluster distance. Partitional methods need the number of clusters k a priori. K-means [10] and K-medoids [11] heuristics are considered the front-men of the partitional methods. They are both based on the concept of finding the best cluster centers, minimizing the distance between each observation and the center of the cluster it is assigned to.

4. Determining optimal number of clusters Clustering methods require the number of clusters k as an input parameter in order to return a clustering. Non-hierarchical methods usually require k to be specified beforehand, whereas, for hierarchical methods, the value of k can be set afterward. Two of the main statistical approaches used for the evaluation of an optimal number of clusters are:

- Elbow Method Is a method that estimates the number of clusters by comparing the within-cluster dispersion.
- Silhouette Method The Silhouette index is proposed by Kaufman et al. [9] and is based on compactness and separation of clusters.

3.2. State-of-the-Art

In Table 1, we summarize the main approaches proposed in the literature to cluster time series of varying lengths. We found that the most favored similarity measure is DTW, and the most popular clustering algorithm is K-medoids. Combining DTW and K-means does not give valid clusters as stated in [12]. The only approach using DTW and K-Means is proposed by Petitjean et al. [13] who introduced a global averaging method called DTW barycenter averaging (DBA), which is a heuristic strategy; however, combining DTW with k-means seems to have a lot of complications, and even with the DBA averaging method, the verdict is left for the testing to see how the DBA fairs with a big length difference compared with the DTW with the k-medoids model.

Table 1. Combined Techniques in the Literature.

Similarity Measure	Clustering Algorithm	Literature
	K-means (DBA)	Zhang et al., 2015 [14]
DTW	K-medoids	Liao et al., 2002 [15] Liao et al., 2006 [16] Hautamaki et al., 2008 [17] Gao et al., 2020 [18]
LCSS	K-medoids	Soleimany et al., 2019 [19]

While this sounds good for the similarity measure (DTW), it is still not clear if this is still true when the similarity measure is used within a machine learning model. In a recent work, Tan et al. [20] explain that there was a little work published in the literature on the classification of time series of varying lengths compared to the "time-warping" problem. They say the problem is comparatively "understudied and unappreciated". When looking at the UCR archive [21], we see also that there are a lot of datasets that are uniform and not much of varying length only very recently in 2018. That is why we believe that the context of our research will help to have a better understanding of the problem. Unfortunately, due to the nature of the data (radiation level), they cannot be rendered public to the UCR archive.

4. Our Approach and Experiments

In this section, we describe the different choices made in our model to cluster gamma dose rate time series. Knowing that we are not contributing to the clustering domain, we are proposing a kind of methodology where we are fine tuning the process of seeking for the best way to do clustering. This led us to the hardest part of our research where we tested all types of combinations between similarity measures and clustering algorithms. In the end, we present our contribution, which is the machine learning model we introduced that achieved the best results through testing. Our approach is depicted in Figure 3. As explained before, machine learning algorithms achieve better performance if the time series data have a consistent scale or distribution. Thus, an important attention has been on incident extraction and data preprocessing. Then, we detail the similarity measure and the clustering algorithm we retain.

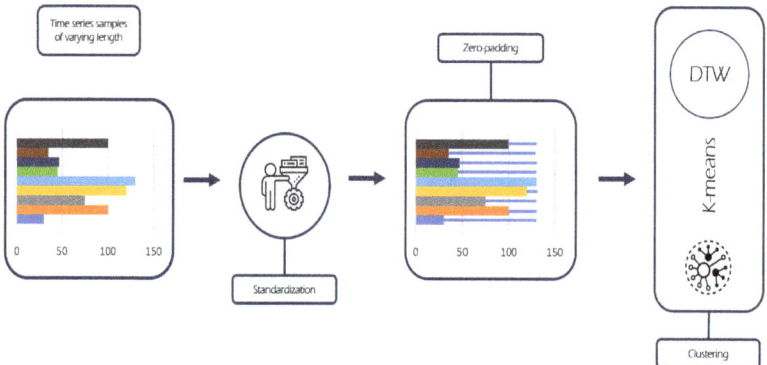

Figure 3. Specific Model for Clustering Sequences of Varying Length.

4.1. Incident Extraction and Preprocessing

In the beginning, we considered all subsequences of the time series where the gamma dose rate went above the threshold as incidents; however, we found that short incidents added much noise to the data set after experimentation. The clustering could not achieve any satisfactory results, so we re-consulted the experts. In the remaining work, we discarded all incidents that did not last at least 30 min above the peak threshold.

1. **Missing Data Imputation:** As we explained previously, the gamma dose rate data are very well susceptible to the missing data problem. That is because we are dealing with data coming from sensors, and these sensors are most probably going to malfunction at one time or another. Because the data we are dealing with are relatively huge and based on the intelligence obtained from experts, we decided to deal with the problem of having missing data by: (1) dropping the whole time series data (one year worth of data) if the missing data are distributed in big patches throughout it; (2) dropping the extracted incident if it encounters a missing data point because this means that the probe is malfunctioning at the time and hence it cannot be trusted.
2. **Scale Standardization:** The extracted incidents resulting from the extraction approach are of varying scale and amplitudes. The gamma dose rate can reach unpre-

dictable levels when affected by a radiation event; we cannot know the maximum and minimum values in order to perform min-max or decimal-scaling normalization. For this reason, we had to discard them. On the other hand, **z-normalization** is highly applied in the time series literature. Its strong point is that it normalizes the samples, so only the *shape* of them is left to compare to each other. A value a of A is standardized to a' by computing:

$$a' = \frac{a - \mu(A)}{\sigma(A)}$$

The fact that it normalized the data to be of a mean equal to zero and standard deviation between 1 and -1 has great advantages, as explained in the next section.

3.   **Length Standardization**. As mentioned before in the state-of-the-art, the elastic measure DTW is very sensitive to outliers, which means that if the variation in length between samples is too high, the clustering is not performed well, as we see later in the evaluation. To solve the varying length problem, a **padding** technique has been used as proposed by Tan et al. [20]. Samples are padded with in-consequential data points such as zero or the mean or the median depending on the data distribution. By padding with zero to the z-normalized data, neither the mean (0) nor the standard deviation was affected since zero is indeed in-consequential for this distribution of data. Notice that without the z-normalization, it would have been impossible to apply the z-padding. Thus, resulting in having all the incidents in the dataset of equal length and without interfering in the characteristics of the data.

The standardization applied in the preprocessing phase was critical for the approach. Without this preprocessing phase, the padding could not have been performed and the other experiments would not yield meaningful clusters.

4.2. The Time Series Clustering Specific Model

1.   **The Similarity Measure**. Among the two elastic measures, we chose DTW as it tolerates slight time axis misalignment. Moreover, DTW is tolerant to samples of varying lengths. The same can be said about LCSS; however, between the two similarity measures, we found that DTW performed better with our data set than LCSS as the latter is more likely to ignore significant data points in the time series, considering them as outliers. You will see in our experiments that our samples are basically made of outliers as they are abnormal behavior of the gamma dose rate, showing up in a stochastic behavior.

2.   **The Clustering Algorithm**. Due to the preprocessing of the data with z-normalization and zero-padding, we opted for the **K-means with DTW Barycenter Averaging:** algorithm for the clustering. Although according to the state-of-the-art, K-medoids is the most popular technique to be used with DTW, we will see that, in our context, K-means performs better as with the zero-padding, samples become of equal length. DBA, which stands for DTW barycenter averaging [14], evaluates the mean of a set of sequences by iteratively refining the potential average sequence to reach the minimum DTW distance between it and the sequences.

3.   **Choosing Optimal Number of Clusters**. Now that we have our clustering model, we have to choose the optimal number of clusters k, which is the maximum number of clusters with no redundancy. In order to do this we had to experiment with different ks and evaluate the results of each. We first tried to do this using the indices mentioned before for determining the optimal number of clusters; however, the results obtained from the algorithms were not helpful and sometime not logical. In our approach, we presented to the experts the computed cluster centers from our experiments for $1 < k < 10$, and, together, we saw that for $k > 3$ we started to have redundant clusters (as shown in Figure 4 for $k = 4$), so we decided that the optimal k for this dataset is 3.

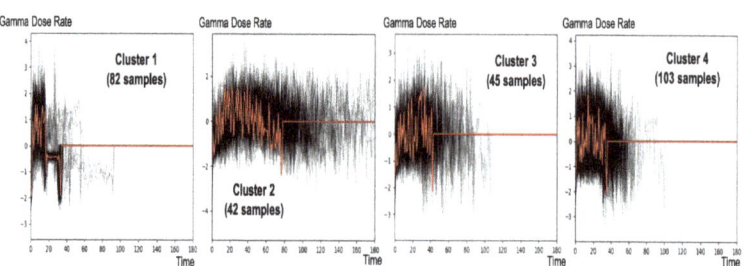

Figure 4. Our model's cluster results for $k = 4$.

4.3. Experimentation

In order to compare the different approaches of the state-of-the-art, as well as to see the benefit of our proposed model, we decide to evaluate, in a systematic way, different combinations of preprocessing phases (with or without z-normalization or zero-padded) with different clustering models (K-means, K-medoids, K-shape) as synthesized in Table 2. The overall number of experiments performed was 24, including the 16 described experiments in Table 2. Due to space limitations, we only give the results obtained with K-medoids or K-means with the same similarity measure and the same preprocessing; however, all evaluations are available by contacting the authors.

Table 2. Model Experiments.

Clustering Algorithm	Similarity Measure	Z-Normalized	Zero-Padded	
			Yes	No
K-means	DTW	Yes	✓	✓
		No	✓	✓
	LCSS	Yes	✓	✓
		No	✓	✓
	Euclidean	Yes	✓	
K-medoids	DTW	Yes	✓	✓
		No	✓	✓
	DTW with length factor	Yes		✓
		No		✓
K-shape	SBD	Yes	✓	

In Figure 5, using K-medoids with DTW with/without padding, we faced the same problem caused by the fact that the K-medoids algorithm tolerates outliers, so the obtained clusters have a lot of misplaced incidents and the centroid of the clusters does not clearly represent the observations in the cluster. On the other hand, observing the results of K-means clustering, we can see how adding up each preprocessing step brought us closer to the best cluster results, shown in Figure 6, which were approved by the experts who found that indeed each cluster (from left to right) can be explained by a different underlying event. Cluster 1's incidents are caused by a **calibration event** performed on the probes. Cluster 2's incidents are caused by a **stormy** rain where the wind causes the very sensitive probes to be affected by vibrations. Cluster 3's incidents are caused by a **normal rain** that causes the elements to go straight down and affect the probe with an immediate sharp increase. Notice that we also tried to increase the number of k, but we found that, when above 3, we started to see redundant clusters.

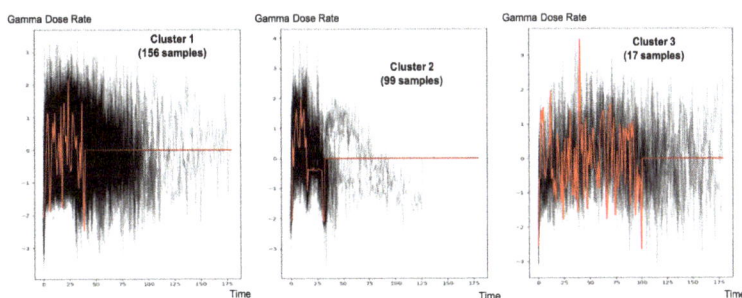

Figure 5. K-medoids with DTW(DBA) and z-normalized data with padding.

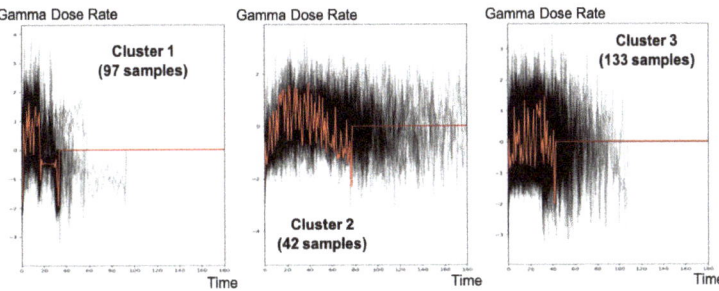

Figure 6. K-means with DTW(DBA) and z-normalized data with padding.

5. Conclusions

In this work, we presented our unsupervised machine-learning-based framework for autonomously identifying underlying events behind high gamma dose rate historical incidents. After extracting and preprocessing the extracted incidents, our machine learning model groups similarly behaving incidents caused by the same underlying event. The experts evaluated the groups, recognized the events, and labeled the incidents. The model that we have proposed is the result of an intense period of evaluations. The systematic methodology has convinced us of the foremost importance of the preprocessing phase. We believe that our proposal could be applied to other application domains, dealing with incidents of varying scale and length. To complete our *Intelligent Radiation Early Warning System*, online incidents should be classified to the proper cluster in real time. We will present our proposed solution in a future publication.

Author Contributions: M.A.S. analyzed and interpreted the need for an intelligent radiation early warning system, introduced the first phase of RIMI framework, and was a major contributor in writing the manuscript. He also queried the AI methodologies and techniques to introduce an approach that can address the shortcomings behind the RIMI first phase. B.F., Y.T., A.J. and R.L. verified the tested techniques and functions for analyzing the data and were major contributors in writing the manuscript. All authors have read and agreed to the published version of the manuscript.

Funding: The first and corresponding author "Mohammed Al Saleh" has a scholarship from the National Council for Scientific Research in Lebanon (CNRS) to continue his Ph.D. degree, including this research.

Institutional Review Board Statement: Not applicable.

Informed Consent Statement: Not applicable.

Data Availability Statement: The datasets used and/or analyzed during the current study are available from the corresponding author on reasonable request.

Acknowledgments: We would like to thank the National Council for Scientific Research (CNRS) in Lebanon for supporting this work. We would like to express our gratitude to the Federal Office for Radiation Protection (BfS) in Germany for allowing us to use the data collected by their REWS for more than 15 years ago. We would also like to thank Roy Issa and Nourhan Bachir for their support in implementing the code behind this research.

Conflicts of Interest: The authors declare no conflict of interest.

Abbreviations

The following abbreviations are used in this manuscript:

REWS	Radiation Early Warning System
DTW	Dynamic Time Warping
DBA	DTW Barycenter Averaging
LCSS	Longest Common Subsequence

References

1. Mann, W.B. The international chernobyl project technical report: Assessment of radiological consequences and evaluation of protective measures. *Appl. Radiat. Isot.* **1993**, *44*, 985–988. [CrossRef]
2. Stöhlker, U.; Bleher, M.; Doll, H.; Dombrowski, H.; Harms, W.; Hellmann, I.; Luff, R.; Prommer, B.; Seifert, S.; Weiler, F. The German Dose Rate Monitoring Network And Implemented Data Harmonization Techniques. *Radiat. Prot. Dosim.* **2019**, *183*, 405–417. [CrossRef] [PubMed]
3. Z-Normalization of Time Series. Available online: https://jmotif.github.io/sax-vsm_site/morea/algorithm/znorm.html. (accessed on 27 January 2022)
4. Gower, J.C.: Properties of Euclidean and non-Euclidean distance matrices. *Linear Algebra Its Appl.* **1985**, *67*, 81–97. [CrossRef]
5. Myers, C.S.; Rabiner, L.R. Connected digit recognition using a level-building DTW algorithm. *IEEE Trans. Acoust. Speech Signal Process.* **1981**, *29*, 351–363 [CrossRef]
6. Liao, T. Clustering of time series data—A survey. *Pattern Recognit.* **2005**, *38*, 1857–1874. [CrossRef]
7. Zervas, G.; Ruger, S. The Curse of Dimensionality and Document Clustering. In Proceedings of the 1999 IEE Colloquium on Microengineering in Optics and Optoelectronics, Glasgow, UK, 11–12 November 1999; Volume 187, pp. 19:1–19:3.
8. Aghabozorgi, S.; Shirkhorshidi, A.S.; Wah, T.Y. Time-series clustering—A decade review. *Inf. Syst.* **2015**, *53*, 16–38. [CrossRef]
9. Kaufman, L.; Rousseeuw, P.J. *Finding Groups in Data: An Introduction to Cluster Analysis*, 1st ed.; John Wiley: New York, NY, USA, 1990.
10. MacQueen, J. Some methods for classification and analysis of multivariate observations. *Comput. Chem.* **1967**, *4*, 257–272.
11. Kaufman, L.; Rousseeuw, P.J. Clustering by means of Medoids. In *Data Analysis based on the L1-Norm and Related Methods*; Springer: Neuchatel, Switzerland, 1987; pp. 405–416.
12. Niennattrakul, V.; Ratanamahatana, C.A. On clustering multimedia time series data using K-means and dynamic time warping. In Proceedings of the International Conference on Multimedia and Ubiquitous Engineering, Seoul, Korea, 26–28 April 2007; pp. 733–738.
13. Petitjean, F., Ketterlin, A., Gançarski, P. A global averaging method for dynamic time warping, with applications to clustering. *Pattern Recognit.* **2011**, *44*, 678–693. [CrossRef]
14. Anh, D.T.; Thanh, L. An efficient implementation of k-means clustering for time series data with DTW distance. *Int. J. Bus. Intell. Data Min.* **2015**, *10*, 213–232. [CrossRef]
15. Liao, T.; Bolt, B.; Forester, J.; Hailman, E.; Hansen, C.; Kaste, R.; O'May, J. Understanding and projecting the battle state. In Proceedings of the 23rd Army Science Conference, Orlando, FL, USA, 2–5 December 2002.
16. Liao, T.W.; Ting, C.F.; Chang, P.-C. An adaptive genetic clustering method for exploratory mining of feature vector and time series data. *Int. J. Prod. Res.* **2006**, *44*, 2731–2748. [CrossRef]
17. Hautamaki, V.; Nykanen, P.; Franti, P. Time-series clustering by approximate prototypes. In Proceedings of the 19th International Conference on Pattern Recognition, Tampa, FL, USA, 8–11 December 2008; pp. 1–4. [CrossRef]
18. Gao, Y., Duan, Y., Liu, Z., Ma, C. Improved K-medoids algorithm-based clustering analysis for handle driving force in automotive manual sliding door closing process. *Proc. Inst. Mech. Eng. Part D J. Automob. Eng.* **2020**, *235*, 871–880. [CrossRef]
19. Soleimany, G.; Abessi, M. A New Similarity Measure for Time Series Data Mining Based on Longest Common Subsequence. *Am. J. Data Min. Knowl. Discov.* **2019**, *4*, 32–45. [CrossRef]
20. Tan, C.W.; Petitjean, F.; Keogh, E.; Webb, G. Time series classification for varying length series. 2019. *Preprints and early-stage research may not have been peer reviewed yet.*
21. Hoang, A.D.; Eamonn, K.; Kaveh, K.; Chin-Chia, M.Y.; Yan, Z.; Shaghayegh, G.; Chotirat, A.R.; Yanping, C.; Bing, H.; Nurjahan, B.; et al. The UCR Time Series Classification Archive. Available online: https://www.cs.ucr.edu/~eamonn/time_series_data_2018/ (accessed on 27 Janurary 2022)

engineering
proceedings

MDPI

Proceeding Paper

A Dynamic Combination of Theta Method and ATA: Validating on a Real Business Case †

Yasin Tadayonrad * and **Alassane Ballé Ndiaye**

Qalinca-Labs, Ecole Polytechnique, Université Libre de Bruxelles, 1050 Brussels, Belgium; alassane.ndiaye@ulb.be
* Correspondence: yasin.tadayonrad@ulb.be; Tel.: +32-494276007
† Presented at the 8th International Conference on Time Series and Forecasting, Gran Canaria, Spain, 27–30 June 2022.

Abstract: In order to make better decisions and take efficient actions in any supply chain system, we need to have better estimation of uncertain parameters, especially the future demands of our customers. To do so we must use a forecasting model which gives the most useful and accurate forecasts. Time series forecasting methods are still one of the most popular approaches used in the business because of their simplicity. One of the most recent methods that caught the attention of researchers and practitioners is Theta method, which was first ranked in M3 competition. This method works based on the decomposition of the deseasonalized original demand data into two components. The first component represents the long-term trend, and the second component indicates the short-term behavior of the data set. ATA method is another method which has been introduced recently. ATA method works like exponential smoothing methods, but in ATA method the smoothing parameter is a function of time point. In this paper we have proposed a new form of Theta method in which we have benefited from the features of ATA and presented a combination of ATA method and Theta method. We have introduced a dynamic model which uses Theta method as the main model and selected from among some alternative methods such as ATA method, simple exponential, and Double Exponential smoothing methods to be used as the theta lines. Also, we optimize the parameters of each method used in the model. Finally, we have tested the mentioned model on a real data set and concluded that the combination of Theta and ATA methods has a better performance compared to the other alternatives in terms of forecast accuracy.

Keywords: forecasting; time series; Theta method; ATA method; simple exponential smoothing (SES); double exponential smoothing (DES); forecasting key performance indicator (KPI); combination

check for
updates

Citation: Tadayonrad, Y.; Ndiaye, A.B. A Dynamic Combination of Theta Method and ATA: Validating on a Real Business Case. *Eng. Proc.* **2022**, *18*, 25. https://doi.org/10.3390/engproc2022018025

Academic Editors: Ignacio Rojas, Hector Pomares, Olga Valenzuela, Fernando Rojas and Luis Javier Herrera

Published: 22 June 2022

Publisher's Note: MDPI stays neutral with regard to jurisdictional claims in published maps and institutional affiliations.

1. Introduction

One of the major concerns in most supply chain systems is finding the best ways to help the managers and decision-makers to make right decisions and take efficient actions [1,2]. Estimating the customers' demand in the most accurate way is one of the most critical issues that affects many decisions in a supply chain system. Therefore, having an efficient and reliable forecasting model plays an important role in this industry. In the past decades, time series forecasting methods have been at the core of attention of researchers and practitioners in this field [3–7]. These methods are usually simple and understandable. That is why those models are still popular in the industry.

1.1. Theta Method

Theta method was introduced and ranked as the first method with the best performance in M3 competition [8]. After that, Theta method has been the benchmark method in the forecasting projects, competitions, and research [9]. The classic Theta method is applied to seasonally adjusted demand data set by decomposing the deseasonalized data into theta lines, extrapolating the theta lines, combining the extrapolated theta lines, and finally seasonalizing the combined line to obtain the forecasts for periods ahead [10]. In the classic form, Theta decomposes the seasonally adjusted data into two theta lines. These two lines refer to long-term and short-term behavior of the original data set. The implementation of classic form of Theta method could be summarized in the following algorithm:

1.1.1. Seasonality Detection

This step can be ignored if our original data set rep-resents demand data in a yearly basis. In case of having quarterly, monthly, weekly, and even daily data we need to detect seasonality patterns in the historical data.

There are several ways for seasonality detection but one of the most common ways is using autocorrelation method. Using the below equations, we can find the existence of seasonality and the seasonal lag in our data.

$$r_k = \frac{\sum_{i=1}^{n-k}\left(d_i - \bar{d}\right)\left(d_{i+k} - \bar{d}\right)}{\sum_{i=1}^{n}\left(d_i - \bar{d}\right)^2} \tag{1}$$

$$|r_m| \geq q_{(1-\frac{\alpha}{2})}\sqrt{\frac{1}{n}\left(1 + 2\sum_{k=1}^{m-1} r_k^2\right)} \tag{2}$$

r_k: Autocorrelation coefficient for lag k.

d_i: Values of original time series at time i.

m: The periodicity of the data (four for quarterly data, twelve for monthly data).

The value of q refers to the $(1 - \alpha/2)\%$ confidence level in a Normal distribution

For any value of m that the absolute value if r_m is greater than the right side of Equation (2), we can say there is a seasonal pattern with lag m. In case of having more than one value for m, we can take the largest value.

1.1.2. Removal of Seasonality

One of the most well-known approaches for removing seasonality from the original data is decomposition methods. Classical multiplicative decomposition and classical additive decomposition are the most popular approaches to decompose seasonal patterns by which we can separate a time series into trend, seasonality, and remainder.

1.1.3. Theta Decomposition

In this step the seasonally adjusted series need to be separated into two components, short-term and long-term components. In Theta method θ is the main parameter that modifies the local curvatures of seasonally adjusted data. Using different values for θ results in different representation of the original data. $\theta = 1$ simply refers to the seasonally adjusted data. $\theta = 0$ refers to the series with no local curvatures, in other words it indicates the linear trend. $0 < \theta < 1$ results in reduction of the local curvatures and, as such, amplification of the long-term behavior. $\theta > 1$ results in amplification of the local curvatures and, as such, amplification of the short-term behavior.

In the classic version of Theta method, two theta lines are used, with $\theta 1 = 0$ and $\theta 2 = 2$, denoted as $t1$ and $t2$. As noted, $t1$ is the linear trend line of the data and corresponds to the long-term component, whereas $t2$ represents the series with double the local curvatures of the nonseasonal data.

The first theta line is $t1$. In the classic Theta method, simple regression is used to fit the nonseasonal data.

$$t1_t(0) = \hat{d} = b_0 + b_1 t \tag{3}$$

b_0: Intercept of seasonality adjusted data

b_1: Slope of seasonality adjusted data

t: Time period

The second theta line is $t2$.

$$t2_t(\theta) = \theta d_t + (1 - \theta)t1_t \tag{4}$$

with $\theta = 2$:

$$t2_t(2) = 2d_t - t1_t \tag{5}$$

1.1.4. Extrapolation

In the standard form, $t1$ is extrapolated by a normal linear regression line, while $t2$ is extrapolated using simple exponential smoothing. Extrapolation of the long-term component using normal linear regression line is as follow:

$$f1_{t+1} = b_0 + b_1(t+1) \tag{6}$$

Extrapolation of the short-term component using SES is:

$$f2_{t+1} = \alpha t2_t + (1 - \alpha)f2_t \tag{7}$$

1.1.5. Combination

The final forecast is a combination of the forecasts of the two theta lines using equal weights. The forecasts of long-term and short-term theta lines should be combined (in the classic version, with equal weights; w_1, $w_2 = 0.5$).

$$f_{t+h} = 0.5\, f1_{t+h} + 0.5\, f2_{t+h} \tag{8}$$

For $\theta > 1$ we can use the following equation for optimizing the weights [11]:

$$w2 = \frac{\theta_2 - 1}{\theta_2 - \theta_1}, \; w1 = 1 - w2 \tag{9}$$

Using the above formula, forecast could be obtained by:

$$f_{t+h} = w_1 f1_{t+h} + w_2 f2_{t+h} \tag{10}$$

1.1.6. Reseasonalization

If the series was identified as seasonal in step one, then the final forecasts are multiplied by the respective seasonal indices. Therefore, we must add/multiply the seasonality indices (calculated in step two) to the forecasts obtained in step five.

1.2. ATA Method

ATA method was introduced by a Turkish team in 2017 [12]. An alternative for two major forecasting approaches: exponential smoothing (ES) and autoregressive integrated moving average (ARIMA). The ATA method works by modifying the smoothing constants of various exponential smoothing models in a way that the smoothing constant becomes a function of t. This modification helps deal with initialization problems and makes the optimization process easier. Also, with ATA it is possible to assign past information equal weights. The ATA method has a similar form to ES, but the smoothing parameters are modified so that when obtaining a smoothed value at a specific time point, the number of observations that can contribute to the value being smoothed is taken into account when the weights among the observations are distributed. Therefore, the smoothing parameter for this method is a function of t, unlike ES where no matter where the value you are smoothing resides on the timeline, the observations receive weights depending only on their distances from the value being smoothed. The standard form of ATA method is given in the following aquations.

$$a_t = \left(\frac{p}{t}\right)d_t + \left(\frac{t-p}{t}\right)(a_{t-1} + b_{t-1}) \tag{11}$$

$$b_t = \left(\frac{q}{t}\right)(a_t - a_{t-1}) + \left(\frac{t-q}{t}\right)b_{t-1} \tag{12}$$

$$f_t(h) = a_t + h\, b_t \tag{13}$$

$p \in \{1,2,\ldots,n\}, q \in \{1,2,\ldots,p\}, t > p \geq q$
For $t \leq p$, $a_t = d_t$
For $t \leq q$, $b_t = d_t - d_{t-1}$
$b_1 = 0$

where:
d_t: the value of the original series
a_t: the smoothed value at time t
b_t: the trend component
p: the smoothing parameter for level
q: the smoothing parameter for trend
$f_t(h)$: the h-step-ahead forecast value for $h = 1, 2, \ldots$
To be able to tackle with dampening trends in the historical patterns, we can us the dampening factor in ATA method as follows:

$$a_t = \left(\frac{p}{t}\right)d_t + \left(\frac{t-p}{t}\right)(a_{t-1} + \varphi b_{t-1}) \tag{14}$$

$$b_t = \left(\frac{q}{t}\right)(a_t - a_{t-1}) + \left(\frac{t-q}{t}\right)\varphi b_{t-1} \tag{15}$$

$$f_t(h) = a_t + \left(\varphi + \varphi^2 + \ldots + \varphi^h\right)b_t \tag{16}$$

$p \in \{1,2,\ldots,n\}, q \in \{1,2,\ldots,p\}, \varphi \in (0,1], t > p \geq q$
For $t \leq p$, $a_t = d_t$
For $t \leq q, b_t = d_t - d_{t-1}$
$b_1 = 0$

where:
d_t: the value of the original series
a_t: the smoothed value at time t
b_t: the trend component
p: the smoothing parameter for level
q: the smoothing parameter for trend
$f_t(h)$: the h-step-ahead forecast value for $h = 1, 2, \ldots$
φ: dampening parameter
The algorithm of implementing ATA method could be summarized as three main steps.
Step 1: Deseasonalize the data by the classical decomposition methods, if necessary.
Step 2: Arbitrary models were used for different data types.
Find an optimal value for the parameter p by minimizing the in-sample one-step-ahead sMAPE using following models and obtain forecast values as desired.
Yearly: ATAadd(p, 1, φ) where $\varphi \in \{0.61, 0.62, \ldots, 1\}$
All other types: (quarterly, monthly, weekly, daily, hourly)
ATAadd(p, 0, 1) and ATAadd(p, 1, 1) were obtained and averaged.
("add" refers to using additive decomposition method in the first step)
Step 3: The forecasts are reseasonalized using seasonal indices from classical decomposition.

2. Materials and Methods

In this work Theta method has been considered as the base model. In Theta method other models need to be used to extrapolate theta lines. As explained in the first section, there are two theta lines in the standard form of Theta method representing the long-term and short-term components of the demand. In the standard form the values of theta parameters are considered as 0 and 2 for the first and second theta lines, respectively. In the proposed model we tested the Theta method with both two and three theta lines. Regarding the mentioned unique features of ATA method and its ability to project the trend in the time series, ATA has been selected to extrapolate the first theta line which represents the long-term component. Therefore, in the third and fourth steps of Theta method, we use the formulas of ATA method (ATA and ATA with damped trend) instead of simple regression model. It means in the proposed method we use Equations (11)–(16) instead of Equations (3) and (6).

Furthermore, exponential smoothing methods (SES and DES methods as well as DES with damped trend) are used as the other candidates to extrapolate the other theta lines.

In order to find the best parameters that result in the most accurate forecasts, all parameters are optimized dynamically. As the demand range varies for different stock keeping units (SKUs), we need to attribute different importance to different products in order to pay more attention to the errors on those products with higher demand. To do so, weighted mean absolute error (wMAE) has been selected as a KPI to measure the performance of the forecasting methods in which we normalize the error based on the scale of demand of each product. Therefore, best values for the related parameters are chosen among the potential values for each model at each iteration (see Appendix A). The possible values that we have considered for each parameter have been listed in Table 1.

Table 1. Potential values for different parameters.

Parameter	Model(s)	Values
θ	Theta	{1.2, 1.4, 1.6, 1.8, 2, 2.2, 2.4, 2.6, 2.8, 3.0}
α	SES, DES	{0.05, 0.1, 0.2, 0.3, 0.5, 0.8, 0.9}
β	DES	{0.1, 0.2, 0.3, 0.8, 0.9}
φ	ATA and DES with damped trend	{0.6, 0.7, 0.8, 0.9}
n	MA	{3, 4, 5, 6, 7}
p	ATA, ATA with damped trend	{2, 3, 4, 5, 6, 7, 8, 9, 10}
q	ATA, ATA with damped trend	{2, ... , p}

3. Results

The given method was implemented on python NumPy library. A large demand dataset from a major international company was used to test the model. The mentioned dataset includes the demand data of 54 months for 19,691 SKUs in their logistics network in the Europe. We implemented the proposed model using NumPy and Pandas libraries on Python 3.7.0 and ran it on the given data set.

In Tables 2 and 3, we have presented the results obtained from different models compared to the results from applying MA and SES (as the benchmarks) on the given data set. We have optimized the value of n and α in MA and SES for each SKU. The first column shows the number of periods that we have considered as the test set. Indeed, we do not train the models on this data set and it remained hidden so as to test the performance of models. The second and third columns show the comparison of the results from classic Theta method in which the first theta line is the simple regression and the second (and third) theta line have been dynamically chosen among SES, DES, and DES with damped trend. The fourth and fifth columns represent the results from ATA and ATA with damped trend methods compared to that of MA. And finally, the last two columns indicate the results from the proposed method in which the first theta line has been fitted and extrapolated using ATA with damped trend method with two and three theta lines, respectively. As we can see in the last row of the tables, the proposed method has a better performance compared to MA and SES as the benchmarks by 5.50% and 3.73%, respectively.

Table 2. Comparing the results obtained from applying different methods on the given data set with the results of the first benchmark (optimized MA).

Number of Test Periods	wMAE Theta2 vs. MA	wMAE Theta3 vs. MA	wMAE ATA vs. MA	wMAE ATA Damped vs. MA	wMAE Theta2 & ATA Damped vs. MA	wMAE Theta3 & ATA Damped vs. MA
8	6.06%	3.03%	7.58%	7.58%	9.09%	7.58%
10	−1.56%	6.25%	9.38%	9.38%	6.25%	3.13%
12	0.00%	−3.57%	−1.79%	0.00%	1.79%	0.00%
14	−1.67%	0.00%	3.33%	5.00%	3.33%	3.33%
18	3.51%	1.75%	1.75%	1.75%	7.02%	5.26%
Average	1.27%	1.49%	4.05%	4.74%	**5.50%**	3.86%

Table 3. Comparing the results obtained from applying different methods on the given data set with the results of the second benchmark (optimized SES).

Number of Test Periods	wMAE Theta2 vs. SES	wMAE Theta3 vs. SES	wMAE ATA vs. SES	wMAE ATA Damped vs. SES	wMAE Theta2 & ATA Damped vs. SES	wMAE Theta3 & ATA Damped vs. SES
8	0.00%	−3.23%	1.61%	1.61%	3.23%	1.61%
10	−4.84%	3.23%	6.45%	6.45%	3.23%	0.00%
12	1.75%	−1.75%	0.00%	1.75%	3.51%	1.75%
14	−1.67%	0.00%	3.33%	5.00%	3.33%	3.33%
18	1.79%	0.00%	0.00%	0.00%	5.36%	3.57%
Average	−0.59%	−0.35%	2.28%	2.96%	**3.73%**	2.05%

4. Conclusions

One of the main concerns of managers and decision-makers in supply chain systems is having accurate estimation of uncertain parameters. Using time series forecasting methods has been always one of the reliable alternatives to obtain the forecasts. In this paper we have benefited from the advantages of some the well-known methods and, combining them, we concluded that we can improve the accuracy of the forecasts using this combined model in which we have used ATA and ATA with damped trend as the first theta line. By testing the performance of other alternative methods (SES, DES, and DES with damped trend), the best method(s) is selected to extrapolate the other theta line(s). The model is also capable of finding the best values for each parameter aiming at minimizing wMAE. We implemented the proposed model on Python and tested it on a real data set. For the future works, we can compare the results from the proposed model with that of machine learning algorithms.

Author Contributions: Both authors contributed to the research paper equally. All authors have read and agreed to the published version of the manuscript.

Funding: Université Libre de Bruxelles.

Institutional Review Board Statement: Not applicable.

Informed Consent Statement: Not applicable.

Data Availability Statement: We cannot provide the original data because of confidential issues.

Acknowledgments: We thank anonymous referees for their insightful comments that have helped improving this paper substantially.

Conflicts of Interest: The authors declare no conflict of interest.

Appendix A

Algorithm A1. This algorithm represents the configuration of python code.

```
for periods in {8, 10, 12, 14, 18}:
    d_test = data_set [ : , - periods: ]
    d_train = data_set [ : , : - periods]
```

```
# 1. Theta classic with 2 theta lines
t1 = regression
for t2 in [SES, DES, DES_damped]:
    for theta, alpha, beta, phi in thetas, alphas, betas, phis:
        f1 = theta2(d = d_train, t1 = regression, 2nd_theta_line = t2, theta =
theta, alpha = alpha, beta = beta, phi = phi)
        kpi_train = wMAE(f1, d_test)
    select the best parameters based on minimum kpi
    select the best model for t2 based on minimum kpi
f_theta2 = theta2(d=d_train, t1=regression, 2nd_theta_line=best_model, theta =
best_theta, alpha = best_alpha, beta = best_beta, phi = best_phi)
kpi_theta2 = wMAE(f_ theta2, d_test)
```

```
# 2. Theta classic with 3 theta lines
t1 = regression
for t2, t3 in [SES, DES, DES_damped]:
    for theta2, theta3, alpha, beta, phi in thetas, alphas, betas, phis:
        f2 = theta3(d = d_train, t1 = regression, 2nd_theta_line = t2,
        3rd_theta_line = t3, theta2 = theta2, theta3 = theta3, alpha = alpha, beta =
        beta, phi = phi)
        kpi_train = wMAE(f2, d_test)
    select the best parameters based on minimum kpi
    select the best models for t2 and t3 based on minimum kpi
f_theta3 = theta3(d = d_train, t1 = regression, 2nd_theta_line = best_model1,
3rd_theta_line = best_model2, theta2 = best_theta2, theta3 = best_theta3 alpha =
best_alpha, beta = best_beta, phi = best_phi)
kpi_theta3 = wMAE(f_ theta3, d_test)
```

```
# 3. ATA
for p, q in ps, qs:
    f3 = ata(d=d_train, p = p, q = q)
    kpi_train = wMAE(f3, d_test)
select the best parameters based on minimum kpi
f_ata = ata(d = d_train, p = best_p, q = best_q)
kpi_ata = wMAE(f_ata, d_test)
```

```
# 4. ATA with damped trend
for p, q, phi in ps, qs, phis:
    f4 = ata_damped(d = d_train, p = p, q = q, phi = phi)
    kpi_train = wMAE(f4, d_test)
select the best parameters based on minimum kpi
f_ata_damped = ata_damped(d = d_train, p = best_p, q = best_q, phi = best_phi)
kpi_ata_damped = wMAE(f_ata_damped, d_test)
```

```
# 5. Theta_ata with 2 theta lines
t1 = ata
for t2 in [SES, DES, DES_damped]:
    for theta, alpha, beta, phi, p, q in thetas, alphas, betas, phis, ps, qs:
        f5 = theta2_ata(d = d_train, t1 = ata, 2nd_theta_line = t2, theta = theta,
        alpha = alpha, beta = beta, phi = phi)
        kpi_train = wMAE(f5, d_test)
    select the best parameters based on minimum kpi
    select the best model for t2 based on minimum kpi
f_theta2_ata = theta2_ata(d = d_train, t1 = ata, 2nd_theta_line = best_model, theta =
best_theta, alpha = best_alpha, beta = best_beta, phi = best_phi)
kpi_theta2_ata = wMAE(f_ theta2_ata, d_test)
```

```
# 6. Theta_ata with three theta lines
t1 = ata
for t2, t3 in [SES, DES, DES_damped]:
    for theta2, theta3, alpha, beta, phi, p, q in alphas, betas, phis, ps, qs:
        f6 = theta3_ata(d = d_train, t1 = ata, 2nd_theta_line = t2, 3rd_theta_line =
        t3, theta2 = best_theta2, theta3 = best_theta3, alpha = alpha, beta = beta,
        phi = phi, p = p, q = q)
        kpi_train = wMAE(f6, d_test)
    select the best parameters based on minimum kpi
    select the best models for t2 and t3 based on minimum kpi
f_theta3_ata = theta3_ata(d = d_train, t1 = ata, 2nd_theta_line = best_model1,
3rd_theta_line = best_model2, theta2 = best_theta2,      theta3 = best_theta3 alpha =
best_alpha, beta = best_beta, phi = best_phi, p = best_p, q = best_q)
kpi_theta3_ata = wMAE(f_ theta3_ata, d_test)
```

Algorithm A1. *Cont.*

for *periods* in {8, 10, 12, 14, 18}:
    d_test = data_set [: , - periods:]
    d_train = data_set [: , : - periods]

# 7. Moving average 	
for *n* in ns:
    f7 = ma(d=d_train, n=n)
    kpi_train = wMAE(f7, d_test)
select the best parameters based on minimum kpi
    f_ma = ma(d = d_train, n = best_n)
    kpi_ma = wMAE(f_ma, d_test)

# 8. Simple exponential smoothing 	
for *alpha* in alphas:
    f8 = ses(d = d_train, alpha = alpha)
    kpi_train = wMAE(f8, d_test)
select the best parameters based on minimum kpi
    f_ses = ses(d = d_train, alpha = best_alpha)
    kpi_ses = wMAE(f_ses, d_test)

Output kpi_theta2, kpi_theta3, kpi_ata, kpi_ata_damped, kpi_theta2_ata, kpi_theta3_ata, kpi_ma, kpi_ses

References

1. Hosseini, S.; Ivanov, D.; Dolgui, A. Review of quantitative methods for supply chain resilience analysis. *Transp. Res. Part E Logist. Transp. Rev.* **2019**, *125*, 285–307. [CrossRef]
2. Chen, H.Y.; Das, A.; Ivanov, D. Building resilience and managing post-disruption supply chain recovery: Lessons from the information and communication technology industry. *Int. J. Inf. Manag.* **2019**, *49*, 330–342. [CrossRef]
3. De Gooijer, J.G.; Hyndman, R.J. 25 years of iif time series forecasting: A selective review. Tinbergen Institute Discussion Papers. *SSRN Electron. J.* **2005**, 5–68. [CrossRef]
4. Hyndman, R.; Koehler, A.B.; Ord, J.K.; Snyder, R.D. *Forecasting with Exponential Smoothing: The State Space Approach*; Springer: Berlin/Heidelberg, Germany, 2008.
5. Hyndman, R.J.; Koehler, A.B.; Snyder, R.D.; Grose, S. A state space framework for automatic forecasting using exponential smoothing methods. *Int. J. Forecast.* **2002**, *18*, 439–454. [CrossRef]
6. Gardner, E.S., Jr.; McKenzie, E. Forecasting trends in time series. *Manag. Sci.* **1985**, *31*, 1237–1246. [CrossRef]
7. Makridakis, S.; Andersen, A.; Carbone, R.; Fildes, R.; Hibon, M.; Lewandowski, R.; Newton, J.; Parzen, E.; Winkler, R. The accuracy of extrapolation (time series) methods: Results of a forecasting competition. *J. Forecast.* **1982**, *1*, 111–153. [CrossRef]
8. Koning, A.J.; Franses, P.H.; Hibon, M.; Stekler, H.O. The M3 competition: Statistical tests of the results. *Int. J. Forecast.* **2005**, *21*, 397–409. [CrossRef]
9. Athanasopoulos, G.; Hyndman, R.J.; Song, H.; Wu, D.C. The tourism forecasting competition. *Int. J. Forecast.* **2011**, *27*, 822–844. [CrossRef]
10. Yapar, G.; Yavuz, I.; Selamlar, H.T. Why and How Does Exponential Smoothing Fail? An In Depth Comparison of ATA-Simple and Simple Exponential Smoothing. *Turk. J. Forecast.* **2017**, *1*, 30–39.
11. Fiorucci, J.A.; Pellegrini, T.R.; Louzada, F.; Petropoulos, F.; Koehler, A.B. Models for optimising the theta method and their relationship to state space models. *Int. J. Forecast.* **2016**, *32*, 1151–1161. [CrossRef]
12. Petropoulos, F.; Nikolopoulos, K. The Theta Method. *Foresight* **2017**, *46*, 11–17.

Proceeding Paper

Limitation of Deep-Learning Algorithm for Prediction of Power Consumption †

Majdi Frikha [1,*]**, Khaled Taouil** [2]**, Ahmed Fakhfakh** [2] **and Faouzi Derbel** [1]

[1] Faculty of Engineering Sciences, Leipzig University of Applied Sciences, 04107 Leipzig, Germany; faouzi.derbel@htwk-leipzig.de

[2] (SM@RT) Laboratory, Digital Research Center of Sfax (CRNS), Sfax 3021, Tunisia; khaled.taouil@enetcom.usf.tn (K.T.); ahmed.fakhfakh@enetcom.usf.tn (A.F.)

* Correspondence: majdi.frikha.doc@enetcom.usf.tn

† Presented at the 8th International Conference on Time Series and Forecasting, Gran Canaria, Spain, 27–30 June 2022.

Abstract: In recent years, electricity consumption has become high due to the use of several domestic applications in the house. On the other hand, there is a trend of using renewable energy in many houses, such as solar energy, energy-storage systems and electric vehicles. For this reason, forecasting household electricity consumption is essential for managing and planning energy use. Forecasting power consumption is a difficult time-series-forecasting task. Additionally, the electrical load has irregular trend elements, which makes it very difficult to predict the demand for electrical energy using simple forecasting techniques. Therefore, several researchers have worked on intelligent algorithms such as machine-learning and deep-learning algorithms to find a solution for this problem. In this work, we demonstrate that deep-learning algorithms are not always reliable and accurate in predicting power consumption.

Keywords: deep learning; prediction; power consumption

check for updates

Citation: Frikha, M.; Taouil, K.; Fakhfakh, A.; Derbel, F. Limitation of Deep-Learning Algorithm for Prediction of Power Consumption. *Eng. Proc.* **2022**, *18*, 26. https://doi.org/10.3390/engproc2022018026

Academic Editors: Ignacio Rojas, Hector Pomares, Olga Valenzuela, Fernando Rojas and Luis Javier Herrera

Published: 22 June 2022

Publisher's Note: MDPI stays neutral with regard to jurisdictional claims in published maps and institutional affiliations.

1. Introduction

Due to economic progress and population growth, global electricity consumption has recently increased. According to the Energy Report realized in 2019, global power demand will increase by 2.1% per year, twice the rate of the primary energy production of the stated policy scenario [1]. Since electricity is used simultaneously in power plant production, it is vital to estimate energy usage ahead of time for a regular supply. Forecasting electricity consumption is a difficult problem to predict over a time series. The data collected by the smart sensor may contain redundancies, outliers, missing values and uncertainties. In addition, forecasting power consumption is a difficult time-series forecasting task. Additionally, the electrical load has irregular trend elements, which makes it very difficult to predict the demand for electrical energy using simple forecasting techniques. Therefore, various forecasting strategies to predict electricity usage have recently been developed. Energy consumption forecasting has been examined using various methodologies, which can be divided into two categories: traditional and artificial techniques [2].

Historically, statistical techniques were mainly used to forecast power demand. In [3], to predict electricity consumption, the SARIMA model (seasonal autoregressive integrated moving average) and the fuzzy neural model were compared to predict power consumption. The study household's hourly and daily electricity use was analyzed using linear regression and quadratic regression models [4]. In [5], a multiple regression approach was proposed using genetic algorithm technology to forecast the daily power consumption of the administration building. Significant drawbacks of both models include the lack of occupancy data and the fact that neither model has been studied to predict the energy demand of comparable homes. In another study, the authors used the bootstrap aggregate autoregressive integrated moving average (ARIMA) and an exponential smoothing method in order to predict energy demand in different countries [6]. In general, statistical methods have shown weaknesses in predicting and capturing the non-linear behavior of energy consumption data long-term. Furthermore, the computational approach has limited predictive capacity due to its non-stationary trend and the sharp patterns in energy consumption. As a result, machine-learning approaches have been used to test a variety of prediction models in order to increase predictive quality [7–9]. For example, Liu et al. [10] created a support vector machine (SVM) model to predict and evaluate the energy consumption of public buildings.

Chen et al. [11] proposed a model that predicts power consumption as a function of ambient temperature, which was driven by the regression capability of the solid non-linear support vector. Pinto et al. [12] proposed a paradigm for ensemble learning that combines three machine-learning methods. Nevertheless, due to the problem of dynamic correlation between the variables and data qualities that change throughout time, existing machine-learning algorithms suffer greatly from overfitting. It is difficult to establish a durable and reliable use in case of overfitting. Similarly, many deep-sequential-learning neural networks are set up to predict power consumption. With one-hour resolution forecasts, a recurrent neural network model was used to estimate energy demand profiles for business and residence databases [13]. A pooling methodology using a recurrent neural network algorithm was developed to solve the task of overfitting by boosting the number of data and the diversity [14]. RNN architecture with LSTM cells was developed to predict power consumption in [15]. Individual household power usage patterns are frequently unpredictable due to a range of factors such as weather conditions and holidays. Therefore, it is unreliable to predict power consumption using methods that are based solely on energy consumption data. Our work in this article shows that deep-learning algorithms are not always reliable and accurate in terms of power-consumption prediction.

2. Deep-Learning Algorithms

2.1. Long Short-Term Memory Neural Network (LSTM)

Long short-term memory neural networks (LSTMs) are an advanced form of recurrent neural networks (RNNs) that replace the original cell neurons. The LSTM inherits the unique features of the RNN, which treats the input as a connected time series. Additionally, the complex structure of the LSTM cell finds a solution to the problem of vanishing gradients and disappearance. The LSTM model flowchart has four key elements: input gates, cell status, forget gates and output gates. The information included in the cell status is maintained, updated and deleted via forget gates, input gates and output gates.

The forget gate, as the name implies, is responsible for deciding what information to discard or retain from the last step. This occurs through the first sigmoid layer. The following step is to determine what information should be stored in the new state of the cell. The update value is determined by a sigmoid function as the input gate layer. Following this, the tanh layer generates a new vector of values that can be injected to the state. The following step is to put them together to make a new status update. The cell state acts as memory for the LSTM. Here, it outperforms vanilla RNNs when processing longer input sequences. The previous state of the cell is coupled to the forget gate at each time step to decide which data to broadcast. It is then combined with the input gate to form a new memory for the cell. Finally, the LSTM cell must provide some output. The cell state obtained above passes through a hyperbolic function named tanh, so the cell state value is filtered between −1 and 1.

2.2. Gated Recurrent Unit (GRU)

The internal structure of an LSTM cell has three gates—input, forget and output—whereas the structure of a GRU cell only has two gates: a reset gate and an update gate [16]. The update gate determines if the preceding cell's memory is still active, and the reset gate combines the next cell's input sequence with the previous cell's memory. However, LSTMs differ slightly in some respects. To begin, the GRU cell has two gates, while the LSTM has three gates. The input and forget gates of the LSTM are then blended with the update gate and applied to the hidden reset gate directly.

2.3. Convolutional Neural Network (CNN)

A convolutional neural network (CNN) is a type of neural network that was created specifically to solve image-classification problems requiring 2D data. A CNN is also used to analyze 1-dimensional data in a time-series task. A CNN uses the principle of weight sharing to provide more performance for difficult problems such as time-series forecasting and power-demand forecasting. When you apply convolutions to the input data, they are converted to a feature map. The pooling layer is used after the convolution layer to model the collected feature maps in order to transform them into a more abstract format.

3. Results and Discussion

Accurate forecasting of electricity consumption improves energy utilization rates and helps building management to make better energy management decisions, and thus, saves significant amounts of energy and money. However, due to the dynamics and random noise of the data, the accurate prediction of power consumption is a difficult goal. In this paper, a framework was designed to obtain accurate results for power-demand prediction. The methodology used in this work involved three steps: data processing, training the data, and evaluation. We designed a three-step system to calculate short-term electricity consumption in this research. First, the incoming data are preprocessed to remove outliers, missing values, and redundant values. To normalize the input dataset to a given range, we used a typical scalar technique. Then, the data are analyzed and sent to the training phase. Then, we perform tests on the CNN, LSTM, GRU and 3-layer LSTM models. Finally, we evaluate our models using metric parameters such as RMSE and MSE. Basically, these measurements calculate the difference between the predicted value and the actual value. Therefore, the MSE calculates the mean squared between the actual and the predicted values. On the other side, RMSE calculates the percentage difference between actual and predicted values. The performance of the models was validated using the IHEPC dataset available on the UCI repository [17]. IHEPC is a household dataset freely accessible from the UCI machine-learning store, containing information on electricity consumption from 2006 to 2010. It contains more than 2 million values, with a total of around 26,000 remaining values. Missing values account for 1.25 percent of the total information and are processed during the preprocessing step. For nearly four years, this dataset has contained power-demand measurements at a 1-min sampling rate. We divided the data into a training set and a test set for our tests. The model is tuned using a training set and the model function predicts the output values for data not seen in the test set. This method is appropriate for home applications and saves time during simulation. In this method, 75% of the data are used as a training set, with the remaining 25% used for testing. In addition, we ran several deep-learning tests. We also performed various tests on different deep-learning models for comparison, such as the LSTM, CNN, GRU, and 3-layer LSTM models. Using the aforementioned methods, the predictive models were trained up to 25 epochs.

The model was trained on an HP Omen PC with a Core i5 intel processor and 16 GB of RAM. The implementation was performed with Python3 software using Keras with TensorFlow libraries in the backend and the Adam optimizer.

In this article, we studied several deep-learning models to find an optimal model for short-term power consumption. We performed tests on deep-learning models including CNN, LSTM, GRU and 3-layer LSTM. The simulation results demonstrate that the 3-layer LSTM model is the best model compared to the other three models.

For example, CNN achieved 0.05 and 0.23 MSE and RMSE, LSTM achieved 0.04 and 0.21 MSE and RMSE, GRU scored 0.04 and 0.22 MSE and RMSE, and 3-layer LSTM attained 0.04 and 0.19 MSE and RMSE, as shown in Table 1.

Table 1. Performance of different deep-learning models over IHEPC dataset.

Deep-Learning Algorithms	RMSE	MSE
CNN	0.23	0.05
LSTM	0.21	0.04
GRU	0.22	0.04
3-layer LSTM	0.19	0.03

Figure 1 presents the prediction performance of the 3-layer LSTM model over the IHEPC dataset. We can see that we correctly predicted the difficult values linked to a strong variation in electricity consumption. Therefore, the results are precise and reliable for the prediction of power consumption.

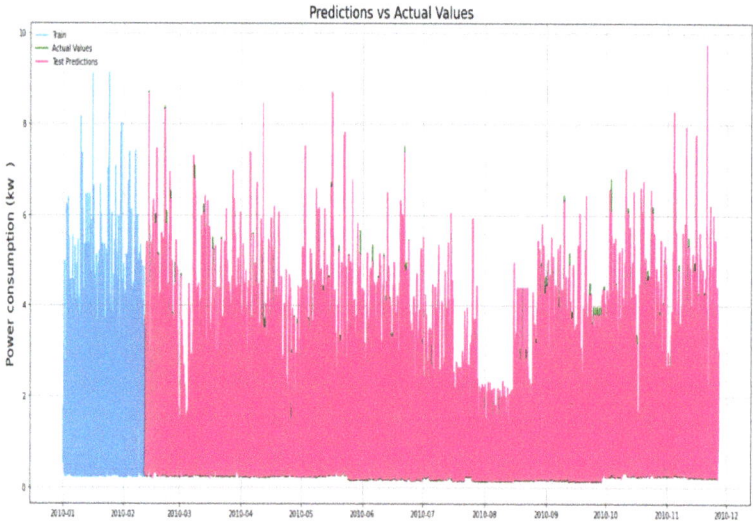

Figure 1. Prediction performance of 3-layer LSTM model over IHEPC dataset.

Figure 2 presents the architecture of the 3-layer LSTM model used in our work. We used three LSTM layers. In the first layer, we used 128 neurons and tanh as the activation function. Next, in the second LSTM layer, we used 128 neurons, linearly, as the activation function, and a dropout equal to 0.25. The third LSTM layer had 64 neurons, Relu as the activation function, and a dropout equal to 0.25. These results present a time stamp prediction of 1 min. However, in the real application, it takes a higher time stamp, such as 15 min or 60 min, because it is used in smart meters. For this reason, we tested the best model, 3-layer LSTM, with different time stamps at 5 min, 15 min and 60 min, in order to show the reliability and accuracy of this model. After the simulation results, it is seen that the performance of the prediction is reduced significantly when the timestamp is increased. This greatly affects the reliability of the 3-layer LSTM model. Table 2 shows the results for each timestamp used.

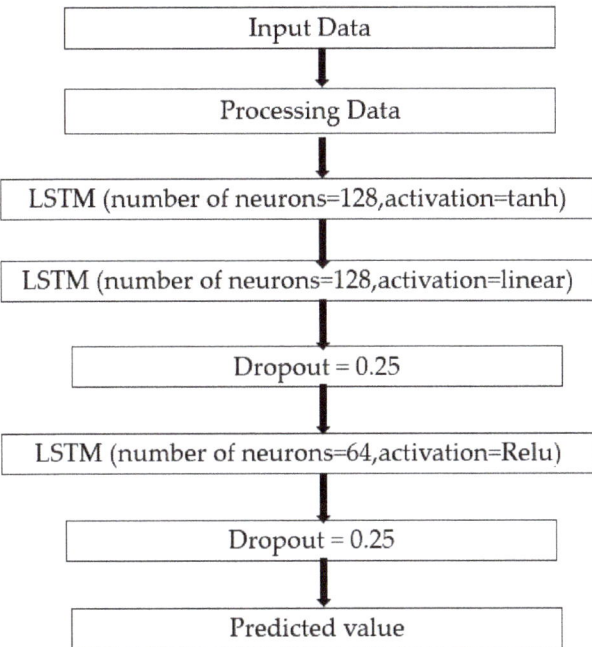

Figure 2. Architecture of 3-layer LSTM model.

Table 2. Performance of different time stamps over 3-layer LSTM model.

Time Stamp	RMSE	MSE
1 min	0.19	0.03
5 min	0.34	0.11
15 min	0.46	0.21
60 min	0.77	0.59

Figures 3 and 4 present the results of the prediction at 15 min and 60 min timestamps. We see that when there is a sudden change or a peak in consumption, the model fails to predict the exact value. The obtained results show that using deep-learning algorithms is not always reliable to predict power consumption. Several factors affect the performance of the prediction, such as reducing the amount of data in the database used in the model. However, in a real application, we would not always be able to use 2 million datapoints for 60 min or 15 min timestamps; this is because we would need to have 60 years of data for a 15 min timestamp. Therefore, we need to obtain an algorithm that can efficiently predict power consumption in all databases at any timestamp.

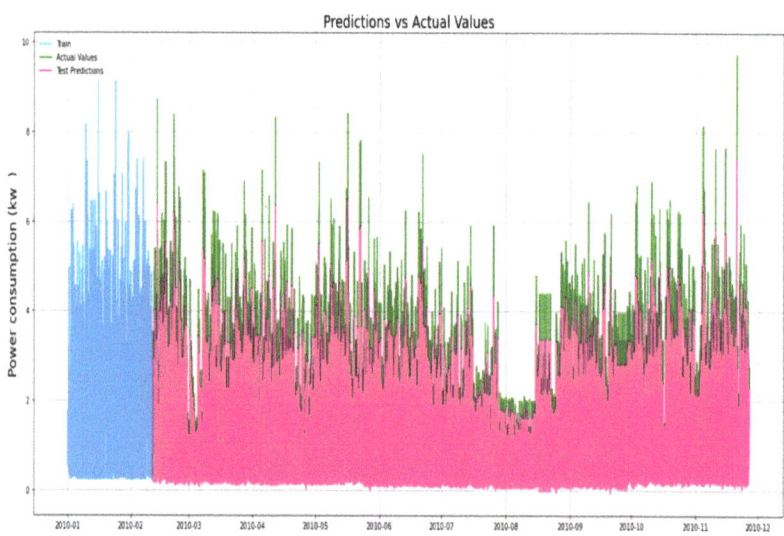

Figure 3. Prediction performance of 3-layer LSTM model over 15 min time stamp.

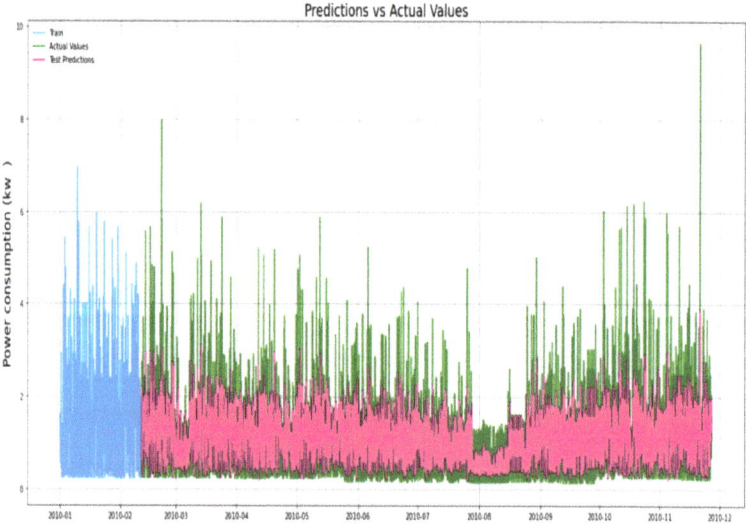

Figure 4. Prediction performance of 3-layer LSTM model over 60 min time stamp.

4. Conclusions

In this work, we proposed a comparative study to predict the power consumption of a specific house. The proposed study has been tested on publicly available IHEPC datasets. We used a typical Min Max Scaler in order to normalize the input data, and then sent the adjusted data into the training step. Following that, we looked at numerous deep-learning models to see how well they performed and how accurate their predictions were using different time stamps. We conclude that deep-learning algorithms are not always reliable and accurate for power-consumption prediction, which confirms the limitation of the deep-learning models to predict power consumption.

Author Contributions: Conceptualization, F.D. and A.F.; methodology, F.D.; software, F.D.; validation, F.D., A.F. and K.T.; formal analysis, F.D.; investigation, M.F.; resources, M.F.; data curation, M.F.; writing—original draft preparation, M.F.; writing—review and editing, M.F.; visualization, M.F.; supervision, F.D.; project administration, F.D.; funding acquisition, A.F. All authors have read and agreed to the published version of the manuscript.

Funding: This research received no external funding.

Institutional Review Board Statement: Not applicable.

Informed Consent Statement: Not applicable.

Data Availability Statement: Not applicable.

Conflicts of Interest: The authors declare no conflict of interest.

References

1. Sajjad, M.; Khan, Z.A.; Ullah, A.; Hussain, T.; Ullah, W.; Lee, M.; Baik, S.W. A Novel CNN-GRU based Hybrid Approach for Short-term Residential Load Forecasting. *IEEE Access* **2020**, *8*, 143759–143768. [CrossRef]
2. Wei, N.; Li, C.; Peng, X.; Zeng, F.; Lu, X. Conventional models and artificial intelligence-based models for energy consumption forecasting: A review. *J. Pet. Sci. Eng.* **2019**, *181*, 106187. [CrossRef]
3. Tran, V.G.; Debusschere, V.; Bacha, S. One week hourly electricity load forecasting using Neuro-Fuzzy and Seasonal ARIMA models. *IFAC Proc. Vol.* **2012**, *45*, 97–102. [CrossRef]
4. Fumo, N.; Biswas, M.A.R. Regression analysis for prediction of residential energy consumption. *Renew. Sustain. Energy Rev.* **2015**, *47*, 332–343. [CrossRef]
5. Amber, K.; Aslam, M.; Hussain, S. Electricity consumption forecasting models for administration buildings of the UK higher education sector. *Energy Build.* **2015**, *90*, 127–136. [CrossRef]
6. De Oliveira, E.M.; Oliveira, F.L.C. Forecasting mid-long term electric energy consumption through bagging ARIMA and exponential smoothing methods. *Energy* **2017**, *144*, 776–788. [CrossRef]
7. Jain, R.K.; Smith, K.M.; Culligan, P.J.; Taylor, J.E. Forecasting energy consumption of multi-family residential buildings using support vector regression: Investigating the impact of temporal and spatial monitoring granu-larity on performance accuracy. *Appl. Energy* **2014**, *123*, 168–178. [CrossRef]
8. Yaslan, Y.; Bican, B. Empirical mode decomposition based denoising method with support vector regression for time series prediction: A case study for electricity load forecasting. *Measurement* **2017**, *103*, 52–61. [CrossRef]
9. Rueda, R.; Cuéllar, M.; Pegalajar, M.; Delgado, M. Straight line programs for energy consumption modelling. *Appl. Soft Comput.* **2019**, *80*, 310–328. [CrossRef]
10. Liu, Y.; Chen, H.; Zhang, L.; Wu, X.; Wang, X.-J. Energy consumption prediction and diagnosis of public buildings based on support vector machine learning: A case study in China. *J. Clean. Prod.* **2020**, *272*, 122542. [CrossRef]
11. Chen, Y.; Xu, P.; Chu, Y.; Li, W.; Wu, Y.; Ni, L.; Bao, Y.; Wang, K. Short-term electrical load forecasting using the Support Vector Regression (SVR) model to calculate the demand response baseline for office buildings. *Appl. Energy* **2017**, *195*, 659–670. [CrossRef]
12. Pinto, T.; Praça, I.; Vale, Z.; Silva, J. Ensemble learning for electricity consumption forecasting in office buildings. *Neurocomputing* **2021**, *423*, 747–755. [CrossRef]
13. Rahman, A.; Srikumar, V.; Smith, A.D. Predicting electricity consumption for commercial and res-idential buildings using deep recurrent neural networks. *Appl. Energy* **2018**, *212*, 372–385. [CrossRef]
14. Kong, W.; Dong, Z.Y.; Jia, Y.; Hill, D.J.; Xu, Y.; Zhang, Y. Short-Term Residential Load Forecasting Based on LSTM Recurrent Neural Network. *IEEE Trans. Smart Grid* **2017**, *10*, 841–851. [CrossRef]
15. Wang, J.Q.; Du, Y.; Wang, J. LSTM based long-term energy consumption prediction with periodicity. *Energy* **2020**, *197*, 117197. [CrossRef]
16. Yan, K.; Li, W.; Ji, Z.; Qi, M.; Du, Y. A Hybrid LSTM Neural Network for Energy Consumption Forecasting of Individual Households. *IEEE Access* **2019**, *7*, 157633–157642. [CrossRef]
17. Dua, D.; Graff, C. *UCI Machine Learning Repository*; University of California, School of Information and Computer Science: Irvine, CA, USA, 2019.

engineering
proceedings

Proceeding Paper

Combination of Post-Processing Methods to Improve High-Resolution NWP Solar Irradiance Forecasts in French Guiana [†]

Rafael Alvarenga [1,*] , Hubert Herbaux [2] and Laurent Linguet [1]

1   UMR Espace-Dev, University of French Guiana, 97300 Cayenne, France; laurent.linguet@univ-guyane.fr
2   Voltalia, 97354 Remire-Montjoly, France; h.herbaux@voltalia.com
*   Correspondence: rafael.alvarenga@etu.univ-guyane.fr; Tel.: +33-7-69-90-38-38
†   Presented at the 8th International Conference on Time Series and Forecasting, Gran Canaria, Spain, 27–30 June 2022.

Abstract: Efforts have been made to improve Numerical Weather Prediction (NWP) forecasts using post-processing techniques, relying on statistical models to refine the weather forecasts. Most approaches used in the literature suffer from two main deficiencies when applied to high-resolution data: (1) they high capacity models to retain nonlinear data fluctuations; (2) some are known to reduce the mean random error; however, they may still generate subsequent biased forecasts. In this study, methods from three different approaches are compared to improve 10-min resolution NWP solar irradiance forecasts, namely a neural network and a linear statistical model as Model Output Statistics, Kalman Filter and Kernel Conditional Density Estimation. The results show that none of the methods, if used individually, improve the mean absolute error (MAE) and mean bias (MBE) jointly. However, a combination of a neural network followed by Kalman filter post-processing results in significant improvements both in the mean random error and the systematic mean bias of original forecasts, reducing the MAE by 45% and the MBE by 91%, respectively.

Keywords: solar irradiance forecast; post-processing; neural network; Kalman filter; conditional kernel density estimation

check for updates

Citation: Alvarenga, R.; Herbaux, H.; Linguet, L. Combination of Post-Processing Methods to Improve High-Resolution NWP Solar Irradiance Forecasts in French Guiana. *Eng. Proc.* **2022**, *18*, 27. https://doi.org/10.3390/engproc2022018027

Academic Editors: Ignacio Rojas, Hector Pomares, Olga Valenzuela, Fernando Rojas and Luis Javier Herrera

Published: 22 June 2022

Publisher's Note: MDPI stays neutral with regard to jurisdictional claims in published maps and institutional affiliations.

1. Introduction

The accurate forecasting of solar irradiance plays an essential role in the management and integration of photovoltaic (PV) systems in transmission grids. The intermittence of solar irradiance, which is highly correlated with the output power, needs to be accurately predicted in advance. It assures the transport system operator that sufficient power will be available to fill the demand throughout the day.

Numerical weather prediction (NWP) models have been widely utilized to generate medium and long-term forecasts of solar irradiance, relying on mathematical equations describing the atmospheric fluid mechanics and thermodynamics [1]. Admittedly, NWP modeling has improved continuously; however, the resulting weather forecasts often present considerable errors. These errors can be divided into two groups: random errors, caused by the insufficient capacity of NWP models to predict the variations of solar irradiance, and systematic bias, caused by defective modeling which will tend to systematically overestimate or underestimate solar irradiance.

Over the past decades, different post-processing techniques were proposed to correct these deviations. Most of the proposed methods follow the approach called model output statistics (MOS) [2–5], where NWP forecast errors are corrected by learning a function that relates the response variable of interest to its predictors. Despite improving the performance of the original forecasts, the approach suffers from two primary deficiencies if applied to high-resolution data: (1) it requires a model with a high capacity to retain nonlinear data fluctuations; (2) it is known to reduce the random error; however, it may still generate subsequent biased forecasts.

Besides MOS, other approaches have also been used in the literature for the same purpose, without sharing the same drawbacks: the Kalman filter (KF) [6–11] recursively improves weather forecasts based on historical errors measured before the forecast generation, and Kernel Conditional Density Estimation (KCDE) [1] allows estimations of the marginal distribution of original forecasts–and consequently, their expected value–conditioned on other explanatory variables.

The objective of this study is to fill the gap in the post-processing of high-resolution forecasts observed in the literature by proposing a global approach to enhance solar irradiance forecasts based on the consecutive combination of post-processing methods, which do not effectively enhance the global performance of the original forecasts when applied individually. Furthermore, the same analysis is proposed for coarser forecasts, revealing differences in the modeling and efficiency of post-processing methods based on temporal resolution.

2. Methodology

The methods to be compared and combined are introduced in this section, namely the MOS, KCDE, and Kalman filters.

2.1. Model Output Statistics

MOS are statistical models that relate observed variables of interest (prediction error, in this case) with the appropriate predictors derived from the outputs of the original model (original NWP predictions). Once calibrated, MOS models are used to estimate the prediction error of WRF forecasts, which are then subtracted from original forecasts, thereby generating improved forecasts. An artificial neural network (ANN) is selected from MOS methods, which are proven to provide better improvements for high-resolution data. A statistical MOS was selected for an additional comparison.

2.1.1. Artificial Neural Network

In ANNs, the function parameters are processing units, called neurons. They are interconnected via a set of weights-analogous to synaptic connections in the nervous system in a manner that allows signals to travel through the network when making predictions or during training. The neurons are grouped in consecutive layers, where each layer is responsible to model patterns of different complexity levels. In this study, a multi-layer perceptron is used as a neural network, where each neuron of one layer is connected to every neuron of the following layer. The output of any neuron is equal to the sum of the outputs of all neurons of the previous layer multiplied by their respective weights, plus a bias term. Subsequently, the net output is passed to an activation function that bounds the activation value to a predefined range. The activation function employed is known as a rectified linear unit (ReLU), which helps the convergence of the model and presents good results. Finally, the model output is equal to the activation value of the only neuron in the output layer.

During training, the weights and biases are updated to reduce the mean square error for each batch of predictions and observations, using the Adam stochastic gradient descent. This process is repeated multiple times, called epochs, that covers the training dataset extensively until the maximum number of epochs is reached.

2.1.2. Lorenz's MOS

As compared to the neural networks, the success of Lorenz's MOS [12] can be partly attributed to its simplicity. In particular, the error was first modeled as a 4th-order polynomial function:

$$e = a_1 \cos^4 Z + a_2 \hat{k}^4 + a_3 \cos^3 Z + \dots + a_8 \hat{k} \tag{1}$$

where e defines the error between the forecasted and measured solar irradiance. The model presented by Lorenz relies on two predictors: Z defining the zenith angle and $\hat{k}$ for the forecasted clear-sky index–the ratio of solar irradiance forecasts to the expected solar irradiance in clear-sky conditions.

The function parameters can be easily estimated using the least squared method over historical forecasts and measurements. Similar to all tested methods, the best group of predictors was selected based on their capability of predicting the original forecast error.

2.2. Kernel Conditional Density Estimation

Kernel density estimation is a probabilistic nonparametric approach for estimating the unknown distribution of a random variable x (e.g., the original forecast error), based on the local estimation of the distribution of its samples $X_1, \ldots, X_n$ [1], as shown in Figure 1.

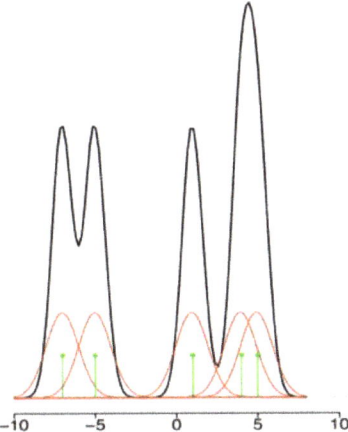

Figure 1. An example of kernel density estimation (black) generated with the help of Gaussian kernels (red) used to define the local distribution of each sample (green).

The kernel, referring to any smooth function K, is used to define the distributions assigned to each sample x, which will then compose the estimated probability function. The most used kernel is the Gaussian kernel, which is defined by:

$$K(x) = \frac{1}{\sqrt{2\pi}} e^{-\frac{x^2}{2}} \qquad (2)$$

It is equivalent to the probability density function of a standard normal distribution. A scaled version allows to handle variables varying in different ranges:

$$K_h(x) = \frac{1}{h} K\left(\frac{x}{h}\right) \qquad (3)$$

where h denotes the bandwith parameter controlling the smoothness of the density estimates. For the density estimation of a dataset presenting n values, the kernel density estimator is defined as follows:

$$\hat{f}(x) = \sum_{n=1}^{n} \frac{1}{n} K(x - X_i) \qquad (4)$$

Ultimately, the conditional version of this density estimation adds a weighting factor proportional to the magnitude of each value along one dimension:

$$\hat{f}(y|x) = \sum_{n=1}^{n} w_i(x)\mathcal{K}_{h_y}(y - Y_i) \tag{5}$$

where

$$w_i(x) = \frac{\mathcal{K}_{h_x}(\|x - X_i\|)}{\sum_{n=1}^{n} \mathcal{K}_{h_x}(\|x - X_i\|)} \tag{6}$$

Interested readers are invited to read the comprehensive definition of the KCDE method provided by Yang [1].

Different methods have been proposed to find the optimal value of the bandwidths h_x and h_y. In this study, a method described in [1] was employed, where the selected bandwidth is the one that minimizes the asymptotic mean integrated squared error (AMISE). For circular data presenting a periodic nature, such as the solar zenith angle, a different kernel is proposed, called the von Mises kernel, which requires adaptations to define an expression for the AMISE during the application of the bandwidth selection method. Finally, for one group of predictors, the point forecasts for the prediction error can be obtained by calculating the expectation of the resulting probability density function generated with the kernel conditional density estimation.

2.3. Kalman Filter

In a general presentation, Kalman filters are used to estimate the error state $x \in \mathbb{R}^n$ of a discrete time-evolving process. At each time step, the first-guess of the error state is as follows:

$$x_t = Ax_{t-1} + w_t \tag{7}$$

where matrix A defines the values of pre-defined predictors at one time step, and the state is a vector representing the effect of each predictor when estimating the prediction error. A nonlinear Kalman filter can be implemented by adding nonlinearities to matrix A, such as predictors in the exponential form.

The observed errors $z \in \mathbb{R}^m$ expressed by a measurement equation that relates the error to measurements for each time step is as follows:

$$z_t = Hx_t + v_t \tag{8}$$

The variable x_{t-1} represents the previous error state, and random variables w_t and v_t are white noises applied to model perturbations in the process and measurements, respectively. The noises are assumed to be independent of each other and follow normal distributions with covariances W and V:

$$p(w) \sim N(0, W)$$
$$p(v) \sim N(0, V) \tag{9}$$

In practice, the process noise covariance W and measurement noise covariance V matrices may change with each time step or measurement and are calculated iteratively with recent values. The same process is applied to the matrices A and H.

The correction procedure involves two groups of equations: time update equations and measurements update equations, time update equations are responsible for making a first guess of the next solar irradiance prediction error, based on the last state of the measured error and error covariance estimates, obtaining an a priori prediction for the next time step; the measurement update equations will then incorporate new measurements into the first guess, obtaining improved a posteriori predictions [13]. The interested reader is referred to [7] for a detailed description of the associated equations.

As mentioned in [1], if the Kalman filter is applied continuously for each lead-time of a day-ahead or intraday prediction, such forecast horizon becomes «resolution-ahead»; e.g, hour-ahead if working in hourly resolution. The procedure needs to be adapted when applied operationally, keeping forecasts in the original horizon. As the original forecasts are issued every day at 00:00 in this study, the first guess at a lead-time L within the horizon of 24 h cannot depend on the previous lead-time L−1 of the same forecast, because the values for the entire forecast are still first guesses, as respective measurements are not yet accessible and update equations cannot be applied. The first guess for the lead-time L should be made based on the same lead-time with available measurements, in this case, the lead-time L of the forecast already improved the day before. A scheme of this procedure is presented in Figure 2.

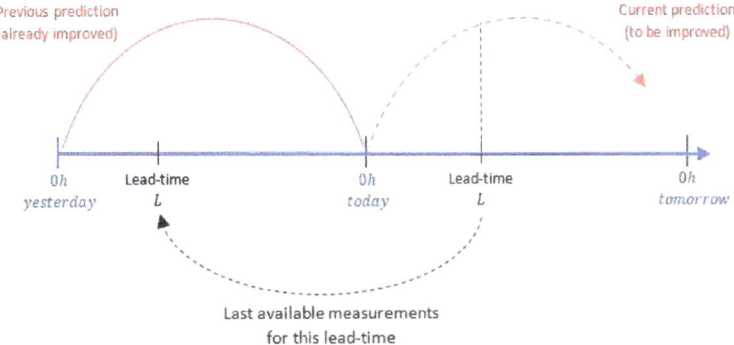

Figure 2. Kalman filter applied operationally for the post-processing of daily-issued predictions.

Unlike MOS methods, Kalman filters do not require parameters to be trained with extensive historical information. However, the method requires recurrent access to observations at each time step, therefore being more efficient in real-time applications rather to improve long-range forecasts.

3. Data

3.1. Weather Forecasts

The weather forecasts used in this study were issued daily at 00:00 by a Weather Research and Forecasting (WRF) numerical model during a year and aggregated in a 10-min resolution.

The WRF forecasts include the global horizontal irradiance to be post-processed and correlated weather variables, which are used as predictors.

Considerable errors were observed in solar irradiance WRF forecasts for low levels of sun elevation (below 15°). These errors can be explained by the approximations made to model the atmosphere within WRF, resulting in more forecast errors when the sunlight crosses larger distances in the atmosphere, like in the early morning and late afternoon. Therefore, the time steps before 8 a.m. and after 5 p.m. were removed from the analysis to avoid such outliers.

3.2. Observations

Ground truth of solar irradiance was obtained with a pyranometer installed at the same location in French Guiana to evaluate and calibrate certain post-processing methods.

The observations were preprocessed with the imputation of outliers or missing values through linear interpolation if they were less than 30% of the day, otherwise the entire day was discarded.

Besides the high-resolution forecasts and observations, a second group of data was obtained by upscaling the same data to an hourly resolution. The objective is to verify the differences in modeling and performance of each method when applying to coarse-grained and fine-grained time series. Figure 3 presents observations in both temporal resolutions for a specific day.

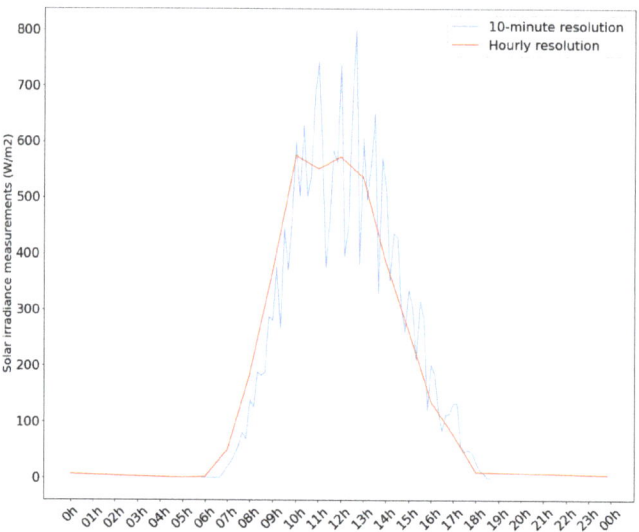

Figure 3. Solar irradiance measured in 10-min resolution (blue) and in-hourly resolution (red) during 20 January 2020.

4. Results and Discussion

The methods described in the previous section and convenient combinations were applied to the post-processing of WRF solar irradiance forecasts in both 10-min resolution and hourly resolution. Accordingly, particularities in the modeling of each time-resolution forecast and obtained results are described in this section.

4.1. Modeling

Post-processing was applied for each method using different combinations of different numbers of predictors. In particular, for ANN, a second search was performed over the parameters of the model, such as the batch size, number of layers, and neurons per layer. The Kalman filter was tested in both linear and nonlinear implementations, with different combinations of exponential predictors in the latter case. The best group of predictors found for each method and for each time-resolution tested are listed in Table 1.

Table 1. Optimal group of predictors per method per resolution.

Resolution	ANN	Lorenz	KCDE	Kalman Filter
10-min	$Irradiance_{pred}$ Wind speed (x) Wind speed (y) Cloud-coverage Temperature Humidity	$Irradiance_{pred}$ Cloud-coverage Sun zenith angle Pressure Temperature Wind speed (x)	$Irradiance_{pred}$ Cloud-coverage Sun zenith angle Pressure	$Irradiance_{pred}$ Cloud-coverage
Hourly	$Irradiance_{pred}$ Wind speed (x) Wind speed (y) Cloud-coverage Temperature Humidity Sun zenith angle	$Irradiance_{pred}$ Cloud-coverage Sun zenith angle Pressure Temperature Wind speed (x)	$Irradiance_{pred}$ Cloud-coverage Sun zenith angle	$Irradiance_{pred}$ Cloud-coverage

MOS and Kalman filter methods were implemented in python, using the Keras library for neural networks, while KCDE was implemented in R using the stats package.

The best groups of predictors used to improve higher resolutions are slightly bigger, which can be explained by the required additional data to explain more sudden variations of solar irradiance. Furthermore, the methods focusing on correcting the random error (e.g., ANN, Lorenz's MOS) tend to require more predictors than methods that focus on the mean bias (e.g., Kalman filter).

In particular, for the Kalman filter, the historical data used in the recursive calculation of predicted bias at each time step is also a parameter to be defined. Basically, the random errors can be better modeled if the historical window is longer, and conversely, a shorter historical window allows for better mean bias modeling. After multiple tests, the optimal window length capable of reducing both the random error and mean bias is 70 days for both time resolutions.

4.2. Improvements on Original Forecasts

All post-processing methods described in this study were tested on the same data and their resulting forecasts are compared by calculating the mean absolute error (MAE) and root mean squared error (RMSE) to assess the random error, and the mean bias error (MBE) to assess the systematic bias:

$$MAE = \left(\frac{1}{n}\right) \sum_{t=1}^{n} |y_t - x_t| \tag{10}$$

$$RMSE = \sqrt{\left(\frac{1}{n}\right) \sum_{t=1}^{n} (y_t - x_t)^2} \tag{11}$$

$$MBE = \left(\frac{1}{n}\right) \sum_{t=1}^{n} y_t - x_t \tag{12}$$

where, y_t denotes the improved prediction and x_t denotes the observation at a time step t.

The MAE of original and resulting forecasts after the application of each method is shown in Figures 4 and 5 for the 10-min resolution and hourly resolution data, respectively.

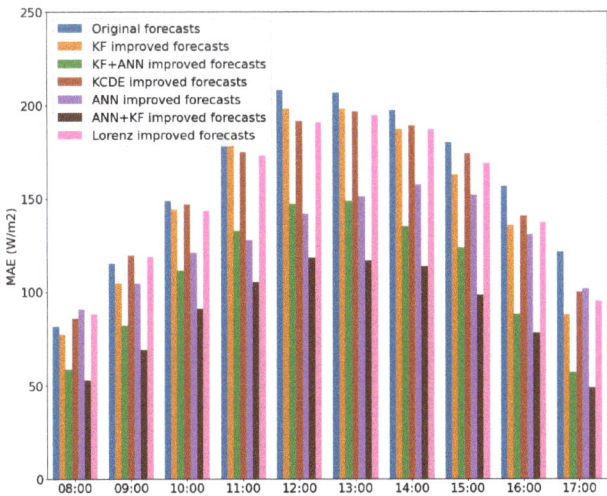

Figure 4. Resulting MAE per hour of the day following the application of each method and convenient combinations of methods on 10-min resolution WRF forecasts.

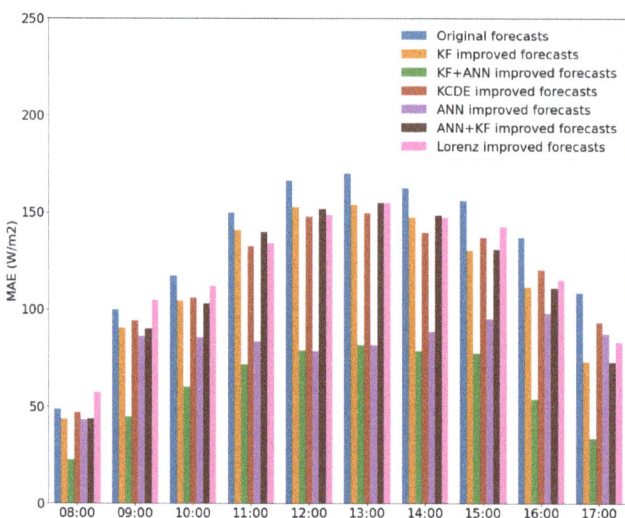

Figure 5. Resulting MAE per hour of the day following the application of each method and convenient combinations of methods on hourly resolution WRF forecasts.

Naturally, as solar irradiance presents increasingly sudden variations, the MAE is higher for fine-grained WRF forecasts.

All tested methods reduce the MAE of original WRF forecasts, the ANN presents the best reduction of the mean error for both time resolutions. However, Figures 6 and 7 illustrate that the ANN is the only method that degrades the mean bias of original WRF forecasts in both time resolutions. The Kalman filter is the best method to reduce the mean bias for both time resolutions, with almost all the bias removed from original WRF forecasts.

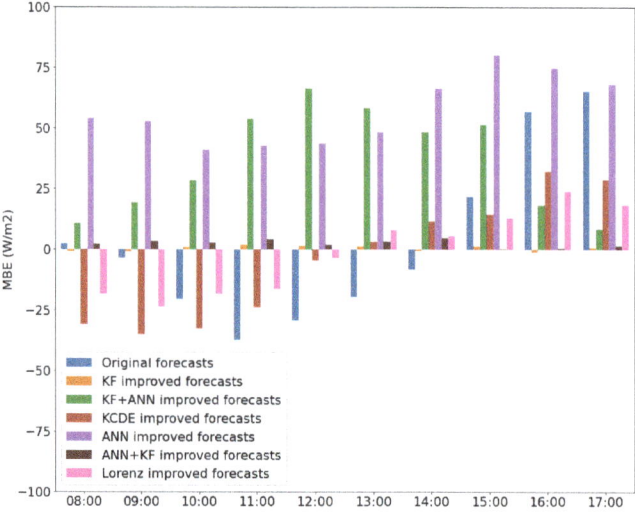

Figure 6. Resulting MBE following the application of each method and convenient combinations of methods over 10-min resolution WRF forecasts.

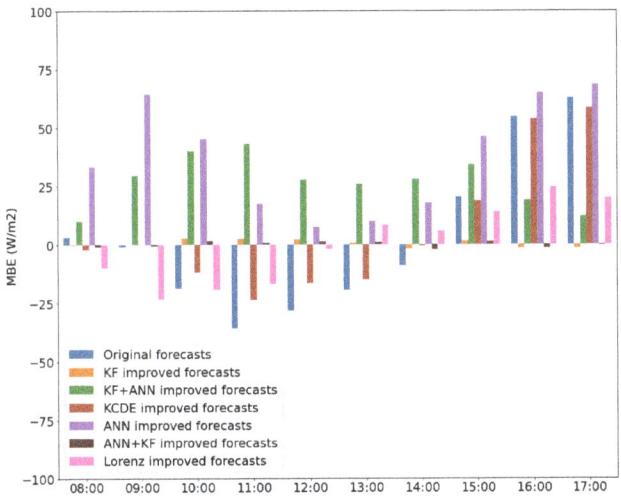

Figure 7. Resulting MBE following the application of each method and convenient combinations of methods over hourly resolution WRF forecasts.

The consecutive combination of these two methods was tested in an attempt to gather the performance of the Kalman filter in reducing the mean bias and the capability of the ANN to reduce the mean error.

The percentage improvement given by each method compared to the original WRF is described in Tables 2 and 3 for a 10-min resolution and hourly resolution forecasts, respectively.

Table 2. Percentage improvement of each method compared to original forecasts in a 10-min resolution (the higher the better, negative values denote degraded results).

Method	MAE	RMSE	MBE
MOS_{ANN}	22	12	−95
MOS_{Lorenz}	7	10	48
KF	8	7	95
KCDE	6	9	27
KF + MOS_{ANN}	32	17	−31
MOS_{ANN} + KF	45	41	91

Table 3. Percentage improvement of each method compared to original forecasts in hourly resolution (the higher the better, negative values denote degraded results).

Method	MAE	RMSE	MBE
MOS_{ANN}	37	36	−49
MOS_{Lorenz}	9	10	43
KF	13	11	94
KCDE	11	12	21
KF + MOS_{ANN}	54	50	−7
MOS_{ANN} + KF	13	11	95

Focusing only on the combinations of ANN and KF methods, the results for both time resolutions reveal that when the ANN is applied lastly, it introduces a bias that was previously removed by the Kalman filter. However, when the Kalman filter is applied after the ANN in high-resolution data, it maintains the reduced mean error and additionally reduces the mean bias firstly introduced by the ANN in a 10-min resolution. Therefore, a consecutive ANN MOS post-processing followed by Kalman filtering yields the best overall results, improving the original MAE by 45% and the original MBE by 91%.

A different type of behavior could be verified in hourly resolution, where for the same combination of methods, the Kalman filter degrades the mean error previously improved by the ANN. In this time resolution, the best approach may depend on the application: if a reduced random error is preferred, a combination of KF+ANN can be used in this order, improving the original MAE by 54% even if the MBE is degraded by −7%, generating positive biased solar irradiance forecasts. On the other hand, if one wants to avoid consecutive biased forecasts (e.g., in PV power plants coupled with batteries, an overestimation of PV production may rapidly fill the batteries in real-time, leaving no capacity to absorb further errors during the day), in which case, the ANN+KF combination is more convenient, improving the MBE of original forecasts by 95% while improving the MAE by 13%.

5. Conclusions and Further Work

This study presents the best combination of post-processing methods to improve high-resolution solar irradiance forecasts generated by a WRF model. The annual meteorological simulation for 2020 at a specific location in French Guiana was analyzed. The evaluation focuses on the capability of each method to improve both the random error and mean bias of original solar irradiance forecasts. Furthermore, an identical analysis is proposed for a lower resolution version of the same forecasts, exhibiting differences in modeling and performance for each method according to the time resolution.

The methods compared in this study are well known to improve systematic and random errors individually, namely Model Output Statistics (MOS), Kalman filter (KF) and KCDE. The results reveal that any of the methods improve both errors simultaneously; however, a combination of a neural network MOS followed by a KF post-processing improves the MAE by 45% and MBE by 91% for high-resolution forecasts. In a coarser time resolution, the same combination of methods improves the MAE by 13% and MBE by 95%, and the combination in the reverse order improves the MAE by 54% independently, degrading the MBE by −7%. In this case, the most valuable combination may depend on the preferred error to be reduced, according to the downstream application.

For future development of the work, a much more extensive analysis can be conducted by comparing the methods on multiple high-resolution forecasts, generated for different locations with different climates.

Author Contributions: Conceptualization, R.A., H.H. and L.L.; methodology, R.A.; software, R.A.; validation, R.A.; formal analysis, R.A.; investigation, R.A.; resources, R.A.; data curation, R.A.; writing—original draft preparation, R.A.; writing—review and editing, H.H. and L.L.; visualization, R.A.; supervision, H.H. and L.L.; project administration, L.L. All authors have read and agreed to the published version of the manuscript.

Funding: This research received no external funding.

Institutional Review Board Statement: Not applicable.

Informed Consent Statement: Not applicable.

Data Availability Statement: Not applicable.

Conflicts of Interest: The authors declare no conflict of interest.

References

1. Yang, D. On post-processing day-ahead NWP forecasts using Kalman filtering. *Sol. Energy* **2019**, *182*, 179–181. [CrossRef]
2. Lauret, P.; Diagne, M.; David, M. A Neural Network Post-processing Approach to Improving NWP Solar Radiation Forecasts. *Energy Procedia* **2014**, *57*, 1044–1052. [CrossRef]
3. Pereira, S.; Canhoto, P.; Salgado, R.; Costa, M.J. Development of an ANN based corrective algorithm of the operational ECMWF global horizontal irradiation forecasts. *Sol. Energy* **2019**, *185*, 387–405. [CrossRef]

4. Lima, F.J.L.; Pereira, E.B.; Martins, F.R. Forecast of Short-term Solar Irradiation in Brazil Using Numerical Models and Statistical Post-processing. In *Proceedings of the EuroSun 2014 Conference*; International Solar Energy Society: Aix-les-Bains, France, 2015; pp. 1–10. [CrossRef]
5. Barutcu, B.; Tanriover, S.T.; Sakarya, S.; Incecik, S.; Sayinta, F.M.; Caliskan, E.; Kahraman, A.; Aksoy, B.; Kahya, C.; Topcu, S. Improving WRF GHI Forecasts with Model Output Statistics. In *Progress in Clean Energy, Volume 1*; Dincer, I., Colpan, C.O., Kizilkan, O., Ezan, M.A., Eds.; Springer International Publishing: Cham, Switzerland, 2015; pp. 291–299. [CrossRef]
6. Diagne, M.; David, M.; Boland, J.; Schmutz, N.; Lauret, P. Post-processing of solar irradiance forecasts from WRF model at Reunion Island. *Sol. Energy* **2014**, *105*, 99–108. [CrossRef]
7. Pelland, S.; Galanis, G.; Kallos, G. Solar and photovoltaic forecasting through post-processing of the Global Environmental Multiscale numerical weather prediction model: Solar and photovoltaic forecasting. *Prog. Photovoltaics Res. Appl.* **2013**, *21*, 284–296. [CrossRef]
8. Rincón, A.; Jorba, O.; Baldasano, J.M.; Monache, L.D. Assessment of short-term irradiance forecasting based on post-processing tools applied on WRF meteorological simulations. In Proceedings of the State-of-the-Art Workshop, COST ES 1002: WIRE: Weather Intelligence for Renewable Energies, Paris, France, 22–23 March 2011; pp. 1–9.
9. Sweeney, C.P.; Lynch, P.; Nolan, P. Reducing errors of wind speed forecasts by an optimal combination of post-processing methods: Comparing and combining post-processing methods. *Meteorol. Appl.* **2013**, *20*, 32–40. [CrossRef]
10. Rincón, A.; Jorba, O.; Frutos, M.; Alvarez, L.; Barrios, F.P.; González, J.A. Bias correction of global irradiance modelled with weather and research forecasting model over Paraguay. *Sol. Energy* **2018**, *170*, 201–211. [CrossRef]
11. Louka, P.; Galanis, G.; Siebert, N.; Kariniotakis, G.; Katsafados, P.; Pytharoulis, I.; Kallos, G. Improvements in wind speed forecasts for wind power prediction purposes using Kalman filtering. *J. Wind. Eng. Ind. Aerodyn.* **2008**, *96*, 2348–2362. [CrossRef]
12. Lorenz, E.; Hurka, J.; Heinemann, D.; Beyer, H.G. Irradiance Forecasting for the Power Prediction of Grid-Connected Photovoltaic Systems. *IEEE J. Sel. Top. Appl. Earth Obs. Remote Sens.* **2009**, *2*, 2–10. [CrossRef]
13. Welch, G.; Bishop, G. An Introduction to the Kalman Filter. *Proc. Siggraph Course* **2006**, *8*, 16.

*engineering
proceedings*

MDPI

Proceeding Paper

Online Classification of High Gamma Dose Rate Incidents †

Mohammed Al Saleh [1,2,3,*], Beatrice Finance [1], Yehia Taher [1], Ali Jaber [2] and Roger Luff [4]

1 David Laboratory, University of Paris-Saclay, 45 Avenue des Etats-Unis, 78035 Versailles, France; beatrice.finance@uvsq.fr (B.F.); yehia.taher@uvsq.fr (Y.T.)
2 Rafic Hariri University Campus, Lebanese University, Beirut 6573, Lebanon; ali.jaber@ul.edu.lb
3 Lebanese Atomic Energy Commission (LAEC), National Council for Scientific Research (CNRS), Airport Road, Beirut 2260, Lebanon
4 Federal Office for Radiation Protection (BfS), 24768 Rendsburg, Germany; rluff@bfs.de
* Correspondence: mhdalsaleh@gmail.com
† Presented at the 8th International Conference on Time Series and Forecasting, Gran Canaria, Spain, 27–30 June 2022.

Abstract: In this paper, we propose a new method for choosing the most suitable time-series classification method that can be applied to online gamma dose rate incidents. We referred to the historical incidents measured in the German Radiation Early Warning Network and clustered them into several classes before testing existing classification methods. This raises the research problem of the online classification of time-series data with varying scales and lengths. Referring to the state-of-the-art methods, we found that no specific classification method can fit our data all the time. This motivated us to introduce our own approach.

Keywords: machine learning algorithms; predictive model; time-series classification; gamma dose rate; Radiation Early Warning Network

check for
updates

Citation: Al Saleh, M.; Finance, B.; Taher, Y.; Jaber, A.; Luff, R. Online Classification of High Gamma Dose Rate Incidents. *Eng. Proc.* **2022**, *18*, 28. https://doi.org/10.3390/engproc 2022018028

Academic Editors: Ignacio Rojas, Hector Pomares, Olga Valenzuela, Fernando Rojas and Luis Javier Herrera

Published: 22 June 2022

Publisher's Note: MDPI stays neutral with regard to jurisdictional claims in published maps and institutional affiliations.

1. Introduction

Time-series analysis is gaining more and more interest in so many domains. That is because, with the proliferation of the use of sensors and IoT devices that continuously produce massive amounts of real-time data, special care has been given for analyzing the data to understand past events and patterns and predict future ones. Medical heart monitor data, stock market prices, weather conditions, etc., are all examples of such time-series data.

In this paper, we are interested in analyzing the gamma dose rate (background radiation level) in the environment. A serious event that occurs and causes an abrupt increase in the gamma dose rate is the leakage or contamination failure of a nuclear reactor, such as what happened in the Chernobyl accident which was the biggest short-term leak of radioactive materials ever recorded in history [1]. Such an event has to be intercepted at the earliest point possible to take the proper measures and precautions and notify the concerned authorities to minimize the effects of such a hazardous situation. It is a very critical task as long-term or acute exposure to a high gamma dose rate can have many hazardous consequences on humans as well as on the ecosystem.

Around the globe, there are thousands of probes (sensors) that collect gamma dose rates in real time. A Radiation Early Warning System (REWS) [2] collects the data and raises the alarm in case of an increase in the local gamma dose rate. Whenever an event occurs (i.e., the gamma dose rate goes above the accepted threshold, provided by experts), an alarm is triggered, and a team of experts and personnel have to unite to investigate the reasons behind this rise. Currently, the analysis of incoming incidents is performed manually with the efforts of experts. Such a method is time-consuming and risky, knowing that the factors affecting the gamma dose rate are not always known immediately. Fortunately, most of the incoming incidents are mainly innocent ones as they remain in an acceptable range value for human health and this value returns to normal after a period of time.

The objective of our research is to propose an *Intelligent Radiation Early Warning System* that finds the cause automatically behind an incident and its classification into *real or innocent* ones at real time. Gaining intelligence is the key aspect of our approach. Therefore, we aimed to transform the static and semi-automatic REWSs into dynamic, fully automatic, and intelligence-driven systems. The proposed system would optimize the ability to analyze any alert generated by an event such as rain.

The two main phases of our *Intelligent REWS* are: (1) building the predictive model and (2) near real-time detection and prediction. In the first phase, the historical data generated by Germany's REWS [3] were analyzed to extract knowledge about the previous incidents that occurred in the past. The historical databases contain raw unlabeled data (i.e., time series) corresponding to the gamma dose rate monitoring at each probe. The data used in this work comprise the past ten years' minute-by-minute gamma dose rate real data for over a thousand probes.

In [4], we already proposed an unsupervised machine learning model that helps us automatically determine the reasons behind the incidents. This task was difficult and required many experiments to find the best time-series clustering algorithm. After tackling all the shortcomings behind the first phase of our *Intelligent REWS*, we now investigate in this paper our contributions for the Online Detection and Prediction phase. As we aim to match unlabeled incidents without any human intervention as soon as possible, our research is in the field of supervised machine learning time-series classification.

The remaining sections of this paper will be organized as follows: Section 2 will state the context and the problems behind our research. The state-of-the-art approaches, similar to our approach in one aspect or another, are described in detail in Section 3. Section 4 will present our approach and contribution. We will evaluate our approach in Section 5. Finally, we will conclude in Section 6.

2. Context and Problem Statement

In this research, we deal with univariate time-series which are unlabeled as shown in Figure 1. Incidents caused by the same event may not have a recognizable temporal trace or characteristics but more common behavior. For example, a particular event may cause peaks of increasing amplitudes that decrease during a longer period of time; another may cause an abrupt increase and maintain its amplitude during a period of time, and so on. Note that incidents caused by the same event can last for a varying length of time and reach different amplitudes.

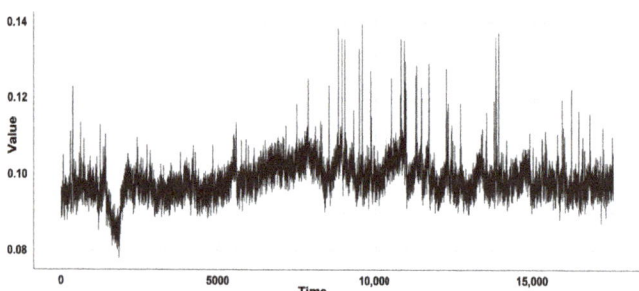

Figure 1. Typical gamma dose rate time series.

In the first phase, we were able to collect nearly 300 innocent incidents from 45 different locations in Germany. Choosing different locations allowed us to have diverse shapes of observations representing the innocent incidents, thus gaining a higher quality dataset to build our investigation upon. Investigating our time-series data revealed important characteristics that need to be handled carefully. Incidents are of highly varying lengths, different scales, and of different levels. The same incidents could have different characteristics. Going further, different incidents could have the same characteristics.

The evolving parameters problem was solved by preparing a catalog of parameters before the extraction process started. A specific algorithm tackled the evolving issue through several calculation steps to ensure that the parameters obtained by the end of each month were accurate. Then, the extracted incidents undergo a unique preprocessing phase to ensure that they are ready to enter the proposed clustering model. This was done using a *z-normalization* method [5] responsible for dealing with the scale issue. The *zero-padding* method was applied to deal with the different length incidents issue.

Once the preprocessing was applied, the best clustering model for our context was formed by combining the similarity measure (DTW) [6] as well as the clustering algorithm (K-means) [7] with its averaging method (DBA). With the help of experts in gamma radiation monitoring, we were able to identify three events after applying our clustering approach that split into three categories: rain, stormy rain, or incidents caused by probe calibration as depicted in Figure 2.

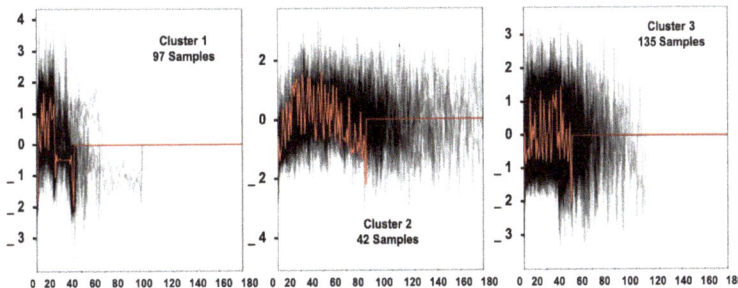

Figure 2. Clusters obtained from our predictive model.

For the online detection and prediction phase, a matching process tries to classify the incoming incidents as depicted in Figure 1 within the labeled clusters depicted in Figure 2. This helps identify the real cause of the current incident. The incoming readings are analyzed to explore the thresholds in real-time. Once an incident is detected, the data preprocessing model used in phase one is also applied to deal with the scale and length issues. Notice that we start analyzing an incident even if the incident is not yet finished. As we aim to match unlabeled incidents without any human intervention as quickly as possible, our research is in the field of supervised machine learning time-series classification.

After investigating the classification algorithms presented in the literature, we noticed several shortcomings that prevented us from relying on a specific algorithm for our online classification model. After going through the classification algorithms introduced in the literature, we noticed that no specific algorithm could perfectly fit our data since our data have unique characteristics and behavior. We noticed that although some algorithms work perfectly for specific types of incidents, they could not classify other types. This problem was enough for us to not trust a specific classification algorithm when dealing with our incoming incidents. Moreover, we noticed that these algorithms were unable to detect incoming incidents that have a unique behavior and should be classified in a new class that will be labeled by the experts later.

In this context, the problem consists of finding a machine-learning-based framework to automate the event identification process to decrease the time and effort spent and increase the efficiency and accuracy of the process. This will result in automatically identifying the incoming incidents as soon as possible and giving the correct impression to the experts to distinguish the innocent incidents from those that are critical. Hence, the main research question behind this paper could be formulated as follows: *"What is the machine learning model that should be used for the online time-series classification of special behavior and how do the different models perform in practice ?".*

3. State of the Art

In this section, we briefly recall the main time-series classification algorithms mentioned in the literature. We compare these techniques based on applicability and effectiveness. In addition to conducting a literature study, we also apply these different techniques to our dataset to test their performance.

For time-series data, there exist several algorithms that consider the time factor, which is essential in our study. A common problematic solution that could happen when dealing with time-series data is to treat each value in the sequence as a separate feature. This is the core difference between time-series data and tabular data. In time-series data, the order of the data is essential and critical. In contrast, in tabular data, the order is ignored and scrambling the order of the features will not affect the prediction process. Therefore, each algorithm dedicated for time-series data is based on a technique and perspective that extracts knowledge from the time-series data concerning the order of the data.

Those algorithms are categorized as follows:

- Distance-based algorithms: This type of algorithms relies on distance metrics to find the optimal class membership. It plays a vital role in pattern recognition problems. The most popular distance measures used are Euclidean [8], Manhattan [9] and Dynamic Time Warping with Barycenter Averaging (DBA) [10] which is the similarity measure used by the K-nearest neighbor algorithm.
- Interval-based algorithms: This algorithm depends—through its classification—on the information retrieved from various series intervals. Time-series forest classifier (TSF) is a classification technique that is built for this type of algorithm [11]. TSF adopts the random forest classifier technique and applies it to time-series data.
- Frequency-based algorithms: classifiers that follow this type of algorithm rely on the frequency of the extracted features from the time-series data. Random interval spectral ensemble known as RISE, is a straightforward classifier that is similar to a time-series forest [12]. Therefore, this algorithm constructs decision trees, and the classification takes place upon the majority of votes.
- Shapelet-based algorithms: the main objective of the shapelet-based algorithm is to identify, for a particular class, the bag of shapelets with discriminatory power. Each shapelet is an interval extracted from a time series and it should follow the same order. During classification, the Shapelet-based algorithm transforms the incoming datasets into "K" shapelets that are yet to be compared by the "K" shapelets extracted for each class in the training phase [13].

In their paper [14], the authors introduced time-series data and time-series classification methods, focusing in their research on the importance of distance-based classifiers. Xing et al. [15], in their paper, divided the time-series classification method into three main categories. Feature-based methods, model-based methods, and distance-based methods. Diving deeply into the literature, we noticed that most of the research works focused on or introduced a specific classification algorithm. As we will see in the experimentation section, when these classification algorithms are applied to our data, they are not able to perform the task in all situations. That is why we propose a novel approach that gives the best results through our testing.

4. Online Detection and Prediction Phase

In Figure 3, we depict the three main components of our online detection and prediction phase. It is composed of: (1) the online incidents extraction, (2) the online preprocessing phase, and finally (3) the online classification phase. First, it is important to mention that the intended result is to reduce the errors and not eliminate all errors. As our data are significant and challenging, removing all errors is impossible.

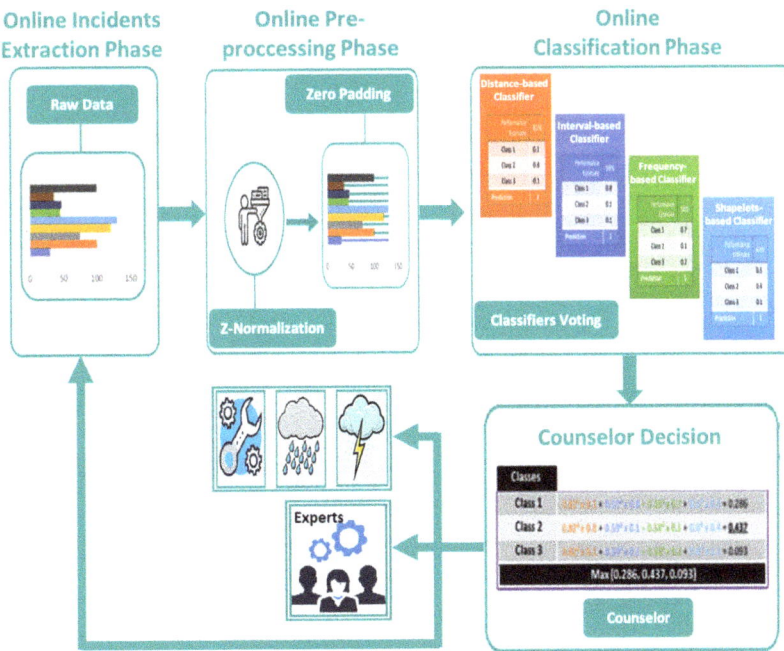

Figure 3. The proposed online detection and prediction phase.

The data that are sent by the probes from different locations are continuously monitored. A high reading that is above the peak threshold will trigger the system to check whether the reading of this probe will remain above the peak for 30 min. If the incoming readings remain high (above the peak threshold), this series will be extracted as an incident starting from the value above the maximum background mean until 30 min have passed.

Extracted incidents cannot directly enter into the classification phase. Preprocessing treatment for the raw incidents should be done. Incidents coming from different probes have different characteristics in terms of length, scale and level. During the preprocessing phase, the data of the incidents are normalized using the z-normalization technique and padded using the zero-padding technique. This preprocessing phase will not affect the shape of the incident; it will only standardize the incidents to become similar to the training dataset that the classifiers have trained over. This will help classifiers identify or predict the class of these unknown incidents.

The classification phase is divided into two phases: the voting phase and the counselor's decision. In the voting phase, four classifiers from the state of the art are implemented separately. All of the previous classifiers were implemented and tested because each one was successful in identifying a particular class. Each classifier will accept as input the incoming incident. The four classifiers will run in parallel:

1. The distance-based classifier is implemented using K-nearest neighbor with dynamic time warping (DTW) + barycenter averaging (DBA) as the similarity measure. This classifier can successfully differentiate between calibration and stormy rain classes with an accuracy reaching 89.28%. However, it faces some difficulty separating between rain and stormy rain classes.

2. The frequency-based classifier was built using the random interval spectral ensemble (RISE) algorithm. This algorithm has proved its ability to differentiate between rain class and stormy rain class; its accuracy reached 85.71%. As for the calibration class,

the algorithm had slight errors in classifying calibration incidents as rain and vice versa.

3. The TSF classifier is implemented based on the interval-based algorithm that is similar to the frequency-based algorithm except in the way it slices the series. Each series is split into intervals of varied length within the same decision tree, while RISE performs a random interval length splitting that varies from one decision tree to another but within the same fixed interval. The TSF classifier supports decision making, especially between calibration and rain classes; its accuracy reached 89.28%.

4. The shapelets-based classifier was implemented, although its accuracy was low as it only reached 50%. However, the significance of this algorithm is in differentiating between the calibration class and rain class. This algorithm failed in separating the other classes because of the high similarity in the shape that some incidents of different classes have. Furthermore, as this algorithm creates a bag of Shaplets (sub-shapes of the series) for each class to be used as discriminatory power, confusion may arise.

In our approach, each classifier will perform its prediction and the output will not just be the predicted class but also the probability of each class upon which it concluded to select the class of higher probability. Then, the second phase of the online classification phase is introduced to take all the classifiers' predictions. Its role is to analyze what the majority has classified this new incoming incident as. The counselor has to choose one of three possible choices:

1. The majority of votes of the classifiers and the aggregated probability is high (above 90%). Thus, the decision is directed to assign the incident to this particular class with the highest probability.

2. If the aggregated probability is between 70% and 89%, the collected data are not enough for the counselor to decide. In this case, one will wait for more time to collect additional readings that can help in the decision making.

3. If the probability was low (less than 70%), this means that the incident occurring should be considered as a new incident and a new class of incidents should be created. Here is the role of the experts in the domain to examine this new incident and attempt to identify the nature and the reasons behind this incident. Furthermore, this new incident could be a new shape for an existing class that the model has not been trained on it yet. Thus, in all cases, this new incident is an added value for the model in the future when re-training the classifiers on identifying such cases.

In summary, combining all classifiers' abilities helped overcome the problems and challenges found in our data. The counselor has three possible choices depending on the highest aggregated probability. Suppose that the probability remains high (above 80%) after three classification attempts. In that case, the incident will be assigned to the class of the highest probability. If the probability varies between 60% and 80%, then the incident will undergo further classification after collecting more incoming data readings. Moreover, the incident is left for the experts to check and verify whether it did not succeed in gaining a probability higher than 60% so that it could be a new incident of a new class to be created or a new shape for the existing class.

5. Experimentation

In order to compare the different approaches of the state of the art, as well as to see the benefit of our proposed model, we decided to evaluate systematically different experiments and evaluations on the labeled time-series data. After investigating all of the mentioned algorithms in the state of the art, we attempted to implement each classifier based on its best practice for selecting the optimal parameters and then apply it over our labeled data. First, the data we have are split into two sets, a training dataset (90% of the dataset) and a testing dataset (forms the rest 10%). When splitting the data between training and testing, we guarantee that the training dataset is balanced and presented well in all three classes so that the classifier will be trained well.

All the implementations are performed using Python libraries. For the best environment performance and for easy implementation, we installed Anaconda, in which we used the Jupyter notebook for writing and testing the code. Anaconda provides us with an isolated environment containing all the needed libraries to perform our tests. Going deeply into the libraries dedicated to time-series data, several methods are defined to handle this type of data. The traditional machine learning algorithms implemented for tabular classifiers cannot be applied in our case of time-series data because these neglect the time factor essential in our data. Thus, in addition to Sklearn, pandas, numpy, and other libraries, we installed and used the Sktime library which contains the time-series classifiers.

In Table 1, we found the evaluation results for the four times series classifiers of the state of the art. Class 0 corresponds to the calibration cluster, Class 1 to the rain class and class 2 to the stormy rain class.

The first classifier is the KNN with DTW, which is a distance-based classifier. By default, this classifier uses the Euclidean distance measure [8] to determine the membership of a class. For our case, the time-series data require a different metric algorithm because incidents are of varying length and are not perfectly aligned in time. Although the accuracy was not bad (89.28%), after training and testing it, some errors still occurred. By investigating what the model failed, we deduced that it could detect the calibration class and the rain class but failed to identify the stormy rain class. The model got confused between the rain class and stormy rain class incidents and classified the stormy rain as rain incidents.

The second classifier is the time-series forest classifier which relies on the interval-based algorithm. This classifier depends on the information retrieved from the various intervals of a series. At first, the classifier splits the series into random intervals; each has a random starting point and length. Then, the algorithm extracts summary features (slope, mean, and standard deviation) from those intervals. The extracted features form the feature vector representing the interval. Since this algorithm is based on the random forest algorithm, it will construct and train a decision tree from the extracted features. Several trees are constructed to support decision making and select the majority of the trees in the forest. After training and testing the TSF classification model, the performance was good (89.3%), but not sufficient. The model was able to identify the calibration class but it faced some errors when identifying the stormy rain class.

Table 1. Applying different classification algorithms to the dataset.

Classification Algorithm	Accuracy	Distinguished Classes	
		Pass	Fail
KNN+DTW	89.28%	Class 0 & Class 1 Class 0 & Class 2	Class 1 and Class 2
TSF	89.3%	Class 0 and Class 2	Class 0 & Class 1 Class 1 & Class 2
RISE	85.71%	Class 1 and Class 2	Class 0 and Class 1 Class 0 and Class 2
Shapelet	50%	Class 0 and Class 2	Class 0 & Class 1 Class 1 and Class 2

The third classifier is the random interval spectral ensemble (RISE) classifier. This classifier is based on the frequency features extracted from the series after splitting it into intervals. It sounds similar to the previous classifier, the TSF, especially because it also uses the random forest algorithm. It differs from TSF in two ways. First is how it splits the series into intervals, where the intervals for each decision tree are of the same length. The second difference is in the type of features that the algorithm extracts from the intervals, where RISE extracts spectral features (series-to-series features) and not summary statistics. The algorithm was significant in classifying the rain class from the data. In the rest of the classes, however, it faced some errors. The accuracy of this model reached (85.71%).

Finally, the last classifier is the shapelet-based classifier. This classifier is very popular and used when dealing with time-series data. A shapelet is a sub-shape of a series. A bag of shapelets is used to represent a particular class. When extracting those shapelets, the algorithm searches for shapes with discriminatory power to identify a class. Shapelets form the identity of each class. When a new unknown incident arrives, the algorithm will extract its shapelets and compare them to the classes' shapelets to confirm which class the incident belongs to. The shapelet-based algorithm was implemented and tested over our data, but the results were unsatisfying. After several tests and attempts to enhance the model's overall accuracy, it nearly reached 50%. However, after we investigated the results, we uncovered the reason for such an outcome. The data that we have are very challenging because they are very similar to each other, which makes their shapes very similar; this is why the model was confused. Even though the classification model was able to identify the rain class, it failed in the other two classes (calibration and stormy rain).

To start evaluating our online classification module, we first tested incoming incidents. These incidents are preprocessed online after being extracted and then prepared to be classified with the classification algorithms. Then, the classification algorithms will work individually in parallel on the incoming incident, trying to classify it as soon as possible. The classification algorithms presented in Table 2 will return their predictions for the incoming incidents as soon as possible. This prediction will be in the form of a probability suggested by each algorithm to each incident while trying to map it to the respective class.

Table 2. Testing our counselorapproach.

	KNN+DTW	TSF	RISE	Shapelet	Counselor Performance	Counselor Decision
Incident 1	C0 (100%) C1 (0%) C2 (0%)	C0 (95%) C1 (0%) C2 (5%)	C0 (63%) C1 (6%) C2 (31%)	C0 (34%) C1 (21%) C2 (45%)	C0 (73%) C1 (6.75%) C2 (20.25%)	Wait for more data
Incident 2	C0 (98%) C1 (2%) C2 (0%)	C0 (96%) C1 (1%) C2 (3%)	C0 (68%) C1 (23%) C2 (9%)	C0 (99%) C1 (0%) C2 (1%)	C0 (90.25%) C1 (6.5%) C2 (3.25%)	C0
Incident 3	C0 (0%) C1 (31%) C2 (69%)	C0 (0%) C1 (0%) C2 (100%)	C0 (0%) C1 (3%) C2 (97%)	C0 (0%) C1 (0%) C2 (100%)	C0 (0%) C1 (8.5%) C2 (91.5%)	C2

Finally, the counselor will start performing the task assigned to it. Thus, the role of the counselor will be to decide which algorithm acts the best and gives the perfect prediction for the incoming incident, as shown in Table 2, where incidents 2 and 3 were assigned to classes 0 and 2, respectively. However, incident 1's probability was not enough for the counselor to make a decision, which it is it suggested waiting for more data.

Our proposed model overcomes the issue that we were concerned about. When tested on its own, the problem with each classification algorithm was its ability to identify a single class and failing in differentiating between the rest of the classes. By combining the outputs of those four algorithms, the counselor was able to either commit the identity of the unknown incoming incident or consider it a new incident related to a new class to be examined by experts. Therefore, the proposed classification model output was satisfying and it supported decision making for predicting the class of incoming incidents.

6. Conclusions

In this work, we presented our machine learning-based framework for autonomously identifying the causes behind the online incoming incidents caused by high gamma dose rate readings. After extracting, preprocessing, and clustering the historical incidents, our approach is to apply a machine learning model that will match online incoming incidents to their similar clustered ones to identify the causes behind them as soon as possible using supervised classification.

In the classification phase, we, specifically, tackled the problem of classifying time series using several classification algorithms at the same time which was properly addressed nowhere in the literature. We researched and experimented with the different classic and state-of-the-art approaches to evaluate their compatibility. When those approaches failed to classify our data when properly testing each approach alone, we proposed our counselor classification model for using all the classification algorithms simultaneously and voting for the one with the best outcome.

Displaying the obtained matching percentages through the experimentation of various algorithms, we were able to highlight how our model comparatively gave the best results. Furthermore, the experts expressed positive and hopeful thoughts upon inspecting the results, which motivated us to publish this contribution in an article. As future work, the next step would be to improve the quality of the overall framework by exploring the evaluation with more datasets to automate the evaluation as well.

Author Contributions: M.A.S. analyzed and interpreted the need for an intelligent radiation early warning system, introduced the second phase of the RIMI framework, and was a major contributor in writing the manuscript. He also queried the AI methodologies and techniques to introduce an approach that can address the shortcomings behind the RIMI second phase. B.F., Y.T., A.J. and R.L. verified the tested techniques and functions for analyzing the data and were major contributors in writing the manuscript. All authors read and agreed to the published version of the manuscript.

Funding: The first and corresponding author "Mohammed Al Saleh" has a scholarship from the National Council for Scientific Research in Lebanon (CNRS) to continue his Ph.D. degree, including this research.

Institutional Review Board Statement: Not applicable.

Informed Consent Statement: Not applicable.

Data Availability Statement: The datasets used and/or analyzed during the current study are available from the corresponding author upon reasonable request.

Acknowledgments: We would like to thank the National Council for Scientific Research (CNRS) in Lebanon for supporting this work. We would like to express our gratitude to the Federal Office for Radiation Protection (BfS) in Germany for allowing us to use the data collected by their REWS since more than 15 years ago. We would also like to thank Roy Issa for his support in implementing the code behind this research.

Conflicts of Interest: The authors declare no conflict of interest.

Abbreviations

The following abbreviations are used in this manuscript:

IoT	Internet of Things
REWS	Radiation Early Warning System
DTW	Dynamic Time Warping
DBA	DTW Barycenter Averaging
KNN	k-Nearest Neighbors
TSF	Time-Series Forest
RISE	Random Interval Spectral Ensemble

References

1. Mann, W.B. The international chernobyl project technical report: Assessment of radiological consequences and evaluation of protective measures. *Appl. Radiat. Isot.* **1993**, *44*, 985–988. [CrossRef]
2. Thieu, D.; Toan, T.N.; My, N.; Sy, N.; Tien, V.; Mai, N.; Cuong, L. Study, Design and Construction of an Early Warning Environmental Radiation Monitoring Station. *Commun. Phys.* **2012**, *22*, 375–382. [CrossRef]
3. Stöhlker, U.; Bleher, M.; Doll, H.; Dombrowski, H.; Harms, W.; Hellmann, I.; Luff, R.; Prommer, B.; Seifert, S.; Weiler, F. The German Dose Rate Monitoring Network Furthermore, Implemented Data Harmonization Techniques. *Radiat. Prot. Dosim.* **2019**, *183*, 405–417. [CrossRef] [PubMed]
4. Al-Saleh, M.; Finance, B.; Haque, R.; Taher, Y.; Jaber, A. *Towards an Autonomous Radiation Early Warning System*; BDCSIntell: Versailles, France, 2019.

5. Z-Normalization of Time Series. Available online: https://jmotif.github.io/sax-vsm_site/morea/algorithm/znorm.html (accessed on 27 January 2022).
6. Myers, C.S.; Rabiner, L.R. Connected digit recognition using a level-building DTW algorithm. *IEEE Trans. Acoust. Speech Signal Process.* **1981**, *29*, 351–363. [CrossRef]
7. MacQueen, J. Some methods for classification and analysis of multivariate observations. *Comput. Chem.* **1967**, *4*, 281–297.
8. Gower, J.C. Properties of Euclidean and non-Euclidean distance matrices. *Linear Algebra Appl.* **1985**, *67*, 81–97. [CrossRef]
9. Suwanda, R.; Syahputra, Z.; Zamzami, E.M. Analysis of Euclidean Distance and Manhattan Distance in the K-Means Algorithm for Variations Number of Centroid K. *J. Phys. Conf. Ser.* **2020**, *1566*. [CrossRef]
10. Anh, D.T.; Thanh, L. An efficient implementation of k-means clustering for time series data with DTW distance. *Int. J. Bus. Intell. Data Min.* **2015**, *10*, 213–232. [CrossRef]
11. Deng, H.; Runger, G.; Tuv, E.; Vladimir, M. A Time Series Forest for Classification and Feature Extraction. *Inf. Sci.* **2013**, *239*, 142–153. [CrossRef]
12. Flynn, M.; Large, J.; Bagnall, T. *The Contract Random Interval Spectral Ensemble (c-RISE): The Effect of Contracting a Classifier on Accuracy*; Hybrid Artificial Intelligent Systems; Springer: Cham, Switzerland, 2019.
13. Zhang, J.; Shen, W.; Gao, L.; Li, X.; Wen, L. Time Series Classification by Shapelet Dictionary Learning with SVM-Based Ensemble Classifier. *Comput. Intell. Neurosci.* **2021**, *2021*, 5586273. [CrossRef]
14. Abanda, A.; Mori, U.; Lozano, J. A review on distance based time series classification. *Data Min. Knowl. Discov.* **2019**, *33*, 378–412. [CrossRef]
15. Xing, Z.Z.; Pei, J.; Keogh, K. A Brief Survey on Sequence Classification. *SIGKDD Explor.* **2010**, *12*, 40–48. [CrossRef]

Proceeding Paper

Comparative Analysis of Residential Load Forecasting with Different Levels of Aggregation †

Ana Apolo Peñaloza *, Roberto Chouhy Leborgne and Alexandre Balbinot

Grupo de Modelagem e Análises de Sistemas de Potência and Laboratório de Instrumentação Eletrônica e Inteligência Artificial, Universidade Federal do Rio Grande do Sul UFRGS, Porto Alegre 90020-000, RS, Brazil; roberto.leborgne@ufrgs.br (R.C.L.); alexandre.balbinot@ufrgs.br (A.B.)
* Correspondence: ana.apolo@ufrgs.br; Tel.: +55-(51)-3308-3129
† Presented at the 8th International Conference on Time Series and Forecasting, Gran Canaria, Spain, 27–30 June 2022.

Abstract: Microgrids need a robust residential load forecasting. As a consequence, this highlights the problem of predicting electricity consumption in small amounts of households. The individual demand curve is volatile, and more difficult to forecast than the aggregated demand curve. For this reason, Mean Absolute Percentage Error (MAPE) varies in a large range (of 1% to 45%), depending on the number of consumers analyzed. Different levels of aggregation of household consumers that can be used in microgrids are analyzed; the load forecasting of the single consumer and aggregated consumers are compared. The forecasting methodology used is the most consolidated of Recurrent Neural Networks, i.e., LSTM. The dataset used contains 920 residential consumers belonging to the Commission for Energy Regulation (CER), a control group that is in the Irish Social Science Data Archive (ISSDA) repository. The result shows that the forecasting of groups of more than 20 aggregated consumers has a lower MAPE that individual forecasting. On the other hand, individual forecasting is better for groups with fewer than 10 consumers.

Keywords: load forecasting; LSTM; residential load forecasting; aggregation

Citation: Peñaloza, A.A.; Leborgne, R.C.; Balbinot, A. Comparative Analysis of Residential Load Forecasting with Different Levels of Aggregation. *Eng. Proc.* **2022**, *18*, 29. https://doi.org/10.3390/engproc2022018029

Academic Editors: Ignacio Rojas, Hector Pomares, Olga Valenzuela, Fernando Rojas and Luis Javier Herrera

Published: 21 June 2022

Publisher's Note: MDPI stays neutral with regard to jurisdictional claims in published maps and institutional affiliations.

1. Introduction

Load forecasting is essential to ensure a balance between demand and generation. Thus, utilities need highly accurate forecasts to maintain the security and stability of power supply [1]. At the same time, the complexity of the distribution network has continued to grow, which has created uncertainty in the grid, especially with the increase in microgeneration from renewable energy, and charging of electric vehicles [2].

Smart meters allow residents to monitor their consumption in real time. In addition to that, these meters provide large amounts of data from utilities [3]. These measurements allow for the enhanced measurement of consumption and energy control, allowing greater flexibility to the distribution network [4].

With this amount of data coming from smart meters, it becomes possible to perform a validation of demand forecasting at household or building levels. At these levels, consumption profiles are volatile [5,6]. Most load forecasting work is focused instead on large substations with tens of MW or transmission grids with tens of GW. Forecasting is assessed by the Mean Absolute Percentage Error (MAPE) metric which is generally below 2% for a substation at transmission level, while it can reach up to 30% for residential consumers [4]. Figure 1 shows aggregated demand curves for different amounts of consumers. This figure expresses that with 100 consumers, the demand curve is quite smoothed.

This work aims to analyze the demand forecasting in the context of microgrids. A dataset of 30 min demand of an individual residential consumer is used. This allows a comparison between demand forecasting of individual and aggregated consumers. This comparison is performed with different numbers of aggregated consumers (5, 10, 20,

30, 50 and 100). The selection of these consumers is random from a set of 256 residential consumers. The error metric used is the MAPE and the forecasting method is the Long Short-Term Memory (LSTM) recurrent neural network. LSTM is a consolidated methodology in load forecasting.

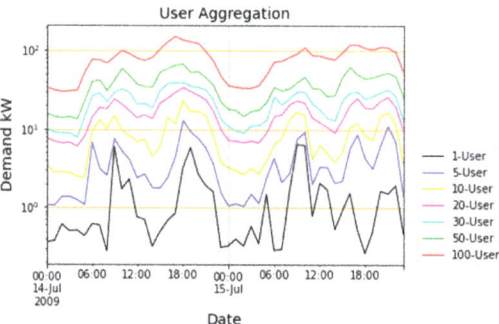

Figure 1. Different number of consumers.

2. Literature Review

The literature for demand forecasting is quite extensive, so it is possible to find statistical or machine learning methods for this purpose. In recent years, deep-learning methods are becoming popular for demand forecasting. Thus, recurrent neural networks, with their variant LSTM and GRU, are the most widely used methodologies for forecasting, as can be found in [2,7–13] for LSTM and [14,15] for GRU.

The forecasting literature is divided into forecasting of energy consumption and forecasting of load demand. Energy consumption forecasting has been used for few consumers, usually households or buildings, as found in [15–19]. On the other hand, load forecasting is used to forecast substations' demand, as found in [5,13,20–22]. These two approaches have completely different forecast errors using the same performance metrics. This is due to the difficulty of predicting power consumption.

Some authors that forecast energy consumption had aggregated individual energy consumption to obtain the building energy consumption [23].

There are few papers in the literature that compare load forecasting results and performance when using individual or aggregated consumers. Methodology performance for different levels of aggregation was evaluated in [7]. The authors found that with an aggregation of 5 consumers, the forecast errors are between 30 and 50%, while with 1000 aggregated consumers, the errors drop to less than 5%. However, the authors have not analyzed the forecasting performance for single users.

One of the first to analyze individual load forecasting is [13]. The individual's demand volatility makes the prediction difficult. Forecasting methodology is using an LSTM neural network. Demand forecasting is done for 69 consumers who belong to a set of 10,000 consumers from Australia for a period of three months. Other quantities of aggregated consumers are not analyzed. Results show that the non-aggregate forecast is better than the aggregate set forecast.

Comparisons of demand forecasting with different levels of aggregation are presented in [4], but the results are ambiguous and do not consider a non-aggregated methodology. Different aggregation levels using LSTM are shown in [24]. Their results suggest that demand forecasting of more than 200 aggregated residential consumers hardly decreases error, with the error curve becoming almost constant. However, the work of [24] only considers the increase in consumers and how this reflects on the aggregate predictor error. Non-aggregated consumers are not considered.

A methodology for demand forecasting of 200 consumers that are divided into groups of 50, 100, and 150 is presented in [25]. Forecasting is performed by LSTM and k-means clustering. The methodology without clustering proved to be better. They do not perform analyses with groups smaller than 50 consumers, which would be a typical microgrid context.

3. Demand Forecasting with RNN

Recurrent Neural Networks (RNNs) have become the most widely used methodology to perform residential demand forecasting [6,8,11,26–28]. The preference for RNNs is due to the fact that their models are sequence-based [6]. RNNs can process large data or text size series [29]. Therefore, RNNs are widely used in text translation and forecasting of time series data [30]. Energy demand is a time series, as observed in Figure 1. Figure 2 shows the typical architecture of RNNs and their unfolding in the earlier and later times.

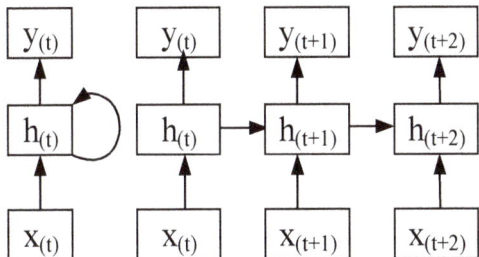

Figure 2. Recurrent neural network architecture. Adapted of [6].

There are two types of RNNs: Long Short-Term Memory (LSTM) and Gated Recurrent Unit (GRU). LSTM and GRU are implemented to solve the problems of gradient bursting, when gradients approach infinity, or gradient fading, with gradients close to zero [30]. These problems are associated with successive multiplications of the weight matrices W [30].

LSTM is a solution to the long-time gradient fading and bursting problems through finite gradient control [30]. GRU, in turn, is a simplified variant of LSTM introduced by Cho [31], which performs the same gradient control using fewer gates.

Long Short-Term Memory

The LSTM is trained by the Backpropagation Through Time (BPTT) algorithm [32]. Figure 3 illustrates a time step with two LSTM cells, showing the internal connection of an LSTM cell. Figure 3 allows one to observe the updates of hidden state (h_t) and cell state (c_t) after a time step [30]. The key to the LSTM cell is cell state (c_t). The cell c_t moves from an earlier time step to the later time step and can be called a long-term memory term.

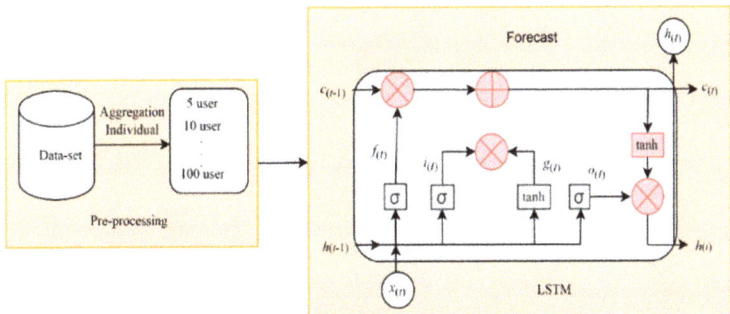

Figure 3. Individual and aggregated load forecasting.

The equation of c_t is shown in (1) and is divided into two parts. The first part is controlled by the forget gate (f_t). The f_t is in charge of defining the elements of the input

x_t to be kept or removed and the elements of the hidden state h_t. Its formula is shown in (2) [6,30]. The input gate (i_t) and input state (g_t) determine the input values that will be kept by the LSTM cell.

The input gate is shown in (3) and the input state (g_t) is shown in (4). So, g_t creates the values that can be added to the cell state while it decides which input values (input x) will be updated. The output gate (o_t) is also divided in two parts. In the first part, the values of the input (x) are placed, and the hidden state (h_t) is used in the output, and in the second part the same happens for the values of ct.

Finally, the sum of the two parts is transformed by the hyperbolic tangent function (tanh) to obtain values in the range from $[-1, 1]$ [6,29,30,33].

$$c_t = g_t \odot i_t + (c_{t-1} \odot f_t) \tag{1}$$

$$f_t = \sigma\left(W_{f \cdot x} x_t + W_{f \cdot h} h_{t-1} + b_f\right) \tag{2}$$

$$i_t = \sigma(W_{i \cdot x} x_t + W_{i \cdot h} h_{t-1} + b_i) \tag{3}$$

$$g_t = tanh\left(W_{g \cdot x} x_t + W_{g \cdot h} h_{t-1} + b_g\right) \tag{4}$$

$$o_t = \sigma(W_{o \cdot x} x_t + W_{o \cdot h} h_{t-1} + b_o) \tag{5}$$

$$h_t = tanh(c_t) \odot o_t \tag{6}$$

where: c_t is the cell state; h is the hidden state; f_t is the forget gate; i_t is the input gate; g_t is the input activation gate; o_t is the output gate. x is the input, W is the weight matrix, b is the bias in gate, σ is the sigmoid function, and *tanh* is the hyperbolic tangent.

4. Methodology for Comparison and Case Study

Figure 4 presents the methodology used to generate the forecasting for the comparison of the performance of the aggregated and individual forecast. The load forecasting is performed by the LSTM Recurrent Neural Network.

Figure 4 shows the methodology divided into two parts. The first is the pre-processing step, which contains normalization and missing data checking. The dataset used in this work belongs to the Smart Metering Electricity Consumer Behavior Trials project, carried out by the Commission for Energy Regulation (CER), Ireland's energy generation and distribution regulatory institution. The project that generated this database aimed to analyze the energy consumption per hour with different residential and industrial consumption tariffs by time of use (ToU). Its concern was to present the behavior of consumers in each of the different price ranges and their adaptation in relation to time of use. The project relied on the use of smart meters with a real-time digital panel, access to consumption via the internet, and detailed bimonthly consumption [34,35].

The dataset CER included 4225 residential consumers. However, this paper focused on the control group that included 657 consumers with measurements over a period of one and a half years, from 14 July 2009 to 31 December 2010. Data acquisition was carried out every 30 min. As the focus of this paper is influence of load aggregation on demand, forecasting groups with 5, 10, 20, 30, 50 and 100 consumers were randomized. The dataset CER does not contain missing data. The sampling period is one hour, and only one season is considered to perform the forecasting. Thus, 1600 samples per user are selected to perform the different forecasts.

In order to verify the performance of the forecast for aggregated and individual consumers, the following set of consumers {5, 10, 20, 30, 50 and 100} is performed. The selection of consumers for each set is randomized among the consumers. In order to verify the influence of consumers on each set, the random selection is repeated 10 times. Once the consumers in the set are selected, their demand is summed to create a single demand curve with 1600 time samples.

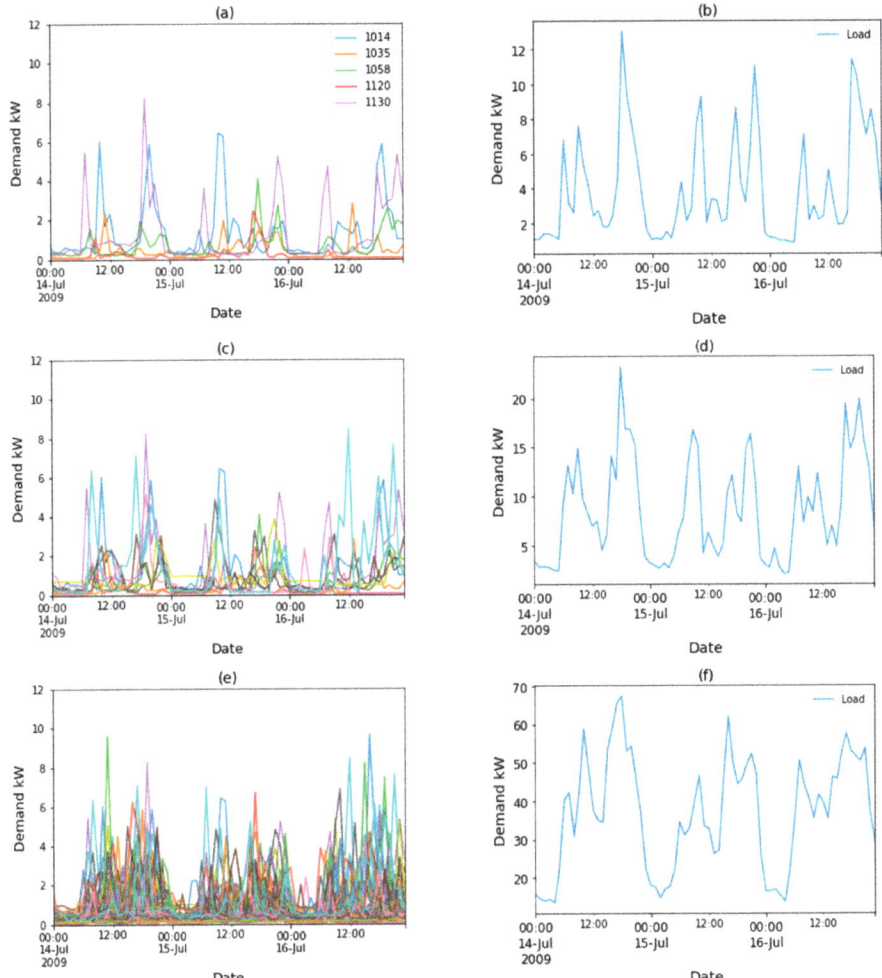

Figure 4. Individual and aggregated demand. (**a**) 5 individual consumers; (**b**) 5 aggregated consumers; (**c**) 10 individual consumers; (**d**) 10 aggregated consumers; (**e**) 50 individual consumers; (**f**) 50 aggregated consumers.

On the other hand, the curve called individual is composed of 1600 samples from each individual in the set (example: from a set with 20 consumers, the number of samples used is 32,000). Next, each individual consumer is predicted and then summed up; finally, the result is compared with the aggregated curve.

Figure 4a,c,e presents on the left the individual demand of 5, 10 and 50 consumers and on the right the aggregated demand of the consumers (see Figure 4b,d,f). Figure 4d,f shows that the demand waveform softens with the increase in the number of consumers, such that with 50 consumers the aggregated peaks (see Figure 4e) are smoother compared to the waveform of 5 consumers (see Figure 4b).

Table 1 shows the LSTM configuration for the aggregated and individual forecasting. The selection of these parameters is based on [8]. The forecast error metric is Mean Absolute Percentage Error (MAPE), which is the most widely used error measure according to the literature.

Table 1. LSTM hyper-parameters.

Hyper-Parameters	Aggregated	Individual
Number of Neurons	512	512
Dropout	0.2	0.2
Epochs	100	100
Optimizer	Adam	RMSProp
Activation Function	tanh	tanh

5. Results

To perform the forecasting, the CER database is divided into 70% for training and 30% for testing. The consumers were aggregated in 5, 10, 20, 30, 50 and 100 consumers to analyze the forecasting performance. The load demand curve of the previous 48 h of each group is used by the algorithm to predict the demand for next hour. In the case of aggregate forecasting, 48 time steps of aggregated demand are used, and the forecast is the aggregated demand of the following hour. In the case of individual forecasting, 48 time steps of individual demand are used for each consumer and the forecast is the individual demand of the next hour for each consumer.

Figure 5a–f show the forecast curve and the actual curve for aggregated and individual consumers, respectively. Figure 5a shows the forecast of individual consumers. Figure 5a–c highlight the difficulty of forecasting microgrids with few consumers (fewer than 10), where uncertainty is relatively more significant due to the volatility of individual consumers. Figure 5d–f show that after 20 aggregated consumers, the volatility decreases, smoothing the curves and facilitating the forecast. Finally, Figure 5f shows the best result because the curve is smoother and therefore less volatile than the curve in Figure 5a.

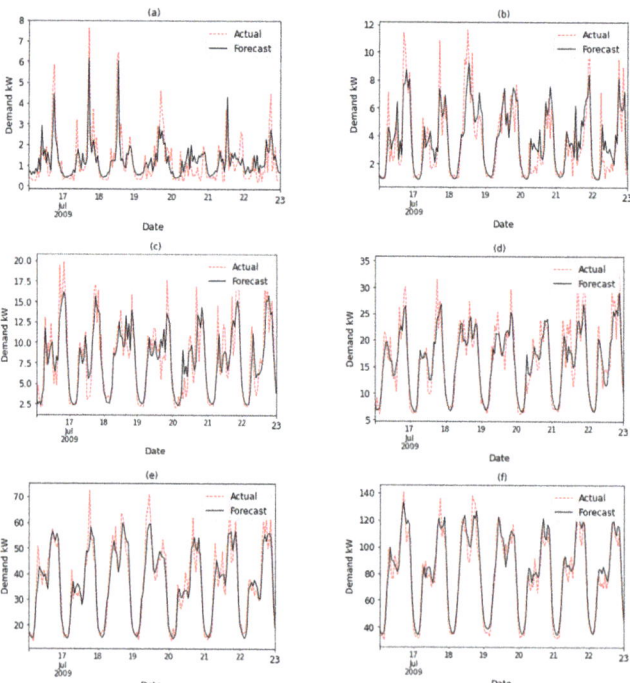

Figure 5. Actual vs. forecast demand curve. (**a**) Individual consumers; (**b**) 5 aggregated consumers; (**c**) 10 aggregated consumers; (**d**) 20 aggregated consumers; (**e**) 50 aggregated consumers; (**f**) 100 aggregated consumers.

Figures 6 and 7 show the average MAPE for the individual and aggregated consumers of the 10 forecast simulations for each group {5, 10, 20, 30, 50 and, 100} consumers. Figure 6 shows the MAPE for training whereas Figure 7 shows the MAPE for testing. Figures 6 and 7 show that MAPE decreases in training and testing when the number of aggregated consumers increases, because the aggregated demand curve is smoother with a larger aggregation of consumers.

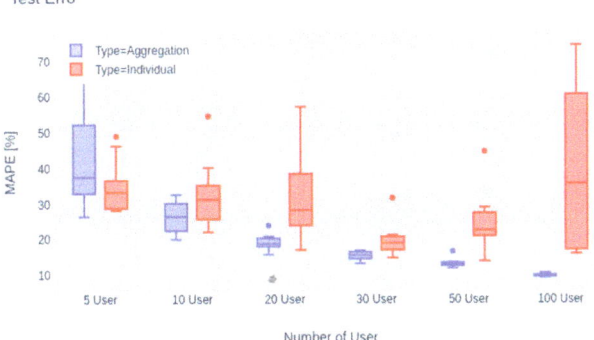

Figure 6. MAPE in the training of individual and aggregated consumers.

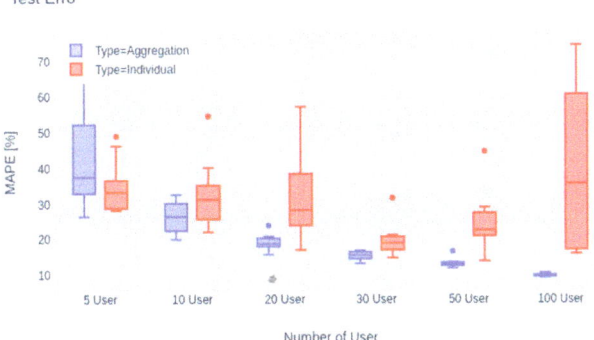

Figure 7. MAPE in the test of individual and aggregated consumers.

The MAPE of individual forecasting is comparable with aggregated forecasting when small number of consumers are considered, less than 10. Therefore, in small micro-grids the individual curve could be more useful than the aggregated one. The MAPE for individual forecasting is due to atypical consumers that tend to affect the individual forecast more than the aggregate. A way to improve the individual forecasting would be to work with consumers with similar consumption profiles. Thus, grouping would be by cluster and not random as was done in this work.

Another paper [36] also works with the CER database, uses a control group with 782 consumers, and his MAPE error is 6%. This work presents a training error of 6.88% when training uses 100 consumers. According to Figures 6 and 7, the error decreases with the increasing number of consumers. With 256 consumers, a 5% training error is found. The error decrease with the increase in consumers is due to the fact that with 256 consumers the demand curve is smoother than with 100 consumers. The error decrease is stable, after 100 consumers, with errors smaller than 3% for 782 consumers.

6. Conclusions

This paper presented a comparison of load forecasting considering an aggregated and an individual demand curve. The load forecasting was performed by the LSTM RNNs that was designed to work with a series of data such as energy demand curves. The analysis was performed with 5, 10, 20, 30, 50 and 100 consumers. The selection of consumers was randomized, and the experiment was repeated 10 times. The aggregated 100-consumer forecasting presented the lowest MAPE. The decrease in the MAPE was due to the smoothed demand curve of the aggregated consumers. The aggregated forecasting reduced the volatility of the electricity consumption. On the other hand, the individual forecast was more susceptible to atypical consumers which produce larger differences in the forecast for small groups (below 20 consumers). However, for small micro-grids, individual consumption is better than aggregate.

Author Contributions: Conceptualization, R.C.L. and A.A.P.; methodology, A.A.P.; validation, A.B.; writing—original draft preparation, A.A.P.; writing—review and editing, R.C.L. and A.B.; All authors have read and agreed to the published version of the manuscript.

Funding: This research was funded by the Coordenação de Aperfeiçoamento de Pessoal de Nível Superior-Brasil (CAPES)–Finance Code 001.

Institutional Review Board Statement: Not applicable.

Informed Consent Statement: Not applicable.

Data Availability Statement: Accessed through the Irish Social Science Data Archive https://www.ucd.ie/issda/data/commissionforenergyregulationcer (accessed on 17 June 2022).

Acknowledgments: This study was financed in part by the Coordenação de Aperfeiçoamento de Pessoal de Nível Superior-Brasil (CAPES)–Finance Code 001. The authors would like to thank the Irish Social Science Data Archive for making the database used in this paper available through "CER Smart Metering Project-Electricity Customer Behaviour Trial, 2009–2010" and also to ISSDA, as follows: "Accessed through the Irish Social Science Data Archive- https://www.ucd.ie/issda/data/commissionforenergyregulationcer (accessed on 17 June 2022).

Conflicts of Interest: The authors declare no conflict of interest. The funders had no role in the design of the study; in the collection, analyses, or interpretation of data; in the writing of the manuscript, or in the decision to publish the results.

References

1. Deng, Z.; Wang, B.; Xu, Y.; Xu, T.; Liu, C.; Zhu, Z. Multi-scale convolutional neural network with time-cognition for multi-step short-Term load forecasting. *IEEE Access* **2019**, *7*, 88058–88071. [CrossRef]
2. Kong, W.; Dong, Z.Y.; Hill, D.J.; Luo, F.; Xu, Y. Short-term residential load forecasting based on resident behaviour learning. *IEEE Trans. Power Syst.* **2018**, *33*, 2017–2018. [CrossRef]
3. Kelly, J.; Knottenbelt, W. The UK-DALE dataset, domestic appliance-level electricity demand and whole-house demand from five UK homes. *Sci. Data* **2015**, *2*, 1–14. [CrossRef] [PubMed]
4. Sevlian, R.; Rajagopal, R. Short Term Electricity Load Forecasting on Varying Levels of Aggregation. 2017, 1–19. Available online: http://arxiv.org/abs/1404.0058 (accessed on 17 June 2022).
5. Elvers, A.; Vos, M.; Albayrak, S. Short-term probabilistic load forecasting at low aggregation levels using convolutional neural networks. In Proceedings of the 2019 IEEE Milan PowerTech, Milan, Italy, 23–27 June 2019. [CrossRef]
6. Kong, W.; Dong, Z.Y.; Jia, Y.; Hill, D.J.; Xu, Y.; Zhang, Y. Short-Term Residential Load Forecasting Based on LSTM Recurrent Neural Network. *IEEE Trans. Smart Grid* **2019**, *10*, 841–851. [CrossRef]
7. Gholizadeh, N.; Musilek, P. Federated learning with hyperparameter-based clustering for electrical load forecasting. *Internet Things* **2022**, *17*, 100470. [CrossRef]
8. Kong, W.; Dong, Z.Y.; Luo, F.; Meng, K.; Zhang, W.; Wang, F.; Zhao, X. Effect of automatic hyperparameter tuning for residential load forecasting via deep learning. In Proceedings of the 2017 Australasian Universities Power Engineering Conference (AUPEC), Melbourne, VIC, Australia, 19–22 November 2017. [CrossRef]
9. Amarasinghe, K.; Marino, D.L.; Manic, M. Deep neural networks for energy load forecasting. *IEEE Int. Symp. Ind. Electron.* **2017**, 1483–1488. [CrossRef]

10. Al Mamun, A.; Hoq, M.; Hossain, E.; Bayindir, R. A hybrid deep learning model with evolutionary algorithm for short-term load forecasting. In Proceedings of the 2019 8th International Conference on Renewable Energy Research and Applications (ICRERA), Brasov, Romania, 3–6 November 2019; pp. 886–891. [CrossRef]

11. Marino, D.L.; Amarasinghe, K.; Manic, M. Building energy load forecasting using Deep Neural Networks. In Proceedings of the IECON 2016-42nd Annual Conference of the IEEE Industrial Electronics Society, Florence, Italy, 23–26 October 2016; pp. 7046–7051. [CrossRef]

12. Somu, N.; MR, G.R.; Ramamritham, K. A hybrid model for building energy consumption forecasting using long short term memory networks. *Appl. Energy* **2020**, *261*, 114131. [CrossRef]

13. Jiao, R.; Zhang, T.; Jiang, Y.; He, H. Short-term non-residential load forecasting based on multiple sequences LSTM recurrent neural network. *IEEE Access* **2018**, *6*, 59438–59448. [CrossRef]

14. Hossen, T.; Nair, A.S.; Chinnathambi, R.A.; Ranganathan, P. Residential Load Forecasting Using Deep Neural Networks (DNN). In Proceedings of the 2018 North American Power Symposium (NAPS), Fargo, ND, USA, 9–11 September 2018; pp. 1–5. [CrossRef]

15. Jiang, Z.; Lin, R.; Yang, F. A hybrid machine learning model for electricity consumer categorization using smart meter data. *Energies* **2018**, *11*, 2235. [CrossRef]

16. Viegas, J.L.; Vieira, S.M.; Sousa, J.M.C. Fuzzy clustering and prediction of electricity demand based on household characteristics. In Proceedings of the 2015 Conference of the International Fuzzy Systems Association and the European Society for Fuzzy Logic and Technology, Asturias, Spain, 30 June–3 July 2015. [CrossRef]

17. Rahman, H.; Selvarasan, I.; Jahitha Begum, A. Short-term forecasting of total energy consumption for India-a black box based approach. *Energies* **2018**, *11*, 3442. [CrossRef]

18. Estebsari, A.; Rajabi, R. Single residential load forecasting using deep learning and image encoding techniques. *Electronics* **2020**, *9*, 68. [CrossRef]

19. Hsiao, Y.H. Household electricity demand forecast based on context information and user daily schedule analysis from meter data. *IEEE Trans. Ind. Inform.* **2015**, *11*, 33–43. [CrossRef]

20. Yan, X.; Abbes, D.; Francois, B. Uncertainty analysis for day ahead power reserve quantification in an urban microgrid including PV generators. *Renew. Energy* **2017**, *106*, 288–297. [CrossRef]

21. Beccali, M.; Cellura, M.; Lo Brano, V.; Marvuglia, A. Short-term prediction of household electricity consumption: Assessing weather sensitivity in a Mediterranean area. *Renew. Sustain. Energy Rev.* **2008**, *12*, 2040–2065. [CrossRef]

22. Moradzadeh, A.; Zakeri, S.; Shoaran, M.; Mohammadi-Ivatloo, B.; Mohammadi, F. Short-term load forecasting of microgrid via hybrid support vector regression and long short-term memory algorithms. *Sustainability* **2020**, *12*, 7076. [CrossRef]

23. Syed, D.; Abu-Rub, H.; Ghrayeb, A.; Refaat, S.S. Household-Level Energy Forecasting in Smart Buildings Using a Novel Hybrid Deep Learning Model. *IEEE Access* **2021**, *9*, 33498–33511. [CrossRef]

24. Peng, Y.; Wang, Y.; Lu, X.; Li, H.; Shi, D.; Wang, Z.; Li, J. Short-term Load Forecasting at Different Aggregation Levels with Predictability Analysis. In Proceedings of the 2019 IEEE Innovative Smart Grid Technologies-Asia (ISGT Asia), Chengdu, China, 21–24 May 2019; pp. 3385–3390. [CrossRef]

25. Hou, T.; Fang, R.; Tang, J.; Ge, G.; Yang, D.; Liu, J.; Zhang, W. A Novel Short-Term Residential Electric Load Forecasting Method Based on Adaptive Load Aggregation and Deep Learning Algorithms. *Energies* **2021**, *14*, 7820. [CrossRef]

26. Tian, C.; Ma, J.; Zhang, C.; Zhan, P. A deep neural network model for short-term load forecast based on long short-term memory network and convolutional neural network. *Energies* **2018**, *11*, 3493. [CrossRef]

27. Yudantaka, K.; Kim, J.S.; Song, H. Dual deep learning networks based load forecasting with partial real-time information and its application to system marginal price prediction. *Energies* **2019**, *13*, 148. [CrossRef]

28. Wang, Z.; Zhao, B.; Guo, H.; Tang, L.; Peng, Y. Deep ensemble learning model for short-term load forecasting within active learning framework. *Energies* **2019**, *12*, 3809. [CrossRef]

29. Goodfellow, I.; Bengio, Y.; Courville, A. *Deep Learning*; MIT Press: Cambridge, MA, USA, 2016.

30. Aggarwal, C.C. *Neural Networks and Deep Learning*, 1st ed.; Springer: New York, NY, USA, 2018; ISBN 978-3-319-94462-3.

31. Chung, J.; Gulcehre, C.; Cho, K.; Bengio, Y. Empirical Evaluation of Gated Recurrent Neural Networks on Sequence Modeling. *arXiv* **2014**, arXiv:1412.3555.

32. Hochreiter, S.; Schmidhuber, J. Long Short-Term Memory. *Neural Comput.* **1997**, *9*, 1735–1780. [CrossRef] [PubMed]

33. Skansi, S. *Introduction to Deep Learning*; Springer: Berlin/Heidelberg, Germany, 2018; ISBN 9783319730035.

34. Exchange, T.; North, B.S. Electricity Smart Metering Customer Behaviour Trials (CBT) Findings Report DOCUMENT TYPE: REFERENCE: DATE. Trial **2011**, 1–58. Available online: https://www.cru.ie/wp-content/uploads/2011/07/cer11080ai.pdf (accessed on 17 June 2022).

35. CER (Commission for Energy Regulation). Available online: hhttps://www.ucd.ie/issda/data/commissionforenergyregulationcer (accessed on 17 June 2022).

36. Humeau, S.; Wijaya, T.K.; Vasirani, M.; Aberer, K. Electricity load forecasting for residential customers: Exploiting aggregation and correlation between households. In Proceedings of the 2013 Sustainable Internet and ICT for Sustainability (SustainIT), Palermo, Italy, 30–31 October 2013; pp. 1–6. [CrossRef]

Proceeding Paper

An Open Source and Reproducible Implementation of LSTM and GRU Networks for Time Series Forecasting †

Gissel Velarde *, Pedro Brañez, Alejandro Bueno, Rodrigo Heredia and Mateo Lopez-Ledezma

Independent Researchers, Cochabamba 06651, Bolivia; pedrobran8@gmail.com (P.B.);
alebuenoaz@gmail.com (A.B.); rodrigoh1205@gmail.com (R.H.); lopezmateo97@yahoo.com (M.L.-L.)
* Correspondence: gv@urubo.org
† Presented at the 8th International Conference on Time Series and Forecasting, Gran Canaria, Spain,
27–30 June 2022.

Abstract: This paper introduces an open source and reproducible implementation of Long Short-Term Memory (LSTM) and Gated Recurrent Unit (GRU) networks for time series forecasting. We evaluated LSTM and GRU networks because of their performance reported in related work. We describe our method and its results on two datasets. The first dataset is the S&P BSE BANKEX, composed of stock time series (closing prices) of ten financial institutions. The second dataset, called Activities, comprises ten synthetic time series resembling weekly activities with five days of high activity and two days of low activity. We report Root Mean Squared Error ($RMSE$) between actual and predicted values, as well as Directional Accuracy (DA). We show that a single time series from a dataset can be used to adequately train the networks if the sequences in the dataset contain patterns that repeat, even with certain variation, and are properly processed. For 1-step ahead and 20-step ahead forecasts, LSTM and GRU networks significantly outperform a baseline on the Activities dataset. The baseline simply repeats the last available value. On the stock market dataset, the networks perform just as the baseline, possibly due to the nature of these series. We release the datasets used as well as the implementation with all experiments performed to enable future comparisons and to make our research reproducible.

Keywords: forecasting; time series; open source; reproducibility

Citation: Velarde, G.; Brañez , P.; Bueno, A.; Heredia, R; Lopez-Ledezma, M. An Open Source and Reproducible Implementation of LSTM and GRU Networks for Time Series Forecasting. *Eng. Proc.* **2022**, *18*, 30. https://doi.org/10.3390/engproc2022018030

Academic Editors: Ignacio Rojas, Hector Pomares, Olga Valenzuela, Fernando Rojas and Luis Javier Herrera

Published: 22 June 2022

Publisher's Note: MDPI stays neutral with regard to jurisdictional claims in published maps and institutional affiliations.

1. Introduction

Artificial Neural Networks (ANNs) and particularly Recurrent Neural Networks (RNNs) gained attention in time series forecasting due to their capacity to model dependencies over time [1]. With our proposed method, we show that RNNs can be successfully trained with a single time series to deliver forecasts for unseen time series in a dataset containing patterns that repeat, even with certain variation; therefore, once a network is properly trained, it can be used to forecast other series in the dataset if adequately prepared.

LSTM [2] and GRU [3] are two related deep learning architectures from the RNN family. LSTM consists of a memory cell that regulates its flow of information thanks to its non-linear gating units, known as the input, forget and output gates, and activation functions [4]. GRU architecture consists of reset and update gates and activation functions. Both architectures are known to perform equally well on sequence modeling problems, yet GRU was found to train faster than LSTM on music and speech applications [5].

Empirical studies on financial time series data reported that LSTM outperformed Autoregressive Integrated Moving Average (ARIMA) [6]. ARIMA [7] is a traditional forecasting method that integrates autoregression with moving average processes. In [6], LSTM and ARIMA were evaluated on $RMSE$ between actual and predicted values on financial data. The authors suggested that the superiority of LSTM over ARIMA was thanks to gradient descent optimization [6]. A systematic study compared different ANNs architectures for stock market forecasting [8]. More specifically, the authors evaluated architectures of the types LSTM, GRU, Convolutional Neural Networks (CNN) and Extreme Learning Machines (ELM). In their experiments, two-layered LSTM and two-layered GRU networks delivered low $RMSE$.

In this study, we evaluate LSTM and GRU architectures because of their performance reported in related work for time series forecasting [6,8]. Our method is described in Section 2. In Sections 2.1–2.3, we review principles of Recurrent Neural Networks (RNN) of the type LSTM and GRU. In Section 2.4, we explain our data preparation, followed by the networks' architecture, training (Section 2.5) and evaluation (Section 2.6). The evaluation was performed on two datasets. In Section 3.1, we describe the S&P BSE-BANKEX or simply BANKEX dataset, which was originally described in [8] and consists of stock time series (closing prices). In Section 3.2, we describe the Activities dataset, a dataset composed of synthetic time series resembling weekly activities with five days of high activity and two days of low activity. The experiments are presented in Section 3. Finally, we state our conclusions in Section 5 and present possible directions for future work. We release the datasets used as well as the implementation with all experiments performed to enable future comparisons and make our research reproducible.

2. Method

The general overview of the method is described as follows. The method inputs time series of values over time and outputs predictions. Every time series in the dataset is normalized. Then, the number of test samples is defined to create the training and testing sets. One time series from the train set is selected and prepared to train an LSTM and a GRU, independently. Once the networks are trained, the test set is used to evaluate $RMSE$ and DA between actual and predicted values for each network. The series are transformed back to unnormalized values for visual inspection. We describe every step in detail. Next, in Sections 2.1–2.3, we review principles of RNNs of the type LSTM and GRU, following the presentation as in [5].

2.1. Recurrent Neural Networks

ANNs are trained to approximate a function and learn the networks' parameters that best approximate that function. RNNs are a special type of ANNs developed to handle sequences. An RNN updates its recurrent hidden state h_t for a sequence $x = (x_1, x_2, \ldots, x_T)$ by:

$$h_t = \begin{cases} 0, & t = 0 \\ \phi(h_{t-1}, x_t), & otherwise, \end{cases} \tag{1}$$

where ϕ is a nonlinear function. The output of an RNN maybe of variable length $y = (y_1, y_2, \ldots, y_T)$.

The update of h_t is computed by:

$$h_t = g(Wx_t + Uh_{t-1}), \tag{2}$$

where W and U are weights' matrices and g is a smooth and bounded activation function such as a logistic sigmoid, or simply called sigmoid function $f(x) = \sigma = \frac{1}{1+e^{-x}}$, or a hyperbolic tangent function $f(x) = tanh(x) = \frac{e^x - e^{-x}}{e^x + e^{-x}}$.

Given a state h_t, an RNN outputs a probability distribution for the next element in a sequence. The sequence probability is represented as:

$$p(x_1, x_2, \ldots, x_T) = p(x_1)p(x_2 \mid x_1)\ldots p(x_T \mid x_1, x_2, \ldots, x_{T-1}). \tag{3}$$

The last element is a so-called end-of-sequence value. The conditional probability distribution is given by:

$$p(x_t \mid x_1, x_2, \ldots x_{t-1}) = g(h_t), \tag{4}$$

where h_t is the recurrent hidden state of the RNN as in expression (1). Updating the network's weights involves several matrix computations, such that back-propagating errors lead to vanishing or exploding weights, making training unfeasible. LSTM was proposed in 1997 to solve this problem by enforcing constant error flow thanks to gating units [2]. GRU is a closely related network proposed in 2014 [3]. Next, we review LSTM and GRU networks. See Figure 1 for illustration.

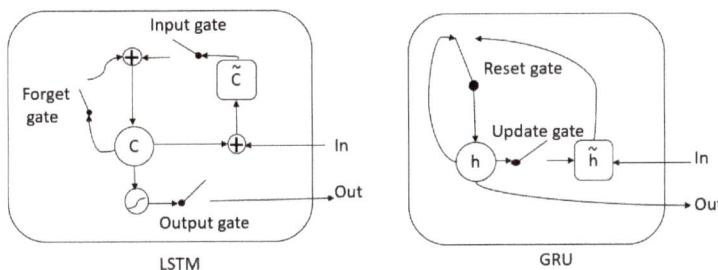

Figure 1. LSTM (**left**) and GRU (**right**). c represents the memory cell and $\tilde{c}$ the new memory cell of the LSTM. h represents the activation and $\tilde{h}$ the new activation of the GRU. Based on [5].

2.2. Long Short-Term Memory

The LSTM unit decides whether to keep content memory thanks to its gates. If a sequence feature is detected to be relevant, the LSTM unit keeps track of it over time, modeling dependencies over long-distance [5].

In Expressions (6)–(8) and (10), W and U represent weights matrices and V represents a diagonal matrix. W, U and V need to be learned by the algorithm during training. The subscripts i, o and f correspond to input, output and forget gates, respectively. For every j-th LSTM unit, there is a memory cell c_t^j at time t, which activation h_t^j is computed as:

$$h_t^j = o_t^j tanh(c_t^j) \tag{5}$$

where o_t^j is the output gate responsible for modulating the amount of memory in the cell. The forget gate f_t^j modulates the amount of memory content to be forgotten and the input gate i_t^j modulates the amount of new memory to be added to the memory cell, such that:

$$o_t^j = \sigma(W_o x_t + U_o h_{t-1} + V_o c_t)^j, \tag{6}$$

$$f_t^j = \sigma(W_f x_t + U_f h_{t-1} + V_f c_{t-1})^j, \tag{7}$$

$$i_t^j = \sigma(W_i x_t + U_i h_{t-1} + V_i c_{t-1})^j. \tag{8}$$

where σ is a sigmoid function. The memory cell c_t^j partially forgets and adds new memory content $\tilde{c}_t^j$ by:

$$c_t^j = f_t^j c_{t-1}^j + i_t^j \tilde{c}_t^j, \tag{9}$$

where:

$$\tilde{c}_t^j = tanh(W_c x_t + U_c h_{t-1})^j. \tag{10}$$

2.3. Gated Recurrent Unit

The main difference between LSTM and GRU is that GRU does not have a separate memory cell, such that the activation h_t^j is obtained by the following expression:

$$h_t^j = (1 - z_t^j) h_{t-1}^j + z_t^j \tilde{h}_t^j. \tag{11}$$

The update gate z_t^j decides the amount of update content given by the previous h_{t-1}^j and candidate activation $\tilde{h}_t^j$. In Expressions (12)–(14), W and U represent weights matrices that need to be learned during training. Moreover, the subscripts z and r correspond to update and reset gates, respectively. The update gate z_t^j and reset gate r_t^j are obtained by the following expressions:

$$z_t^j = \sigma(W_z x_t + U_z h_{t-1})^j, \tag{12}$$

$$r_t^j = \sigma(W_r x_t + U_r h_{t-1})^j, \tag{13}$$

where σ is a sigmoid function. The candidate activation $\tilde{h}_t^j$ is obtained by:

$$\tilde{h}_t^j = tanh(W x_t + r_t \odot (U h_{t-1}))^j. \tag{14}$$

where $\odot$ denotes element-wise multiplication.

2.4. Data Preparation

Every time series or sequence in the dataset is normalized as follows. Let v be a sequence $v = (v_1, v_2, \ldots, v_Q)$ of Q samples that can be normalized between 0 and 1:

$$x = v' = \frac{v - v_{min}}{v_{max} - v_{min}}. \tag{15}$$

We define the number of samples in the test set as $test_s$. The number of samples N for training is obtained by $N = Q - test_s - w$. Then, a sequence x is selected arbitrarily and prepared to train each network as follows. We define a window of size w and a number of steps ahead f, where $f < w < N < Q$, such that:

$$X = \begin{bmatrix} x_1 & x_2 & \cdots & x_w \\ x_2 & x_3 & \cdots & x_{w+1} \\ x_3 & x_4 & \cdots & x_{w+2} \\ \cdots & \cdots & \cdots & \cdots \\ x_{Q-(w-1+f)} & x_{Q-(w-2+f)} & \cdots & x_{Q-f} \end{bmatrix},$$

X becomes a $Q - (w - 1 + f)$ by w matrix, and:

$$Y = \begin{bmatrix} x_{w+1} & x_{w+2} & \cdots & x_{w+f} \\ x_{w+2} & x_{w+3} & \cdots & x_{w+2+f} \\ x_{w+3} & x_{w+4} & \cdots & x_{w+3+f} \\ \cdots & \cdots & \cdots & \cdots \\ x_{Q-(f-1)} & x_{Q-(f-2)} & \cdots & x_Q \end{bmatrix} \tag{16}$$

becomes a $Q - (w - 1 + f)$ by f matrix containing the targets. The first N rows of X and Y are used for training. The remaining $Q - N$ elements are used for testing. The settings for our experiments are described in Section 3, after we introduce the characteristics of the dataset used.

2.5. Networks' Architecture and Training

We tested two RNNs. One with LSTM memory cells and one with GRU memory cells. In both cases, we use the following architecture and training:

- A layer with 128 units,
- A dense layer with size equal to the number of steps ahead for prediction,

with recurrent sigmoid activations and *tanh* activation functions as explained in Sections 2.2 and 2.3. The networks are trained for 200 epochs with Adam optimizer [9]. The number of epochs and architecture were set empirically. We minimize Mean Squared Error (*MSE*) loss between the targets and the predicted values, see Expression (17). The networks are trained using a single time series prepared as described in Section 2.4. The data partition is explained in Section 3.3.

2.6. Evaluation

We use Mean Squared Error (MSE) to train the networks:

$$MSE = n^{-1} \sum_{t=1}^{n} (x_t - y_t)^2, \tag{17}$$

where n is the number of samples, x_t and y_t are actual and predicted values at time t. Moreover, we use Root Mean Squared Error ($RMSE$) for evaluation between algorithms:

$$RMSE = \sqrt{MSE}. \tag{18}$$

Both metrics, MSE and $RMSE$, are used to measure the difference between actual and predicted values, and therefore, smaller results are preferred [10]. We also use Directional Accuracy (DA):

$$DA = \frac{100}{n} \sum_{t=1}^{n} d_t, \tag{19}$$

where:

$$d_t = \begin{cases} 1 & (x_t - x_{t-1})(y_t - y_{t-1}) \geq 0 \\ 0 & otherwise. \end{cases}$$

such that x_t and y_t are the actual and predicted values at time t, respectively, and n is the sample size. DA is used to measure the capacity of a model to predict direction as well as prediction accuracy. Thus, higher values of DA are preferred [10].

3. Experiments

In this section, we report experiments performed with both datasets.

3.1. The S&P BSE BANKEX Dataset

This dataset was originally described in [8]; however, our query retrieved a different number of samples as in [8]. We assume it must have changed since it was originally retrieved. We collected the time series on 20 January 2022, using Yahoo! Finance's API [11] for the time frame between 12 July 2005, and 3 November 2017, see Table 1. Most time series had 3035 samples, and some time series had 3032 samples; therefore, we stored each time series's last 3032 samples. Figure 2 presents the time series of BANKEX without and with normalization.

Table 1. Entities in the S&P BSE-BANKEX Dataset.

Number	Entity	Symbol
1	Axis Bank	AXISBANK.BO
2	Bank of Baroda	BANKBARODA.BO
3	Federal Bank	FEDERALBNK.BO
4	HDFC Bank	HDFCBANK.BO
5	ICICI Bank	ICICIBANK.BO
6	Indus Ind Bank	INDUSINDBK.BO
7	Kotak Mahindra	KOTAKBANK.BO
8	PNB	PNB.BO
9	SBI	SBIN.BO
10	Yes Bank	YESBANK.BO

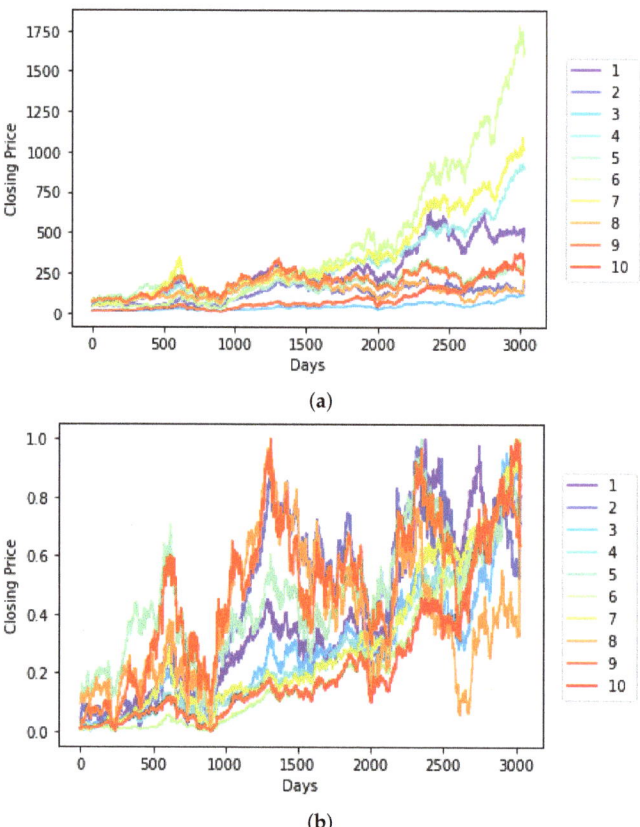

Figure 2. (**a**) Time series in the BANKEX dataset without normalization. Closing Price in Indian Rupee (INR). Daily samples retrieved between 12 July 2005 and 3 November 2017 using Yahoo! Finance's API [11]. All time series with 3032 samples. (**b**) Same time series as in (**a**), but with normalization; closing price normalized between 0 and 1. The numbers from 1 to 10 correspond to the numbers (first column) for each series in Table 1.

3.2. The Activities Dataset

The Activities dataset is a synthetic dataset created resembling weekly activities with five days of high activity and two days of low activity. The dataset has ten time series with 3584 samples per series. Initially, a pattern of five ones followed by two zeros was repeated to obtain a length of 3584 samples. The series was added a slope of 0.0001. The original series was circularly rotated for the remaining series in the dataset, to which noise was added, and each sequence was arbitrarily scaled, so that the peak-to-peak amplitude of each series was different, see Figure 3.

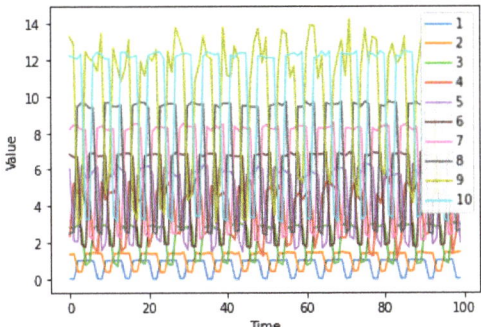

Figure 3. Time series in the Activities dataset without normalization, first 100 samples.

3.3. Datasets Preparation and Partition

Following Section 2.4, every time series was normalized between 0 and 1. We used a window of size $w = 60$ days. We tested for $f = 1$ and $f = 20$ steps ahead. We used the last 251 samples of each time series for testing. We selected arbitrarily the first time series of each dataset for training our LSTM and GRU networks.

3.4. Results

The results are presented in Tables 2–5. Close-to-zero *RMSE* and close-to-one *DA* are preferred. On the Activities dataset, two-tailed Mann–Whitney tests show that for 1-step ahead forecasts, *RMSE* achieved by any RNN is significantly lower than that delivered by the baseline (LSTM & Baseline: $U = 19, n = 10, 10, p < 0.05$. GRU & Baseline: $U = 0, n = 10, 10, p < 0.05$). In addition, GRU delivers significantly lower *RMSE* than LSTM ($U = 91, n = 10, 10, p < 0.05$). In terms of *DA*, both RNN perform equally well and significantly outperform the baseline. For 20-step ahead forecasts, again both RNNs achieve significantly lower *RMSE* than the baseline (LSTM & Baseline: $U = 0, n = 10, 10, p < 0.05$. GRU & Baseline: $U = 0, n = 10, 10, p < 0.05$). This time, LSTM achieves lower *RMSE* than GRU ($U = 10, n = 10, 10, p < 0.05$) and higher *DA* ($U = 81, n = 10, 10, p < 0.05$).

Table 2. One-step ahead forecast on Activities dataset. *RMSE*: columns 2 to 4. *DA*: columns 5 to 7.

	RMSE			*DA*		
	LSTM	**GRU**	**Baseline**	**LSTM**	**GRU**	**Baseline**
Mean	0.2949	0.1268	0.3730	0.6360	0.6236	0.4212
SD	0.0941	0.0425	0.0534	0.0455	0.0377	0.0403

Table 3. Twenty-step ahead forecast on Activities dataset. *RMSE*: columns 2 to 4. *DA*: columns 5 to 7.

	RMSE			*DA*		
	LSTM	**GRU**	**Baseline**	**LSTM**	**GRU**	**Baseline**
Mean	0.1267	0.2048	0.4551	0.6419	0.6261	0.4805
SD	0.0435	0.0683	0.0678	0.0331	0.0255	0.0413

Table 4. One-step ahead forecast on BANKEX dataset. *RMSE*: columns 2 to 4. *DA*: columns 5 to 7.

	RMSE			*DA*		
	LSTM	**GRU**	**Baseline**	**LSTM**	**GRU**	**Baseline**
Mean	0.0163	0.0163	0.0161	0.4884	0.4860	0.4880
SD	0.0052	0.0056	0.0056	0.0398	0.0385	0.0432

Table 5. Twenty-step ahead forecast on BANKEX dataset. *RMSE*: columns 2 to 4. *DA*: columns 5 to 7.

	RMSE			DA		
	LSTM	**GRU**	**Baseline**	**LSTM**	**GRU**	**Baseline**
Mean	0.0543	0.0501	0.0427	0.5004	0.5004	0.4969
SD	0.0093	0.0064	0.0113	0.0071	0.0087	0.0076

On the BANKEX dataset, two-tailed Mann–Whitney tests show that for 1-step ahead forecasts there is no difference among approaches considering *RMSE* (LSTM & Baseline: $U = 51, n = 10, 10, p > 0.05$. GRU & Baseline: $U = 55, n = 10, 10, p > 0.05$. LSTM & GRU: $U = 49, n = 10, 10, p > 0.05$). Similar results are found for 20-step ahead forecasts (LSTM & Baseline: $U = 76, n = 10, 10, p > 0.05$. GRU & Baseline: $U = 67, n = 10, 10, p > 0.05$. LSTM & GRU: $U = 66, n = 10, 10, p > 0.05$). *DA* results are consistent with those obtained for *RMSE*. Figure 4a,b show examples of 20-step ahead forecasts and Figure 5 presents an example of 1-step ahead forecasts. Visual inspection helps understand the results.

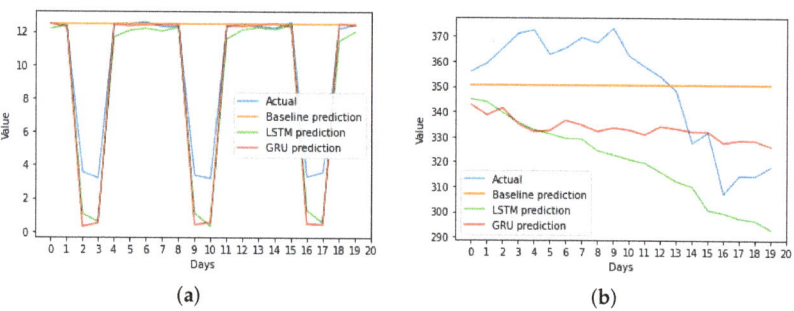

Figure 4. Examples of 20-step ahead forecast. (**a**) Activities dataset. (**b**) BANKEX dataset.

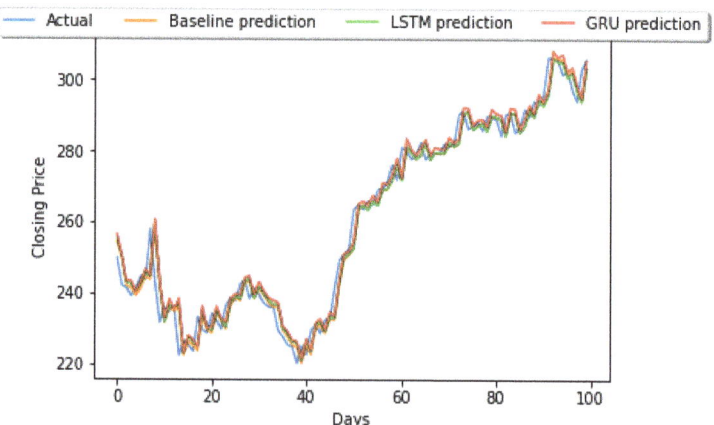

Figure 5. Example of 1-step ahead forecast. Actual and predicted closing price over the first 100 days of the test set Yes Bank. Closing Price in Indian Rupee (INR).

4. Discussion

The motivation for developing a reproducible and open-source framework for time series forecasting relates to our experience in trying to reproduce previous work [6,8]. We found it challenging to find implementations that are simple to understand and replicate. In addition, datasets are not available. We discontinued comparisons with [8], since the dataset we collected was slightly different, and we were unsure if the reported results referred to normalized values or not. If the algorithms are described but the implementations are not available, a dataset is necessary to compare forecasting performance between two algorithms, such that a statistical test can help determine if one algorithm is significantly more accurate than the other [12] (pp. 580–581).

5. Conclusions

We proposed a method for time series forecasting based on LSTM and GRU and showed that these networks can be successfully trained with a single time series to deliver forecasts for unseen time series in a dataset containing patterns that repeat, even with certain variation. Once a network is properly trained, it can be used to forecast other series in the dataset if adequately prepared. We tried and varied several hyperparameters. On sequences, such as those resembling weekly activities that repeat with certain variation, we found an appropriate setting; however, we failed to find an architecture that would outperform a baseline on stock market data; therefore, we assume that we either failed at optimizing the hyperparameters of the networks, the approach is unsuitable for this application, or we would need extra information that is not reflected in stock market series alone. For future work, we plan to benchmark different forecasting methods against the method presented here. In particular, we want to evaluate statistical methods as well as other machine learning methods that have demonstrated strong performance on forecasting tasks [13]. We release our code as well as the dataset used in this study to allow this research to be reproducible.

Author Contributions: P.B., A.B., R.H. and M.L.-L. designed, implemented, and trained the networks, G.V. advised on the project, optimized the networks and code, and wrote the paper. All authors have read and agreed to the published version of the manuscript.

Funding: This research received no external funding.

Data Availability Statement: The code and datasets to reproduce this research are available at: https://github.com/Alebuenoaz/LSTM-and-GRU-Time-Series-Forecasting (accessed on 22 May 2022).

Acknowledgments: We would like to thank the anonymous reviewers for their valuable observations.

Conflicts of Interest: The authors declare no conflict of interest.

References

1. Rumelhart, D.E.; Hinton, G.E.; Williams, R.J. Learning representations by back-propagating errors. *Nature* **1986**, *323*, 533–536. [CrossRef]
2. Hochreiter, S.; Schmidhuber, J. Long short-term memory. *Neural Comput.* **1997**, *9*, 1735–1780. [CrossRef] [PubMed]
3. Cho, K.; Van Merriënboer, B.; Bahdanau, D.; Bengio, Y. On the properties of neural machine translation: Encoder-decoder approaches. *arXiv* **2014**, arXiv:1409.1259.
4. Greff, K.; Srivastava, R.K.; Koutník, J.; Steunebrink, B.R.; Schmidhuber, J. LSTM: A search space odyssey. *IEEE Trans. Neural Netw. Learn. Syst.* **2016**, *28*, 2222–2232. [CrossRef] [PubMed]
5. Chung, J.; Gulcehre, C.; Cho, K.; Bengio, Y. Empirical evaluation of gated recurrent neural networks on sequence modeling. *arXiv* **2014**, arXiv:1412.3555.
6. Siami-Namini, S.; Tavakoli, N.; Namin, A.S. A comparison of ARIMA and LSTM in forecasting time series. In Proceedings of the 2018 17th IEEE International Conference on Machine Learning and Applications (ICMLA), Orlando, FL, USA, 17–20 December 2018; pp. 1394–1401.
7. Box, G.; Jenkins, G. *Time Series Analysis: Forecasting and Control*; Holden-Day: San Francisco, CA, USA, 1970.
8. Balaji, A.J.; Ram, D.H.; Nair, B.B. Applicability of deep learning models for stock price forecasting an empirical study on BANKEX data. *Procedia Comput. Sci.* **2018**, *143*, 947–953. [CrossRef]
9. Kingma, D.P.; Ba, J. Adam: A method for stochastic optimization. *arXiv* **2014**, arXiv:1412.6980.
10. Wang, J.J.; Wang, J.Z.; Zhang, Z.G.; Guo, S.P. Stock index forecasting based on a hybrid model. *Omega* **2012**, *40*, 758–766. [CrossRef]
11. Yahoo. Yahoo! Finance's API. 2022. Available online: https://pypi.org/project/yfinance/ (accessed on 20 January 2022).
12. Alpaydin, E. *Introduction to Machine Learning*; The MIT Press: Cambridge, MA, USA; London, UK, 2014.
13. Makridakis, S.; Spiliotis, E.; Assimakopoulos, V. M5 accuracy competition: Results, findings, and conclusions. *Int. J. Forecast.* **2022**. [CrossRef]

Proceeding Paper

Outliers Impact on Parameter Estimation of Gaussian and Non-Gaussian State Space Models: A Simulation Study †

Fernanda Catarina Pereira [1,*] , **Arminda Manuela Gonçalves** [2,‡] and **Marco Costa** [3,‡]

1   Centre of Mathematics, University of Minho, 4710-057 Braga, Portugal
2   Department of Mathematics and Centre of Mathematics, University of Minho, 4710-057 Braga, Portugal;
    mneves@math.uminho.pt
3   Centre for Research and Development in Mathematics and Applications, Águeda School of Technology and
    Management, University of Aveiro, 3810-193 Aveiro, Portugal; marco@ua.pt
*   Correspondence: id9976@alunos.uminho.pt
†   Presented at the 8th International Conference on Time Series and Forecasting, Gran Canaria, Spain,
    27–30 June 2022.
‡   These authors contributed equally to this work.

Abstract: State space models are powerful and quite flexible tools that allow systems that vary significantly over time due to their formulation to be dealt with, because the models' parameters vary over time. Assuming a known distribution of errors, in particular the Gaussian distribution, parameter estimation is usually performed by maximum likelihood. However, in time series data, it is common to have discrepant values that can impact statistical data analysis. This paper presents a simulation study with several scenarios to find out in which situations outliers can affect the maximum likelihood estimators. The results obtained were evaluated in terms of the difference between the maximum likelihood estimate and the true value of the parameter and the rate of valid estimates. It was found that both for Gaussian and exponential errors, outliers had more impact in two situations: when the sample size is small and the autoregressive parameter is close to 1, and when the sample size is large and the autoregressive parameter is close to 0.25.

Keywords: state space models; parameter estimation; outliers; simulation study

1. Introduction

There are several books in the literature that describe state space models in detail [1–5]. A major advantage of these models is the possibility of explicitly integrating the unobservable components of a time series by relating to each other stochastically.

State space models have in their structure a latent process, the state, which is not observed. The Kalman filter is typically used to estimate it, as it is a recursive algorithm that, at each time, computes the optimal estimator in the sense that it has the minimum mean squared error of the state when the model is fully specified, and one-step-ahead predictions by updating and improving the predictions of the state vector in real time when new observations become available. The Kalman filter was originally developed by control engineering in the 1960s in one of Kalman's papers [6] describing a recursive solution to the linear filter problem for discrete time. Today, this algorithm is applied in various areas of study.

Usually, to estimate the unknown parameters of the model, the maximum likelihood method is used by assuming normality of the errors; however, this assumption cannot always be guaranteed. Non-parametric estimation methods can be a strong contribution when it comes to the initial values of iterative methods used to optimize the likelihood function, which often do not verify the convergence of the algorithms due to the initial choice of these parameters. For example, ref. [7] propose estimators based on the generalized method of moments, the distribution-free estimators, where these estimators do not depend on the distribution of errors.

Nevertheless, even if the assumption of normality of errors is not verified, the Kalman filter still returns optimal predictions within the class of all linear estimators. However, the optimal properties of Kalman filter predictors can only be ensured when all state space models' parameters are known. When the unknown parameter vector is replaced by its estimate, the mean squared error of the estimators is underestimated.

The analysis and modeling of dynamic systems through state space models has been quite useful given its flexibility. In its formulation, the state process is assumed to be a Markov process, allowing optimal predictions of the states and, consequently, observations based only on the optimal estimator of the current state to be obtained.

Despite these advantages, any prediction model is dependent on the quality of the data. Particularly, in many cases, meteorological time series are subject to higher uncertainties, and Kalman filter solutions can be biased [8].

In particular, outliers are an important issue in time series modeling. Time series data are typically dependent on each other and the presence of outliers can impact parameter estimates, forecasting and also inference results [9]. In the presence of incomplete data and outliers in the observed data, ref. [10] developed a modified robust Kalman filter. Ref. [11] showed that linear Gaussian state space models are suitable for estimating the unknown parameters and can consequently affect the state predictions, especially when the measurement error was much larger than the stochasticity of the process. Ref. [12] proposed a non-parametric estimation method based on statistical data depth functions to obtain robust estimates of the mean and the covariance matrix of the asset returns, which is more robust in the presence of outliers, and also does not require parametric assumptions.

This work arose from the project "TO CHAIR—The Optimal Challenges in Irrigation", in which short-term forecast models, with the state space representation, were developed to model the time series of maximum air temperature. For this project, we analyzed data provided by the University of Trás-os-Montes and Alto Douro, corresponding to the maximum air temperature observed in a farm, located in the district of Bragança, between 20 February and 11 October 2019, and data from the website weatherstack.com, corresponding to the forecasts with a time horizon of 1 to 6 days of the same meteorological variable for the same location. The main goal focused on improving the accuracy of the forecasts for the farm. However, there were some modeling problems, particularly regarding the convergence of the numerical method, which arose in the presence of outliers.

Therefore, to evaluate and compare the quality of the estimates of the unknown parameters of the linear invariant state space model in the presence of outliers, this paper presents four simulation studies: the first is based on the linear Gaussian state space model; the second is based on the linear Gaussian state space model with contaminated observations; the third is based on the linear non-Gaussian state space model with exponential errors; and the last one is based on the linear non-Gaussian state space model with exponential errors and contaminated observations. For each of the four studies, several scenarios were tested, in which 2000 samples with valid estimates of size n $(n = 50, 200, 500)$ were simulated. The results obtained were evaluated in terms of the difference between the maximum likelihood estimate and the true value of the parameter and the rate of valid estimates.

2. Simulation Design

In general, the linear univariate state space model is given as follows:

$$Y_t = \beta_t W_t + e_t, \text{ observation equation} \tag{1}$$
$$\beta_t = \mu + \phi(\beta_{t-1} - \mu) + \varepsilon_t, \text{ state equation} \tag{2}$$

where $t = 1, \ldots, n$ is the discrete time and

- Y_t is the observed data;
- W_t is a factor, assumed to be known, that relates the observation Y_t to the state β_t at time t;

- $\{\beta_t\}_{t=1,\ldots,n} \sim AR(1)$, $-1 < \phi < 1$, $E(\beta_t) = \mu$, and $var(\beta_t) = \dfrac{\sigma_\varepsilon^2}{1-\phi^2}$;
- $E(e_t) = 0$, $E(e_t e_s) = 0$, $\forall t \neq s$, and $var(e_t) = \sigma_e^2$;
- $E(\varepsilon_t) = 0$, $E(\varepsilon_t \varepsilon_s) = 0$, $\forall t \neq s$, and $var(\varepsilon_t) = \sigma_\varepsilon^2$;
- $E(e_t \varepsilon_s) = 0$, $\forall t, s$.

This paper aims to investigate under what conditions the presence of outliers affects the estimation of parameters and states in the state space model. Thus, we simulate time series of size n ($n = 50, 200, 500$) using the model defined by Equations (1) and (2). For simplicity's sake, we consider for all simulation studies $W_t = 1$, $\forall t$, and $\mu = 0$, that is

$$Y_t = \beta_t + e_t, \tag{3}$$
$$\beta_t = \phi\beta_{t-1} + \varepsilon_t, \ \ t = 1,\ldots,n. \tag{4}$$

To create the contamination scenario, we study real time series concerning maximum air temperature. We used data from two different sources: the first corresponds to daily records of maximum air temperature between 20 February and 11 October 2019 (234 observations) through a portable weather station installed on a farm located in the Bragança district in northeastern Portugal; the second database corresponds to forecasts from the weatherstack.com website. These forecasts have a time horizon of up to 6 days; this means that, for a certain time t, we have forecasts given at times $t - 6, t - 5, \ldots, t - 1$.

So, first we took the difference between the recorded/observed maximum temperature and the website's forecasts, say, $\Lambda_{t,(h)}$, where t is the time, in days, and h is the time horizon of the forecasts, $h = 1, \ldots, 6$ days. Next, we calculated the percentage of outliers of $\Lambda_{t,(h)}$, whose percentage was on average 5%. Regarding the variable $\Lambda_{t,(h)}$, outliers were removed and replaced by linear interpolation, say, $\Lambda_{t,(h)}^*$, in order to remove the contamination present in the data, and its mean was subtracted, $\Lambda_{t,(h)}^* - mean(\Lambda_{t,(h)}^*)$, so that it had zero mean. Then, for each time horizon h ($h = 1, \ldots, 6$), the model with a state space representation presented by Equations (3) and (4) was fitted to the data $\Lambda_{t,(h)}^* - mean(\Lambda_{t,(h)}^*)$.

In order to establish a relationship between the estimates of parameters ϕ, σ_ε^2 and σ_e^2, that were obtained from the "non-contaminated" data, and the magnitude of the outliers of $\Lambda_{t,(h)}$, the linear regression model was fitted, whose relationship is given by

$$k = 1.8874 + 3.5161\sqrt{\dfrac{\sigma_\varepsilon^2}{1-\phi^2} + \sigma_e^2} \tag{5}$$

where $k = |\text{outliers of } \Lambda_{t,(h)} - \text{mean of } \Lambda_{t,(h)} \text{ without outliers}|$, is the magnitude of the outliers, and $\dfrac{\sigma_\varepsilon^2}{1-\phi^2} + \sigma_e^2$ is the total variance of Y_t. In total, $\Lambda_{t,(h)}$ ($h = 1, \ldots, 6$) shows 59 outliers.

In this work, four simulation scenarios were tested:

1. The first is based on the linear Gaussian state space model given by

$$Y_t = \beta_t + e_t, \ e_t \sim \mathcal{N}(0, \sigma_e^2)$$
$$\beta_t = \phi\beta_{t-1} + \varepsilon_t, \ \varepsilon_t \sim \mathcal{N}(0, \sigma_\varepsilon^2), \ \ t = 1,\ldots,n$$

2. The second is based on the linear Gaussian state space model with contaminated observations.
   To contaminate the model, the deterministic factor k, given in (5), is added in this way

$$Y_t = \beta_t + e_t + I_t k, \ e_t \sim \mathcal{N}(0, \sigma_e^2)$$
$$\beta_t = \phi \beta_{t-1} + \varepsilon_t, \ \varepsilon_t \sim \mathcal{N}(0, \sigma_\varepsilon^2),$$

where $I_t \sim \mathcal{B}(1, 0.05)$.

3. The third is based on the linear non-Gaussian state space model with exponential errors defined by

$$Y_t = \beta_t + e_t, \ e_t \sim \text{Exp}(\lambda_e) - \frac{1}{\lambda_e}$$
$$\beta_t = \phi \beta_{t-1} + \varepsilon_t, \ \varepsilon_t \sim \text{Exp}(\lambda_\varepsilon) - \frac{1}{\lambda_\varepsilon}, \ t = 1, \ldots, n$$

4. The last one is based on the linear non-Gaussian state space model with exponential errors and contaminated observations. Similar to scenario 2, we have

$$Y_t = \beta_t + e_t + I_t k, \ e_t \sim \text{Exp}(\lambda_e) - \frac{1}{\lambda_e}$$
$$\beta_t = \phi \beta_{t-1} + \varepsilon_t, \ \varepsilon_t \sim \text{Exp}(\lambda_\varepsilon) - \frac{1}{\lambda_\varepsilon}, \ t = 1, \ldots, n$$

where $I_t \sim \mathcal{B}(1, 0.05)$, and k given in (5).

For each of the four scenarios, sample sizes of $n = 50, 200, 500$ were simulated. In this study, a range of values were simulated for ϕ (0.25, 0.75), and σ_ε^2 and σ_e^2 (0.10, 1.00, 5.00, 0.10, 2.00, 0.05). For each parameter combination, 2000 replicates with valid estimates were considered, i.e., estimates within the parameter space: $-1 < \phi < 1$, $\sigma_\varepsilon > 0$, and $\sigma_e > 0$. In all simulations, we take the initial state $\beta_0 = 0$ in the Kalman filter.

To evaluate the quality of the parameter estimates, we considered the Root Mean Square Error (RMSE),

$$\text{RMSE}(\Theta) = \sqrt{\frac{1}{2000} \sum_{i=1}^{2000} \left(\Theta_i - \widehat{\Theta}_i \right)^2}$$

the Mean Absolute Error (MAE),

$$\text{MAE}(\Theta) = \frac{1}{2000} \sum_{i=1}^{2000} \left| \Theta_i - \widehat{\Theta}_i \right|$$

the Mean Absolute Percentage Error (MAPE),

$$\text{MAPE}(\Theta) = \frac{1}{2000} \sum_{i=1}^{2000} \left| \frac{\Theta_i - \widehat{\Theta}_i}{\Theta_i} \right| \times 100$$

$\Theta = (\phi, \sigma_\varepsilon^2, \sigma_e^2)$ and the convergence rate. The convergence rate provides information about the percentage of valid estimates among all simulations (simulations with valid and non-valid estimates). The convergence rate is given by the number of valid simulated estimates (in this case, 2000) divided by the number of total simulations.

To estimate the unknown parameters of the state space model (3) and (4) $\Theta = (\phi, \sigma_\varepsilon^2, \sigma_e^2)$ of each simulation, the maximum likelihood method was used by assuming the normality of the disturbances for all four scenarios. Log-likelihood maximization was performed by the Newton–Raphson numerical method. In this study, the R package "astsa" was used [3,13,14].

3. Results

In this section, the simulation results are presented. Tables 1–3 present the results of the simulations in terms of the RMSE, MAE, MAPE (%) and the convergence rate (%) for sample sizes $n = 50$, $n = 200$ and $n = 500$, respectively, considering both non-contaminated (NC) and contaminated Gaussian errors. Tables 4–6 show the simulation results considering contaminated and non-contaminated exponential errors.

Table 1. RMSE, MAE, MAPE and convergence rate of Θ with 2000 simulations of sample sizes $n = 50$, considering Gaussian errors (NC = Non-Contaminated; C = Contaminated).

Parameters				RMSE			MAE			MAPE (%)			Convergence Rate
ϕ	σ_ε^2	σ_e^2		ϕ	σ_ε^2	σ_e^2	ϕ	σ_ε^2	σ_e^2	ϕ	σ_ε^2	σ_e^2	(%)
	0.10 0.05		NC	0.2542	0.0563	0.0502	0.1894	0.0484	0.0452	75.7423	48.3383	90.4927	$2000/2679 \simeq 75\%$
			C	0.3823	0.3325	0.3095	0.2983	0.2375	0.2052	119.3057	237.5420	410.4236	$2000/3059 \simeq 65\%$
	1.00 0.10		NC	0.2598	0.4638	0.3699	0.1934	0.3634	0.2632	77.3528	36.3408	263.1570	$2000/2466 \simeq 81\%$
			C	0.3514	1.3520	1.2319	0.2717	1.0957	0.7552	108.6993	109.5651	755.1521	$2000/2295 \simeq 87\%$
	5.00 2.00		NC	0.2880	2.7078	2.2864	0.2184	2.2837	1.9787	87.3520	45.6746	98.9341	$2000/2515 \simeq 80\%$
			C	0.3820	6.3580	5.6467	0.2994	5.1446	4.1499	119.7610	102.8927	207.4966	$2000/2223 \simeq 90\%$
0.25	0.10 1.00		NC	0.3320	0.6580	0.6630	0.2634	0.4794	0.5380	105.3703	479.3548	53.7974	$2000/3520 \simeq 57\%$
			C	0.4851	1.5345	1.1760	0.3916	1.0672	0.9876	156.6558	1067.1860	98.7612	$2000/2533 \simeq 79\%$
	2.00 5.00		NC	0.3097	3.3616	3.3738	0.2404	2.6656	2.7813	96.1717	133.2785	55.6251	$2000/3137 \simeq 64\%$
			C	0.4735	6.8657	5.6124	0.3706	4.8976	4.7397	148.2420	244.8814	94.7940	$2000/2265 \simeq 88\%$
	0.05 0.10		NC	0.2672	0.0750	0.0727	0.2077	0.0621	0.0620	83.0659	124.1018	62.0471	$2000/3015 \simeq 66\%$
			C	0.4473	0.3198	0.3676	0.3585	0.2216	0.2602	143.4173	443.1005	260.2065	$2000/3033 \simeq 66\%$
	0.10 0.05		NC	0.1595	0.0503	0.0367	0.1228	0.0413	0.0309	16.3687	41.2797	61.7597	$2000/2265 \simeq 88\%$
			C	0.4356	0.3444	0.5165	0.3019	0.1916	0.3533	40.2592	191.5928	706.5637	$2000/3843 \simeq 52\%$
	1.00 0.10		NC	0.1190	0.3430	0.1885	0.0917	0.2728	0.1408	12.2261	27.2783	140.7727	$2000/2374 \simeq 84\%$
			C	0.3056	1.3890	2.3812	0.2071	0.9184	1.7949	27.6161	91.8402	1794.8840	$2000/2552 \simeq 78\%$
	5.00 2.00		NC	0.1364	2.2249	1.5857	0.1062	1.8382	1.3111	14.1653	36.7633	65.5527	$2000/2220 \simeq 90\%$
			C	0.2899	6.8220	10.8105	0.1897	4.5106	8.5797	25.2983	90.2117	428.9829	$2000/2192 \simeq 91\%$
0.75	0.10 1.00		NC	0.3152	0.4849	0.4972	0.2410	0.3009	0.3666	32.1341	300.8559	36.6612	$2000/2695 \simeq 74\%$
			C	0.5611	1.4225	1.4693	0.3981	0.8159	1.2037	53.0740	815.9315	120.3714	$2000/2751 \simeq 73\%$
	2.00 5.00		NC	0.2362	2.6149	2.4755	0.1784	1.8878	1.9114	23.7931	94.3914	38.2272	$2000/2228 \simeq 90\%$
			C	0.4479	6.7006	7.5337	0.3085	4.2198	6.1402	41.1287	210.9902	122.8036	$2000/2302 \simeq 87\%$
	0.05 0.10		NC	0.2296	0.0582	0.0526	0.1743	0.0429	0.0414	23.2456	85.7212	41.3812	$2000/2223 \simeq 90\%$
			C	0.5148	0.3089	0.4349	0.3731	0.1787	0.3175	49.7412	357.4894	317.4564	$2000/3234 \simeq 62\%$

As expected, contamination had an impact on the performance of the maximum likelihood estimators.

First, it is seen that for small sample sizes and non-contaminated errors, the convergence rate tends to decrease. For example, for $n = 500$ in the case of non-contaminated Gaussian errors, the convergence rate was over 72%, while for $n = 50$, it was over 57%. For contaminated Gaussian and exponential errors, the convergence rate decreased compared to non-contaminated errors.

Overall, an improvement in the rate of valid estimates (convergence rate) is noticeable when $\phi = 0.75$ compared to $\phi = 0.25$ in the case of non-contaminated Gaussian and exponential errors. In the case of contaminated Gaussian and exponential errors, this behavior only occurred when $n = 500$.

Table 2. RMSE, MAE, MAPE and convergence rate of Θ with 2000 simulations of sample sizes $n = 200$, considering Gaussian errors (NC = Non-Contaminated; C = Contaminated).

Parameters				RMSE			MAE			MAPE (%)			Convergence Rate
ϕ	σ_ε^2	σ_e^2		ϕ	σ_ε^2	σ_e^2	ϕ	σ_ε^2	σ_e^2	ϕ	σ_ε^2	σ_e^2	(%)
	0.10 0.05		NC	0.2125	0.0533	0.0486	0.1552	0.0481	0.0445	62.0843	48.0637	89.0227	$2000/2142 \simeq 93\%$
			C	0.4414	0.2937	0.3973	0.3511	0.2170	0.3170	140.4550	216.9786	634.0003	$2000/3415 \simeq 59\%$
	1.00 0.10		NC	0.1827	0.3872	0.3342	0.1263	0.2890	0.2466	50.5172	28.8980	246.6108	$2000/2158 \simeq 93\%$
			C	0.3302	1.2494	1.3655	0.2531	1.1183	0.8983	101.2448	111.8291	898.3335	$2000/2339 \simeq 86\%$
	5.00 2.00		NC	0.2257	2.4857	2.2298	0.1647	2.1584	1.9656	65.8709	43.1676	98.2816	$2000/2114 \simeq 95\%$
			C	0.3210	6.0353	5.7585	0.2525	5.2843	4.1940	101.0001	105.6860	209.6988	$2000/2171 \simeq 92\%$
0.25	0.10 1.00		NC	0.3294	0.5910	0.5952	0.2693	0.4203	0.4418	107.7206	420.3230	44.1772	$2000/3064 \simeq 65\%$
			C	0.5079	1.1490	1.2565	0.4159	0.7094	1.1202	166.3406	709.3999	112.0214	$2000/2934 \simeq 68\%$
	2.00 5.00		NC	0.2942	3.1051	3.0346	0.2352	2.4888	2.4204	94.0959	124.4377	48.4077	$2000/2432 \simeq 82\%$
			C	0.4888	5.2005	5.9769	0.3932	3.6031	5.3909	157.2640	180.1539	107.8174	$2000/2355 \simeq 85\%$
	0.05 0.10		NC	0.2512	0.0690	0.0672	0.1992	0.0574	0.0555	79.6690	114.7299	55.4981	$2000/2353 \simeq 85\%$
			C	0.4992	0.2898	0.3841	0.4026	0.1951	0.3182	161.0268	390.1951	318.2143	$2000/3550 \simeq 56\%$
	0.10 0.05		NC	0.0791	0.0306	0.0223	0.0613	0.0243	0.0177	8.1741	24.2574	35.4005	$2000/2020 \simeq 99\%$
			C	0.3249	0.1774	0.6307	0.1998	0.1042	0.5622	26.6395	104.1552	1124.3160	$2000/5655 \simeq 35\%$
	1.00 0.10		NC	0.0557	0.1838	0.1057	0.0442	0.1468	0.0859	5.8966	14.6823	85.8500	$2000/2175 \simeq 92\%$
			C	0.2726	0.7185	2.5998	0.1459	0.5113	2.3158	19.4529	51.1345	2315.7740	$2000/3564 \simeq 56\%$
	5.00 2.00		NC	0.0763	1.4259	0.9946	0.0596	1.1414	0.7971	7.9484	22.8271	39.8563	$2000/2022 \simeq 99\%$
			C	0.1241	3.4324	10.9591	0.0944	2.3950	10.0756	12.5843	47.8992	503.7812	$2000/2054 \simeq 97\%$
0.75	0.10 1.00		NC	0.2457	0.3409	0.3348	0.1779	0.1836	0.2116	23.7169	183.5833	21.1571	$2000/2139 \simeq 94\%$
			C	0.4690	0.8662	1.5181	0.3137	0.4036	1.3994	41.8257	403.6151	139.9393	$2000/2673 \simeq 75\%$
	2.00 5.00		NC	0.1293	1.4609	1.3363	0.0943	1.0084	0.9691	12.5672	50.4175	19.3819	$2000/2012 \simeq 99\%$
			C	0.3233	3.2270	7.9895	0.1826	1.8840	7.3360	24.3493	94.1989	146.7208	$2000/2320 \simeq 86\%$
	0.05 0.10		NC	0.1246	0.0326	0.0291	0.0927	0.0232	0.0216	12.3547	46.3956	21.6304	$2000/2025 \simeq 99\%$
			C	0.3633	0.2014	0.4895	0.2410	0.1021	0.4373	32.1288	204.1943	437.3301	$2000/4233 \simeq 47\%$

When the errors are not contaminated, the RMSE, MAE and MAPE tend to decrease with increasing sample size. However, this premise is not true when the errors are contaminated. In fact, it was found that for both Gaussian and exponential errors, outliers had more impact in two situations: when $\phi = 0.75$ and $n = 50$ (Tables 1 and 4); and when $\phi = 0.25$ and $n = 500$ (Tables 3 and 6). This impact is reflected in the RMSE, MAE and MAPE, which produced very high values.

Furthermore, there are many cases where, for example, the RMSE of the estimators of the contaminated errors are 3 times higher than the RMSE of the non-contaminated errors. For example, in the case of the Gaussian errors with $n = 500$, $\phi = 0.25$, $\sigma_\varepsilon^2 = 0.10$ and $\sigma_e^2 = 0.05$, the RMSE of ϕ, σ_ε^2 and σ_e^2 of the contaminated Gaussian errors were about 3, 6 and 11 times higher, respectively, compared to the non-contaminated Gaussian errors (Table 3).

On the other hand, comparing both the Gaussian and exponential error cases, we find that there are no significant differences in the convergence rate, as well as in the efficiency of the autoregressive ϕ estimator. However, the RMSE, MAE and MAPE of the variance estimators, σ_ε^2 and σ_e^2, are in general higher in the case of exponential errors.

Table 3. RMSE, MAE, MAPE and convergence rate of Θ with 2000 simulations of sample sizes $n = 500$, considering Gaussian errors (NC = non-contaminated; C = contaminated).

Parameters				RMSE			MAE			MAPE (%)			Convergence Rate
ϕ	σ_ε^2	σ_e^2		ϕ	σ_ε^2	σ_e^2	ϕ	σ_ε^2	σ_e^2	ϕ	σ_ε^2	σ_e^2	(%)
0.25	0.10 0.05		NC	0.1670	0.0487	0.0451	0.1246	0.0440	0.0410	49.8262	43.9675	81.9983	2000/2090 ≃ 96%
			C	0.5099	0.2843	0.4946	0.4266	0.2027	0.4261	170.6503	202.6937	852.1144	2000/3936 ≃ 51%
	1.00 0.10		NC	0.1322	0.3212	0.2834	0.0926	0.2411	0.2142	37.0469	24.1096	214.2324	2000/2073 ≃ 96%
			C	0.3757	1.0511	1.6760	0.2954	0.9210	1.3679	118.1795	92.1025	1367.9340	2000/2309 ≃ 87%
	5.00 2.00		NC	0.1665	2.1973	2.0204	0.1219	1.9401	1.8018	48.7737	38.8022	90.0924	2000/2015 ≃ 99%
			C	0.3571	5.2313	7.1197	0.2745	4.4927	6.0116	109.7836	89.8549	300.5794	2000/2154 ≃ 93%
	0.10 1.00		NC	0.3186	0.5157	0.5157	0.2655	0.3497	0.3555	106.1993	349.7172	35.5477	2000/2793 ≃ 72%
			C	0.5660	1.0072	1.2870	0.4735	0.5918	1.1856	189.3834	591.7733	118.5649	2000/2666 ≃ 75%
	2.00 5.00		NC	0.2596	2.7002	2.6426	0.2080	2.1282	2.0529	83.2062	106.4111	41.0575	2000/2102 ≃ 95%
			C	0.4327	4.9215	5.7057	0.3449	3.4861	5.2227	137.9698	174.3029	104.4536	2000/2347 ≃ 85%
	0.05 0.10		NC	0.2375	0.0645	0.0628	0.1900	0.0528	0.0510	75.9833	105.5881	50.9948	2000/2082 ≃ 96%
			C	0.5787	0.2691	0.4908	0.5039	0.1635	0.4430	201.5559	326.9245	443.0177	2000/4751 ≃ 42%
0.75	0.10 0.05		NC	0.0477	0.0195	0.0142	0.0373	0.0154	0.0114	4.9771	15.3516	22.7729	2000/2003 ≃ 100%
			C	0.1696	0.0817	0.6618	0.1106	0.0549	0.6455	14.7532	54.8753	1291.0500	2000/2501 ≃ 80%
	1.00 0.10		NC	0.0395	0.1343	0.0782	0.0318	0.1081	0.0647	4.2341	10.8147	64.6665	2000/2090 ≃ 96%
			C	0.0732	0.3663	2.5760	0.0587	0.2834	2.5003	7.8213	28.3405	2500.3230	2000/2815 ≃ 71%
	5.00 2.00		NC	0.0474	0.9427	0.6600	0.0371	0.7485	0.5228	4.9477	14.9700	26.1379	2000/2005 ≃ 100%
			C	0.0744	1.9273	10.4652	0.0578	1.4293	10.1291	7.7126	28.5863	506.4527	2000/2020 ≃ 99%
	0.10 1.00		NC	0.1732	0.2068	0.2027	0.1219	0.1011	0.1174	16.2546	101.1061	11.7441	2000/2001 ≃ 100%
			C	0.2439	0.5109	1.5706	0.2001	0.2151	1.5087	26.6834	215.1086	150.8725	2000/2390 ≃ 84%
	2.00 5.00		NC	0.0723	0.7514	0.7300	0.0554	0.5623	0.5663	7.3812	28.1170	11.3252	2000/2000 ≃ 100%
			C	0.1162	1.6095	7.9601	0.0903	1.0526	7.6541	12.0342	52.6321	153.0817	2000/2014 ≃ 99%
	0.05 0.10		NC	0.0689	0.0175	0.0159	0.0528	0.0131	0.0122	7.0341	26.2519	12.2090	2000/2002 ≃ 100%
			C	0.1914	0.1201	0.5832	0.1534	0.0547	0.5635	20.4470	109.4875	563.4770	2000/2293 ≃ 87%

Table 4. RMSE, MAE, MAPE and convergence rate of Θ with 2000 simulations of sample sizes $n = 50$, considering exponential errors (NC = non-contaminated; C = contaminated).

Parameters				RMSE			MAE			MAPE (%)			Convergence rate
ϕ	σ_ε^2	σ_e^2		ϕ	σ_ε^2	σ_e^2	ϕ	σ_ε^2	σ_e^2	ϕ	σ_ε^2	σ_e^2	(%)
0.25	0.10 0.05		NC	0.2403	0.0621	0.0520	0.1799	0.0504	0.0457	71.9672	50.3763	91.4927	2000/2635 ≃ 76%
			C	0.3995	0.3399	0.3274	0.3134	0.2428	0.2110	125.3731	242.7797	422.0013	2000/3048 ≃ 66%
	1.00 0.10		NC	0.2591	0.5315	0.3983	0.1934	0.4320	0.2635	77.3567	43.2020	263.5235	2000/2442 ≃ 82%
			C	0.3516	1.3525	1.3138	0.2744	1.0954	0.7735	109.7515	109.5363	773.5130	2000/2313 ≃ 86%
	5.00 2.00		NC	0.2810	3.0601	2.4320	0.2140	2.4909	1.9947	85.6126	49.8187	99.7367	2000/2489 ≃ 80%
			C	0.3788	6.3086	5.6419	0.2971	5.0720	4.0209	118.8333	101.4390	201.0444	2000/2221 ≃ 90%
	0.10 1.00		NC	0.3352	0.7070	0.7121	0.2656	0.4958	0.6145	106.2327	495.7865	61.4506	2000/3845 ≃ 52%
			C	0.4979	1.4952	1.2090	0.4045	1.0352	1.0202	161.7847	1035.2270	102.0164	2000/2500 ≃ 80%
	2.00 5.00		NC	0.3036	3.5020	3.6159	0.2359	2.7018	3.0956	94.3541	135.0912	61.9127	2000/3273 ≃ 61%
			C	0.4756	7.4254	5.7965	0.3764	5.2303	4.8901	150.5748	261.5164	97.8024	2000/2281 ≃ 88%
	0.05 0.10		NC	0.2712	0.0818	0.0775	0.2089	0.0644	0.0676	83.5522	128.8785	67.6088	2000/3045 ≃ 66%
			C	0.4505	0.3498	0.3421	0.3573	0.2485	0.2372	142.9146	496.9232	237.1900	2000/3014 ≃ 66%

Table 4. *Cont.*

Parameters				RMSE			MAE			MAPE (%)			Convergence Rate
ϕ	σ_ε^2	σ_e^2		ϕ	σ_ε^2	σ_e^2	ϕ	σ_ε^2	σ_e^2	ϕ	σ_ε^2	σ_e^2	(%)
	0.10 0.05		NC	0.1611	0.0564	0.0398	0.1246	0.0450	0.0322	16.6099	45.0059	64.3029	$2000/2273 \simeq 88\%$
			C	0.4359	0.3223	0.5405	0.3033	0.1875	0.3750	40.4453	187.5322	750.0313	$2000/3694 \simeq 54\%$
	1.00 0.10		NC	0.1175	0.4488	0.1929	0.0925	0.3574	0.1397	12.3275	35.7367	139.7342	$2000/2364 \simeq 85\%$
			C	0.3433	1.3662	2.5133	0.2284	0.9272	1.8790	30.4537	92.7218	1879.0050	$2000/2470 \simeq 81\%$
	5.00 2.00		NC	0.1448	2.7020	1.7189	0.1120	2.1216	1.3609	14.9294	42.4323	68.0429	$2000/2181 \simeq 92\%$
0.75			C	0.3000	6.8179	11.0149	0.1977	4.5487	8.6278	26.3555	90.9748	431.3905	$2000/2176 \simeq 92\%$
	0.10 1.00		NC	0.3093	0.4945	0.5622	0.2368	0.3007	0.4524	31.5769	300.7228	45.2368	$2000/2672 \simeq 75\%$
			C	0.5765	1.3806	1.5393	0.4103	0.7817	1.2490	54.7124	781.7267	124.9006	$2000/2792 \simeq 72\%$
	2.00 5.00		NC	0.2394	2.8641	2.9144	0.1801	1.9810	2.3408	24.0172	99.0487	46.8162	$2000/2221 \simeq 90\%$
			C	0.4688	6.9340	7.5328	0.3241	4.3006	6.0393	43.2112	215.0307	120.7854	$2000/2277 \simeq 88\%$
	0.05 0.10		NC	0.2345	0.0614	0.0594	0.1767	0.0437	0.0484	23.5599	87.3926	48.3987	$2000/2246 \simeq 89\%$
			C	0.5399	0.3405	0.4259	0.4039	0.2083	0.3024	53.8548	416.5115	302.3952	$2000/3314 \simeq 60\%$

Table 5. RMSE, MAE, MAPE and convergence rate of Θ with 2000 simulations of sample sizes $n = 200$, considering exponential errors (NC = non-contaminated; C = contaminated).

Parameters				RMSE			MAE			MAPE (%)			Convergence Rate
ϕ	σ_ε^2	σ_e^2		ϕ	σ_ε^2	σ_e^2	ϕ	σ_ε^2	σ_e^2	ϕ	σ_ε^2	σ_e^2	(%)
	0.10 0.05		NC	0.2195	0.0567	0.0502	0.1605	0.0501	0.0458	64.1779	50.0747	91.6168	$2000/2185 \simeq 92\%$
			C	0.4489	0.2919	0.4062	0.3589	0.2159	0.3230	143.5695	215.8788	645.9832	$2000/3303 \simeq 61\%$
	1.00 0.10		NC	0.1942	0.4247	0.3510	0.1343	0.3304	0.2550	53.7222	33.0384	255.0102	$2000/2194 \simeq 91\%$
			C	0.3275	1.2229	1.3829	0.2520	1.0916	0.8967	100.8199	109.1563	896.7205	$2000/2299 \simeq 87\%$
	5.00 2.00		NC	0.2352	2.6233	2.2958	0.1709	2.2450	2.0030	68.3418	44.8991	100.1478	$2000/2120 \simeq 94\%$
0.25			C	0.3157	6.0485	5.8589	0.2491	5.2427	4.2303	99.6284	104.8537	211.5132	$2000/2170 \simeq 92\%$
	0.10 1.00		NC	0.3263	0.6068	0.6071	0.2698	0.4264	0.4734	107.9090	426.4313	47.3421	$2000/3235 \simeq 62\%$
			C	0.5063	1.1797	1.2615	0.4136	0.7430	1.1099	165.4252	743.0232	110.9928	$2000/2793 \simeq 72\%$
	2.00 5.00		NC	0.2871	3.0873	3.0756	0.2286	2.4294	2.4630	91.4476	121.4710	49.2608	$2000/2409 \simeq 83\%$
			C	0.4800	5.3433	5.8893	0.3878	3.7179	5.2539	155.1106	185.8963	105.0775	$2000/2349 \simeq 85\%$
	0.05 0.10		NC	0.2547	0.0706	0.0689	0.2040	0.0582	0.0576	81.5998	116.3832	57.6243	$2000/2381 \simeq 84\%$
			C	0.4861	0.2824	0.3672	0.3959	0.1923	0.3042	158.3634	384.6917	304.2286	$2000/3600 \simeq 56\%$
	0.10 0.05		NC	0.0796	0.0350	0.0233	0.0617	0.0274	0.0186	8.2315	27.4339	37.1357	$2000/2037 \simeq 98\%$
			C	0.3272	0.2014	0.6101	0.1953	0.1114	0.5404	26.0350	111.3510	1080.8030	$2000/5646 \simeq 35\%$
	1.00 0.10		NC	0.0597	0.2508	0.1085	0.0474	0.1994	0.0873	6.3241	19.9427	87.2755	$2000/2177 \simeq 92\%$
			C	0.2891	0.7251	2.6068	0.1467	0.5148	2.3368	19.5576	51.4762	2336.7630	$2000/3530 \simeq 57\%$
	5.00 2.00		NC	0.0746	1.6329	1.0466	0.0594	1.3146	0.8439	7.9157	26.2910	42.1946	$2000/2025 \simeq 99\%$
0.75			C	0.1272	3.6999	10.6605	0.0940	2.5298	9.7850	12.5288	50.5952	489.2506	$2000/2058 \simeq 97\%$
	0.10 1.00		NC	0.2397	0.3397	0.3613	0.1728	0.1807	0.2566	23.0433	180.7138	25.6634	$2000/2212 \simeq 90\%$
			C	0.4477	0.8176	1.5542	0.3042	0.3849	1.4218	40.5591	384.9222	142.1828	$2000/2667 \simeq 75\%$
	2.00 5.00		NC	0.1296	1.5155	1.5429	0.0951	1.0538	1.1744	12.6814	52.6910	23.4870	$2000/2015 \simeq 99\%$
			C	0.3411	3.2286	8.1396	0.1906	1.8699	7.4604	25.4199	93.4933	149.2072	$2000/2354 \simeq 85\%$
	0.05 0.10		NC	0.1199	0.0326	0.0327	0.0888	0.0235	0.0253	11.8369	46.9942	25.2911	$2000/2029 \simeq 99\%$
			C	0.4057	0.1971	0.4953	0.2636	0.0980	0.4410	35.1415	196.0500	440.9552	$2000/4253 \simeq 47\%$

Table 6. RMSE, MAE, MAPE and convergence rate of Θ with 2000 simulations of sample sizes $n = 500$, considering exponential errors (NC = non-contaminated; C = contaminated).

Parameters				RMSE			MAE			MAPE (%)			Convergence Rate
ϕ	σ_ε^2	σ_e^2		ϕ	σ_ε^2	σ_e^2	ϕ	σ_ε^2	σ_e^2	ϕ	σ_ε^2	σ_e^2	(%)
0.25													
	0.10	0.05	NC	0.1774	0.0502	0.0459	0.1295	0.0449	0.0415	51.8133	44.9298	83.0451	2000/2101 ≃ 95%
			C	0.5105	0.2796	0.4923	0.4312	0.2000	0.4234	172.4715	200.0235	846.7976	2000/3882 ≃ 52%
	1.00	0.10	NC	0.1360	0.3393	0.2890	0.0925	0.2583	0.2157	37.0141	25.8315	215.7496	2000/2068 ≃ 97%
			C	0.3751	1.0426	1.6910	0.2938	0.9117	1.3735	117.5078	91.1686	1373.5180	2000/2331 ≃ 86%
	5.00	2.00	NC	0.1704	2.2503	2.0470	0.1234	1.9625	1.8020	49.3534	39.2493	90.0986	2000/2017 ≃ 99%
			C	0.3479	5.3039	7.0687	0.2679	4.5285	5.9227	107.1780	90.5707	296.1330	2000/2129 ≃ 94%
	0.10	1.00	NC	0.3131	0.5300	0.5411	0.2597	0.3703	0.3968	103.8980	370.3198	39.6789	2000/2816 ≃ 71%
			C	0.5597	1.0212	1.2769	0.4684	0.6074	1.1618	187.3698	607.3962	116.1793	2000/2652 ≃ 75%
	2.00	5.00	NC	0.2601	2.7288	2.7233	0.2073	2.1620	2.1463	82.9108	108.0979	42.9251	2000/2126 ≃ 94%
			C	0.4306	4.9082	5.7249	0.3452	3.5071	5.1919	138.0972	175.3540	103.8379	2000/2317 ≃ 86%
	0.05	0.10	NC	0.2376	0.0645	0.0627	0.1901	0.0524	0.0510	76.0432	104.7235	50.9923	2000/2074 ≃ 96%
			C	0.5858	0.2454	0.4984	0.5118	0.1446	0.4560	204.7275	289.2989	456.0194	2000/4715 ≃ 42%
0.75													
	0.10	0.05	NC	0.0475	0.0231	0.0155	0.0372	0.0181	0.0123	4.9720	18.1002	24.5343	2000/2004 ≃ 100%
			C	0.1591	0.0842	0.6609	0.1062	0.0545	0.6454	14.1550	54.5197	1290.8090	2000/2474 ≃ 81%
	1.00	0.10	NC	0.0384	0.1704	0.0773	0.0307	0.1373	0.0643	4.0941	13.7260	64.3178	2000/2080 ≃ 96%
			C	0.0721	0.3674	2.5627	0.0581	0.2882	2.4862	7.7527	28.8233	2486.2120	2000/2794 ≃ 72%
	5.00	2.00	NC	0.0466	1.0946	0.6805	0.0370	0.8577	0.5377	4.9267	17.1536	26.8825	2000/2003 ≃ 100%
			C	0.0724	1.9116	10.6844	0.0572	1.4456	10.3496	7.6297	28.9121	517.4798	2000/2039 ≃ 98%
	0.10	1.00	NC	0.1725	0.1945	0.2149	0.1211	0.0988	0.1473	16.1486	98.8105	14.7318	2000/2010 ≃ 100%
			C	0.2492	0.5142	1.5627	0.1972	0.2080	1.4974	26.2946	208.0308	149.7398	2000/2384 ≃ 84%
	2.00	5.00	NC	0.0760	0.8252	0.9283	0.0576	0.6068	0.7308	7.6842	30.3421	14.6165	2000/2001 ≃ 100%
			C	0.1204	1.7123	7.9869	0.0934	1.0745	7.6659	12.4592	53.7261	153.3177	2000/2013 ≃ 99%
	0.05	0.10	NC	0.0684	0.0185	0.0190	0.0524	0.0138	0.0149	6.9855	27.6962	14.9040	2000/2001 ≃ 100%
			C	0.1908	0.1162	0.5854	0.1535	0.0531	0.5665	20.4642	106.2381	566.4536	2000/2334 ≃ 86%

4. Discussion

In this work, outliers were found to impact the performance of the Maximum Likelihood estimators. In particular, it was found through the simulation study that outliers have a very significant impact in both cases: when the sample size is small and the autoregressive parameter is close to 1, and when the sample size is large and the autoregressive parameter is close to 0.25. This impact was reflected in the RMSE, MAE and MAPE values which, in many cases, were higher compared to the case of non-contaminated errors.

Moreover, we notice that the rate of valid estimates (convergence rate) is higher for large sample sizes, and is more evident for non-contaminated Gaussian and exponential errors. On the other hand, it is also important to have large sample sizes to avoid problems related to parameter estimation [11]. In general, the convergence rate is lower when Gaussian and exponential errors are contaminated.

Therefore, our next step is to develop methods to detect outliers in time series and/or to establish other estimation methods that are more robust, in the sense that they do not assume a distribution of the data and are less sensitive to outliers.

In this work, the outliers were generated from a regression model that established a linear relationship between the magnitude of the outliers and the total variance of the model with the state space representation of maximum air temperature real data. The rate of outliers from the real data was 5%; thus, this was the percentage used in this work.

In the literature, we did not find a unanimous approach for doing this. For example, ref. [15] contaminated the error of the zero-mean Gaussian equation of state by replacing the standard deviation of the observation error with a 10-times-higher standard deviation with a probability of 10% (symmetric outliers). They also considered the case of asymmetric outliers, where the zero mean of the observation error was replaced with a value 10 times higher than the standard deviation with a probability of 10%. Ref. [16] followed the same line as [15], but in this case they call symmetric outliers "zero-mean" and asymmetric outliers "non-zero", considering the probability of contamination to be 5%. Ref. [9] contaminated both the observation and state equation errors, considering the magnitude of the outliers equal to 2.5 the standard deviation from the diagonal elements of the observation and state covariance matrices, respectively.

Author Contributions: F.C.P., A.M.G. and M.C. contributed to this work. All authors have read and agreed to the published version of the manuscript.

Funding: This research was funded by FEDER/COMPETE/NORTE 2020/POCI/FCT funds through grants UID/EEA/-00147/20 13/UID/IEEA/00147/006933-SYSTEC project and To CHAIR - POCI-01-0145-FEDER-028247. A. Manuela Gonçalves was partially financed by Portuguese Funds through FCT (Fundação para a Ciência e a Tecnologia) within the Projects UIDB/00013/2020 and UIDP/00013/2020 of CMAT-UM. Marco Costa was partially supported by The Center for Research and Development in Mathematics and Applications (CIDMA) through the Portuguese Foundation for Science and Technology (FCT - Fundação para a Ciência e a Tecnologia), references UIDB/04106/2020 and UIDP/04106/2020. F. Catarina Pereira was financed by national funds through FCT (Fundação para a Ciência e a Tecnologia) through the individual PhD research grant UI/BD/150967/2021 of CMAT-UM.

Institutional Review Board Statement: Not applicable.

Informed Consent Statement: Not applicable.

Data Availability Statement: Not applicable.

Conflicts of Interest: The authors declare no conflict of interest.

References

1. Hamilton, J.D. *Time Series Analysis*; Princeton University Press: Princeton, NJ, USA, 1994.
2. Harvey, A.C. *Forecasting, Structural Time Series Models and the Kalman Filter*; Cambridge University Press: Cambridge, UK, 2009.
3. Shumway, R.H.; Stoffer, D.S. *Time Series Analysis and its Applications: With R Examples*; Springer: New York, NY, USA, 2017.
4. Petris, G.; Petrone, S.; Campagnoli, P. *Dynamic Linear Models with R*; Springer: Berlin/Heidelberg, Germany, 2009.
5. Durbin, J.; Koopman, S. *Time Series Analysis by State Space Methods*; Oxford University Press: Oxford, UK, 2001.
6. Kalman, R. A New Approach to Linear Filtering and Prediction Problems. *ASME J. Basic Eng.* **1960**, *82*, 35–45. [CrossRef]
7. Costa, M.; Alpuim, T. Parameter estimation of state space models for univariate observations. *J. Stat. Plan. Inference* **2010**, *140*, 1889–1902. [CrossRef]
8. Costa, M.; Monteiro, M. Bias-correction of kalman filter estimators associated to a linear state space model with estimated parameters. *J. Stat. Plan. Inference* **2016**, *176*, 22–32. [CrossRef]
9. You, D.; Hunter, M.; Chen, M.; Chow, S.M. A diagnostic procedure for detecting outliers in linear state-space models. *Multivar. Behav. Res.* **2020**, *55*, 231–255. [CrossRef] [PubMed]
10. Cipra, T.; Romera, R. Kalman filter with outliers and missing observations. *Test* **1997**, *6*, 379–395. [CrossRef]
11. Auger-Méthé, M.; Field, C.; Albertsen, C.M.; Derocher, A.E.; Lewis, M.A.; Jonsen, I.D.; Flemming, J.M. State-space models' dirty little secrets: Even simple linear Gaussian models can have estimation problems. *Sci. Rep.* **2016**, *6*, 26677. [CrossRef] [PubMed]
12. Pandolfo, G.; Iorio, C.; Siciliano, R.; D'Ambrosio, A. Robust mean-variance portfolio through the weighted L^p depth function. In *Annals of Operations Research*; Springer: Berlin/Heidelberg, Germany, 2020; Volume 292, pp. 519–531.
13. Shumway, R.H.; Stoffer, D.S. *Time Series: A Data Analysis Approach Using R*; CRC Press: Boca Raton, FL, USA, 2019.
14. R Core Team. *R: A Language and Environment for Statistical Computing*; R Foundation for Statistical Computing: Vienna, Austria, 2021.
15. Crevits, R.; Croux, C. Robust estimation of linear state space models. *Commun. Stat.-Simul. Comput.* **2019**, *48*, 1694–1705. [CrossRef]
16. Ali, K.; Tahir, M. Maximum likelihood-based robust state estimation over a horizon length during measurement outliers. *Trans. Inst. Meas. Control* **2021**, *43*, 510–518. [CrossRef]

Proceeding Paper

Time Series Sampling [†]

Florian Combes [1,2,*,‡] , **Ricardo Fraiman** [3,‡] and **Badih Ghattas** [2,‡]

1 Renault Group, Customer Usage, 78297 Guyancourt, France
2 CNRS, Aix Marseille University, I2M, 13009 Marseille, France; badihghattas@gmail.com
3 Centro de Matemática, Universidad de la República, Montevideo 11200, Uruguay; fraimanricardo@gmail.com
* Correspondence: combes.florian13@gmail.com
† Presented at the 8th International Conference on Time Series and Forecasting, Gran Canaria, Spain, 27–30 June 2022.
‡ These authors contributed equally to this work.

Abstract: Some complex models are frequently employed to describe physical and mechanical phenomena. In this setting, we have an input X, which is a time series, and an output $Y = f(X)$ where f is a very complicated function, whose computational cost for every new input is very high. We are given two sets of observations of X, S_1 and S_2 of different sizes such that only $f(S_1)$ is available. We tackle the problem of selecting a subsample $S_3 \in S_2$ of a smaller size on which to run the complex model f and such that distribution of $f(S_3)$ is close to that of $f(S_1)$. We adapt to this new framework five algorithms introduced in a previous work "Subsampling under Distributional Constraints" to solve this problem and show their efficiency using time series data.

Keywords: optimal sampling; Kolmogorov–Smirnov; time series; encoding; dynamic time warping

1. Introduction

The study of the damage caused over time and stress on a mechanical part allows for prediction of the failure of this part [1,2]. For this, it is necessary, on the one hand, to have reliable data and, on the other hand, to have a model that is faithful to reality. Such models are used to generate some scenarios using the solution of partial derivative equations (PDEs). Their input is often composed of different variables in the form of a time series denoted by X, and their output $f(X)$ may be multidimensional and depend on space and time. The use of such models consists of solving complicated PDEs, and each generated scenario corresponds in the machine learning paradigm to an inference for a new input X, and, therefore, to the computation of $f(X)$. The more complex that these models are, and the closer they are to reality, the more expensive they are in terms of computing time and power. In practice, these calculations can take days or weeks.

Consider a set $S_1 = \{X_1, \dots, X_{n_1}\}$ with a distribution similar to that of the time series X lying in a separable metric space $(\mathcal{E}, \rho)$. To each observation, we apply a deterministic smooth function. This function, $f : \mathcal{E} \to \mathbb{R}$, is expensive and complex and may be seen as a black box. Moreover, we have a large sample S_2 of size n_2 with the same distribution as X. We do not know the values $f(S_2)$. The goal is to find a subsample $S_3 \subset S_2$ of a size n_3 smaller than n_2 in such a way that the distribution of $f(S_3)$ is close to that of $f(S_1)$.

At first sight, this is a classic sampling problem. We can use sampling techniques identical to those used in surveys as well as unsupervised [3] or supervised techniques [4–6]. Some recent algorithms were proposed in [7] to solve this problem for the general case of variable X that lies in any metric space. We are interested, in this paper, in adapting such algorithms for the case in which X is a time series. We explore, in this paper, two possible adaptations; the first consists of encoding the time series X by independent features, and the second using appropriate distances between time series and adjusting the sampling algorithms to use such distances.

This manuscript is organized as follows. In Section 2, we fix some notations that will be used throughout the manuscript, and we specify the framework of the problem to be solved. In Section 3, we describe the algorithms used in [7] to solve the problem. In Section 4, we suggest alternative adaptations for these algorithms for their application to time series. Section 5 gives an industrial application of these approaches. In Section 6, some concluding remarks are provided.

2. The Problem Setting

Let $S_1 = \{X_1, \ldots, X_{n_1}\}$ as a set of n_1 time series following the same distribution μ as X, and $S_2 = \{X'_1, \ldots, X'_{n_2}\}$ as a second set of time series of size n_2 coming from the same distribution μ. Let $f : \mathcal{E} \to \mathbb{R}$ as a deterministic function that is very complicated and hard to compute. The unknown distribution of $f(X)$ will be denoted by F. Moreover, we dispose of

$$\mathcal{Y}_1 =: \{Y_i = f(X_i) \text{ for } i = 1, \ldots n_1\}$$

of the images of the first sample S_1 denoted $f(S_1)$. The images of S_2 by f are not available.

From this information, we want to determine a subsample $S_3 \subset S_2$ of size $n_3 \ll n_2$ in such a way that the empirical distribution of $f(S_3) := \{f(X_j) : X_j \in S_3\}$ will be close to the distribution of $f(X_1)$.

Several approaches are possible for this problem in a general setting in which X is a random variable in a separable metric space.

If μ_1 stands for the empirical distribution of S_1 and μ_3 for that of a subset $S_3 \subset S_2$, and the function f is regular, we look for a subset S_3 such that a :

$$d(\mu_1, \mu_3), \tag{1}$$

is minimal among all possible subsets. Here, d is a distance metrizing weak convergence, similar to the Prokhorov distance. In the next section, we will describe some algorithms proposed in [7] to solve this problem and that we aim to adapt to the time series.

3. Sampling Algorithms

We describe briefly some existing algorithms designed to solve our problem in a general context where X is a random variable that lies in any metric space. A more detailed description of these approaches may be found in [7].

Let $S_1 = \{X_1, \ldots X_{n_1}\}$ and $S_2 = \{X'_1, \ldots X'_{n_2}\}$ be two independent samples with $n_2 > n_1$ that come from the same distribution of X.

Among the following algorithms, some make use of $\mathcal{Y}_1$, and others do not.

3.1. Extended Nearest Neighbors Approach

This algorithm does not make use of $\mathcal{Y}_1$. The selected subset S_3 is simply the set of the nearest extended neighbors of S_1 in S_2. Consider the nearest neighbors of S_1 in S_2, $d_1, \ldots, d_{n_1}$, their ordered distances and $j(1), \ldots j(n_1)$ their indices.

Suppose that two elements of S_1, called X_i and X_j, have identical nearest neighbors, X'_l, with respective distances d_i and d_j, and suppose that if $d_i < d_j$, then X'_l will be the nearest neighbor of X_i, while for X_j we will have to take its second nearest neighbor, and so on. This approach is based on the idea that if the elements of S_2 are close to those of S_1, then the images of S_3 by f should be close to those of S_1.

3.2. A Partition-Based Algorithm

For this algorithm, a partition of the set $\mathcal{Y}_1$ into L clusters of size m is built s.t. $n = mL$. Denote the clusters by C_k, their complements by $C_{n-k} = S_1 \setminus C_k$ and F_k the empirical cdf of Y in C_k. Denote by $\hat{C}_k$ the cluster which minimizes $\|F_k - F_{n-k}\|$, and the subset $\tilde{C}_k = \{X_{i1}, \ldots X_{ik}\} \subset S_1$ fulfilling $f(\tilde{C}_k) = \hat{C}_k$ which is a subset of S_1. S_3 is defined as the set of the nearest neighbors of $\tilde{C}_k$ from $S2$. The partition used in this algorithm may be any random partition, or any partition obtained from a clustering algorithm similar to k-means.

3.3. A Histogram-Based Approach

The idea in this algorithm is to use the empirical distribution of the sample $\mathcal{Y}_1$. First, $\mathcal{Y}_3$ is obtained by a stratified sampling from $\mathcal{Y}_1$ where the stratas are obtained using the bins of the histogram built on $\mathcal{Y}_1$. S_3 is then taken to be the set of the nearest neighbors of $f^{-1}(\mathcal{Y}_3)$ from S_2. The empirical distribution of $f(S_3)$ is close to that of $f(S_1)$, S_1, and the S_3 distributions are expected to be close if f is smooth. Two alternatives to this algorithm have been proposed in [7], replacing the stratified sampling to get $\mathcal{Y}_3$ with either the support points approach [3] or the D-optimality [4].

4. Adaptation of Algorithms to Time Series

We suppose that the time series available in both samples S_1 and S_2 have different lengths. In this section, we will show how the algorithms presented in Section 3 may be adjusted to be used when X is a time series. For this purpose, two approaches are considered, encoding and choosing appropriate distances for time series. For the first approach, each time series in the data is embedded in a vectorial metric space through feature extraction; features may be used arbitrarily or obtained from an autoregressive linear model applied to each time series.

4.1. Encoding

We experiment with two types of encodings.

- Simple statistical feature extraction
  The p statistical characteristics are computed for each time series. These include the minimum, maximum, sum, number of times a threshold is crossed, length of zero periods, and so on. These engineering features depend on the dataset at hand and its characteristics.
- Using linear autoregressive (AR) models
  A linear autoregressive model is adjusted to each time series with a maximum order *pmax*. Once the optimal orders p_j are obtained for all time series in any sample, we fix the final desired order as $p = max_j\{p_j\}$. Finally, each time series is represented by its p estimated coefficients.

4.2. Using Appropriate Distance

Most of the algorithms described in Section 3 are based on neighborhood and, thus, distances. Here, we suggest replacing the Euclidean distance used in the general framework with dynamic time warping (DTW).

DTW allows for comparison of two time series by measuring their similarity, even if they have different lengths [8,9].

Consider the two time series $A = \{A_1, \ldots, A_n\}$ and $B = \{B_1, \ldots, B_m\}$ with $n \neq m$, which lie in the same dimensional space. The goal of DTW is to find the optimal temporal alignment between A and B; each point from A is associated with at least one point from B (and reciprocally), as shown in Figure 1. The optimal alignment, corresponding to the DTW distance between A and B, is the one giving the minimum total length between the couples of aligned points. This may be computed by resolving a linear programming problem.

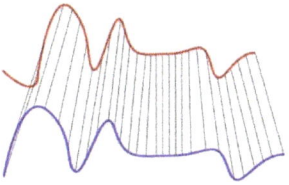

Figure 1. Time points alignment between two time series [10].

For a long time series, the DTW may be very complex to compute. The computation may be simplified using fast versions of the underlying optimization algorithm or by sampling the time series using arbitrary frequencies.

5. Real Dataset Application

We apply now the proposed approach to a time series dataset concerning real customers provided by RENAULT (the French car industry). All experiments were run using the R software [11] together with packages [12,13].

5.1. Driving Behavior Dataset

The variable X in our dataset is the time series of driver's speed. A large number of time series are available sampled at 5 Hz with a recording duration varying from a few days to a few weeks. Sampling at 5 Hz represents 86,400 points per day. This means that the time series studied are very large and different. An example of such time series is provided in Figure 2. We have used a selected sample of 691 customers.

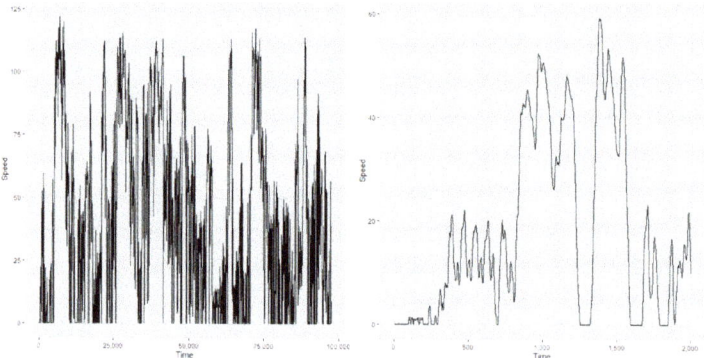

Figure 2. Complete driver's speed (**left**) and zoomed part (**right**) .

As these time series are speed traces of real customers, they vary from 0 to 150 km/h in our sample. Long and short stays at zero may be observed in these time series, corresponding to either night periods or shorter periods that correspond to car pauses, such as those for red lights. The lengths of the time series in our sample vary from 25,000 points to several million. Figure 3 shows the distribution of the time series lengths and the distribution of the zero values among the time series.

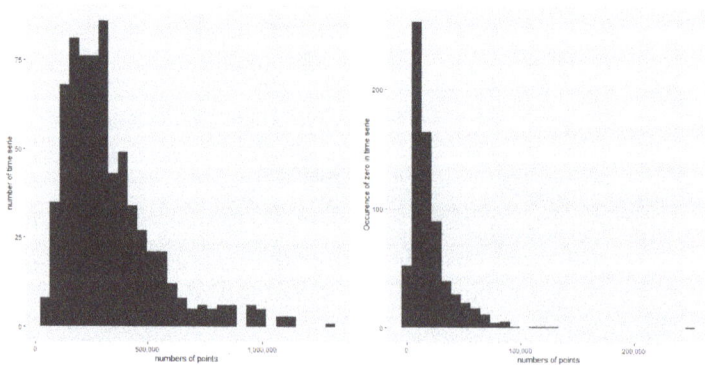

Figure 3. Histograms of time series length (**right**) and number of zeroes in each time series (**left**) .

In addition, for the 691 customers, a complex numerical model f was run in order to estimate the maximum soot released from each customer's vehicle. This model requires as input x the speed data time series together with many other characteristics of the vehicle. The maximum soot is the output of interest. As this model requires very long time computations (several hours for each customer depending on its parametrization), the objective is to select from among a dataset not used with the model, such as a sample of customers, for which the model would issue a similar distribution for the maximum soot to that already modeled for the customers.

5.2. Results

In this section, we provide the results of the algorithms proposed in Section 3: the extended nearest neighbors, the partition-based algorithm, the histogram-based approach and both variants using the support point and D-optimality.

To test these algorithms, the sample was randomly split into two parts with S_1 having 100 customers, and S_2 having the other 591. Each algorithm was run 100 times, and, from each run, the obtained optimal subsample S_3 was compared to S_1 using the Kolmogorov–Smirnov (KS) two samples test between $f(S_1)$ and $f(S_3)$, as the output of the model is known for all the samples in our dataset. Table 1 gives the average values of the KS statistics and the p-values over the 100 runs. We can observe that, depending on the encoding used, the algorithms do not react in the same way. We can see that the histogram-based algorithm provides the same results for the AR coefficients and feature extraction, though it is less efficient with the DTW. For the partition-based algorithms, the DTW performs much better than the two encoding approaches. While for the nearest neighbors and the support point, we get very close results for both encodings. Finally, for the D-optimality, we can see that the DTW and AR features provide the same results, which are better than those for feature extraction.

Table 1. Average results for each encoding and for each algorithm over 100 runs. NN = nearest neighbors.

Encoding Algorithm	Autoregressive			Feature Extraction			Dynamic Time Warping		
	N_3	Stat	p-Value	N_3	Stat	p-Value	N_3	Stat	p-Value
Extended NN	88	0.12	0.53	91	0.11	0.60	100	0.11	0.59
Partition-based	10	0.27	0.57	10	0.27	0.55	69	0.13	0.53
Histogram-based	48	0.44	0.0001	48	0.44	0.0001	48	0.46	0.0001
D-optimality	100	0.12	0.54	16	0.21	0.61	100	0.11	0.59
Support point	50	0.15	0.50	50	0.14	0.59	50	0.14	0.57

Figure 4 shows the distribution of the p-values and the KS statistics over the 100 runs for all algorithms, the two encodings and DTW.

We can see that the deviation of the computed statistics are different for the three approaches: the AR, feature extraction and DTW. We can see that, for all algorithms, the AR encoding results are more unstable than those of the two other approaches.

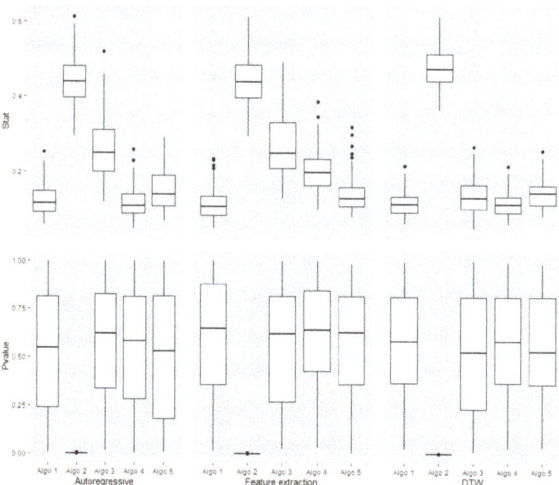

Figure 4. Results of all algorithms by encoding from left to right: AR features, feature extraction and DTW. Algo 1 = Extended nearest neighbors; Algo 2 = Histogram-based; Algo 3 = Partition-based; Algo 4 = D-optimality; Algo 5 = Support point.

6. Discussion and Conclusions

In this work, we have tackled the problem of selecting a subsample of time series to satisfy some distributional constraints. We have adapted several algorithms proposed recently in a more general framework to our context. All of the proposed approaches were tested over a real dataset of a car's speed time series. The results obtained show that our algorithms work as expected, except for one approach: the histogram-based one. To adapt the existing algorithms we have suggested various numerical representations for the time series and shown that different choices for encoding may affect the results significantly. More complex models than the autoregressive approach, or more refined statistical representations for the time series, might be more efficient. One idea under investigation is to use supervised embedding through recurrent neural networks.

Author Contributions: Conceptualization, R.F. and B.G.; software, F.C.; writing—original draft preparation, R.F. and B.G.; writing—review and editing, F.C. and B.G.; supervision, B.G. All authors have read and agreed to the published version of the manuscript.

Funding: This research received no external funding.

Institutional Review Board Statement: Not applicable.

Informed Consent Statement: Not applicable.

Data Availability Statement: The data is not accessible because it is the property of Renault Group.

Conflicts of Interest: The authors declare no conflict of interest.

References

1. García Márquez, F.P.; Pedregal, D.; Roberts, C. Time series methods applied to failure prediction and detection. *Reliab. Eng. Syst. Saf. - Reliab. Eng Syst Saf.* **2010**, *95*, 698–703. [CrossRef]
2. Khatkhate, A.; Ray, A.; Keller, E.; Gupta, S. Symbolic Time Series Analysis of Mechanical Systems for Anomaly Detection. *ASME/IEEE Trans. Mechatron.* **2006**, *11*, 439–447. [CrossRef]
3. Joseph V.R.; Mak, S. Support points. *Ann. Stat.* **2018**, *46*, 2562–2592. [CrossRef]
4. Wang, H.Y.; Min, Y.; John, S. Information-Based Optimal Subdata Selection for Big Data Linear Regression. *J. Am. Stat. Assoc.* **2019**, *114*, 393–405. [CrossRef]
5. Wang, H.Y.; Rong, Z.; Ping, M. Optimal Subsampling for Large Sample Logistic Regression. *J. Am. Stat. Assoc.* **2018**, *113*, 829–844. [CrossRef] [PubMed]

6. Joseph, V.R.; Mak, S. Supervised compression of big data. *Stat. Anal. Data Min. Asa Data Sci. J.* **2021**, *14*, 217–229. [CrossRef]

7. Combes, F.; Fraiman, R.; Ghattas, B. Subsampling under Distributional Constraints. Working Paper. Available online: https://hal.archives-ouvertes.fr/hal-03666898/file/OptimalSampling.pdf (accessed on 15 April 2022).

8. Sakoe, H.; Chiba, S. Dynamic programming algorithm optimization for spoken word recognition. *IEEE Trans. Acoust. Speech, Signal Process.* **1978**, *26*, 43–49. [CrossRef]

9. Vintsyuk, T.K. Speech discrimination by dynamic programming. *Cybernetics* **1968**, *4*, 52–57. [CrossRef]

10. Martin, D.; Serrano, A.; Bergman, A.W.; Wetzstein, G.; Masia, B. ScanGAN360: A Generative Model of Realistic Scanpaths for 360° Images between Two Sequences to Minimize Their Distance. *arxiv* **2013**, arxiv:2103.13922.

11. R Core Team. *R: A Language and Environment for Statistical Computing*; R Foundation for Statistical Computing: Vienna, Austria, 2022.

12. Mak, S. Support: Support Points. R Package Version 0.1.5. 2021. Available online: https://CRAN.R-project.org/package=support (accessed on 15 April 2022).

13. Giorgino, T. Computing and Visualizing Dynamic Time Warping Alignments in R: The dtw Package. *J. Stat. Softw.* **2009**, *31*, 1–24. [CrossRef]

Proceeding Paper

Modelling a Continuous Time Series with FOU(*p*) Processes †

Juan Kalemkerian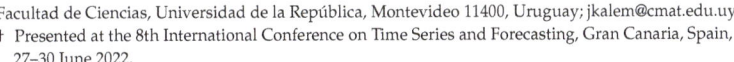

Facultad de Ciencias, Universidad de la República, Montevideo 11400, Uruguay; jkalem@cmat.edu.uy

† Presented at the 8th International Conference on Time Series and Forecasting, Gran Canaria, Spain, 27–30 June 2022.

Abstract: In this work we summarize the knowledge about FOU(*p*) processes (fractional iterated Ornstein–Uhlenbeck processes of order emphp). Fractional Ornstein–Uhlenbeck processes are a particular case of FOU(*p*) processes (when $p = 1$). FOU(*p*) processes are able to model time series with both long- and short-range dependence. We give the definition, the main theoretical properties, and a procedure for estimating the parameters consistently. We also show how to model a continuous time series with FOU(*p*) processes, and we give an example of an application.

Keywords: fractional Brownian motion; long-range dependence; fractional Ornstein–Uhlenbeck process

1. Introduction

Usually, in time series, the researcher has a series of measurements evenly spaced in time (for example, measurements per minute, every thirty seconds, or weekly measurements). In these cases the underlying process is continuous time. The fractional iterated Ornstein–Uhlenbeck processes of order p (that we call FOU(*p*) and which are defined in [1]) are stationary and centred Gaussian continuous-time processes. By construction, the FOU(*p*) process depends on the two parameters defining the underlying fractional Brownian motion, namely, the Hurst exponent (H) and the scale parameter σ. From the relationship between the variogram and the Hölder index of the process trajectories, using a result given in [2], it is proved in [1] that H is the Hölder index of a FOU(*p*), giving information about the irregularity of the trajectories. If the process is observed in a discretized and equispaced interval $[0, T]$, by applying a procedure suggested in [3] it is possible to estimate H and σ consistently. Apart from H and σ, a FOU(*p*) process is determined by a set of additional parameters, the so-called λ parameters, giving information about the local dependence. The theoretical properties of any FOU(*p*) process and a methodology for estimating its parameters consistently (including the asymptotic behaviour) are given in [1]. The estimation method and the asymptotic results for the λ parameters were obtained under the assumption that the process is observed over the entire interval $[0, T]$, where $T \to \infty$. In [4], a consistent method can be found for estimating the λ parameters in the discretized case. An interesting property of the FOU(*p*) process is that it exhibits short-range dependence when $p \geq 2$, even though $H > 1/2$ (in this case, the generating fractional Brownian motion has long-range dependence). In addition, when $p = 1$ we have the result that FOU(1) is the classical fractional Ornstein–Uhlenbeck process (fOU) defined in [5], which has long-range dependence when $H > 1/2$. Another interesting property is that as p grows, the autocorrelation function of the process goes more quickly to zero. In addition, FOU(1) (fOU) processes can be approximated by FOU(2) (simply taking $\lambda_1 \to 0$, where $\lambda = (\lambda_1, \lambda_2)$). Thus, FOU(*p*) processes can be viewed as a generalization of fOU processes and are able to model a time series with short-range dependence or long-range dependence. The main objective of this work is to summarize the results obtained in [1,4,6] for modeling a time series through FOU(*p*) processes. In Section 2, we give the definition of a FOU(*p*) process. The method for estimating its parameters is given in Section 3. In Section 4, we give a method of modeling a time series through the FOU(p) process, including an example. Some conclusions are given in Section 5.

2. Definition of FOU(p) Processes

FOU(p) processes are built from the fractional Brownian motion.

Definition 1. *A fractional Brownian motion with Hurst parameter $H \in (0,1]$ is an almost surely continuous centred Gaussian process $\{B_H(t)\}_{t \in \mathbb{R}}$ such that its auto-covariance function is*

$$\mathbb{E}(B_H(t)B_H(s)) = \frac{1}{2}\left(|t|^{2H} + |s|^{2H} - |t-s|^{2H}\right) \text{ for every } t,s \in \mathbb{R}.$$

To use a fractional Brownian motion with a scale parameter σ, we use the notation $\{\sigma B_H(t)\}_{t \in \mathbb{R}}$.

Now, we can define a fractional iterated Ornstein–Uhlenbeck process of order p (FOU(p)), as found in [1].

Definition 2. *Let $\{\sigma B_H(s)\}_{s \in \mathbb{R}}$ be a fractional Brownian motion with Hurst parameter H and scale parameter σ. Suppose further that $\lambda_1, \lambda_2, \ldots, \lambda_q$ are pairwise different and positive numbers and $p_1, p_2, \ldots, p_q \in \mathbb{N}$ such that $p_1 + p_2 + \ldots + p_q = p$. Then, the fractional iterated Ornstein–Uhlenbeck process of order p is defined as*

$$X_t := T_{\lambda_1}^{p_1} \circ T_{\lambda_2}^{p_2} \circ \ldots \circ T_{\lambda_q}^{p_q}(\sigma B_H)(t) = \sum_{i=1}^{q} K_i(\lambda) \sum_{j=0}^{p_i-1} \binom{p_i-1}{j} T_{\lambda_i}^{(j)}(\sigma B_H)(t),$$

where the numbers $K_i(\lambda)$ are defined by

$$K_i(\lambda) = K_i(\lambda_1, \lambda_2, \ldots, \lambda_q) := \frac{1}{\prod\limits_{j \neq i}(1 - \lambda_j/\lambda_i)} \tag{1}$$

and the operators $T_{\lambda_i}^{(j)}$ are defined by

$$T_{\lambda}^{(h)}(y)(t) := \int_{-\infty}^{t} e^{-\lambda(t-s)} \frac{(-\lambda(t-s))^h}{h!} dy(s) \text{ for } h = 0,1,2,\ldots \tag{2}$$

We define T_λ simply for the $h = 0$ case, that is

$$T_\lambda(y)(t) := \int_{-\infty}^{t} e^{-\lambda(t-s)} dy(s). \tag{3}$$

Remark 1. *The equality $T_{\lambda_1}^{p_1} \circ T_{\lambda_2}^{p_2} \circ \ldots \circ T_{\lambda_q}^{p_q} = \sum_{i=1}^{q} K_i(\lambda) \sum_{j=0}^{p_i-1} \binom{p_i-1}{j} T_{\lambda_i}^{(j)}$ that appears in Definition 2 is proved in [7].*

Remark 2. *The equality $T_{\lambda_1}^{p_1} \circ T_{\lambda_2}^{p_2} \circ \ldots \circ T_{\lambda_q}^{p_q} = \sum_{i=1}^{q} K_i(\lambda) \sum_{j=0}^{p_i-1} \binom{p_i-1}{j} T_{\lambda_i}^{(j)}$ implies that the composition $T_{\lambda_1}^{p_1} \circ T_{\lambda_2}^{p_2} \circ \ldots \circ T_{\lambda_q}^{p_q}$ is commutative. Then, we assume that $\lambda_1 < \lambda_2 < \ldots < \lambda_q$. This will be helpful for estimating $\lambda = (\lambda_1, \lambda_2, \ldots, \lambda_q)$, to avoid ambiguity.*

Notation 1. $\{X_t\}_{t \in \mathbb{R}} \sim FOU\left(\lambda_1^{(p_1)}, \lambda_2^{(p_2)}, \ldots, \lambda_q^{(p_q)}, \sigma, H\right)$, where $0 < \lambda_1 < \lambda_2 < \ldots < \lambda_q$, or more simply, $\{X_t\}_{t \in \mathbb{R}} \sim FOU(p)$.

Remark 3. *The notation* $FOU\left(\lambda_1^{(p_1)}, \lambda_2^{(p_2)}, \ldots, \lambda_q^{(p_q)}, \sigma, H\right)$ *implies that* $0 < \lambda_1 < \lambda_2 < \ldots < \lambda_q$. *On the other hand, the notation* $FOU(p)$ *means that we have taken p times the composition of operators* T_λ *for different or equal values of* λ.

Remark 4. *Every* $FOU\left(\lambda_1^{(p_1)}, \lambda_2^{(p_2)}, \ldots, \lambda_q^{(p_q)}, \sigma, H\right)$ *is a Gaussian, centred, almost surely continuous process and is almost surely non-differentiable at any point (the proof of these results can be found in [1]).*

Remark 5. *When* $p = 1$, $FOU(\lambda, \sigma, H)$ *is the classical fractional Ornstein–Uhlenbeck process.*

Remark 6. *In the case in which* $p_1 = p_2 = \ldots = p_q = 1$, *we have*

$$X_t = T_{\lambda_1} \circ T_{\lambda_2} \circ \ldots \circ T_{\lambda_q}(\sigma B_H)(t) = \sum_{i=1}^{q} K_i(\lambda) T_{\lambda_i}(\sigma B_H)(t) \qquad (4)$$

and we simply write $\{X_t\}_{t \in \mathbb{R}} \sim FOU(\lambda_1, \lambda_2, \ldots, \lambda_q, \sigma, H)$.

Remark 7. *From Equation (4) we have that any* $FOU(\lambda_1, \lambda_2, \sigma, H)$ *where* $0 < \lambda_1 < \lambda_2$ *can be writing as*

$$X_t = \frac{\lambda_1}{\lambda_1 - \lambda_2} X_t^{(1)} + \frac{\lambda_2}{\lambda_2 - \lambda_1} X_t^{(2)} \qquad (5)$$

being $X_t^{(i)} = \sigma \int_{-\infty}^{t} e^{-\lambda_i(t-s)} dB_H(s)$ *for* $i = 1, 2$. *That is,* $X_t^{(i)}$ *is a classical fractional Ornstein–Uhlenbeck process with* $\lambda = \lambda_i$. *Then a* $FOU(2)$ *process is a linear combination of two fOU processes with different values of* λ.

Remark 8. *From Equation (5), if* $\lambda_1 \to 0$, *we have that* $X_t \to X_t^{(2)}$, *that is, every fractional Ornstein–Uhlenbeck processes can be approximated by a FOU(2) process (by taking* λ_1 *small).*

Remark 9. *In [1] it is shown that every* $FOU(p)$ *process has a short-range dependence for* $p \geq 2$ *and every* $H \in (0,1)$. *On the other hand, it is well-known that if* $H > 1/2$, *every classical Ornstein–Uhlenbeck process has long-range dependence. Therefore, if* $H > 1/2$, *according with previous remark, we have that the short-range dependence FOU(2) processes can able to approximate a long-range dependence fOU process.*

Remark 10. *From remarks 5 and 9, we can say that the* $FOU(p)$ *processes are a generalization of fOU processes and are able to model a time series with short-range dependence or long-range dependence.*

3. Parameter Estimation

In this section, we summarize a procedure that allows the estimation of the parameters of any $FOU(p)$ in a consistent way. Similarly to the estimators for (λ, σ, H) proposed in [8] for the fractional Ornstein–Uhlenbeck process, the procedure for estimating the parameters in any $FOU(p)$ process has two steps. As a first step, we estimate σ and H independently of the values of the λ parameters. As a second step, using the explicit formula for the spectral density (see Equation (8)) and substituting $(\widehat{H}, \widehat{\sigma})$ instead of (H, σ), we can estimate $\lambda = (\lambda_1, \lambda_2, \ldots, \lambda_q)$ using Whittle estimators.

Throughout this section, we assume that we have an equispaced sample in $[0, T]$ of a $FOU(p)$ process, that is, $X_{T/n}, X_{2T/n}, \ldots, X_T$, which we simply call $X_1, X_2, \ldots, X_n$.

3.1. Estimation of H and σ

We start by recalling the definition of a filter of length $k + 1$ and order L.

Definition 3. $a = (a_0, a_1, \ldots, a_k)$ *is a filter of length* $k + 1$ *and order* $L \geq 1$ *when the following conditions are fulfilled:*

- $\sum_{i=0}^{k} a_i i^l = 0$ *for all* $0 \leq l \leq L - 1$.
- $\sum_{i=0}^{k} a_i i^L \neq 0$.

Remark 11. *Given* a, *a filter of order* L *and length* $k + 1$, *the new filter* a^2 *defined by* $a^2 = (a_0, 0, a_1, 0, a_2, 0, \ldots, 0, a_k)$ *has order* L *and length* $2k + 1$.

Given a filter a, we can define the quadratic variation of a sample associated with a.

Definition 4. *Given a filter* a *of length* $k + 1$ *and a sample* $X_1, X_2, \ldots, X_n$, *we define*

$$V_{n,a} := \frac{1}{n} \sum_{i=0}^{n-k} \left(\sum_{j=0}^{k} a_j X_{i+j} \right)^2.$$

If we use a filter a of order $L \geq 2$ and length $k + 1$, and we take $\Delta_n = n^{-\alpha}$ for some $\alpha > 0$ such that $T = n\Delta_n \to +\infty$, then if $H > 1/2$, the estimators of H and σ are given by

$$\hat{H} = \frac{1}{2} \log_2 \left(\frac{V_{n,a^2}}{V_{n,a}} \right), \tag{6}$$

$$\hat{\sigma} = \left(\frac{-2V_{n,a}}{\Delta_n^{2\hat{H}} \sum_{i=0}^{k} \sum_{j=0}^{k} a_i a_j |i - j|^{2\hat{H}}} \right)^{1/2}. \tag{7}$$

In [1,4], the theoretical details for the asymptotic normality and consistency of $\hat{H}$ and $\hat{\sigma}$ can be found.

3.2. Estimation of the λ Parameters

If $X = \{X_t\}_{t \in \mathbb{R}} \sim FOU(\lambda_1^{(p_1)}, \ldots, \lambda_q^{(p_q)}, \sigma, H)$, where $\sum_{i=1}^{q} p_i = p$, the spectral density of X is given by (see [1])

$$f^{(X)}(x, \lambda, \sigma, H) = \frac{\sigma^2 \Gamma(2H + 1) \sin(H\pi) |x|^{2p-1-2H}}{2\pi \prod_{i=1}^{q} (\lambda_i^2 + x^2)^{p_i}}. \tag{8}$$

From (8), we can estimate $\lambda = (\lambda_1, \lambda_2, \ldots, \lambda_q)$ using a modified Whittle contrast. Consider (for any fixed $T > 0$) the function

$$U_T^{(n)}(\lambda, \sigma, H) = \frac{T}{n} \sum_{i=1}^{n} h_T^{(n)}(iT/n, \lambda, \sigma, H)$$

where $h_T^{(n)}$ is defined by

$$h_T^{(n)}(x, \lambda, \sigma, H) = \frac{1}{2\pi} \left(\log f^{(X)}(x, \lambda, \sigma, H) + \frac{I_T^{(n)}(x)}{f^{(X)}(x, \lambda, \sigma, H)} \right) w(x)$$

where

$$I_T^{(n)}(x) = \frac{T}{2\pi} \left| \frac{1}{n} \sum_{j=1}^{n} e^{\frac{ijTx}{n}} X_{\frac{iT}{n}} \right|^2$$

is the discretization of the periodogram of the process and w is some weight function. Then, the vector λ can be estimated by

$$\hat{\lambda}_T^{(n)} = \arg\min_{\lambda \in \Lambda} U_T^{(n)}\left(\lambda, \hat{\sigma}, \hat{H}\right) \tag{9}$$

where $\hat{\sigma}$ and $\hat{H}$ are defined by (7) and (6), respectively, and Λ is some compact set. Details about the consistency of this estimator, including how to choose the w function, can be found in [4].

Remark 12. *When $q = 1$, that is, $\{X_t\}_{t \in \mathbb{R}} \sim \text{FOU}\left(\lambda^{(p)}, \sigma, H\right)$, the λ parameter can be estimated more easily by the following formula:*

$$\hat{\lambda} = \left(\frac{n\hat{\sigma}^2 \hat{H} \Gamma\left(2\hat{H}\right) \prod_{i=1}^{p-1}\left(i - \hat{H}\right)}{(p-1)! \sum_{i=1}^{n} X_i^2} \right)^{\frac{1}{2\hat{H}}}. \tag{10}$$

Theorems on the consistency and asymptotic normality of $\hat{\lambda}$ can be found in [6].

4. Modelling an Observed Time Series Using FOU(p) Processes

Of course, before starting to model with FOU(p) it is necessary to subtract the mean value and remove the seasonal component if it has one. Given $X_1, X_2, \ldots, X_n$ observations of a stationary centred time series that we wish to model using a FOU(p) process, we firstly assume that the observations form an equispaced sample on $[0, T]$, that is, $X_{T/n}, X_{2T/n}, \ldots, X_T$ for some value of T. According to what was seen in the previous section, we need to estimate (λ, σ, H), whose estimators depend on T. Thus, firstly we need to know the value of T.

4.1. Choosing the Value of T

To give the value of T is equivalent to give the unit of measurement of time in which the observations are taken. In general, it is natural to take some value of T (for example, if the observations are weekly and we have 104 observations, it is natural to take $T = 104$ weeks or $T = 2$ years), but we can take any value of T and interpret it (in terms of the original time measure of the data). Therefore, we can choose a value of T that optimizes a certain criterion. According to theoretical results (see [1,4,6]), in order to model a time series dataset using FOU(p) processes, it is necessary to have values of n and T such that $n, T \to +\infty$ and $T/n \to 0$ at a certain rate. Now, n is the sample size, and the observations lie in the range of $[0, T]$ for some value of T. In [4], it is suggested that a certain value of T should be chosen to optimize some criterion, for example, MAE, RMSE, AIC, BIC, or the Willmott index.

4.2. An Application to Real Data

In this section, we work with the well-known Series A (a record of 197 chemical process concentration readings, taken every two hours). To model this with a FOU(p) process, we use values of $p = 2, 3, 4$. As a first step, for each one of these models, we select a suitable value of T. We minimize the error forecasts for the last m observations

$$\sqrt[h]{\frac{1}{m} \sum_{i=1}^{m} \left| X_{n-m+i} - \hat{X}_{n-m+i} \right|^h}$$

for $h = 1$ (mean absolute error, MAE) and $h = 2$ (the root mean square error prediction, RMSE) and maximize the Willmott index defined by

$$W_h = 1 - \frac{\sum_{i=1}^{m} \left| X_{n-m+i} - \hat{X}_{n-m+i} \right|^h}{\sum_{i=1}^{m} \left(\left| \hat{X}_{n-m+i} - \overline{X}(m) \right| + \left| X_{n-m+i} - \overline{X}(m) \right| \right)^h}$$

where $\overline{X}(m) := \frac{1}{m} \sum_{i=1}^{m} X_{n-m+i}$ and $X_1, X_2, \ldots, X_n$ (or $X_{T/n}, X_{2T/n}, \ldots, X_T$) are the real observations, for $h = 1$ and $h = 2$. Observe that W_h takes values between 0 and 1, and the predictions improve as W_h grows (W_2 is called Willmott index and W_1 is called the

Willmott L^1 index). In Table 1, we show the values of the four forecast quality measures for the AR(7), ARMA(1,1) models and every adjusted FOU(p) models for $p = 2,3,4$. Every considered FOU(p) model, performs similarly and near to AR(7) in the four measures. In Figure 1, we show the values of the four forecast quality measures in the function of T for the FOU($\lambda^{(2)}, \sigma, H$) model (the other FOU(p) models behave similarly) for $m = 50$ predictions. That is, for every value of T and every model, we estimate the parameters of the FOU(p) model and then we obtain the m predictions for the last m observations (at one step) and compute the RMSE, MAE, W_1, and W_2. In every case, the optimal value is reached in the neighbourhood of $T = 11$. To estimate (σ, H), we used a Daubechies filter of order 2:

$$a = \frac{1}{\sqrt{2}}(0.482962, -0.836516, 0.224143, 0.129409).$$

ARMA $(1,1)$ and AR(7) are suggested for modeling the Series A dataset (see [9] where this dataset was introduced) [10,11]. In Figure 2, we show that the adjusted FOU($\lambda^{(3)}, \sigma, H$) and FOU($\lambda^{(4)}, \sigma, H$) have a better fit than the two ARMA models considered.

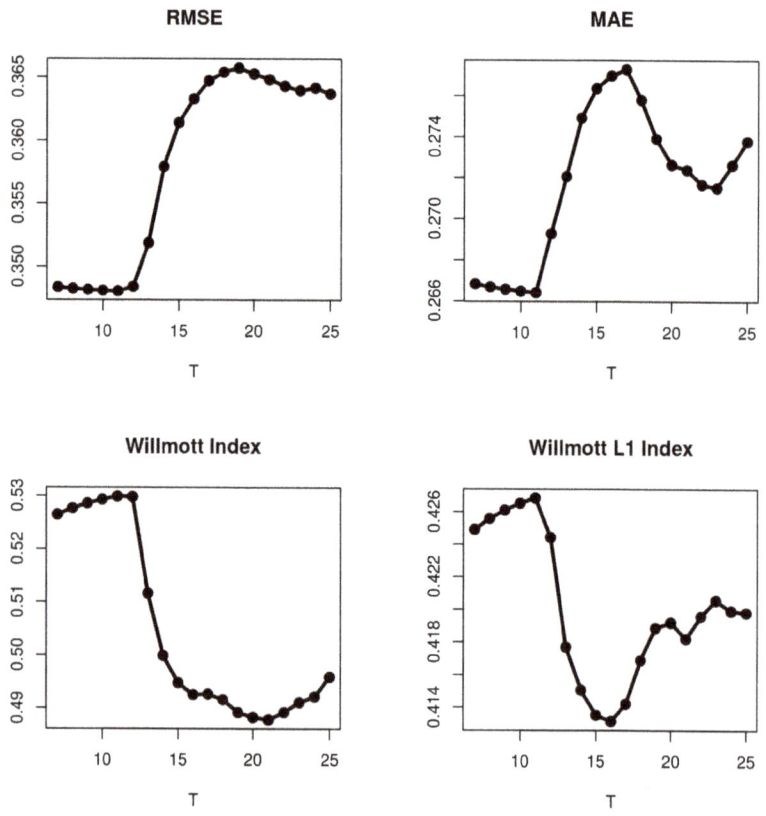

Figure 1. RMSE, MAE, W_1, and W_2 (for $m = 50$ predictions) when the model used is FOU($\lambda^{(2)}, \sigma, H$) as a function of T.

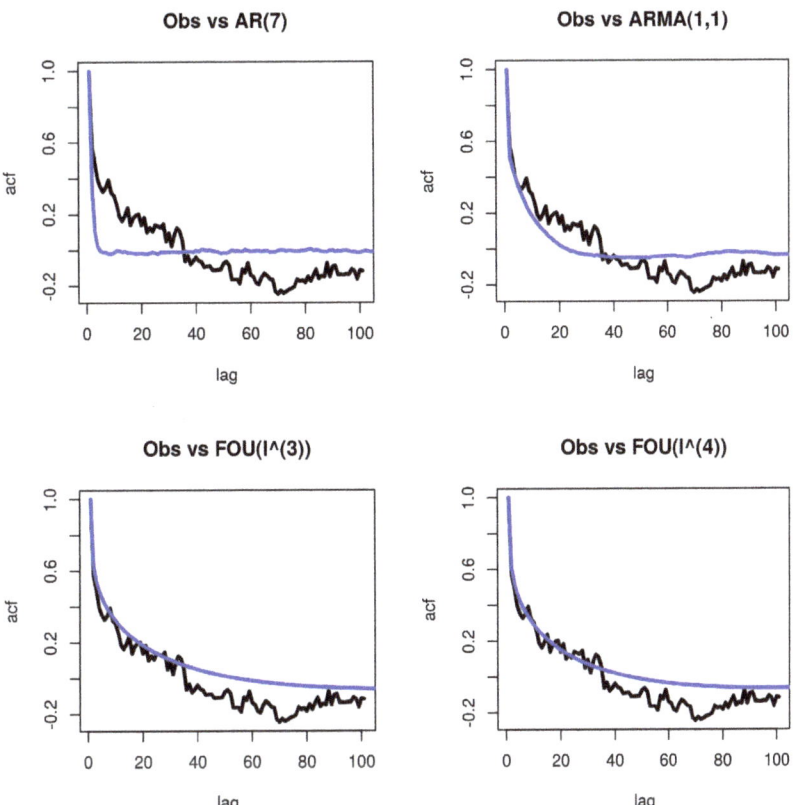

Figure 2. In black, the empirical auto-covariance function and in blue, the fitted auto-covariance function, according to the adjusted model for the Series A dataset.

Table 1. Values of W_2, W_1, *RMSE*, and *MAE* for different models adjusted to Series A. In bold the optimum value.

Model	W_2	W_1	*RMSE*	*MAE*
AR(7)	0.6184	**0.4943**	**0.2995**	**0.2167**
ARMA(1, 1)	0.5883	0.4620	0.3120	0.2343
FOU$(\lambda_1, \lambda_2, \sigma, H)$	0.6263	0.4743	0.3076	0.2372
FOU$(\lambda_1, \lambda_2, \lambda_3, \sigma, H)$	0.6260	0.4743	0.3076	0.2371
FOU$(\lambda_1, \lambda_2, \lambda_3, \lambda_4, \sigma, H)$	0.6244	0.4733	0.3074	0.2369
FOU$\left(\lambda^{(2)}, \sigma, H\right)$	0.6247	0.4712	0.3086	0.2393
FOU$\left(\lambda^{(3)}, \sigma, H\right)$	**0.6277**	0.4750	0.3078	0.2373
FOU$\left(\lambda^{(4)}, \sigma, H\right)$	0.6264	0.4742	0.3076	0.2372

5. Some Concluding Remarks

We summarize below the main conclusions obtained (details can be found in [1,4,6]):

1. FOU(p) processes are a Gaussian family of continuous-time stochastic processes that generalize (by taking $p = 1$) the classical fractional Ornstein–Uhlenbeck processes.

2. When $p \geq 2$, any FOU(p) has short-range dependence for every value of H, whereas for $p = 1$ and $H > 1/2$, it is well known that the classical fractional Ornstein–Uhlenbeck process has a long-range dependence. In addition, any long-range dependence fractional Ornstein–Uhlenbeck process ($H > 1/2$) can be approximate for some FOU(2) (short-range dependence).

3. As p grows, the FOU(p) process has a shorter memory (in the sense that the autocorrelation function goes more quickly to zero).

4. Under general conditions, it is possible to estimate all the parameters of any FOU(p) process in a consistent way.

5. FOU(p) processes are able to model a wide range of time series. In [4,6], four examples of real datasets with small and large sample sizes and with short-range and long-range dependence can be found (one of them is the Series A dataset used in Section 4).

6. Another possible advantage (that should be studied) of using a FOU(p) process to model a continuous-time dataset (rather than a discrete-time model) is the Hölder index (H), since H gives a measure of the irregularity of the trajectories. Smaller values of H indicate more irregular trajectories.

Funding: This research received no external funding.

Institutional Review Board Statement: Not applicable.

Informed Consent Statement: Not applicable.

Data Availability Statement: Samples of the compounds are available from the basic R packages.

Conflicts of Interest: The author declares no conflict of interest.

References

1. Kalemkerian, J.; León, J.R. Fractional iterated Ornstein-Uhlenbeck Processes. *ALEA* **2019**, *16*, 1105–1124. [CrossRef]
2. Ibragimov, I.A.; Rozanov, Y.A. *Gaussian Random Processes*; Springer: Berlin/Heidelberg, Germany, 1978.
3. Istas, I.; Lang, G. Quadratic variations and estimation of the local Hölder index of a Gaussian process. *Ann. L'inst. Henry Poincaré* **1997**, *23*, 407–436. [CrossRef]
4. Kalemkerian, J. Modelling and Parameter Estimation for Discretely Observed Fractional iterated Ornstein-Uhlenbeck Processes. *arXiv* **2020**, arXiv:2004.10369.
5. Cheridito, P.; Kawaguchi, H.; Maejima, M. Fractional Ornstein-Uhlenbeck Processes. *Electron. J. Probab.* **2003**, *8*, 1–14. [CrossRef]
6. Kalemkerian, J. Parameter Estimation for the FOU(p) Processes with the same lambda. *arXiv* **2022**, arXiv:2202.00642.
7. Arratia, A.; Cabaña, A.; Cabaña, E. A construction of Continuous time ARMA models by iterations of Ornstein-Uhlenbeck process. *SORT* **2016**, *40*, 267–302.
8. Brouste, A.; Iacus, S.M. Parameter estimation for the discretely observed fractional Ornstein-Uhlenbeck process and the Yuima R package. *Comput. Stat.* **2013**, *28*, 1529–1547. [CrossRef]
9. Box, G.E.P.; Jenkins, G.M.; Reinsel, G.C. *Time Series Analysis, Forecasting and Control*; Prentice Hall: Hoboken, NJ, USA, 1994.
10. Cleveland, W.S. The inverse autocorrelations of a time series and their applicattions. *Technometrics* **1971**, *14*, 277–298. [CrossRef]
11. McLeod, A.I.; Zang, Y. Partial autocorrelation parametrization for subset autoregression. *J. Time Ser. Anal.* **2006**, *27*, 599–612. [CrossRef]

Proceeding Paper

PV Energy Prediction in 24 h Horizon Using Modular Models Based on Polynomial Conversion of the L-Transform PDE Derivatives in Node-by-Node-Evolved Binary-Tree Networks †

Ladislav Zjavka * and Václav Snášel

Department of Computer Science, Faculty of Electrical Engineering and Computer Science, VŠB-Technical University of Ostrava, 708 00 Ostrava, Czech Republic; vaclav.snasel@vsb.cz
* Correspondence: ladislav.zjavka@vsb.cz
† Presented at the 8th International Conference on Time Series and Forecasting, Gran Canaria, Spain, 27–30 June 2022.

Abstract: Accurate daily photovoltaic (PV) power predictions are challenging as near-ground atmospheric processes include complicated chaotic interactions among local factors (ground temperature, cloudiness structure, humidity, visibility factor, etc.). Fluctuations in solar irradiance resulting from the cloud structure dynamics are influenced by many uncertain parameters, which can be described by differential equations. Recent artificial intelligence (AI) computational tools allow us to transform and post-validate forecast data from numerical weather prediction (NWP) systems to estimate PV power generation in relation to on-site local specifics. However, local NWP models are usually produced each six hours to simulate the progress of main weather quantities in a medium-scale target area. Their delay usually covers several hours, further increasing the inadequate operational quality required in PV plants. All-day prediction models perform better, if they are developed with the last historical weather and PV data. Differential polynomial neural network (D-PNN) is a recently designed computational method, based on a new learning approach, which allows us to represent complicated data relations contained in local weather patterns to account for irregular phenomena. D-PNN combines two-input variables to split the partial differential equation (PDE), defined in the general order k and n variables, into partition elements of two-input node PDEs of recognized order and type. The node-determined sub-PDEs can be easily converted using operator calculus (OC), in several types of predefined convert schemes, to define unknown node functions expressed in the Laplace images form Application of the inverse L-transformation formula to the L-converts results in obtaining the prime function originals. D-PNN elicits a progressive modular tree structure to assess one-by-one the optimal PDE node solutions to be inserted in the sum output of the overall expanded computing model. Statistical modular models are the result of learning schemes of preadjusted day data records from various observational localities. They are applied after testing to the rest of unseen daily series of known data to compute estimations of clear-sky index (CSI) in the 24 h input-delayed time-sequences.

Keywords: modelling dynamics; differential learning; multinomial tree; operator calculus; conversion scheme; Laplace image

Citation: Zjavka, L.; Snášel, V. PV Energy Prediction in 24 h Horizon Using Modular Models Based on Polynomial Conversion of the L-Transform PDE Derivatives in Node-by-Node-Evolved Binary-Tree Networks. *Eng. Proc.* **2022**, *18*, 34. https://doi.org/10.3390/engproc2022018034

Academic Editors: Ignacio Rojas, Hector Pomares, Olga Valenzuela, Fernando Rojas and Luis Javier Herrera

Published: 27 June 2022

Publisher's Note: MDPI stays neutral with regard to jurisdictional claims in published maps and institutional affiliations.

1. Introduction

Stochastic photovoltaic power (PVP) production can hardly be predicted when relying solely on NWP data units, which cannot fully account for local anomalies in the near-ground surface terrain [1]. NWP utilities try to integrate their output with sky- or ground-produced image data patterns to localize and identify the development of cloud structure formations on a regional scale [2]. Middle-time horizon NWP forecasting can be fused with clear sky data modelling and re-analyzed to determine the optimal interval sizes of training samples.

Distribution data based on forecast errors, obtained for various cloudiness situations, can be used to define probability intervals in prediction days and to represent inhomogeneous weather states. An increase in the modular temperature of photovoltaic panels results in a decrease in efficient power production and irradiance conversion [3]. AI computing is not focused on the direct recognition of particular physical development on multilayer atmosphere scales. They usually use the available size of data records in modelling or analyzing local atmospheric progress. Statistics can be applied in short-time prediction of, or need to fuse combine their data processing with, NWP forecasting in a larger day horizon. Irradiance inputs and target PVP output sequences in a day-determined range can be used in statistical analyses or AI learning. The statistics models were applied to 24–48 h middle-scale data to post-process the system forecasts and compute PVP at all input–output-related sequence times. The conversion of NWP data has some drawbacks; the model functionality shows a great dependency on the applicability and reliability of the forecast data in processing [4]. The quality of AI-based learning predictions can essentially differ; the statistical procedure must undergo appropriate initialization and testing. Many AI methods show some limitations, for example, model unfitting or inadequate generalization related to local constraints of PVP plant designs. AI solutions can process additional data features or use extra units (cloudiness motion, spectral analysis) to recognize character of fluctuations or type structures in cloudiness formation processes. Popular hybrid techniques fuse different computing or processing approaches, additionally combining the unique key-model features to innovate the inadequate performance. Multistep forecasting can be direct or iterative (or a combination). In the first, the values are forecasted all at once at different times, contrary to the second approach, where iteratively predicted data at the previous time steps are supplied for the input vectors at the following computing time sequences. Additional solar features can be used, e.g., clearness factor, cloudiness index, aerosol and visibility parameter, turbidity, sun angle, or azimuth. The summation ensembles form a weighted model output to compute the final result according to the predetermined weather type or probabilistic reliability. If single-model forecasts differ in a large measure, the overall output is given a significant uncertainty. In contrast, when the results of the ensemble models show a large similarity, the uncertain character of the output model is greatly reduced. Probability intervals in the model output define an uncertainty range in computing reliable data estimations under different initial constraint statistics density.

The new differential learning is used to gradually elicit structures based on the form of a polynomial neural network (PNN), initially using one node, to partition and transform the general PDE of n variables into summation modules of single PDEs in blocks of two-variable nodes. The rational components are obtained in the form of Laplace transform images of unknown node functions, formed according to operator calculus (OC) procedures [5]. The inverse L-operation is applied to the node-produced rational components, based on the OC expression. Unknown node originals are obtained to be summed in the overall output of the n-variable PDE model. D-PNN combines and extracts the most applicable node input couples in each layer, step by step, to generate modular subcomponents from the originally defined PDEs and extend with them the iterative solution to reach the output error minima. The appropriate testing procedure can employ the external complement scheme to allow adaptation and adjustment of those node components, minimizing all computed errors in training and testing defined by the modelling constraint of a problem [6]. Historical observations with 24 h delay between input and output data are processed to pre-assess the optimal lengths of daily intervals, which enable us to obtain the operable statistics predictions in a day horizon. Finally, the tested models can compute their output sequences in the defined time horizon in relation to the processed last-day input data and the learned patterns included in the determined data sample range.

2. 24 h Sequenced PV-Output Prediction Based on Data Record Statistics

AI regression was used in training the 24 h delay between input–output data patterns (blue, left), selected in the optimal day-range sequences, by the initial assessment model.

The statistic models were developed in multisite data processing to apply the last known observation input series to forecast the complete day light cycle of PV power production in the applied 24 h trained prediction horizon (red, right). PVP production in the next 24 h is calculated by processing series at the related times in sequence data in the previous day. Initial assessment models examine data intervals, gradually increasing their days, to pre-define the optimal training process. Their computed output is compared one by one with the time-related data of the target CSI in the reserved part, to obtain the best accuracy. Error minima determine the approximate number of applicable day records that can be used in training. The recognized day-data patterns show mostly a degree of similarity compared to the latest observational hours used in the final testing. This procedure can successfully obtain up-to-date models that can process the unknown last-day input series (Figure 1) in most day-experiment instances.

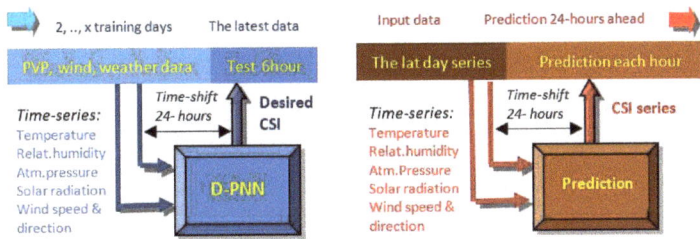

Figure 1. CSI day-sequence forecasting by models (red **right**) resulting from training for the initially assessed day-data patterns in an all-day input–output horizon (blue **left**).

The clear-sky index (CSI) is a relative solar parameter defined by ratio of the real to the ideal PVP considering total clear sky at any day time cycles. It is necessary to compute the output of the model in training and prediction [7] regardless of changes in the actual values, directly related to the PVP cycles in a time. PVP pattern change considerably as a result of different atmospheric conditions and local anomalies (e.g., cloudiness type, humidity character, wind gusts, etc. Overnight sudden changes in the previous pattern can cause difficulties in training. The statistically developed model may be completely out of date, unable to process unrecognized data series in prediction. NWP processing data can be applied in these sudden cases [5]. Figure 2 shows the frontal change in PVP patterns on 3 May.

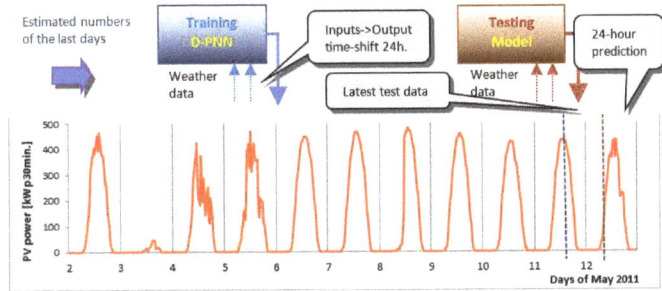

Figure 2. Model development, testing and CSI final output computing (red, right) related to changing PVP day patterns in the fixed 24 h input–output time delay (blue, left).

3. PDE Conversion and L-Transformation Using Operator Calculus

D-PNN evolves binary-tree structures to partition the generally defined PDE of n variables into determined-order sub-PDEs of two variables (using data samples). The simple PDEs are L-transformed using OC definitions into rational components, forming the Laplace images for the node-searched unavailable summation term series. Inverse members determined by L-restoration are used to calculate the overall output to model the separable function of n variables, initially defined only by the PDE [8].

$$a + bu + \sum_{i=1}^{n} c_i \frac{\partial u}{\partial x_i} + \sum_{i=1}^{n} \sum_{j=1}^{n} d_{ij} \frac{\partial^2 u}{\partial x_i \partial x_j} + \dots = 0 \tag{1}$$

$$u = \sum_{k=1}^{\infty} u_k \tag{2}$$

where the following are defined: $u(x_1, x_2, \dots, x_n)$—unknown separable function of n-input variables; $a, b, c_i, d_{ij}, \dots$—weights of terms; u_i—partial sum functions.

The general form of PDE (1) can be used to describe a problem-separable u function of n inputs, which can be formulated as a non-limited convergent series (2) of simplified functions u_k of two variables initially defined by sub-PDEs (3) in an equality of eight variables.

$$F\left(x_1, x_2, u, \frac{\partial u}{\partial x_1}, \frac{\partial u}{\partial x_2}, \frac{\partial^2 u}{\partial x_1^2}, \frac{\partial^2 u}{\partial x_1 \partial x_2}, \frac{\partial^2 u}{\partial x_2^2}\right) = 0 \tag{3}$$

where u_k are node partial sum functions of an unknown separable function u.

The adapted polynomial conversion using OC formulas for the derivatives $f(t)$ described by an ordinary differential equation (ODE) is based on the proposition that the Laplace transformation is applicable in the case of known initial conditions (4).

$$L\left\{f^{(n)}(t)\right\} = p^n F(p) - \sum_{k=1}^{n} p^{n-i} f_{0+}^{(i-1)} \quad L\{f(t)\} = F(p) \tag{4}$$

where the following are defined: $f(t), f'(t), \dots, f^{(n)}(t)$—originals continuous in $<0+, \infty>$; p, t—complex and real variables.

Polynomial conversion applied to ODE derivatives results in a set of Equation (4), where the Laplace transform $F(p)$ can be formulated through the complex conjugate p. $F(p)$ is separated in a rational term (5) to define the L-image of the function $f(t)$. The inverse transform of OC of the ration term restores the original $f(t)$ of a real variable t (5).

$$F(p) = \frac{P(p)}{Q(p)} = \frac{Bp + C}{p^2 + ap + b} = \sum_{k=1}^{n} \frac{A_k}{p - \alpha_k} \tag{5}$$

where the following are defined: B, C, A_k—coefficients of elementary fractions; a, b—polynomial parameters.

$$F(p) = \frac{P(p)}{Q(p)} = \sum_{k=1}^{n} \frac{P(\alpha_k)}{Q_k(\alpha_k)} \frac{1}{p - \alpha_k} \quad f(t) = \sum_{k=1}^{n} \frac{P(\alpha_k)}{Q_k(\alpha_k)} e^{\alpha_k \cdot t} \tag{6}$$

where the following are defined: α_k—simple real roots of the multinomial; $Q(p), F(p)$—L-transform image.

Rational components (8), formed to express the Laplace image terms of u_k functions (2), which are not available, result from the GMDH polynomials (7) composed of binary nodes of a PNN tree structure (Figure 3) in the PDE converting procedure. The inverse L operation is necessary (8) in the PNN nodes according to the definition of OC (6). The sum of originals determined by binary nodes in the partial u_k is used to calculate the overall model u (2) [8]. Each D-PNN node, using the GMDH output, groups possible simple or composite member solutions (8) for specific two-input sub-PDEs. The selected components are included in the D-PNN output sum to better converge to the target output.

$$y = a_0 + a_1 x_i + a_2 x_j + a_3 x_i x_j + a_4 x_i^2 + a_5 x_j^2 \tag{7}$$

where the following are defined: x_i, x_j—two input variables of neuron nodes.

$$y_i = w_i \frac{b_0 + b_1x_1 + b_2sig(x_1^2) + b_3x_2 + b_4sig(x_2^2)}{a_0 + a_1x_1 + a_2x_2 + a_3x_1x_2 + a_4sig(x_1^2) + a_5sig(x_2^2)} \cdot e^{\varphi} \quad (8)$$

where the following are defined: $\varphi = arctg(x_1/x_2)$—phase representation of two input variables; x_1, x_2, a_i, b_i—polynomial parameters; w_i—weights; sig—sigmoidal transform.

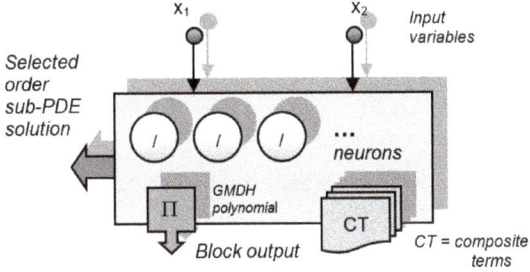

Figure 3. Block nodes of produce and group simple (/) and composite PDE member solutions.

The Euler formulation of conjugates in complex form (9), represents the conversion $f(t)$ in OC (6). The radius r is defined as a rational element, while the angle ($arctg(x_2/x_1)$) of two real inputs is related to the inverse restoration L of $F(p)$.

$$p = \underbrace{x_1}_{Re} + i \cdot \underbrace{x_2}_{Im} = \sqrt{x_1^2 + x_2^2} \cdot e^{i \cdot arctan(\frac{x_2}{x_1})} = r \cdot e^{i \cdot \varphi} = r \cdot (\cos\varphi + i \cdot \sin\varphi) \quad (9)$$

4. PDE Partition in Backward Tree Structures of D-PNN Layers

D-PNN forms progressive binary-tree structures, using composite processing functions (7) in PNN nodes, by extending/modifying the last added/processed layer with selected blocks nodes, one by one. Node blocks in secondary subsequent tree layers can form composite term (CT) products, in addition to one-fraction neurons (8). CTs are products consisting of adjustable neurons, i.e., sub-PDE converts, selected in the back-attached production blocks in the backward linked tree structure layers (Figure 4). CTs represent composite sub-PDE solutions for the node-unavailable u_k function series in the form of a product that includes images of external and internal functions commonly expressed by the derivation rules (11).

$$F(x_1, x_2, \ldots, x_n) = f(z_1, z_2, \ldots, z_m) = f(\phi_1(X), \phi_2(X), \ldots, \phi_m(X)) \quad (10)$$

$$\frac{\partial F}{\partial x_k} = \sum_{i=1}^{m} \frac{\partial f(z_1, z_2, \ldots, z_m)}{\partial z_i} \cdot \frac{\partial \phi_i(X)}{\partial x_k} \quad k = 1, \ldots, n \quad (11)$$

For example, a block in the third layer can form additional CTs using products of sub-PDE ratio converts (12), that is, the simple neuron images of two and four back-linked tree blocks in the previous two layers (Figure 4).

$$y_{31} = w_{31} \cdot \frac{b_0 + b_1x_{21} + b_2x_{21}^2 + b_3x_{22} + b_4x_{22}^2}{a_0 + a_1x_{21} + a_2x_{22} + a_3x_{21}x_{22} + a_4x_{21}^2 + a_5x_{22}^2} \cdot \frac{b_0 + b_1x_{12} + b_2x_{12}^2}{a_0 + a_1x_{11} + a_2x_{12} + a_3x_{11}x_{12} + a_4x_{11}^2 + a_5x_{12}^2} \cdot \frac{P_{12}(x_1, x_2)}{Q_{12}(x_1, x_2)} \cdot e^{\varphi_{31}} \quad (12)$$

where the following are defined: Q_{ij}, P_{ij} = output and reduced multi-nomial of n and $n - 1th$ degree; y_{kp}—pth Composite Term (CT); $\varphi_{21} = arctg(x_{11}/x_{13})$; $\varphi_{31} = arctg(x_{21}/x_{22})\varphi$.

The number of possible CT combinations in blocks doubles along with each back-joined preceding layer (Figure 4). Neurons in each next layer can produce more composite partial model components, using the block node outputs and PDE converts.

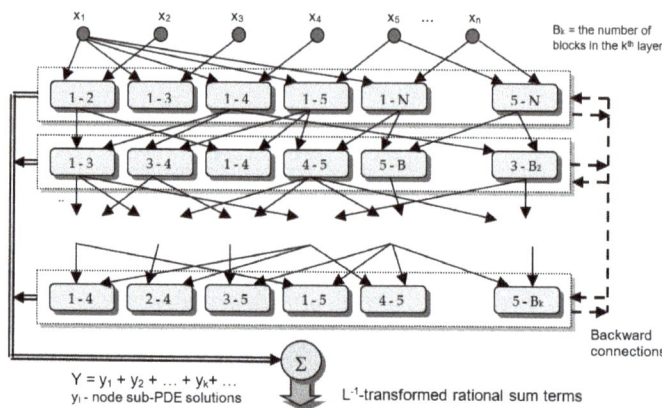

Figure 4. D-PNN searches for the most valuable input couple node blocks to generate sum PDE components, neurons and CTs, possible to insert in the overall model.

The summation model output Y is the arithmetic mean of active neurons + CT, produced in node blocks, which optimizes the adjustment and selection of PDE terms (13).

$$Y = \frac{1}{k}\sum_{i=1}^{k} y_i \qquad (13)$$

where k = the number of active neurons or CTs (node PDE solutions).

Multi-objective models based on procedures can be used to optimize performance of the back-production of selected neurons and CTs in the tree-like block structure (Figure 4). D-PNN searches for the most relevant combination couples in each input layer, analogously to the principles of GMDH [6], to form and rearrange adequate PDE components acceptable by the model. Polynomial coefficients and weights of terms are partially optimized using the gradient method [9] in each iteration tree cycle. The algorithm randomly skips the block nodes, one by one, to select and update the applied neurons or CTs involved in the complete model. The training error is calculated in relation to a continuously performed test based on the external complement restraint evaluation. This approach allows only inserting or adapting PDE components that comply with the testing restrictions. The root mean squared error (RMSE) is a gradually minimized measure of the model approximation ability at each step of training (Figure 1).

5. PVP Prediction Using the AI Pre-Determined Training Sequences in 24 h Horizon

PVP was forecasted at the Starojcka Lhota plant located in the North-East Moravian region of the Czech Republic, using historical measurements of ground environment temperature, PVP, and irradiance along with multisite spatial meteorological data of wind parameters from three nearby regional wind farms located in Maletin, Drahany, and Veseli nad Moravou. These data sets were supplied with free access airport weather observations (avg. ground temperature, avg. humidity, avg. atm. pressure, avg. wind parameters and visibility conditions) of two ground-based stations located in Brno-Turany and Ostrava-Monov (Figure 5). These standard variables were used in the development of models to predict the complete day-ahead PVP cycle data in the 24 h input–output delay. Detailed minute power measurements of the PV plant and wind farms were averaged and extrapolated to correspond to a half-hour meteorological data series from airport weather observation stations [10].

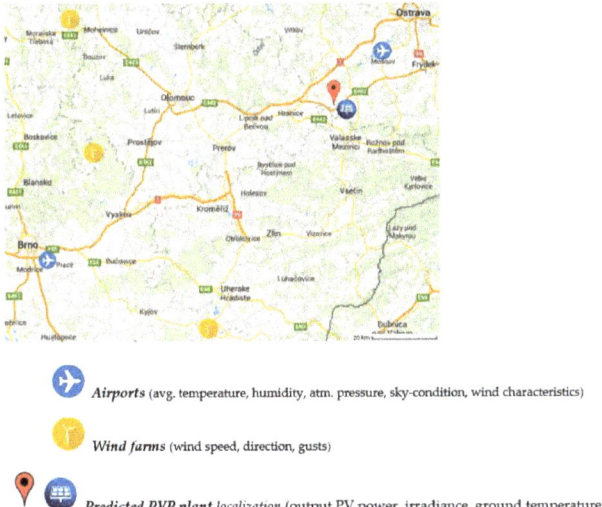

Airports (avg. temperature, humidity, atm. pressure, sky-condition, wind characteristics)

Wind farms (wind speed, direction, gusts)

Predicted PVP plant *localization* (output PV power, irradiance, ground temperature)

Figure 5. PVP plant and wind farm allocation in measurements and meteo-observations.

Figure 6 shows PVP forecast results of the D-PNN, Statistics and Machine Learning Tool-Box (SMLT) for Matlab regression [11], and persistent models in the 24 h horizon in specific demonstration days of the examined 2-week interval from 12–25 May 2011. The SMLT day-ahead final forecasting models were chosen considering their test error minima, obtained from the reserved part of available set data. The optimal training days, including applicable data patterns, were predetermined initially by examination of data in the previous gradually increasing training-day intervals, using a simplified model form, the same as using D-PNN (Figure 1). The SMLT forecast models resulting from Gaussian Process Regression (GPR), Support Vector Machine (SVM), and Ensemble Boosted/Bagged Tree (EBT), using the same input–output data sample variables in the next day 24 h CSI sequence prediction, obtained with the testing RMSE minima which differ only in a slight measure. Persistent comparative models, average CSI in processing series over the determined number of the last-day intervals, were used to estimate the approximation series at the responding PVP cycle day time. These oversimplified forecast benchmark solutions could be considered as daily error-reference minima.

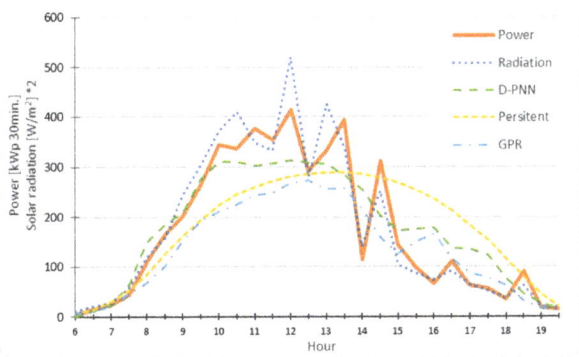

Figure 6. St. Lhota, 16 May 2011: variable cloudiness (catching and sunny periods follow); RMSE: D-PNN = 60.09; Persistent = 89.51; SMLT = 78.1 kWp 30 min.

The ratios of the averaged PVP series and the difference values show the relative involvement in the day PV patterns (Figure 7). Slight variations in the data indicate a smooth plain in PVP cycles in settled sunny weather. These phenomena are contrary to the ramping fluctuations in PVP day series, mostly in cloudy weather (Figure 6). The prediction errors in day ahead PVP estimations may be related to relative ratios and absolute differences obtained on PVP data series (Figure 7; they can denote a pattern complexity in daily PVP cycle series in consideration of the PV power average/maxima. Figure 8 presents the mean R^2 determination parameter in the prediction of PV power 24 h in advance. The models of D-PNN and SMLT better perform in case of different estimations in the optimal training data sample sequences in comparison to the benchmark reference solutions (Figure 9), i.e., the varying number of the training data records can result in analogous prediction series (Figure 8).

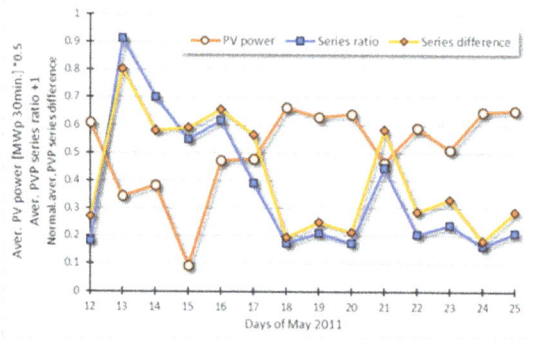

Figure 7. The daily average PV series ratios are dimensionless and characterize daily data patterns regard-less of the absolute power values, 12–25 May 2011.

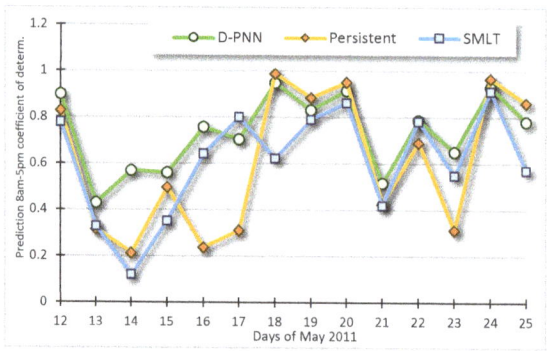

Figure 8. The 2-week daily average PVP prediction coefficient of determination R^2: D-PNN = 084, Persistent = 0.787, SMLT = 0.79.

The reference models mostly perform worse in changeable cloudy weather; however, lower errors in the 24 h persistent prediction can be obtained in days with a higher degree of similarity in patterns indicated by smooth plain PVP cycles (no ramping events). The applied AI models show slight inaccuracies in this specific condition if the last-day unsettled changeable weather intervals are suddenly broken by an overnight front, resulting in a sunny-day character (the second week in the examined data period). SMLT models obtain more accurate prediction data, as compared to D-PNN, in days of settled stable weather conditions, including a few previous days. The AI predictions can sometimes obtain an increase in the final model accuracy in the early afternoon (Figure 6). These phenomena are directly related to particular weather patterns and characteristics of training data samples in days of forecasts. An increase in forecast errors in the first week data is related to unsettled weather conditions resulting in more complex data patterns not fully applicable to AI learning. Output errors denote the operability of finally tested prediction models in processing the reserved last observed data sequences applied on the 24 h horizon.

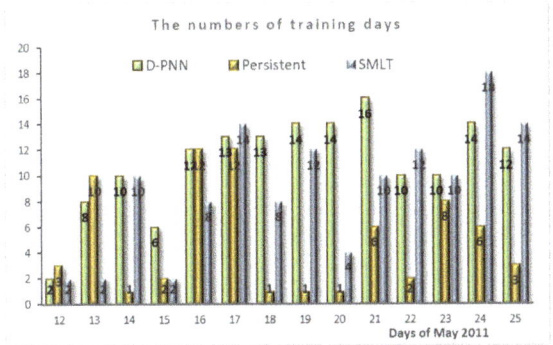

Figure 9. Daily initialization time of the 24 h PVP prediction models.

6. Conclusions

Estimated day sequence optima in the training data eliminate sudden variations and rapid changes in local weather situations. New approaches applicable in a more adequate selection of data sample records can try to recognize the frontal overnight change breaks in weather progress. The following data intervals can be applied in training, in place of the initial model identification scheme. Data patterns can be re-analyzed in a longer time interval (if available the observations) to extract adequate training data records according to the pattern similarity, one by one, in order to obtain the test error minima, not necessarily considering the sequence in the day time.

Author Contributions: Conceptualization, L.Z. and V.S.; methodology, L.Z.; software, L.Z.; validation, V.S.; formal analysis, L.Z.; investigation, V.S.; resources, V.S.; data curation, L.Z.; writing—original draft preparation, L.Z.; writing—review and editing, L.Z.; visualization, L.Z.; supervision, V.S.; project administration, V.S.; funding acquisition, V.S. All authors have read and agreed to the published version of the manuscript.

Funding: This research received no external funding.

Institutional Review Board Statement: Not applicable.

Informed Consent Statement: Not applicable.

Data Availability Statement: Data and software: https://drive.google.com/drive/folders/1ZAw8 KcvDEDM-i7ifVe_hDoS35nI64-Fh.

Acknowledgments: The work was supported by SGS, VSB—Technical University of Ostrava, Czech Republic, under the grant "Parallel processing of Big Data IX" [No\SGS2022/12].

Conflicts of Interest: The authors declare no conflict of interest.

References

1. Vannitsem, S. Dynamical properties of mos forecasts: Analysis of the ecmwf operational forecasting system. *Weather. Forecast.* **2008**, *23*, 1032–1043. [CrossRef]
2. Inman, R.H.; Pedro, H.T.; Coimbra, C.F. Solar forecasting methods for renewable energy integration. *Prog. Energy Combust. Sci.* **2013**, *39*, 535–576. [CrossRef]

3. Shi, J.; Lee, W.-J.; Liu, Y.; Yang, Y.; Wang, P. Forecasting power output of photovoltaic systems based on weather classification and support vector machines. *IEEE Trans. Ind. Appl.* **2012**, *148*, 1064–1069. [CrossRef]

4. Zjavka, L.; Krömer, P.; Mišák, S.; Snášel, V. Modeling the photovoltaic output power using the differential polynomial network and evolutional fuzzy rules. *Math. Model. Anal.* **2017**, *22*, 78–94. [CrossRef]

5. Zjavka, L.; Sokol, Z. Local improvements in numerical forecasts of relative humidity using polynomial solutions of general differential equations. *Q. J. R. Meteorol. Soc.* **2018**, *144*, 780–791. [CrossRef]

6. Nikolaev, N.Y.; Iba, H. *Adaptive Learning of Polynomial Networks*; Genetic and evolutionary computation; Springer: New York, NY, USA, 2006.

7. Coimbra, C.; Kleissl, J.; Marquez, R. *Overview of Solar Forecasting Methods and a Metric for Accuracy Evaluation*; Elsevier: Amsterdam, The Netherlands, 2013; pp. 171–194.

8. Zjavka, L.; Mišák, S. Direct wind power forecasting using a polynomial decomposition of the general differential equation. *IEEE Trans. Sustain. Energy* **2018**, *9*, 1529–1539. [CrossRef]

9. Zjavka, L.; Snášel, V. Constructing ordinary sum differential equations using polynomial networks. *Inf. Sci.* **2014**, *281*, 462–477. [CrossRef]

10. Weather Underground Historical Data. Available online: https://www.wunderground.com/history/daily/LKTB/date/2016-7-22 (accessed on 24 June 2022).

11. Matlab-Statistics and Machine Learning Tool-Box for Regression. Available online: www.mathworks.com/help/stats/choose-regression-model-options.html (accessed on 24 June 2022).

Proceeding Paper

Modelling the Number of Daily Stock Transactions Using a Novel Time Series Model [†]

Sunecher Yuvraj

Department of Accounting, Finance and Economics, Faculty of Business Management and Finance, University of Technology Mauritius, Port-Louis 11108, Mauritius; ysunecher@umail.utm.ac.mu

† Presented at the 8th International Conference on Time Series and Forecasting, Gran Canaria, Spain, 27–30 June 2022.

Abstract: This paper focusses on the impact of the COVID-19 on the Stock Exchange of Mauritius (SEM) by modelling the number of daily stock transactions of two banks. Hence, a non-stationary bivariate integer-valued autoregressive and moving average of order 1 (BINARMA (1,1)) process with COM-Poisson (CMP) innovations (BINARMA (1,1) CMP) is introduced. The conditional maximum likelihood (CML) approach is used to estimate the model parameters. The novel model is applied on the intra-day trading of two banking stocks.

Keywords: non-stationary; autoregressive; moving average; COM-poisson; CML

Citation: Yuvraj, S. Modelling the Number of Daily Stock Transactions Using a Novel Time Series Model. *Eng. Proc.* **2022**, *18*, 35. https://doi.org/10.3390/engproc2022018035

Academic Editors: Ignacio Rojas, Hector Pomares, Olga Valenzuela, Fernando Rojas and Luis Javier Herrera

Published: 27 June 2022

Publisher's Note: MDPI stays neutral with regard to jurisdictional claims in published maps and institutional affiliations.

1. Introduction

The Stock Exchange of Mauritius Ltd. (SEM, Port-Louis, Mauritius) started trading on 30 March 1989 as a private limited company with the responsibility of promoting a proficient and well-regulated stock market in Mauritius. The SEM changed its status on 6 October 2008 to operate as a public company and has all these years left any stone unturned to be the leading stock exchange market in the African continent. To date, the SEM has positioned itself as an essential capital raising platform for nearly 61 companies operating in the financial, construction, leisure, agricultural and other sectors of the economy. In its internationalization process, the SEM has set-up a multi-currency listing, trading and financial platform and has modernized its listing framework with different multi-asset class financial products. In 2010, the SEM embarked in a new journey by changing its strategic direction and started an internationalization of its operational and regulatory framework. To date, the market capitalization and the annual turnover of the SEM are approximately USD 7.5 billion and USD 302 billion, respectively.

The start of the financial year 2020–2021 was affected by the direct impact of the COVID-19 followed by the first nationwide sanitary confinement from March 2020 to May 2020. With the upliftment of the confinement, the Mauritian economy gradually started its recovery pathway. However, a second nationwide confinement was announced in March 2021 due to the resurgence of the COVID-19 cases with a partial de-confinement plan as from May 2021 up till now. Undeniably, the impact of the COVID-19 was severe such that the SEM has been navigating mostly in the red zone during this pandemic period. In the year 2021, the market started recovering following the announcements of the vaccines against the COVID-19, but the recovery was again affected by the second confinement. Hence, modelling the number of intra-day transactions on the stock market is of upmost importance. Several researchers have also elaborated on the potential covariates that affect these daily stock transactions: the impact of news entering the market, the time of day effect and the day effect [1,2]. Time of the day effect and the impact of news on the market have proved to influence the intensity of daily trading on the stock market [3]. However up till now, there has not been any studies that have incorporated the cross-correlation between two competing companies affected by the above covariates as well as the COVID-19 news effect.

Quoreshi [4,5] is the first author who tried to model the number of intra-day transactions in the literature by developing a BINMA(p) process and applying the latter on the number of intra-day transactions of AstraZeneca and Ericsson B based on the Generalized Poisson distribution of the innovation series due to the over-dispersed nature of the data. Several authors have recently introduced bivariate processes under the non-stationary negative binomial (NB) and CMP innovations in the literature under either autoregressive or moving average structures (see Jowaheer et al. [6], Mamodekhan et al. [7] and Sunecher et al. [8,9]). As for the estimation of parameters, Quoreshi [4,5] estimated the regression effects using the feasible generalized least squares (FGLS) technique and concluded that the estimates of the model parameters are efficient, but the efficiency of these estimates have been questioned (see Sunecher et al. [8]). Another estimation method which has been frequently used in the literature is the generalized quasi-likelihood (GQL) method which has proved to yield more reliable estimates than FGLS. However, the likelihood-based approach provides the best estimates [10].

Based on the above findings, this paper proposes a novel bivariate integer-valued autoregressive and moving average of order 1 (BINARMA (1,1)) process under non-stationary COM-Poisson (CMP) innovation series where the model parameters are estimated using the conditional maximum likelihood (CML) approach. This novel model is then applied to the intra-day series of two banks listed on the SEM.

Hence, the paper is laid out as follows: In Section 2, the BINARMA (1,1) process with CMP innovations is developed. In Section 3, the CML approach is derived and Section 4 presents the forecasting equations. In Section 5, the BINARMA (1,1) model is applied on the number of intra-day transactions of two banks listed in SEM and is compared with two other competing models. The conclusion is presented in the last section.

2. The Non-Stationary BINARMA (1,1) Process with COM-Poisson Innovations (BINARMA (1,1) CMP)

Consider

$$Y_t^{[1]} = \gamma_{11} * Y_{t-1}^{[1]} + \gamma_{12} * R_{t-1}^{[2]} + R_t^{[1]} \tag{1}$$

$$Y_t^{[2]} = \gamma_{21} * Y_{t-1}^{[2]} + \gamma_{22} * R_{t-1}^{[2]} + R_t^{[2]} \tag{2}$$

where $\gamma_{kj} \in (0,1)$ and $\gamma_{kj}*$ are mutually independent binomial thinning operators such that $\gamma_{kj} * Y_{t-1}^{[k]} = \sum_{i=0}^{Y_{t-1}^{[k]}} Z_i$ where $Z_i \sim Bernoulli(\gamma_{kj})$.

'$\circ$' indicates the binomial thinning operator [11,12] such that $\{\gamma_{kk} \circ Y_{t-1}^{[k]} | Y_{t-1}^{[k]}\} \sim$ Binomial$(Y_{t-1}^{[k]}, \gamma_{kk})$ where:

1. $E(\gamma \circ Y) = \gamma E(Y)$;
2. $Var(\gamma \circ Y) = \gamma(1-\gamma)E(Y) + \gamma^2 Var(Y)$;
3. $Cov(\gamma_1 \circ Y^{[1]}, \gamma_2 \circ Y^{[2]}) = \gamma_1 \gamma_2 Cov(Y^{[1]}, Y^{[2]})$.

As for the innovation terms, $Corr(R_t^{[1]}, R_t^{[2]}) = \alpha_{12}$ where $(R_t^{[1]}, R_t^{[2]})$ follows a bivariate COM-Poisson distribution with $R_t^{[k]} \sim COM - Poisson(\lambda_t^{[k]}, \bar{\nu}_k)$. Note that $\lambda_t^{[k]} = (\theta_t^{[k]})^{1/\bar{\nu}_k} - (\frac{\bar{\nu}_k - 1}{2\bar{\nu}_k})$, where $\theta_t^{[k]} = \exp(x_t'\beta^{[k]})$ with $x_t = [x_{t1}, x_{t2}, \ldots, x_{tj}, \ldots, x_{tp}]'$ and $\beta^{[k]} = [\beta_1^{[k]}, \beta_2^{[k]}, \ldots, \beta_j^{[k]}, \ldots, \beta_p^{[k]}]'$ for $k \in \{1,2\}$.

Based on the above conditions, the moments are derived as follows:

$$E(Y_t^{[1]}) = E(\gamma_{11} \circ Y_{t-1}^{[1]} + \gamma_{12} \circ R_{t-1}^{[1]} + R_t^{[1]})$$
$$= E(\gamma_{11} \circ Y_{t-1}^{[1]}) + E(\gamma_{12} \circ R_{t-1}^{[1]}) + E(R_t^{[1]})$$
$$= \gamma_{11} E(Y_{t-1}^{[1]}) + \gamma_{12} E(R_{t-1}^{[1]}) + E(R_t^{[1]})$$
$$\mu_t^{[1]} = E(Y_t^{[1]}) = \gamma_{11} \mu_{t-1} + \gamma_{12} \lambda_{t-1}^{[1]} + \lambda_t^{[1]}, \tag{3}$$

$$E(Y_t^{[2]}) = E(\gamma_{21} \circ Y_{t-1}^{[2]} + \gamma_{22} \circ R_{t-1}^{[2]} + R_t^{[2]})$$
$$= E(\gamma_{21} \circ Y_{t-1}^{[2]}) + E(\gamma_{22} \circ R_{t-1}^{[2]}) + E(R_t^{[2]})$$
$$= \gamma_{21} E(Y_{t-1}^{[2]}) + \gamma_{22} E(R_{t-1}^{[2]}) + E(R_t^{[2]})$$
$$\mu_t^{[2]} = E(Y_t^{[2]}) = \gamma_{21} \mu_{t-1} + \gamma_{22} \lambda_{t-1}^{[1]} + \lambda_t^{[1]}, \tag{4}$$

$$Var(Y_t^{[1]}) = Var(\gamma_{11} \circ Y_{t-1}^{[1]} + \gamma_{12} \circ R_{t-1}^{[1]} + R_t^{[1]})$$
$$= Var(\gamma_{11} * Y_{t-1}^{[1]}) + Var(\gamma_{12} * R_{t-1}^{[1]}) + Var(R_t^{[1]}) + 2Cov(\gamma_{11} * Y_{t-1}^{[1]}, \gamma_{12} * R_{t-1}^{[1]})$$
$$= \gamma_{11}(1 - \gamma_{11})E(Y_{t-1}^{[1]}) + \gamma_{11}^2 Var(Y_{t-1}^{[1]}) + \gamma_{12}(1 - \gamma_{12})E(R_{t-1}^{[1]})$$
$$+ \gamma_{12}^2 Var(R_{t-1}^{[1]}) + Var(R_t^{[1]}) + 2Cov(\gamma_{11} * Y_{t-1}^{[1]}, \gamma_{12} * R_{t-1}^{[1]})$$
$$= \gamma_{11}(1 - \gamma_{11})\mu_{t-1}^{[1]} + \gamma_{11}^2 Var(Y_{t-1}^{[1]}) + \gamma_{12}(1 - \gamma_{12})\lambda_{t-1}^{[1]}$$
$$+ \gamma_{12}^2 \left[\frac{\lambda_{t-1}^{[1]}}{\tilde{v}_k} + \frac{\tilde{v}_k - 1}{2\tilde{v}_k^2} \right] + \left[\frac{\lambda_{t-1}^{[1]}}{\tilde{v}_k} + \frac{\tilde{v}_k - 1}{2\tilde{v}_k^2} \right] + 2\gamma_{11}\gamma_{12}Cov(Y_{t-1}^{[1]}, R_{t-1}^{[1]})$$
$$= \gamma_{11}(1 - \gamma_{11})\mu_{t-1}^{[1]} + \gamma_{11}^2 Var(Y_{t-1}^{[1]}) + \gamma_{12}(1 - \gamma_{12})\lambda_{t-1}^{[1]}$$
$$+ (1 + \gamma_{12}^2 + 2\gamma_{11}\gamma_{12}) \left[\frac{\lambda_{t-1}^{[1]}}{\tilde{v}_1} + \frac{\tilde{v}_1 - 1}{2\tilde{v}_1^2} \right], \tag{5}$$

where

$$Cov(Y_{t-1}^{[1]}, R_{t-1}^{[1]}) = Cov(\gamma_{11} \circ Y_{t-2}^{[1]} + \gamma_{12} \circ R_{t-2}^{[1]} + R_{t-1}^{[1]}, R_{t-1}^{[1]})$$
$$= Cov(R_{t-1}^{[1]}, R_{t-1}^{[1]})$$
$$= Var(R_{t-1}^{[1]})$$
$$= \frac{\lambda_{t-1}^{[1]}}{\tilde{v}_1} + \frac{\tilde{v}_1 - 1}{2\tilde{v}_1^2}. \tag{6}$$

Similarly,

$$Var(Y_t^{[2]}) = Var(\gamma_{21} * Y_{t-1}^{[2]}) + Var(\gamma_{22} * R_{t-1}^{[2]}) + Var(R_t^{[2]}) + 2Cov(\gamma_{21} * Y_{t-1}^{[2]}, \gamma_{22} * R_{t-1}^{[2]})$$
$$= \gamma_{21}(1 - \gamma_{21})\mu_{t-1}^{[2]} + \gamma_{21}^2 Var(Y_{t-1}^{[2]}) + \gamma_{22}(1 - \gamma_{22})\lambda_{t-1}^{[2]}$$
$$+ (1 + \gamma_{22}^2 + 2\gamma_{21}\gamma_{22}) \left[\frac{\lambda_{t-1}^{[2]}}{\tilde{v}_2} + \frac{\tilde{v}_2 - 1}{2\tilde{v}_2^2} \right]. \tag{7}$$

As for the covariance for the same series,

$$\begin{aligned}
\text{Cov}(Y_t^{[1]}, Y_{t+h}^{[1]}) &= \text{Cov}[Y_t^{[1]}, (\gamma_{11} \circ Y_{t+h-1}^{[1]} + \gamma_{12} \circ R_{t+h-1}^{[1]} + R_{t+h}^{[1]})] \\
&= \gamma_{11} \text{Cov}[Y_t^{[1]}, Y_{t+h-1}^{[1]}] \\
&= \gamma_{11} \text{Cov}[Y_t^{[1]}, (\gamma_{11} \circ Y_{t+h-2}^{[1]} + \gamma_{12} \circ R_{t+h-2}^{[1]} + R_{t+h-1}^{[1]})] \\
&= \gamma_{11}^2 \text{Cov}[Y_t^{[1]}, Y_{t+h-2}^{[1]}] \\
&\;\;\vdots \\
&= \gamma_{11}^{h-1} \text{Cov}[Y_t^{[1]}, (\gamma_{11} \circ Y_t^{[1]} + \gamma_{12} \circ R_t^{[1]} + R_{t+1}^{[1]})] \\
&= \gamma_{11}^h \text{Var}(Y_t^{[1]}) + \gamma_{11}^{h-1} \gamma_{12} \text{Var}(R_t^{[1]}) \\
&= \gamma_{11}^h \text{Var}(Y_t^{[1]}) + \gamma_{11}^{h-1} \gamma_{12} \left[\frac{\lambda_{t-1}^{[1]}}{\tilde{v}_1} + \frac{\tilde{v}_1 - 1}{2\tilde{v}_1^2} \right]
\end{aligned}$$
(8)

and

$$\text{Cov}(Y_t^{[2]}, Y_{t+h}^{[2]}) = \gamma_{21}^h \text{Var}(Y_t^{[2]}) + \gamma_{21}^{h-1} \gamma_{22} \left[\frac{\lambda_{t-1}^{[2]}}{\tilde{v}_2} + \frac{\tilde{v}_2 - 1}{2\tilde{v}_2^2} \right].$$
(9)

The cross-covariance are derived as follows:

$$\begin{aligned}
\text{Cov}(Y_t^{[1]}, Y_t^{[2]}) &= \text{Cov}(\gamma_{11} \circ Y_{t-1}^{[1]} + \gamma_{12} \circ R_{t-1}^{[1]} + R_t^{[1]}, \gamma_{21} \circ Y_{t-1}^{[2]} + \gamma_{22} \circ R_{t-1}^{[2]} + R_t^{[2]}) \\
&= \gamma_{11}\gamma_{21}\text{Cov}(Y_{t-1}^{[1]}, Y_{t-1}^{[2]}) + \gamma_{11}\gamma_{22}\text{Cov}(Y_{t-1}^{[1]}, R_{t-1}^{[2]}) \\
&\quad + \gamma_{12}\gamma_{21}\text{Cov}(R_{t-1}^{[1]}, Y_{t-1}^{[2]}) + \text{Cov}(R_{t-1}^{[1]}, R_{t-1}^{[2]}) + \text{Cov}(R_t^{[1]}, R_t^{[2]}) \\
&= \gamma_{11}\gamma_{21}\text{Cov}(Y_{t-1}^{[1]}, Y_{t-1}^{[2]}) + (\gamma_{11}\gamma_{22} + \gamma_{12}\gamma_{21} + \gamma_{12}\gamma_{22})\alpha\sqrt{\lambda_{t-1}^{[1]}}\sqrt{\lambda_{t-1}^{[2]}} \\
&\quad + \alpha\sqrt{\lambda_t^{[1]}}\sqrt{\lambda_t^{[2]}},
\end{aligned}$$
(10)

$$\begin{aligned}
\text{Cov}(Y_t^{[1]}, Y_{t+h}^{[2]}) &= \text{Cov}[Y_t^{[1]}, (\gamma_{21} \circ Y_{t+h-1}^{[2]} + \gamma_{22} \circ R_{t+h-1}^{[2]} + R_{t+h}^{[2]})] \\
&= \gamma_{21}\text{Cov}[Y_t^{[1]}, Y_{t+h-1}^{[2]}] \\
&= \gamma_{21}\text{Cov}[Y_t^{[1]}, (\gamma_{21} \circ Y_{t+h-2}^{[2]} + \gamma_{22} \circ R_{t+h-2}^{[2]} + R_{t+h-1}^{[2]})] \\
&= \gamma_{21}^2 \text{Cov}[Y_t^{[1]}, Y_{t+h-2}^{[2]}] \\
&\;\;\vdots \\
&= \gamma_{21}^{h-1}\text{Cov}[Y_t^{[1]}, (\gamma_{21} \circ Y_t^{[2]} + \gamma_{22} \circ R_t^{[2]} + R_{t+1}^{[2]})] \\
&= \gamma_{21}^h \text{Cov}(Y_t^{[1]}, Y_t^{[2]}) + \gamma_{21}^{h-1}\gamma_{22}\text{Cov}(R_t^{[1]}, R_t^{[2]}) \\
&= \gamma_{21}^h \text{Cov}(Y_t^{[1]}, Y_t^{[2]}) + \gamma_{21}^{h-1}\gamma_{22}\alpha\sqrt{\lambda_t^{[1]}}\sqrt{\lambda_t^{[2]}}
\end{aligned}$$
(11)

and

$$\text{Cov}(Y_t^{[2]}, Y_{t+h}^{[1]}) = \gamma_{11}^h \text{Cov}(Y_t^{[1]}, Y_t^{[2]}) + \gamma_{11}^{h-1}\gamma_{12}\alpha\sqrt{\lambda_t^{[1]}}\sqrt{\lambda_t^{[2]}}.$$
(12)

Remark 1. *Under stationary moment conditions, replacing* $t = 1$ *in Equations (3)–(7) and Equation (10), we have*

$$\mu_1^{[1]} = E(Y_t^{[1]}) = \frac{(\gamma_{12} + 1)\lambda_1^{[1]}}{1 - \gamma_{11}}$$
(13)

$$\mu_1^{[2]} = E(Y_t^{[2]}) = \frac{(\gamma_{22} + 1)\lambda_1^{[2]}}{1 - \gamma_{21}} \tag{14}$$

$$Var(Y_1^{[1]}) = \left(\frac{1}{1 - \gamma_{11}^2}\right)\{\gamma_{11}(1 - \gamma_{11})\mu_1^{[1]} + \gamma_{12}(1 - \gamma_{12})\lambda_1^{[1]}$$
$$+ (1 + \gamma_{12}^2 + 2\gamma_{11}\gamma_{12})\left[\frac{\lambda_1^{[1]}}{\tilde{v}_1} + \frac{\tilde{v}_1 - 1}{2\tilde{v}_1^2}\right]\}, \tag{15}$$

$$Var(Y_1^{[2]}) = \left(\frac{1}{1 - \gamma_{21}^2}\right)\{\gamma_{21}(1 - \gamma_{21})\mu_{t-1}^{[2]} + \gamma_{22}(1 - \gamma_{22})\lambda_{t-1}^{[2]}$$
$$+ (1 + \gamma_{22}^2 + 2\gamma_{21}\gamma_{22})\left[\frac{\lambda_{t-1}^{[2]}}{\tilde{v}_2} + \frac{\tilde{v}_2 - 1}{2\tilde{v}_2^2}\right]\}, \tag{16}$$

$$Cov(Y_1^{[1]}, Y_1^{[2]}) = \frac{(\gamma_{11}\gamma_{22} + \gamma_{12}\gamma_{21} + \gamma_{12}\gamma_{22} + 1)\alpha\sqrt{\lambda_1^{[1]}}\sqrt{\lambda_1^{[2]}}}{1 - \gamma_{11}\gamma_{21}} \tag{17}$$

Remark 2. *Using the initial values for $t = 1$ in Equations (12)–(16), we compute the values of $\mu_t^{[1]}, \mu_t^{[2]}, Var(Y_t^{[1]}), Var(Y_t^{[2]})$ and $Cov(Y_t^{[1]}, Y_t^{[2]})$ in Equations (3)–(11) iteratively for $t = 2, \ldots, T$.*

3. Conditional Maximum Likelihood Method

In this section, we derive the CML method for estimating the parameters of the BINARMA (1,1) model based on thinning and convolution properties [13]. The conditional density of the proposed BINARMA (1,1) model with COM-Poisson innovations is derived as follows:

$$f_1(k) = \sum_{j_1=0}^{k}\binom{y_{t-1}^{[1]}}{j_1}\binom{r_{t-1}^{[1]} = y_{t-1}^{[1]} - k}{k - j_1}$$
$$\gamma_{11}^{j_1}(1 - \gamma_{11})^{y_{t-1}^{[1]} - j_1}\gamma_{12}^{k-j_1}(1 - \gamma_{12})^{y_{t-1}^{[1]} - 2k + j_1}, \tag{18}$$

$$f_2(s) = \sum_{j_2=0}^{s}\binom{y_{t-1}^{[2]}}{j_2}\binom{r_{t-1}^{[2]} = y_{t-1}^{[2]} - s}{s - j_2}$$
$$\gamma_{21}^{j_2}(1 - \gamma_{21})^{y_{t-1}^{[2]} - j_2}\gamma_{22}^{s-j_2}(1 - \gamma_{22})^{y_{t-1}^{[2]} - 2s + j_2}, \tag{19}$$

and a bivariate distribution of the innovation terms $f_3(r_t^{[1]} = y_{t-1}^{[1]} - k, r_t^{[2]} = y_{t-1}^{[2]} - s) = P_{(R_t^{[1]} = r_t^{[1]}, R_t^{[2]} r_t^{[2]})}$, where

$$f_3(r_t^{[1]} = y_{t-1}^{[1]} - k, r_t^{[2]} = y_{t-1}^{[2]} - s) = \left[\frac{(\lambda_t^{[1]})^{y_{t-1}^{[1]} - k}}{((y_{t-1}^{[1]} - k)!)^{\tilde{v}_1}}\right]\left[\frac{1}{Z(\lambda_t^{[1]}, \tilde{v}_1)}\right]\left[\frac{(\lambda_t^{[2]})^{y_{t-1}^{[2]} - k}}{((y_{t-1}^{[2]} - k)!)^{\tilde{v}_2}}\right]\left[\frac{1}{Z(\lambda_t^{[2]}, \tilde{v}_2)}\right] \tag{20}$$

where the normalizing constant $Z(\lambda_t^{[k]}, \tilde{v}_k) = \sum_{j=0}^{\infty}\frac{\lambda_t^{[k]j}}{(j!)^{v_k}}$.

The conditional density is written as $f((y_t^{[1]}, y_t^{[2]})|(y_{t-1}^{[1]}, y_{t-1}^{[2]}, r_{t-1}^{[1]}, r_{t-1}^{[2]}), \theta) = \sum_{k=0}^{g_1}\sum_{s=0}^{g_2} f_1(k)f_2(s)f_3(r_t^{[1]} = y_{t-1}^{[1]} - k, r_t^{[2]} = y_{t-1}^{[2]} - s)$, where $\theta = [\gamma_{11}, \gamma_{12}, \gamma_{21}\gamma_{22}, \tilde{v}_1, \tilde{v}_2, \beta^{[k]}]$ is the vector of unknown parameters, $g_1 = \min(y_t^{[1]}, y_{t-1}^{[1]})$ and $g_2 = \min(y_t^{[2]}, y_{t-1}^{[2]})$.

The conditional likelihood function is given by

$$L(\theta|y) = \prod_{t=1}^{T} f((y_t^{[1]}, y_t^{[2]})|(y_{t-1}^{[1]}, y_{t-1}^{[2]}, r_{t-1}^{[1]}, r_{t-1}^{[2]}), \theta) \tag{21}$$

and after maximizing Equation (22)

$$\log[L(\theta|y)] = \log\left[\sum_{t=1}^{T} f((y_t^{[1]}, y_t^{[2]})|(y_{t-1}^{[1]}, y_{t-1}^{[2]}, r_{t-1}^{[1]}, r_{t-1}^{[2]}), \theta)\right] \tag{22}$$

we obtain the maximum likelihood estimators of θ for some starting value of y_0.

4. Forecasting Equations

Based on the proposed model, the forecasting equations are derived as follows:

$$E(Y_{t+1}^{[1]}|y_t^{[1]}, r_t^{[1]}) = E(\gamma_{11} \circ Y_t^{[1]}|y_t^{[1]}) + E(\gamma_{12} \circ R_t^{[1]}|r_t^{[1]}) + E(R_{t+1}^{[1]})$$
$$= \gamma_{11}y_t^{[1]} + \gamma_{12}r_t^{[1]} + \lambda_{t+1}^{[1]} \tag{23}$$

$$E(Y_{t+1}^{[2]}|y_t^{[2]}, r_t^{[2]}) = E(\gamma_{21} \circ Y_t^{[2]}|y_t^{[2]}) + E(\gamma_{22} \circ R_t^{[2]}|r_t^{[2]}) + E(R_{t+1}^{[2]})$$
$$= \gamma_{21}y_t^{[1]} + \gamma_{22}r_t^{[2]} + \lambda_{t+1}^{[2]} \tag{24}$$

and

$$\text{Var}(Y_{t+1}^{[1]}|y_t^{[1]}, r_t^{[1]}) = \text{Var}(\gamma_{11} \circ y_t^{[1]}|y_t^{[1]}) + \text{Var}(\gamma_{12} \circ R_t^{[1]}|r_t^{[1]}) + \text{Var}(R_{t+1}^{[1]})$$
$$= \gamma_{11}(1-\gamma_{11})y_t^{[1]} + \gamma_{12}(1-\gamma_{12})r_t^{[1]} + \frac{\lambda_{t+1}^{[1]}}{\tilde{v}_1} + \frac{\tilde{v}_1 - 1}{2\tilde{v}_1^2} \tag{25}$$

$$\text{Var}(Y_{t+1}^{[2]}|y_t^{[2],r_t^{[2]}}) = \text{Var}(\gamma_{21} \circ y_t^{[2]}|y_t^{[2]}) + \text{Var}(\gamma_{22} \circ R_t^{[2]}|r_t^{[2]}) + \text{Var}(R_{t+1}^{[2]})$$
$$= \gamma_{21}(1-\gamma_{21})y_t^{[2]} + \gamma_{22}(1-\gamma_{22})r_t^{[2]} + \frac{\lambda_{t+1}^{[2]}}{\tilde{v}_2} + \frac{\tilde{v}_2 - 1}{2\tilde{v}_2^2} \tag{26}$$

5. Modelling Daily Stock Transactions

This section focusses on the number of daily stock transactions of the two most eminent banking institutions in Mauritius, namely Mauritius Commercial Bank Group Limited (MCB) and State Bank of Mauritius Holdings Ltd. (SBMH), that are listed on SEM. The daily stock transactions refers to the number of times stocks are bought and sold at the prevailing price during the trading session. MCB and SBMH are licensed by the Bank of Mauritius and have the biggest market share in the country. MCB was founded in 1838 and is the oldest and largest banking institution in Mauritius, while SBMH is the second largest commercial bank established in 1973. The total assets of MCB is nearly USD 15.8 billion, with a market capitalization on the SEM of USD 1.5 billion. MCB is owned by almost 22,000 domestic and foreign shareholders, has over 1.1 million individual and institutional clients and employs approximately 3700 staff. On the other hand, the total assets of SBMH is nearly USD 6.6 billion, with a market capitalization on the SEM of USD 253 million. SBMH is owned by almost 18,518 domestic and international shareholders, has over 0.75 million individual and institutional customers and employs approximately 2845 staff. The COVID-19 pandemic since the year 2020 has caused unprecedented disruptions and created innumerable challenges for both commercial banks. In the wake of this difficult time, many investors of the SEM have been negatively affected and has been navigating in the red zone for quite some time because of the uncertainty prevailing due to the COVID-19 pandemic. MCB and SBMH have not been spared by the pandemic and their performance on the SEM has been affected negatively since the pandemic. Hence, it is of upmost importance to model the number of daily stock transactions of these two banks and provide reliable estimates to the investors so that they can decide whether they need to hold or sell the shares of MCB and SBMH.

The transactions of MCB and SBMH must be inter-related as they operate in the same sector, namely the banking sector and provides the same line of services and financial activities. Thus, we collected data from the several brokers on the number of daily transactions of these two banking institutions from 4 October to 10 December 2021 over 30 min intervals. As far the covariates are concerned, based on previous researchers [1,3–5], the following variables were identified as those influencing the number of daily stock transactions on the SEM: the intervention of any COVID-19 news that affect the financial market, the time of day effect and the day effect.

Hence, in this section, we analyze the intra-day stock transactions of MCB and SBMH using a novel time series model, namely the BINARMA (1,1) model with CMP innovations. The Stock market data for the number of daily transactions were collected from the SEM for MCB and SBMH within 30 min interval from 4 October to 10 December 2021, amounting to 450 paired observations. In the same line, the covariates that influence these daily stock transactions were recorded as follows: information on COVID-19 news (x_{t1}) where 1 refers for any new COVID-19 information which influence the stock trading of SBMH and MCB and 0 for no COVID-19 information, Friday effect (x_{t2}) where 1 refers to trading conducted on Fridays and 0 for trading conducted on Mondays, Tuesdays, Wednesdays and Thursdays and time of the day effect (x_{t3}) where 1 refers to the trading effected during the time period 12:00–13:30 and 0 for the trading between 09:00 and 12:00. Normally, the SEM operates from Monday to Friday only between 09:00 to 13:30 and is closed on public holidays. Based on 450 paired observations, the time series plots and the descriptive statistics are shown in Figures 1–4 and Table 1.

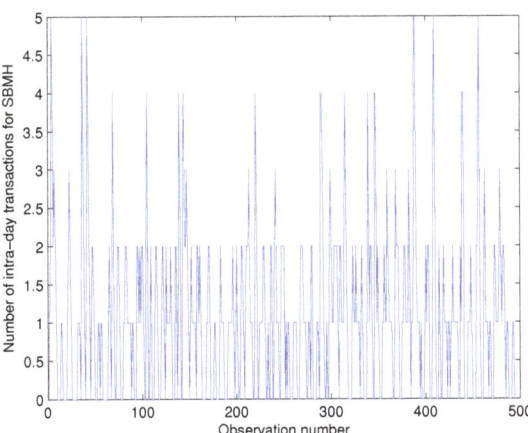

Figure 1. Time series plot for SBMH.

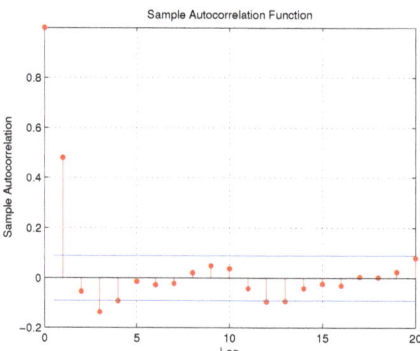

Figure 2. ACF plot for SBMH.

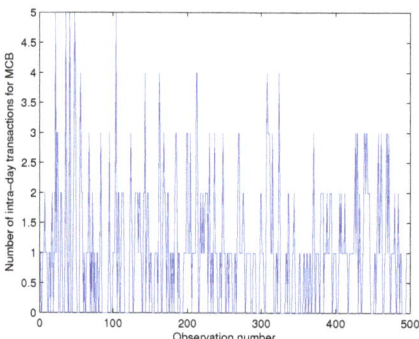

Figure 3. Time series plot for MCB.

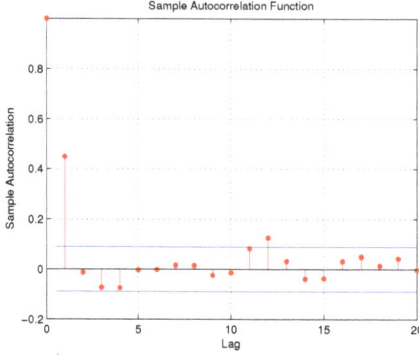

Figure 4. ACF plot for MCB.

Table 1. Summary statistics for the intra-day transactions of SBMH and MCB.

	Sample Mean	**Sample Variance**	**Sample Lag-1**	**Sample Cross-Correlation**
SBMH	1.0765	1.4191	0.5867	0.1617
MCB	1.0393	1.0154	0.5116	

From Table 1, we can conclude that the SBMH data series is slightly over-dispersed while the MCB data series is slightly under-dispersed. Both series have an average sample lag-1 correlation, with a sample cross-correlation of 0.1617, which confirms both the existence of relationship between as well as within the two series. As for the ACF plots, we observe that for both series that lag-1 has the highest peak. Thus, the proposed BI-NARMA (1,1) model with CMP innovations is used to model the in-sample daily trading of SBMH ($Y_t^{[1]}$) and MCB ($Y_t^{[2]}$) between 4 October and 3 December 2021, totalling 405 paired observations, while the out-sample from 5 December to 10 December 2021 is used to validate the model. We also apply the bivariate integer-valued autoregressive model of order 1 with CMP innovations (BINAR(1)CMP) developed by Jowaheer et al. [6] and the bivariate integer-valued moving average model of order 1 with CMP innovations (BINMA(1)) developed by Mamodekhan et al. [7] on the intra-day series. Under $\lambda_t^{[k]} = \exp(\hat{\beta}_0^{[k]} + \hat{\beta}_1^{[k]} x_{t1} + \hat{\beta}_2^{[k]} x_{t2} + \hat{\beta}_3^{[k]} x_{t3})$, the estimates of the covariate effects under the application of the three models are shown in Table 2.

Table 2. Intra-day transactions for MCB and SBMH: Estimates of the regression parameters.

Models	Series	$\hat{\beta}_0$	$\hat{\beta}_1$	$\hat{\beta}_2$	$\hat{\beta}_3$
BINARMA (1,1) CMP	$Y_t^{[1]}$	0.2268	0.2633	0.1482	0.1399
	s.e	(0.1975)	(0.0581)	(0.0288)	(0.0295)
	$Y_t^{[2]}$	0.1543	0.2456	0.1297	0.1193
	s.e	(0.2259)	(0.0447)	(0.0350)	(0.0587)
BINMA(1)CMP	$Y_t^{[1]}$	0.2122	0.2530	0.1533	0.1264
	s.e	(0.2089)	(0.0615)	(0.0314)	(0.0322)
	$Y_t^{[2]}$	0.1650	0.2627	0.1074	0.1317
	s.e	(0.2451)	(0.0566)	(0.0416)	(0.0661)
BINAR(1)CMP	$Y_t^{[1]}$	0.2412	0.2490	0.1231	0.1211
	s.e	(0.2159)	(0.0691)	(0.0375)	(0.0388)
	$Y_t^{[2]}$	0.1856	0.2659	0.0926	0.1262
	s.e	(0.2517)	(0.0612)	(0.0487)	(0.0701)

From the regression coefficients Table 2, we observe that the estimates of the covariates obtained using the BINARMA (1,1) CMP have lower standard errors compared to those obtained using BINAR(1)CMP and BINMA(1)CMP and hence, we interpret only the estimates of the BINARMA (1,1) CMP model. We can also notice that all the explanatory variables are significant, thus confirming their influence on the number of intra-day transactions of MCB and SBMH. Since the pandemic of COVID-19 started in the year 2020, any news entering the domestic market pertaining to confinement, number of COVID-19 cases in Mauritius, potential vaccines against COVID-19, the gradual recovery of the economy and the lifting of the confinement have caused an increase in the number of inra-day stock transactions of both MCB and SBMH. For SBMH, as news filter in the market, we expect an increase in the stock transactions of 30.1 percent and 27.8 percent for MCB. From these figures, we can conclude that there are more trading for SBMH stocks than MCB stocks as MCB is a more robust bank than SBMH. The other two explanatory variables, namely the Friday and time effects, have also affected the number of intra-day transactions of MCB and SBMH, but their influence were lower than the COVID-19 news effect. From the correlation Table 3, we can confirm that there exists a relationship within and between the number of daily trading of MCB and SBMH.

Table 3. Intra-day transactions for MCB and SBMH: Estimates of the dependence parameters.

Models	Parameters	$\hat{\gamma}_{11}$	$\hat{\gamma}_{22}$	$\hat{\gamma}_{12}$	$\hat{\gamma}_{21}$
BINARMA (1,1) CMP	Correlation	0.3117	0.1096	0.0825	0.3988
	s.e	(0.0440)	(0.0322)	(0.0533)	(0.0564)
BINMA(1)CMP	Correlation	0.3182	0.1112	0.0875	0.3893
	s.e	(0.0488)	(0.0351)	(0.0561)	(0.0590)
BINAR(1)CMP	Correlation	0.3021	0.1178	0.0802	0.4049
	s.e	(0.0498)	(0.0377)	(0.0581)	(0.0595)

Using the forecasting Equations (23) and (24), we compute the one-step ahead forecast of the number of stock trading of SBMH and MCB based on the out-sample trading data between 5 December to 10 December 2021, totalling 45 paired observations and the corresponding root mean square errors (RMSEs) for three models with CMP innovations are shown in Table 4:

Table 4. RMSEs for the out-sample number of intra-day transactions of MCB and SBMH.

Models	RMSE $Y_t^{[1]}$	RMSE $Y_t^{[2]}$
BINARMA (1,1) CMP	0.1511	0.1285
BINMA(1)CMP	0.1598	0.1357
BINAR(1)CMP	0.1655	0.1469

From Table 4, we observe that the BINARMA (1,1) CMP provide better RMSEs than BINAR(1)CMP and BINMA(1)CMP.

6. Conclusions

This paper considers the modeling of the intra-day transactions of two most prestigious banking companies: MCB and SBMH in Mauritius and how the COVID-19 pandemic has affected the stock transactions of these two commercial banks. Since the time series data of one bank is over-dispersed and the other one is under-dispersed, we develop a BINARMA (1,1) process with CMP innovation terms to model these data. In this paper, a CML approach is used to estimate the regression and correlation parameters for the two series. This novel BINARMA (1,1) CMP model together with the CML were then applied to estimate the regression and correlation effects of the intra-day transactions where it was found to yield significant estimates for the time of trade, Friday and COVID-19 news effect. The forecasting equations were also developed and they yield reliable estimates for the volume of transaction for the two series based on the real figures.

Funding: This research received no external funding.

Institutional Review Board Statement: Not applicable.

Informed Consent Statement: Not applicable.

Data Availability Statement: Not applicable.

Conflicts of Interest: The author declares no conflict of interest.

References

1. Bundoo, S. *An Analysis of Stock Market Anomalies and Momentum Strategies on the Stock Exchange of Mauritius*; Technical Report; African Economic Research Consortium: Nairobi, Kenya, 2011.
2. Subadar, A. Seasonal Pattern and Volatility in the Mauritian's Official and Development Enterprise Stock Market. *Univ. Maurit. Res. J.* **2013**, *19*, 146–159.
3. Easley, D.; O'Harra, M. Time and the process of security price adjustment. *J. Financ.* **1992**, *47*, 905–927. [CrossRef]
4. Quoreshi, A. A Vector Integer-Valued Moving Average Model for High Frequency Financial Count Data. *Econ. Lett.* **2008**, *101*, 258–261. [CrossRef]
5. Quoreshi, A. Bivariate Time Series Modeling of Financial Count Data. *Commun. Stat. Theory Methods* **2006**, *35*, 1343–1358. [CrossRef]
6. Jowaheer, V.; Mamode Khan, N.; Sunecher, Y. A BINAR(1) Time series model with Cross-correlated COM-Poisson innovations. *Commun. Stat. Theory Methods* **2017**, *47*, 1133–1154. [CrossRef]
7. Mamode Khan, N.; Jowaheer, V.; Sunecher, Y. BINMA(1) Model with COM-Poisson Innovations: Estimation and Application. *Commun. Stat. Simul. Comput.* **2018**, *49*, 1631–1652.
8. Sunecher, Y.; Mamodekhan, N.; Jowaheer, V. Estimating the parameters of a BINMA Poisson model for a non-stationary bivariate time series. *Commun. Stat. Simul. Comput.* **2016**, *46*, 6803–6827. [CrossRef]
9. Sunecher, Y.; Mamodekhan, N.; Jowaheer, V. A GQL estimation approach for analysing non-stationary over-dispersed BINAR(1) time series. *J. Stat. Comput. Simul.* **2017**, *87*, 1911–1924. [CrossRef]
10. Sutradhar, B.; Jowaheer, V.; Rao, P. Remarks on asymptotic efficient estimation for regression effects in stationary and non-stationary models for panel count data. *Braz. J. Probab. Stat.* **2014**, *28*, 241–254. [CrossRef]
11. Steutel, F.; Van Harn, K. Discrete analogues of self-decomposability and stability. *Ann. Probab.* **1979**, *7*, 3893–3899. [CrossRef]
12. Weiβ, C. Thinning Operations for modelling time series of counts-a survey. *AStA Adv. Stat. Anal.* **2008**, *92*, 319–341.
13. Pedeli, X.; Karlis, D. On estimation of the bivariate Poisson INAR process. *Commun. Stat. Simul. Comput.* **2013**, *35*, 514–533. [CrossRef]

Proceeding Paper

Improving the Predictive Power of Historical Consistent Neural Networks †

Rockefeller Rockefeller [1,2,*] , **Bubacarr Bah** [1,2,‡], **Vukosi Marivate** [3,‡] and **Hans-Georg Zimmermann** [4,‡]

1   African Institute for Mathematical Sciences, Cape Town 7945, South Africa; bubacarr@aims.ac.za
2   Department of Mathematical Sciences, Stellenbosch University, Cape Town 7945, South Africa
3   Department of Computer Sciences, University of Pretoria, Pretoria 0028, South Africa;
    vukosi.marivate@cs.up.ac.za
4   Fraunhofer Society, 200703 Munich, Germany; hans.georg.zimmermann@iis.fraunhofer.de
*   Correspondence: rockefeller@aims-senegal.org
†   Presented at the 8th International Conference on Time Series and Forecasting, Gran Canaria, Spain,
    27–30 June 2022.
‡   The first author did most of the work as the student, which was jointly supervised by the other authors.

Abstract: The Historical Consistent Neural Networks (HCNN) are an extension of the standard Recurrent Neural Networks (RNN): they allow the modeling of highly-interacting dynamical systems across multiple time scales. HCNN do not draw any distinction between inputs and outputs, but model observables embedded in the dynamics of a large state space. In this paper, we propose to improve the predictive power of the (Vanilla) HCNN using three methods: (1) HCNN with Partial Teacher Forcing, (2) HCNN with Sparse State Transition Matrix, and (3) a Long Short Term Memory Formulation of HCNN. We investigated the effect of those long memory improvement methods on three chaotic time-series mathematically generated from the Rabinovich–Fabrikant, the Rossler System and the Lorenz system. To complement our study, we compared the accuracy of the different HCNN variants with well-known recurrent neural networks methods such as Vanilla RNN and LSTM for the same prediction tasks. Overall, our results show that the Vanilla HCNN is superior to RNN and LSTM. This is even more the case if you include the above long memory extensions (1), (2) and (3). We demonstrate that (1) and (3) are superior for the modeling of our chaotic dynamical systems. We show that for these deterministic systems, the ensembles are narrowed.

Keywords: recurrent neural networks; historical consistent neural networks; time series forecasting; chaotic dynamical systems

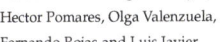

Citation: Rockefeller, R.; Bah, B.; Marivate, V.; Zimmermann, H.-G. Improving the Predictive Power of Historical Consistent Neural Networks. *Eng. Proc.* **2022**, *18*, 36. https://doi.org/10.3390/engproc2022018036

Academic Editors: Ignacio Rojas, Hector Pomares, Olga Valenzuela, Fernando Rojas and Luis Javier Herrera

Published: 27 June 2022

Publisher's Note: MDPI stays neutral with regard to jurisdictional claims in published maps and institutional affiliations.

1. Introduction

Over the recent years, data-driven approaches, including deep learning techniques have played an instrumental role in the way we model, predict, and control dynamical systems [1]. Thanks to the help of modern mathematical methods, the availability of data and computational resources, Neural Networks have been increasingly used to understand complex systems (non linear and high dimensional systems) [2]. In 1989, Hornik, Stinchcombe, and White proved through the Universal Approximation theorem that Multi-layer feedforward Networks are Universal Approximators [3]. The Universal Approximation for RNN is stated in [2]. Recurrent neural networks (or RNN) are a family of Neural networks designed for processing sequential data. They are increasingly being used to understand, analyze and forecast the evolution of complex dynamical systems due to the explicit modeling of time and memory they offer [4]. RNN fulfill the universal approximation properties and allow the identification of dynamical systems in form of high dimensional, non-linear state space models [5]. Simple in architectures with sophisticated learning algorithms, they have emerged as one of the first class candidates for modeling dynamical systems [6]. The benefits they offer to deal with the typical challenges associated with forecasting in general, make them suitable for learning non-linear dependencies from observed time series data [7].

Throughout the training process, RNN rely on external inputs, which make them suitable for the modeling of open dynamical systems. However, they assume constant environmental conditions as from present time on, which make them temporarily inconsistent [7]. HCNN do not have this inconsistency between past and future modeling. Introduced by [8], HCNN is based upon the assumption that dynamical systems must be seen in a context of large systems in which various (non-linear) dynamics interact with each other in time. HCNN do not only model the individual dynamics of interest, but also the external drivers in the same manner, by embedding them in the dynamics of a large state space [8].

This paper brings about three contributions: Firstly, we modeled three well-known chaotic dynamical systems by the use of Vanilla HCNN: namely the Lorenz, the Rabinovich–Fabrikant and the Rossler Systems. Secondly, we improved the forecast accuracy and the length of the forecast horizon of the Vanilla HCNN using three methods: HCNN with Partial Teacher Forcing, HCNN with Sparse constraint on state transition matrix, and a Long Short Term Memory Formulation of HCNN. Thirdly, we ran a comparative analysis between those different strands of HCNN and well-known deep learning neural network models such as Vanilla Recurrent Neural Networks (RNN) and long-short term memory based model (LSTM). The rest of this paper is organized as follows.

The Sections 2 and 3 provide respectively a review of the mathematical description of RNN and an architectural description of HCNN as well as its learning algorithm. In Section 4, we discussed the intuition behind and the architecture of the different HCNN improvement methods. The focus of Section 5 is on the data generation of the three chaotic dynamical systems. Section 6 shows the different results and comparative analysis between the pre-cited methods and the existing well-known recurrent neural networks namely RNN and LSTM. In Section 7, we demonstrate that our results are reproducible for different HCNN instances. Finally, we present the conclusion and future work in the Section 8.

2. Reminder of Recurrent Neural Networks for Dynamical Systems

Let us consider, as in Figure 1, a dynamical system driven by an external signal u_t.

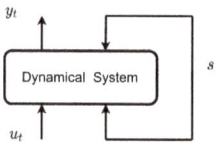

Figure 1. RNN Identification of a (folded) dynamical system using a discrete time description.

$$s_t = f(s_{t-1}, u_t) \tag{1}$$
$$y_t = g(s_t) \tag{2}$$

Let us assume that, at each time t, an output y_t is recorded. A dynamical system can be described for discrete time grids by a state space model, consisting respectively of a state transition and an output equation. The recursive Equation (1) describes the current state of the system s_t with respect to the previous state of the system s_{t-1} and the external signals u_t. The expected output y_t is computed as a function of the current state of the system (2). Key in the success of RNN, is their ability to generalized well, due to the fact that it is trained using parameter sharing [9]. Without loss of generality, we can approximate the state space model with the state transition (3) and the related output Equation (4):

$$s_t = \tanh(As_{t-1} + Bu_t) \tag{3}$$
$$y_t = Cs_t \tag{4}$$

where A, B and C are the weight matrices, respectively, for hidden-to-hidden, input-to-hidden and hidden-to-output connections. This makes a simple Recurrent Neural Network (RNN) with recurrent connections between hidden units across the whole time range [4]. By performing a finite unfolding in time, we transform the temporal equations above into the spatial architecture as shown in the Figure 2 above [8].

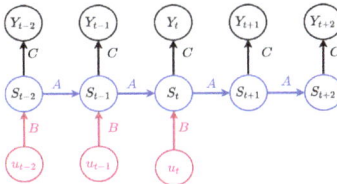

Figure 2. Vanilla RNN architecture.

The Vanilla RNN explains the dynamics observed on the y_t at each time point by splitting its complexity into two parts: the external driven part represented by the external influences u_t and the autonomous driven part (or hidden dynamics) represented by the internal states s_t. If the internal states of the system play an important role into understanding the dynamics of the observables, then an overshooting extends the autonomous part of the system several steps in the future and enable a reliable forecast of the y_t. For a given sequence of u_t and computed y_t values, we pair the corresponding observed values y_t^d and find the optimal set of shared parameters (the matrices A, B and C) by solving the following optimization problem in the Equation (5) here after [7]:

$$\min_{A,B,C} \frac{1}{T} \sum_{t=1}^{T} ||y_t - y_t^d||$$

(5)

The training of the RNN can be conducted using the error-back-propagation-through-time (BPTT) algorithm. This is a natural extension of standard back-propagation that performs gradient descent on a network unfolded in time. More details on BPTT are given in [4]. However, despite its success over the past years, and especially on short term forecasts, the missing external inputs u_t in the future (which can be interpreted as a constant environment, i.e., $u_t \simeq 0$), makes a vanilla RNN temporarily inconsistent [7].

3. Historical Consistent Neural Networks

The HCNN were designed to address the temporal inconsistency in RNN. A dynamical system is often viewed in the context of large systems in which various (non-linear) dynamics interact with one another in time. However, we can only measure/observe a small subset of those variables. Therefore, HCNN reconstruct (at least part of) the hidden variables in order to understand the dynamics of the whole system [7,10]. Here the input and output variables are combined and termed as observables ($Y_t := (u_t, y_t), (Y_t \in \mathbb{R}^N)$). Together with the hidden variables, they form the state of the system at each time τ (see Figure 3) and are treated by the model in the same manner. The corresponding state transition Equation (6) and output Equation (7) are also provided below.

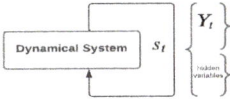

Figure 3. HCNN identification of a (folded) dynamical system using a discrete time description.

$$st = A \tanh(s_{t-1}) \tag{6}$$
$$Y_t = [Id, 0]s_t \tag{7}$$

The joint dynamics for all observables is characterized in the HCNN by the sequence of states s_t. The observables $(i = 1, \ldots, N)$ are arranged on the first N state neurons of s_t and followed by non-observable (hidden) variables as subsequent neurons. The object $[Id, 0]$ is a fixed matrix that reads out the observables from the state vector s_t [7]. At the initial time, the state s_0 is described as a bias/random vector and the matrix A contains the only free parameters [7].

Similar to a standard RNN, HCNN fulfils the universal approximation theorem, as highlighted in [7,10]. However, the lack of any input signals and an unfolding across the complete data makes it difficult to train in practice [8]. As proposed by [4], the models that have recurrent connections from their outputs leading back into the model may be trained with teacher forcing.

This is a procedure that emerges from the maximum likelihood criterion. It makes the best possible use of the data from the observables and therefore accelerates the training of the HCNN [2,10]. Throughout the fitting procedure, the teacher forcing mechanism introduces a hidden layer r_t that is a copy of the internal state s_t, with the exception that its first N components which correspond to the computed expected values Y_t are replaced with the observed values Y_t^d as shown in the Equation (8).

$$Y_t = [Id, 0]s_t$$
$$r_t = s_t - [Id, 0]^\top (Y_t - Y_t^d) \tag{8}$$
$$s_{t+1} = A \tanh(r_t) \tag{9}$$

From the temporal equations above, we can also derive its spatial representation, through the resulting network architecture of the HCNN with integrated teacher forcing mechanism as illustrated in the Figure 4 below.

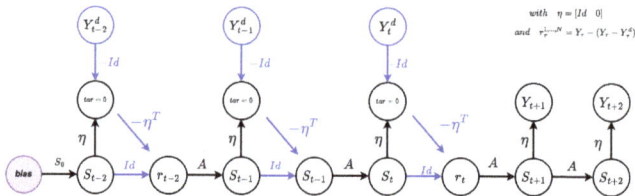

Figure 4. HCNN identification of a (folded) dynamical system using a discrete time description.

At each time t during training, the output layer of the HCNN is replaced by a cluster that is given a fixed target value of zero. This forces the HCNN to create the expected values Y_t at each time t, to compensate for the negative observed values $-Y_t$ coming from the top node [8]. The content of that cluster, i.e., $(Y_t - Y_t^d)$, with a minus symbol is transferred to the upper part (the first N neurons) of the hidden layer r_t. Furthermore, a copy of the state s_t is also transferred to the intermediate hidden layer r_t on a component-by-component basis. As a result of that, the expected values Y_t on the first N components of the hidden layer r_t are replaced by the observed values [8] and the subsequent state s_{t+1} is computed using the state transition Equation (9).

4. Long-Term Memory Improvement Methods

To improve the long-term memory of the Vanilla HCNN model, three different improvement methods have been designed: HCNN with Partial Teacher Forcing, with Large

Sparse State Transition Matrices and a Long Short-Term Memory Formulation. The intuitions behind each of the methods are shown below.

4.1. HCNN with Partial Teacher Forcing

To enforce the long-term learning of the HCNN, we endow the output layers of the HCNN with a dropout filter, guided by a probability, as illustrated in the Equation (10).

$$\text{dropout}_{(p)}(x_i) = \begin{cases} 0 & \text{if dropout}_{(p)} \\ x_i & \text{if no dropout}_{(1-p)} \end{cases} \tag{10}$$

At time t, when the filter is activated (which means for a probability p), the HCNN randomly suppress elements in the time series that come from the cluster containing the difference between expectations and observations $(Y_t - Y_t^d)$. Thus, in the upper part (the first N components) of the r_t vector, the network is enforced to replace the observations with its internal expectations. The architecture is represented in the Figure 5 below.

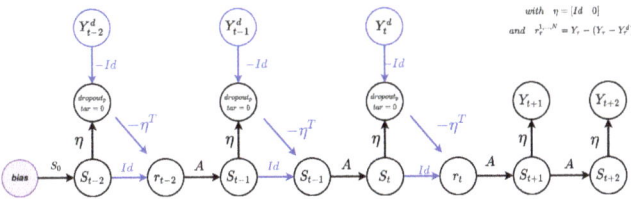

Figure 5. HCNN architecture with partial teacher forcing mechanism.

4.2. HCNN with Large Sparse State Transition Matrix

HCNN may often use large state vectors to model large dynamical systems (number of observables > 100). During training time, the iteration with a fully connected state transition matrix A could cause an information overload, leading to two risks:

- The matrix–vector computation between A and $\tanh(s_t)$, which includes the addition of randomly generated (and learned) scalar values will likely blow up to infinity (∞).
- The superposition of additional information brought in by the large dimensionality of A could destroy the longer memory information acquired throughout.

In order to overcome that, we can choose to set the transition matrix A sparse to a chosen degree. As a result of that, the spread of the information peak through the network is damped by the sparsity too. Another approach, as proposed by [7], consists of a heuristic approach that represents the sparsity of A, as inversely proportional to the state dimensionality of the system, as shown in the Equation (11) below:

$$\text{Sparsity }(A) = \min(1, \frac{50}{\dim(s)}) \tag{11}$$

4.3. HCNN with LSTM Formulation

The third approach to improve the long-term memory of the vanilla HCNN is through an exponential smoothing embedding of the HCNN with a learnable diagonal matrix [11], subject to the following constraints $0 \leq D_{ii} \leq 1$. The resulting state transition Equation (12) and output Equation (13) are provided below:

$$\begin{aligned} s_t &= (Id - D)s'_{t-1} + DA \tanh(s'_{t-1}) \\ &= s'_{t-1} + D(A \tanh(s'_{t-1}) - s'_{t-1}) \end{aligned} \tag{12}$$

$$Y_t = [Id, 0]s_t \tag{13}$$

where $s'_{t-1} = TeacherForcing(s_{t-1})$

Built upon the ideas of the LSTM formulation of RNN [12], the resulting architecture of the LSTM formulation of HCNN is provided in the Figure 6 below.

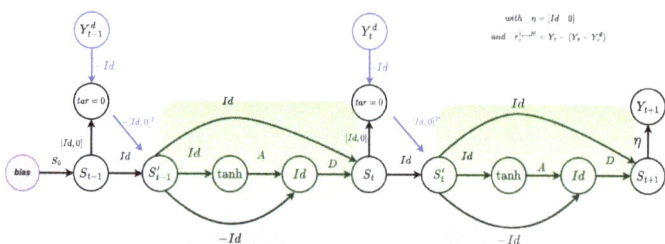

Figure 6. Architectural description of HCNN with an LSTM Formulation.

The next section will focus on the different dynamical systems that will be used to generate the data for the fitting procedure of the HCNN models.

5. Experimental Setup

The experiments we carried out in this work aimed at forecasting the dynamics of three fully observable, chaotic and deterministic systems, namely the Rabinovich–Fabrikant, Rossler System and the Lorenz system. Their chaotic properties come from the fact that they are very sensitive to their initial conditions, which smallest changes completely modify the respective trajectories. They are also well known to show aperiodic behaviour which is apparently random and unpredictable [1,13].

5.1. The Rabinovich–Fabrikant System

The Rabinovich–Fabrikant system is represented by the system of Equation (14) below:

$$\begin{cases} \frac{dx}{dt} & = y(z - 1 + x^2) + \gamma x \\ \frac{dy}{dt} & = x(3z + 1 - x^2) + \gamma y \\ \frac{dz}{dt} & = -2z(\alpha + xy) \end{cases} \tag{14}$$

where we set $\alpha = 0.2, \gamma = 0.1$. Introduced by Mikhail Rabinovich and Anatoly Fabrikant, the set of equations describes the stochasticity arising from the modulation instability in a non-equilibrium dissipative medium [14]. The corresponding attractor is shown in the Figure 7 below.

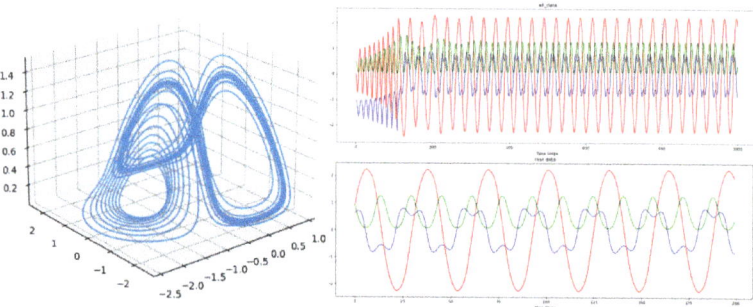

Figure 7. The Rabinovich–Fabrikant attractor and the corresponding time series, split into training and test data.

5.2. The Rossler System

The Rossler system is represented by the system of Equation (15) below:

$$\begin{cases} \frac{dx}{dt} = -y - z \\ \frac{dy}{dt} = x + ay \\ \frac{dz}{dt} = b + z(x - c) \end{cases} \tag{15}$$

where we set $a = 0.2$, $b = 0.2$ and $c = 6.3$. Studied first by Otto Rössler in the 1970s, these non-linear ordinary differential equations define a continuous-time dynamical system that exhibits chaotic dynamics associated with the fractal properties as it is shown by the corresponding attractor in the Figure 8 below [15].

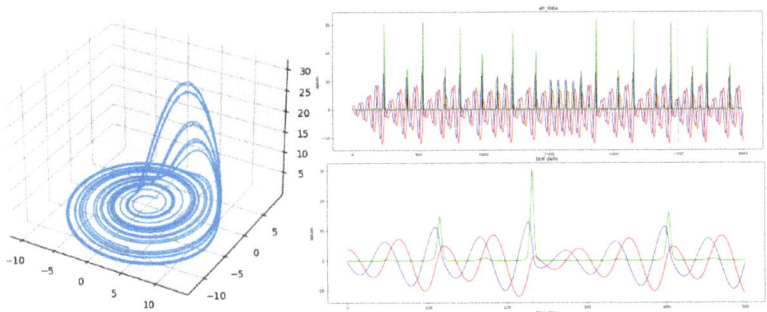

Figure 8. The Rossler attractor and the corresponding time series, split into training and test data.

5.3. The Lorenz System

The Lorenz system is represented by the system of Equation (16) below:

$$\begin{cases} \frac{dx}{dt} = \sigma(y - x) \\ \frac{dy}{dt} = (\rho - z) - y \\ \frac{dz}{dt} = xy - \beta z \end{cases} \tag{16}$$

where we set $\rho = 10$, $\sigma = 28$ and $\beta = 2.667$. The equations above describe the rate of change of three quantities, namely the rate of convection, the horizontal temperature variation and the vertical temperature variation. First studied by Edward Lorenz, the Lorenz system is a simplified mathematical model for the atmospheric convection [16,17]. The graphical representation of its attractor is provided in the Figure 9 below.

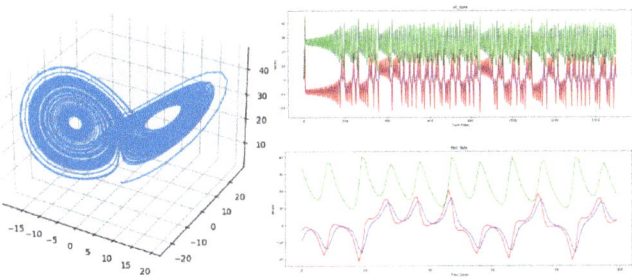

Figure 9. The Lorenz attractor and the corresponding time series, split into training and test data.

5.4. Traning Strategies

We solved each of the systems above by numerical approximation, with the configurations summarized in the Table 1 below.

Table 1. Configuration of the training data for each of the chaotic dynamical systems.

System	Initial Conditions	Sample Size	Step Size	Truncation Parameter	Training Size	Test Size
Rossler	$(1,1,1)$	10,000	0.01	5	1800	200
Lorenz	$(0,1,1.05)$	12,000	0.01	8	1400	100
Rab-Fabrikant	$(-1,0,0.5)$	20,000	0.01	10	1800	200

Here, the truncation parameter refers to the down-sampling that has been applied on the initial sample size. On the Lorenz time series for instance, we recorded values only every 8th time step and obtained a new sample size of 2000 observations, which has been divided into 1400 for the training and 100 observations for the forecast period as it is shown in the Figure 9 above. The truncation parameter was chosen carefully to make sure that for each system, from a graphical view point, the shapes of the corresponding attractors are preserved as exemplified in the Figures 7–9 above.

The different HCNN models were instantiated with 20 variables. Three accounting for the observables and 17 hidden variables, modeled in the same manner, to explain the dynamics of the different chaotic dynamical systems at hand. For the HCNN model with Sparse constraints, we chose the state dimensionality value as 100 ($\dim(s) = 100$), which implies the transition matrix A will be half sparse as stated in the Equation (11) above. For The HCNN with Partial Teacher Forcing, the dropout filter was set with a incremental probability to ensure that the dropout probability will reach 25% at the end of the training. The diagonal matrix D of the LSTM Formulation of HCNN was constrained between 0 and 1 at each stage of the training. For comparison purpose, we also instantiated a Recurrent Neural Network model and an LSTM formulation of it with 20 hidden states each.

5.5. Evaluation Metrics

As evaluation metric, we chose the Logarithm of Hyperbolic Cosine as our Loss Function, represented by the equation below:

$$\text{LogCosh Loss} = \frac{1}{T}\sum_{t=1}^{T}\frac{1}{p}\ln\cosh\left(p\left(Y_t - Y_t^d\right)\right) \tag{17}$$

6. Results and Analysis

The different models were trained and the results are shown in the different plots below.

6.1. On the Rabinovich-Fabrikant System

The plots below consist of both the actual observations and the predicted values of the three trajectories along the forecast period for each of the models as shown in pairs below the Vanilla HCNN and Vanilla RNN models (Figure 10), the HCNN with partial Teacher Forcing and with Sparse Constraints models (Figure 11), the LSTM Formulation of HCNN and of RNN models (Figure 12).

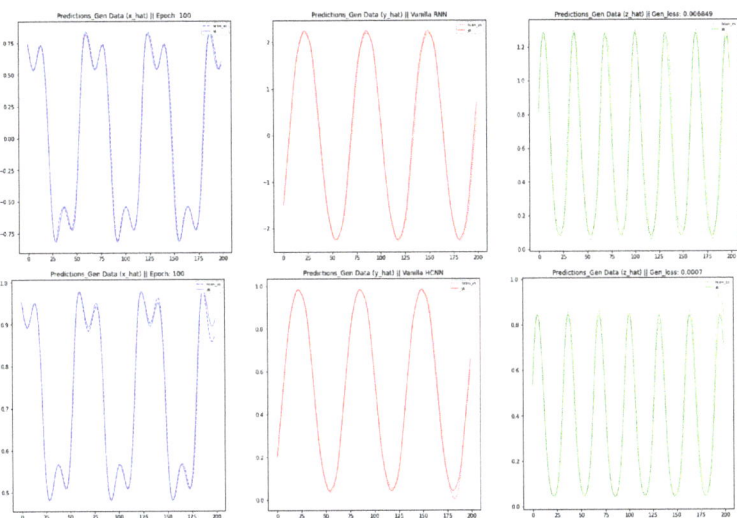

Figure 10. Generalization: Vanilla HCNN (**top**) and Vanilla RNN (**bottom**).

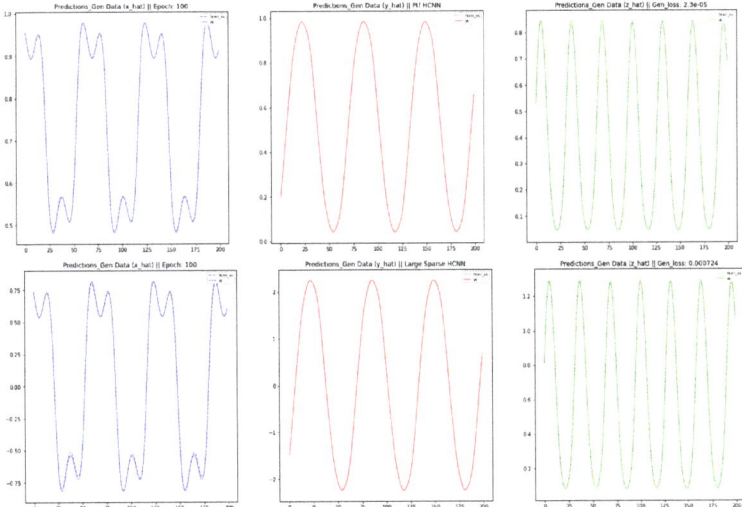

Figure 11. Generalization: HCNN pTF (**top**) and HCNN Large Sparse (**bottom**).

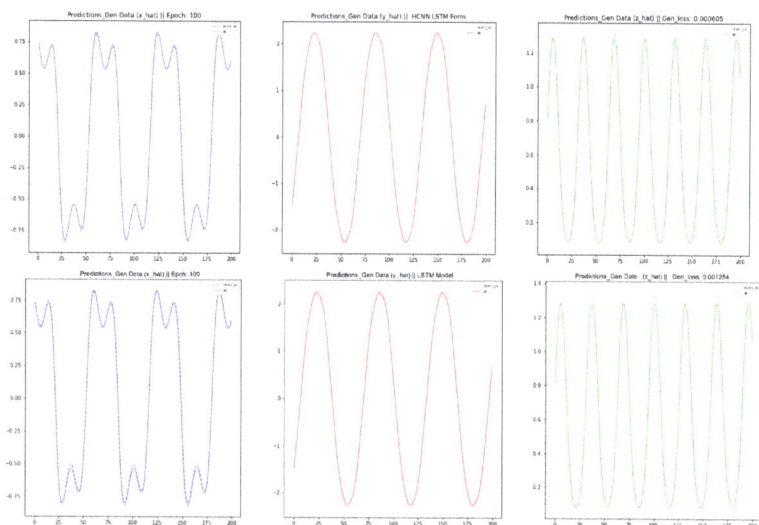

Figure 12. Generalization: HCNN with LSTM Form (**top**) and LSTM Based Model (**bottom**).

6.2. On the Rossler System

The plots below consist of both the actual observations and the predicted values of the three trajectories along the forecast period for each of the models as shown in pairs below the Vanilla HCNN and Vanilla RNN models (Figure 13), the HCNN with partial Teacher Forcing and with Sparse Constraints models (Figure 14), the LSTM Formulation of HCNN and of RNN models (Figure 15).

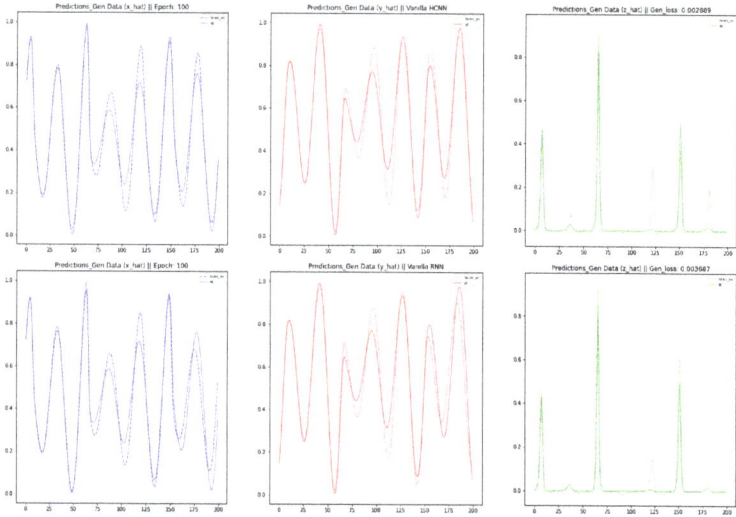

Figure 13. Generalization: Vanilla HCNN (**top**) and Vanilla RNN (**bottom**).

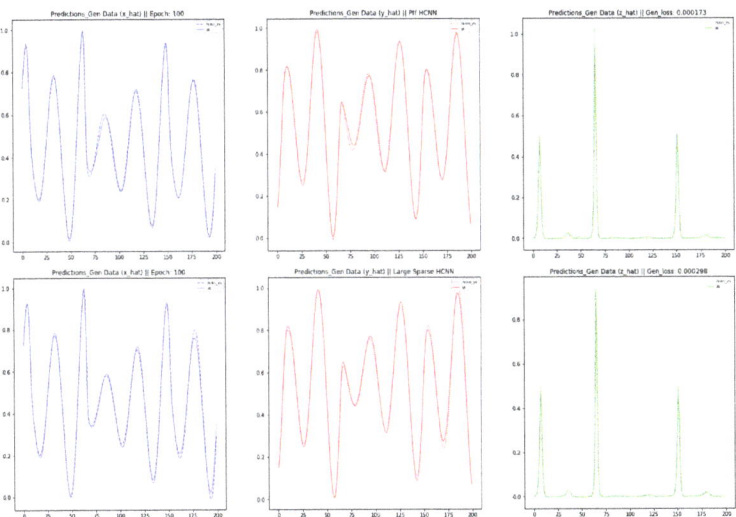

Figure 14. Generalization: HCNN pTF (**top**) and HCNN Large Sparse (**bottom**).

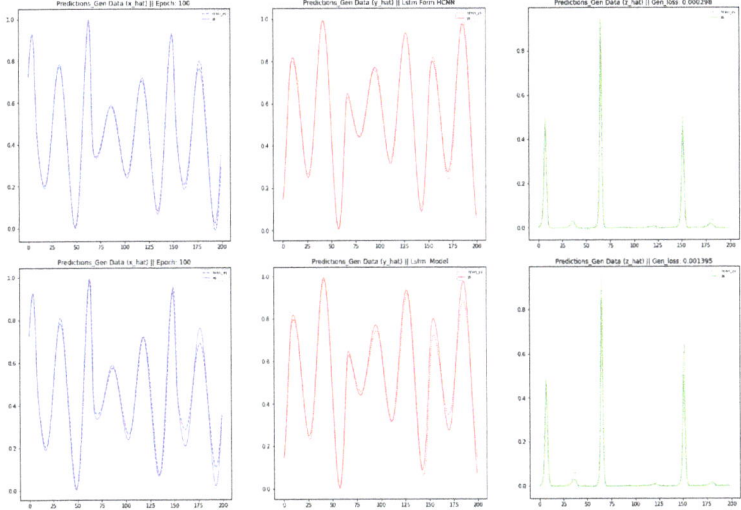

Figure 15. Generalization: HCNN with LSTM Form (**top**) and LSTM Based Model (**bottom**).

6.3. On the Lorenz System

The plots below consist of both the actual observations and the predicted values of the three trajectories along the forecast period for each of the models as shown in pairs below the Vanilla HCNN and Vanilla RNN models (Figure 16), the HCNN with partial Teacher Forcing and with Sparse Constraints models (Figure 17), the LSTM Formulation of HCNN and of RNN models (Figure 18).

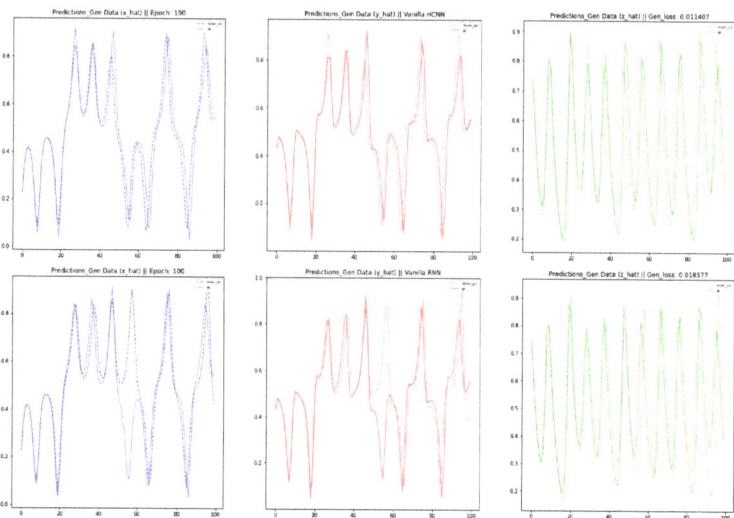

Figure 16. Generalization: Vanilla HCNN (**top**) and Vanilla RNN (**bottom**).

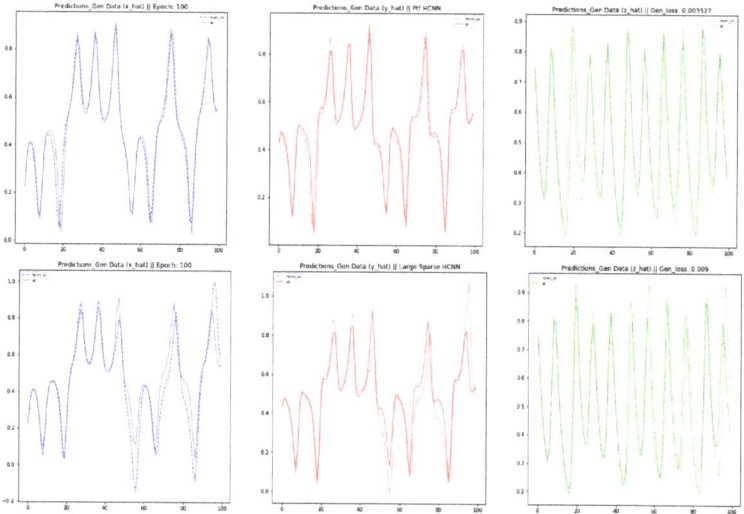

Figure 17. Generalization: HCNN pTF (**top**) and HCNN Large Sparse (**bottom**).

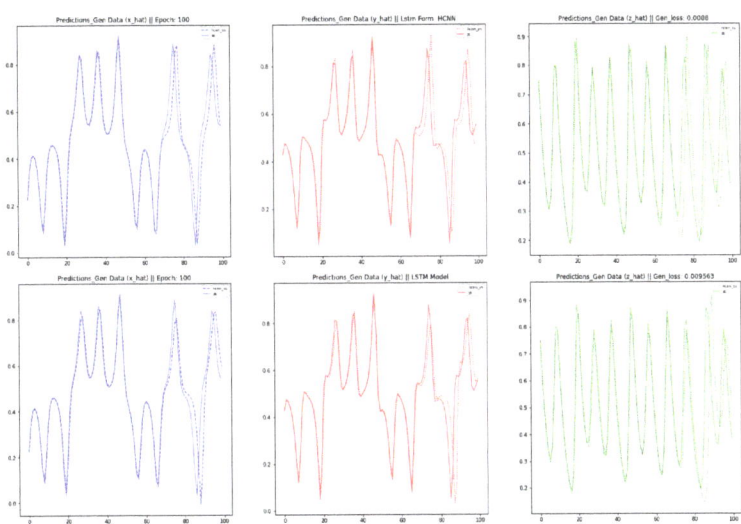

Figure 18. Generalization: HCNN with LSTM Form (**top**) and LSTM Based Model (**bottom**).

For each of the experiments, HCNN with partial Teacher Forcing is the superior method. To summarize our findings, we grouped the results for every model in the Table 2 below.

Table 2. Forecast error made by the different models on the different chaotic dynamical systems.

Model	Rabi-Fabrikant $(\times 10^{-3})$	Rossler $(\times 10^{-3})$	Lorenz $(\times 10^{-3})$
Vanilla HCNN	0.7	2.88	3.52
Vanilla RNN	6.84	3.68	18.5
HCNN p-Teacher Forcing	**0.023**	**0.17**	**0.173**
HCNN Lar-Sparse Tran. Mat	0.072	0.29	9.01
HCNN with LSTM Form.	0.6	0.22	8.07
RNN with LSTM Form.	1.25	1.39	9.56

As a general remark, the vanilla HCNN model outperformed the Vanilla RNN model on the three forecasting exercises. Out of the three HCNN improvement methods, not only the HCNN with partial Teacher Forcing is the superior one, it has also improved the forecast error made by the existing well-known RNN and LSTM models (provided by the PyTorch library).

7. Ensemble Computations

To ensure that our results are reproducible, we instantiate an ensemble of HCNN with 10 members and train them simultaneously to forecast the dynamics of the Lorenz system. The Figure 19 below consists of both the actual observations and the 10 instances of the HCNN model, and median of the ensembles.

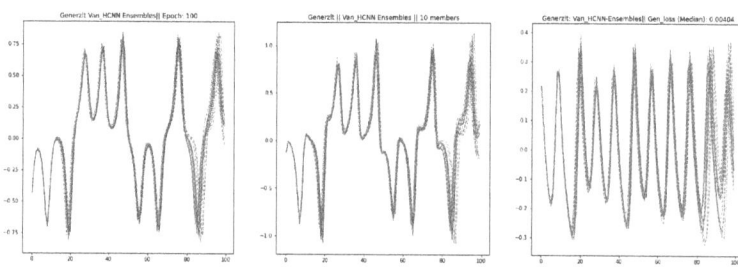

Figure 19. Vanilla HCNN ensemble computations.

Looking at the picture above, we can see that for the 10 different instances of Vanilla HCNN, the shape of the three time series are preserved. At each time step, we computed the median and average out of each the 10 forecasts. The result we obtained show a balance between both generalization errors with the values being respectively 4.04×10^{-3} for the ensemble's median forecast and 4.09×10^{-3} for the ensemble's average forecast. This shows that HCNN are able to model High dimensional non linear systems in a consistent way and that both the ensemble's median and average forecast are also reliable candidates for the forecast the dynamics of such systems. .

8. Conclusions

Throughout this paper, we have seen that HCNNs are able to model High dimensional deterministic non linear systems in a consistent way. The different improvement methods have been instrumental in enforcing a long term learning of the dynamics of the multivariate time-series generated from the Lorenz, the Rossler and the Rabinovich-Fabrikant Systems. Among the three improvement methods, measuring by the generalization error, the Partial Teacher Forcing method is the superior way to improve both the long memory and the extent of the forecast horizon. The Large Sparse HCNN method is mostly aligned to biological methods. The LSTM Formulation Method has a linear sub-structure to overcome the vanishing/exploding gradient problems which sometimes creates numerical instability. The results obtained from the ensemble computation graphically show that the shape of the three time series are near each other throughout the whole forecast horizon. Hence, this shows that for different instances of HCNN, the results are ensured to be reproducible. Moving forward, it is worth noting that the datasets were generated mathematically. This gives to those dynamical systems the attribute of fully observables. Since the final goal of this ongoing research is on the analysis of climate data, those are rather high-dimensional and noisy measurements: such kind of system are called partially observables. There is currently a work in progress to extend these techniques to wind forecasting as a basis for wind turbine control. Analysing such systems will require transferring the long memory insights gained from this experiment to that new task. Furthermore, the identification of the optimal HCNN meta-parameters and the formulation of additional improvement techniques for the learning of HCNN will also be probable directions to look at. On another hand, the ensemble forecasts (median and average of the ensemble forecasts) seem to be a promising direction to navigate into, for such forecasting exercise.

Author Contributions: Conceptualization, R.R., B.B., H.-G.Z. and V.M.; methodology, R.R., B.B., H.-G.Z. and V.M.; software, R.R.; validation, R.R., B.B., H.-G.Z. and V.M.; formal analysis, R.R.; investigation, R.R.; resources, R.R.; data curation, R.R.; writing—original draft preparation, R.R.; writing—review and editing, R.R., B.B., H.-G.Z. and V.M.; visualization, R.R.; supervision, R.R., B.B., H.-G.Z. and V.M.; project administration, R.R., B.B., H.-G.Z. and V.M.; All authors have read and agreed to the published version of the manuscript.

Funding: This work was carried out with the aid of a grant from the International Development Research Centre, Ottawa, Canada, and with financial support from the Government of Canada, provided through Global Affairs Canada (GAC).

Acknowledgments: A special thanks to the African Institute for Mathematical Sciences, AIMS South Africa, which is my host institution, through the Next Einstein Initiative.

Conflicts of Interest: The authors declare no conflict of interest.

References

1. Brunton, S.L.; Kutz, J.N. *Data-Driven Science and Engineering: Machine Learning, Dynamical Systems, and Control*; Cambridge University Press: Cambridge, UK, 2022.
2. Schäfer, A.M.; Zimmermann, H.G. Recurrent neural networks are universal approximators. In Proceedings of the 16th International Conference, Athens, Greece, 10–14 September 2006; Springer: Berlin/Heidelberg, Germany, 2006.
3. Hornik, K.; Stinchcombe, M.; White, H. Multilayer feedforward networks are universal approximators. *Neural Netw.* **1989**, *2*, 359–366. [CrossRef]
4. Goodfellow, I.; Bengio, Y.; Courville, A. *Deep Learning*; MIT Press: Cambridge, MA, USA, **2017**.
5. Rumelhart, D.E.; Hinton, G.E.; Williams, R.J. Learning representations by back-propagating errors. *Nature* **1986**, *323*, 533–536. [CrossRef]
6. Haykin, S.; Network, N. A comprehensive foundation. *Neural Netw.* **2004**, *2*, 41.
7. Zimmermann, H.G.; Tietz, C.; Grothmann, R. Forecasting with recurrent neural networks: 12 tricks. In *Neural Networks: Tricks of the Trade*; Springer: Berlin/Heidelberg, Germany, 2012; pp. 687–707.
8. Zimmermann, H.G.; Grothmann, R.; Tietz, C.; Jouanne-Diedrich, H.V. Market modelling, forecasting and risk analysis with historical consistent neural networks. In *Operations Research Proceedings 2010*; Springer: Berlin/Heidelberg, Germany, 2011; pp. 531–536.
9. Mvubu, M.; Kabuga, E.; Plitz, C.; Bah, B.; Becker, R.; Zimmermann, H.G. On Error Correction Neural Networks for Economic Forecasting. In Proceedings of the 2020 IEEE 23rd International Conference on Information Fusion (FUSION), Rustenburg, South Africa, 6–9 July 2020.
10. Zimmermann, H.G.; Neuneier, R.; Grothmann, R. Multi-agent modelling of multiple FX-markets by neural networks. *IEEE Trans. Neural Netw.* **2001**, *12*, 735–743. [CrossRef] [PubMed]
11. Danny, P.; Allon, J. Multivariate exponential smoothing: Method and practice. *Int. J. Forecast.* **1989**, *5*, 83–98.
12. Hochreiter, S.; Schmidhuber, J. Long short-term memory. *Neural Comput.* **1997**, *9*, 1735–1780. [CrossRef] [PubMed]
13. Serrano-Pérez, J.D.; Fernández-Anaya, G.; Carrillo-Moreno, S.; Yu, W. New results for prediction of chaotic systems using deep recurrent neural networks. *Neural Process. Lett.* **2021**, *53*, 1579–1596. [CrossRef]
14. Rabinovich, M.I.; Fabrikant, A.L. Stochastic self-modulation of waves in nonequilibrium media. *J. Exp. Theor. Phys.* **1979**, *77*, 617–629.
15. Rössler, O.E. An equation for continuous chaos. *Phys. Lett. A* **1976**, *57*, 397–398. [CrossRef]
16. Curry, J.H. A generalized Lorenz system. *Commun. Math. Phys.* **1978**, *60*, 193–204. [CrossRef]
17. Edward, O.; Sauer, T.; Yorke, J.A. *Coping with Chaos. Analysis of Chaotic Data and the Exploitation of Chaotic Systems*; Wiley Series in Nonlinear Science; John Wiley and Sons: Hoboken, NJ, USA, 1994.

Proceeding Paper

Exploration of Different Time Series Models for Soccer Athlete Performance Prediction †

Siarhei Kulakou [1], **Nourhan Ragab** [1,2], **Cise Midoglu** [1,*], **Matthias Boeker** [1], **Dag Johansen** [3], **Michael A. Riegler** [1,3] and **Pål Halvorsen** [1,2,4]

1   Simula Metropolitan Center for Digital Engineering (SimulaMet), 0167 Oslo, Norway; siarheik@ifi.uio.no (S.K.); s351643@oslomet.no (N.R.); matthias@simula.no (M.B.); michael@simula.no (M.A.R.); paalh@simula.no (P.H.)
2   Department of Computer Science, Oslo Metropolitan University (OsloMet), 0130 Oslo, Norway
3   Department of Computer Science, UIT The Arctic University of Norway, 9037 Tromsø, Norway; dag.johansen@uit.no
4   Forzasys AS, 0164 Oslo, Norway
*   Correspondence: cise@simula.no
†   Presented at the 8th International Conference on Time Series and Forecasting, Gran Canaria, Spain, 27–30 June 2022.

Abstract: Professional sports achievements combine not only the individual physical abilities of athletes but also many modern technologies in areas such as medicine, equipment production, nutrition, and physical and mental health monitoring. In this work, we address the problem of predicting soccer players' ability to perform, from subjective self-reported wellness parameters collected using a commercially deployed digital health monitoring system called PmSys. We use 2 years of data from two Norwegian female soccer teams, where players have reported daily ratings for their readiness-to-play, mood, stress, general muscle soreness, fatigue, sleep quality, and sleep duration. We explore various time series models with the goal of predicting readiness, employing both a univariate approach and a multivariate approach. We provide an experimental comparison of different time series models, such as purely recurrent models, models of mixed recursive convolutional types, ensemble of deep CNN models, and multivariate versions of the recurrent models, in terms of prediction performance, with a focus on detecting peaks. We use different input and prediction windows to compare the accuracy of next-day predictions and next-week predictions. We also investigate the potential of using models built on data from the whole team for making predictions about individual players, as compared to using models built on the data from the individual player only. We tackle the missing data problem by various methods, including the replacement of all gaps with zeros, filling in repeated values, as well as removing all gaps and concatenating arrays. Our case study on athlete monitoring shows that a number of time series analysis models are able to predict readiness with high accuracy in near real-time. Equipped with such insight, coaches and trainers can better plan individual and team training sessions, and perhaps avoid over training and injuries.

Keywords: athlete training; data imputation; injury prevention; performance prediction; self-reporting; soccer; time series analysis

Citation: Kulakou, S.; Ragab, N.; Midoglu, C.; Boeker, M.; Johansen, D.; Riegler, M.A.; Halvorsen, P. Exploration of Different Time Series Models for Soccer Athlete Performance Prediction. *Eng. Proc.* **2022**, *18*, 37. https://doi.org/10.3390/engproc2022018037

Academic Editors: Ignacio Rojas, Hector Pomares, Olga Valenzuela, Fernando Rojas and Luis Javier Herrera

Published: 29 June 2022

Publisher's Note: MDPI stays neutral with regard to jurisdictional claims in published maps and institutional affiliations.

1. Introduction

Team sports are gaining traction with association football (soccer) in the lead as the most watched sport on television [1]. In 2018, 3.572 billion viewers tuned in to watch the FIFA World Cup [2]. This is equivalent to half of the population on the globe [2]. Soccer is played by amateurs and professionals globally and is a sport that brings people together across the world.

For most professional sports achievements, athletes' individual physical abilities are combined with many modern technologies from fields such as medicine, equipment production, nutrition, and physical and mental health monitoring. Proper diet, rest, and training regimens, as well as continuous monitoring and analysis of wellness and performance metrics can make a big difference for both individual and team sports. Soccer players constantly adhere to a strict nutrition plan, training process, and rest regime so that their body is in the required state at particular moments. The athletes' condition is influenced not only by the amount of consumed and burned calories, or the duration and intensity of the training process, but also by parameters such as the duration and quality of their sleep and their general mental state including mood and stress level.

The increasing popularity and adoption of Machine Learning (ML) approaches has led to more evidence-based decision making [3]. In this context, it is possible to compile a set of parameters describing the general state of the athlete at a certain point of time, collect objective or subjective measurements of these parameters, and try to predict the state/behavior of the athlete's body in the near future using ML. For instance, according to Fuller et al. [4], an average soccer team can expect around 50 injuries per season. Using ML, it might be feasible to make evidence-based decisions for reducing injuries at a chosen period in the future using time series analysis and predictions. The desired outcome of implementing such technologies into sports science is that injuries will be reduced, performance will be improved, and better decisions will be made. Similar technologies have already been approved by organizations such as FIFA and are used by several teams in the Norwegian top league.

In this work, we address the problem of predicting soccer players' ability to perform, from subjective self-reported wellness parameters collected using a commercially deployed digital health monitoring system called PmSys. We focus on *readiness to play*, which is a measure of a player's ability to complete a training session or play in a match. We address the research question: Can we predict readiness for elite female soccer athletes using ML on data collected using an athlete monitoring system? More specifically, we try to answer the following. Which time series models are capable of capturing adequate information for accurate predictions? Is it more accurate to predict a player's readiness using data from an individual player or team based data? How far back in the historical data should we go and how far into the future can we predict? Does the training dataset size have an impact on the results? Which hyperparameter configurations result in the most accurate predictions?

We design and implement a software framework for undertaking time series predictions which can be configured extensively [5], and run multiple iterations of experiments to answer the above questions. Our results show that a number of time series analysis models are able to predict readiness with high accuracy in near real-time. Equipped with such insight, coaches and trainers can better plan individual and team training sessions, and perhaps avoid over training and injuries.

The rest of this paper is organized as follows. In Section 2, we provide background information and an overview of related work. In Section 3, we describe our dataset and methodology. In Section 4, we present selected results from our analysis of the above research questions, and discuss our findings. In Section 5, we conclude the paper.

2. Background and Related Work

2.1. Time Series Prediction

A time series is described as an ordered collection of data points where each data point is an observation in time [6–8]. Time series are sample realizations of stochastic processes [6]. Stochastic processes can be found in various fields, such as temperature measurements or a stock market index. Time series have an inherent dependence in time. Successive observations are dependent and thus not randomly sampled [6]. Time as an additional dimension distinguishes time series data from the more generally known cross-sectional data. The time series analysis describes a set of statistical models that aim to model the underlying stochastic process. The objectives of time series analysis are forecasting and control [6]. Forecasting is considered as a regression problem and is defined as the prediction of values based on the time series model beyond the present. The main tasks of time series analysis are: (i) understand under the influence of which parameters the value of the time series is formed, (ii) build a mathematical model for each parameter or combination. Any time series can be decomposed into a trend, seasonal, cyclical, and random components. The first three components form the non-random component of the time series. The random component is present in any time series, but components of a non-random constituent in the time series structure are not necessary [9].

The development of Recurrent Neural Networks (RNNs) made a significant contribution to the study and help solve regression problems associated with time series. RNNs are applicable in tasks where something holistic is broken into parts. One of the most popular types of recurrent neural networks is the Long Short-Term Memory (LSTM) network. Some of the most outstanding achievements of using LSTM are the revolutionizing of speech recognition, outperforming traditional models in specific speech applications [10], improving large-vocabulary speech recognition [11,12], and breaking records for improved machine translation [13]. The LSTM extends the traditional time series analysis models such as autoregressive integrated moving average models or exponential smoothing methods. Saimi et al. [14] demonstrated the superiority of the LSTM over the traditional approaches. In addition, in 2014, a gate mechanism was introduced, called Gated Recurrent Units (GRU), for recurrent neural networks. One found that its effectiveness in solving problems of modeling music and speech signals is comparable to the use of long short-term memory [15]. Compared to LSTM, this mechanism has fewer parameters because there are no output gates [16].

2.2. The PmSys Athlete Monitoring System

PmSys is a digital monitoring system that was developed for the collection, storage, analysis, and visualization of athletes' health data [17,18]. The intention for creating this system was to replace the manual method of collecting information, and its storage on paper, with a digital one. According to the creators, the primary users are soccer players, coaches, and medical personnel [19]. The primary tool for information registration is a questionnaire that the players could easily and quickly fill out each day using a mobile application [20]. This approach allows athletes to manage their own time when filling out the questionnaire without the coach's insistent control of the process.

Several experiments have been carried out to see if ML can be used to forecast future values of soccer player readiness to play in previous work. Wiik et al. [18] conducted a study with the purpose of reducing sports injuries and predicting readiness to play. Based on a dataset from two male high division soccer teams in Norway (one team from January 2017 until late August 2017 including 19 players, the other team from February 2018 to mid June 2018 including 22 players, with an overall dataset of 6000 entries), they demonstrated the value of utilizing a LSTM RNN to predict reported training load. They were able to train the model to predict positive peaks and negative peaks. Positive peaks are categorized as values above 8 and negative peaks are categorized as values below 3. Both of the datasets did not have values for all days. As a result, they had to account for the issue of missing data. The missing data were not replaced or deleted to provide a realistic use scenario. This was performed to provide a more realistic use case, as data gaps would always exist due to vacations, injury time, and other factors. To keep the simplicity of reproducing and interpreting the results, the model was kept small. This allowed to explore the underlying possibilities in the data. To assess and confirm the data, two distinct methodologies were used. The initial strategy was to train the entire team and then predict when the player would be ready to play. The second strategy involves training the model on the player who will be predicted. When the entire team was used to train the model, the predictions were more accurate, and the graphs closely tracked the peaks. Wiik et al. [18] attempted another experiment with traditional ML methods such as linear regression and random forest, but the results were not significantly improved.

Another research performed by Johansen et al. [21] demonstrated the impact of employing current technologies in sports to detect injuries and train optimally. In this study they have seen the advantages of incorporating technology into elite athlete performance.

Their decade of expertise has culminated in a smartphone-based application with a backend system for cutting-edge athlete monitoring. A cooperation between computer scientists, sport scientists, and medical professionals has helped to discover gaps that technology can address, allowing athletes to progress in the proper direction. PmSys was well received by both athletes and staff, making it simpler to advocate for earlier bedtimes and modified training days.

3. Dataset and Methodology

3.1. Dataset

Over the course of 2 years, players from 2 participant elite female soccer teams in the PmSys system have contributed to the collection of subjective reports through a mobile application, where they used questionnaires for registering their individual subjective responses to a list of metrics daily. In this work, we use a subset of these metrics as listed below.

- Readiness to play (rated 1–10).
- Mood (rated 1–5).
- Stress level (rated 1–5).
- General muscle soreness (rated 1–5).
- Fatigue (rated 1–5).
- Sleep quality (rated 1–5).

3.2. Proposed Investigations

Time series models: We propose to benchmark different time series models, such as purely recurrent models (RNN, LSTM, GRU, RNNPlus, LSTMPLus, GRU-Plus), models of mixed recursive convolutional types (RNN-FCNPlus, LSTM-FCNPlus, GRU-FCNPlus), ensemble of deep CNN models (InceptionTime), and multivariate versions of the recurrent models (MRNN-FCNPlus, MLSTM-FCNPlus, MGRU-FCNPlus).

Univariate vs. multivariate prediction: A univariate time series has a single time-dependent variable. Using only the readiness parameter from our dataset to predict readiness is an example of a univariate time series. A multivariate time series, on the other hand, has more than one time-dependent variable. We propose to use mood, stress, soreness, and fatigue, along with readiness, as a multivariate time series, to compare univariate vs. multivariate prediction performance of the readiness parameter.

Window size: We propose to compare the performance of running trained models on test data with different sliding window sizes, both in terms of input window (indicating the amount of data to be used for making predictions) and output window (indicating the amount of data to be predicted).

Training on team vs. training on player: Motivated by the findings of Wiik et al. [18], we propose to compare the accuracy of predicting the readiness parameter for a single player, using a model trained on data from the same player only versus using a model trained on data from the player's entire team.

Hyperparameter configuration: We propose to investigate the influence of hyperparameters on prediction accuracy, in particular batch size, number of epochs in training, and data shuffling.

Data imputation: As our dataset is composed of subjectively reported metrics, a common problem is missing data (i.e., responses not being recorded every day). Missing data causes time series to have gaps. Several solutions can address this challenge: (i) replacing all gaps with 0, (ii) filling in the gaps with the value from the previous day, and (iii) removing all gaps and concatenating the data array.

3.3. Implementation

Python is a suitable language for working with large data sets since it is easy to use and has many already implemented libraries related to machine learning. We use **pandas** to extract data from file and preprocessing. Pandas' data functionality is built on the NumPy library, a lower-level tool. Includes special techniques for working with numeric tables and time series. **Tsai** is a state-of-the-art deep learning library for time series and sequences (https://timeseriesai.github.io/tsai/ (accessed on 1 June 2022)). It is an open-source deep learning package built on top of Pytorch and fastai [22], focusing on state-of-the-art techniques for time series tasks such as classification, regression, forecasting, and imputation. This library contains a number of ready-to-use deep learning models that are possible to run directly in Python for time series prediction, which we use. To test the performance of various models, we also use the process and system utilities library (**psutil**). Table 1 presents the specifications of the hardware and software components of the benchmark implementation of our proposed framework.

Table 1. System specifications for the benchmark implementation.

Category	Name	Version	Description
Software	Ubuntu	18.04.6 LTS	OS
	Python	3.6.9	Programming language
	Tsai	0.2.22	ML library
	Fastai	2.5.2	ML library
	Torch	1.9.0 + cu102	ML library
	Pandas	1.1.5	Data analysis library
	Psutil	5.8.0	Performance measurement library
Hardware	Memory	DDR4 46.9 GiB	
	Harddisk	SSD 491.2 GiB	
	CPU	Intel Core i7-9700 (8 cores)	

3.4. Metrics

Prediction performance: The metrics used to evaluate prediction models operate on a set of continuous values (with an infinite number of items) and therefore differ slightly from the metrics used for classification tasks. The most popular metrics for regression models are Mean Squared Error (MSE), Root Mean Square Error (RMSE), and Mean Absolute Error (MAE). In the following, we primarily use MSE. MSE measures the average sum of the square of the difference between the actual value and the predicted value for all data points. Exponentiation is performed, so negative values are not compensated with positive ones. Compared to the MAE, MSE has several advantages: it emphasizes big mistakes over more minor mistakes. It is differentiable, which allows it to be more efficiently used to find the minimum or maximum values using mathematical methods. The lower the MSE, the higher the prediction accuracy.

$$MSE = \frac{1}{n} \sum_{i=1}^{n} (y_i - \hat{y}_i)^2$$

System performance: The primary metrics for measuring performance are usually time spent on training and testing models, processor, memory, disk, and Graphics Processing Unit (GPU) usage. We primarily focus on computation without the requirement for a GPU, therefore we measure all other parameters except the GPU usage: *(i) Time usage:* Time is measured in seconds. For measuring the time to train and test each model, we use the `time` module (https://docs.python.org/3/library/time.html (accessed on 1 June 2022)) from the Python standard library, which provides various time-related functions. *(ii) CPU, memory and disk usage:* To measure CPU, memory, and disk usage, we use a cross-platform library called psutil (https://pypi.org/project/psutil/ (accessed on 1 June 2022)). This library has a set of utilities for obtaining information about system performance (since our processor consists of 8 cores, we use the utility `cpu_percent()` to obtain information about a load of each core in percentage. We also use psutil to measure memory and disk usage. The `virtual_memory()` utility function provides information about various memory parameters. We are interested in the parameter used, which shows the amount of memory used at a given time. The `disk_usage()` function also has the parameter used that provides information about the used disk space at a given time). We measure the used memory and disk in GiB. We measure CPU, memory, and disk usage with an interval of one second.

4. Selected Results

4.1. Benchmarking Different Time Series Models

We ran the 13 different models listed in Section 3 on data from one team, predicting the readiness parameter for a single player using the model trained on the player's own data. Initial values for the hyperparameters batch size and number of epochs were chosen based on examples in the Tsai code repository (https://github.com/timeseriesAI/tsai/tree/main/tutorial_nbs (accessed on 1 June 2022)). For the sliding window size, multiple values (3, 5, 7, 14, 21, 28, 35, 42, 49) were considered. Missing data were treated with and without gaps. Table 2 presents the best performing models and their corresponding MSE for univariate prediction. The best results were obtained using a sliding window of size 3 and data without gaps. The initial value for the number of epochs (200) was suitable for almost all models, except for the GRU, where overfitting was observed in the training, and the value reduced to 100. Almost all models could predict the ground truth contour of readiness over time quite well with a slight deviation, except for GRUPlus. Some models also were able to predict positive and negative peaks successfully, especially the InceptionTime, MGRU-FCNPlus, MLSTM-FCNPlus, RNN-FCNPlus, MRNN-FCNPlus, GRU-FCNPlus, and LSTM-FCNPlus.

Table 2. MSE values for top models. Univariate prediction for single player, input window size: 3, no zero-padding.

Model	MSE
InceptionTime	1.191
MGRU-FCNPlus	1.280
MLSTM-FCNPlus	1.299
RNN-FCNPlus	1.321
LSTM	1.331
MRNN-FCNPlus	1.350
GRU-FCNPlus	1.369
GRU	1.375
LSTM-FCNPlus	1.409
LSTMPlus	1.480
GRUPlus	1.763

4.2. Univariate vs. Multivariate Prediction

We ran the same configurations to carry out the initial experiments for multivariate scenario, with the difference that multivariate times series consisting of readiness, mood, stress, soreness, and fatigue, where the target parameter to predict is readiness, are used. After initial observations of multivariate prediction, 200 epochs turned out to be too high and influenced the results of predictions. As the plots of the training and validation loss function for various models showed, many of them were already trained after 20 epochs; therefore, we decided to correct the number of epochs for all models and rerun the initial experiments with sliding window sizes of 3, 5, 7, 28, and 49.

Table 3 presents the best performing models and their corresponding MSE for multivariate prediction with a higher number of epochs (top), and a lower number of epochs (bottom). With a large number of epochs, only three neural networks had an MSE below 2. Where MSE for the top ten models for univariate prediction was within the range 1191–1480, the MSE for only the four best models with multivariate prediction was within 1325–1603, which meant that employing univariate prediction was more accurate. The best results for both multivariate and univariate prediction were obtained for a sliding window of size 3 and data without gaps. Overfitting influenced multivariate prediction to a greater extent. Similar to univariate prediction, InceptionTime was among the best models, with LSTMPlus and InceptionTime predictions closest to ground truth overall, and the plots of predicted against actual values of readiness for most models adequate for following peaks.

Table 3. MSE for top models. Multivariate prediction for single player, input window size: 3, no zero-padding. Number of epochs: 200 (top), 20 (bottom).

Model	MSE
LSTMPlus	1.668
InceptionTime	1.721
LSTM	1.735
LSTM-FCNPlus	1.325
InceptionTime	1.567
GRU-FCNPlus	1.600
MLSTM-FCNPlus	1.603

4.3. Input and Output Window Size

To investigate how the input window and output window sizes influence prediction in a more practical context, we focused on a daily and weekly predictions as might be relevant to soccer clubs during a game season. We ran experiments using a period of 2 years to train on the entire team and predict the readiness for one player for (7, 14, 21) days as the input window, and 1 and 7 days as the output window. Table 4 presents the MSE values for univariate prediction with LSTMPlus as a representative model, with different window sizes, for Team A. We note that similar results are obtained for Team B, and the MSE value increases for each day predicted in the future (see Figure 1), which was against our initial expectation of a somewhat weekly pattern (and therefore reduced MSE for 7 days). The increase in inaccuracy is possibly due to readiness being a continuous rather than periodically peaking parameter, meaning that the days immediately leading up to a day are important. If the peaks were more periodic, the predictions for future days which are ahead by multiple days (e.g., same day of the week in the upcoming week) would be possible to predict without relying on the whole of the leading week.

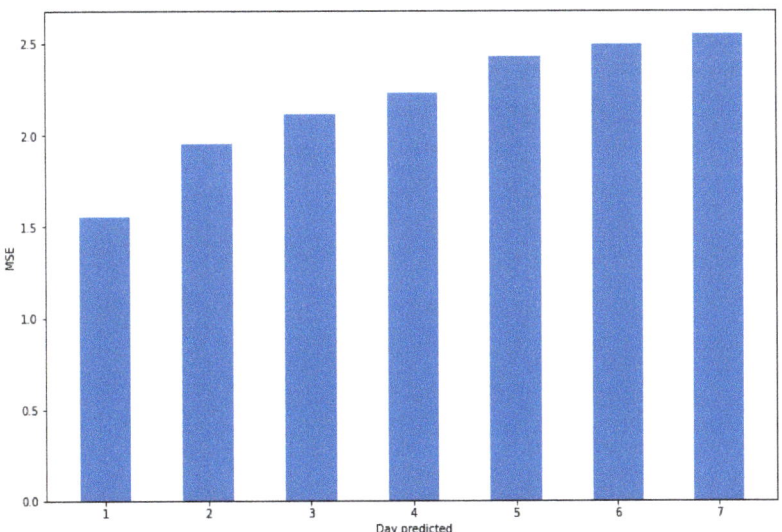

Figure 1. MSE per predicted day. Training on the entire team and testing on single player from Team B, number of epochs: 30, batch size: 5, input window: 21, output window: 7.

Table 4. MSE for LSTMPlus with different input and output window sizes (Team A).

Year	Epoch	Batch Size	Input Window	Output Window	Train on	Shuffle	MSE
2020	30	5	7	1	Team	False	1.54
2020	30	5	14	1	Team	False	1.37
2020	30	5	21	1	Team	False	1.31
2021	30	5	7	7	Team	False	1.54–1.57
2021	30	5	14	7	Team	False	1.51–1.64
2021	30	5	21	7	Team	False	1.87–2.61

4.4. Training on Team vs. Training on Player

Previous related work has proven that training on the entire team and predicting readiness for a single player can give promising results [18,21,23]. In Table 5, we present the results from experiments on Team A with 30 epochs and a batch size of 5, comparing the performance of models trained on the entire team and trained on a single player for predicting the readiness for the player. Overall, training on the entire team and predicting for one player show lower MSE values.

Table 5. MSE for LSTMPlus trained on single player vs. trained on entire team (Team A).

Epoch	Batch Size	Input Window	Output Window	Train on	Shuffle	MSE
30	5	7	1	Team	False	1.54
30	5	7	1	Player	False	1.64
30	5	14	1	Team	False	1.37
30	5	14	1	Player	False	1.49
30	5	21	1	Team	False	1.31
30	5	21	1	Player	False	1.25

Figure 2 demonstrates the viability of training on the entire team, where the predictions follow the actual values quite accurately and the peaks are anticipated correctly. We also observe that the MSE value increases as the input window increases, possibly indicating that predicting the next day using data from the last week (input window: 7, output window: 1) might be the optimal use case for our scenario.

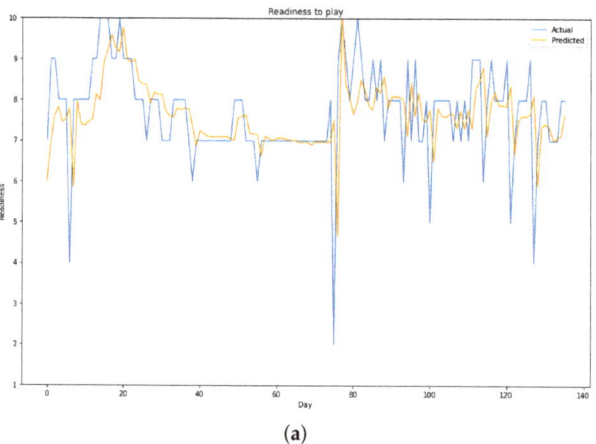

(a)

Figure 2. *Cont.*

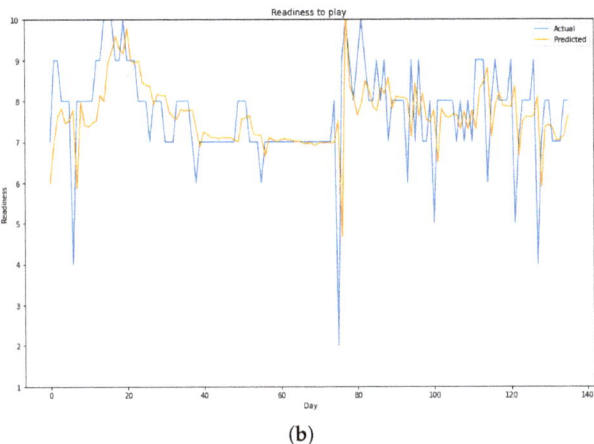

(b)

Figure 2. Actual and predicted values for readiness for player from Team A. Training on entire team, number of epochs: 30, batch size: 5. (**a**) input window: 7; (**b**) input window 21.

4.5. Hyperparameter Configuration

Model optimization depends on hyperparameters, which include number of epochs, batch size and data shuffle. We pick a single player from a team, modify the hyperparameters and train the model on the entire team to predict on the player using univariate prediction with LSTMPLus. Table 6 presents the MSE values for different hyperparameter settings. The result showed that enabling shuffle led to a reduced MSE. The plots of actual and predicted values, however, were almost identical for different values for other hyperparameters. For all cases, the predicted peaks were quite close to the actual values. The only hyperparameter modification that reduced the MSE value was enabling data shuffle, and its influence was not significant.

Table 6. MSE for LSTMPlus with different hyperparameter values.

Epoch	Batch Size	Input Window	Output Window	Train on	Shuffle	MSE
30	5	7	1	Team	True	0.68
30	5	7	1	Team	False	0.72
40	5	7	1	Team	True	0.72
40	5	7	1	Team	False	0.73
30	25	7	1	Team	True	0.68
30	25	7	1	Team	False	0.69
50	5	7	1	Team	True	0.86
50	5	7	1	Team	False	0.76
50	25	7	1	Team	True	0.70
50	25	7	1	Team	False	0.73

4.6. System Performance

Table 7 reports system performance metrics as recorded on the benchmark implementation specified in Table 1 for selected models for univariate and multivariate prediction.

Table 7. System performance metrics for benchmark implementation: univariate (top) and multivariate (bottom) prediction.

Model	Training Time (s)	Testing Time for 10 Repetitions (s)	CPU (Min/Max)	Memory (Min/Max)	Disk (Min/Max)
MRNN-FCNPlus	381	0.370	45/100	18.450/18.540	34.040/34.048
InceptionTime	554	0.539	60/100	18.130/18.200	34.060/34.068
LSTM-FCNPlus	341	0.324	50/100	18.330/18.400	34.044/34.054
MGRU-FCNPlus	387	0.306	45/100	18.500/18.570	34.046/34.056
LSTMPlus	216	0.261	60/100	18.210/18.270	34.044/34.051
InceptionTime	46	0.295	80/100	17.875/17.895	34.048/34.050
GRU-FCNPlus	111	0.204	85/100	17.772/17.787	34.053/34.055
LSTM-FCNPlus	147	0.240	75/100	17.762/17.784	34.050/34.051

InceptionTime and LSTM have the best training time (200 epochs) for multivariate and univariate prediction, respectively. The testing time for all models (7100 data points) turned out to be approximately the same, and we see that testing proceeded very quickly. To calculate the CPU usage, we used a utility that measured the utilization for each core separately. The CPU utilization was measured only in the process of training the models. As a result, it turned out that the usage increased several times at the start of the training process and remained at the level of 75–100% (multivariate) and 65–100% (univariate) for all models. After the end of the training, the CPU utilization also immediately decreased. The values of memory and disk usage in the training process turned out to be insignificant. The minimum and maximum amount of memory and disk usage differed by about a few hundred MB. Overall, our preliminary analysis indicates that a framework as we have proposed in this work can be run in near real time without requiring a lot of resources.

5. Conclusions

In this work, we addressed the problem of predicting soccer players' ability to perform, from subjective self-reported wellness parameters collected using a commercially deployed digital health monitoring system called PmSys. We focused on readiness to play, which is a measure of a player's ability to complete a training session or play in a match, and experimented with a software framework for undertaking time series predictions to derive insights regarding the influence of different factors on prediction accuracy.

As an initial study, we investigated and presented our results regarding the following: (1) We tested various time series models to see which were capable of capturing adequate information for accurate predictions. (2) We compared univariate and multivariate approaches to see if we can leverage different wellness parameters in the dataset to predict readiness? (3) We looked at the impact of different input and output sizes to see how far back in the historical data it is necessary to go for training, and how far into the future it is possible to predict with acceptable accuracy. (4) We looked at how training on a single player versus training on the entire team affected the results, to see if prediction frameworks can leverage data from teams for making predictions on individual players. (5) We investigated the influence of different hyperparameters such as the number of epochs, batch size, and data shuffle on prediction accuracy.

We found out that most of the tested ML models are able to yield a reasonable accuracy in prediction, provided that training parameters are adjusted to avoid overfitting. In terms of performance, the best model for the multivariate prediction turned out to be InceptionTime, and for the univariate prediction, LSTM. We could not find evidence that multivariate predictions perform better within the context of our dataset and scenario, however, further analysis of the other parameters available from the PmSys dataset are necessary. We saw that daily predictions performed better than weekly predictions, indicating that the readiness parameter might not be as strongly periodic as initially assumed.

Training on the entire team and predicting for a single player resulted in more accurate overall results, especially when a team has high consistency across players, and the correct prediction of peaks. This is a first step toward determining the system's generalizability so that it may be used in other sports. Hyperparameter tuning did not have significant influence within our testing range, except for data shuffling, which improved performance.

In this work, we have tried to address various research aspects independently, and using different parts of the PmSys dataset at times; however, there are many investigations that need to be continued in a more systematic manner over the complete and extended dataset for a more comprehensive understanding of the potentially complex interplay between influencing factors on prediction performance. Dataset and pipeline standardization, including the evaluation of libraries other than Tsai, are also necessary for a large-scale analysis covering a wide range of parameter values and system settings. Other future work topics include the investigation of the contextual relevance of the samples (e.g., what effects does it have on the predictions when using off-season vs. on-season, weekday vs. weekend, match day vs. regular training), more advanced methods for handling missing data, and a deeper analysis of multivariate prediction with an augmented set of supplementary wellness and health parameters.

Overall, we demonstrated that it is possible to make relatively accurate predictions about elite soccer player readiness using ML algorithms such as LSTM, using the kind of datasets collected by athlete monitoring platforms such as PmSys. ML-based time series prediction pipelines, integrated with such platforms, can have a huge impact in the field of sports science and computer science, and our approach can be extended to various health, wellness, injury, and training parameters, as well as different sports as well.

Author Contributions: Conceptualization, D.J., M.A.R., and P.H.; methodology, D.J., M.A.R., P.H., and C.M.; software, S.K. and N.R.; validation, S.K., N.R., P.H., and C.M.; investigation, S.K., N.R., P.H., and C.M.; resources, D.J., M.A.R., and P.H.; data curation, M.B., C.M., and P.H.; writing—original draft preparation, C.M.; writing—review and editing, C.M., M.B., and P.H.; visualization, N.R.; supervision, C.M., D.J., M.A.R., and P.H.; project administration, P.H.; funding acquisition, D.J., M.A.R., and P.H. All authors have read and agreed to the published version of the manuscript.

Funding: The work is partially funded by Tromsø Research Foundation. The funding body had no role in the study itself or in the writing of this paper.

Institutional Review Board Statement: Not applicable.

Informed Consent Statement: Informed consent was obtained from all subjects involved in the study. The study was approved by both the Norwegian Privacy Data Protection Authority (reference number: 296155) and exempted from further user consent because the data were fully anonymous. All metadata were removed, and all files renamed to randomly generated file names before the original PmSys system exported the files from the cloud server. The study was also exempted from approval from the Regional Committee for Medical and Health Research Ethics—South East Norway and the Regional Committee for Medical and Health Research Ethics—Northern Norway since the collection of the data did not include a bio-bank, medical, or health data related to illness or interfere the normal operation of the players. Since the data are anonymous, the dataset is publicly shareable based on Norwegian and General Data Protection Regulation (GDPR) laws.

Data Availability Statement: The resources for reproducing the results can be found under https://github.com/simula/pmsys (accessed on 26 June 2022).

Conflicts of Interest: Authors D.J. and P.H. both own shares in the Forzasys AS company developing among other things data collection systems and solutions for AI-based analysis of sports data. The PmSys system from Forzasys was used to collect the subjective reports, but there is no commercial interest from Forzasys regarding this publication and dataset. Otherwise, the authors declare no competing interests.

References

1. Bandyopadhyay, K. *Legacies of Great Men in World Soccer: Heroes, Icons*; Routledge: Abingdon-on-Thames, UK , 2017.
2. FIFA. More than Half the World Watched Record-Breaking 2018 World Cup. 2022. Available online: https://www.fifa.com/tournaments/mens/worldcup/2018russia/media-releases/more-than-half-the-world-watched-record-breaking-2018-world-cup (accessed on 11 May 2022).
3. Pugliese, R.; Regondi, S.; Marini, R. Machine learning-based approach: Global trends, research directions, and regulatory standpoints. *Data Sci. Manag.* **2021**, *4*, 19–29. [CrossRef]
4. Fuller, C.W.; Ekstrand, J.; Junge, A.; Andersen, T.E.; Bahr, R.; Dvorak, J.; Hägglund, M.; McCrory, P.; Meeuwisse, W.H. Consensus statement on injury definitions and data collection procedures in studies of football (soccer) injuries. *Br. J. Sports Med.* **2006**, *40*, 193–201. [CrossRef] [PubMed]
5. Kulakou, S.; Ragab, N.; Midoglu, C. PmSys. 2022. Available online: https://github.com/simula/pmsys (accessed on 23 May 2022).
6. Box, G.E.; Jenkins, G.M.; Reinsel, G.C.; Ljung, G.M. *Time Series Analysis: Forecasting and Control*; John Wiley & Sons: Hoboken, NJ, USA, 2015.
7. Adhikari, R.; Agrawal, R.K. An introductory study on time series modeling and forecasting. *arXiv* **2013**, arXiv:1302.6613.
8. Shumway, R.H.; Stoffer, D.S.; Stoffer, D.S. *Time Series Analysis and Its Applications*; Springer: Berlin/Heidelberg, Germany, 2000; Volume 3.
9. Hamilton, J.D. *Time Series Analysis*; Princeton University Press: Princeton, NJ, USA, 2020.
10. Fernández, S.; Graves, A.; Schmidhuber, J. An application of recurrent neural networks to discriminative keyword spotting. In Proceedings of the International Conference on Artificial Neural Networks, Porto, Portugal, 9–13 September 2007; pp. 220–229.
11. Sak, H.; Senior, A.W.; Beaufays, F. Long Short-Term Memory Recurrent Neural Network Architectures for Large Scale Acoustic Modeling. 2014. Available online: https://static.googleusercontent.com/media/research.google.com/en//pubs/archive/43905.pdf (accessed on 26 June 2022).
12. Li, X.; Wu, X. Constructing long short-term memory based deep recurrent neural networks for large vocabulary speech recognition. In Proceedings of the 2015 IEEE International Conference on Acoustics, Speech and Signal Processing (ICASSP), Brisbane, Australia, 19–24 April 2015; pp. 4520–4524.
13. Sutskever, I.; Vinyals, O.; Le, Q.V. Sequence to sequence learning with neural networks. In Proceedings of the Twenty-Seventh Conference on Neural Information Processing Systems (NIPS'14), Montreal, QC, Canada, 8–13 December 2014; pp. 3104–3112.
14. Siami-Namini, S.; Tavakoli, N.; Namin, A.S. A comparison of ARIMA and LSTM in forecasting time series. In Proceedings of the 2018 17th IEEE International Conference on Machine Learning and Applications (ICMLA), Orlando, FL, USA, 17–20 December 2018; pp. 1394–1401.
15. Chung, J.; Gulcehre, C.; Cho, K.; Bengio, Y. Empirical evaluation of gated recurrent neural networks on sequence modeling. *arXiv* **2014**, arXiv:1412.3555.
16. Britz, D. Recurrent Neural Network Tutorial, Part 4 Implementing a GRU/LSTM RNN with Python and Theano. 2015. Available online: https://sites.google.com/site/nttrungmtwiki/home/it/machine-lear/neural-networks/recurrent-neural-network/recurrent-neural-network-tutorial-part-4-implementing-a-gru-lstm-rnn-with-python-and-theano (accessed on 26 June 2022).
17. Pettersen, S.A.; Johansen, H.D.; Baptista, I.A.M.; Halvorsen, P.; Johansen, D. Quantified Soccer Using Positional Data: A Case Study. *Front. Physiol.* **2018**, *9*, 866. [CrossRef]
18. Wiik, T.; Johansen, H.D.; Pettersen, S.A.; Baptista, I.; Kupka, T.; Johansen, D.; Riegler, M.; Halvorsen, P. Predicting Peek Readiness-to-Train of Soccer Players Using Long Short-Term Memory Recurrent Neural Networks. In Proceedings of the 2019 International Conference on Content-Based Multimedia Indexing (CBMI), Dublin, Ireland, 4–6 September 2019; pp. 1–6. [CrossRef]
19. Hoang, T.T. pmSys: Implementation of a Digital Player Monitoring System. Master's Thesis, University of Oslo, Oslo, Norway, 2015 .
20. Nguyen, C.N. Implementation of a Digital Player Monitoring System: PmSys. Master's Thesis, University of Oslo, Oslo, Norway, 2015.
21. Johansen, H.D.; Johansen, D.; Kupka, T.; Riegler, M.A.; Halvorsen, P. Scalable Infrastructure for Efficient Real-Time Sports Analytics. In Proceedings of the ICMI'20 Companion: Companion Publication of the 2020 International Conference on Multimodal Interaction, Virtual, 25–29 October 2020; Association for Computing Machinery: New York, NY, USA, 2020; pp. 230–234. [CrossRef]
22. Howard, J.; Gugger, S. Fastai: A layered API for deep learning. *Information* **2020**, *11*, 108. [CrossRef]
23. Kulakou, S. Exploration of Time-Series Models on Time Series Data. Master's Thesis, University of Oslo, Oslo, Norway, 2021.

Proceeding Paper

The Bootstrap for Testing the Equality of Two Multivariate Stochastic Processes with an Application to Financial Markets [†]

Ángel López-Oriona [1,*] and José A. Vilar [1,2]

1   Research Group MODES, Research Center for Information and Communication Technologies (CITIC), University of A Coruña, 15071 A Coruña, Spain; jose.vilarf@udc.es
2   Technological Institute for Industrial Mathematics (ITMATI), 15705 Santiago de Compostela, Spain
*   Correspondence: oriona38@hotmail.com
†   Presented at the 8th International Conference on Time Series and Forecasting, Gran Canaria, Spain, 27–30 June 2022.

Abstract: The problem of testing the equality of generating processes of two multivariate time series is addressed in this work. To this end, we construct two tests based on a distance measure between stochastic processes. The metric is defined in terms of the quantile cross-spectral densities of both processes. A proper estimate of this dissimilarity is the cornerstone of the proposed tests. Both techniques are based on the bootstrap. Specifically, extensions of the moving block bootstrap and the stationary bootstrap are used for their construction. The approaches are assessed in a broad range of scenarios under the null and the alternative hypotheses. The results from the analyses show that the procedure based on the stationary bootstrap exhibits the best overall performance in terms of both size and power. The proposed techniques are used to answer the question regarding whether or not the dotcom bubble crash of the 2000s permanently impacted global market behavior.

Keywords: multivariate time series; quantile cross-spectral density; frequency domain; moving block bootstrap; stationary bootstrap; dotcom bubble

Citation: López-Oriona, Á.; Vilar, J.A. The Bootstrap for Testing the Equality of Two Multivariate Stochastic Processes with an Application to Financial Markets. *Eng. Proc.* **2022**, *18*, 38. https://doi.org/10.3390/engproc2022018038

Academic Editors: Ignacio Rojas, Hector Pomares, Olga Valenzuela, Fernando Rojas and Luis Javier Herrera

Published: 8 July 2022

Publisher's Note: MDPI stays neutral with regard to jurisdictional claims in published maps and institutional affiliations.

1. Introduction

Comparison of time series often arises in multiple fields including machine learning, finance, economics, computer science, biology, medicine, physics, and psychology, among many others. For instance, it is not uncommon for an investor to have to determine if two particular assets show the same dynamic behavior over time based on historical data. In the same way, a physician often needs to find out to what extent two ECG signals recorded from different subjects exhibit similar patterns. There exist a wide variety of tools that have been used for these and similar purposes, including cluster analysis [1], classification [2], outlier detection [3], and comparisons through hypotheses tests [4]. It is worth highlighting that these techniques have mainly focused on univariate time series (UTS) [5], while the study of multivariate time series (MTS) has been given limited consideration [6].

In the context of hypotheses tests for time series, spectral quantities have played an important role. Specifically, testing for the equality of spectral densities has found substantial interest in the literature. Ref. [7] proposed a test for comparing spectral densities of stationary time series with unequal sample sizes. The procedure generalizes the class of tests presented in [8], which are based on an estimate of the L^2-distance between the spectral density and its best approximation under the null hypothesis. Ref. [9] constructed a non-parametric test for the equality of spectral density matrices based on an L^2-type statistic.

This work is devoted to constructing procedures to test for the equality of the so-called quantile cross-spectral density (QCD) between two independent MTS. Specifically, let $X_t^{(1)}$ and $X_t^{(2)}$ be two independent, d-variate, real-valued, strictly stationary stochastic processes. We fix a frequency $\omega \in [-\pi, \pi]$ and a pair of probability levels, $\tau, \tau' \in [0, 1]$, and we denote the corresponding QCD matrices by $\mathbf{f}^{(i)}(\omega, \tau, \tau')$, $i = 1, 2$. The hypotheses we consider can be stated as

$$H_0 : \mathfrak{f}_{X_t^{(1)}} = \mathfrak{f}_{X_t^{(2)}} \quad \text{against} \quad H_1 : \mathfrak{f}_{X_t^{(1)}} \neq \mathfrak{f}_{X_t^{(2)}}, \tag{1}$$

where $\mathfrak{f}_{X_t^{(1)}}$ and $\mathfrak{f}_{X_t^{(2)}}$ are the corresponding sets of QCD matrices defined as

$$\mathfrak{f}_{X_t^{(i)}} = \{\mathbf{f}^{(i)}(\omega, \tau, \tau'), \omega \in [-\pi, \pi], \tau, \tau' \in [0, 1]\}. \tag{2}$$

where $i = 1, 2$. In order to perform the test in (1), we rely on a distance measure between stationary stochastic processes, so-called d_{QCD}, which has already being utilized in several MTS data mining tasks [6,10–12]. This metric is simply the Euclidean distance between two complex vectors constructed by concatenating the terms in each collection of matrices (2) for some finite set of frequencies and probability levels. Hence, an equivalence occurs between the null hypothesis in (1) and the distance d_{QCD} being zero for every possible set, making an estimate of this metric an appropriate tool to carry out the test in (1). The high ability of d_{QCD} to detect every possible discrepancy between stochastic processes was shown in our previous work [10].

Two methods to perform the test in (1) are introduced in this manuscript. They are based on the moving block bootstrap (MBB) (see [13,14]) and the stationary bootstrap (SB) (see [15]). Both approaches are compared in terms of size and power by means of a broad simulation study. Finally, the tests are applied to answer the question regarding whether or not the dotcom bubble burst of 2000 changed the global behavior of financial markets.

The rest of the paper is organized as follows. The distance d_{QCD} between stochastic processes is defined in Section 2. The two techniques to carry out the test in (1) are presented in Section 3. The results from the simulation study performed to compare the proposed tests are reported in Section 4. Section 5 contains the financial application and Section 6 concludes.

2. A Distance Measure between Stochastic Processes

Let $\{X_t, t \in \mathbb{Z}\} = \{(X_{t,1}, \dots, X_{t,d}), t \in \mathbb{Z}\}$ be a d-variate real-valued strictly stationary stochastic process. Denote by F_j the marginal distribution function of $X_{t,j}$, $j = 1, \dots, d$, and by $q_j(\tau) = F_j^{-1}(\tau)$, $\tau \in [0, 1]$, the corresponding quantile function. Fix $l \in \mathbb{Z}$ and an arbitrary pair of quantile levels $(\tau, \tau') \in [0, 1]^2$, and consider the cross-covariance of the indicator functions $I\{X_{t,j_1} \leq q_{j_1}(\tau)\}$ and $I\{X_{t+l,j_2} \leq q_{j_2}(\tau')\}$ given by

$$\gamma_{j_1, j_2}(l, \tau, \tau') = \text{Cov}(I\{X_{t,j_1} \leq q_{j_1}(\tau)\}, I\{X_{t+l,j_2} \leq q_{j_2}(\tau')\}),$$

for $1 \leq j_1, j_2 \leq d$. Taking $j_1 = j_2 = j$, the function $\gamma_{j,j}(l, \tau, \tau')$, with $(\tau, \tau') \in [0, 1]^2$, so-called quantile autocovariance function (QAF) of lag l, generalizes the traditional autocovariance function.

Under suitable summability conditions (mixing conditions), the Fourier transform of the cross-covariances is well-defined and the *quantile cross-spectral density* (QCD) is given by

$$f_{j_1, j_2}(\omega, \tau, \tau') = (1/2\pi) \sum_{l=-\infty}^{\infty} \gamma_{j_1, j_2}(l, \tau, \tau') e^{-il\omega}, \tag{3}$$

for $1 \leq j_1, j_2 \leq d$, $\omega \in \mathbb{R}$ and $\tau, \tau' \in [0, 1]$. Note that $f_{j_1, j_2}(\omega, \tau, \tau')$ is complex-valued so that it can be represented in terms of its real and imaginary parts, which will be denoted by $\Re(f_{j_1, j_2}(\omega, \tau, \tau'))$ and $\Im(f_{j_1, j_2}(\omega, \tau, \tau'))$, respectively.

For fixed quantile levels (τ, τ'), QCD is the cross-spectral density of the bivariate process $(I\{X_{t,j_1} \leq q_{j_1}(\tau)\}, I\{X_{t,j_2} \leq q_{j_2}(\tau')\})$. Therefore, QCD measures dependence between two components of the multivariate process over different ranges of their joint distribution and across frequencies. This quantity can be evaluated for every couple of components on a range of frequencies Ω and of quantile levels $\mathcal{T}$ in order to obtain a complete representation of the process, i.e., consider the set of matrices

$$f_{X_t}(\Omega, \mathcal{T}) = \{f(\omega, \tau, \tau'), \ \omega \in \Omega, \ \tau, \tau' \in \mathcal{T}\},$$

where $f(\omega, \tau, \tau')$ denotes the $d \times d$ matrix in $\mathbb{C}$ given by

$$f(\omega, \tau, \tau') = (f_{j_1, j_2}(\omega, \tau, \tau'))_{1 \leq j_1, j_2 \leq d}.$$

Representing X_t through f_{X_t}, complete information on the general dependence structure of the process is available. Comprehensive discussions about the favorable properties of the quantile cross-spectral density are given in [10,16].

According to the prior arguments, a dissimilarity measure between two multivariate processes, $X_t^{(1)}$ and $X_t^{(2)}$, could be established by comparing their representations in terms of the QCD matrices, $f_{X_t^{(1)}}$ and $f_{X_t^{(2)}}$, evaluated on a common range of frequencies and quantile levels. Specifically, for a given set of K different frequencies $\Omega = \{\omega_1, \dots, \omega_K\}$, and r quantile levels $\mathcal{T} = \{\tau_1, \dots, \tau_r\}$, each stochastic process $X_t^{(u)}$, $u = 1, 2$, is characterized by means of a set of r^2 vectors $\{\Psi_{\tau_i, \tau_{i'}}^{(u)}, 1 \leq i, i' \leq r\}$ given by

$$\Psi_{\tau_i, \tau_{i'}}^{(u)} = (\Psi_{1, \tau_i, \tau_{i'}}^{(u)}, \dots, \Psi_{K, \tau_i, \tau_{i'}}^{(u)}), \tag{4}$$

where each $\Psi_{k, \tau_i, \tau_{i'}}^{(u)}$, $k = 1, \dots, K$ consists of a vector of length d^2 formed by rearranging by rows the elements of the matrix $f(\omega_k, \tau_i, \tau_{i'})$.

Once the set of r^2 vectors $\Psi_{\tau_i, \tau_{i'}}^{(u)}$ is obtained, they are all concatenated in a vector $\Psi^{(u)}$ in the same way as vectors $\Psi_{k, \tau_i, \tau_{i'}}^{(u)}$ constitute $\Psi_{\tau_i, \tau_{i'}}^{(u)}$ in (4). Then, we define the dissimilarity between $X_t^{(1)}$ and $X_t^{(2)}$ by means of:

$$d_{QCD}(X_t^{(1)}, X_t^{(2)}) = \Psi^{(1)} - \Psi^{(2)}, \tag{5}$$

where $v = (\sum_{k=1}^{n} |v_k|^2)^{1/2}$, with $v = (v_1, \dots, v_n)$ being an arbitrary complex vector in $\mathbb{C}^n$, and $|\cdot|$ stands for the modulus of a complex number. Note that d_{QCD} in (5) can also be expressed as

$$d_{QCD}(X_t^{(1)}, X_t^{(2)}) = \left[\Re_v(\Psi^{(1)}) - \Re_v(\Psi^{(2)})^2 + \Im_v(\Psi^{(1)}) - \Im_v(\Psi^{(2)})^2 \right]^{1/2},$$

where $\Re_v$ and $\Im_v$ denote the element-wise real and imaginary part operators, respectively.

Since, in practice, we only have finite-length realizations of the stochastic processes $X_t^{(1)}$ and $X_t^{(2)}$, the value of d_{QCD} is unknown and a proper estimate must be obtained.

Let $\{X_1, \dots, X_T\}$ be a realization from the process $(X_t)_{t \in \mathbb{Z}}$ so that $X_t = (X_{t,1}, \dots, X_{t,d})$, $t = 1, \dots, T$. For arbitrary $j_1, j_2 \in \{1, \dots, d\}$ and $(\tau, \tau') \in [0, 1]^2$, the authors of [16] propose to estimate $f_{j_1, j_2}(\omega, \tau, \tau')$ considering a smoothed cross-periodogram based on the indicator functions $I\{\hat{F}_{T,j}(X_{t,j})\}$, where $\hat{F}_{T,j}(x) = T^{-1} \sum_{t=1}^{T} I\{X_{t,j} \leq x\}$ denotes the empirical distribution function of $X_{t,j}$. This approach extends to the multivariate case for the estimator proposed by [17] in the univariate setting. More specifically, the *rank-based copula cross periodogram* (CCR-periodogram) is defined by

$$I_{T,R}^{j_1, j_2}(\omega, \tau, \tau') = \frac{1}{2\pi T} d_{T,R}^{j_1}(\omega, \tau) d_{T,R}^{j_2}(-\omega, \tau'),$$

where

$$d_{T,R}^{j}(\omega, \tau) = \sum_{t=1}^{T} I\{\hat{F}_{T,j}(X_{t,j}) \leq \tau\} e^{-i\omega t}.$$

The asymptotic properties of the CCR-periodogram are established in Proposition S4.1 of [16]. Like the standard cross-periodogram, the CCR-periodogram is not a consistent estimate of $f_{j_1,j_2}(\omega, \tau, \tau')$. To achieve consistency, the CCR-periodogram ordinates (evaluated on the Fourier frequencies) are convolved with weighting functions $W_T(\cdot)$. The *smoothed CCR-periodogram* takes the form

$$\hat{G}_{T,R}^{j_1,j_2}(\omega, \tau, \tau') = \frac{2\pi}{T} \sum_{s=1}^{T-1} W_T(\omega - \frac{2\pi s}{T}) I_{T,R}^{j_1,j_2}(\frac{2\pi s}{T}, \tau, \tau'), \tag{6}$$

where

$$W_T(u) = \sum_{v=-\infty}^{\infty} \frac{1}{h_T} W(\frac{u + 2\pi v}{h_T}),$$

with $h_T > 0$ being a sequence of bandwidths such that $h_T \to 0$ and $Th_T \to \infty$ as $T \to \infty$, and W is a real-valued, even weight function with support $[-\pi, \pi]$. Consistency and asymptotic performance of the smoothed CCR-periodogram $\hat{G}_{T,R}^{j_1,j_2}(\omega, \tau, \tau')$ are established in Theorem S4.1 of [16].

By considering the smoothed CCR-periodogram in every component of the vectors $\Psi^{(1)}$ and $\Psi^{(2)}$, we obtain their estimated counterparts $\hat{\Psi}^{(1)}$ and $\hat{\Psi}^{(2)}$, which allow us to construct a consistent estimate of d_{QCD} by defining

$$\hat{d}_{QCD}(X_t^{(1)}, X_t^{(2)}) = \hat{\Psi}^{(1)} - \hat{\Psi}^{(2)}. \tag{7}$$

Quantity $\hat{d}_{QCD}(X_t^{(1)}, X_t^{(2)})$ has been successfully applied to perform clustering of MTS in crisp [6] and fuzzy [10–12] frameworks.

3. Testing for Equality of Quantile Cross-Spectral Densities of two MTS

In this section, two procedures to address the problem of testing (1) are constructed. They are based on the distance d_{QCD} defined in (5). Both approaches consider well-known bootstrap methods for dependent data. The key principle is to draw pseudo-time series capturing the dependence structure in order to approximate the distribution of $\hat{d}_{QCD}$ under the null hypothesis.

3.1. A Test Based on the Moving Block Bootstrap

In this section, we introduce a bootstrap test based on a modification of the classical moving block bootstrap (MBB) method proposed by [13,14]. MBB generates replicates of the time series by joining blocks of fixed length, which have been drawn randomly with replacement from among blocks of the original realizations. This approach allows us to mimic the underlying dependence structure without assuming specific parametric models for the generating processes.

Given two realizations of the d-dimensional stochastic processes $X_t^{(1)}$ and $X_t^{(2)}$, denoted by $\overline{X}_t^{(1)} = \{X_1^{(1)}, \dots, X_T^{(1)}\}$ and $\overline{X}_t^{(2)} = \{X_1^{(2)}, \dots, X_T^{(2)}\}$, respectively, the procedure proceeds as follows.

Step 1. Fix a positive integer, b, representing the block size, and take k equal to the smallest integer greater than or equal to T/b.

Step 2. For each realization, define the block $B_j^{(i)} = \{X_j^{(i)}, \dots, X_{j+b-1}^{(i)}\}$, for $j = 1, \dots, q$, with $q = T - b + 1$. Let $\overline{B} = \{B_j^{(1)}, \dots, B_q^{(1)}, B_j^{(2)}, \dots, B_q^{(2)}\}$ be the set of all blocks, those coming from $\overline{X}_t^{(1)}$ and those coming from $\overline{X}_t^{(2)}$.

Step 3. Draw two sets of k blocks, $B^{(i)*} = \{B_1^{(i)}, \dots, B_k^{(i)}\}$, $i = 1, 2$, with equiprobable distribution from the set $\overline{B}$. Note that each $B_j^{(i)}$, $j = 1, \dots, k, i = 1, 2$, is a b-dimensional MTS.

Step 4. Construct the pseudo-time series $\overline{X}_t^{(i)*}$ by considering the first T temporal components of $B^{(i)*}$, $i = 1, 2$. Compute the bootstrap version $\hat{d}_{QCD}^*$ of $\hat{d}_{QCD}$ based on the pseudo-time series $\overline{X}_t^{(1)*}$ and $\overline{X}_t^{(2)*}$.

Step 5. Repeat Steps 3 and 4 a large number B of times to obtain the bootstrap replicates $\hat{d}_{QCD}^{(1)*}, \ldots, \hat{d}_{QCD}^{(B)*}$.

Step 6. Given a significance level α, compute the quantile of order $1 - \alpha$, $q_{1-\alpha}^*$, based on the set $\{\hat{d}_{QCD}^{(1)*}, \ldots, \hat{d}_{QCD}^{(B)*}\}$. Then, the decision rule consists of rejecting the null hypothesis H_0 if $\hat{d}_{QCD}(X_t^{(1)}, X_t^{(2)}) > q_{1-\alpha}^*$.

Note that, by considering the whole set of blocks $\overline{B}$ in Step 2, both pseudo-time series $\overline{X}_t^{(1)*}$ and $\overline{X}_t^{(2)*}$ contain information about the original series $\overline{X}_t^{(1)}$ and $\overline{X}_t^{(2)}$ in equal measure. This way, the bootstrap procedure is able to approximate correctly the distribution of the test statistic $\hat{d}_{QCD}$ under the null hypothesis even if this hypothesis is not true.

From now on, we will refer to the test presented in this section as MBB.

3.2. A Test Based on the Stationary Bootstrap

The second bootstrap mechanism to approximate the distribution of $\hat{d}_{QCD}$ is an adaptation of the classical stationary bootstrap (SB) proposed by [15]. This resampling method is aimed at overcoming the lack of stationarity of the MBB procedure. Note that the distance measure d_{QCD} is well-defined only for stationary processes, so it is desirable that a bootstrap technique based on this metric generates stationary pseudo-time series.

Given two d-dimensional realizations, denoted by $\overline{X}_t^{(1)} = \{X_1^{(1)}, \ldots, X_T^{(1)}\}$ and $\overline{X}_t^{(2)} = \{X_1^{(2)}, \ldots, X_T^{(2)}\}$, from the stochastic processes $X_t^{(1)}$ and $X_t^{(2)}$, respectively, the SB method proceeds as follows.

Step 1. Fix a positive real number $p \in [0, 1]$.

Step 2. Consider the set $\widetilde{X}_t = \{\overline{X}_t^{(1)}, \overline{X}_t^{(2)}\}$. Draw randomly two temporal observations from $\widetilde{X}_t$. Note that each one of these observations is of the form $X_{j^i}^{(k^i)}$ for some $k^i = 1, 2$ and $j^i = 1, \ldots, T$, $i = 1, 2$. Observation $X_{j^i}^{(k^i)}$ is the first element of the pseudo-series $\overline{X}_t^{(i)*}$, $i = 1, 2$.

Step 3. For $i = 1, 2$, given the last observation $X_{j^i}^{(k^i)}$, the next bootstrap replication in $\overline{X}_t^{(i)*}$ is defined as $X_{j^i+1}^{(k^i)}$ with probability $1 - p$, and drawn from the set $\widetilde{X}_t$ with probability p. When $j^i = T$, the selected observation is $X_1^{(2)}$ if $k^i = 1$ and $X_1^{(1)}$ if $k^i = 2$.

Step 4. Repeat Step 3 until the pseudo-series $\overline{X}_t^{(1)*}$ and $\overline{X}_t^{(2)*}$ contain T observations. Based on the pseudo-series $\overline{X}_t^{(1)*}$ and $\overline{X}_t^{(2)*}$, compute the bootstrap version $\hat{d}_{QCD}^*$ of $\hat{d}_{QCD}$.

Step 5. Repeat Steps 3–4 B times to obtain $\hat{d}_{QCD}^{(1)*}, \ldots, \hat{d}_{QCD}^{(B)*}$.

Step 6. Given a significance level α, compute the quantile of order $1 - \alpha$, $q_{1-\alpha}^*$, based on the set $\{\hat{d}_{QCD}^{(1)*}, \ldots, \hat{d}_{QCD}^{(B)*}\}$. Then, the decision rule consists of rejecting the null hypothesis H_0 if $\hat{d}_{QCD}(X_t^{(1)}, X_t^{(2)}) > q_{1-\alpha}^*$.

It is worth remarking that, like the MBB procedure, a proper approximation of the distribution of $\hat{d}_{QCD}$ under the null hypothesis is also ensured here due to considering the pooled time series $\widetilde{X}_t$ in the generating mechanism.

From now on, we will refer to the test presented in this section as SB.

4. Simulation Study

In this section, we carry out a set of simulations with the aim of assessing the performance with finite samples of the testing procedures presented in Section 3. After describing the simulation mechanism, the main results are discussed.

4.1. Experimental Design

The effectiveness of the testing methods was examined with pairs of MTS realizations, $\overline{X}_t^{(1)} = \{X_1^{(1)}, \ldots, X_T^{(1)}\}$ and $\overline{X}_t^{(2)} = \{X_1^{(2)}, \ldots, X_T^{(2)}\}$, simulated from bivariate processes selected to cover different dependence structures. Specifically, three types of generating models were considered, namely VARMA processes, nonlinear processes, and dynamic conditional correlation models [18]. In all cases, the deviation from the null hypothesis of equal underlying processes was established by means of differences in the coefficients of the generating models. In each scenario, the degree of deviation between the simulated realizations is regulated by a specific parameter δ included in the formulation of the models. The specific generating models concerning each scenario are given below, taking into account that, unless otherwise stated, the error process $(\epsilon_{t,1}, \epsilon_{t,2})^\mathsf{T}$ consists of iid realizations following a bivariate Gaussian distribution.

Scenario 1. VAR(1) models given by

$$\begin{pmatrix} X_{t,1} \\ X_{t,2} \end{pmatrix} = \begin{pmatrix} 0.1+\delta & 0.1+\delta \\ 0.1+\delta & 0.1+\delta \end{pmatrix} \begin{pmatrix} X_{t-1,1} \\ X_{t-1,2} \end{pmatrix} + \begin{pmatrix} \epsilon_{t,1} \\ \epsilon_{t,2} \end{pmatrix}.$$

Scenario 2. TAR (threshold autoregressive) models given by

$$\begin{pmatrix} X_{t,1} \\ X_{t,2} \end{pmatrix} = \begin{pmatrix} (0.9-\delta)X_{t-1,2}I_{\{|X_{t-1,1}|\leq 1\}} + (\delta-0.3)X_{t-1,1}I_{\{|X_{t-1,1}|>1\}} \\ (0.9-\delta)X_{t-1,1}I_{\{|X_{t-1,2}|\leq 1\}} + (\delta-0.3)X_{t-1,2}I_{\{|X_{t-1,2}|>1\}} \end{pmatrix} + \begin{pmatrix} \epsilon_{t,1} \\ \epsilon_{t,2} \end{pmatrix}.$$

Scenario 3. GARCH models in the form $(X_{t,1}, X_{t,2})^\mathsf{T} = (\sigma_{t,1}\epsilon_{t,1}, \sigma_{t,2}\epsilon_{t,2})^\mathsf{T}$ with

$$\sigma_{t,1}^2 = 0.01 + 0.05X_{t-1,1}^2 + 0.94\sigma_{t-1,1}^2,$$

$$\sigma_{t,2}^2 = 0.5 + 0.2X_{t-1,2}^2 + 0.5\sigma_{t-1,2}^2,$$

$$\begin{pmatrix} \epsilon_{t,1} \\ \epsilon_{t,2} \end{pmatrix} \sim N\left[\begin{pmatrix} 0 \\ 0 \end{pmatrix}, \begin{pmatrix} 1 & \rho_t \\ \rho_t & 1 \end{pmatrix}\right],$$

where the correlation between the standardized shocks is given by $\rho_t = 0.9 - \delta$.

Series $\overline{X}_t^{(1)}$ is always generated by taking $\delta = 0$, while $\overline{X}_t^{(2)}$ is generated using different values of δ, thus allowing us to obtain simulation schemes under the null hypothesis, when $\delta = 0$ also for $\overline{X}_t^{(2)}$, and under the alternative hypothesis otherwise.

In each trial, $B = 200$ bootstrap replicates were considered to approximate the distribution of the test statistic under the null hypothesis. In all cases, we selected the bandwidth $h_T = T^{-1/3}$ to compute $\hat{d}_{QCD}$ and its bootstrap replicates. This choice ensures the consistency of the smoothed CCR-periodogram as an estimate of QCD (Theorem S4.1 in [16]). As for the two key hyperparameters, we chose $b = T^{1/3}$ and $p = T^{-1/3}$ for the block size in MBB and the probability in SB, respectively, since both values led to the best overall behavior of both procedures in our numerical experiments. Note that these choices are also consistent with the related literature. For instance, ref. [19] addressed the issue of selecting b in the context of bias and variance bootstrap estimation, concluding that the optimal block size is of order $T^{1/3}$. However, since the mean block size in SB corresponds to $1/p$, it is reasonable to select p of order $T^{-1/3}$.

Simulations were carried out for different values of series length T. Our results show that both bootstrap procedures exhibit relatively high power when low-to-moderate sample sizes are used. However, larger sample sizes are necessary to reach a reasonable approximation of the nominal level. For this reason, the results included in the next section correspond to $T \in \{500, 1000\}$, in the case of the null hypothesis, and $T \in \{100, 200, 300\}$, in the case of the alternative hypothesis. In all cases, the results were obtained for a significance level $\alpha = 0.05$.

4.2. Results and Discussion

The results under the null hypothesis are summarized in Table 1, where the simulated rejection probabilities of the proposed bootstrap tests are displayed.

Table 1. Simulated rejection probabilities under the null hypothesis for $\alpha = 0.05$.

T	Method	Scenario		
		1	2	3
500	MBB	0.080	0.070	0.080
	SB	0.055	0.055	0.050
1000	MBB	0.070	0.095	0.130
	SB	0.040	0.060	0.060

Table 1 clearly shows that both bootstrap techniques exhibit different behaviors under the null hypothesis. The MBB method provides rejection probabilities greater than expected for both values of T. In fact, the deviation from the theoretical significance level is more marked when $T = 1000$, particularly for Scenario 3. The technique SB seems to adjust the significance level quite well in all the analyzed scenarios, which makes this test the most accurate one in terms of size approximation.

The estimated rejection probabilities under the set of considered alternative hypotheses are provided in Table 2.

Table 2. Simulated rejection probabilities of the bootstrap tests under several alternative hypotheses determined by the deviation parameter δ.

T	Method	Scenario 1			Scenario 2			Scenario 3		
		δ			δ			δ		
		0.1	0.2	0.3	0.2	0.4	0.6	0.4	0.8	1.2
100	MBB	0.160	0.575	0.980	0.540	0.775	0.990	0.080	0.395	0.950
	SB	0.100	0.465	0.960	0.325	0.690	0.910	0.055	0.230	0.870
200	MBB	0.185	0.790	0.995	0.780	0.925	1	0.185	0.725	1
	SB	0.095	0.695	0.990	0.625	0.885	0.985	0.080	0.455	0.965
300	MBB	0.225	0.835	1	0.885	0.990	1	0.255	0.840	1
	SB	0.130	0.770	1	0.805	0.955	1	0.155	0.695	1

In short, MBB shows the best performance in terms of power but an overrejecting behavior in terms of size.

5. Case Study: Did the Dotcom Bubble Change the Global Market Behavior?

This section is devoted to analyzing the effect that the dotcom bubble crash produced over the global economy. Specifically, the described bootstrap procedures are used to determine whether this landmark event had a permanent effect on the behavior of financial markets worldwide.

5.1. The Dotcom Bubble Crash

Historically, the dotcom bubble was a rapid rise in U.S. technology stock equity valuations exacerbated by investments in Internet-based companies during the bull market in the late 1990s. The value of equity markets grew substantially during this period, with the Nasdaq index rising from under 1000 to more than 5000 between the years 1995 and 2000. Things started to change in 2000, and the bubble burst between 2001 and 2002 with equities entering a bear market [20]. The crash that followed saw the Nasdaq index tumble from a peak of 5048.62 on 10 March 2000, to 1139.90 on 4 October 2002, a 76.81% fall [21]. By the end of 2001, most dotcom stocks went bust.

Concerning the time period of the dotcom bubble, the majority of authors consider the dotcom bubble to take place in the period 1996–2000 [22]. In addition, it is assumed that the bubble-burst period was between 2000 and 2002, since, as stated before, the Nasdaq index fell by 76.81% in 4 October 2002.

5.2. The Considered Data

To analyze the effects of the dotcom bubble in the global economy, we considered three well-known stock market indexes, which are briefly described below.

- **S&P 500**. This index comprises 505 common stocks issued by 500 large-cap companies and traded on stock exchanges in the United States. The S&P 500 gives weights to the companies according to their market capitalization.
- **FTSE 100**. This market index includes the 100 companies listed in the London Stock Exchange with the highest market capitalization. It is also a weighted index with weights depending on the market capitalization of the different firms.
- **Nikkei 225**. This index is a price-weighted, stock market index for the Tokyo Stock Exchange. It measures the performance of 225 large, publicly owned companies in Japan from a wide array of industry sectors.

We focus on the trivariate time series formed by the daily stock prices of the three previous indexes. The data were sourced from the finance section of the Yahoo website (https://es.finance.yahoo.com, accessed on 20 July 2021). As our goal is to determine whether the dotcom bubble distorted the global market behavior, we split this MTS into two separate periods: before and after the bubble-burst period. To this end, we consider the periods from 1987 to 2002 and from 2003 to 2018. In addition, we only select dates corresponding to trading days for the three indexes and forming two periods of the same length. Based on these considerations, the first period covers the simultaneous trading days from 2 January 1987 to 25 July 2002, and the second period includes the simultaneous trading days from 26 July 2002 to 28 December 2018. In this way, each MTS is constituted by 3928 daily observations.

Since the series of closing prices are not stationary in mean, we proceed to take the first difference of the natural logarithm of the original values, thus obtaining series of so-called daily returns, which are depicted in Figure 1. The new series exhibit common characteristics of financial time series, so-called "stylized facts", as heavy tails, volatility clustering, and leverage effects.

Two MTS were constructed by considering simultaneously the three UTS in Figure 1 before and after the dotcom bubble crash (vertical line). Then, the equality of the generating processes of both MTS was checked using the bootstrap tests proposed throughout the manuscript based on $B = 500$ bootstrap replicates.

5.3. Results

The p-values obtained by means of the methods MBB and SB were all 0. Therefore, both bootstrap techniques indicate rejection of the null hypothesis at any reasonable significance level. This suggests that the whole MTS exhibits a different dependence structure in each of the considered periods. A direct implication of this fact could be that the dotcom bubble crash in the early 2000s provoked a permanent change in the behavior of the global economy.

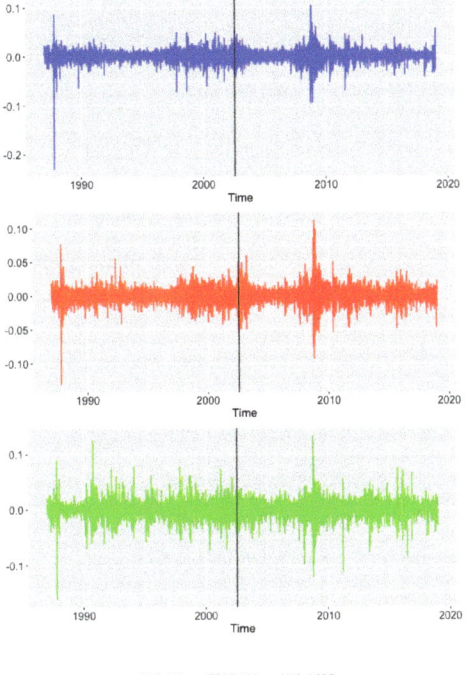

Figure 1. Daily returns of the S&P 500 (top panel), FTSE 100 (middle panel), and Nikkei 225 (bottom panel) stock market indexes from 2 January 1987 to 28 December 2018. The vertical line indicates the end of the dotcom bubble burst.

6. Conclusions

In this work, we addressed the problem of testing the equality of the stochastic processes generating two multivariate time series. For that purpose, we first defined a distance measure between multivariate processes based on comparing the quantile cross-spectral densities, called d_{QCD}. Then, two tests considering a proper estimate of this dissimilarity ($\widehat{d}_{QCD}$) were proposed. Both approaches are based on bootstrap techniques. Their behavior under the null and the alternative hypotheses was analyzed through a simulation study. The techniques were also used to answer the question regarding whether or not the dotcom bubble crash of the 2000s affected global market behavior.

Author Contributions: Conceptualization, Á.L.-O. and J.A.V.; methodology, Á.L.-O. and J.A.V.; software, Á.L.-O.; writing—review and editing, Á.L.-O. and J.A.V. All authors have read and agreed to the published version of the manuscript.

Funding: This research has been supported by MINECO (MTM2017-82724-R and PID2020-113578RB-100), the Xunta de Galicia (ED431C-2020-14), and "CITIC" (ED431G 2019/01).

Institutional Review Board Statement: Not applicable.

Informed Consent Statement: Not applicable.

Data Availability Statement: Not applicable.

Acknowledgments: The authors thank ITISE 2022 organisers for allowing them to submit this paper to the proceedings.

Conflicts of Interest: The authors declare no conflict of interest.

References

1. Liao, T.W. Clustering of time series data—A survey. *Pattern Recognit.* **2005**, *38*, 1857–1874. [CrossRef]
2. Wu, J.; Yao, L.; Liu, B. An overview on feature-based classification algorithms for multivariate time series. In Proceedings of the 2018 IEEE 3rd International Conference on Cloud Computing and Big Data Analysis (ICCCBDA), Chengdu, China, 20–22 April 2018, pp. 32–38.
3. Blázquez-García, A.; Conde, A.; Mori, U.; Lozano, J.A. A Review on outlier/Anomaly Detection in Time Series Data. *ACM Comput. Surv. (CSUR)* **2021**, *54*, 1–33. [CrossRef]
4. Tsay, R.S. Nonlinearity tests for time series. *Biometrika* **1986**, *73*, 461–466. [CrossRef]
5. Lafuente-Rego, B.; Vilar, J.A. Clustering of time series using quantile autocovariances. *Adv. Data Anal. Classif.* **2016**, *10*, 391–415. [CrossRef]
6. López-Oriona, Á.; Vilar, J.A. Quantile cross-spectral density: A novel and effective tool for clustering multivariate time series. *Expert Syst. Appl.* **2021**, *185*, 115677. [CrossRef]
7. Preuß, P.; Hildebrandt, T. Comparing spectral densities of stationary time series with unequal sample sizes. *Stat. Probab. Lett.* **2013**, *83*, 1174–1183. [CrossRef]
8. Dette, H.; Kinsvater, T.; Vetter, M. Testing non-parametric hypotheses for stationary processes by estimating minimal distances. *J. Time Ser. Anal.* **2011**, *32*, 447–461. [CrossRef]
9. Jentsch, C.; Pauly, M. Testing equality of spectral densities using randomization techniques. *Bernoulli* **2015**, *21*, 697–739. [CrossRef]
10. López-Oriona, Á.; Vilar, J.A.; D'Urso, P. Quantile-based fuzzy clustering of multivariate time series in the frequency domain. *Fuzzy Sets Syst.* **2022**, *443*, 115–154. [CrossRef]
11. López-Oriona, Á.; D'Urso, P.; Vilar, J.A.; Lafuente-Rego, B. Quantile-based fuzzy C-means clustering of multivariate time series: Robust techniques. *arXiv* **2021**, arXiv:2109.11027.
12. Lopez-Oriona, A. Spatial weighted robust clustering of multivariate time series based on quantile dependence with an application to mobility during COVID-19 pandemic. *IEEE Trans. Fuzzy Syst.* **2021**, 1. [CrossRef]
13. Kunsch, H.R. The jackknife and the bootstrap for general stationary observations. *Ann. Stat.* **1989**, *17*, 1217–1241. [CrossRef]
14. Liu, R.Y.; Singh, K. Moving blocks jackknife and bootstrap capture weak dependence. *Explor. Limits Bootstrap* **1992**, *225*, 248.
15. Politis, D.N.; Romano, J.P. The stationary bootstrap. *J. Am. Stat. Assoc.* **1994**, *89*, 1303–1313. [CrossRef]
16. Baruník, J.; Kley, T. Quantile coherency: A general measure for dependence between cyclical economic variables. *Econom. J.* **2019**, *22*, 131–152. [CrossRef]
17. Kley, T.; Volgushev, S.; Dette, H.; Hallin, M. Quantile spectral processes: Asymptotic analysis and inference. *Bernoulli* **2016**, *22*, 1770–1807. [CrossRef]
18. Engle, R. Dynamic conditional correlation: A simple class of multivariate generalized autoregressive conditional heteroskedasticity models. *J. Bus. Econ. Stat.* **2002**, *20*, 339–350. [CrossRef]
19. Hall, P.; Horowitz, J.L.; Jing, B.Y. On blocking rules for the bootstrap with dependent data. *Biometrika* **1995**, *82*, 561–574. [CrossRef]
20. Geier, B. What Did We Learn from the Dotcom Stock Bubble of 2000. Available online: https://time.com/3741681/2000-dotcom-stock-bust/ (accessed on 20 July 2021).
21. Clarke, T. e Dot-Com Crash of 2000–2002. Available online: https://moneymorning.com/2015/06/12/the-dot-com-crash-of-2000-2002/ (accessed on 20 July 2021).
22. Morris, J.J.; Alam, P. Value relevance and the dot-com bubble of the 1990s. *Q. Rev. Econ. Financ.* **2012**, *52*, 243–255. [CrossRef]

Proceeding Paper

Using Forecasting Methods on Crime Data: The SKALA Approach of the State Office for Criminal Investigation of North Rhine-Westphalia †

Kai Seidensticker * and Katharina Schwarz

State Office for Criminal Investigation of North Rhine-Westphalia, 40221 Düsseldorf, Germany;
katharina01.schwarz@polizei.nrw.de
* Correspondence: kai.seidensticker@polizei.nrw.de
† Presented at the 8th International Conference on Time Series and Forecasting, Gran Canaria, Spain,
27–30 June 2022.

Abstract: In this article, we introduce the topic of crime forecasting performed in North Rhine-Westphalia, Germany. We give a brief overview of three forecasting methods used in theory and practice: predictive policing, risk terrain modeling, and time series analysis. As a result, spatio-temporally-based statistical techniques offered high potential to optimize operational and strategic planning for policing.

Keywords: crime forecasting; predictive policing; risk terrain modeling; time series analysis

Citation: Seidensticker, K.; Schwarz, K. Using Forecasting Methods on Crime Data: The SKALA Approach of the State Office for Criminal Investigation of North Rhine-Westphalia. *Eng. Proc.* **2022**, *18*, 39. https://doi.org/10.3390/engproc 2022018039

Academic Editors: Ignacio Rojas, Hector Pomares, Olga Valenzuela, Fernando Rojas and Luis Javier Herrera

Published: 11 July 2022

Publisher's Note: MDPI stays neutral with regard to jurisdictional claims in published maps and institutional affiliations.

1. Introduction

Crime is a complex social phenomenon that has a lasting impact on the population's sense of security and can burden society. The complexity of this phenomenon makes it difficult to predict. Every day, new crimes of different types occur because of different decisions and the routine activities of perpetrators, victims, and capable guardians, resulting in many new trends in crime. Investigating these crime characteristics, crime patterns, and criminal behavior is a major objective of criminology. In the last decades, many new options in criminal investigation have arisen as a result of rapid technological development and newly designed technologies. Because of the difficulty in dealing with the massive amount of data produced every day, data mining techniques have also become increasingly crucial in terms of criminal investigation. The digitalization of society also led to the development of different policing strategies and philosophies, which are often based on extensive data systems (Big Data). In addition, the importance of system-related decision-making processes in policing increases [1]. Nowadays, in the investigation, prosecution, and prevention of crime, crime analysis and the use of big data play a significant role.

Attempting to anticipate the future is not a new way of thinking in the context of policing, but rather a standard approach. For example, prevention efforts—which are a foremost task of the police—aim to prevent potential future threats in a pre-emptive manner. Two insights are essential for the idea of crime forecasting: First, human actions can vary due to different values and preferences and also due to the influence of spatial/temporal changes [2]; and second, crimes do not occur uniformly or randomly in space and time [3] (p. 5). What is new is the systematic use of technical solutions, big data, and the gaining complexity of data analytics in policing. With the police trying to explore what they might already know based on their existing data, police open the door to using big data and linking data to intelligence. In this spirit of optimism, a wide variety of data analysis methods have been implemented in German police forces since 2014. These include methods such as predictive policing. The State Office for Criminal Investigation of North Rhine-Westphalia (LKA NRW) tested and implemented its own predictive policing model as part of a holistic crime analysis and forecasting approach, called SKALA (System for Crime Analysis and Anticipation). The SKALA approach intends to understand the main use of crime analysis and forecast algorithms, such as predictive policing methods, risk terrain modeling, and time series analysis, to investigate crime patterns at different spatial and temporal scales to support crime prevention. Currently, the focus is on residential burglaries, commercial burglaries, and motor vehicle offenses. This is because numerous theoretical and empirical scientific works are already available both on the phenomenology and explanation of these particular offenses and on the distribution of crime phenomena in space and time. These formed an essential cornerstone for the conception and evaluation of the models and of the forecast development.

This paper gives an overview of the different methods used to forecast crimes in the context of SKALA. The crime-forecasting project in North Rhine-Westphalia is presented in the first part. The second part presents the three forecasting procedures, crime forecasting, risk terrain modeling, and time series analysis. We present the (classical) forecasting approach of the LKA NRW, which has already been in operational use since 2015. Afterward, we discuss the spatial risk assessment of crime for NRW, including risk terrain modeling. The temporal component is then considered, taking into account the time series decomposition and ARIMA modeling of crime data. Finally, the conclusions on the three procedures are drawn, and the potential and limitations of each are discussed.

2. Crime Forecasting in North Rhine-Westphalia

In Germany, crime rates of residential burglaries increased rapidly between 2009 (113,800 cases) and 2015 (167,136 cases) [4] (p. 70). This increase and the high level of public and political attention to the issue of a residential burglary led to the need for innovative approaches to tackling this crime phenomenon. Because predictive policing ought to be a successful method for reducing crime in countries, this approach was tested in Germany. Predictive policing is still an umbrella term that describes methodological processes utilized by law enforcement agencies to predict crime and aid in planning operational responses [5] (p. 47). Available definitions range from calculating the probability of future crimes to specific methods to investigate crimes already omitted [6] (pp. 8–9). Pearsall defines predictive policing as " ... taking data from disparate sources, analyzing them, and then using results to anticipate, prevent and respond more effectively to future crime" [7] (p. 16). In Germany, predictive policing is commonly defined as a computer-assisted method for spatially-based probability calculations of crime [8]. This method aims to identify risk areas so that the police can plan appropriate policing measures and optimally allocate their limited forces.

In North Rhine-Westphalia, predictive policing was tested between 2015 and 2018 within the project SKALA to study the spatio-temporal dimension of crime phenomena. In detail, the objectives of the project were (1) to examine the possibilities and limits of predicting crime hot spots, and (2) to examine the efficiency and effectiveness of police interventions based on them [9]. For this purpose, an attempt was made to calculate the crime risks using spatial data for each residential district of the participating cities. The method used was initially simple decision tree models and later random forest models. After successfully completing the project in 2018, SKALA was expanded into an independent research area within the Criminological Research Department of the LKA NRW, and the crime forecasts were extended to the entire state of NRW in 2021. Several tests of other forecasting methods followed these initial experiences with the predictive policing method to support police work in NRW by SKALA. These methods include a variant of the classic predictive policing approach for operational planning, risk terrain modeling, and trend analysis for long-term predictions. Although there is a difference between prediction and forecasting, for the purpose of this study, we use them inter-changeably. Perry et al. [6] (p. xiii) argued that the most common distinction is that forecasting is objective, scientific, and reproducible, whereas prediction is subjective, mostly intuitive, and non-reproducible.

3. Material and Methods

3.1. Crime Forecasting

The classical crime forecasting approach in the SKALA project focuses on using predictive policing as a method to compute spatial crime risks. In practice, predictive policing involves several steps and processes that build on each other, starting with analyzing the specific offense and the collection and processing of data required for crime prediction. The illustrated methodical process (Figure 1) allows an insight into the individual steps for implementing predictive policing from the police department's point of view, as it also took place in SKALA. Deviations are conceivable, but at least similar designs are likely to be present whenever machine learning technologies are used.).

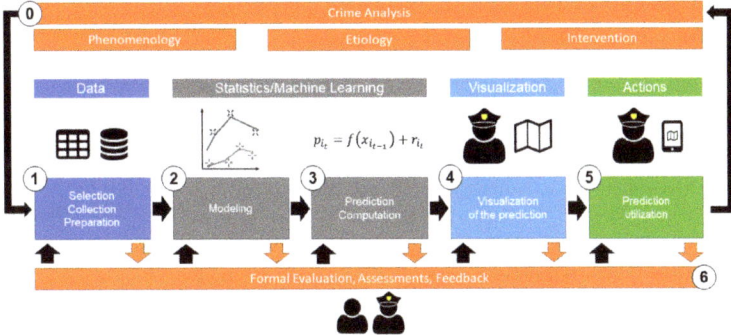

Figure 1. The predictive policing process. Adapted with permission from Ref. [10]. 2017, Bode/Stoffel/Keim.

All process steps depend on the available data, the data acquisition, and the preparation of the data for further processing. For predictive policing, data quality is therefore of crucial importance. In this context, data acquisition problems are conceivable, for example, when recording a residential burglary's suspected and not precisely determinable time. Moreover, data uncertainties can arise on the side of the police forces if crimes are legally misjudged or reported late by the victims, which cannot be ruled out for the crime of residential burglary, for example. In addition, the fundamental problem is that crime phenomena cannot usually be fully described with the available data, especially when unobservable or unquantifiable effects are important. Thus, when making crime forecasts, the question must be asked whether the anticipated crime event occurred independently of the criminological and mathematical models used.

A deliberate decision was made to avoid an exclusively data-driven approach in order to produce crime forecasts, and a theory-driven approach was adopted. Specifically, due to the increasing digital availability of data and the further development in the field of big data processing, data mining approaches—for the prediction of feature characteristics or data points—are also increasingly represented in the methodological discussion on predictive policing [11] (p. 8). Data mining covers (partially) automated methods for analyzing data sets, which can find statistical correlations and provable patterns [12]. Data mining approaches go beyond assumption-driven multivariate data analysis. They can also find non-linear or only partially existing correlations that might have remained undetected during the theoretical derivation of hypotheses from tentatively proven theories. An exclusively data-driven approach must be viewed critically, especially in the context of predictive policing, since plausible assumptions about possible causal relationships already exist for the vast majority of criminal phenomena, which cannot simply be ignored. Likewise, methods of data-driven approaches are subject to the assumption that the input data describe the phenomenon to be analyzed to the degree that automatic pattern and group identification do not occur based on spurious correlations. Especially with regard to data protection, principles such as data economy, and the difficulty of analyzing highly complex phenomena such as crime, it becomes clear that purely data-driven methods should not be used alone in the area of predictive policing. This is based on the fact that crime cannot always be clearly objectified and thus represented within a data set [13].

The theory-driven approach ensured that the used model was based on robust scientific theories and research findings. This distinguished the approach from many other predictive policing methods, which are often based only on the near-repeat approach, which refers to the empirically-proven observation that crime recurs in the same or adjacent locations within a given period [14] (p. 414) [15] (pp. 368 ff.). In practice, the probabilities of residential burglaries, burglaries from commercial properties, and motor vehicle offenses were calculated based on spatial data for residential quarters in selected police districts of NRW.

A three-stage procedure was chosen for this purpose. First, spatio-temporal clusters of crime data were calculated based on the near-repeat approach, which refers to a period of 14 days and a radius of 500 m for the residential burglary. The collected crime data mainly included the time and location of the offense, the modus operandi, and the proceeds of the crimes (property stolen). The calculated spatio-temporal clusters were transferred to the residential district level. The residential districts were areas characterized by a number of 400 households per quarter (see Figure 2). For NRW, this resulted in 18,875 residential districts. A uniform size at the household level was chosen because grid cells can lead to over- or underestimation of offenses.

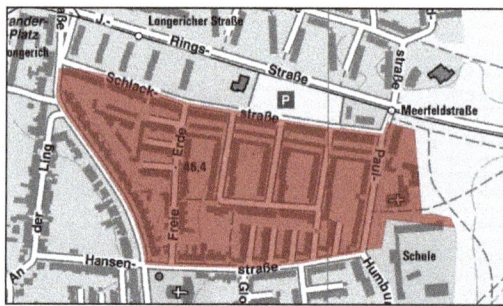

Figure 2. Example of a residential district. Reprinted with permission from Ref. [9]. 2018, LKA NRW.

Second, random forest models got a subset of influencing variables out of the socio-economic data. These data were chosen because of their statistical impact on the occurrence of crime. They included information on the residential location, such as population structure, building construction, income, infrastructure connections, and mobility indicators. In this step, random forest models were used to avoid overfitting [16,17]. The advantage of this application is the relatively easy operability and the possibility to perform initial data analysis tasks in a short time, including model and forecast generation. The decision tree models had a comparatively good performance. In addition, they are transparent and comprehensible, so they were favored within this framework. Third, the modeling and forecasting were performed based on the previous results and selected data within a linear regression model.

The areas for which the highest crime probabilities were calculated compared with other areas of the entire forecast area are defined as forecast areas. Their share was limited to about 1.5 percent of the total number of quarters in each police district for practical reasons, such as planning policy measures and allocating and distributing limited police resources.

The calculation of crime probabilities was based on the total area of every single police authority. This procedure ensured that the individual risk of residential burglary for each residential quarter could be determined in the forecast week, as many other predictive policing methods only refer to sub-areas of cities or regions.

The methodological implementation of the model and forecast generation described above focuses primarily on long-term statistical considerations. In the course of SKALA, the pilot authorities repeatedly criticized that future crime series, such as a particular modus operandi, was not reflected in the forecasts. Analyses based on the available series of crimes from the police authorities showed that differentiation from other series or individual crimes was not possible based on the available data material. However, the homogeneity of the characteristics within the respective series was always high. Nevertheless, as a supplement to the statistical and decision tree-based approach of the model and prognosis generation, a second forecast model was developed, which focused on possible series of crimes. This so-called analytical model was independent of the more comprehensive statistical model and supplemented it, depending on the data situation.

3.2. Risk Terrain Modelling

The Risk Terrain Modelling (RTM) approach is a method used to compute the future risk of crime in specific places. Unlike other methods such as hotspot mapping, the calculations with RTM are not, or rather not only, based on crime data but also include geographical characteristics of places [6] (p. 50). RTM is a classification approach that characterizes an area's risk for crime based on its environmental characteristics [6] (p. 51). Therefore, new hotspots are predicted based on their similarities to other 'known' hotspots. The result might be a map of places that did not see any crime but should be considered risky places because of their similar spatial risks compared to crime hotspots. The spatial risk profiles generated are derived from the respective geographic characteristics of the space, which can be identified as risk factors for crime. Studies suggest that the prediction accuracy of the RTM models is better than that of classic hotspot models [18]. However, the correlations found in such models do not necessarily imply a meaningful and substantively justifiable causality. They are usually the results of the "unsupervised learning" method, intended to identify previously unknown correlations or patterns without categorizing the data [19].

In SKALA, the RTM instrument should primarily be made available to police forces with a deficient number of cases in relation to their area (rural regions), as this makes it difficult to use the previously described crime forecasting model, which particularly results from the fact that the models are primarily based on patterns of crime events that are close in time and space. Therefore, alternative model approaches were sought that are more strongly based on the influence and distribution of socio-economic, building-specific, and infrastructural attributes and their distribution in space.

In the classical RTM, risk factors are determined from a large number of space-specific attributes using statistical methods, which significantly influence the risk burden (number of events per unit of space and time) for a selected offense. The mathematical model underlying the relationship between the significant characteristics and the risk burden enables a forecast calculation of the expected risk of crime. Following this, a risk map can be generated for the entire space of a selected authority. The temporal validity of such a map is strictly linked to changes in the area-specific characteristics and the number of cases, which in rural regions are subject to relatively minor changes on short time scales.

The existing socio-economic and other freely available data, such as point data of bus stops, banks, and supermarkets, were processed, calculated, and aggregated for a uniform grid of 100 × 100 m to test the RTM approach. Figure 3 shows example density maps of different variables for the same city. In the classic RTM approach, the individual input variables are processed in binary form for each raster cell. This means that for each variable and raster cell, it is determined whether the variable is present in the raster cell or not. In the course of development, it quickly became apparent that this approach was insufficient to provide satisfactory results. Therefore, a modified approach was used to convert the existing variables to density-based units, allowing better differentiation of the individual variables' spatial distribution. Another deviation from the classical RTM is the inclusion of variables calculated from the characteristics of the historical processes, such as the average distance of residential burglary to the three nearest residential burglaries (relative to the center of each grid cell).

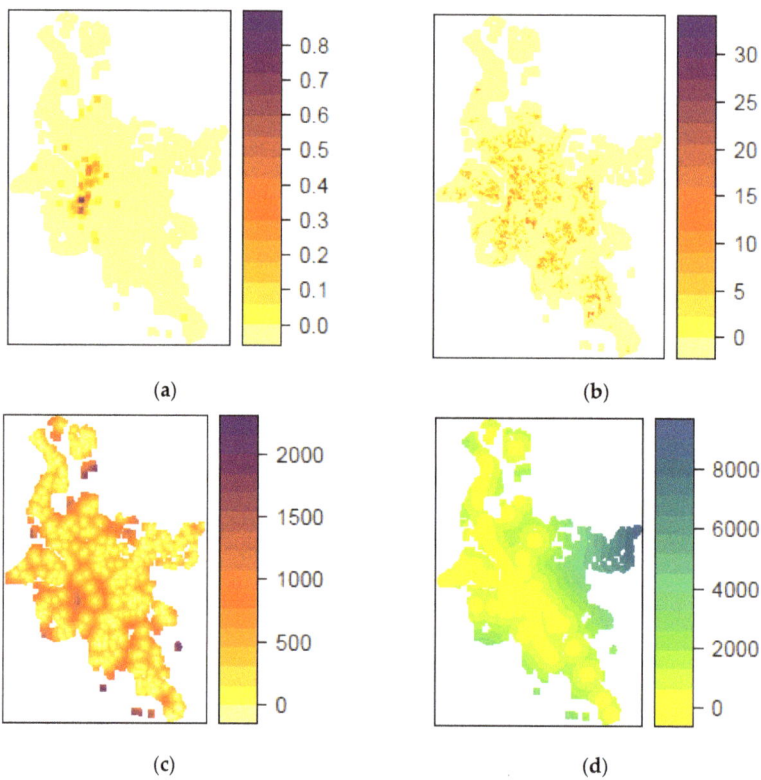

Figure 3. Input variables using the example of Düsseldorf with the (**a**) variability of parking lots, (**b**) street light density, (**c**) car density, and (**d**) minimum distance to train stops taken from Open Street Map (OSM).

The result for a risk map depends significantly on the assumed relationship between the target variable and the input variables. The different model algorithms realize the mathematical formulation of this problem. The classical RTM formulation is based on Poisson regression. Figure 4 shows an example of a risk map based on Poisson regression. Alternatively, the risk determination can be conceived as a classification problem using common methods such as RF (random forest) or SVM (support vector machine). The main difference between the two formulations in a risk map is the interpretation of the risk load. While a Poisson regression gives a non-scalable risk number for a grid cell that is only valid for the respective authority (for example, a grid cell with a risk number of 5.7 in one city would have a different meaning than a grid cell with the same risk number in another city), the classification gives a probability for the occurrence of an event for each grid cell similar to the previous forecast model used in SKALA (see Figure 5).

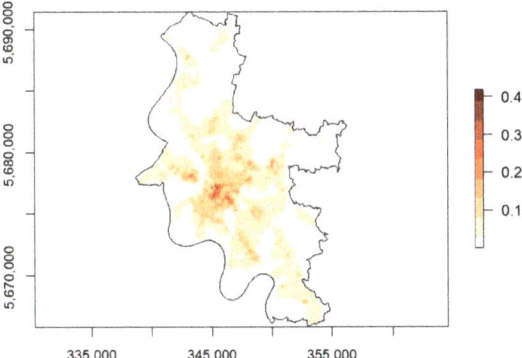

Figure 4. RTM (Poisson model) for 100×100 m grid cells in risk classes over six main percentiles for the police authority Düsseldorf.

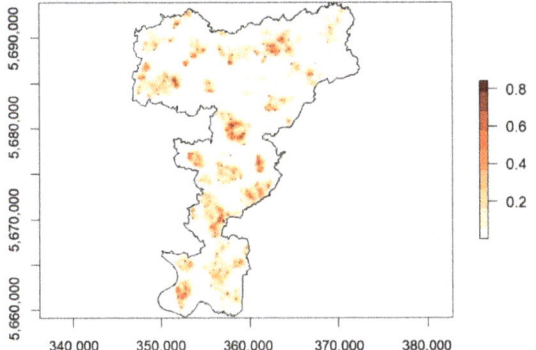

Figure 5. RTM (classification model) of the police authority Mettmann.

As quality criteria for the comparison of the different models, the quality measure of deviance was chosen for the Poisson regression. Deviance indicates how well the significant variables and model parameters determined in the model can describe or reproduce the original statistical distribution of the target variable. For the RF and SVM classification models, the quality measures AUC and PrecRec were chosen. For the AUC value, the closer the AUC value is to 1, the better the model prediction. An AUC value of 0.5 would mean that the model does not predict better than chance. A maximum AUC value of 1 means that all areas were predicted exactly correctly. PrecRec stands for the sum of the quality measures Precision and Recall.

3.3. Time Series Analysis

Time series analysis offers the possibility to detect patterns in the temporal change of crime data, which play a major role, especially in crime prediction and prevention. Methods such as time series decomposition and autoregressive integrated moving average (ARIMA) modeling can be used for this purpose. A decomposed crime time series consists of the original time series and the three decomposed parts with the estimated trend component, seasonal component, and remainder component. The calculation of trends and seasonality are used for the long-term prediction of crime events to facilitate strategic planning in police agencies [20,21]. Several studies, e.g., Malik et al. [22] and Borges et al. [23], use STL as an initial time series analysis for later modeling a predictive policing approach. Furthermore, this approach allows statements about recurring and changing temporal components of crime without considering socioeconomic or demographical information.

ARIMA modeling is a powerful tool for time series analysis and short-term forecasting. Since ARIMA was successfully applied for predictions in economics, marketing, industry production, and social problems, it was also applied for forecasting property crime [20]. In this study, the ARIMA model was used to predict one week in advance from the observations on property crime, but only for the whole city and not for districts. ARIMA has the potential to enable crime prediction by only using offense data, as well as analyzing temporal crime patterns on different spatial scales by spatial data aggregation [24]. In crime research and strategic planning in police work, information on possible future events in crime data enables short- and long-term orientation and the recognition of changes and recurring patterns.

For time series analysis, a raw time-series signal was constructed out of the criminal records for each analyzed offense, e.g., residential burglary, over a period of five years from 1 January 2017 to 31 December 2021. The number of cases per offense per time unit was aggregated for a sub-region. Thus, only the time and location information of the offense were used. Weekly aggregated offense data on residential district and city level were considered for the time series analysis. Analyses based on daily data were considered problematic due to the small offense numbers.

In the first step, a time series decomposition was performed on daily aggregated offense data. The Seasonal Time Series Decomposition based on Loess (STL) is a filtering method for separating three components from a seasonal time series, namely trend (T), season (S), and the remainder (R) [25]. The first component, the trend at the time, indicates the series' long-term increase or decrease. The second component, the seasonality, indicates whether the time series is modified by seasonal influences, referring to one cycle per year in this case. The third component, the remainder, represents any residual noise in the data. Since STL is an additive model, the time series (Y) at the time (t) can be described as follows [23]:

$$Y_T = T_t + S_t + R_t \tag{1}$$

The output of this process is the separation of the original time series of criminal record entries into two distinct derivatives: the trend and the season.

Daily aggregated offense data on residential districts were used for time series decomposition.

Time series analysis can also be utilized in the process of prediction. In a second step, the autoregressive integrated moving average (ARIMA) model introduced by Box and Jenkins [26] was used to forecast the number of crime events for periods of one week and one month. This model can provide accurate forecasts over relatively short periods [20].

The autoregressive (AR) models attribute current observations only to past observations. In moving average (MA) processes, however, observations are attributed not only to the observations but also to the non-observed error of the past periods, which also influences future observations. Thus, ARIMA models take advantage not only of the observed past observations but also of information that is not described directly in the time series but is defined as the error of the prediction. ARIMA models combine AR models and MA processes as follows:

$$y_t = \alpha + \emptyset_1 y_{dt-1} + \emptyset_p y_{dt-p} + \theta_1 \varepsilon_{t-1} + \theta_q \varepsilon_{t-1} + \varepsilon_\tau \tag{2}$$

Here, y_d is the d-fold differentiated observations that can follow an AR process with p orders and an MA process with q orders. Therefore, the task is to specify the parameters d, i.e., the order of the necessary integration or differentiation, as well as p and q in the ARIMA (p, d, and q) model [20,27].

The ARIMA model was applied for weekly aggregated offense data at the residential district and city levels.

4. Results and Discussion

4.1. Crime Forecasting

By testing predictive policing as a theory-based approach, the primary purpose of this study was to support strategic and target-oriented police work that identified potential hotspots at an early stage based on known crime-relevant factors. The aim was to achieve a resource-efficient deployment of police forces and, ideally, reduce the frequency of crime. The results show that it is often possible to calculate higher crime probabilities in the chosen spatial reference for residential burglaries, commercial burglaries, and motor vehicle offenses compared with the basic statistical probabilities. Depending on the modeling, the probabilities of residential burglaries in selected residential districts were, on average, about ten times higher than those of a random area selection. Nevertheless, it was found that the compilation of weekly crime forecasts in more rural districts was ineffective due to a relatively low number of cases. However, analyses focusing on the structural differences between urban and rural regions have found approaches that make it possible to determine the probability of burglary in more rural regions so that it was possible to compute crime forecasts for the entire state.

In addition, the influence of the socio-structural data on residential burglaries was also examined. In summary, the results show that the influencing strengths of the variables varied greatly depending on the season and district. Accordingly, the results are not automatically transferable to other districts or periods. Furthermore, it was shown in this context that the model quality crucially depended on the quality and temporal availability of the data.

4.2. Risk Terrain Modelling

In both cases, modifying the classical RTM approach to classification and Poisson models led to significantly better model performance. For example, a Poisson model showed a model improvement of about 35 to 40 percent. Deviance with dynamic variables (calculated based on historical police data) was significantly lower than deviance with purely static variables like sociostructural data. Conversely, this finding means that a RTM map created with only static variables is less reliable in its informative value than a RTM map with dynamic and static variables. The quality of the dynamic variables, on the other hand, decreases with decreasing density of the number of cases, i.e., with progression from urban to rural regions.

In addition, the analyses showed that the weighting of the variables among each other is an important aspect of variable selection. The rough distribution of weights between two different model approaches is largely similar. For example, the dynamic variables are often in the upper weight range. The analyses have also shown that both the weighting of the variables among each other and the selection of the variables themselves can be subject to strong local variations. Depending on the selected period, both model approaches enable a statement to be made for the same temporal scope in each case. For example, a model that has been trained with historical data from the last six months enables a forecast for the following six months. Due to the very slowly changing socio-structural data and strongly fluctuating local dynamic variables, there is a compelling lower temporal horizon limit for which a RTM map can be generated reliably. However, no universally valid lower boundary can be defined due to the strong local fluctuations.

In summary, it can be shown that a spatial risk assessment is also possible for more rural police departments in NRW. Due to the high computation times of the model for the large spaces and the desire for a fine-scale grid, a seasonal risk assessment is necessary to support strategical decision-making processes in the police authorities.

4.3. Time Series Analysis

The results of the time series decomposition of the weekly aggregated offense data on the residential district level for NRW are presented in Figure 6, exemplarily for residential burglary. The estimated trend component revealed a decrease in residential district level residential burglaries from 2017 until December 2021. Regarding the seasonal component, an increase in the winter terms was detected, and a decrease in the summer terms throughout the entire analysis period was also detected. These temporal and spatial patterns can be applied to metropolitan cities. The procedure cannot be transferred to more rural regions due to the small number of cases.

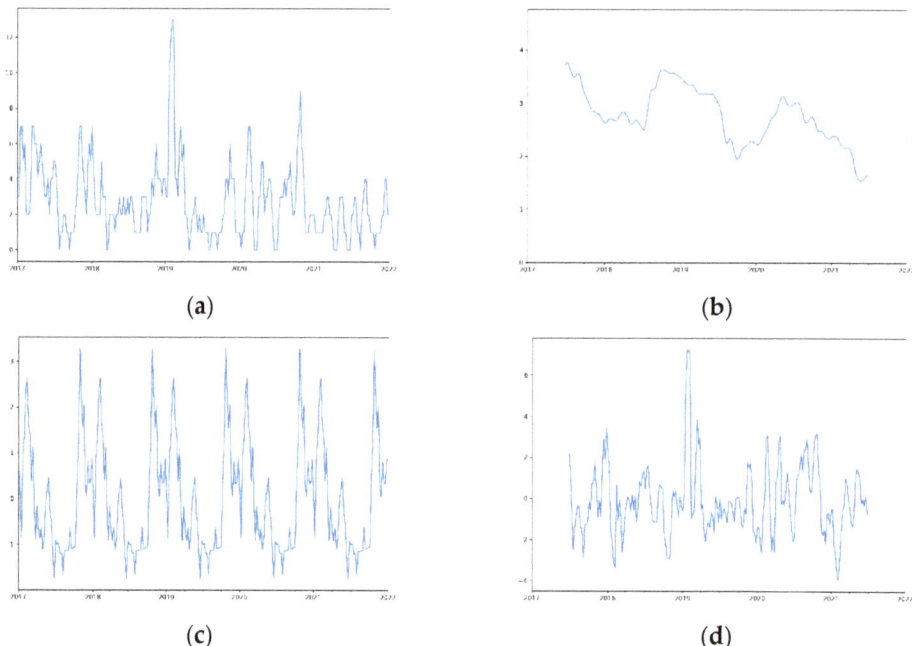

(a)

(b)

(c)

(d)

Figure 6. Time series decomposition of residential burglary in one exemplary residential district in Dusseldorf from 2017 to 2021 with (**a**) raw time series, (**b**) trend, (**c**) season, and (**d**) remainder.

The results can likewise be transferred to all residential districts. In general, areas close to the city center, which are densely populated, show similar temporal patterns, as shown in Figure 6. The procedure cannot be transferred to peri-urban areas, which tend to be characterized by a lower population density and thus have lower offense numbers. In these areas, approaches such as integrating the spatio-temporal clusters or residential district aggregation can help make valid calculations.

The experimental results produced for the cities and residential districts in NRW using an ARIMA model of the weekly aggregated offense time series support the value of crime time series analysis. The results for residential burglary are shown exemplarily for a selected residential district in Dusseldorf in Figure 7. The fitting of the ARIMA model shows that both seasonal components and the initially increasing and subsequently decreasing trend could be captured. The higher case numbers in the winter months could also be mapped. The prediction of offense numbers for the following 16 weeks and one year show that both the decreasing trend and the seasonal component are included. The offense numbers recorded by the police fall within the confidence intervals of the predicted values. Thus, this method is promising, for example, for the prediction of residential burglaries and long-term planning and strategic orientation of the police authorities. The ARIMA model is a way to look at both long-term changes and seasonal components of crime. The use of the model is advantageous for crime data, as studies have shown that ARIMA works better than complex Artificial New Networks, for example, in the case of a small number of datasets [28]. The fitted ARIMA model can forecast future points in a series [20].

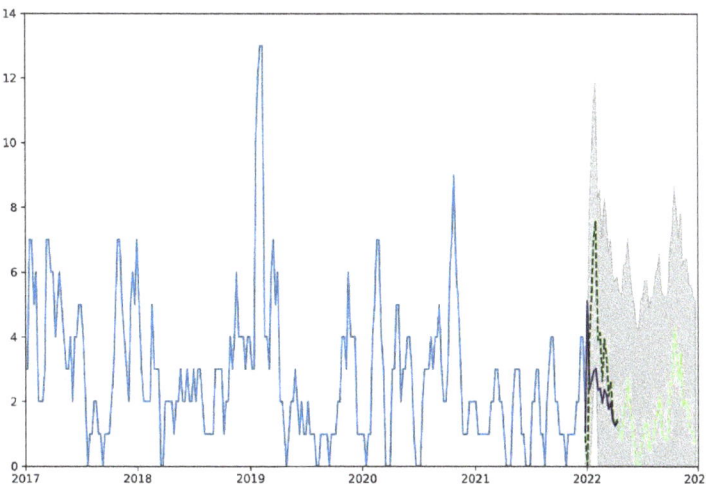

Figure 7. Time series of residential burglary events in a residential district in Dusseldorf with the ARIMA-modelled prediction for the first 16 weeks (dashed dark-green line) and 52 weeks (dashed light-green line) in 2023.

In general, time series analysis is a helpful approach to analyzing seasonal and long-term patterns of offense numbers. The conclusions can be drawn from these results for the following weeks or months as to what extent offense numbers are likely to increase, decrease, or remain constant. Therefore, long-term strategic decision-making processes in the police authorities can be supported.

5. Potential and Limitations

Spatio-temporally-based statistical techniques offer police agencies the potential to optimize their operational and strategic planning based on predictions and to take necessary action before a crime occurs. Targeted control of the forces or the alignment of operational focal points in specific crime areas is possible. Changes in crime can be detected earlier based on such calculations.

In evaluating crime forecasting methods, data quality is crucial concerning data uncertainty. Data uncertainty refers to the problem that it is usually unknown as to what extent errors are contained in the collected and utilized data. In this context, data collection problems such as measurement uncertainties are conceivable, e.g., when re-cording the suspected time of a burglary. For data collection in the context of police forces, a source of uncertainty is the fact that criminal offenses are either legally misjudged or are reported late by the victims, which is not uncommon for the criminal charges of burglaries [8]. In addition, the data quality of the data collected in the field of policing is often low, as periods and localities are not (or cannot) always be precisely defined. Similarly, it is challenging to predict offenses that should be prevented by increased police presence. There is often a lack of knowledge about whether police presence has prevented offenses or whether the predictive models are outputting inaccurate risk estimates.

Overall, crime forecasting methods offer a wide range of possible applications that enable criminal expertise to be enriched by scientific findings.

Author Contributions: Conceptualization, K.S. (Kai Seidensticker) and K.S. (Katharina Schwarz); methodology, K.S. (Kai Seidensticker) and K.S. (Katharina Schwarz); software, K.S. (Katharina Schwarz); validation, K.S. (Katharina Schwarz); formal analysis, K.S. (Kai Seidensticker) and K.S. (Katharina Schwarz); investigation, K.S. (Kai Seidensticker) and K.S. (Katharina Schwarz); resources, K.S. (Kai Seidensticker) and K.S. (Katharina Schwarz); data curation, K.S. (Kai Seidensticker) and K.S.

(Katharina Schwarz); writing—original draft preparation, K.S. (Katharina Schwarz); writing—review and editing, K.S. (Kai Seidensticker); visualization, K.S. (Kai Seidensticker) and K.S. (Katharina Schwarz); supervision, K.S. (Kai Seidensticker); project administration, K.S. (Kai Seidensticker); funding acquisition, K.S. (Kai Seidensticker). All authors have read and agreed to the published version of the manuscript.

Funding: This research received no external funding.

Institutional Review Board Statement: Not applicable.

Informed Consent Statement: Not applicable.

Data Availability Statement: Not applicable.

Conflicts of Interest: The authors declare no conflict of interest.

References

1. Seidensticker, K.; Bode, F. Good policing in times of abstract police. In *The Abstract Police*; Terpstra, J., Salet, R., Fyfe, N., Eds.; Eleven International Publishing: Den Haag, The Netherlands, 2022; pp. 169–182.
2. Fotheringham, A.S.; Brunsdon, C.; Charlton, M. *Geographically Weighted Regression. The Analysis of Spatially Varying Relationships*; John Wiley & Sons Ltd.: West Sussex, UK, 2002.
3. Ratcliffe, J. Crime mapping: Spatial and temporal challenges. In *Handbook of Quantitative Criminology*; Piquero, A.R., Weisburd, D., Eds.; Springer: New York, NY, USA, 2010; pp. 5–24.
4. Bundeskriminalamt (BKA). *PKS Jahrbuch 2018, Band 4, Version 3.0*; BKA: Wiesbaden, Germany, 2019.
5. Seidensticker, K. SKALA—Predictive Policing in North Rhine-Westphalia. *Eur. Law Enforc. Res. Bull.* **2021**, *21*, 47–60.
6. Perry, W.; McInnis, B.; Price, C.; Smith, S.; Hollywood, J. *Predictive Policing. The Role of Crime Forecasting in Law Enforcement Operations*; RAND Corporation: Santa Monica, CA, USA, 2013.
7. Pearsall, B. Predictive Policing: The future of law enforcement. *Natl. Inst. Justice J.* **2010**, *266*, 16–19.
8. Seidensticker, K.; Bode, F.; Stoffel, F. Predictive Policing in Germany. Konstanzer Online-Publikationssystem (KOPS). 2018. Available online: http://nbn-resolving.de/urn:nbn:de:bsz:352-2-14sbvox1ik0z06 (accessed on 5 July 2022).
9. Landeskriminalamt Nordrhein-Westfalen (LKA NRW). *Abschlussbericht Projekt SKALA*; LKA NRW: Düsseldorf, Germany, 2018.
10. Bode, F.; Stoffel, F.; Keim, D. *Variabilität und Validität von Qualitätsmetriken im Bereich von Predictive Policing*; KOPS: Konstanz, Germany, 2017.
11. Pollich, D.; Bode, F. Predictive Policing: Zur Notwendigkeit eines (sozial)wissenschaftlich basierten Vorgehens. *Poliz. Wiss.* **2017**, *3*, 2–12.
12. Fayyad, U.; Piatetsky-Shapiro, G.; Smyth, P. The KDD Process for Extracting Useful Knowledge from Volumes of Data. *Commun. ACM* **1996**, *39*, 27–34. [CrossRef]
13. Seidensticker, K. Predictive Policing—Herausfordernde Polizeiarbeit der Zukunft? In *Zukunft Digitaler Polizeiarbeit*; Rüdiger, T., Ed.; Verlag für Polizeiwissenschaft: Frankfurt am Main, Germany, 2021; pp. 41–76.
14. Bernasco, W. Them Again? Same-Offender Involvement in Repeat and Near Repeat Burglaries. *Eur. J. Criminol.* **2008**, *5*, 411–431. [CrossRef]
15. Gluba, A.; Heitmann, S.; Hermes, N. Reviktimisierung bei Wohnungseinbrüchen. Eine empirische Untersuchung zur Bedeutung des Phänomens der (Near) Repeat Victimisation im Landkreis Harburg. *Kriminalistik* **2015**, *6*, 368–375.
16. Barnard, D.; Germino, M.; Pilliod, D.; Arkle, R.; Applestein, C.; Davidson, B.; Fisk, M. Cannot see the random forest for the decision trees: Selecting predictive models for restoration ecology. *Restor. Ecol.* **2019**, *27*, 1–11. [CrossRef]
17. Bellman, R. A Markovian decision process. *J. Math. Mech.* **1957**, *6*, 679–684. [CrossRef]
18. Wang, X.; Brown, D. The spatio-temporal modeling for criminal incidents. *Secur. Inform.* **2012**, *1*, 1. [CrossRef]
19. Hastie, T.; Tibshirani, R.; Friedman, J. *The Elements of Statistical Learning. Data Mining, Inference, and Prediction*, 2nd ed.; Springer: Berlin/Heidelberg, Germany, 2009.
20. Chen, P.; Yuan, H.; Shu, X. Forecasting crime using the arima model. In Proceedings of the 5th International Conference on Fuzzy Systems and Knowledge Discovery, Shandong, China, 18–20 October 2008; IEEE: Piscataway Township, NJ, USA, 2008; pp. 627–630.
21. Islam, K.; Raza, A. Forecasting crime using ARIMA model. *arXiv* **2020**, arXiv:2003.08006.
22. Malik, A.; Maciejewski, R.; Towers, S.; McCullough, S.; Ebert, D.S. Proactive spatiotemporal resource allocation and predictive visual analytics for community policing and law enforcement. *IEEE Trans. Vis. Comput. Graph.* **2014**, *20*, 1863–1872. [CrossRef]
23. Borges, J.; Ziehr, D.; Beigl, M.; Cacho, N.; Martins, A.; Araujo, A.; Bezerra, L.; Geisler, S. Time-series features for predictive policing. In Proceedings of the IEEE International Smart Cities Conference (ISC2), Kansas City, MO, USA, 16–19 September 2018; IEEE: Piscataway Township, NJ, USA, 2018; pp. 1–8.
24. Roy, S.; Bhunia, G.S.; Shit, P.K. Spatial prediction of COVID-19 epidemic using ARIMA techniques in India. *Model. Earth Syst. Environ.* **2021**, *7*, 1385–1391. [CrossRef] [PubMed]

25. Cleveland, R.B.; Cleveland, W.S.; McRae, J.E.; Terpenning, I. STL: A seasonal-trend decomposition procedure based on loess. *J. Off. Stat.* **1990**, *6*, 3–73.
26. Box, G.E.; Jenkins, G. *Time Series Analysis: Forecasting and Control*; Holdan-Day: San Francisco, CA, USA, 1970.
27. Tariq, H.; Hanif, M.K.; Sarwar, M.U.; Bari, S.; Sarfraz, M.S.; Oskouei, R.J. Employing Deep Learning and Time Series Analysis to Tackle the Accuracy and Robustness of the Forecasting Problem. *Secur. Commun. Netw.* **2021**, *2021*, 5587511. [CrossRef]
28. Jha, S.; Yang, E.; Almagrabi, A.O.; Bashir, A.K.; Joshi, G.P. Comparative analysis of time series model and machine testing systems for crime forecasting. *Neural. Comput. Appl.* **2021**, *33*, 10621–10636. [CrossRef]

Proceeding Paper

Reconstructed Phase Spaces and LSTM Neural Network Ensemble Predictions †

Sebastian Raubitzek * and **Thomas Neubauer**

Information and Software Engineering Group, Institute of Information Systems Engineering,
Faculty of Informatics, TU Wien, Favoritenstrasse 9-11/194, 1040 Vienna, Austria; thomas.neubauer@tuwien.ac.at
* Correspondence: sebastian.raubitzek@tuwien.ac.at
† Presented at the 8th International Conference on Time Series and Forecasting, Gran Canaria, Spain,
27–30 June 2022.

Abstract: We present a novel approach that combines the concept of reconstructed phase spaces with neural network time-series predictions. The presented methodology aims to reduce the parametrization problem of neural networks and improve autoregressive neural network time-series predictions. First, the idea is to interpolate a dataset based on its reconstructed phase space properties and then filter an ensemble prediction based on its phase space properties. The corresponding ensemble predictions are made using randomly parameterized LSTM (Long Short-Term Memory) neural networks. These neural networks then produce a multitude of auto-regressive predictions, which are then filtered to achieve a smooth reconstructed phase space trajectory. Thus, we can circumvent the problem of parameterizing the neural network for each dataset individually. Here, the interpolation and the ensemble prediction aim to produce a smooth trajectory in a reconstructed phase space. The best results are compared to a single hidden layer LSTM neural network and benchmark results from the literature. The results show that the baseline predictions are outperformed for all three discussed datasets, and one of the benchmark results from the literature is bested by the presented approach.

Keywords: phase space reconstruction; LSTM; neural networks; ensemble prediction; stochastic interpolation

Citation: Raubitzek, S.; Neubauer, T. Reconstructed Phase Spaces and LSTM Neural Network Ensemble Predictions. *Eng. Proc.* **2022**, *18*, 40. https://doi.org/10.3390/engproc2022018040

Academic Editors: Ignacio Rojas, Hector Pomares, Olga Valenzuela, Fernando Rojas and Luis Javier Herrera

Published: 25 July 2022

1. Introduction

The rise of artificial intelligence, i.e., machine learning and deep learning, motivates many researchers to perform predictions and analyses based on historical data using these methods, rather than employing mechanistic expert models. The reason for making predictions in the first place is to answer important questions, e.g., future population estimates, predicting epileptic seizures, and estimating future stock market prices. The outcomes of these predictions are encouraging, e.g., solar radiation can be predicted using machine learning methods [1].

One reason for machine learning's poor performance is an overall lack of data. A means of overcoming the lack of data for time-series analysis approaches is to employ an interpolation technique to increase the amount of data. Here, one can choose from many different techniques, such as polynomial, fractal [2], or stochastic interpolation methods [3]. In this article, we use an improved version of the Brownian multi-point bridges developed by [3], which is discussed and validated in detail in ref. [4]. For simplicity, we refer to this method as PhaSpaSto interpolation, which is an abbreviation for **pha**se **spa**ce trajectory smoothing **sto**chastic interpolation.

Next, when it comes to the autoregressive prediction of time-series data, we want to consider the properties of the reconstructed phase space trajectories of a given set of time-series data, i.e., we want the reconstructed phase space trajectory of our prediction to be as smooth as possible.

Thus, we want to find out to what extent the idea of the reconstructed phase spaces of time-series data can be used to improve neural network time-series predictions. For this reason, we present the following scheme, depicted in Figure 1. We first interpolate a given time series using the discussed PhaSpaSto interpolation (Section 4); next, we employ the randomly parameterized neural networks developed in ref. [5] (Section 6), thus generating a multitude of different autoregressive predictions for each set of time-series data. Finally, we filter these predictions based on the smoothness of their reconstructed phase space trajectories, i.e., we want to keep only the smoothest phase space trajectories (Section 6.2).

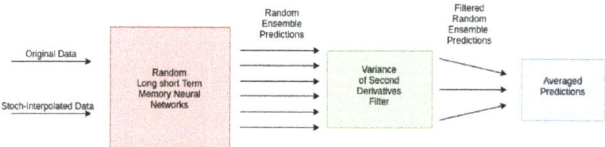

Figure 1. Schematic depiction of the filtering process. The whole pipeline is applied, first, to the original non-interpolated data, and second, to the stoch.-interpolated data set.

This article is structured as follows. The current section, i.e., Section 1, provides a brief introduction and explains the developed scheme. Section 2 lists related work and briefly describes the connections to this article. Section 3 discusses the idea of reconstructed phase spaces and introduces the used terminology and notations. Next, Section 4 introduces the employed stochastic interpolation method, whereas Section 6 describes the employed neural network approach for autoregressive time-series prediction and the prediction filter. All datasets are described and plotted with their interpolation and corresponding phase space reconstructions in Section 5. Section 7 gives all prediction results. Section 8 concludes this article and gives ideas for future research.

2. Related Work

The presented research is mainly motivated by the findings of [2,4–6]. This section will briefly describe the mentioned publications, list them chronologically, i.e., by their publication date, and put them into context.

- Ref. [7]: This publication presents a method to determine if images are blurry. For this purpose, the second derivatives of grey-scale images are taken, and the corresponding variance over all pixels is analyzed. This concept is used in the presented article. We adapted the idea of variances of second derivatives, which is discussed in Section 4.2.
- Ref. [3]: This publication presents a novel stochastic interpolation technique where the idea of a Brownian bridge, i.e., a constrained fractional Brownian motion (fBm), is extended to more than two points, i.e., to *multi-point fractional Brownian bridges*. This method is the basis for the employed interpolation techniques and provides the population of random interpolations for the genetic algorithm.
- Ref. [2]: In this publication, a fractal interpolation to interpolate univariate time-series data is presented. This research suggests that different interpolation methods for univariate time-series data may yield predictions of different quality. Thus, as presented here, employing an attractor-based interpolation is an obvious next step compared to a fluctuation-based interpolation.
- Ref. [5]: This publication is a continuation of [2]. The fractal interpolation and LSTM neural network approach is continued as ensembles of predictions. Randomly parameterized LSTM neural networks are generated from non-, linear-, and fractal-interpolated data. Afterward, these predictions are filtered based on their signal complexities. Contrary to this publication, we test LSTM neural network predictions of stochastically interpolated data.
- Ref. [4]: This publication validates a stochastic interpolation based on the smoothness of reconstructed phase space trajectories and Brownian Bridges, i.e., the PhaSpaSto

interpolation. The basic idea is to filter/improve a multitude of stochastic interpolations of the same time-series data using a genetic algorithm and the variance of second derivatives along a reconstructed phase space trajectory to generate smooth phase space embeddings.

The interpolation technique developed in this paper is briefly described in Section 4 and used to improve the presented predictions.

3. Phase Space Reconstruction

First, we need to introduce the concept of reconstructed phase spaces [8,9].

We estimate a phase space embedding for all data under study. To find a suitable phase space embedding, one has to determine two parameters, the embedding dimension d_E and the time delay τ.

To estimate the time delay τ, i.e., the delay between two consecutive time steps, we use the method based on the average information between two signals [10].

To estimate the embedding dimension d_E, we use the algorithm of false nearest neighbors [11].

The phase space embedding for a given signal $[x_1, x_2, \ldots, x_n]$, thus, is

$$\vec{y}(i) = \left[x_i, x_{i+\tau}, \ldots, x_{i+(d_E-1)*\tau} \right] \quad , \tag{1}$$

and a corresponding three-dimensional phase space embedding, thus, is

$$\vec{y}(i) = [x_i, x_{i+\tau}, x_{i+2\tau}]. \tag{2}$$

4. PhaSpaSto Interpolation

The used interpolation technique consists of two parts: first, the multi-point fractional Brownian Bridges from [3], and second, a corresponding genetic algorithm choosing the best parts of the so-created fractional Brownian bridges.

4.1. Multi-Point Fractional Brownian Bridges

The employed genetic algorithm is fueled by a population of stochastically interpolated time-series data—in our case, multi-point fractional Brownian bridges. To generate these stochastically interpolated time-series data, multi-point fractional Brownian bridges [3] were used. Thus, we briefly summarize this approach.

We consider a Gaussian random process $X(t)$, whose covariance is defined as $C(t, t') = \langle X(t)X(t') \rangle$. In the following, we focus on fractional Browian motion where the covariance is given according to $\langle X(t)X(t') \rangle = \frac{1}{2}(t^{2H} + t'^{2H} - |t - t'|^{2H})$, where H is the Hurst exponent. To elucidate our interpolation scheme, we first define a so-called fractional Brownian bridge [12,13], which is a construction of fBm starting from 0 at $t = 0$ and ending at X_1 at $t = t_1$, i.e.,

$$X^B(t) = X(t) - (X(t_1) - X_1)\frac{\langle X(t)X(t_1) \rangle}{\langle X(t_1)^2 \rangle} . \tag{3}$$

This construction ensures that $X^B(t_1) = X_1$, which is also depicted in Figure 1. This single bridge can now be generalized to an arbitrary number of (non-equidistant) prescribed points X_i at t_i by virtue of a multi-point fractional Brownian bridge [3]

$$X^B(t) = X(t) - (X(t_i) - X_i)\sigma_{ij}^{-1}\langle X(t)X(t_j) \rangle , \tag{4}$$

where $\sigma_{ij} = \langle X(t_i)X(t_j) \rangle$ denotes the covariance matrix. Furthermore, we imply summation over identical indices. The latter linear operation on the Gaussian random process $X(t)$ ensures that the bridge takes on exactly the values X_k at t_k, which can be seen from $X^B(t_k) = X(t_k) - (X(t_i) - X_i)\sigma_{ij}^{-1}\sigma_{kj} = X(t_k) - (X(t_i) - X_i)\delta_{ik} = X_k$, where δ_{ik} denotes the Kronecker delta. Hence, this method allows for the reconstruction of a sparse signal, where small-scale correlations are determined by the choice of the Hurst exponent H.

4.2. Genetic Algorithm

We build a simple genetic algorithm to find the best possible interpolation given the data's phase space reconstruction using Taken's theorem. We want our reconstructed phase space curve to be as smooth as possible and thus define the trajectory's fitness as follows.

The basic idea is to use a concept from image processing, i.e., the blurriness of a picture, and apply it to phase space trajectories. We want our trajectory to be as blurry, i.e., as smooth, as possible. In image processing, the blurriness is determined via second-order derivatives of grey-scale images at each pixel [7]. We employ this concept, but instead of using it at each pixel, we calculate the variance of second-order derivatives along our phase space trajectories. Similar to the idea from image processing, where the low variance of second-order derivatives implies more blurriness, curves with a low variance of second-order derivatives exhibit comparatively smooth trajectories. The reason here is intuitively apparent: whereas curves with a high variance of second-order derivatives have a range of straight and pointy sections, curves with a low variance of second-order derivatives have a similar curvature along the trajectory and thus are smoother. Hence, in order to guarantee smoothness along the trajectory, we want this variance to be as low as possible, which thus is our loss L. Concluding, our fitness is maximal when our loss L is minimal.

Again, we start with the phase space vector and the corresponding embedding dimension d_E and time delay τ (see Section 3) of each signal as

$$\vec{y}(i) = \left[x_i, x_{i+\tau}, \dots, x_{i+(d_E-1)\cdot\tau} \right] \quad . \tag{5}$$

Thus, we have one component for each dimension of the phase space. Consequently, we can write the individual components as

$$y_j(i) = x_{i+(j-1)*\tau} \quad , \tag{6}$$

where $j = 1, 2, \dots, d_E$. We then take the second-order finite difference central derivative of a discrete function [14]

$$u_j''(i) = x_{i+(j-1)*\tau+1} - 2x_{i+(j-1)*\tau} + x_{i+(j-1)*\tau-1} \quad , \tag{7}$$

at each point, and for each component. Next, we add up all the components as

$$u''(i) = \sqrt{\sum_{j=1}^{d_E} u_j''(i)^2} \quad . \tag{8}$$

Then, finally, we use the variance of the absolute values of second derivatives along the phase space curve as our loss L of a phase space trajectory:

$$L = \mathrm{Var}_i\left[u''(i) \right] . \tag{9}$$

The employed genetic algorithm consists of the following building blocks.

A candidate solution is an interpolated time series using a random Hurst exponent $H \in (0; 1)$. The corresponding population of candidates is, e.g., 1000 of these stochastically interpolated time-series data with random Hurst exponents. A population of interpolated time-series data is generated using the multi-point Brownian bridges such that, for each member of the population, a random Hurst exponent with $H \in (0; 1)$ is chosen, which then defines the interpolation of the member of the population. After generating the population, all members are sorted with respect to their fitness, i.e., the lower the loss L, the better an interpolation is. The mating is implemented such that only the best 50%, with respect to fitness, can mate to produce new offspring. The mating is done such that, for every gene, i.e., each interpolation between two data points, there is a 50:50 chance to inherit it from either one of the parents. The mutation was implemented such that, in each generation, there is a 20% chance that a randomly chosen interpolated time series is replaced with a new interpolated time series within a corresponding randomly chosen new Hurst exponent. Moreover, we implemented a criterion for aborting the program, which was fulfilled if the population fitness mean did not change for ten generations. This described procedure was then performed for 1000 generations. However, the 1000 generations were never reached, as the criterion for abortion was always triggered, and the program was ended, thus yielding the best interpolation with respect to the fitness of the phase space trajectories before reaching the 1000th generation.

5. Datasets

We chose three datasets to test and demonstrate our approach. Two of the featured datasets are from the Time Series Data Library [15] and thus are known test datasets and provide us with benchmark results, which are discussed in Section 7.4.

The third dataset is the annual maize yields in Austria, which can be obtained from http://www.fao.org/faostat/, accessed on 21 July 2022. This third dataset is considered the most challenging of the three datasets for two reasons. First, it is an agricultural dataset, i.e., it is affected by the weather, genetic improvements of the plants, varying fertilization strategies, etc., meaning that we will most likely not discover any reasonable seasonalities and or trends, despite the apparent increase in maize yields due to various improvements in agriculture. Second, this dataset is collected annually for all of Austria, i.e., a lot of the information contained in the dataset is lost due to the annual and regional averaging. Thus, we conclude that it will be challenging or impossible to predict annual maize yields several years ahead effectively.

5.1. Car Sales in Quebec Dataset

This is a dataset from the Time Series Data Library [15]. It depicts monthly car sales in Quebec from January 1960 to December 1968, with an overall 108 data points.

The corresponding phase space embedding, with a time delay $\tau = 1$, was detrended by subtracting a linear fit from the data and normalized such that the range of all data is between $[0, 1]$. The interpolated time series and the corresponding reconstructed phase space are depicted in Figure 2.

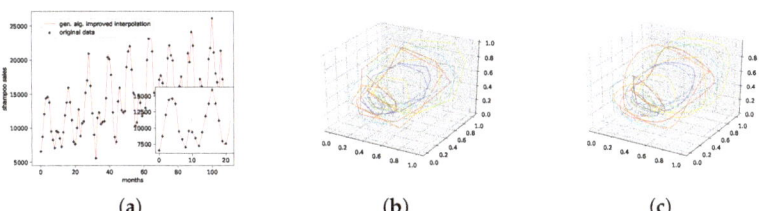

(a)   (b)   (c)

Figure 2. Time-series and attractor plots for the annual car sales in Quebec dataset. (**a**) Stoch. interpolated, 13 interpolation points, time-series plot; (**b**) non-interpolated, reconstructed attractor plot, detrended, normalized; (**c**) stoch.-interpolated, 13 interpolation points, reconstructed attractor plot, detrended, normalized. The rainbow colors in the phase space plots correspond to different steps in time. The spectrum starts with blue (early) and ends with red (later).

5.2. Monthly International Airline Passengers Dataset

This is a dataset from the Time Series Data Library [15]. It depicts monthly international airline passengers from January 1949 to December 1960, with an overall 144 data points, given in units of 1000.

The corresponding phase space embedding, with a time delay $\tau = 1$, was detrended by subtracting a linear fit from the data and normalized such that the range of all data is between $[0,1]$. The interpolated time series and the corresponding reconstructed phase space are depicted in Figure 3.

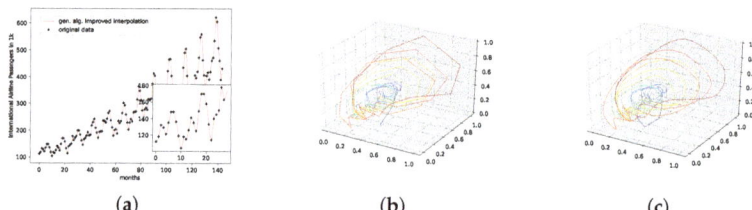

(a)   **(b)**   **(c)**

Figure 3. Time-series and attractor plots for the monthly international airline passengers dataset. (**a**) Stoch.-interpolated, 13 interpolation points, time-series plot; (**b**) non-interpolated, reconstructed attractor plot, detrended, normalized; (**c**) stoch.-interpolated, 13 interpolation points, reconstructed attractor plot, detrended, normalized. The rainbow colors in the phase space plots correspond to different steps in time. The spectrum starts with blue (early) and ends with red (later).

5.3. Annual Maize Yields in Austria

This is a dataset of the annual yields of maize in Austria ranging from 1961 to 2017, with an overall 57 data points. This dataset can be downloaded at http://www.fao.org/faostat/, accessed on 21 July 2022. The corresponding phase space embedding, with a time delay $\tau = 1$ and an embedding dimension of $d_E = 3$, was detrended by subtracting a linear fit from the data and normalized such that the range of all data is between $[0,1]$. The interpolated time series and the corresponding reconstructed phase space are depicted in Figure 4.

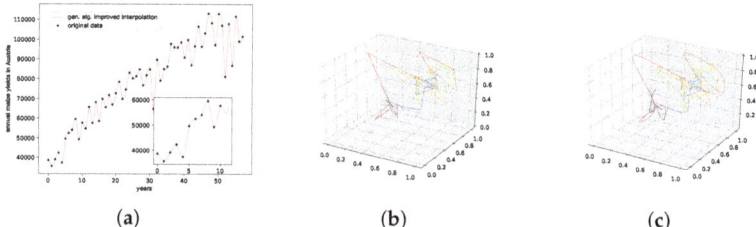

(a)   **(b)**   **(c)**

Figure 4. Time-series and attractor plots for the annual maize yields in Austria data set. (**a**) Stoch.-interpolated, 13 interpolation points, time-series plot; (**b**) non -interpolated, reconstructed attractor plot, detrended, normalized; (**c**) stoch.-interpolated, 13 interpolation points, reconstructed attractor plot, detrended, normalized. The rainbow colors in the phase space plots correspond to different steps in time. The spectrum starts with blue (early) and ends with red (later).

5.4. Data Preprocessing

Two steps of preprocessing were performed before forecasting the featured datasets. First, each dataset was made stationary by subtracting a linear fit. Second, each dataset was scaled to $[0.1, 0.9]$.

Finally, each dataset was split into a train and test dataset with an 80%/20% ratio.

6. LSTM Neural Network Time-Series Prediction

LSTMs are a category of recurrent neural networks (*RNNs*). RNNs are capable of using feedback or *recurrent* connections to cope with time-series data.

LSTMs [16] feature a component called a *memory block* to enhance their capability to model long-term dependencies. This memory block is a recurrently connected subnet containing two functional modules, i.e., the memory cell and the corresponding gates. The task of the memory cell is to remember the temporal state of the neural network. On the other hand, the gates are responsible for controlling the information flow and consist of multiplicative units.

6.1. Randomly Parameterized Neural Networks

In this article, we are using an approach developed in [5]. The idea is to generate many randomly parameterized neural networks to build ensemble predictions based on the phase space properties of the autoregressively produced predictions. An autoregressive prediction is a one-step-at-a-time prediction, whereas old outputs are used as inputs for the next step.

These randomly parameterized neural networks feature one to five hidden LSTM layers, a *hard sigmoid* activation function in the hidden and input layers, and a rectified linear unit as the output activation function. No dropout criterion or regularization was used.

We used the following ranges for the parameters for our randomly parameterized neural network implementation.

- Number of input nodes: $1 \rightarrow$ size of the training data $- 1$
- Number of neurons for each hidden layer: $1 \rightarrow 50$
- Batchsizes: $2 \rightarrow 128$
- Epochs: $1 \rightarrow 50$

We used LSTM architectures for this research, one can use any type of neural network cell for this approach.

6.2. Prediction Filter

The so-generated autoregressive predictions are then filtered using the criterion for smooth phase space trajectories from Section 4.2, i.e., we want the variance of second derivatives along a reconstructed phase space trajectory to be as low as possible. We thus randomly chose 1 to 10 predictions from the whole set of predictions. Next, these predictions are averaged to form an ensemble prediction. This ensemble prediction is merged with the training data. Then, the variance of second derivatives along the phase space trajectory is analyzed. This process is repeated 1 million times. The set of averaged predictions with the lowest variance of second derivatives is kept. On all plots, this procedure is referred to as `loss_rand`.

7. Experiments and Results

In this Section, we provide the experimental setup and the corresponding results.

First, each dataset was interpolated using PhaSpaSto interpolation (Section 4) with varying interpolation points. For the monthly international airline passengers and the car sales in Quebec datasets, interpolations with the following numbers of interpolation points were performed: $N_I = \{1, 3, 5, 7, 9, 11, 13\}$. For the annual maize yields in Austria, this range was changed to $N_I = \{9, 11, 13, 15\}$ to save computational resources. Further, we produced 500 randomly parameterized neural network predictions for the monthly international airline passengers and car sales in Quebec datasets. In contrast, for the annual maize yields in Austria dataset, 1000 of these predictions were produced. These multitudes of predictions were created for the non-interpolated and the interpolated datasets. As initially mentioned, the whole scheme is depicted in Figure 1.

All of these predictions were analyzed using the root mean squared error (RMSE). Here, we used the RMSE on both a normalized dataset, i.e., the dataset and the prediction are scaled to be $\in [0, 1]$ (denoted as **RMSE [0, 1]**, Equation (10)), and the regular dataset and prediction (denoted as **RMSE**, Equation (10)).

All errors for all datasets are collected in Table 1. The corresponding plots for the car sales in Quebec dataset are collected in Figure 5, the results for the monthly international airline passengers are plotted in Figure 6, and finally, the results for the annual maize yields in Austria are depicted in Figure 7. Further, we discuss each dataset separately in the following.

$$RMSE = \left(\frac{1}{n}\sum_{i=1}^{n}[\hat{x}_i - x_i]^2\right)^{\frac{1}{2}},\tag{10}$$

Here, $\hat{x}_i$ are the predicted values, x_i is the ground truth, and n is the number of samples.

Table 1. Results for all datasets and experiments, i.e., interpolated, non-interpolated, filtered, and unfiltered.

Data	Approach	RMSE [0, 1]	RMSE
Car Sales in Quebec	not interpolated, unfiltered	0.31148	6395.04838
Car Sales in Quebec	not interpolated, filtered	0.11635	1927.52494
Car Sales in Quebec	stoch. interpolated, $N_I = 13$, unfiltered	0.24762	5104.42560
Car Sales in Quebec	stoch. interpolated, $N_I = 1$, filtered	0.07958	1617.40461
Monthly International Airline Passengers	not interpolated, unfiltered	0.19676	101.92294
Monthly International Airline Passengers	not interpolated, filtered	0.06823	35.34095
Monthly International Airline Passengers	stoch. interpolated, $N_I = 13$, unfiltered	0.17180	86.28560
Monthly International Airline Passengers	stoch. interpolated, $N_I = 9$, filtered	0.05286	21.20474
Annual Maize Yields Austria	not interpolated, unfiltered	0.23536	18,253.10327
Annual Maize Yields Austria	not interpolated, filtered	0.16424	12,737.42487
Annual Maize Yields Austria	stoch. interpolated, $N_I = 15$, unfiltered	0.20499	15,442.32505
Annual Maize Yields Austria	stoch. interpolated, $N_I = 15$, filtered	0.14563	11,227.39159

7.1. Car Sales in Quebec Dataset

All errors for the car sales in Quebec dataset are collected in Table 1, and the corresponding plots are collected in Figure 5.

When comparing the errors for the results with and without interpolation, we see that the interpolated results are reduced, i.e., the unfiltered, interpolated results have a lower error than the unfiltered, not interpolated ones. The same is true for the filtered results.

Next, the filtered results consistently drastically outperformed the unfiltered ones. Exactly this behavior is depicted in Figure 5. The overall best result is the interpolated and filtered prediction approach, which can be seen in Figure 5d.

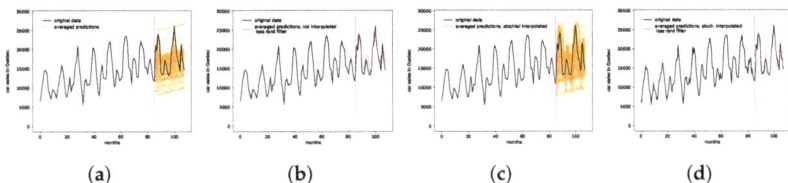

(a)   (b)   (c)   (d)

Figure 5. Autoregressive prediction results for the car sales in Quebec dataset. (**a**) Non-interpolated, non-filtered; (**b**) non-interpolated, filtered; (**c**) stoch. interpolated, 13 interpolation points, non-filtered; (**d**) stoch. interpolated, 1 interpolation point, filtered.

7.2. Monthly International Airline Passengers

All errors for the monthly international airline passengers dataset are collected in Table 1, and the corresponding plots are collected in Figure 6.

When comparing the errors for the results with and without interpolation, we see that the errors for the interpolated results are reduced, i.e., the unfiltered interpolated results have a lower error than the unfiltered, not interpolated ones. The same is true for the filtered results.

Next, the filtered results always drastically outperformed the unfiltered ones. Exactly this behavior is depicted in Figure 6. The overall best result is the interpolated and filtered prediction approach, which can be seen in Figure 6d.

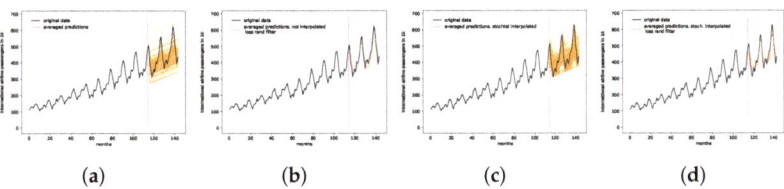

(a)   (b)   (c)   (d)

Figure 6. Autoregressive prediction results for the car sales in Quebec dataset. (**a**) Non-interpolated, non-filtered; (**b**) non-interpolated, filtered; (**c**) stoch. interpolated, 13 interpolation points, non-filtered; (**d**) stoch. interpolated, 9 interpolation points, filtered.

7.3. Annual Maize Yields in Austria Dataset

All errors for the monthly international airline passengers dataset are collected in Table 1, and the corresponding plots are collected in Figure 7.

When comparing the errors for the results with and without interpolation, we see that the interpolated results are reduced, i.e., the unfiltered, interpolated results have a lower error than the unfiltered, not interpolated ones. The same is true for the filtered results.

Next, the filtered results consistently drastically outperformed the unfiltered ones. Exactly this behavior is depicted in Figure 7. The overall best result is the interpolated and filtered prediction approach, which can be seen in Figure 7d.

This dataset is considered to be the most difficult of the three featured datasets, and although our predictions are still off, as can be seen in Figure 7d, the performed procedures, i.e., PhaSpaSto interpolation and the prediction filter, do improve the accuracy of the forecast. Further, the result depicted in Figure 7d suggests that the employed neural networks learned some inherent behavior, especially when taking into account the initial variations after the train/test cut.

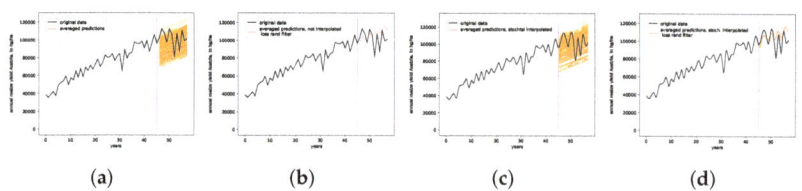

Figure 7. Autoregressive prediction results for the car sales in Quebec dataset. (**a**) Non-interpolated, non-filtered; (**b**) non-interpolated, filtered; (**c**) stoch. interpolated, 15 interpolation points, non-filtered; (**d**) stoch. interpolated, 15 interpolation points, filtered.

7.4. Benchmark and Baseline Predictions

We finally provide some baseline and benchmark results for the conducted experiments. We used an LSTM neural network with one hidden layer as a baseline prediction. Each neural network was trained with a batch size of 2 and varying epochs. Further, `verbose` was set to 2. For the activation of the neural network, `hard_sigmoid` was chosen, and the activation function of the output layer was `relu`. For the initialization, `glorot_uniform` was used for the LSTM layer, `orthogonal` was used as the recurrent initializer, and `glorot_uniform` for the Dense layer. For the LSTM layer, the bias was set to `use_bias=True`, with a corresponding `bias_initializer="zeros"`. Further, no constraints, regularizers, or dropout criteria were used for the recurrent and the Dense layers. As an optimizer, `rmsprop` was used and the loss was calculated using `mean_squared_error`. The output node returned only one result, i.e., the next time step. The varying architectures are collected in Table 2 and the corresponding predictions are depicted in Figure 8.

Table 2. Errors for the baseline predictions for each dataset.

Data	Architecture	RMSE [0, 1]	RMSE
Car Sales in Quebec	20 input nodes 30 hidden layer neurons 45 training epochs	0.08593	1764.38996
Monthly International Airline Passengers	20 input nodes 30 hidden layer neurons 40 training epochs	0.05899	30.56100
Annual Maize Yields Austria	20 input nodes 30 hidden layer neurons 18 training epochs	0.16617	12,886.99962

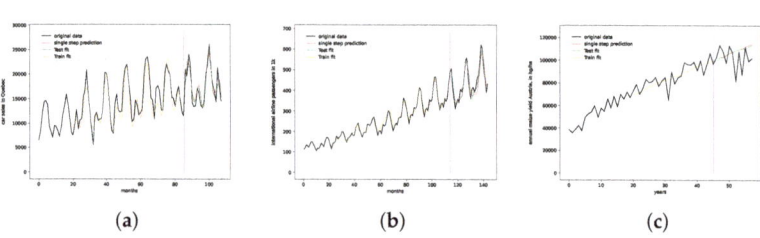

Figure 8. LSTM baseline predictions. The red line denotes the autorgressive single step-by-step prediction, which is featured in Table 2. (**a**) Car sales in Quebec dataset; (**b**) monthly international airline passengers dataset; (**c**) annual maize yields in Austria dataset.

The featured baseline predictions, though reasonable, are consistently outperformed by the interpolated filtered results from our main experiments—see Table 1—in terms of RMSE. Here, we want to highlight that the baseline neural network did not capture the characteristics of the annual maize yields dataset. This may be due to poor parameterization or the fact that a single hidden layer is not sufficient to capture the dynamics of this dataset. Still, we tuned the employed neural networks by hand, and the results for the other dataset show that neural networks of these sizes are sufficient for univariate time-series data of this length. The best ensemble result, in comparison, provides a drastically improved result compared to the baseline prediction.

When it comes to benchmark results from the literature, we found the best result for the monthly international airline passengers dataset in ref. [17], with an RMSE of 13.0 for a hybrid MLP-ARIMA approach, which is superior to our baseline of 30.6 and our best ensemble result of 21.2. Thus, we conclude that our ensemble approach with the presented specifications cannot outperform state-of-the-art methods for this dataset.

For the monthly car sales in Quebec dataset, we found a comparable result in ref. [18], with an RMSE $[0, 1]$ of 0.08143 for the additive Holt–Winters method. Our baseline LSTM result for this dataset has an RMSE $[0, 1]$ of 0.08593 and our best ensemble results is at 0.07958. We conclude that our ensemble prediction is able to outperform the best results from ref. [18] for this dataset.

As far as the authors know, there is no benchmark result for the annual maize yields in Austria dataset. Thus, we stick to the previously presented baseline prediction, which is outperformed by the presented ensemble prediction.

7.5. Summary

We briefly summarize our findings and point out the main results below.

1. The presented stochastic interpolation method—for simplicity, referred to as *PhaSpaSto* interpolation—can be used to improve retrogressive neural network time-series predictions. This is supported by the findings of Table 1. Here, we can see that both the filtered and unfiltered interpolated results outperformed those without interpolation. The same is true for all filtered results, i.e., the interpolated results always outperformed the unfiltered ones. These results are depicted in Figures 5–7.
2. Filtering the multitude of predictions based on the second derivatives along their reconstructed phase space portraits drastically improved the results for all datasets. The corresponding results are, again, collected in Table 1 and Figures 5–7.
3. The presented interpolated and filtered approach outperformed the baseline and benchmark predictions for the monthly car sales in Quebec dataset, discussed in Section 7.4.

   Though the interpolated and filtered ensemble approach did outperform a given baseline prediction for the monthly international airline passengers dataset, the featured benchmark prediction from the literature still outperformed our approach on this dataset.

   We provide a baseline prediction for the annual maize yields in Austria dataset, which was outperformed using our interpolated and filtered ensemble approach, discussed in Section 7.4. We cannot provide a benchmark result from the literature for this dataset.
4. The employed neural network ensembles were not individually parameterized for each dataset. Instead, we filtered the predictions according to the phase space properties of each dataset. Thus, we could circumvent the problem of parameterizing neural networks.

8. Conclusions

This article presents an experiment to test the applicability of a novel interpolation method—for simplicity, abbreviated as PhaSpaSto interpolation—combined with randomly parameterized neural network autoregressive predictions. These predictions are then filtered using the variance of second derivatives along a reconstructed phase space trajectory to only keep forecasts that ensure a smooth phase space trajectory.

First, a given time series is interpolated using the featured interpolation method. It is forecast by generating multiple differently parameterized neural networks, each providing an autoregressive prediction of the data under study. Finally, this multitude of predictions is filtered such that the result guarantees a smooth reconstructed phase space trajectory.

The results show that this novel approach outperforms the provided baseline predictions. Further, we were able to best a given benchmark result from the literature for one of the three discussed datasets.

The concept of reconstructed phase spaces can be applied to interpolate time series to guarantee a smooth phase space trajectory, which, in turn, improves the accuracy of our neural network predictions. Further, filtering ensemble predictions based on their phase space properties, i.e., the smoothness of their phase space trajectories, improves the presented ensemble predictions. Moreover, we can circumvent the problem of parameterizing neural networks by generating many predictions and filtering them based on their phase space properties.

Ideas for future research in this field are, e.g., to test the presented filter on other state-of-the-art ensemble approaches or to test the robustness of neural network predictions using the presented PhaSpaSto and related interpolation techniques. We further want to highlight that the proposed methodology improves the accuracy on the featured annual maize yields dataset, which the authors expected to be a challenging dataset. Thus, another idea for future research might be to specifically target challenging time-series prediction problems, such as forecasting agricultural or financial time-series data.

Author Contributions: Conceptualization, S.R.; Data curation, S.R.; Funding acquisition, T.N.; Investigation, S.R.; Methodology, S.R.; Project administration, T.N.; Resources, T.N.; Software, S.R.; Supervision, T.N.; Validation, S.R.; Visualization, S.R.; Writing—original draft, S.R.; Writing—review and editing, S.R. All authors have read and agreed to the published version of the manuscript.

Funding: The authors acknowledge the funding of the project "DiLaAg—Digitalization and Innovation Laboratory in Agricultural Sciences", by the private foundation "Forum Morgen", the Federal State of Lower Austria, and by the FFG; Project AI4Cropr, No. 877158.

Institutional Review Board Statement: Not applicable.

Informed Consent Statement: Not applicable.

Data Availability Statement: Not applicable.

Conflicts of Interest: The authors declare no conflict of interest.

References

1. Voyant, C.; Notton, G.; Kalogirou, S.; Nivet, M.L.; Paoli, C.; Motte, F.; Fouilloy, A. Machine learning methods for solar radiation forecasting: A review. *Renew. Energy* **2017**, *105*, 569–582. [CrossRef]
2. Raubitzek, S.; Neubauer, T. A fractal interpolation approach to improve neural network predictions for difficult time series data. *Expert Syst. Appl.* **2021**, *169*, 114474. [CrossRef]
3. Friedrich, J.; Gallon, S.; Pumir, A.; Grauer, R. Stochastic Interpolation of Sparsely Sampled Time Series via Multipoint Fractional Brownian Bridges. *Phys. Rev. Lett.* **2020**, *125*, 170602. [CrossRef] [PubMed]
4. Raubitzek, S.; Neubauer, T.; Friedrich, J.; Rauber, A. Interpolating Strange Attractors via Fractional Brownian Bridges. *Entropy* **2022**, *24*, 718. [CrossRef] [PubMed]
5. Raubitzek, S.; Neubauer, T. Taming the Chaos in Neural Network Time Series Predictions. *Entropy* **2021**, *23*, 1424. [CrossRef] [PubMed]
6. Raubitzek, S.; Neubauer, T. Combining Measures of Signal Complexity and Machine Learning for Time Series Analyis: A Review. *Entropy* **2021**, *23*, 1672. [CrossRef] [PubMed]
7. Pech-Pacheco, J.; Cristobal, G.; Chamorro-Martinez, J.; Fernandez-Valdivia, J. Diatom autofocusing in brightfield microscopy: A comparative study. In Proceedings of the 15th International Conference on Pattern Recognition, ICPR-2000, Barcelona, Spain, 3–7 September 2000; Volume 3, pp. 314–317. [CrossRef]
8. Takens, F. Detecting strange attractors in turbulence. In *Dynamical Systems and Turbulence, Warwick 1980, Lecture Notes in Mathematics*; Rand, D., Young, L.S., Eds.; Springer: Berlin/Heidelberg, Germany, 1981; Volume 898, pp. 366–381.
9. Packard, N.H.; Crutchfield, J.P.; Farmer, J.D.; Shaw, R.S. Geometry from a Time Series. *Phys. Rev. Lett.* **1980**, *45*, 712–716. [CrossRef]
10. Fraser, A.M.; Swinney, H.L. Independent coordinates for strange attractors from mutual information. *Phys. Rev. A* **1986**, *33*, 1134–1140. [CrossRef] [PubMed]

11. Rhodes, C.; Morari, M. The false nearest neighbors algorithm: An overview. *Comput. Chem. Eng.* **1997**, *21*, S1149–S1154. [CrossRef]
12. Delorme, M.; Wiese, K.J. Extreme-value statistics of fractional Brownian motion bridges. *Phys. Rev. E* **2016**, *94*, 052105. [CrossRef] [PubMed]
13. Sottinen, T.; Yazigi, A. Generalized Gaussian bridges. *Stoch. Process. Appl.* **2014**, *124*, 3084–3105. [CrossRef]
14. Quarteroni, A.; Sacco, R.; Saleri, F. *Numerical Mathematics*, 2nd ed.; Springer: Berlin/Heidelberg, Germany, 2007; Volume 37. [CrossRef]
15. Hyndman, R.; Yang, Y. Time Series Data Library v0.1.0. 2018. Available online: pkg.yangzhuoranyang.com/tsdl (accessed on 1 July 2022).
16. Hochreiter, S.; Schmidhuber, J. Long Short-term Memory. *Neural Comput.* **1997**, *9*, 1735–1780. [CrossRef]
17. Domingos, S.d.O.; de Oliveira, J.F.; de Mattos Neto, P.S. An intelligent hybridization of ARIMA with machine learning models for time series forecasting. *Knowl.-Based Syst.* **2019**, *175*, 72–86.
18. Shah, V. A Comparative Study of Univariate Time-Series Methods for Sales Forecasting. Master's Thesis, University of Waterloo, Waterloo, ON, Canada, 2020.

Proceeding Paper

Dynamic Asymmetric Causality Tests with an Application †

Abdulnasser Hatemi-J

College of Business and Economics, UAE University, Al Ain P.O. Box 1551, United Arab Emirates;
ahatemi@uaeu.ac.ae
† Presented at the 8th International Conference on Time Series and Forecasting, Gran Canaria, Spain,
27–30 June 2022.

Abstract: Testing for causation—defined as the preceding impact of the past value(s) of one variable on the current value of another when all other pertinent information is accounted for—is increasingly utilized in empirical research using the time-series data in different scientific disciplines. A relatively recent extension of this approach has been allowing for potential asymmetric impacts, since this is harmonious with the way reality operates, in many cases. The current paper maintains that it is also important to account for the potential change in the parameters when asymmetric causation tests are conducted, as several reasons exist for changing the potential causal connection between the variables across time. Therefore, the current paper extends the static asymmetric causality tests by making them dynamic via the use of subsamples. An application is also provided consistent with measurable definitions of economic, or financial bad, as well as good, news and their potential causal interactions across time.

Keywords: dynamic causality; asymmetric causality; positive changes; negative changes; oil; stock market; the US

JEL Classification: C32; C51; D82; G15; E17

check for
updates

Citation: Hatemi-J, A. Dynamic Asymmetric Causality Tests with an Application. *Eng. Proc.* **2022**, *18*, 41. https://doi.org/10.3390/engproc 2022018041

Academic Editors: Ignacio Rojas, Hector Pomares, Olga Valenzuela, Fernando Rojas and Luis Javier Herrera

Published: 2 August 2022

Publisher's Note: MDPI stays neutral with regard to jurisdictional claims in published maps and institutional affiliations.

1. Introduction

From cradle to grave, one of the most prevalent and persistent questions in life is figuring out what is the cause and what is the effect when certain pertinent events are observed. This subject must have been one of the most inspirational and important issues since the dawn of humankind. Throughout history, many philosophers have devoted their pondering to causality as an abstraction. Yet there is no common definition of causality, and above all, there is no common or universally accepted approach for detecting or measuring causality. Since the pioneer notion of [1] and the seminal contribution of [2], testing for the predictability impact of one variable on another has increasingly gained popularity and practical usefulness in different fields when the variables are quantified across time. This approach is known as Granger causality in the literature, and it describes a situation in which the past values of one variable (i.e., the cause variable) are statistically significant in an autoregressive regression model of another variable (i.e., the effect variable) when all other relevant information is also accounted for. The null hypothesis is defined as zero restrictions imposed on the parameters of the cause variable in the autoregressive model when the dependent variable is the potential effect variable. If the null hypothesis is not accepted empirically, it is taken as empirical evidence for causality, according to the Wiener–Granger method (alternative designs exist, such as those detailed by [3,4]). There have been several extensions of this method, especially since the discovery of unit roots and stochastic trends, which is a common property of many time-series variables, that quantify economic or financial processes across time. Refs. [5–7] suggested testing for causality via an error correction model if the variables are integrated. Ref. [8] proposed a modified [9] test statistic in order to take into account the impact of unit roots when causality tests are conducted within the vector autoregressive (VAR) model by adding additional unrestricted lags. Ref. [10,11] suggested bootstrapping with leverage adjustments in order to generate accurate critical values for the modified Wald test, since the asymptotical values are not precise when the desirable statistical assumptions for a good model are not satisfied, according to the Monte Carlo simulations conducted by the authors. The bootstrap corrected tests appear to have better size and power properties compared to the asymptotic tests, especially in small sample sizes.

However, there are numerous reasons for the potential causal connection between the variables to have an asymmetric structure. It is commonly agreed to in the literature that markets with asymmetric information prevail (based on the seminal contributions of [12–14]). People frequently react more strongly to a negative change, in contrast to a comparable positive one (According to [15–18], among others, there is indeed an asymmetric behavior by the investors in the financial markets, since they have a tendency to respond more strongly to negative compared to positive news). There are also natural restrictions that can lead to the asymmetric causation phenomenon. For instance, there is a limit on the potential price decrease of any normal asset or commodity, since the price cannot drop below zero. However, there is no restriction on the amount of the potential price increase. In fact, if the price decreases by a given percentage point and then increases again by the same percentage point; it will not end up at the initial price level, but at a lower level. This is true even if the process occurs in the reverse order. There are also moral and/or legal limitations that can lead to an asymmetric behavior. For example, if a company manages to increase its profit by the P% at a given period, it is feasible and easy to expand the business by that percentage point. However, if the mentioned company experiences a loss by the P%, it is not that easy to implement an immediate contraction of the business operation by the P%. The contraction is usually less than the P%, and it can take a longer time to realize this contraction compared to the corresponding expansion. It is naturally easier for the company to hire people than to fire them. In the markets for many commodities, it can also be clearly observed that there is an inertia effect for price decreases compared to price increases. Among others, the fuel market can be mentioned. When the oil price increases, there seems to be an almost immediate increase in fuel prices, and by the same proportion, if not more. However, when the oil price decreases, there is a lag in the decrease in fuel prices, and the adjustment might not be fully implemented. This indicates that the fuel prices adjustments are asymmetric with regard to the oil price changes under the ceteris paribus condition. In order to account for this kind of potential asymmetric causation in the empirical research based on time-series data, ref. [19] suggests implementing asymmetric causality tests, which the author introduces. However, these asymmetric causality tests are static by nature.

The objective of the current paper is to extend these asymmetric causality tests to a dynamic context by allowing for the underlying causal parameters to vary across time, which can be achieved by using subsamples. There are several advantages for using this dynamic parameter approach. One of the advantages of the time-varying parameter approach is that it takes into account the well-known [20] critique, which is an essential issue from the policy-making point of view. Peoples' preferences can change across time, resulting in a change in their behavior, thereby changing the economic or financial process. There are ground-breaking technological innovations and progresses that happen with time. Major organizational restructuring can take place across time. Unexpected major events, such as the current COVID-19 pandemic, can occur. All these events can result in a change in the potential causal connection between the underlying variables in a model. Thus, a dynamic parameter model can be more informative, and it can better present the way things operate in reality. Moreover, from a correct model specification perspective, the dynamic parameter approach can be preferred to the constant parameter approach, as it is also more informative. Since the dynamic testing of the potential causation connection is more informative than the static approach, it can shed light on the extent of the pertinent phenomenon known, in the financial literature, as the correlation risk. According to [21], correlation risk is defined as the potential risk that the strength of the relationship between financial assets varies unfavorably across time. This issue can have crucial ramifications for investors, institutions, and the policy makers.

The rest of the paper is organized as follows. Section 2 introduces the methodology of dynamic asymmetric causality testing. Section 3 provides an application of the potential causal impact of oil prices on the world's largest stock market, accounting for rising and falling prices, using both the static and the dynamic asymmetric causality tests. Conclusions are offered in the final section.

2. Dynamic Asymmetric Causality Testing

The subsequent definitions are utilized in this paper.

Definition 1. *An n-dimensional stochastic process* $(x_t)_{t=1,\cdots,T}$ *measured across time is integrated of degree 1, signified as I(1), if it must be differenced once for becoming a stationary process. That is,* $x_t \sim\sim I(1)$ *if* $\Delta x_t \sim\sim I(0)$*, where the denotation* Δ *is the first difference operator.*

Definition 2. *Define* $(\varepsilon_t)_{t=1,\cdots,T}$ *as an n-dimensional stochastic process. Thus, during any time period* $t \in \{1,\cdots,T\}$*, the positive and negative shocks of this random variable* ε_t *(i.e.,* ε_t^+ *and* ε_t^-*) are identified as the following:*

$$\varepsilon_t^+ := max(\varepsilon_t, 0) := (max(\varepsilon_{1t}, 0), \cdots, max(\varepsilon_{nt}, 0)) \tag{1}$$

and

$$\varepsilon_t^- := min(\varepsilon_t, 0) := (min(\varepsilon_{1t}, 0), \cdots, min(\varepsilon_{nt}, 0)) \tag{2}$$

The definition of the positive and negative shocks was suggested by [22] for testing for hidden cointegration.

The implementation of the causality tests in the sense of the Wiener–Granger method is operational within the vector autoregressive (VAR) model of [23]. The asymmetric version of this test method is introduced by [19] (Ref. [24] extends the test to the frequency domain). Consider the following two I(1) variables with deterministic trend parts (For the simplicity of expression, we assume that $n = 2$. However, it is straightforward to generalize the results):

$$x_{1t} = a + bt + x_{1t-1} + \varepsilon_{1t}, \tag{3}$$

and

$$x_{2t} = c + dt + x_{2t-1} + \varepsilon_{2t}, \tag{4}$$

where a, b, c, and d are parametric constants and t is the deterministic trend term. The positive and negative partial sums of the two variables can be recursively defined as the following, based on the definitions of shocks presented in Equations (1) and (2):

$$x_{1t}^+ := \frac{at + \left[\frac{t(t+1)}{2}\right]b + x_{10}}{2} + \sum_{i=1}^{t} \varepsilon_{1i}^+ \tag{5}$$

$$x_{1t}^- := \frac{at + \left[\frac{t(t+1)}{2}\right]b + x_{10}}{2} + \sum_{i=1}^{t} \varepsilon_{1i}^- \tag{6}$$

$$x_{2t}^+ := \frac{ct + \left[\frac{t(t+1)}{2}\right]d + x_{20}}{2} + \sum_{i=1}^{t} \varepsilon_{2i}^+ \tag{7}$$

$$x_{2t}^- := \frac{ct + \left[\frac{t(t+1)}{2}\right]d + x_{20}}{2} + \sum_{i=1}^{t} \varepsilon_{2i}^- \tag{8}$$

where x_{10} and x_{20} are the initial values. Note that the required conditions of having $x_{1t} = x_{1t}^+ + x_{1t}^-$ and $x_{2t} = x_{2t}^+ + x_{2t}^-$ are fulfilled (For the proof of these results and for the transformation of I(2) and I(3) variables into the cumulative partial sums of negative and positive components see [25]). Interestingly, the values expressed in Equations (5)–(8) also have economic or financial implications in terms of measuring good or bad news that can affect the markets. It should be mentioned that the issue of whether to include the deterministic trends in the data generating process for a given variable is an empirical issue. In some cases, there might be the need for both a drift and a trend, and in other cases, it might be sufficient to include a drift without any trend. It is also possible to have no drift and no trend. For the selection of the deterministic trend components, the procedure suggested by [26] can be useful.

The asymmetric causality tests can be implemented via the vector autoregressive model of order p, as originally introduced by [22], i.e., the VAR(p). Let us consider testing for the potential causality between the positive components of these two variables. Then, the vector consisting of the dependent variables is defined as $x_t^+ = (x_{1t}^+, x_{2t}^+)$, and the following VAR($p$) can be estimated based on this vector:

$$x_t^+ = B_0^+ + B_1^+ x_{t-1}^+ + \cdots + B_p^+ x_{t-p}^+ + B_{p+1}^+ x_{t-p-1}^+ + v_t^+ \tag{9}$$

where B_0^+ is the 2×1 vector of intercepts, B_r^+ is a 2×2 matrix of parameters to be estimated for lag length r ($r = 1, \dots, p$), and v_t^+ is a 2×1 vector of the error terms. An important issue consideration before using the VAR(p) for drawing inference is to determine the optimal lag order p. This can be achieved, among other methods, by minimizing the information criterion suggested by [27], which is expressed as the following:

$$HJC = \ln\left(\left|\hat{\Pi}_p{}^+\right|\right) + p\left(\frac{n^2 \ln T + 2n^2 \ln(\ln T)}{2T}\right), p = 1, \dots, p_{\max}. \tag{10}$$

where $\left|\hat{\Pi}_p{}^+\right|$ is the determinant of the variance–covariance matrix of the error terms in the VAR model that is estimated based on the lag length p, ln is the natural logarithm, n is the number of time-series included in the VAR model, and T is the full sample size used for estimating the parameters in that model (The Monte Carlo simulations conducted by [28] demonstrate clearly that the information criterion expressed in equation (10) is successful in selecting the optimal lag order when the VAR model is used for forecasting purposes. In addition, the simulations show that this information criterion is robust to the ARCH effects and performs well when the variables in the VAR model are integrated. See also [29] for more information on this criterion). The lag order that results in the minimum value of the information criterion is to be selected as the optimal lag order. It is also important that the off-diagonal elements in the variance-covariance matrix are zero. Therefore, tests for multivariate autocorrelation need to be performed in order to verify this issue. The null hypothesis that the jth element of x_t^+ does not cause the kth element of x_t^+ can be tested via a [9] test statistic (It should be mentioned that the additional unrestricted lag has been added to the VAR model for taking into account the impact of one unit root, consistent with the results of [8]. Multivariate tests for autocorrelation also need to be implemented to make sure that the off-diagonal elements in the variance and covariance matrix are zero). The null hypothesis of non-causality can be formulated as the following:

$$H_0 : \text{The row } k, \text{ column } j \text{ element in } B_r^+ \text{ equals zero for } r = 1, \dots, p. \tag{11}$$

For a dense representation of the Wald test statistic, we need to make use of the following denotations (It should be pointed out that this formulation requires that the p initial values for each variable in the VAR model are accessible. For the particulars on this requirement, see [30]):

$X^+ := (x_1^+, \ldots, x_T^+)$ as a $(n \times T)$ matrix, $D^+ := \left(B_0^+, B_1^+, \ldots, B_{p+1}^+ \right)$ as a $(n \times (1 + n \times (p+1)))$ matrix, $Z_t^+ := \left[1, x_t^+, x_{t-1}^+, \ldots, x_{t-p}^+ \right]'$ as a $((1 + n \times (p+1)) \times 1)$ matrix, $Z^+ := (Z_0^+, \ldots, Z_{T-1}^+)$ as a $((1 + n \times ((p+1)+1)) \times T)$ matrix and $V^+ = (v_1^+, \ldots, v_T^+$ as a $(n \times T)$ matrix. Via these denotations, we can express the VAR model and the Wald test statistic compactly as the following:

$$X^+ = D^+ Z^+ + V^+ \tag{12}$$

$$Wald^+ = (C\beta^+)' \left[C \left((Z^{+\prime} Z^+)^{-1} \otimes \hat{\Pi}_u^+ \right) C' \right]^{-1} (C\beta^+) \tag{13}$$

The parameter matrix D^+ is estimated via the multivariate least squares as the following:

$$\hat{D}^+ = X^+ Z^{+\prime} (Z^+ Z^{+\prime})^{-1} \tag{14}$$

Note that $\beta^+ = vec(\hat{D}^+)$ and vec is the column-stacking operator. That is

$$\beta^+ = vec(\hat{D}^+) = \left((Z^+ Z^{+\prime})^{-1} \otimes I_n \right) vec(X^+) \tag{15}$$

The denotation $\otimes$ is the Kronecker product operator, and C is a $((p+1) \times n) \times (1 + n \times (p+1))$ indicator matrix that includes one and zero elements. The restricted parameters are defined by elements of ones, and the elements of zeros are used for defining the unrestricted parameters under the null hypothesis. I_n is an $(n \times n)$ identity matrix. $\hat{\Pi}_u^+$ represents the variance–covariance matrix of the unrestricted VAR model as expressed by Equation (12), which can be estimated as the following:

$$\hat{\Pi}_u^+ = \frac{\hat{V}_u^+{}' \hat{V}_u^+}{T - q} \tag{16}$$

Note that the constant q represents the number of parameters that are estimated in each equation of the VAR model. By using the presented denotations, the null hypothesis of no causation might also be formulated as the following expression:

$$H_0 : C\beta^+ = 0 \tag{17}$$

The Wald test statistic expressed in (13) that is used for testing the null hypothesis of non-causality, as defined in (11) based on the estimated VAR model in Equation (12), has the following distribution, asymptotically:

$$Wald^+ \xrightarrow{d} \chi_p^2 \tag{18}$$

This is the case if the assumption of normality is fulfilled. Thus, the Wald test statistic for testing for potential asymmetric causal impacts has a χ^2 distribution, with the number of degrees of freedom equal to the number of restrictions under the null hypothesis of non-causality, which is equal to p in this particular case. This result also holds for a corresponding VAR model for negative components, or any other combinations. For the proof, see Proposition 1 in [25].

However, if the assumption of the normal distribution of the underlying dataset is not fulfilled, the asymptotical critical values are not accurate, and bootstrap simulations need to be performed in order to obtain accurate critical values. If the variance is not constant, or if the ARCH effects prevail, then the bootstrap simulations need to be conducted with leverage adjustments. The size and power properties of the test statistics, based on the bootstrap simulation approach with leverage corrections, has been investigated by [10,11] via the Monte Carlo simulations. The simulation results provided by the previously mentioned authors show that the causality test statistic based on the leveraged bootstrapping exhibits correct size and higher power, compared to a causality test based on the asymptotic distributions, especially when the sample size is small or when the assumption of normal distribution and constant variance of the error terms are not fulfilled.

The bootstrap simulations can be conducted as the following. First, estimate the restricted model based on regression Equation (12). The restricted model imposes the restrictions under the null hypothesis of non-causality. Second, generate the bootstrap data, i.e., X^{+*}, via the estimated parameters from the regression, the original data, and the bootstrapped residuals. This means generating $X^{+*} = \hat{D}^+ Z^+ + V^{+*}$. Note that the bootstrapped residuals (i.e., V^{+*}) are created by T random draws, with replacement from the modified residuals of the regression. Each of these random draws, with replacement, has the same likelihood, which is equal a probability of $1/T$. The bootstrapped residuals need to be mean-adjusted in order to ensure that the residuals have zero expected value in each bootstrap sample. This is accomplished via subtracting the mean value of the bootstrap sample from each residual in that sample. Note that the residuals need to be adjusted by leverages in order to make sure that the variance is constant in each bootstrap sample. Next, repeat the bootstrap simulations 10,000 times and estimate the Wald test each time (For more information on the leverage adjustments in univariate cases, see Davison and [31], and in multivariate cases, see [10]). Use these test values in order to generate the bootstrap distribution of the test. The critical value at the α significance level via bootstrapping (denoted by c^*_α) can be acquired by taking the (α)th upper quantile of the distribution of the Wald test that is generated via the bootstrapping. The final step is to estimate the Wald test value based on the original data and compare it to the bootstrap critical value at the α level of significance. The null hypothesis of non-causation is rejected at the α significance level if the estimated Wald test value is higher than the c^*_α (i.e., the bootstrap critical value at α level).

In order to account for the possibility of the potential change in the asymmetric causal connection between the variables, these tests can be conducted using subsamples. A crucial issue within this context is to determine the minimum subsample size that is required for testing for the dynamic asymmetric causality. The following formula, developed by [32], can be used for determining the smallest subsample size (S):

$$S = \left[T \left(0.01 + \frac{1.8}{\sqrt{T}} \right) \right] \tag{19}$$

where T is the original full sample size. Note that S needs to be rounded up.

Two different approaches regarding the subsamples can be implemented for this purpose. The first one is the fixed rolling window approach, which is based on repeated estimation of the model, with a subsample size of S each time, and the window is moved forward by one observation each time. That is, we need to estimate the time varying causality for the following subsamples, where each number represents a point in time:

$$1, 2, 3, \cdots, S$$
$$2, 3, 4, \cdots, (S+1)$$
$$3, 4, 5, \cdots, (S+1), (S+2)$$
$$4, 5, 6, \cdots, (S+1), (S+2), (S+3)$$
$$\vdots$$
$$(T-S+1), (T-S+2), (T-S+3), \cdots, (T-S+S)$$

This means that the first subsample consists of the range covering the first observation to the S observation. The next subsample removes the first observation from S and adds the one after S. The process is continued until the full range is covered. For example, assume that $T = 10$ and then we have $S = 6$ based on Equation (19) when S is rounded up (Obviously, the sample size normally needs to be bigger than 10 observations in the empirical analysis. Here, a very small sample size is assumed for the sake of the simplicity of the expression).

Thus, we have the following subsamples (where each number represents the corresponding time):

$$1, 2, 3, \cdots, S = 1, 2, 3, 4, 5, 6$$
$$2, 3, 4, \cdots, (S+1) = 2, 3, 4, 5, 6, 7$$
$$3, 4, 5, \cdots, (S+1), (S+2) = 3, 4, 5, 6, 7, 8$$
$$4, 5, 6, \cdots, (S+1), (S+2), (S+3) = 4, 5, 6, 7, 8, 9$$
$$(T-S+1), (T-S+2), (T-S+3), \cdots, (T-S+S) = (10-6+1), (10-6+2),$$
$$(10-6+3), (10-6+4), (10-6+5), (10-6+6) = 5, 6, 7, 8, 9, 10$$

The graphical illustration of this approach for the current example is depicted in Figure 1.

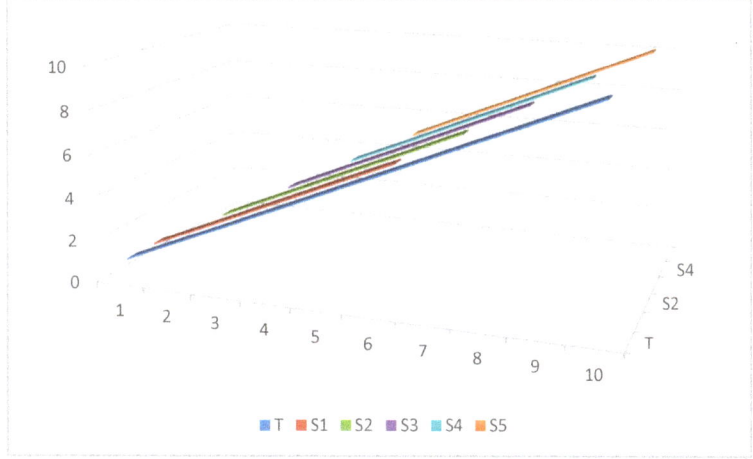

Figure 1. The illustration of the subsamples compared to the entire sample based on the fixed rolling window approach. Notes: T represents the full sample size, and S_i represents subsample i (for $i = 1$, ..., 5.), in this case.

The second method for determining multiple subsamples is to start with S and recursively add an observation to S each time for obtaining the next subsample without removing any observation from the beginning. In this approach, the sample size increases by one observation in each subsample until it covers the full range. That is, the size of the first subsample is equal to S and the size of the last one is equal to T. This is a recursive rolling window approach that is anchored at the start. The graphical drawing of this method for the mentioned example is shown in Figure 2.

The next step in order to implement the dynamic asymmetric causality tests is to calculate the Wald test statistic for each subsample and produce its bootstrap critical value at a given significance level. Then, the following ratio can be calculated for each subsample:

$$TVpCV = \frac{Wald\ Test\ Value\ Based\ on\ the\ Given\ Subsample}{Bootstrap\ Critical\ Value\ at\ the\ Given\ Significance\ Level\ and\ Subsample} \quad (20)$$

where $TVpCV$ signifies the test value per the critical value at a given significance level using a particular subsample. If this ratio is higher than one, it implies that the null hypothesis of no causality is rejected at the given significance level for that subsample. The 5% and the 10% significance levels can be considered. A graphical illustration of (20) for different subsamples can be informative to the investigator in order to detect the potential change of the asymmetric causal connection between the underlying variables in the model.

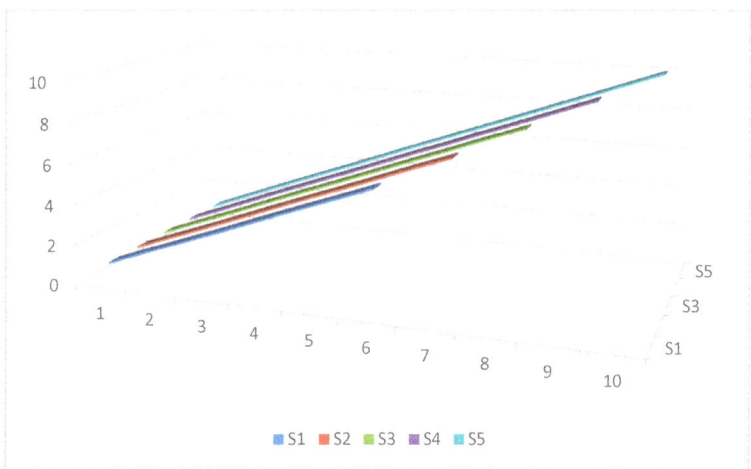

Figure 2. The graphical presentation of the subsamples based on the recursive rolling window approach. Notes: S_i represents subsample i (for $i = 1, \ldots, 5.$), in this example. Note that the $S_5 = T$, in this case.

An alternative method for estimating and testing the time-varying asymmetric causality tests is to make use of the [33] filter within a multivariate setting. However, this method might not be operational if the dimension of the model is rather high and/or the lag order is large.

3. An Application

An application is provided for detecting the change in the potential causal impact of oil prices and the world's largest financial market. Two indexes are used for this purpose. The first one is the total share prices index for all shares for the US. The second index is the global price of Brent Crude in USD per barrel. The frequency of the data is yearly, and it covers the period of 1990–2020. The source of the data is the FRED database, which is provided by the Federal Reserve Bank of St. Louis. Let us denote the stock price index by S and the oil price index by O. The aim of this application is to investigate whether the potential impact of rising or falling oil prices on the performance of the world's largest stock market is time dependent or not. Interestingly, the US market is not only the largest market and its financial market is the most valuable in the word, but the US is also the biggest oil producer in the world. These combinations might make the empirical results of this pragmatic application more useful and general.

The variables are expressed in the natural logarithm format. The unit root test results of the conducted Phillips–Perron test confirm that each variable is integrated at the first order (The unit root test results are not reported, but they are available on request). First, the following linear regression is estimated via the OLS technique for the stock price index (i.e., $x_{1t} = lnS_t$):

$$(lnS_t - lnS_{t-1}) = a + bt + \varepsilon_{1t}, \tag{21}$$

Next, the residuals of the above regression are estimated. That is

$$\hat{\varepsilon}_{1t} = (lnS_t - lnS_{t-1}) - \hat{a} - \hat{b}t.$$

Note that the circumflex implies the estimated value. The positive and negative shocks are measured as the following, based on the definitions presented in Equations (1) and (2):

$$\hat{\varepsilon}_{1t}^{+} := max(\hat{\varepsilon}_{1t}, 0) \qquad \text{and} \qquad \hat{\varepsilon}_{1t}^{-} := min(\hat{\varepsilon}_{1t}, 0) \tag{22}$$

The positive and negative partial sums for this variable are defined as the following, based on the results presented in Equations (5) and (6):

$$(lnS_t)^{+} := \frac{\hat{a}t + \left[\frac{t(t+1)}{2}\right]\hat{b} + (lnS_0)}{2} + \sum_{i=1}^{t} \hat{\varepsilon}_{1i}^{+} \tag{23}$$

$$(lnS_t)^{-} := \frac{\hat{a}t + \left[\frac{t(t+1)}{2}\right]\hat{b} + (lnS_0)}{2} + \sum_{i=1}^{t} \hat{\varepsilon}_{1i}^{-} \tag{24}$$

where lnS_0 signifies the initial value of the stock price index in the logarithmic format, which is assumed to be zero, in this case. Note that the equivalency condition $lnS_t = (lnS_t)^{+} + (lnS_t)^{-}$ is fulfilled. It should be mentioned that the value expressed by Equation (22) represents the good news with regard to the stock market, while the value expressed by Equation (23) signifies the bad news pertaining to the same market. The oil price index can also be transformed into cumulative partial sums of positive and negative components in an analogous way. Note that a drift and a trend were included in the equation of each variable, since it seems to be needed, based on the graphs presented in Figure 3.

The dataset can be transformed by a number of user-friendly statistical software components. Prior to implementing causality tests, diagnostic tests were also implemented. The results of these tests are presented in Table A1, which indicate that the assumption of normality is not fulfilled, and the conditional variance is not constant, in most cases. Thus, making use of the bootstrap simulations with leverage adjustments is necessary in order to produce reliable critical values. This is particularly the case for subsamples, since the degrees of freedom are lower.

Both symmetric and the asymmetric causality tests are implemented in a dynamic setting using the statistical software component created by [34] in Gauss. The results for the symmetric causality tests are presented in Tables A2 and A3, based on the 5% and the 10% significance levels. Based on these results, it can be inferred that the oil price does not cause the results of the stock market price index, not even at the 10% significance level.

The results are also robust regarding the choice of the subsamples because the same results are obtained with all subsamples. An implication of this empirical finding is that the market is informationally efficient in the semi-strong form with regard to oil prices, as defined by [35]. However, when the tests for dynamic asymmetric causality are implemented, the results show that an oil price decrease does not cause a decrease in the stock market price index, and these results are the same across subsamples, even at the 10% significance level (see Tables A4–A6). Conversely, the null hypothesis that an oil price increase does not cause an increase in the stock market price index is rejected during four subsamples.

It is interesting that by using only three fewer observations, the null hypothesis of non-causality would be rejected at the 10% significance level, in contrast to the result for the entire sample period, which does not reject the underlying null hypothesis (see Figure 4 and Table A7).

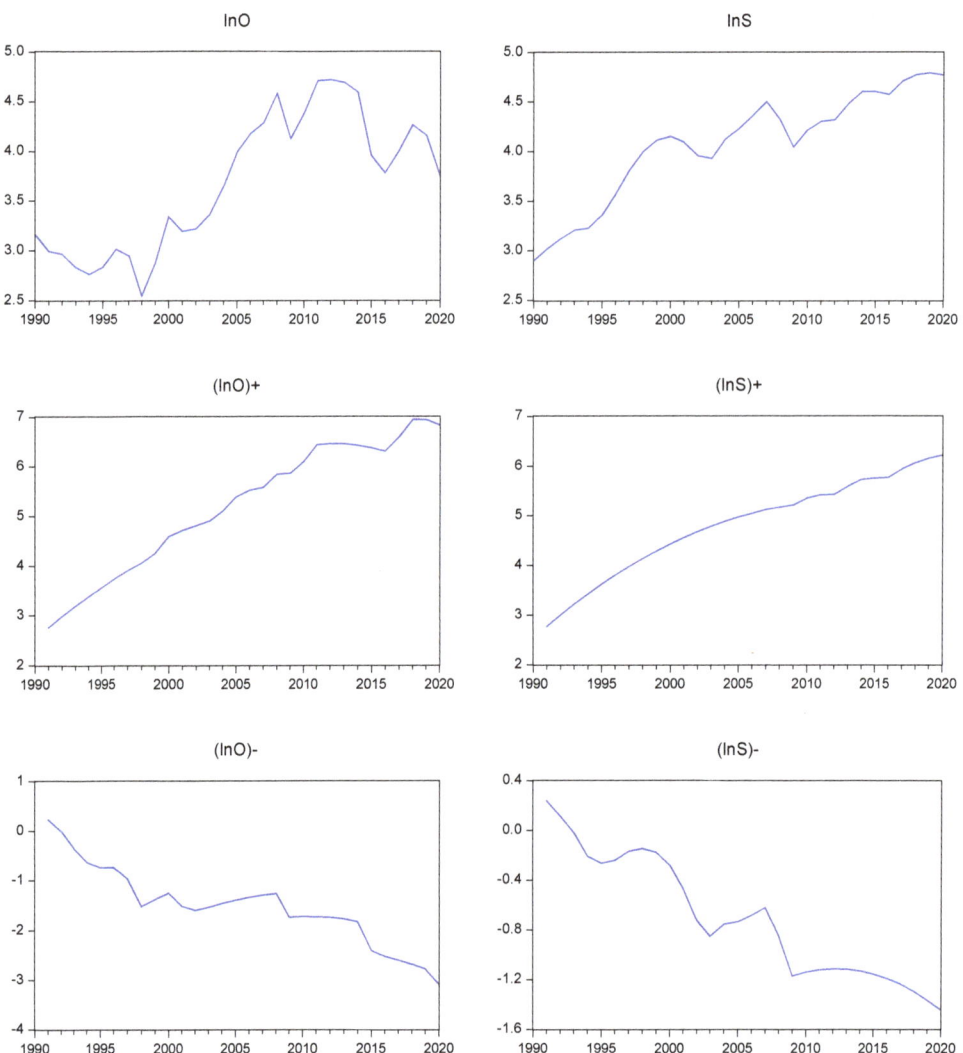

Figure 3. The time plot of the variables, along with the cumulative partial components for positive and negative parts. Notes: The notation $\ln O_t$ represents the oil price index, and $\ln S_t$ represents the US stock market price index for all shares. The corresponding sign indicates the positive and negative components.

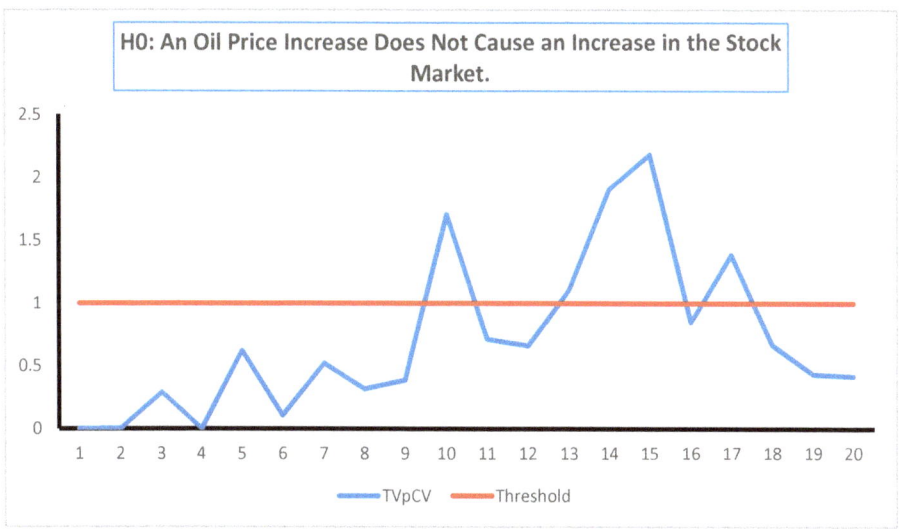

Figure 4. The time plot of the causality test results for the positive components at the 10% significance level.

4. Conclusions

Tests for causality in the Wiener–Granger method are regularly used in empirical research regarding the time series data in different scientific disciplines. A popular extension of this approach is the asymmetric casualty testing approach, as developed by Hatemi-J (2012). However, this approach is static by nature. A pertinent issue within this context is whether the potential asymmetric causal impacts between the underlying variables in a model are steady or not over the selected time span. In order to throw light on this issue, the current paper suggests implementing asymmetric causality tests across time to see whether the potential asymmetric causal impact is time dependent or not. This can be achieved by using subsamples via two different approaches.

An application is provided in order to investigate the potential causal connection of oil prices with the stock prices of the world's largest financial market within a time-varying setting. The results of the dynamic symmetric causality tests show that the oil prices do not cause the level of the market price index, regardless of the subsample size. However, when the dynamic asymmetric causality tests are implemented, the results show that positive oil price changes cause a positive price change in the stock market using certain subsamples. In fact, if only three fewer observations are used compared to the full sample size, the results show that there is causality from the oil price increase to the stock market price increase. Conversely, if the full sample size is used (i.e., only three more degrees of freedom), no causality is found. This shows that it can indeed be important to make use of the dynamic causality tests in order to see whether or not the causality result is robust across time.

It should be pointed out that an alternative method for estimating and testing the time-varying asymmetric causality tests is to make use of the [33] filter within a multivariate setting. However, this method might not be operational if the dimension of the VAR model is rather high and/or the lag order is large.

The time-varying asymmetric causality tests results can shed light on whether the causal connection between the variables of interest is general or time dependent. This has important practical implications. If the causal connection changes across time, then the decision or policy based on this causal impact needs to be time dependent as well. This is the case because a static strategy is likely to be inefficient within a dynamic environment.

At the end, the following English proverb that has been quoted by Wiener (1956) [1] says it all.

"For want of a nail, the shoe was lost;
For want of a shoe, the horse was lost;
For want of a horse, the rider was lost;
For want of a rider, the battle was lost;
For want of a battle, the kingdom was lost!"

Funding: This research received no external funding.

Institutional Review Board Statement: Not applicable.

Informed Consent Statement: Not applicable.

Data Availability Statement: FRED DATA BASE, https://fred.stlouisfed.org (accessed on 26 June 2021).

Acknowledgments: This paper was presented at the 8th International Conference on Time Series and Forecasting (ITISE 2022), Spain. The author would like to thank the participants for their comments. The usual disclaimer applies, nevertheless.

Conflicts of Interest: The author declares no conflict of interest.

Appendix A

Table A1. Test results for multivariate normality and multivariate ARCH in the VAR model.

Variables in the Model	The p-Values of the Multivariate Normality Tests	The p-Values of the Multivariate ARCH Tests
$[\ln S_t,\ \ln O_t]$	0.0814	0.3743
$\left[(\ln S_t)^+,\ (\ln O_t)^+\right]$	0.5555	0.0028
$\left[(\ln S_t)^-,\ (\ln O_t)^-\right]$	0.0087	0.0150

Notes: (1) $\ln O_t$ signifies the oil price index and $\ln S_t$ indicates the US stock price index for all shares. The vector $\left[(\ln S_t)^+,\ (\ln O_t)^+\right]$ denotes the cumulative partial sum of the positive changes, and the vector $\left[(\ln S_t)^-,\ (\ln O_t)^-\right]$ indicates the cumulative partial sum of the negative changes. (2) The multivariate test of [36] was implemented for testing the null hypothesis of multivariate normality in the residuals in each VAR model. (3) The multivariate test of [37] was conducted for testing the null hypothesis of no multivariate ARCH (1).

Table A2. Dynamic symmetric causality test results at the 5% significance level. (H$_0$: The oil price does not cause the stock market price index).

SSP	Test Value	10% Bootstrap CV	TVpCV
1	1.788	572.528	0
2	1.431	52.787	0.034
3	0.832	20.977	0.068
4	0.863	13.312	0.062
5	0.112	10.484	0.082
6	0.317	4.592	0.024
7	0.365	5.385	0.059
8	0.429	5.135	0.071
9	0.239	4.678	0.092

Table A2. *Cont.*

SSP	Test Value	10% Bootstrap CV	TVpCV
10	0.525	4.502	0.053
11	0.5	4.76	0.11
12	0.538	4.054	0.123
13	0.642	4.561	0.118
14	0.757	4.606	0.139
15	0.591	4.859	0.156
16	0.281	4.211	0.14
17	0.623	3.68	0.076
18	0.635	4.571	0.136
19	0.638	4.252	0.149
20	0.627	4.403	0.145
21	0.627	4.129	0.152

DENOTATIONS: SSP: The subsample period. CV: the critical value; TVpCV: the test value per the critical value; TVpCV = (test value)/(bootstrap critical value at the given significance level). If the value of TVpCV > 1, it implies that the null hypothesis of no causality is rejected at the given significance level.

Table A3. Dynamic symmetric causality test results at the 10% significance level. (H_0: The oil price does not cause the stock market price index).

SSP	Test Value	10% Bootstrap CV	TVpCV
1	0.187	139.42	0.001
2	1.788	22.105	0.081
3	1.431	10.186	0.14
4	0.832	8.851	0.094
5	0.863	7.811	0.11
6	0.112	2.957	0.038
7	0.317	3.574	0.089
8	0.365	3.231	0.113
9	0.429	3.188	0.135
10	0.239	3.043	0.079
11	0.525	3.011	0.174
12	0.5	2.876	0.174
13	0.538	3.083	0.174
14	0.642	2.95	0.218
15	0.757	3.218	0.235
16	0.591	2.835	0.209
17	0.281	2.623	0.107
18	0.623	3.04	0.205
19	0.635	2.894	0.219
20	0.638	2.981	0.214
21	0.627	3.05	0.206

DENOTATIONS: SSP: the subsample period; CV: the critical value; TVpCV: the test value per the critical value; TVpCV = (test value)/(bootstrap critical value at the given significance level). If the value of TVpCV > 1, it implies that the null hypothesis of no causality is rejected at the given significance level.

Table A4. Dynamic asymmetric causality test results at the 10% significance level. (H$_0$: An oil price increase does not cause an increase in the stock market price index).

SSP	Test Value	10% Bootstrap CV	TVpCV
1	0	0.104	0
2	0	0	0.001
3	0.003	0.01	0.287
4	0	10.351	0
5	5.292	8.517	0.621
6	0.838	7.86	0.107
7	2.89	5.562	0.52
8	1.052	3.335	0.315
9	1.124	2.905	0.387
10	10.014	5.873	1.705
11	2.309	3.245	0.712
12	3.688	5.594	0.659
13	6.353	5.749	1.105
14	9.888	5.188	1.906
15	11.778	5.392	2.184
16	2.607	3.074	0.848
17	7.435	5.378	1.382
18	2.136	3.2	0.667
19	1.279	2.965	0.432
20	1.288	3.085	0.417

DENOTATIONS: SSP: the subsample period; CV: the critical value; TVpCV: the test value per the critical value; TVpCV = (test value)/(bootstrap critical value at the given significance level). If the value of TVpCV > 1, it implies that the null hypothesis of no causality is rejected at the given significance level.

Table A5. Dynamic asymmetric causality test results at the 5% significance level. (H$_0$: An oil price decrease does not cause a decrease in the stock market price index).

SSP	Test Value	10% Bootstrap CV	TVpCV
1	40.802	415.432	0.098
2	1.021	34.228	0.030
3	1.001	19.468	0.051
4	1.245	14.706	0.085
5	0.44	11.328	0.039
6	0.525	9.4	0.056
7	0.616	10.372	0.059
8	0.036	5.526	0.007
9	0	5.221	0
10	0.353	4.948	0.071
11	0.362	4.86	0.075
12	0.373	4.692	0.080
13	0.382	4.387	0.087
14	0.387	4.717	0.082

Table A5. *Cont.*

SSP	Test Value	10% Bootstrap CV	TVpCV
15	0.372	4.664	0.080
16	0.081	4.374	0.019
17	0.085	4.338	0.020
18	0.087	5.029	0.017
19	0.084	4.757	0.018
20	0.078	4.499	0.017

DENOTATIONS: SSP: the subsample period; CV: the critical value; TVpCV: the test value per the critical value; TVpCV = (test value)/(bootstrap critical value at the given significance level). If the value of TVpCV > 1, it implies that the null hypothesis of no causality is rejected at the given significance level.

Table A6. Dynamic asymmetric causality test results at the 10% significance level. (H_0: An oil price decrease does not cause a decrease in the stock market price index).

SSP	Test Value	10% Bootstrap CV	TVpCV
1	40.802	93.964	0.434
2	1.021	19.269	0.053
3	1.001	10.783	0.093
4	1.245	9.204	0.135
5	0.44	7.935	0.055
6	0.525	6.316	0.083
7	0.616	6.836	0.09
8	0.036	3.601	0.01
9	0	3.339	0
10	0.353	3.275	0.108
11	0.362	3.048	0.119
12	0.373	3.248	0.115
13	0.382	3.076	0.124
14	0.387	3.199	0.121
15	0.372	2.938	0.127
16	0.081	2.862	0.028
17	0.085	2.784	0.031
18	0.087	3.205	0.027
19	0.084	2.884	0.029
20	0.078	3.066	0.025

DENOTATIONS: SSP: the subsample period; CV: the critical value; TVpCV: the test value per the critical value; TVpCV = (test value)/(bootstrap critical value at the given significance level). If the value of TVpCV > 1, it implies that the null hypothesis of no causality is rejected at the given significance level.

Table A7. Dynamic asymmetric causality test results at the 5% significance level. (H$_0$: An oil price increase does not cause an increase in the stock market price index.).

SSP	Test Value	5% Bootstrap CV	TVpCV
1	0	0.157	0
2	0	0	0
3	0.003	0.039	0.072
4	0	16.548	0
5	5.292	12.61	0.42
6	0.838	11.836	0.071
7	2.89	8.299	0.348
8	1.052	5.009	0.21
9	1.124	4.334	0.259
10	10.014	8.446	1.186
11	2.309	4.543	0.508
12	3.688	7.523	0.49
13	6.353	7.967	0.797
14	9.888	7.387	1.339
15	11.778	7.529	1.564
16	2.607	5.282	0.494
17	7.435	7.514	0.989
18	2.136	4.334	0.493
19	1.279	4.311	0.297
20	1.288	4.536	0.284

DENOTATIONS: SSP: the subsample period; CV: the critical value; TVpCV: the test value per the critical value; TVpCV (test value)/(bootstrap critical value at the given significance level). If the value of TVpCV > 1, it implies that the null hypothesis of no causality is rejected at the given significance level.

References

1. Wiener, N. The Theory of Prediction. In *Modern Mathematics for Engineers*; Beckenbach, E.F., Ed.; McGraw-Hill: New York, NY, USA, 1956; Volume 1.
2. Granger, C.W. Investigating Causal Relations by Econometric Models and Cross-spectral methods. *Econometrica* **1969**, *37*, 424–439. [CrossRef]
3. Sims, C.A. Money, Income and Causality. *Am. Econ. Rev.* **1972**, *62*, 540–552.
4. Geweke, J. Measurement of Linear Dependence and Feedback between Multiple Time Series. *J. Am. Stat. Assoc.* **1982**, *77*, 304–324. [CrossRef]
5. Granger, C.W. Developments in the Study of Cointegrated Economic Variables. *Oxf. Bull. Econ. Stat.* **1986**, *48*, 213–228. [CrossRef]
6. Granger, C.W. Some Recent Development in a Concept of Causality. *J. Econom.* **1988**, *39*, 199–211. [CrossRef]
7. Engle, R.F.; Granger, C.W. Co-integration and error correction: Representation, estimation, and testing. *Econometrica* **1987**, *55*, 251–276. [CrossRef]
8. Toda, H.Y.; Yamamoto, T. Statistical Inference in Vector Autoregressions with Possibly Integrated Processes. *J. Econom.* **1995**, *66*, 225–250. [CrossRef]
9. Wald, A. Contributions to the Theory of Statistical Estimation and Testing Hypotheses. *Ann. Math. Stat.* **1939**, *10*, 299–326. [CrossRef]
10. Hacker, S.; Hatemi-J, A. Tests for Causality between Integrated Variables using Asymptotic and Bootstrap Distributions: Theory and Application. *Appl. Econ.* **2006**, *38*, 1489–1500. [CrossRef]
11. Hacker, S.; Hatemi-J, A. A Bootstrap Test for Causality with Endogenous Lag Length Choice: Theory and Application in Finance. *J. Econ. Stud.* **2012**, *39*, 144–160. [CrossRef]
12. Akerlof, G. The Market for Lemons: Quality Uncertainty and the Market Mechanism. *Q. J. Econ.* **1970**, *84*, 488–500. [CrossRef]
13. Spence, M. Job Market Signalling. *Q. J. Econ.* **1973**, *87*, 355–374. [CrossRef]
14. Stiglitz, J. Incentives and Risk Sharing in Sharecropping. *Rev. Econ. Stud.* **1974**, *41*, 219–255. [CrossRef]
15. Longin, F.; Solnik, B. Extreme correlation of international equity markets. *J. Financ.* **2001**, *56*, 649–676. [CrossRef]

16. Ang, A.; Chen, J. Asymmetric correlations of equity portfolios. *J. Financ. Econ.* **2002**, *63*, 443–494. [CrossRef]
17. Hong, Y.; Zhou, G. Asymmetries in stock returns: Statistical test and economic evaluation. *Rev. Financ. Stud.* **2008**, *20*, 1547–1581. [CrossRef]
18. Alvarez-Ramirez, J.; Rodriguez, E.; Echeverria, J.C. A DFA approach for assessing asymmetric correlations. *Phys. A Stat. Mech. Its Appl.* **2009**, *388*, 2263–2270. [CrossRef]
19. Hatemi-J, A. Asymmetric Causality Tests with an Application. *Empir. Econ.* **2012**, *43*, 447–456. [CrossRef]
20. Lucas, R.E. Econometric Policy Evaluation: A Critique. In *The Phillips Curve and Labor Markets. Carnegie-Rochester Conference Series on Public Policy*; Brunner, K., Meltzer, A., Eds.; Elsevier: New York, NY, USA, 1976; Volume 1, pp. 19–46.
21. Meissner, G. *Correlation Risk Modelling and Management*; Wiley Financial Series; Wiley: Hoboken, NJ, USA, 2014.
22. Granger, C.W.; Yoon, G. *Hidden Cointegration*; Department of Economics Working Paper; University of California: San Diego, CA, USA, 2002.
23. Sims, C.A. Macroeconomics and Reality. *Econometrica* **1980**, *48*, 1–48. [CrossRef]
24. Bahmani-Oskooee, M.; Chang, T.; Ranjbarc, O. Asymmetric causality using frequency domain and time-frequency domain (wavelet) approaches. *Econ. Model.* **2016**, *56*, 66–78. [CrossRef]
25. Hatemi-J, A.; El-Khatib, Y. An Extension of the Asymmetric Causality Tests for Dealing with Deterministic Trend Components. *Appl. Econ.* **2016**, *48*, 4033–4041. [CrossRef]
26. Hacker, S.; Hatemi-J, A. *The Properties of Procedures Dealing with Uncertainty about Intercept and Deterministic Trend in Unit Root Testing*; Working Paper Series in Economics and Institutions of Innovation 214; Royal Institute of Technology, CESIS—Centre of Excellence for Science and Innovation Studies: Stockholm, Sweden, 2010.
27. Hatemi-J, A. A new method to choose optimal lag order in stable and unstable VAR models. *Appl. Econ. Lett.* **2003**, *10*, 135–137. [CrossRef]
28. Hatemi-J, A. Forecasting properties of a new method to choose optimal lag order instable and unstable VAR models. *Appl. Econ. Lett.* **2008**, *15*, 239–243. [CrossRef]
29. Mustafa, A.; Hatemi-J, A. A VBA Module Simulation for Finding Optimal Lag Order in Time Series Models and Its Use on Teaching Financial Data Computation. *Appl. Comput. Inform.* **2022**, *18*, 208–220. [CrossRef]
30. Lutkepohl, H. *New Introduction to Multiple Time Series Analysis*; Springer: Berlin/Heidelberg, Germany, 2005.
31. Davison, A.C.; Hinkley, D.V. *Bootstrap Methods and Their Application*; Cambridge University Press: Cambridge, UK, 1999.
32. Phillips, P.C.; Shi, S.; Yu, J. Testing for multiple bubbles: Historical episodes of exuberance and collapse in the S&P 500. *Int. Econ. Rev.* **2015**, *56*, 1043–1078.
33. Kalman, R.E. A New Approach to Linear Filtering and Prediction Problems. *J. Basic Eng.* **1960**, *82*, 35–45. [CrossRef]
34. Hatemi-J, A.; Mustafa, A. DASCT01: Gauss Module for estimating Dynamic Asymmetric and Symmetric Causality Tests, Statistical Software Components D00001, Boston College Department of Economics. 2021. Available online: https://ideas.repec.org/c/boc/bocode/d00001.html (accessed on 11 May 2021).
35. Fama, E.F. Efficient Capital Markets: A Review of Theory and Empirical Work. *J. Financ.* **1970**, *25*, 383–417. [CrossRef]
36. Doornik, J.A.; Hansen, H. An omnibus test for univariate and multivariate normality. *Oxf. Bull. Econ. Stat.* **2008**, *70*, 927–939. [CrossRef]
37. Hacker, S.; Hatemi-J, A. A multivariate test for ARCH effects. *Appl. Econ. Lett.* **2005**, *12*, 411–417. [CrossRef]

*engineering
proceedings*

MDPI

Proceeding Paper

Coarse Grain Spectral Analysis for the Low-Amplitude Signature of Multiperiodic Stellar Pulsators [†]

Sebastià Barceló Forteza [1,*], Javier Pascual-Granado [2], Juan Carlos Suárez [1], Antonio García Hernández [1] and Mariel Lares-Martiz [2]

[1]   Department of Theoretical Physics and Cosmology, University of Granada (UGR), 18071 Granada, Spain
[2]   Instituto de Astrofísica de Andalucía (CSIC), Glorieta de la Astronomía s/n, 18008 Granada, Spain
[*]   Correspondence: sbarceloforteza@ugr.es
[†]   Presented at the 8th International Conference on Time Series and Forecasting, Gran Canaria, Spain, 27–30 June 2022.

Abstract: Coarse Grain Spectral Analysis (CGSA) can explain the possible multiscaling nature of the thousands of low-amplitude peaks observed in the power spectra of some pulsating stars. Space-based observations allowed for the scientific community to find this kind of structure thanks to their long-duration, high-photometric precision and duty cycle compared to observations from the ground. Although these time series are far from perfect (outliers, trends, gaps, etc.), we used our own data preprocessing method, known as the 2K+1 stage interpolation method, to improve the background noise up to a factor 14, avoiding spurious effects. We applied both techniques, the 2K+1 stage method and the CGSA analysis, to shed some light on a real problem regarding stellar seismology: finding the physical nature of the low-amplitude signature for multiperiodic stellar pulsators.

Keywords: time series analysis; data preprocessing methods; spectrum analysis; multiscaling; applications in real problem (stellar seismology)

Citation: Barceló Forteza, S.; Pascual-Granado, J.; Suárez, J.C.; García Hernández, A.; Lares-Martiz, M. Coarse Grain Spectral Analysis for the Low-Amplitude Signature of Multiperiodic Stellar Pulsators. *Eng. Proc.* **2022**, *18*, 42. https://doi.org/10.3390/engproc2022018042

Academic Editors: Ignacio Rojas, Hector Pomares, Olga Valenzuela, Fernando Rojas and Luis Javier Herrera

Published: 22 August 2022

Publisher's Note: MDPI stays neutral with regard to jurisdictional claims in published maps and institutional affiliations.

1. Introduction: Harmonic or Fractal Time Series?

The observed flux in a classical multiperiodic pulsating star time series can be considered as the contribution of several harmonic terms i,

$$F \approx \sum_i A_i \sin\left(2\pi\nu_i t + \phi_i\right) + N \tag{1}$$

characterized by their frequency ν_i, amplitude A_i, and phase ϕ_i; and noise (N). Once space-based telescopes allowed for long-duration, high-precision and duty-cycle time series to be obtained, the number of detected low-amplitude harmonics explosively increased [1]. The debate of their nature not only includes a physical origin but also a cascade error due to a flawed analysis [2]. One of these cases may be the presence of a self-affine signal, $y(t)$,

$$F \approx \sum_i A_i \sin\left(2\pi\nu_i t + \phi_i\right) + \lambda^H y(\lambda t) \tag{2}$$

where λ is the scale factor, and H is the so-called Hausdorff exponent, characterizing long-term correlations and the type of self-affinity in a time series. This term has to be taken as a statistical meaning, so that the scaling relationship holds when one performs appropriate measures on mean values over pairs of points at the same distance or over equal-length subseries or windows. It also includes white noise.

Using the Coarse Grain Spectral Analysis (CGSA), we can separate the harmonic from the fractal contribution and calculate their percentage on the time series [3]. Nevertheless, a constant cadence is required, without gaps, which cannot be achieved in real, raw observations.

2. Methodology: Fractal Analysis of a Gaped Time Series

To study their power spectra, we subtracted the pulsations with an improved method based on iterative sine wave fitting [4] called the 2K+1 stage method [5,6]. We used the subtracted signal,

$$S_i \equiv \frac{rms_i - rms_{i+1}}{rms_0}, \tag{3}$$

where rms_{i+1} is the root mean square of the residuals to stop the iterative process and finish each stage [5]. This alarm avoids a cascade error since its value should always be positive. The first 2K interpolation stages filled the gaps with the information subtracted for the previous stage, but started the frequency analysis from the beginning, avoiding spurious peaks due to minimum differences (see Figure 1). The last stage considers all datapoints for the frequency analysis. Three stages allow an improvement up to a factor 14 of the background noise for real, high-duty-cycle light curves (≈ 0.9) [7]. More stages are needed for lower cases. Figure 1 shows the improvement in the detection of simulated time series with ≈ 1400 typical oscillations with different expected duty cycles.

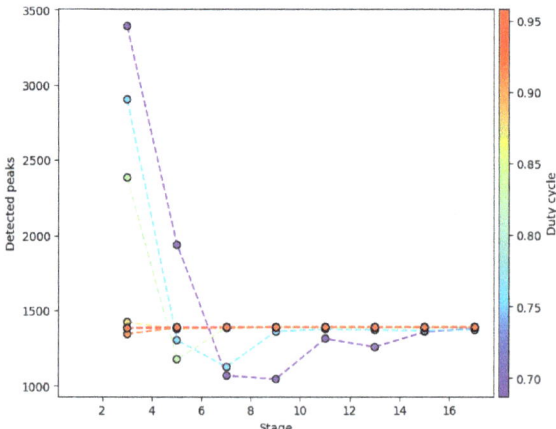

Figure 1. Number of detected peaks at each stage for our interpolation method. Each line is a simulated time series with ≈ 1400 typical oscillations from high (0.95, red) to low (0.68, purple) duty cycles. From [6].

At the final stage, we were able to properly study a higher number of lower-amplitude harmonics with lower S_i. The CGSA should increase if we subtracted a legitimate harmonic [8]. However, this should decrease if we found a fractal contribution, since a new sinusoid would be added instead of subtracted.

We calculated the CGSA after the subtraction of all peaks with consecutive lower S_i level to observe if the contribution of the remaining is harmonic, especially for the lowest ($logS_i \leq -2$), which corresponds to the low-amplitude signature for this kind of pulsating star [9].

3. Results: Applying the Method to a Real Pulsating Star

We analysed a real star observed with the TESS space telescope for approximately one year (see Figure 2). Around 65% of the remaining signal becomes fractal before low-amplitude peaks are subtracted. Nevertheless, the CGSA does not decrease for those low-amplitude subtracted signal. Therefore, no fractal signature is detected down to noise. Repeating this analysis for more multiperiodic stars observed by TESS will allow for us to characterize these variations and ascertain their nature [6].

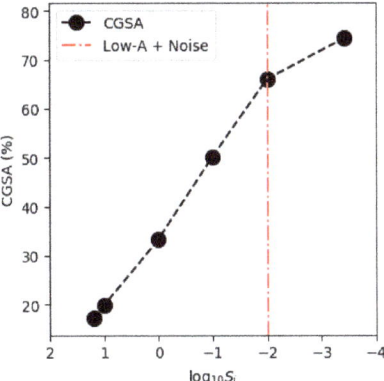

Figure 2. CGSA for the remaining signature after subtracting all peaks with signals higher than $logS_i$ (black). The red dashed–dotted line points to the remaining signature of low-amplitude peaks and noise after removing intermediate-amplitude variations.

Author Contributions: Conceptualization, S.B.F., J.P.-G., J.C.S.; methodology, S.B.F., J.P.-G.; investigation, all authors; original draft preparation, S.B.F.; review and editing, all authors. All authors have read and agreed to the published version of the manuscript.

Funding: S.B.F. and J.C.S. received financial support from the Spanish State Research Agency (AEI) Projects No. PID2019-107061GB-C64: "Contribution of the UGR to the PLATO2.0 space mission. Phases C/D-1". J.P.-G. and M.L.-M. acknowledge funding support from Spanish public funds for research under project ESP2017-87676-C5-5-R. A.G.H. acknowledges funding support from 'European Regional Development Fund/Junta de Andalucía-Consejería de Economía y Conocimiento' under project E-FQM-041-UGR18 by Universidad de Granada.

Acknowledgments: The authors wish to thank *TESS* team whose efforts made these results possible. Funding for the TESS mission is provided by the NASA Explorer Program. S.B.F. also thanks the resources received from the PLATO project collaboration with Centro de Astrobiología (PID2019-107061GB-C61). J.P.-G. and M.L.-M. acknowledge financial support from the State Agency for Research of the Spanish MCIU through the "Center of Excellence Severo Ochoa" award to the Instituto de Astrofísica de Andalucía (SEV-2017-0709).

Conflicts of Interest: The authors declare no conflict of interest.

Abbreviations

The following abbreviations are used in this manuscript:

CGSA	Coarse Grain Spectral Analysis
TESS	Transiting Exoplanet Survey Satellite

References

1. Poretti, E.; Michel, E.; Garrido, R.; Lefèvre, L.; Mantegazza, L.; Rainer, M.; Rodríguez, E.; Uytterhoeven, K.; Amado, P.J.; Martín-Ruiz, S.; et al. HD 50844: A new look at δ Scuti stars from CoRoT space photometry. *Astron. Astrophys.* **2009**, *506*, 85–93. [CrossRef]
2. Pascual-Granado, J.; Garrido, R.; Suárez, J.C. Limits in the application of harmonic analysis to pulsating stars. *Astron. Astrophys.* **2015**, *581*, A89. [CrossRef]
3. Yamamoto, Y.; Hughson, R.L. Extracting fractal components from time series. *Phys. D Nonlinear Phenom.* **1993**, *68*, 250. [CrossRef]
4. Ponman, T. The analysis of periodicities in irregularly sampled data. *Mon. Not. R. Astron. Soc.* **1981**, *196*, 583–596. [CrossRef]
5. Barceló Forteza, S.; Michel, E.; Roca Cortés, T.; García, R.A. Evidence of amplitude modulation due to resonant mode coupling in the δ Scuti star KIC 5892969. *Astron. Astrophys.* **2015**, *579*, A133. [CrossRef]
6. Barceló Forteza, S.; Pascual-Granado, J.; Suárez, J.C.; García Hernández, A.; Lares-Martiz, M. Unveiling rotation through fractal analysis of the grass for delta Scuti stars. 2022, *in preparation*.

7.   Barceló Forteza, S.; Moya, A.; Barrado, D.; Solano, E.; Martín-Ruiz, S.; Suárez, J.C.; García Hernández, A. Unveiling the power spectra of δ Scuti stars with TESS. The temperature, gravity, and frequency scaling relation. *Astron. Astrophys.* **2020**, *638*, A59. [CrossRef]
8.   de Franciscis, S.; Pascual-Granado, J.; Suárez, J.C.; Hernández, A.G.; Garrido, R.; Lares-Martiz, M.; Rodón, J.R. A fractal analysis application of the pre-whitening technique to δ Scuti stars time series. *Mon. Not. R. Astron. Soc.* **2019**, *487*, 4457–4463. [CrossRef]
9.   Barceló Forteza, S.; Roca Cortés, T.; García Hernández, A.; García, R.A. Evidence of chaotic modes in the analysis of four δ Scuti stars. *Astron. Astrophys.* **2017**, *601*, A57. [CrossRef]

MDPI

St. Alban-Anlage 66

4052 Basel

Switzerland

Tel. +41 61 683 77 34

Fax +41 61 302 89 18

www.mdpi.com

Engineering Proceedings Editorial Office

E-mail: engproc@mdpi.com

www.mdpi.com/journal/engproc

www.ingramcontent.com/pod-product-compliance
Lightning Source LLC
LaVergne TN
LVHW070124100526
838202LV00016B/2227